LANDLORD AND TENANT

LAW IN CONTEXT

Editors: Robert Stevens (Haverford College, Pennsylvania), William Twining (University of Warwick) and Christopher McCrudden (Balliol College, Oxford)

Landlord and Tenant

Text and Materials on Housing and Law

Second edition

MARTIN PARTINGTON

Professor of Law at Brunel University

WEIDENFELD AND NICOLSON

London

To the memory of my parents

George Weidenfeld and Nicolson Ltd
91 Clapham High Street, London sw4

ISBN 0 297 77790 4 cased
ISBN 0 297 77791 2 paperback

Printed in Great Britain by
Butler & Tanner Ltd, Frome and London

CONTENTS

CASES

Note: Page references to cases from which extracts have been taken are given in **bold** type.

STATUTES

Note: Page references to extracts from statutes are shown in **bold** type.

Statutory Instruments

STATISTICAL TABLES

ACKNOWLEDGEMENTS

Grateful acknowledgement is made to the following for permission to reproduce material from their publications:

The Controller of Her Majesty's Stationery Office; The Editor, All England Law Reports; The Incorporated Council of Law Reporting for England and Wales; The Editor, Local Government Reports; The Editor, *Estates Gazette*; Times Newspapers Ltd; Sweet & Maxwell for W.F. Holdsworth, *History of English Law*; R.E. Megarry, *The Rent Acts*; R.E. Megarry and H.W.R. Wade, *The Law of Real Property*, and J.R. Lewis and J.A. Holland, *Landlord and Tenant*; B.T. Batsford for J.D. Chambers and G.E. Mingay, *The Agricultural Revolution*; Penguin Books for D.V. Donnison, *The Government of Housing*; Oxford University Press for A.W.B. Simpson, *Introduction to the History of Land Law*; Oxford University Press and the Institute of Race Relations for J. Rex and R. Moore, *Race, Community and Conflict*; Butterworth for A.J. Hawkins, *Law Relating to Owners and Occupiers of Land*; Martin Robertson for A.J. Culyer, *The Economics of Social Policy*; Croom Helm for S. Lansley, *Housing and Public Policy*; Macmillan for N. Ginsberg, *Class, Capital and Social Policy*; Institute of Economic Affairs for F.G. Pennance, *Verdict on Rent Control*; University of California Press for Wallace F. Smith, *Housing, The Social and Economic Elements*; *The Solicitors' Journal*; *The Conveyancer*; *Journal of Social Welfare Law*; *Journal of Planning and Environment Law*; *Legal Action Group*; *Modern Law Review*; *New Law Journal*; *Lloyds Bank Review*; *Public Administration*; and Rogers (Printers) Birmingham Ltd for *Chirms Rent Book*.

PREFACE TO THE SECOND EDITION

One of the privileges afforded to those who have written for the 'Law in Context' series is that, in preparing second editions, they have been given great freedom by the publishers and encouragement by the editors to re-structure and re-write their books. In the light of comments and criticisms on the first edition, and of my own experience in using it, I have taken full advantage of this privilege. My principal reason for doing this is to develop the book's function as an educational tool. Although the first edition was conceived mainly as a students' text, I also attempted to make it practically useful for those engaged in various kinds of housing advice agency. This led to space being taken up describing a number of questions which, from a teaching point of view, were of marginal importance; and a number of themes were only touched on in the Preface to the first edition which should have been expanded in the body of the text.

This edition is substantially revised; much new material has been incorporated, existing material re-written and the order of its presentation altered. In its revised form, I hope that it will be suitable for law students who are studying landlord and tenant as part of land law courses, or who take separate options in landlord–tenant law or housing law. It is also intended for students who need to study this area of law as part of courses on estate management or land or housing administration. In addition, it may be of assistance in the training of various groups of practitioners such as housing advisers, tenancy relation officers and rent officers. More generally, I hope that those who study urban policy, social policy, or social administration will find useful a rather more detailed discussion of the legal issues relating to the landlord and tenant relationship than is usually available in their existing literature. Finally, although the text deals principally with English law, I hope that it will offer some insight into the contribution of law to the regulation of housing markets in any Western industrialized society.

*　　　*　　　*

Although the book is designed to be useful both to lawyers and non-lawyers, it is nonetheless important to stress that it remains predominantly a law book. The rules of law and the functions of those rules in the context of the landlord–tenant relationship provide the central focus for the materials contained in it. It is not a book on land policy in general or housing policy in particular.

At the same time, it is not a wholly traditional law text book. Most books on land law concentrate solely on analysis of the law itself.[1] For example, in their standard text Megarry and Wade (1975) state (p. 2) that:

the objects of learning the law of real property [land law] are
(i)   to acquire a knowledge of the rights and liabilities attached to interests in land;
(ii) to lay a foundation for the study of conveyancing.

To a degree, these objectives, particularly (i), are incorporated here. As will be seen, much of the material used is designed to develop familiar legal skills such as analysis of case law and (still too frequently underplayed) statute law. However, the educational limitations of these objectives are now widely accepted; the range of questions posed is too narrow. This book, therefore, attempts to expand the study of the law of landlord and tenant by encouraging students to consider, either explicitly or implicitly, further questions such as: How and why have the existing rules of landlord and tenant arisen? What is the importance of intervention by government in landlord–tenant relationships? How effective can law be as a means of regulating the relationship between landlords and tenants? What is the attitude of judges to such law? How do landlords and tenants regard the law? To what extent do recent developments challenge traditional notions of 'property rights' or 'freedom of contract'? There is still a lack of texts designed to give the student the opportunity not only to learn the law but also to think about it; this book is designed to fill that gap.

In the first edition, I set the discussion of the law relating to the landlord–tenant relationship in the context of residential lettings. The decision to limit the approach adopted in this book to housing is, as I suggested in the first edition, partly pragmatic. It would have been possible to incorporate materials relating to business tenancies or agricultural leases; but this would take up space and prevent considera-

1. A brave exception is Harwood (1977).

tion of other issues that I regard as important. In addition, there are at least three good educational reasons for such an approach. Firstly, experience suggests that analysis of landlord–tenant law in the context of housing is more interesting to students when they first approach this area of land law. Second, it enables them to study in some detail material which they may not be able to study in other courses. More generally, an examination of the law of landlord and tenant in the context of housing has an especial justification in that it illustrates the difficulties of attempting to advance social policy goals by regulating the private sector of the economy.

The book was originally planned as a cases and materials book rather than a straight text book. I have continued this approach in this edition, though, as will be seen, there is rather more narrative than in the first edition. However it should be stressed that the book is designed to be *worked at*, not just *worked through*. In other words, materials are presented which are designed to be thought about by the student; the issues are not clear-cut and are not presented so as to appear as if they are clear-cut. Difficult legal doctrines, conflicting cases, controversial materials are provided. Some questions are raised in the text for consideration. But by no means all the answers are offered.

Two particular educational objectives were borne in mind when selecting the materials that have gone into this book. The first is that, in presenting extracts from cases, I hope that students will consider not only the narrow points of principle but also more theoretical questions about juristic method that underlie the material. (For an introduction to these questions see Twining and Miers (1976), especially ch. 8.) The second is that much of the non-legal material is designed to show the law not working as it was designed to. Lawyers often adopt a somewhat law-centred view of the world and assume that everyone acts on the same information that they have; by contrast, non-lawyers are often surprisingly overawed by discussion of law and may thus assume it has an impact that it does not have.

Although it is now some years since I taught at the University of Warwick, I think it right to re-state that this book derives from a course that was pioneered there and that the approach adopted in it is still intended to reflect the philosophy of the Warwick law school that the study of law should be broadened from within. Fortunately, the

Law Department of the London School of Economics, while not perhaps having as articulated an educational philosophy as Warwick, nevertheless provides a more than encouraging atmosphere in which I have been able to develop these materials.

In addition to those mentioned in the first .edition whose help I was pleased to acknowledge, numerous other friends and colleagues have continued to offer advice and encouragement. In particular, I should like to thank Tim Murphy, Richard de Friend, Andrew Arden and Malcolm Grant for their, often unwitting, assistance; the Staff Research Fund at the L.S.E. which enabled me to employ occasional research assistance; to Greta and Philip, who stuck pages; and to Daphne and Adam whose diversions always helped when things were not going well. Despite her change of name and status – which I am delighted to record – Susan Hunt remains the only person who can both read my writing and produce immaculate typescript; my indebtedness to her is enormous.

Finally, I should like to thank successive generations of students at Warwick and L.S.E. Their continued interest in the subject has been tremendously supportive, and, in the case of those who have produced research papers, a source of most valuable information, much of which is reflected in the pages that follow. As always defects are entirely my responsibility.

23 March 1980   *London School of Economics*
                                             and Political Science

Author's Note: Housing Act 1980

The publisher's deadlines for the production of this book have meant that it was necessary to rely on copies of the Housing Bill as it passed through its various Parliamentary stages. Final proofs have been corrected as against the version of the Bill, amended after the Report stage in the House of Lords, printed on 22 July 1980. No substantial changes to the Bill, as relevant to this book, were made after that date, but there may have been minor textual amendments. Thus there may be slight discrepancies between material contained in this volume and the Queen's Printers' copy of the Act.

I

Setting the Context

'The objects which men aim at when they become possessed of land in the British Isles may, I think, be enumerated as follows: (1) political influence; (2) social importance, founded on territorial possession, the most visible and unmistakable form of wealth; (3) power exercized over tenantry; the pleasure of managing, directing and improving the estate itself; (4) residential enjoyment, including what is called sport; (5) the money return – the rent.'

(Earl of Derby, 1881, quoted in Douglas (1976, p. 17).)

Introduction

If we are to understand the social function of law in general, and of landlord–tenant law in particular, we need to have both a knowledge of the details of the law and some idea of the context from which that law developed and in which it currently operates. In studying this context it may be possible to develop some theory about the nature of the landlord–tenant relationship which again may assist us in analysing the social function of the law. In this chapter, we start by offering two contrasting hypotheses about the nature of the landlord–tenant relationship. We attempt to test those hypotheses by looking, briefly, at the historical development of the lease. Then we examine the main features of the housing market today, and of the landlords and tenants who operate within that market. Finally, in the light of this, we offer some suggestions that may help our understanding of the functions of law in this area, and also our understanding of the limits of the law.

1. The essential nature of the landlord–tenant relationship

In legal theory, the landlord–tenant relationship utilizes two of the most potent verbal symbols (Kahn-Freund, 1977, p. 13) of the common law: 'property rights', and 'freedom of contract'. If asked to characterize the essential nature of landlord–tenant relationships, most lawyers would state that it is an example of the principle that private owners of land should have the right to dispose of interests in their land as they wish – in this case, for limited periods of time. During the period of the lease, the tenant acquires a legally recognized, but necessarily restricted, interest in that land; and the terms on which his use and enjoyment of that land are based are contained in collateral contractual arrangements (covenants) which have been negotiated and agreed between the parties. Such a description, framed in terms of the apparently fundamental values of 'rights' and 'freedom', gives the impression of a relationship founded on consensus and agreement (Stein & Shand, 1974, ch. 9).

However, the very notion of 'property rights' points to the alternative proposition that for the non-propertied, there may exist no rights; the principle of 'freedom of contract' may conceal the fact that it is the person with the stronger bargaining power who has the 'freedom' to impose contractual terms on the weaker. In other words, the landlord–tenant relationship, far from being based on consensus, may contain within it fundamental conflicts. It may be characterized as a relationship that is founded on power – the power of property – set against the weakness and insecurity of those who do not have that property.

The posing of these alternative models – the 'consensus' and 'conflict' models – is not at all original; sociologists and political theorists, for example, have argued about this issue for many years. However, for law students, used to concentrating in positivistic fashion on the law as it now stands, without considering how it developed or how it might change, it may be helpful to offer these two alternatives. The next section, on the history of landlord–tenant relations, develops the point.

2. An historical outline of the landlord–tenant relationship

Space permits only a short account of the history of the development of the lease. We know that the lease for years was being used as early as the twelfth century (Holdsworth, 1923, vol. 3, p. 213). Even though the feudal system of land tenure was still in operation, the lease was never part of this system. Rather it developed as a means whereby landowners came to use their land more commercially,[1] and at the same time evade their feudal incidents and deprive their lords of the profits they made (Bean, 1968, pp. 20–25).

At first, lessees only had a personal action for damages, were they to lose possession of their land. It was not till 1499 that a decision of the Common Pleas, confirmed by the King's Bench, finally settled the law that a lessee had a right to recover the land against ejectors in general. The reasons for this development are explained by Holdsworth (*ibid.*, pp. 216–17):[2]

It is quite clear that such lessees, if ejected, would not have been compensated adequately if they had only been given damages. We have seen, too, that the government desired to stop the depopulation of the country caused by the conversion of arable land into pasture for sheep. It is obvious that a rule that the ejected lessee could not recover the land would have facilitated the operations of the landlords, who were pursuing this undesirable policy. These were no doubt the decisive reasons which brought about the enlargement of the remedy which could be obtained by the writ of *ejectio firmae*...

The writ of *ejectio firmae* and the action of ejectment to which it gave rise won their greatest victory in the following period when, by a series of legal fictions, they were made to do the work of the real actions so efficaciously that they gradually reduced them to the rank of antiquarian curiosities. We have seen that by that date the writ and the action had also become available to the copyholder, so that through them the common law at length acquired a uniform remedy for the protection of all kinds of interests in land.

These legal developments resulted in the widespread use of the lease, as Simpson (1961, pp. 233 ff, notes omitted) describes:

With the decay of the feudal tenurial system and the full recognition of the lease for years as an adequately protected interest in land, albeit a chattel interest, the lease for years became the legal institution under which a very great proportion of the land of the country was farmed; the landowners

---

1. The circumstances surrounding the decline of feudalism are a matter of considerable controversy, see, e.g., Hilton (ed.) (1978); also Miller & Hatcher (1978).
2. See too Milsom (1969, pp. 127–32).

exploited the land at one remove, and left a class of tenant farmers in actual occupation of the soil. At its best this system could be an admirable one. The landlord and tenant divided between them the burden of providing capital for agriculture, and a progressive landlord could do a great deal to encourage and indeed insist upon good husbandry. The system at its worst can be seen in the melancholy history of Ireland, where a large proportion of the English landlords rarely even visited their estates, and were only concerned to extract from their tenants rents which would enable them to live in affluence in England. In the course of time the Legislature has found it necessary to intervene to protect tenants against the abuses which rapacious landlords could readily perpetrate under the common law. In particular the Legislature has intervened to give tenants a security of tenure beyond the term fixed by their lease, and to enable limited owners, particularly life tenants, to grant leases of longer duration than would have been possible at common law. With the exception of a Statute of 1540, of restricted scope, these interventions begin in the nineteenth century with the series of Statutes dealing with Settled Land. At an earlier period the difficulties inherent in the lease could be dealt with only by private action. Thus settlements could include a grant of leasing powers to the life tenant, so that he could grant leases to endure beyond his life; covenants for renewal could be inserted into leases to give security to the tenant farmer. In one respect conveyancing practice in the sixteenth century curiously anticipated the modern position of the tenant farmer, for it was customary to grant leases for life rather than for years, a custom which long survived on conservatively managed estates.

In the sixteenth century the practice of granting farming leases for periods of twenty-one years became increasingly common. There are vague hints that extremely long leases were void at common law, but in the seventeenth century it is clear that there were no restrictions upon the possible length of terms. Very long terms, however, are usually employed only as conveyancing devices. The longest customary period for a lease which is not merely a device is the building lease, customarily fixed in the nineteenth century at ninety-nine years. Local conveyancing custom has settled the usual terms for other purposes, and it varies today in different parts of the country and in different estates, as it has always differed.

Chambers and Mingay (1966, pp. 17 ff, notes omitted) describe the groups of people who owned land, those who rented it, and some of the political consequences of this situation:

Finally, an essential function of land was to support a body of landlords, who together with the urban middle classes, constituted the governing class. Because of their wealth, influence and command of patronage, the few hundred great landlords, whose extensive but scattered estates ran into many thousands of acres, were able to control Parliament and dominate government. The far more numerous class of lesser landlords or gentry owned together about half of the land in the country but were content with a subsidiary role in government. Although the majority of seats in the Commons were occupied by country gentlemen, only a few of the more talented and wealthy among them, gifted politicians like Walpole, managed to attain high office; the generality of squires could not even afford to contest an election, and devoted their energies to the care of their estates and local affairs. As Justices, however, many of them were persons of consequence in their own neighbourhood, having responsibility for maintaining law and order and the power to try offenders at Petty and Quarter Sessions. The importance of the Justices was enhanced by their administrative authority over the poor law, over markets and fairs, weights and measures, roads and bridges and a multitude of other matters – matters affecting much more the day-to-day life of the country than the Acts passed in Parliament...

In England and Wales the farmers proper numbered about 330,000 according to Gregory King. Nearly half of them, 150,000 he estimated, were tenants who farmed the land belonging to the great landlords and gentry. The remaining 180,000 were owner-occupiers, farming their own land, and sometimes renting additional land from a landlord. The vast majority of the independent owners King placed in the category of 'lesser', and the amount of land owned by each of these was probably small, averaging perhaps less than 20 acres. Below the small owners were of course the cottagers and labourers. It is impossible to say exactly how numerous they were, but from King's figures it has been estimated that they were not very much greater in number than the farmers – perhaps only seven labourers to every four occupiers of land. Even in 1831, when farms had grown in size and many small occupiers had disappeared, the proportion of labourers to land-occupiers was still only eleven to four. The picture sometimes presented of English farming, with a select band of large capitalist farmers employing a vast army of landless labourers, is patently a false one.

Gradually large estates began to develop as the larger owners bought up small estates. Much technical innovation in farming took place on the estates of these larger freeholders. However, as Chambers and Mingay continue:

The large tenant-farmers of the landlords were also important as progressive farmers, although we hear less about them. Indeed, as farmers they enjoyed some advantages over the owner-occupiers. The tenants of reputable landlords had little fear of being turned out, even when they had no lease; and the bargaining power of farmers capable of managing large farms enabled them to obtain their land at a moderate rent and obliged the landlords to provide suitable buildings, fences, roads, protection against flooding, and perhaps a part of the expenses incurred in marling or manuring the soil. These large tenant-farmers could devote their own capital entirely to stocking the farm and buying good beasts and equipment; and if the times proved unfavourable and they made losses, the landlords could often be induced to abate their rents and help them through a lean period.

The English system of landlord and tenant, therefore, was one of partnership in which the costs and risks of farming were shared.[3] The landlords provided the basic necessities for good farming, ideally an enclosed, convenient farm, with the buildings well maintained and the land in good heart, and the farmer provided the stock and working capital, and the vital element of skill and enterprise. And in exceptional circumstances the landlord might keep his tenants up to the mark by a carefully detailed and strictly-enforced lease, or might bind the tenants to follow the advice of his steward in the management of the land. Of course many estates fell short of this ideal, the farms too small, run-down and inconvenient, the farmers backward, ignorant or lazy, their landlords incompetent or indifferent. But at its best the English landlord-tenant system was reasonably efficient and flexible – far more so than the conservative peasant farming of the continent – and it provided the essential framework for the great leap forward of agriculture in the eighteenth and nineteenth centuries.

Later (*ibid.*, pp. 44–9) they discuss the use made of leases, which was not as frequent as many contemporary writers suggested. Many tenants were able to trust their landlords to give them security of tenure.[4] In an era of fluctuating prices, long leases tended to be too rigid, for example on rent levels. Some of the larger and more efficient landlords used leases to try to ensure, through the use of covenants, that their tenants farmed in particular ways; but the mere existence of such covenants could not guarantee that they would be observed. They conclude (*ibid.*, p. 49):

[Some] landlords preferred not to grant leases in order that they might have a closer control over those of their tenants who were entitled to vote at the county elections. But probably only a small minority of landlords were prepared to keep their tenants in a state of constant insecurity for political motives, refusing them leases and depriving them of the conventional security enjoyed by the majority of annual tenants. Such a policy was bound to affect

3. Some data on levels of investment by, respectively, landlords and tenant farmers is to be found in Holderness (1974).

4. This was, however, certainly not always so. Smith (1970, pp. 160 ff) notes examples of serious, sometimes violent, conflicts between landlords and tenants. And the threat of insecurity gave landlords considerable influence over their tenants' voting behaviour; see Thompson (1963, pp. 201 ff). Mass evictions of tenant farmers by landlords in Wales following the 1868 General Election played an important part in the introduction of the secret ballot in 1872 (Douglas, 1976, p. 97).

the farming of the estate, and before long the landlord would be obliged to recognize its effects on his rentals. Except therefore for its use in areas of large-scale and progressive farming like Norfolk, it does not seem that in general we can regard the lease as a very important instrument in agricultural improvement, nor its absence as a great obstacle to efficiency. Its most valuable role was probably in encouraging farmers to undertake the risks of cultivating newly-enclosed waste lands by guaranteeing them low rents for the early years of the tenancy. Even here, however, we need more knowledge of its actual use before we can be sure just how important it really was.

In addition to agricultural holdings, the landlord–tenant relationship was also the form of tenure for the provision of residential accommodation. In the country, some landlord farmers were prepared to build cottages on their land for their employees, at any rate during periods when agricultural labour was badly needed – i.e. during the French wars, which brought a continuing demand for corn at high prices. However, as Gauldie notes (1974, pp. 30–31):

After Waterloo, when prices fell, [farmers] found it impossible to absorb the increased population ... Because there was a surplus of labour and a shortage of house accommodation in the country from the last decades of the eighteenth and throughout the nineteenth centuries it became possible, even advisable, to choose which section of the population should be allowed to stay. It is not surprising that farming landlords chose ... the least offensive of the rural community.

Some evidence of the supply of building land by estate owners in the eighteenth century, based on records from about fifteen British towns, is given by Chalklin[5] (1968):

While the rise in the value of land on its conversion from agricultural use into building sites was an obvious incentive to estate owners, it was offset in part by the high initial cost of providing the basic amenities, and the frequent delay in obtaining a substantial return on this outlay. In England and Wales land was either sold, or conveyed on building lease, the latter being preferred by the large private owners and corporations, and by 1800 ninety-nine years was becoming an increasingly common term. In the case of leasehold developments landlords preferred that builders should erect better-class rather than artisan dwellings, although the demand for the former was limited apart from London, Edinburgh and Bath. Their main means of controlling development lay in the covenants inserted in the leases, which varied greatly in number and detail.

5. Chalklin (1974) has a useful account of the development of Georgian towns and contains much information on the forms of tenure used.

McDonald notes (1969, p. 185, notes omitted) that while enlightened landlords could use the lease to ensure very good building developments which were properly planned and efficiently run, yet:

> The altruism of even the best landlords was limited – a result of their providing almost exclusively for the middle and upper classes. One aspect of maintaining the character of an area was the exclusion of poorer classes. It was impossible for them to afford the leases unless the landlord had overinvested in large properties and the rents fell. Attempts were also made to prevent traders and working-class people from even passing through the area. Thus on the Bedford estate gates were erected in order to exclude people from adjacent but less salubrious districts. Similarly when a slum developed on an estate, the solution was not to make any improvement in the conditions, but to clear the houses when the leases fell in and build new ones for a better class of people. This exacerbated the problem of the slum dwellers as the total stock of cheap accommodation was reduced and overcrowding would increase elsewhere. The value of maintaining the character of an area must be questioned when it is gained at such a cost. The main exception to this pattern was that several estates towards the end of the nineteenth century started to provide land at moderate rents for the erection of working-class tenements by philanthropic organizations.

In the middle-to-late nineteenth century a number of issues highlighted the elements of conflict that could exist between landlords and tenants. In the country, tenant-farmers agitated increasingly for 'tenant-right': the right to compensation for any unexhausted improvements made by them and remaining on their agricultural holdings at the end of their tenancies.[6] (This was already a customary practice in Lincolnshire; what was demanded was for this practice to extend to the whole country.) In Ireland, there was considerable rural agitation, which in turn encouraged protest among the crofters of Scotland, and amongst farmers in Wales (Douglas, 1976, *passim*). Capitalist entrepreneurs showed their antagonism towards the landed class through the movement for free trade in land (Perkin, 1969, p. 451). And first disease, and later fear of social unrest amongst the urban working class, focused attention on the appalling conditions of the tenanted accommodation in which the urban poor had to live (Stedman-Jones, 1976, Part II).

The political responses to each of these pressures were varied. For example, the tenant-right movement led to the Agricultural Holdings Act 1875, and a later, more effective, piece of legislation in 1883. The

6. See, e.g., McQuiston (1973); Fisher (1978).

Irish Land Act 1881 incorporated the 'three Fs': Fixity of Tenure, Free Sale and Fair Rents. Attempts to improve the conditions of the urban poor were contained in measures such as the Public Health Act 1848, and the Torrens and Cross Acts of 1868 and 1875. Many of these measures did not achieve what their advocates sought; indeed in the case of measures to improve the position of urban tenants the results were frequently counter-productive, at least in the relatively short term (Wohl, 1971). However, these measures, combined with other proposals including those for leasehold enfranchisement (discussed by, among others, the Select Committee on Town Holdings (1889)), for the taxation of site values of land (suggested by Henry George), or for the nationalization of land (advocated by the Land Nationalization Society under Alfred Russell Wallace) were all clear indications of the social pressures that were developing which led governments to devise ways of attempting to regulate the landlord–tenant relationship.

In a more general context, these issues can be seen as just one aspect of the 'land question', which relates to the problem of whether land is to be treated just like other forms of property, whose use is to be determined solely by the owner of the property, or whether, because each piece of land is unique and land as a whole is available only in finite amounts, land should be regarded as a social asset that should be made available to all. Looked at in an even wider context, intervention in the landlord–tenant relationship may be seen as an example of 'corporatism' whereby governments have intervened increasingly in the private sector of the economy (Winkler, 1975).

Interpreting the nature of the response of governments to these questions in the specific context of the landlord–tenant relationship is inevitably a matter of considerable debate. Some have argued that these interventions have amounted to an effective destruction of private property. Others suggest that property has been re-structured so that ownership of land is no longer a source of rights, but of social obligations as well. Yet others say that to look at changes in legal forms is misleading; that the imbalance of power inherent in landlord–tenant relationships remains and will not be removed until the capitalist system has been destroyed and the social relationships based on capitalism are replaced by social relationships founded on different political–economic structures.

It is not the purpose of this book to resolve these debates, which in any event cannot be adequately summarized here. However, a number of points may be made on the above. The first is that although the landlord–tenant relationship was often regarded as beneficial to both sides, especially in the context of agricultural holdings, nonetheless there was often the possibility, and sometimes the reality of conflict resulting from an imbalance of power in the landlord–tenant relationship. This conflict might take the form of direct exploitation of tenants; or be indirect, based on the political control landlords might have over their tenantry.

Second, the landlord–tenant relationship did not emerge as an efficient way of ensuring that the very poorest were given opportunities for decent housing. This became a source of increasing social tension, and is a key factor in understanding how housing law and housing policy developed in the twentieth century.

A third, more general point can also be made. I suggest that the foregoing indicates that property rights should not be regarded with quasi-religious awe. Many students, particularly of property law, are inclined to do this. However, far from being a magic bundle of unchanging rights, property has been subjected to considerable political, social and economic pressures. The extent to which lawyers understand and come to terms with those pressures is likely to be an important factor in any analysis of the social function of law in general, and of landlord–tenant law in particular.

3. The landlord–tenant relationship: contemporary data

It was noted above (p. 9) that the overall effect of the legislative interventions that began in the middle-to-late nineteenth century, and which have continued to the present day, is the subject of considerable debate; the materials later in this book, which discuss the mix between traditional private law and more recent statute law, are presented with the view of getting readers to think about how, if at all, the nature of landlord–tenant relationship has changed over the years. One point may be made here, however, which is that, unlike other areas of social policy, such as education, health or social insurance, where what was originally provided privately came to be taken over predominantly by government, housing has remained the one area of social policy in which the private sector of the economy has continued to dominate. Although (as Table 1.1 opposite shows) about a third of homes are now provided by local authorities, the ideology of private property, and those whose interests were protected by that ideology, have helped to ensure that there should be no serious challenge to the predominance of the private sector.

In this section, after first presenting the current structure of tenure patterns, I offer some of the available data on landlords and tenants. Before so doing, a word about the nature of the data used.

In the tables that follow there are some problems with the comparability of data. For example, *Housing and Construction Statistics* are based on the 1971 census figures, and extrapolation therefrom. *General Household Survey* and *National Dwelling and Housing Survey* figures are both

Table 1.1   Housing tenure, England and Wales (millions of houses and percentage of stock)

Year	Owner-occupied		Local authority and new towns		Private rented and miscellaneous*		Total number
	Number	%	Number	%	Number	%	
(a) 1914	0.8	10	0.02	0.2	7.1	89.8	7.9
(a) 1938	3.7	32	1.1	10	6.6	58	11.4
(b) 1951	3.9	31	2.2	17	6.4	52	12.5
(a) 1960	6.4	44	3.6	25	4.6	31	14.6
(c) 1966	7.8	49	4.3	27	3.9	24	16.0
(c) 1971	8.9	52	4.9	29	3.3	19	17.1
(c) 1976	10.1	56	5.3	29	2.8	15	18.1

* Includes housing associations.

Sources: (a) *Housing Policy: Technical Volume 1* (1977), p. 38, Table 1.23; (b) *Housing Policy: A Consultative Document* (1977), p. 14, Fig. 2; (c) *Housing and Construction Statistics* (1972, 1978), nos 1 & 22.

Reprinted from Ginsburg (1979), p. 113.

based on interviews of samples of the population; but the samples used are different. The Paley study (1978) relates only to 'densely rented areas'. Further, while some of the studies relate only to England, others relate to England and Wales. Thus none of the sets of data is strictly comparable, and each is subject to its own form of error and bias. However, the purpose of using these data in this text is not to give exact, definitive numbers, but to indicate orders of magnitude. For this reason, the data are presented in raw, untreated form, even though this will mean that there are some inconsistencies which should be guarded against.

Table 1.2(a). Tenure by region: numbers ('000s), end of 1977

Region	Owned outright	Owned with mortgage or loan	Rented from council	Rented from housing association	Rented privately unfurnished	Rented privately furnished	All households
North	215	283	467	18	125	13	1,120
Yorkshire/Humberside	399	503	587	13	196	43	1,741
East Midlands	323	455	407	9	156	20	1,371
East Anglia	187	197	184	9	75	25	678
South East	1,329	1,977	1,706	117	733	340	6,203
Greater London	442	733	831	87	366	200	2,660
Rest of South East	887	1,244	875	30	367	140	3,544
South West	493	484	367	16	160	63	1,583
West Midlands	382	575	624	21	155	35	1,792
North West	614	748	670	23	229	51	2,336
England	3,943	5,222	5,013	225	1,830	590	16,824

Table 1.2(b) Tenure by region: percentages, end of 1977

Region	Owned outright	Owned with mortgage or loan	Rented from council	Rented from housing association	Rented privately		All households
					unfurnished	furnished	
North	19.2	25.2	41.7	1.6	11.2	1.2	100.0
Yorkshire/Humberside	22.9	28.9	33.7	0.7	11.3	2.5	100.0
East Midlands	23.6	33.2	29.7	0.7	11.4	1.5	100.0
East Anglia	27.7	29.1	27.2	1.3	11.1	3.7	100.0
South East	21.4	31.9	27.5	1.9	11.8	5.5	100.0
Greater London	16.6	27.6	31.3	3.3	13.8	7.5	100.0
Rest of South East	25.0	35.1	24.7	0.8	10.4	3.9	100.0
South West	31.2	30.6	23.1	1.0	10.1	4.0	100.0
West Midlands	21.3	32.1	34.9	1.2	8.7	1.9	100.0
North West	26.3	32.0	28.7	1.0	9.8	2.2	100.0
England	23.4	31.0	29.8	1.3	10.9	3.5	100.0

Source: National Dwelling and Housing Survey (1978), Table 38.

A Current tenure patterns

The first point to note is the dramatic change in the pattern of tenure shown by Table 1.1 which shows the sharp rise in the levels of owner-occupation and renting from local authorities, combined with a fall in the level of private sector renting.

Further estimates for England (Table 1.2) are now available from the *National Dwelling and Housing Survey* (1978), which break the general categories presented in Table 1.1 into more detail.

Table 1.3   Major subdivisions of the 'privately rented and other tenures' sector, England and Wales 1966–76

	(thousands)		
	1966 (April)	1971 (April)	1976 (End-year)
Housing associations	130	180	250
Rented with job or business and by virtue of employment*	800	810	700
Rented unfurnished from a private landlord:			
Controlled	1,700	1,200	375
Regulated	1,070	840	1,115
Rented furnished (excluding 'tied' accommodation)	250	330	350
Total	*3,950*	*3,360*	*2,790*

* Nearly 100,000 are armed services married quarters (see *Annual Abstract of Statistics* 1976, Table 187, for comprehensive figures for the United Kingdom).

Source: Department of the Environment estimates. *Housing Policy* 3 (1977), p. 62.

Even this apparent detail does not indicate the further subdivisions which exist within the privately rented sector. Table 1.3, largely derived from the *General Household Survey*, offers more information on this and shows how the subdivisions have altered over a ten-year period.

Furthermore, as Table 1.4 shows, the owner-occupied sector in fact contains a considerable percentage of leasehold properties. In addition, it has been estimated (Dunn & White, 1979) that in 1977 approximately 20% of residential sector sales and 30% of commercial sales were of leasehold interests. In the residential sector most such sales were below £15,000. Properties with only a few years to run on the lease frequently sold for much less. Over 80% of sales where the lease had less than thirty-five years to run were for amounts less than £5,000. About 30% of residential leasehold sales related to new leases; the rest were of existing leases. For new leases, the bulk were for periods of over thirty-five years and in most cases the annual rent was less than £150.

Table 1.4   Leasehold/freehold tenures by region, end of 1977

Region	Owned leasehold		Owned freehold		All owner-occupiers
	('000s)	(Percent-age)	('000s)	(Percent-age)	
North	95	19.0	403	81.0	498
Yorkshire/Humberside	106	11.8	796	88.2	902
East Midlands	23	2.9	755	97.1	778
East Anglia	10	2.5	374	97.5	384
South East	314	9.5	2,992	90.5	3,306
Greater London	183	15.6	992	84.4	1,175
Rest of South East	129	6.1	2,002	93.9	2,131
South West	91	9.3	886	90.7	977
West Midlands	188	19.6	769	80.4	957
North West	564	41.4	798	58.6	1,362
England	1,391	15.1	7,773	84.9	9,165

Source: National Dwelling and Housing Survey (1978), Table 39. [The data must be treated with great caution. They represent the replies given by owner-occupiers to a question as to whether the properties were lease- or freehold. However a more detailed analysis of the data suggests that the question may have been misunderstood.]

Three obvious conclusions may be drawn from these figures:

(*i*)   despite frequent references to the decline in the private rented sector, total numbers of leases and tenancies remain very substantial;

(*ii*)   the total numbers owning their house outright is still relatively small. It can be argued that those who own with a mortgage are in a position analogous to tenants; the analogy will not be pursued here, but there is a case for comparing the position of mortgagors with those of tenants and comparing developments in the regulation of mort-gagees with those relating to landlords;

(*iii*)   regional differences in forms of tenure are significant, reflecting not only different levels of prosperity and distribution of income and wealth, but also, perhaps, the power of conveyancers.

Table 1.5   Households in privately rented accommodation by type of landlord and region, end of 1977

Region	Type of landlord												All households privately renting
	Property company		Employer-company		Employer-person		Relative		Other person		Other		
	'000s	%	'000s	%	'000s	%	'000s	%	'000s	%	'000s	%	'000s
North	10	7.5	18	13.0	14	10.4	11	8.0	71	51.4	13	9.7	138
Yorkshire/Humberside	21	8.8	42	17.9	17	7.1	11	4.4	125	52.5	23	9.5	239
East Midlands	15	8.7	34	19.2	17	9.9	7	4.0	91	51.4	12	6.9	176
East Anglia	7	6.6	17	16.7	12	11.7	3	3.5	53	53.4	8	8.1	100
South East	187	17.4	115	10.8	68	6.4	58	5.5	560	52.2	83	7.8	1,073
Greater London	143	25.2	45	8.0	21	3.8	24	4.3	298	52.6	34	6.1	566
Rest of South East	44	8.7	70	13.9	47	9.3	34	6.7	262	51.7	49	9.7	507
South West	16	7.1	32	14.5	18	8.2	16	7.2	119	53.4	22	9.7	224
West Midlands	25	1.5	29	17.6	11	6.6	13	7.6	103	61.8	8	4.9	190
North West	53	18.9	27	9.6	7	2.6	13	4.8	158	56.4	22	7.8	281
England	335	13.8	315	13.0	166	6.8	133	5.5	1,281	52.9	192	7.9	2,421

Source: National Dwelling and Housing Survey (1978), Table 40.

B Data on landlords and tenants

The data presented here relate, first, to the private rented sector; second to the local authority sector; third to housing associations.

(i) THE PRIVATE SECTOR

Landlords

In the past, there has been a lack of information about landlords in the private rented sector (*Housing Policy* (3), 1977, pp. 72–4). Recently, however, a more detailed picture has begun to emerge. As Table 1.5 shows, the predominant type of landlord is the individual: employer-person, relative, or other person. The vast majority of those are non-resident; but some are resident, sharing space, and others are resident, not sharing space, as Table 1.6 shows. (These distinctions are important for the purposes of Rent Act protections.)

Table 1.6   Individual private landlords by region, end of 1977

	Households renting from individual						All households renting from individual
	Resident landlord sharing space		Resident landlord not sharing space		No resident landlord		
Region	'ooos	%	'ooos	%	'ooos	%	
North	1	1.1	4	4.3	91	94.5	97
Yorkshire/Humberside	7	4.6	4	2.4	142	93.0	153
East Midlands	3	2.4	2	1.6	110	95.9	115
East Anglia	6	8.1	4	6.2	59	85.7	69
South East	66	9.6	60	8.6	562	81.8	687
Greater London	39	11.4	37	10.6	268	77.9	344
Rest of South East	27	7.8	23	6.6	294	85.6	343
South West	13	8.4	16	10.3	125	81.2	154
West Midlands	9	7.4	3	2.6	114	90.0	127
North West	9	4.9	6	3.5	164	91.5	179
England	114	7.2	99	6.3	1,366	86.5	1,579

Source: National Dwelling and Housing Survey (1978), Table 41.

More personal details about individual landlords are to be found in Paley's study of 'densely rented areas of England and Wales, 1976'[7] (Paley, 1978, p. 10):

7. For definition and rationale, see Paley (1978, ch. 7).

In about two thirds of cases the individual landlord was a man rather than a woman and this was true whether the landlord was resident or non-resident.

In nearly half of all cases of lettings with individual landlords, this landlord was aged sixty or over and very often, especially where resident, he or she was aged seventy or over. This explains the low proportion of cases, 45% where an individual landlord was in full time employment. However, in 13% of cases where the individual landlord was resident, compared with only 2% of cases where he or she was not, the landlord's age was less than thirty.

Non-resident individual landlords tended to be of higher social class and income than resident individual landlords. In 46% of the cases where the individual landlord was not resident, this individual was in either Social Class I or II of the Registrar General's classification but this was true in only 28% of the cases where the individual landlord was resident. For lettings with non-resident individual landlords, the median landlord income from all sources was £61 gross per week compared with only £33 gross per week for lettings with resident individual landlords.

Although a high proportion of individual landlords were elderly, they had not in general become landlords while elderly. Where the individual landlord of a letting was aged seventy or over, in 57% of cases he or she had been letting accommodation for more than twenty years and, where such a landlord was aged between sixty and seventy, in 72% of cases he or she had been letting for more than ten years. In a later chapter, we shall see that in 38% of cases of lettings made by resident individuals and in 23% of cases of lettings made by non-resident individuals, the landlord had started to let accommodation within the six years previous to interview. Only in 15% of cases were these 'newly letting' landlords aged sixty or over when interviewed.

On company landlords, Table 1.5 (above) shows that in 1977 on average throughout the country 13.8% of lettings were by property companies, though this fluctuated widely in different parts of the country. By contrast, Paley's study of densely rented areas in 1976 showed that, on average in those areas (*ibid.*, p. 9), companies were responsible for 25% of lettings. Her figures for London correspond closely with the figures in Table 1.5. For areas outside London the discrepancy may be due to the fact that she was studying only densely rented areas, where one would expect more company involvement. She further discovered that 'of these company lettings, two-thirds were by private companies and one-third by public companies. Property companies letting mainly residential accommodation accounted for two-thirds of the company lettings, that is for 17% of all the sampled lettings. Companies concerned mainly with non-residential

Table 1.7 Lettings by type of landlord by size of landlord's holding. Densely rented areas of England and Wales 1976

Number of lettings in England and Wales 1976	Type of landlord making the letting						
	Resident individual	Non-resident individual	Company	Charity/ housing association	Non-charitable trust executors	Public body etc	All types
	%	%	%	%	%	%	%
1	36	18	2	–	–	5	12
2–4	42	22	4	2	15	2	15
5–9	10	20	5	2	4	3	10
10–24	12	26	16	2	14	–	16
25–49	–	8	16	4	17	7	9
50–99	–	3	14	3	19	–	6
100–499	–	3	6	10	25	10	8
500–999	–	–	14	13	6	2	4
1,000–9,999	–	–	18	36	–	33	12
10,000 or more	–	–	5	28	–	38	8
100	100	100	100	100	100	100	100
Information not obtained	4	18	26	3	6	18	75
Lettings for which landlord interview obtained	119	355	251	160	58	78	1021

Source: Paley (1978), p. ii.

property accounted for 2% of all the lettings, while companies whose main business was something other than property accounted for 6%.'

Some indication of the size of holdings of the different categories of private landlord can be seen in Table 1.7 which shows, not surprisingly, that many individual landlords had only a small number of lettings. More surprising perhaps were the often substantial holdings of dwellings by companies. Furthermore, despite frequent attacks on the effect of the Rent Acts on landlords, Paley showed that 71% of the lettings surveyed had been bought or built by their current landlords, which shows that some landlords have continued to be prepared to invest in rented accommodation; further, 23% of the lettings surveyed had been acquired (whether by purchase or otherwise) since 1971 (*ibid.*, pp. 11–12). It should not be concluded from this that company landlordism is going to increase; but equally it can be seen that not all landlords are willy-nilly abandoning the private rented sector (Harloe *et al.*, 1974, pp. 102 ff).

Tenants

There have been a number of studies of the characteristics of private tenants, and continuing information is now available through the *General Household Survey* and the *Family Expenditure Survey*. A number of features of this sector stand out:

(*a*) Couples aged 60 or over, or individuals (mainly widows and widowers) are much more likely to be tenants of private landlords than are younger couples (Holmans, 1979, p. 12). In 1971, nearly one-third of all household heads renting unfurnished had lived in their present home for more than 30 years; many have thus survived from the days when this was the majority tenure (*Housing Policy* (3), 1977, p. 69).

(*b*) Furnished rented accommodation is the tenure of the small young household: '70 per cent of the households . . . who were renting furnished were individuals or two-adult households under age 60, and only 10 per cent of households renting furnished accommodation included children . . .' (Holmans, *ibid.*).

(*c*) A substantial number of married couples still set up home first in rented accommodation as a temporary arrangement, with the intention of buying a house when they can afford it (Holmans, *ibid.*).

(*d*) Among single men and women aged 30 and over, owner-occupation is the commonest tenure though (by comparison with couples) a relatively high proportion of them are tenants of private landlords (Holmans, *op. cit.*, p. 14).

(*e*) The turnover of tenants, especially in the furnished sector, is very rapid in relation to the size of the sector. In 1971 there appear to have been over 300,000 households entering the private-rented sector, and about 350,000 departures to other tenures (*Housing Policy* (3), 1977, p. 69).

(*f*) However, apart from the older people ((a) above) there are others who stay for a considerable time. They include a disproportionate number of poorer people. For example, in households with 'economically active' heads, average incomes were lower among tenants renting unfurnished from private landlords than among local authority tenants or owner-occupiers (Holmans, 1979, Tables A.8 and A.10). The proportion of householders in semi-skilled or unskilled manual work who are tenants of private landlords is considerably higher than the proportion of householders in skilled manual occupations who rent from private landlords (*National Dwelling and Housing Survey*, 1978, Tables 3 and 4). Even though the size of the owner-occupied sector is considerably larger than the size of the privately rented sector, a substantial number of tenants below pensionable age are in receipt of supplementary benefits as compared with owner occupiers. (In 1975 the figures were respectively 172,000 and 94,000 (*Housing Policy* (3), 1977, p. 70).)

(ii) THE LOCAL AUTHORITY SECTOR

Landlords

Table 1.1 (above) provides estimates of the total number of local authority rented dwellings in England and Wales; Table 1.2 shows (for England) the wide variations in the ways in which they are distributed on a regional basis. The extent to which particular local authorities have built housing for letting partly reflects local demand; but local political attitudes have also influenced the extent to which public sector housing programmes have been advanced.

Two assumptions have underlain the provision of public sector housing which are of particular relevance to this book, and which have come in for considerable criticism. The first is that local authorities will be 'model' landlords; the second is that they will be 'social' landlords.

Behind the notion of 'model' landlordism is the idea that local authorities will behave towards their tenants in a benevolent, even paternalistic way. The arbitrary evictions, the poor quality of accommodation, the failure to do repairs, the charging of extortionate rents that were said to be characteristics of the private sector were all to be re-moved from public sector housing. In recent years, however, many attacks have been made on the role of local authorities as landlords. The discretions that they formerly had regarding their choice of tenants and allocation of accommodation, their policies for manage-ment of estates and defining the terms of lettings, have all been subject to increasingly insistent demands for control. As this book was being prepared, legislation was being passed through Parliament to create a 'Tenants' Charter' which is designed to increase legal controls over housing practices. Perhaps this is the clearest indication yet of what has been seen as the failure of many local authority housing depart-ments to act in a socially responsive way. The argument that, being elected bodies, they would exercise their powers in the interests of the local electorate has not necessarily meant that they have pursued sensible or just housing policy goals. (See further below, pp. 512–31.)

In so far as local authorities were to be 'social' landlords, the idea was that they would offer housing opportunities to those who were hardest hit by the operation of the free market in housing. The extent to which these social goals have been achieved is examined in the data on local authority tenants (below).

Tenants

Data on the characteristics of local authority tenants suggest that they are very diverse (*Housing Policy* (1), 1977, ch. 2; Holmans (1979)). A number of specific points may, however, be made:

(*a*) Local authority tenants include a distinctly higher proportion of larger families (those with 3+ children) than other tenures.

(*b*) There is also a higher proportion of older tenants than for other tenures (except for those renting unfurnished from private landlords) reflecting increased investment in old people's homes, sheltered accommodation and the like.

(*c*) Widowhood and divorce is frequently the occasion for a move into local authority tenure, and local authorities have been providing increasingly for widowed, divorced and deserted women with chil-dren (*Housing Policy* (3), 1977, p. 12).

(*d*) In terms of incomes, although there is considerable overlap with owner-occupiers, the average income of families with an 'eco-nomically active' head is about 25% below that for owner occupiers, but markedly higher than that of tenants in the private rented sector (Holmans, 1979, Table A.8).

(*e*) However, in the case of households with 'economically inactive' heads, there has been an increasing proportion of local authority lettings made available for them. 'In the very broadest terms, local authorities have been taking over from private landlords the housing of the poor' (*Housing Policy* (3), 1977, p. 12).

(*f*) The vast majority of local authority tenant households have heads who are, or were, in manual occupations. Even though 'for the working classes' was removed from the law in 1949 (below, pp. 477–8) as the group for whom housing was to be provided, there has been little change in the class of those getting council tenancies.

(*g*) The numbers who have moved from local authority renting to owner-occupation have been few: about 3% a year in the early 1970s (*Housing Policy* (3), 1977, p. 12). Whether this figure remains at that level, now council tenants have been given the 'right to buy' (Housing Act 1980, s. 1) remains to be seen (Schifferes, 1980a).

(*h*) There is considerable evidence that black families are allocated to the poorest local authority estates (Community Relations Commission, 1976, 1977a, 1977b).

(iii) HOUSING ASSOCIATIONS

Landlords

Housing associations come in a bewildering variety of forms. They have long been regarded as a potentially very important source of accommodation. Some have argued that they may ultimately replace the private landlord: while this potential has yet to be fully realized, Table 1.3 gives an indication of the growth in this sector.

Since the Housing Act 1974 came into effect, housing associations wishing to receive grants and loans from public funds have been required to register with the Housing Corporation (Housing Act 1974, s. 18). The vast majority of housing associations are therefore registered. Housing Corporation records show that in mid 1978 there were 1,260 registered 'fair rent' and 'hostel' housing associations: 96% in England and 4% in Wales. They managed an estimated 240,000 dwellings plus 5,000 hostel bed-spaces. (In addition there were about 1,500 registered almshouses, co-ownership and co-operative associations.) The housing stock consists of both purpose-built accommodation and older properties which have been improved.

Part 1 of the Housing Act 1974 gives the Corporation extensive powers to provide dwellings itself (s. 1(2)(*d*)); to acquire land (s. 3), and to develop it (s. 4). But in practice its most important tasks are the promotion and regulation of the activities of housing associations (s. 1(2)). On the promotion side, it is given substantial borrowing powers, including the power to borrow abroad and from the European Investment Bank and the Commission of the EEC (s. 7 as amended by Housing Act 1980, s. 120); and can lend money to housing associations (s. 9). Further the Corporation can act as agent for the Secretary of State for the Environment in administering the various subsidies that are available from central government (ss. 29–35). As regards regulation, the Corporation has broad powers to inquire into the affairs of housing associations and act for their protection (ss. 19–20, as amended Housing Act 1980, Schedule 17; see too Housing Act 1980, ss. 124–5 and Schedule 16). The adequacy of these powers of regulation was the subject of recent controversy (Public Accounts Committee, 1979; Noble, 1979).

Associations also vary considerably in type. In particular there is a crucial distinction between 'specialist associations', which allocate more than 50% of their available accommodation to a particular type of tenant, and general-purpose associations. Specialist associations may offer sheltered accommodation for the elderly, hostels for single people, accommodation for the socially or economically vulnerable – e.g. one-parent families, ex-psychiatric patients, the handicapped, ex-offenders – or groups indentified by a job or activity, such as nurses or students. The general-purpose associations are self-explanatory.

Tenants

The most recent estimates (Housing Corporation, 1979, p. 2) show there were some 225,000 households, containing half a million people, living in accommodation rented from housing associations. About 20% of these households became tenants within the twelve months prior to May 1978, a further indication of the rapid growth of the sector.

Some indication of the types of person who are being allocated to housing association dwellings can be gained from a study of new housing association tenants in a two-week period in May 1978 (Housing Corporation, 1979). The main findings are:

Of the 1,775 new housing association tenants identified in the survey, 125 (7 per cent) were occupying older properties purchased for rebuilding or modernisation ... These sitting tenants did not become tenants because of associations' selection policies, but because of the type of development being undertaken. The remaining 1,650 tenants were allocated housing as a result of deliberate procedures on the part of housing associations ... In comparison with the household structure and characteristics of the population in England and Wales as a whole, new tenants are significantly more likely to be:

'single persons of all ages; small families with children under 16, and particularly single parent families; retired from full time employment; employed in junior and other non-manual, skilled and semi-skilled manual occupations; unemployed.'

As a consequence of the relatively high proportion of retired or unemployed household heads, gross incomes tended to be low, with a median for all new tenants of £2,080 per annum (£40 per week) compared with a national median for household heads working full-time in all tenures of between £4,000 and £4,100 (about £78 per week).

Almost one third of the new tenants had rented accommodation from a private landlord previously, about 25 percent had shared with relatives or friends, and 18 percent had been tenants of a local authority. 11 percent had been owner-occupiers. For about ten percent of the new tenants, the grant of a housing association tenancy was the first time they had lived as separate households.

12 percent of the new tenants had lacked one or more of the basic amenities in their previous accommodation, slightly above the national average. 38 percent of new tenants had shared one of the basic amenities, compared with only two percent nationally. 18 percent of new tenants said that they had been overcrowded in their previous home, while 9 percent had found their previous accommodation too large.

Unsatisfactory or unsuitable housing was the reason given most frequently by association staff for allocating accommodation to new tenants (43 percent of cases). Other common reasons given for allocating accommodation were that the tenant had been nominated for housing by a local authority and a variety of reasons connected with homelessness or insecurity. Reasons connected with the lack of alternative housing solutions were also frequently given.

Over half the new tenants were housed as a result of making a direct application to an individual housing association, while over a quarter were housed as a result of being nominated by a local authority. The characteristics of tenants housed as a result of these two practices were very similar. 8 percent of the new tenants were referred to housing associations by other agencies.

Referred tenants were more likely to be families with children compared with tenants from other sources, and household heads were likely to be manual workers on low wages. Rates of unemployment amongst household heads who were economically active were 38 percent, almost ten times the national average. Referred tenants were also more likely to have been sharing accommodation with relatives or friends, or to have been living in a hostel or institution than other groups of tenants. Two thirds of them had shared one or more of the basic amenities in their previous accommodation, compared with under one third of the direct applicants and nominated tenants.

Sitting tenants were more likely to be elderly single people, almost all of
whom rented their accommodation from a non-resident private landlord.
Two thirds of the sitting tenants had lacked one or more of the basic amenities
in their previous accommodation, and over half mentioned other deficiencies
including damp, rot and faulty wiring, and underoccupation of the space.

One fifth of the new tenants were allocated accommodation by specialist
associations, which comprised 46 percent of the associations taking part in
the survey. The range of housing needs being met by these associations was
wide, but two groups of people in particular were more highly represented
amongst new tenants of specialist associations than amongst new tenants of
general purpose associations. The first group were elderly single people, two
thirds of whom were housed by three large national associations. The second
significant group were single people of working age, 85 percent of whom were
housed by small specialist associations with fewer than 250 dwellings.

Four fifths of the new tenants were housed by general purpose housing
associations who housed a wider range of people overall; and significantly
more families with children, who formed over half the new tenants of these
associations.

Tenants housed by specialist associations were more likely to have applied
direct for housing than in general purpose associations and over half the new
tenants in specialist associations were allocated sheltered housing. Almost half
the new tenants of general purpose associations also applied direct, and a
third were nominated by local authorities. Only 6 per cent of general purpose
association tenants were allocated sheltered housing, and over a quarter of
the new tenants were allocated improved older housing.

Tenants housed in Greater London were more likely to be single people
of working age, whereas those in metropolitan or non-metropolitan areas were
more likely to be over retirement age. However, within each area, major differences were observed between people housed by specialist associations and
those by general purpose associations, and it is clear from the survey data
that it is the type of association rather than the type of area of operation
which has the determining influence on who is housed.

Although these findings indicate that housing associations are
assisting socially vulnerable groups who often fall outside the scope
of most local authority allocation policies, there have been criticisms
that the general-purpose associations, in particular, are too restrictive
in their allocation policies and are not therefore providing a true
alternative for those outside local authority housing provision (Porter,
1979; Niner, 1979).

As with local authority tenants, housing association tenants have been given the 'right to buy' (Housing Act 1980, s. 1). The impact of this change of policy is impossible to judge at the time of writing, though there are considerable fears that it may divert the housing association movement from its principle aim of providing accommodation to rent.

4. The function of landlord–tenant law

In the final section of this chapter, I wish to raise for discussion some questions about the function of landlord–tenant law as a method of regulating the landlord–tenant relationship. (See, too, Partington, 1980a.)

A The 'gap' problem

The body of law that is discussed in the following chapters may seem to have a number of quite different objectives:

(*i*) it may *prescribe procedures* for effecting certain transactions, e.g. in relation to the creation of a lease;

(*ii*) it may attempt to *create rights* to protect certain groups, e.g. security of tenure for tenants, or certain duties regarding the homeless;

(*iii*) it may offer *modes of enforcement* which underpin those rights, e.g. in the law on harassment and unlawful eviction;

(*iv*) it may have a *constitutional function*, e.g. authorizing the expenditure of public funds on housing provision;

(*v*) it may attempt to *lay down standards*, e.g. by providing definitions of unfitness of certain accommodation for human habitation.

But as we shall also see, the 'success' of that law in achieving those apparent objectives is extremely mixed. Rights go by default or are not enforced; standards are not met; procedures are ignored. So it is important to ask why there is this apparent gap between the objectives of the law and its achievements. (This problem is not, of course, unique to landlord–tenant law, but is one of the general issues raised by the study of law.) A number of explanations may be suggested.

(i) THE IMBALANCE OF POLITICAL STRENGTH

One of the important lessons to be drawn from the data presented in the last section of this chapter is that, taken as a whole, tenants are relatively poor, or otherwise disadvantaged. Many are elderly; others are highly mobile. These factors may help to explain why tenants' organizations, especially in the private sector and housing association sector, have tended to be politically ineffective (Barnett, 1969, pp. 125–6; Partington, 1980b). A Federation of Private Residents Associations was founded in 1973, to represent 'all groupings of residents' and tenants' associations in the private housing sector'. It claims a number of successful legislative innovations, e.g. over control of service charges (see below, p. 327). But the thrust of this group's work has related more to the concerns of middle-class tenants of blocks of flats, particularly in London, than working-class tenants in the more vulnerable sectors of the market.

Amongst council tenants there is a longer tradition of tenants' organizations. The fact that most council tenants live on council estates has eased the problems of organization and communication, as compared with tenants in the private sector. A national group, the National Tenants' Organisation, has recently emerged attempting to coordinate and advance the views of council tenants in government circles. While tenants' organizations have on occasion been very active and effective in fighting particular issues (for details of particular campaigns see, e.g., the journal *Community Action*), their overall impact has also been somewhat limited (Corrigan & Ginsburg, 1975).

This is not to say that the tenants' case has been wholly unrepresented. Charitable pressure groups such as SHELTER, or the Campaign for the Homeless and Rootless, have been extremely active in putting forward the claims of tenants to government. But these groups have not generally been able to claim massive 'grassroot' support.

One important recent development which might have some impact in raising the collective consciousness and strength of council tenants' organizations is the establishment of Tenants' Charters. This idea has been discussed for a number of years (see, e.g., Ward, 1974; Richardson, 1977) and there have been experiments with Tenants' Charters in particular local authorities (Franey, 1979a). The Housing Act 1980 goes some way towards formalizing the concept by giving many council tenants security of tenure (Housing Act 1980, ss. 28–41; see below, pp. 510–31) and requiring local authorities to consult with their tenants about various aspects of housing management (*ibid.*, ss. 42–44; though consultation on rent levels is specifically excluded, s. 42(3)).

Sceptics have argued, however, that, far from encouraging genuine tenant participation, the concept will be used by local authorities as an additional method of controlling the lives of tenants. Certainly Franey argues (1979a) that the idea of a tenants' charter can only work with a considerable amount of effort and goodwill on the part of the local authorities involved.

By contrast, landlords are relatively well organized. Local auth-- ority landlords have developed powerful pressure groups, both at the political level (e.g. the Association of Municipal Authorities, the Association of District Councils) and at official level (e.g. the Institute of Housing Managers). Most housing associations belong to the National Federation of Housing Associations, an 'independent' body funded by the Department of the Environment. The Federation and its parent body, the Housing Corporation, obviously represent another powerful group. In the private sector, we have seen that there are still a number of substantial company landlords in business. The British Property Federation spends much of its time advancing the claims of these larger landlords (Ambrose & Colenutt, 1975). There is also the Small Landlords' Association, whose purpose is clear from its title, and around the country there are a number of local landlords' representative bodies. The working of these smaller pressure groups have not, as yet, been adequately researched.

The influence of these groupings on the development of particular policies, and any consequent legislation, is hard to assess. Despite their apparent weakness, a number of measures have been passed designed to protect the interests of tenants. In parliamentary terms, tenants' interests have been represented with some success. (For a use- ful, and rather broader, introduction to the political context of hous- ing policy see McKay & Cox, 1979, ch. 4.) Nonetheless, as has already been remarked, the laws that have been enacted have by no means always operated as intended. Does the apparent political imbalance between landlords and tenants help to explain this? Is it possible to assess the extent to which laws are effective as a means of controlling the economically or politically powerful?

(ii) JUDICIAL ATTITUDES

Another suggestion as to why laws in the landlord–tenant area do not appear to operate as intended is that this is due to judicial atti- tudes, which are said to be hostile to the aims of the legislation. Con- sider, in particular, the cases on the lease–licence distinction cited in chapter 3. (For a more general discussion see Griffith, 1978.) The diffi- culty with this line of argument is that although it may be possible to detect apparently hostile remarks in the pages of reported cases in landlord and tenant law, this does not necessarily *prove* that all judges – in particular those county court judges who deal with the bulk of cases in this area – share the same attitudes. Casual empiricism may suggest that this is the case; but the lower courts have not been adequately studied for the validity of the hypothesis to be sustained.

One remarkable case that is worth considering in this context is the House of Lords decision in *Johnson* v. *Moreton* [1978] 1 All E.R. 37 in which the issue under discussion was whether a landlord and an agricultural tenant could (by clause 27 of the lease) contract out of the statutory protections contained in the Agricultural Holdings Act 1948, s. 24. Consider the following remarks of Lord Salmon:

During the 1939–45 war, the submarine menace was such that it would have been virtually impossible to import into this country any more goods vital for our survival than we in fact did. Accordingly, it is extremely doubtful whether we could have survived had it not been for the food produced by our own farms. Even in 1947 when the Agriculture Act of that year was passed, food rationing was still in existence. It must have been clear to all that it was then and always would be of vital importance, both to the national economy and security, that the level of production and the efficiency of our farms should be maintained and improved. This could be achieved only by the skill and hard work of our farmers and the amount of their earnings which they were prepared to plough back into the land from which those earnings had been derived. A very large proportion of those farmers were tenant farmers. They were tenants because they did not have the necessary capital to buy land or could not find any land which they wanted that was for sale, or for sale at a price which they could afford. In spite of ss. 23 and 25 of the [Agriculture] 1923 Act which had put them in a somewhat better position than did the common law, the sword of Damocles was always hanging over their heads. If they were tenants for a term of years, they might receive an effective notice to quit on the date when the term expired, and this term was rarely for more and usually for less than ten years. If they were tenants from year to year, and very many of them were, they might in any year receive an effective notice to quit at the end of the next ensuing year. Accordingly there was no great inducement for these farmers to work as hard as they could, still less to plough money back into land which they knew they might well lose sooner or later.

The security of tenure which tenant farmers were accorded by the 1947 Act was not only for their own protection as an important section of the public, nor only for the protection of the weak against the strong; it was for the protection of the nation itself. This is why s. 31(1) of the 1947 Act, reproduced by s. 24(1) of the 1948 Act, gave tenant farmers the option to which I have referred and made any agreement to the contrary void. If any clause such as cl 27 was valid landlords might well insist on a similar clause being introduced into every lease; and prospective tenants, having no money with which to buy the land they wanted to farm, would, in reality, have had little choice but to agree. Accordingly, if cl 27 is enforceable the security of tenure which Parliament clearly intended to confer, and did confer on tenant farmers for the public good would have become a dead letter ...

Lord Hailsham said (in part):

It seems to me that the whole validity of the landlords' argument depends on his being able to establish, to borrow the words of Lord Westbury LC in *Hunt v Hunt* ((1862) 4 De GF & J 221 at 223), that the remedy and right conferred on the tenant by s 24(1) of the 1948 Act is '*nothing more* that a private remedy and a private right', or, to use the phrase of Lord Simon of Glaisdale quoted above, that the procedure prescribed by s 24(1) is one *entirely* in the favour of a particular tenant, without any element of public policy ... I myself am satisfied that this is not so on at least two separate but closely connected heads.

The first is the nature of farming itself. At least since the 1880s successive Parliaments have considered the fertility of the land and soil of England and the proper farming of it as something more than a private interest. Fertility is not something built up as the result of a mere six months' activity on the part of the cultivator, which was all the period of notice given by the common law to the individual farming tenant, by whom in the main the land of England was cultivated then, as now, mainly under a yearly tenancy. It takes years (sometimes generations) of patient and self-abnegating toil and investment to put heart into soil, to develop and gain the advantage of suitable rotations of crops, and to provide proper drains, hedges and ditches. Even to build up a herd of dairy cattle, between whose conception and first lactation at least three years must elapse, takes time and planning, whilst to disperse the work of a lifetime of careful breeding is but the task of an afternoon by a qualified auctioneer. Even within the space of a single year the interval between seed time and harvest, between expenditure and return, with all the divers dangers and chances of weather, pest or benignity of climate is sufficient to put an impecunious but honest cultivator at risk without adding to his problems any uncertainty as to his next year's tenure. At first Parliament was concerned simply with compensation for cultivation, manuring and improvement. But it never regarded these as matters simply for private contract, or something wholly unconnected with any public interest. From the first, Parliament was concerned with the management of the soil, the land of England which had grown gradually into its present fertility by the toil of centuries of husbandmen and estate owners. By the 1920s Parliament similarly concerned itself with the length of notice to which the yearly tenant was entitled. Such provisions are now to be found in ss 3 and 23 of the 1948 Act. But they date from this time. In 1947 a new and momentous step was taken. The landlord's notice to quit, save in certain specified instances', was at the option of the tenant to be subject to consent, at first of the Minister, but latterly of a quasi-judicial tribunal, the agricultural land tribunal, whose jurisdiction cl 27 of this lease seeks by its express terms to eliminate and oust. Even the consent of the agricultural land tribunal is carefully regulated by s 25 of the 1948 Act (consolidating and amending the 1947 provisions). The circumstances in which its consent may be accorded are thus defined and limited by objective and justiciable criteria. These are not simply matters of private contracts from which the landlord can stipulate that the tenant can deprive himself as if it were a 'jus pro se introductum'. It is a public interest introduced for the sake of the soil and husbandry of England of which both landlord and tenant are in a moral, though not of course a legal, sense the trustees for posterity. Silence is not an argument, particularly when the words are prima facie mandatory, for excusing a term in a contract introduced for the purpose of annulling the protection given to the tenant by s 24.

But there is another ground, closely related to the first, for disagreeing with the landlords' contention. It is not only the tenants of agricultural holdings that Parliament has increasingly sought to protect by statute from an improvident use of their contractual powers. The policy of the law has been repeatedly used to protect the weaker of two parties who do not contract from bargaining positions of equal strength. The protection given to minors by the courts is, of course, immemorial but has been reinforced by statute. The exigencies of war have provided a whole bundle of interferences with contractual obligations, and these have often developed into permanent features of peace-time legislation. The Rent Restriction Acts are an example. We were referred to the momentous decision of Astbury J, under the 1915 Act, in *Artizans, Labourers and General Dwellings Co Ltd v Whitaker* ([1919] 2 K.B. 301), subsequently embodied by Parliament in the 1920 Act.

There was also the line of cases beginning with *Salford Union of Guardians v Dewhurst* ([1926] A.C. 619) . . . which fortified the robust treatment by Farwell J of the war time emergency legislation of 1939 in *Soho Square Syndicate Ltd v E Pollard & Co Ltd*. Farwell J's reasoning was subsequently endorsed by the Court of Appeal in *Bowmaker Ltd v Tabor* ([1941] 2 K.B. 1) . . . The truth is that it can no longer be treated as axiomatic that, in the absence of explicit language, the courts will permit contracting out of the provisions of an Act of Parliament where that Act, though silent as to the possibility of contracting out, nevertheless is manifestly passed for the protection of a class of persons who do not negotiate from a position of equal strength, but in whose well-being there is a public as well as a private interest. Such acts are not necessarily to be treated as simply 'jus pro se introductum', a 'private remedy and a private right' which an individual member of the class may simply bargain away by reason of his freedom of contract. It is precisely his weakness as a negotiating party from which Parliament wishes to protect him ... I would not have it supposed that the examples I have given of the policy of recent Parliaments to limit freedom of contract in the interest of the weaker party to contracts of a particular class are limited to the examples I have given. Almost every session of Parliament provides fresh examples in the field, for instance, of consumer protection, or employer and employee. I have limited myself, however, to classes of legislation examples of which were cited in argument in the instant case. It is not for the courts to decide whether the policy underlying these statutes is always wise or productive of the results intended. The point is that, once the court has identified the point of such legislation, it should be cautious about permitting 'contracting out' ...

Lord Simon said (in part):

The landlords rely on the principle of law expressed in the maxim 'quilibet potest renunciare juri pro se introducto' ('anyone may, at his pleasure, renounce the benefit of a stipulation or other right introduced entirely in his own favour'). The right to serve a counter-notice was, the landlords argue, a statutory provision entirely in favour of the agricultural tenant (it is completely up to him whether or not he serves a counter-notice) and he can therefore contract not to do so. In argument this has been referred to as 'contracting out of the statute' ...

The maxim exemplifies Maine's famous observation that the movement of progressive societies had thitherto been a movement from status to contract, that is, from on the one hand societies where legal relationships between persons arise from their membership of classes to which the law ascribes peculiar rights and obligations, capacities and incapacities, to on the other hand societies where those relationships arise from private agreements between the parties which will be enforced by the law. It was natural for Maine, writing in the middle of the 19th century, to discern such a movement. The laissez-faire laissez-aller ideology was dominant. Human felicity, it was argued, was best promoted by leaving to every person to seek his own maximum advantage in competition with his fellows. A free market, including a free labour market, would ensure that the individual's effort was directed to anticipating and satisfying with maximum efficiency the wants of his fellows. The most powerful motive force in the universe, man's pursuit of his own interest, would thus be harnessed to drive a whole society forward. 'Man's selfishness is God's providence', they said.

The development of the law, as so often, reflected the dominant ideology. Freedom and sanctity of contract tended to be considered as pre-eminent legal values. It is unnecessary to expatiate after Dicey's classic study: it is sufficient to note, for example, equity's increasing reluctance to relieve against contractual forfeitures and Jessel MR's representative pronouncement in *Printing and Numerical Registering Co v Sampson* ((1875) L.R. 19 Eq. 462 at 465):

> '... if there is one thing which more than another public policy requires it is that men of full age and competent understanding shall have the utmost liberty of contracting, and that their contracts when entered into freely and voluntarily shall be held sacred and shall be enforced by courts of justice.'

But well within the lifetimes of Maine and Jessel MR the ideology which lay behind their juristic views was questioned. By some it was directly attacked: society's objective should be not wealth but welfare (with the implication that the pursuit and achievement of wealth were destructive of welfare), which was best promoted by the direct intervention of the organ of the state and could not be left to the bargain of the market-place. 'Competition' came to have the cliché 'cut-throat' attached to it. Others, more subtly, argued that, for the laissez-faire system to work felicitously as claimed, there must be a genuinely free, open and abundant market in which there is equality of bargaining power: equality of knowledge of the market and of staying-power in holding out for a bargain. This called for at least a limited intervention by the state to prevent or counteract rigging of the market by monopolies or oligopolies and to redress inequalities of bargaining power. And consonantly, even in the 19th century, the law began to back-pedal. The 'quilibet' maxim was held to be inapplicable to a matter in which the public had an interest.

There was one economic and social relationship where it was claimed that there were palpably lacking the prerequisites for the beneficent operation of laissez-faire, that of landlord and tenant. The market was limited and sluggish: the supply of land could not expand immediately and flexibly in response to demand, and even humble dwellings took more time to erect than those in want of them could spare. Generally, a man became a tenant rather than an owner-occupier because his circumstances compelled him to live hand-to-mouth; the landlord's purse was generally longer and his command of knowledge and counsel far greater than the tenant's. In short, it was held, the constriction of the market and the inequality of bargaining-power enabled the landlord to dictate contractual terms which did not necessarily operate to the general benefit of society. It was to counteract this descried constriction of the market and to redress this descried inequality of bargaining-power that the law, specifically, in the shape of legislation, came to intervene repeatedly to modify freedom of contract between landlord and tenant. Since Maine the movement of many 'progressive' societies has been reversed. The holding of a statutory or a protected tenancy is rather a status than a pure creature of contract. The Agricultural Holdings Act 1948 exemplifies such legislative activity specifically where the tenancy is of agricultural land.

The movement from status to contract was largely a creature of the common law. The reverse movement has been largely a creature of legislation. As a result lawyers sometimes tend to regard freedom and sanctity of contract as still of special and supervening juristic value. But freedom of contract and its consequences are quite likely to be 'mischiefs' as that word is used in statutory construction. Courts of law do not nowadays hold themselves out to judge public policy in the light of ideologies. But since statutory construction almost always calls for consideration of the statutory objective, it is incumbent to hold in mind the palpable objective of s 24(1), namely, to vouchsafe to the good tenant-husbandman a security of tenure which went beyond the lease he had bargained for ...

The principle which, in my view, emerges from this line of authority is as follows. Where it appears that the mischief which Parliament is seeking to remedy is that a situation exists in which the relations of parties cannot properly be left to private contractual regulation, and Parliament therefore provides for statutory regulation, a party cannot contract out of such statutory regulation (albeit exclusively in his own favour), because so to permit would be to reinstate the mischief which the statute was designed to remedy and to render the statutory provision a dead letter.

I think that this principle applies to s 24(1) of the 1948 Act.

Comment

Do you regard these as statements of principle that should be clearly applied to the residential landlord–tenant relationship as well? Or are they mere expressions of liberal sentiments that should not be applied more widely? To what extent are the kinds of consideration that appear to have influenced their lordships here, applied in other cases discussed in this book? In particular, do you regard these statements as relevant to the discussion of the various devices that have emerged as attempted methods to evade the Rent Acts? (See chapters 3 and 4.)

One suggestion that has been made is that housing law would be more sensitively applied if there were to be created a specialist housing court or housing tribunal. A number of groups made this suggestion to the, now apparently defunct, Department of the Environment's *Review of the Rent Acts*. (See, e.g., LAG, 1977; SHAC, 1977; Law Centre's Working Group, 1977.) Would specialist judges be more likely to understand the underlying social issues in landlord–tenant cases? Would such a reform inevitably result in a closing of the gap between the law in the books and the law in practice?

(iii) LACK OF LEGAL AND OTHER ADVISORY SERVICES

Another reason for the failure of the law to meet its apparent objectives is the fact that there are insufficient lawyers prepared to under-stand the relevant legislation and to take on cases in this area. Two particular points may be noted. First, in so far as empirical evidence is available, it does seem that solicitors in private practice do not do much work in the landlord–tenant area (Royal Commission on Legal Services, 1979, *Users' Survey*, 1979, Table 8.14). Yet in those areas where neighbourhood law centres have been established, landlord–tenant issues have tended to dominate their case-loads (e.g. Byles & Morris, 1977, p. 33). These two points, taken together, suggest that there is extensive unmet need for additional legal services on such issues. It is therefore suggested that, were such services available, the apparent 'gap' between the letter of the law and its use would be nar-rowed. An extension of this argument suggests that if housing advice services were more generally available this could result in more effec-tive use of the legislation (Harloe, 1976; Mylan, 1979). But what general inpact would massive increases in such services have? How far is it likely that there will ever be adequate services to advise all those potentially affected by landlord–tenant law?

(iv) COMPLEXITY OF THE LAW

Whatever facilities for assisting with the use of law may be created, a further argument as to why the law has failed to achieve its apparent objectives is that it is far too complex for the layman to comprehend. The complexity of the law will, no doubt, be conceded by anyone who has studied the contents of this book. However, although calls to simplify the law are frequently made, it must be asked to what extent this is a realistic possibility. Is not the law attempting to balance a complex and varied range of interests? If that is so, is it not inevitable that the *legal* provisions required to achieve this political objective will be complicated?

This is not to say, however, that the language used could not be made more straightforward (see below, p. 38). One theme touched on in a number of places in this book is the impact of policies designed to get information over to tenants (e.g. pp. 58–64, 272–3).

B Limits of the law

Whatever response is made to the issues raised above, the inherent limits of the law must also be appreciated.

First, however much protective legislation may exist, this cannot guarantee that private landlords in particular will wish to continue renting accommodation. It is frequently asserted that the decline in the availability of privately rented accommodation is exclusively attributable to the passing of the Rent Acts. This crude hypothesis is simply not sustainable; the decline in the size of the private rented sector appears to have begun even before the first Rent Act was passed in 1915, and many other factors have encouraged the shift to owner-occupation (availability of mortgage finance, tax concessions, better rates of return on investments than housing and so on) (*Housing Policy* (3), 1977, pp. 62–8). (In some respects, what is surprising is that there are still private landlords left at all (Eversley, 1975; Finnis, 1977).) However, it cannot be denied that the enactment of protective legislation has contributed to the decline of this sector of the market. So another limitation on the function of landlord–tenant law is that landlords may vote with their feet and abandon this form of enterprise. (Significantly, perhaps, the widely held assumption that owner-occupation is now always the best buy has begun to come under some critical scrutiny: see, e.g., Whitehead, 1979b; Karn, 1979; Harrison & Lomas, 1980. The implications of this debate are beyond the scope of this book, but may suggest that a change in attitudes to renting will develop in the next few years.)

Second, and even more important to stress, whether there are enough houses of adequate standard, at a price people can afford, is essentially the result of political and economic decisions relating to the distribution of resources in society. The law may assist in very many cases to prevent tenants being arbitrarily evicted, or to improve housing conditions, but whatever functions the law may have in regulating the landlord–tenant relationship and providing forums for the settlement of disputes, these crucial questions relating to the availability of accommodation must not be regarded as exclusively legal issues (CDP, 1977; Abel, 1973, pp. 184–9).

2

An Outline of the Law of Landlord and Tenant

Introduction

The starting point for any discussion of the law of landlord–tenant in Britain must be traditional common law and equitable principles relating to landlord and tenant. Thus, after a look at the vocabulary of this area of law, this chapter provides a basic account of these principles.

1. Legal language and professional power: the problem of mystification

Lawyers, like other professional groups, have developed an extensive vocabulary of technical terms to describe the concepts they employ. Such vocabulary consists partly of words or phrases (e.g. fee simple) which are obviously incomprehensible without further explanation; partly of words or phrases (e.g. year, term of years) which look straightforward but are in fact used in a specialist sense, often quite different from ordinary use. Again there may be concepts which at one time could be understood literally, but because of changes in the law have become positively misleading; the most notorious example in landlord–tenant law is 'notice to quit' which, because of statutory changes, does not usually mean that tenants have to leave. (See below, pp. 412–13.) Finally there is the more general issue, but one that is of great importance in the context of landlord–tenant law, of the complexity of language to be found in our statute law which results from the conventional rules under which such law is drafted; whether or not they should be altered is not a question to be discussed here, but is one that should be considered by any student of law (see Twining & Miers, 1976, chapter 10).[1]

Views on the complexity of legal language are mixed. Some say it is a necessary evil – something that ought to be done away with but which cannot be accomplished in practice. Alternatively, legal language is said to have some positive virtues in that it provides a sensible way of facilitating, by use of a kind of linguistic shorthand, discussion of complex concepts. A third view is that the development of a specialist language is a sinister means to enable professional people to exert power and control over those who do not understand the language, and, more practically, to justify their charging high fees for engaging in the process of interpretation. (See, e.g., Johnson, 1972, esp. ch. 3; Abel, 1979.) What is your view?

Whatever one thinks of these arguments, one consequence of the complexity of legal language is to make law inaccessible and mysterious to lay people. Since the student, at least at the outset of his studies, is more lay person than lawyer, the following section attempts to make the basic vocabulary used in landlord–tenant law more accessible and less mysterious. This is an essential prerequisite to any understanding of the literature in the area.

2. Basic vocabulary

A The 'term of years'

Section 1(1) of the Law of Property Act 1925 provides that only two 'estates in land' are capable of subsisting or of being conveyed or created 'at law'. One of these is the 'term of years'.

The doctrine of the 'estate in land', deriving from the Latin *status*, has been used from feudal days to refer to the time period during which a person's rights to land were to last. The phrase 'term of years' appears self-explanatory. However the Law of Property Act 1925, s. 205(1)(xxvii) defines it in a far from obvious way to include 'a term for less than a year, or for a year or years and a portion of a year or from year to years'.[2] Thus, all kinds of arrangement, from weekly tenancies to 999-year leases, fall within the definition.

---

1. The increasing use of computers may have some role to play in the tidying up of legal language (Tapper, 1974).

2. This definition will not automatically apply when the phrase 'term of years' is used in other statutes: *Re Land and Premises at Liss, Hants.* [1971] Ch. 986.

B Lease : tenancy : demise

Under conventional usage, a tenancy usually refers to relatively short-term landlord–tenant relationships; lease to more formal, longer-term relationships. They are not, however, terms of art, and there are no hard and fast rules. 'Demise' is another more technical word, frequently appearing in conveyancing documents, which also means lease.

C Landlord : Tenant

The person who grants a lease is the landlord/lessor; the person to whom it is granted is the lessee/tenant.

D Reversion

When a lease/tenancy is created, the landlord will always retain a reversion. This constitutes that part of the lessor's interest in the land which he has not disposed of when granting the tenancy. Thus, when the tenancy ends, the land reverts to the grantor. (This principle is now subject to considerable statutory amendments, see below, chapter 8.)

E Assignment

It is possible both for the landlord to assign his reversion and for the tenant to assign his lease. The effect of this is that a new landlord or a new tenant steps into the shoes of the original landlord or tenant. Frequently the tenant's right to assign is restricted or even excluded by a covenant against assignment (see below, pp. 80–90).

F Sub-letting

Instead of assigning, the tenant may create a sub-lease (or under-lease), whereby a new letting, for a shorter period than that held by the original tenant, is created. The original tenancy is sometimes called the 'mesne' tenancy. Again, the power to sub-let is commonly curtailed (see below, pp. 80–90).

Illustration (from Megarry & Wade (1975, pp. 616–17))

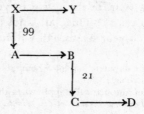

This diagram is the usual way of representing the following events. X grants a 99-years lease to A and then assigns the reversion to Y. B takes an assignment of A's lease and grants a sub-lease to C for 21 years, and C assigns his sub-lease to D. As to the 99-years lease, X is the 'lessor,' Y is the 'assignee of the reversion' or 'landlord,' and A the 'lessee.' B is in a dual position: as to the 99-years lease, he is the 'assignee' or 'tenant'; as to the 21-years lease, he is 'sub-lessor' or 'landlord.' The 99-years lease is then called the 'head lease,' so as to distinguish it from the sub-lease. C is the 'sub-lessee,' and D the 'assignee' of the sub-lease, or the 'sub-tenant.' By annexing the dates of each transaction to each link in the diagram the sequence of events may be shown.

It will be appreciated that it is possible for very extensive chains of leases to be created. 'In parts of Lancashire in particular there are tiers of leases comprising one or more houses. At one and the same time there may exist leases for 999 years, for 999 years less 10 days, for 990 years, for 990 years less 10 days, for 99 years, for 99 years less 10 days and so on until eventually at the bottom of the ladder there is an actual tenant in occupation' (*Royal Commission on Legal Services*, 1979, p. 283, para. 4). They recommended compulsory enfranchisement by statute of all the leases except the actual occupation tenancy.

G Leasehold covenants

Covenants in the lease are promises made by the parties to the lease. Covenants commonly found in a lease are those to pay rent, or to repair. Covenants may be *express* – specifically written into a formal document – or *implied* by the courts. The most important example of the latter kind is the landlord's covenant for quiet enjoyment (see below, pp. 452–5) which will be implied if not specifically mentioned in the lease.

H Privity of contract : privity of estate

As between the original parties to a lease, all covenants are enforceable under normal contractual principles based on privity of contract.

However, where one party to a lease has *assigned* (but not sub-let) his interest, covenants may be directly enforceable by or against the assignee because of the principle of privity of estate. Only covenants that 'touch and concern' the land are so enforceable.

Examples (from Megarry and Wade (1975, pp. 725–7, footnotes omitted))

Covenants by a lessee

Touching and concerning	*Not touching and concerning*
To pay rent.	To pay an annual sum to a third person.
To repair the property or fixtures on it.	To pay rates in respect of other land.
To pay £40 towards redecoration on quitting.	Not to employ persons living in other parishes to work in the demised mill (the landlord's motive being to benefit his other property in the parish).
To insure against fire.	
To use as a private dwelling-house only.	
Not to assign the lease without the landlord's consent.	To repair and renew the tools of a smithy standing on the land (the tools were movable chattels, not fixtures).
Not to let X be concerned in the conduct of the business carried on upon the premises.	
To buy beer for a public-house or petrol for a filling station only from the lessor.	

Covenants by a lessor

Touching and concerning	*Not touching and concerning*
To renew the lease (the inclusion of this is somewhat anomalous).	To sell the reversion at a stated price, at the tenant's option.
To supply the demised premises with water.	To pay at the end of the lease for chattels not amounting to fixtures.
Not to build on a certain part of the adjoining land.	To pay the tenant £500 at the end of the lease unless a new lease is granted.
Not to determine a periodic (quarterly) tenancy during its first three years.	To keep in repair a large number of houses in the district.
	To allow the tenant to display advertising signs on other premises.

I Protected tenancy : statutory tenancy : regulated tenancy

A protected tenancy is one subject to full Rent Act protection. No simple definition is possible (see the discussion in chapters 3 and 4 below).

A statutory tenancy arises on the termination of a protected tenancy (see below, p. 207).

Regulated tenancy is defined by Rent Act 1977, s. 18 (as amended by Housing Act 1980):

18. (1) Subject to sections 24(3) and 143³ of this Act, a 'regulated tenancy' is, for the purposes of this Act, a protected or statutory tenancy.

(2) Where a regulated tenancy is followed by a statutory tenancy of the same dwelling-house, the two shall be treated for the purposes of this Act as together constituting one regulated tenancy.

3. Essential prerequisites for creation of lease

A Two parties

Since one of the features of the leasehold interest is that, except where statute law operates, it is founded on a contract, there must be two parties to such contract. A lease cannot be made with oneself (*Rye* v. *Rye* [1962] A.C. 496).

B 'Land'

The subject matter of a lease must be 'land', a term widely defined by Law of Property Act 1925, s. 205(1)(ix). It includes minerals and other strata under the surface, buildings erected upon the surface, technically called 'corporeal hereditaments', and 'incorporeal hereditaments', such as easements, *profits à prendre* (which include sporting rights) and franchises (such as fairs or markets).

C Reversion

A lease must always be granted out of a larger estate; there must always be a reversion. If there are no interests to revert to a landlord at any stage, the legal result is that there has been an assignment of that lease.

D Certain term

It is an old principle that the term for which the lease is made must be certain. This easily applies where the term of the lease is defined in the agreement. One problem arose during World War II, where

---

3. Section 24(3) is discussed below, p. 159; s. 143 refers to the power contained in the Rent Act given to the Secretary of State to release areas of the country from Rent Regulation where he is satisfied there is no scarcity of accommodation. This power has not yet been exercised.

a lease 'for the duration of the war' was held to be invalid since the term was uncertain in length (*Lace* v. *Chantler* [1944] K.B. 368). As a result, Parliament hurriedly passed the Validation of War-Time Leases Act 1944, which converted such tenancies into ones for a fixed period of ten years, determinable after the end of the war, usually on one month's notice.

This principle obviously is harder to apply in the case of periodic tenancies. Simpson (1961, pp. 235–7, notes omitted) has shown how, with some hesitation, the judges adapted the principle to cope with such tenancies:

In Littleton's time it was clearly settled that a fixed duration was essential to a lease. A person who was let into possession of land by the freeholder but who was not granted any certain term was ranked as a tenant at will, and a tenancy at will could be determined at any time. Tenants at will were given some degree of protection by the law relating to emblements; if ejected after they had sown a crop they had a liberty to enter and reap what they had sown. Otherwise they had a wholly precarious interest, and this made tenancies at will extremely unsatisfactory. Now in the developed law the periodic tenancy is recognized as a form of lease; the typical example is the yearly tenancy, which will continue until it is determined by six months' notice on either side, and such tenancies are extremely common. Such periodic or 'running' leases obviously pose a problem in legal analysis which is glossed over in modern textbooks, for in a sense they do not conform to the rule which requires a lease to be for a fixed term – they are in effect leases for an uncertain duration, determinable by notice. They are not leases for a fixed term with an option to renew; such an analysis is quite unrealistic. In short they are anomalous, and when they first came before the courts at the end of the fifteenth and the beginning of the sixteenth centuries they provoked a great deal of controversy. In 1506 a lease for one year, and then from year to year as the parties pleased, at a fixed rent, was held to be a lease at will only. A case in 1523 on the same type of lease provoked a long discussion in the Common Pleas, and the judges were divided. Upon grounds of convenience, for such arrangements were common, Brudenell CJ and Pollard J. were prepared to hold that by such an arrangement a lease for one year was created at once, followed by successive one-year terms for each year in which the arrangement was continued; if the tenant, with the consent of the landlord, continued in possession for one day of a new year, then a fixed term for the whole of that year was created. Fitzherbert and Brooke JJ. were not so sympathetic. Such an arrangement, in their view, created a lease for one year and no more; thereafter the tenant who remained in possession became a tenant at will only. If the arrangement was expressed as a lease for *years* 'at the will of the parties', or 'for as long as the parties pleased', then they would treat it as a lease for a fixed term of two years (to give effect to the plural 'years') followed by a tenancy at will. For two centuries thereafter the dispute as to the nature of periodic tenancies continued its arid course. In 1601 Gawdy and Fenner JJ. adopted the view of Brudenell CJ and Pollard J. Popham CJ introduced another quaint construction, for he held that a lease 'from year to year as the parties pleased' created a term of two years (from year to year = two years) followed by a tenancy at will. Popham's view was adopted in 1606, where the court was confronted with a lease 'for a period of one year and so from year to year for as long as both parties should please'; three years are mentioned, and these are added up to confer a term of three years followed by a tenancy at will. This sort of absurd construction would lead one to say that a lease from 'year to year to year to year' would create a term of four years; neither common-sense nor logic recommends it. Eventually the view of Brudenell and Pollard triumphed when the great Holt CJ adopted it in 1702, and in the course of the eighteenth century the dispute died out. This paved the way for a new and important development. In the absence of an express arrangement for a periodic tenancy the courts were ready to imply one instead of a mere tenancy at will, so long as this could be justified, as it could be if rent had been paid and accepted by the year. Thus Blackstone says:

'The law is however careful, that no sudden determination of the will by one party shall tend to the manifest and unforeseen prejudice of the other ... courts of law have of late years leaned as much as possible against construing demises, where no certain term is mentioned, to be tenancies at will; but have rather held them to be tenancies from year to year so long as the parties so please, especially where an annual rent is reserved; in which case they will not suffer either party to determine the tenancy even at the end of the year, without reasonable notice to the other, which is generally understood to be six months.'

The position now reached, somewhat pragmatically, is that these tenancies fall within the law of leases since the term, though originally indeterminate, is determinable by either party (Woodfall, 1978, para. 1-0508). In two recent cases the question has arisen of how arrangements, determinable by one side only, are to be decided.

Re Midland Railway Company's Agreement [1971] Ch. 725 (C.A.)

RUSSELL LJ: This is an appeal from a decision of Foster J, in which he held that a notice given by the British Railways Board ('the board') purporting to determine a tenancy granted in December 1920 by its predecessor the Midland Ry Co. was ineffective, because the terms of the tenancy contained a proviso that the tenancy should not be terminated by the landlord company 'until they shall require the said premises for the purposes of their undertaking', a proviso which the judge held was binding and effective. The board admittedly do not so require the premises; they want a more realistic rent than the £1 per annum negotiated in 1920... Clause 2 was as follows:

'This agreement may be determined by either party on giving to the other three months' notice such notice to be in writing and to expire at any time hereafter without reference to the commencement of the Tenancy. The Tenants shall have no claim upon the Company for any damage or loss that he may sustain by giving up the said Premises pursuant to such Notice (except the reasonable value of any growing crops which may be then unfit to get) and shall pay a proportionate part of the said rent for the fraction of the current half year up to the day of the expiration of such notice. Provided that this Agreement shall not be so terminated by the Company until they shall require the said premises for the purposes of their undertaking.'

The board contends that the proviso to cl. 2 conflicted with a general principle that for a tenancy to be valid there must be a certainty as to the maximum duration of the estate. Consequently (it was argued) the only tenancy that existed was one which arose from the facts of the entry into possession and payment and receipt of rent; such tenancy was a half yearly tenancy which included a right in the landlord to give three months' notice expiring at any time, the terms of cl. 2 being inferred as part of the tenancy but shorn of the proviso; alternatively that if such tenancy did not incorporate the provisions of cl. 2, it was terminable by a half year's notice expiring on a half yearly date. If that alternative was correct it was accepted that the notice actually given was ineffective; but a new and valid notice could be given by the board. For the board it was alternatively contended that this was a creation of a periodic half yearly tenancy; that the proviso was wholly repugnant to the nature of such a tenancy and must therefore be rejected, leaving the periodic tenancy subject only to the variation of the ordinary common law rules as to determination found in the rest of cl. 2, i.e. a three months' notice expiring on any date.

... It has been quite clearly and for long established that if a term of years is to be validly created the maximum duration must be ascertained before the term takes effect. A purported lease 'for the duration of the war' is no lease (see *Lace* v. *Chantler*) because there is no present knowledge how many years will elapse while that undesirable situation continues. It is too late to enquire why this aspect of the particular estate was considered essential to its existence or to question the doctrine. A lease for life was outside the requirement, probably because this was recognized as an estate of freehold. Moreover, if it was desired to achieve a result in substance the same as a lease until an event the date of whose occurrence could not be forecast, this could be done by the grant of a lease for (say) 90 years determinable on the

event. We mention this only to show that the subject-matter under consideration has an air of artificiality, of remoteness from practical considerations; and
in such circumstances we think the court should be unwilling to be moved
by some process of logic to travel further than authority compels in the direction of holding that what parties to a transaction in plain English agreed
is something impossible in law and therefore void. In *Lace* v. *Chantler* the landlord sought possession of a dwelling house. The county court judge ordered
possession on grounds not presently material. The defendant tenant in terms
pleaded that 'The said dwellinghouse was let to the defendant for the duration
of the war'. The defendant appealed. This court obviously took the point
... that the letting pleaded did not create a leasehold interest at all, since
the maximum duration of the estate was quite uncertain when it purported
to take effect. Now it appears to us that the decision is confined to a case
in which that which was purported to be done was simply to create a leasehold
interest for a single and uncertain period. The applicability of this matter
of certainty to a periodic tenancy was not under consideration. If the case
of *Lace* v. *Chantler* had been one in which there was simply a periodic tenancy
with a proviso that the landlord would not give notice during the continuance
of the war, this court might not have concluded that such an agreement,
which would of course have left the tenant free to determine on notice at
any time, was inoperative to create a leasehold. There is nothing in the reasoning of the judgments to lead to the necessary conclusion that such must have
been so.

If one has an ordinary case of a periodic tenancy (e.g. a yearly tenancy),
it is plain that in one sense at least it is uncertain at the outset what will
be the maximum duration of the term created, which term grows year by
year as a single term springing from the original grant. It cannot be predicated
that in no circumstances will it exceed, for example, 50 years; there is no
previously ascertained maximum duration for the term; its duration will depend on the time that will elapse before either party gives notice of determination. The simple statement of the law that the maximum duration of a term
must be certainly known in advance of its taking effect cannot therefore have
direct reference to periodic tenancies. The question therefore is whether authority or principle should lead us to mould or enlarge that simple statement
of the law so as to adapt and apply it to such a tenancy. It is argued that
the principle of avoidance through uncertainty is only not applicable to an
ordinary periodic tenancy because of the ability of either party at any time
to define the maximum by giving notice of determination. This, it is suggested,
provides the necessary degree of certainty; because of this power neither party
is left in a state of unknowing what is his maximum commitment to the other.
But where (it is said) one or other party is, by the terms of the document,
deprived of that power until a future event or the fulfilment of a condition
the date of whose occurrence (if at all) is uncertain, that person is in such
a state of unknowing. Therefore it is said the term should be held void; and

reference is made to the statement in Hill and Redman, *Law of Landlord and Tenant* which suggests that an ordinary periodic tenancy does not conflict with the ancient doctrine, because although the maximum duration of the term be originally indefinite, it can be made subject to a definite limit by either party giving notice to determine.

In the course of the argument we found this approach logically attractive. Here is one term growing period by period and there is no knowing (on one side) its maximum length, if (on that side) there is no power to determine save in an event whose occurrence is in point of time uncertain. Why logically should that differ from a lease directly for a term of which the maximum duration is uncertain? But in the end we are persuaded that, there being no authority to prevent us, it is preferable as a matter of justice to hold parties to their clearly expressed bargain rather than to introduce for the first time in 1971 an extension of a doctrine of land law so as to deny the efficacy of that bargain. We were referred to a number of decided cases, but in none of them was it held that a curb on the power to determine a periodic tenancy infringed the principle that an estate of leasehold to be effective must be certain in its maximum duration; rather they were cases in which the question in debate was whether the curb was repugnant to the nature of a periodic tenancy.

Accordingly we hold that in the present case the proviso in cl. 2 is not such as to negative the tenancy on the ground of uncertainty of duration. Moreover, we do this on the broad ground, and not on the narrow ground that the particular proviso leaves it open to the landlord by adjustment of the requirements of its undertaking to assume the power to determine the leasehold interest. . . .

There remains the question whether the proviso must in law be rejected as repugnant to the nature of the estate created – a half-yearly periodic tenancy. Our instinct, as previously indicated, is to give effect if possible to the bargain made by the parties. It may well be that if in a periodic tenancy an attempt was made to prevent the lessor ever determining the tenancy, that would be so inconsistent with the stated bargain that either a greater estate must be found to have been constituted or the attempt must be rejected as repugnant. But short of that we see no reason why an express curb on the power to determine which the common law would confer upon the lessor should be rejected as repugnant to the nature of the leasehold interest granted. In *Breams Property Investment Co. Ltd.* v. *Stroulger* [1948] 2 K.B. 1 a curb on the lessors for three years unless they required the premises for their own use was upheld in this court, notwithstanding the earlier cases of *Doe d. Warner* v. *Browne* (1807) 8 East 165 and *Cheshire Lines Committee* v. *Lewis & Co.* (1880) 50 L.J.Q.B. 121. It follows that in a periodic tenancy a similar curb for 10, 20 or 50 years should not be rejected as repugnant to the concept of a periodic tenancy: and once the argument based on uncertainty is rejected we see no distinction in the present case. Accordingly in our judgment this appeal should be dismissed. We say nothing as to the situation which might arise in law should the defendants sell the reversion to another, when it might be arguable that the proviso would be no longer relevant.

Centaploy v. *Matlodge* [1974] Ch. 1 (Ch. D.)

This case involved deciding whether leases of two garages were valid or not. The facts were not clear, but it was held that there was an oral agreement that only the plaintiffs (lessees) could determine the arrangement. There were also two memoranda (P.1 and P.2) which were in the following terms: 'Ground floor garage. Received from Centaploy Ltd. the sum of £12 being one week's rent on 39/41 Ashburn Mews, S.W.7, and to continue until determined by the lessee . . .' and 'Received from Redshire Ltd. [predecessor in title to Centaploy] the sum of £1 15s od being one week's rent on 25 Ashburn Mews, S.W.7, the tenancy to continue thus on the same terms until determined by the lessee'.

Whitford J. said (in part):

The next point taken by the defendants is of more substance. They say that if there is a lease it is void because it lacks certainty. The defendants accept that a normal weekly tenancy was granted, but submit that P.1 and P.2 do not, in terms, refer to a weekly tenancy at all. While the words 'weekly tenancy' do not appear in either case, in both these documents there are references to 'one week's rent' and the words 'and to continue' are also to be found. The defendants say it is impossible to infer that there is a weekly tenancy under P.1 and P.2 because the provision for determination is inconsistent with such a periodic tenancy.

I was referred to *Gladstone* v. *Bower* [1960] 1 Q.B. 170 where a question arose as to whether a particular agreement took effect as an agreement for the letting of a farm on a tenancy from year to year. Diplock J. said, at p. 178:

'A tenancy from year to year at common law is an interest which does possess certain invariable characteristics without which it is not a tenancy from year to year and which constitute a standard by which the magnitude of other interests may be judged; it must last for one year and, unless determined at the end of the first year by notice (either six months' notice or whatever other length of notice, if any, is expressly provided for in the contract of tenancy), will be renewed by operation of law for successive periods of one year each, until determined at the end of one such yearly period by such a notice.'

It seems to me that on their true construction the documents in question provide for a tenancy from week to week unless determined, but the judgment of Diplock J. to which I have referred makes it clear that there may be some variation in the terms on which a periodic tenancy may be determined without it ceasing to be a periodic tenancy. It cannot, in my view, be said that the term is uncertain on the basis of the finding of Lord Greene M.R. in *Lace* v. *Chantler* [1944] K.B. 368, the next case to which the defendants referred. In that case the premises were let 'for the duration of the war,' so that when the agreement took effect there was a lease for a single term the duration of which was wholly uncertain. No doubt in one sense it can be said that there is an artificiality in referring to certainty of term even, for example, in the case of what counsel for the defendants was prepared to describe as an ordinary weekly tenancy, a weekly tenancy at, for example, £12 a week with nothing said about determination. At the moment when the first £12 is paid over, unless one of the parties there and then gives notice to determine, the tenancy is going to run for two weeks, for if nothing is said the rule is that determination shall be on one week's notice on either side. Thereafter, if nothing is said on either side, the tenancy may run on for a wholly indefinite period, but it stands accepted that this fact does not lead to the result that the tenancy is void for uncertainty. The Court of Appeal has held in *In re Midland Railway Co.'s Agreement* [1971] Ch. 725 that the simple statement of the law that if a term is to be validly created the maximum duration of that term must be ascertained before the term takes effect, cannot have direct application to periodic tenancies. It is, apparently, enough if you know when it could be brought to an end even if you do not know exactly when it will be brought to an end.

The law is evolutionary. In the evolution of life it is common enough to find that forms which were at one time successful have died out completely or changed radically. The defendants accept that a fetter can be placed on the right to determine a periodic tenancy for a certain period. They also accept, in this court, though they expressly reserve the point for a higher court, that, on the authority of *In re Midland Railway Co.'s Agreement*, it must be accepted here such a fetter can be placed upon the right to determine for an uncertain period. The defendants base themselves further on a decision given by the Court of King's Bench in *Doe d. Warner* v. *Browne* (1807) 8 East 165, where it was decided that it was repugnant to the nature of a tenancy from year to year that the right to determine should rest solely with the tenant, a decision approved by the Court of Appeal in *Cheshire Lines Committee* v. *Lewis & Co.* (1880) 50 L.J.Q.B. 121.

Uncertainty and repugnancy were the defendants' main ground of attack assuming agreements in other respects unimpeachable ... In fact both the plaintiffs and the defendants relied upon the judgment of the Court of Appeal in *In re Midland Railway Co.'s Agreement* ...

Whitford J. reviewed that case, and went on:

In the present case the position on uncertainty is somewhat different. Here we have a period growing week by week and there is never going to be any possibility of knowing, on the landlord's side, its maximum length, for there is never going to be a right in the landlords to determine.

In *In re Midland Railway Co.'s Agreement*, counsel for the defendants submitted that a periodic tenancy is only an exception to the uncertainty rule, because if both sides are going to be able to determine there is no relevant uncertainty: see [1971] Ch. 725, 730. In the present case a stronger case can be made out on the defendants' side than was made out in *In re Midland Railway Co.'s Agreement*. It can be urged that as the landlord cannot ever be certain when the agreement is going to be brought to an end there must be a relevant uncertainty. As I understand the judgment in the Court of Appeal, what has been held in relation to the issue of uncertainty is that it is better to enforce a clearly expressed bargain than to attempt to introduce yet further refinements into a field where the lines have perhaps already been rather overfinely drawn. On this basis I have reached the conclusion, having regard to what was said in the Court of Appeal in *In re Midland Railway Co.'s Agreement*, that I must reject the defendants' argument on the basis of uncertainty which, but for *In re Midland Railway Co.'s Agreement*, I would have been prepared to accept...

On the repugnancy point, Whitford J. said:

In *In re Midland Railway Co.'s Agreement* the point which I have to consider – the ghost of the past – was expressly left unlaid. Here we have a case where the tenant is saying that on the bargain struck the landlord cannot ever determine the tenancy.

Now counsel for the plaintiffs was able to say, and to say quite rightly, that great inroads have been made on the application of this idea of repugnancy since 1807, as the passage I have just read shows, and there is no need for me to go into the cases between *Doe d. Warner* v. *Browne* and *In re Midland Railway Co.'s Agreement*, for it is now plain that a fetter for a period, even a period of uncertain duration, cannot necessarily be considered as repugnant to the grant of a periodic tenancy. It nevertheless appears to me that it must be basic to a tenancy that at some stage the person granting the tenancy shall have the right to determine and a tenancy in which the landlord is never going to have the right to determine at all is, as I see, it, a complete contradiction in terms. Unless, therefore, some greater estate than a weekly tenancy was created by the agreements, the determination provisions must, in my view, be regarded as repugnant and on this aspect the defendants are entitled to succeed...

The result was that the argument that the tenancy was wholly void failed; even though the determination provisions were struck down, the plaintiffs were protected as business tenants under the Landlord and Tenant Act 1954, Part II (see below, pp. 441–4).

Comment

What do you learn from Russell L.J.'s judgment about the judicial approach to the question of certainty? Is the doctrine of repugnancy a ghost of the past that really should be laid to rest?

E Exclusive possession must be granted

Finally, for a lease to be created the right to exclusive possession of the premises must be given to the tenant. Because a lease is an estate in land, i.e. a property right that should be enforceable against the whole world including the landlord, the tenant must be given the right to exclude all other persons from the premises during the period of the lease.

This principle has become the source of considerable litigation in recent years, because much of the legislation passed by Parliament to protect tenants, whether residential or business tenants, only operates when property has been 'let'. The courts have interpreted this to mean that such legislation only applies to arrangements that can be characterized according to common law principles as tenancies (*Barton* v. *Fincham* [1921] 2 K.B. 291 (C.A.)), and not to other arrangements based on the fact of occupation which will be classified as *licences*. Since this is a difficult and controversial conceptual issue, it merits a separate chapter (see below, chapter 3).

4. The classification of tenancies

Reflecting the broad definition of the phrase 'term of years', the law recognizes a great range of tenancies and gives different names to the different types. A fundamental distinction is that between a 'specific' or 'fixed term' tenancy, which lasts for a fixed period; and a 'periodic' tenancy, which lasts until brought to an end by one of the parties.

A Fixed-term tenancies : different types

(i) *'Tenancy for a term of years'*. This is self-explanatory.

(ii) *'Tenancy determinable with life'*. At common law it was possible to create a tenancy for the period of one's life or, indeed, *pur autre vie*,

during the lifetime of another. This used to be a legal estate. Section
1(1) of the Law of Property Act 1925, however, has changed this rule.
By s. 149(6) of the Act, such a lease is usually converted into one for
a fixed period of 90 years, determinable after the death by at least
one month's notice in writing, if the lease is granted at a rent.[4]

(iii) *'Reversionary lease'*. It is now possible to create a lease that takes
effect at some future date. Originally, this was not possible because
of the doctrine of *interesse termini* which meant that actual entry onto
the property was usually necessary before the lease could be effective.
This doctrine was, however, abolished by s. 149(1) of the Law of Property Act 1925. Note, though, s. 149(3): 'A term, at a rent or granted
in consideration of a fine, limited after the commencement of this Act
to take effect more than 21 years from the date of the instrument purporting to create it, shall be void ...' (see *Re Strand and Savoy Properties*
[1960] 2 All E.R. 327; *Weg Motors Ltd* v. *Hales* [1961] 3 All E.R.
181.)

(iv) *'Perpetually renewable leases'*. If a lease is created giving the tenant
the right to renew it as often as it expires, this is now converted by
the Law of Property Act 1922, s. 145, into a term of 2,000 years. A
sub-lease which is perpetually renewable is converted into one of 2,000
years less one day. (See *Northchurch Estates* v. *Daniels* [1947] Ch. 117.)

(v) *'Concurrent leases'*. It is even possible to have leases of the same
premises, at the same time, to different lessees. There is little evidence
on how much these are used, and little case-law.

(vi) *'Shorthold Tenancies'*. A new kind of fixed-term tenancy, relating
to residential accommodation only, has been created by the Housing
Act 1980, s. 52; see further below, pp. 205, 439.

B Use of fixed-term tenancies

Long fixed-term tenancies are often referred to as 'building leases'.[5]
Under such an arrangement, the lessee pays a low ground rent to
his landlord for a period of (say) 99 years; in addition he covenants
to erect on the site and keep in repair specified buildings. This form

---

4. Distinguish this type of tenancy from the phrase 'tenant for life' which can arise
under the Settled Land Act 1925, but which has nothing to do with the law of leasehold.
5. The features of the building lease were described by Uthwatt–Jenkins, 1950, paras.
22–24.

of lease may be used by a landowner who wishes to lease the land to a property developer who will come onto the land and build accommodation. It is sometimes also used where the lessee is to be the occupier of premises already built on the site. Using a 'building lease' in these circumstances is of course a fiction but is the result of conveyancing practice in different parts of the country.

Use of leases as the form of tenure for owner-occupation varies significantly in different parts of the country (Table 1.4, above, p. 15).

Short fixed-term tenancies (say for 7, 14 or even 21 years) are often referred to as 'occupation leases'. A major difference between these and 'building leases' is that a full market rent (subject to any Rent Act limitations) will more often be paid.

C Periodic tenancies : different types

(i) '*Tenancy from year to year*'. This is one possible type. It can be created expressly by the grant of a lease to run 'from year to year' or 'as a yearly tenancy'. In addition, such a tenancy may be created by inference. This may happen for example when a fixed term of years comes to an end, and the tenant holds over with the landlord's consent. (*Tickner* v. *Buzzacott* [1965] Ch. 426.) Whether or not such a tenancy can in fact be inferred may be a difficult question of fact.

A feature of the yearly tenancy, as opposed to other periodic tenancies, is that the common law period of notice to bring it to an end is half a year (unless there is any express arrangement to the contrary).

(ii) '*Tenancies for less than a year*'. These may be quarterly, monthly or weekly. The best way of distinguishing these short, periodic tenancies is to ask how the rent is to be paid. If weekly, then the tenancy is a weekly one and so on. In the absence of express agreement, the period of notice to terminate such a tenancy is the full period of the tenancy. This principle is now subject to the Protection from Eviction Act 1977, s. 5(1) (see below, p. 412). The possibility of a daily tenancy has been doubted (*Appah* v. *Parncliffe Investments* [1964] 1 W.L.R. 1064).

This category of tenancy, in particular the weekly tenancy, is the one most commonly used in Britain for housing purposes (see Tables 1.1 and 1.2, pp. 11–13).

D Other tenancies

In addition to the above, there are a number of other types of tenancy to be mentioned here.

(i) STATUTORY TENANCIES

The most important category of tenancy, which is not created by the agreement of two parties, comes into existence by operation of statute, usually to give a tenant security of tenure. We shall examine the details of the provisions of the Rent Acts in relation to security of tenure for residential accommodation later (see below, pp. 417–41). There are also statutory provisions to protect tenants where a long tenancy at a low rent comes to an end under Part I of the Landlord and Tenant Act 1954 and the Leasehold Reform Act 1967. It has often been said that such tenancies give no estate in land but only a personal right of occupation to the statutory tenant. (See, e.g., *Keeves* v. *Dean* [1924] 1 K.B. at 694 *per* Bankes L.J.; for the contrasting position under Landlord and Tenant Act 1954, Part II, see below, p. 442).

(ii) LEGAL RAG-BAG

Finally, mention may be made of three interests known to the law which are not within the definition of 'terms of years' nor are part of the statutory framework, and which are hard to classify strictly as tenancies but which can be mentioned here as they are called tenancies.

'*Tenancy at will*'. This concept originally developed to cover 'tenant' farmers who had no fixed term or formal lease. Here, the lessee has no defined estate in the land, i.e. he holds it for no fixed period, but 'at will'. The lessor can put him out at any time. This may arise by express grant or by implication. Today the courts are not keen on such tenancies because they are so vague and the tenant's rights are so ill-defined. The modern reluctance of the courts to recognize a tenancy at will is discussed by the Court of Appeal in *Heslop* v. *Burns* [1974] 3 All E.R. 406 (see below, pp. 111–16); and in *Hagee* v. *Erikson* [1975] 3 All E.R. 234 (C.A.) it was noted that although tenancies at will are not covered by Landlord and Tenant Act 1954, Part II, the courts will look carefully before deciding that such a tenancy exists.

'*Tenancy at sufferance*'. This arises where X, once in lawful possession of land, holds over after his tenancy has expired, without the landlord's consent. In effect, this is similar to squatting, except that the tenant had previous rights. Essentially it is a legal device to prevent the tenant being regarded as a trespasser. (The distinction between this and the tenancy at will is discussed by Viscount Simonds in *Wheeler* v. *Mercer* [1957] A.C. 416 at 426.)

At common law it was well established that both these categories of tenancy could be expanded to become periodic tenancies where rent was paid and accepted. The length of the tenancy would be related to the period in respect of which the rent was paid (*Dougal* v. *McCarthy* [1893] 1 Q.B. 736; *Young* v. *Hargreaves* (1963) 186 E.G. 355). One result of this principle was that the tenant on sufferance could not be sued for rent; if the landlord acknowledged that rent was owing, this would amount to recognition of a new tenancy. Instead, the landlord would have to bring an action for possession, together with a claim for 'mesne profits' for the use and occupation of the property.

In the case of tenancies falling within the scope of the Rent Acts, it appears that these principles have been modified. The issue was discussed by the Court of Appeal in *Harvey* v. *Stagg* (1978) 247 E.G. 463. In this case, a tenancy had expired by effluxion of time on 19 October 1975. Stagg asked the landlord if he and fellow tenants could stay on; the landlord agreed if they paid an additional £10 per month rent. In the words of Orr L.J., the county court judge decided that

all that was agreed by the parties in law was that, as the tenants wanted to stay on and as costs had gone up, the rent should be increased by £10 a month and otherwise no attempt was made to vary the existing terms or make a new tenancy. That, in his view, was all that took place and he concluded that it did not constitute a new tenancy.

Orr L.J. then proceeded to discuss whether this conclusion was correct. He cited *Morrison* v. *Jacobs* [1945] K.B. 577, where Scott L.J. had said (at p. 580):

It is erroneous, I think, to hold, in the case of a dwelling-house to which the Rent Restrictions Acts apply, that where the tenant has remained in possession after a term of years and the landlord has accepted rent from the tenant, any such inference of a consensus *ad idem* between the parties to a new common law tenancy arises, because before the passing of those Acts, in certain circumstances such an inference could be drawn. The relevant consideration is that in the case of a dwelling-house to which the Rent Restrictions Acts apply, where a term of years has expired, the landlord cannot obtain possession of the house unless he brings himself within the terms of certain provisions of those Acts...

Orr L.J. concluded:

[In] my judgment, it is not possible to say, having regard to the Rent Restrictions Acts background, that the only inference as a matter of law which the county court judge could have properly drawn in the present case was that there had been an agreement to a renewal of a contractual tenancy. The fact of the flat being subject to the Rent Acts was a consideration which the judge was entitled, and in my view bound, to take into account. Doing so, it seems to me impossible to say that he erred in law and equally impossible to say that he came, as a matter of fact and of inference – since the matter was in this case really one of inference – to a wrong conclusion.

Comment. Is this a legitimate re-interpretation of the common law? Why do the judges appear to have altered the circumstances in which the inference of a new tenancy at common law could be drawn?

'*Tenancy by estoppel*'. Megarry & Wade (1975, p. 646, notes omitted):

If a person with no estate in land purports to grant a tenancy of the land, the grant can pass no actual estate. Yet, even though the lessor's want of title is apparent to the parties, both the parties and their successors in title will be estopped from denying that the grant was effective to create the tenancy that it purported to create. There is thus brought into being a tenancy by estoppel under which the parties and their successors in title have (as against another) most of the rights and liabilities of an estate in land, although no estate is actually granted...

For an example, see *Quennell* v. *Maltby* (below, p. 230).

5. Creation of leases : formal leases

A Requirement of writing

The Law of Property Act 1925, provides:

s. 52(1)   All conveyances of land or of any interest therein are void for the purpose of conveying or creating a legal estate unless made by deed.

s. 52(2)   This section does not apply to:
(d) leases or tenancies ... not required by law to be made in writing; ...

s. 54(2)   Nothing in the foregoing provision ... shall affect the creation by parol of leases taking effect in possession for a term not exceeding three years (whether or not the lessee is given power to extend the term) at the best rent which can be reasonably obtained without taking a fine.[6]

6. *Kushner* v. *Law Society* [1952] 1 K.B. 214.

s. 55   Nothing in the last ... section shall...
           (d) affect the operation of the law relating to part performance...
s. 205(1)(ii) 'Conveyance' includes ... lease ...

One result of these rules is that while writing is necessary to create long-term leases, short-term tenancies (including the very common weekly tenancy) *prima facie* need no writing at all. The requirement of writing in theory ensures that both parties to the leasehold agreement have given some thought to their mutual rights and obligations, and there is clear evidence of their agreement. Where there is no writing, tenants (or landlords) may be put at a severe disadvantage if landlords (or tenants) decide unilaterally to alter terms which have been orally agreed. This will give the more powerful side of the landlord–tenant relationship considerable scope for abuse. Although oral agreements for weekly tenancies are legally binding, nevertheless lack of writing may cause severe problems if cases come to court and a judge is required to decide which party is telling the truth.

In addition, the purpose of much of the legislation relating to the residential landlord–tenant relationship which is discussed in this book, is to create a 'Poor Man's Lease'[7] defining the rights and obligations of landlords and tenants, and, in some cases, shifting the balance of those obligations. One of the major reasons why this law is not used more is that tenants, in particular, are ignorant of their legal rights. Further, as Abel-Smith, Zander and Brooke showed (1973), many prospective tenants fail to seek legal advice on their legal rights (Zander, 1978, p. 281). While acquisition of knowledge does not necessarily lead to its use, it is nonetheless an essential prerequisite for its use. It is therefore necessary to devise effective means of passing on this information.

B Rent books[8]

The law on rent books is one of the methods that has been adopted. The Landlord and Tenant Act 1962 provides:

s. 1(1)   Where a person (hereafter in this Act referred to as the 'tenant')

---

7. A useful phrase coined by Nevitt (1970).

8. Provision of rent books was first made a statutory requirement in certain circumstances by the Increase of Rent and Mortgage Interest (Restrictions) Act 1938, s. 6. The ineffectiveness of this provision was commented on by the *Interdepartmental Committee on Rent Control* (1945, pp. 35–6), who recommended that the provision of rent books be made obligatory for all periodic tenancies not exceeding one month (except furnished lettings).

has a right granted to him or any predecessor in title of his by a contract or conferred by an enactment to occupy any premises as a residence in consideration of a rent, and that rent is payable weekly, it shall be the duty of the landlord to provide a rent book or other similar document for use in respect of the premises.

(2) The foregoing subsection shall not apply to any premises if the rent includes a payment in respect of board and the value of that board to the tenant forms a substantial proportion of the whole rent.

The Act then provides that the name and address of the landlord be given on the rent book (s. 2(1)(a) and s. 6(2)). The Department of the Environment is given powers to require other information to be incorporated into rent books relating to tenancies covered by the Rent Act 1977[9] (s. 2(1)(b)–(d)). Penalties are prescribed for failure to comply with the rules (s. 4). Offences may be prosecuted by local authorities (s. 5(2)). In addition, the Housing Finance Act 1972, s. 24(10)–(12) provides that information about rent allowances should be given with rent books. Failure to do this is also a criminal offence punishable by a fine.

For tenancies falling within the Rent Act 1977, the required information is contained in the Rent Book (Forms of Notice) Regulations 1976 (S.I. 1976 No. 378). There are three forms prescribed; since they are somewhat similar, only the form relating to regulated tenancies is set out here.

RENT BOOK FOR REGULATED TENANCY

Form of notice to be included in every rent book or other similar document used in connection with a regulated tenancy under which the rent is payable weekly.

INFORMATION FOR TENANT

1. Address of premises...

2. Name and address of landlord ....

3. Name and address of agent (if any) ....

4. The rent inclusive/exclusive of rates is £ .... per week.
   If a fair rent is registered, paragraph 5 and, where it applies, paragraph 7 must be filled in.

5. The registered rent (which excludes rates) is £ .... per week.
   The word 'variable' should be added after the amount of registered rent if the

9. There is also power to prescribe a notice for tenancies protected under the Rent (Agriculture) Act 1976, but this power has not yet been exercised.

entry in the register permits the landlord to vary the rent, in accordance with the cost of providing services or maintaining or repairing the premises in accordance with the terms shown in the register, without having to have a new rent registered.

6. As a result of the provisions for phasing rent increases following the registration of a fair rent, the maximum rent (exclusive of rates) which the landlord may for the time being charge may be less than the registered rent.

7. In addition to the registered rent £............per week is payable by way of rates borne by the landlord or a superior landlord.

IF A RENT HAS NOT BEEN REGISTERED

8. You or your landlord or both of you acting together may at any time apply to the Rent Officer to have a fair rent registered for the premises. Your local authority may also apply to the Rent Officer, but only to have a reduced rent registered.

9. Where no rent has been registered and your contractual term has ended then, except in the case where you enter into the new agreement referred to in paragraph 10 below, only limited increases in the rent are permitted, for example for rates increases or improvements (but see paragraph 11 below).

10. You and your landlord may agree to increase the rent under the existing contractual tenancy or to enter into a new tenancy agreement at an increased rent. Any such agreement must be in writing and signed by both you and the landlord, and must contain a statement at the head of the agreement, in conspicuous characters, to the effect that:–

(i) your security of tenure will not be affected if you refuse to enter into the agreement, and

(ii) entry into the agreement will not deprive you or the landlord of the right to apply at any time to the Rent Officer for the registration of a fair rent.

11. There are special provisions where grant-aided improvement works have been carried out, and where a tenancy, including a statutory tenancy, has been converted from rent control. Your local authority, a Housing Aid Centre or a Citizens' Advice Bureau can give you further information and tell you the address of the Rent Officer.

IF A RENT HAS BEEN REGISTERED

12. The landlord may not charge more rent (exclusive of rates) than is shown in the register, or if an increase of rent must be phased, more than is permitted under the relevant phasing provisions. He may add to this the amount of the rates that he pays for the premises if there is a note on the register that he pays the rates (see paragraph 7 above). In certain cases the registered rent may vary in accordance with the cost of providing services

or maintaining or repairing the premises, but only if there is a note on the register to this effect (see paragraph 5 above).

13. The registered rent cannot be changed without applying to the Rent Officer. He will not register a new rent applying within the three years after a registration takes effect, unless an application is made by you and the landlord acting together, or there has been a change in the circumstances taken into account when the rent was registered – for example a change in the terms of the tenancy or the furniture supplied, or in the condition of the premises.

14. Further information on rents of regulated tenancies is set out in a booklet available free of charge at rent offices, Housing Aid Centres, Citizens' Advice Bureaux and local Council Offices.

SUB-LETTING

15. If you sub-let part of the premises and you are not permitted to do this under your tenancy agreement, your landlord may apply to the county court for an order to evict you.

16. If you sub-let part of the premises, then:–

(a) if the sub-tenancy is protected under the Rent Act 1968 you must give the landlord, within 14 days, a statement in writing of the sub-letting, giving particulars of occupancy, including the rent charged. The penalty for failing to do this without reasonable excuse, or for giving false particulars, is a fine not exceeding £10. When you have once given the landlord the particulars, you need not do so again if the only change is a change of sub-tenant; and

(b) if you overcharge your sub-tenant, the landlord may apply to the county court for an order to evict you.

SECURITY OF TENURE

17. If you have a contractual tenancy the landlord must first bring it to an end before he can exercise any of his other rights. If he does so by means of a notice to quit, he must give you at least four weeks' notice in writing and that notice must contain certain prescribed information about tenants' rights.

18. Even after your contractual term ends, your landlord cannot evict you without a court order, which except in certain special cases will be granted only if the court thinks it reasonable to do so and either there is suitable accommodation for you to go to or one of a limited number of conditions is satisfied (for example, you have failed to pay rent, or you or your family have been a nuisance or annoyance to neighbours).

19. It is a criminal offence for your landlord or anyone else to try to make you leave by using force, by harassing you or your family, or by interfering with your home or your possessions unless authorised by the court. If anyone does this, you should complain to your local authority.

RENT ALLOWANCES

20. If you have difficulty in paying your rent you may apply to your local authority for a rent allowance. When the rent is payable weekly, the landlord is obliged to insert in this rent book appropriate particulars of your local authority's rent allowance scheme. You may obtain further details of the scheme, and also details of your local authority's rate rebate scheme, from your local Council Offices.

In the case of tenancies covered by the Rent Act 1977 (though not 'restricted contracts'), or of protected occupancies or statutory tenancies under the Rent (Agriculture) Act 1976, it is a criminal offence punishable by a fine of up to £50 for 'any person' to show a tenant as being in arrears in respect of any amount which is irrecoverable by the landlord because of the rent-fixing rules contained in the legislation (see below, chapter 5) unless the landlord has a bona fide claim to recover the sum. If the tenant requests such an entry to be removed, the landlord will be personally liable (whoever made the entry in the book) for a further offence, if the entry is not removed within 7 days (Rent Act 1977, s. 57(4) and (5), s. 126(8) and (9); Rent (Agriculture) Act 1976, s. 21(4) and (5)). In certain cases where the level of recoverable rent has been determined by a court, it may also call for the production of the rent book and order its rectification by the registrar or clerk of the court (Rent Act 1977, ss. 40 and 58; Rent (Agriculture) Act 1976, s. 42).

These provisions raise a number of questions. Although the Forms of Notice are incorporated into commercially available rent books, are they in a language that people will understand? Even if comprehensible, there is some evidence that landlords fail to provide rent books (Francis, 1971, p. 216), or if they do provide them they fail to ensure that the information is correct (*ibid.*, p. 256; see also Caplan (1975, paras. 5.19 and 8.34–8.46)). The Select Committee on Race Relations and Immigration (1971, para. 177) noted:

We spoke to several tenants with either no rent book or an improperly kept one. The senior rent officer at Lewisham said: 'I think I have rarely seen a rent book properly made out in all respects' and the Citizens Advice Bureau there had 'never heard of anyone being fined for not providing a rent book'. Although Bedford Corporation thought the legislation on rent books satisfactory, the Department of the Environment said: 'It is very much the feeling in the Department that the law about rent books should be tightened up'.

So far we have discussed rent books as a medium of education. But

as Hoath has argued (1978–9, pp. 4–6), they have other functions
as well. They can be useful evidence in cases of dispute about payment
of rent (Cutting, 1979, p. 29); tenants who have applied for a council
tenancy can use them to show their reliability as tenants. The existence of a rent book may tip the balance between deciding that an
occupier is a tenant as opposed to a licensee (see below, pp. 97–119),
or in deciding whether a supplementary benefit claimant is a 'house-
holder'.[10]

Despite their potential usefulness, a careful look at the provisions
of the Act shows that the scope of the legislation is limited. Landlords
may quite simply evade the law by requiring the rent to be paid fort-
nightly or monthly. And there are many gaps in the information that
has to be provided. To overcome these issues, Francis (1971, pp.
226–7) recommended:

The Landlord and Tenant Act 1962 relating to rent books should be
amended in the following respects:

(*a*) The provision of a rent book (or similar document) should be made
obligatory not only where the rent is payable weekly, but whenever
the rent is payable at intervals not exceeding two months.

(*b*) The rent book should be supplied to and remain in the custody of
the tenant, without prejudice to the right of the landlord to keep
a duplicate, and subject to the right of the landlord to call for production of it where necessary, e.g. to make any proper entry therein
or amendment thereto.

(*c*) A rent book (or similar document) relating to a furnished tenancy
should contain an inventory of the furniture (including fixtures and
fittings) supplied by the landlord for the use of the tenant at the
commencement of the tenancy.

Local authorities should have a general power to call for production of rent
books, and should from time to time, through an appropriate officer carry
out spot checks, especially in furnished multi-occupied houses, for the purpose
of ascertaining whether the law is being complied with.

More recently, Hoath (1978–9, p. 12) has suggested that landlords
should be required to make it clear whether rent is payable in advance
or arrear; where services are provided, these should be specified; and
a summary of the landlord's repairing obligations under the Housing

---

10. 'Householders' are paid benefit at a higher rate than non-householders. Supplementary Benefits Act 1976 (as amended by Social Security Act 1980), Schedule 1, para.
2 and regulations made thereunder.

Act 1961, s. 32 (see below, pp. 350–51) should be given. Notwithstanding these suggestions, reform appears to be a low priority; at the time of writing there are no plans for major alterations to the rent book rules.

Even if the rules were changed, the problem of their enforcement would remain. Given that breach of the rules is a criminal offence, one possible sanction (if local authorities will not use their powers of prosecution) would be to deny landlords their right to rent while they are committing the offence. This argument was raised in *Shaw* v. *Groom* [1970] 1 All E.R. 702:

HARMAN L.J.: This is an appeal by leave from the judgment of his Honour Judge Dow, sitting at Clerkenwell, on 1 August 1969 whereby he refused the plaintiff landlord's application for arrears of rent against the defendant tenant in respect of a weekly tenancy of a room at 38 Lofting Road, London N1, which the tenant had occupied for some 20 years as a weekly tenant at a rent of 7s. 11d. plus 2s. 6d. for electricity. The claim was for some £100 and was in part disputed by the tenant as to amount, but by way of supplemental defence the point was taken that no rent at all was recoverable by the landlord in that she was in breach of s. 4 of the Landlord and Tenant Act 1962, which makes the provision of a rent book or other similar document obligatory on all landlords in cases where there exists a contract to occupy any premises as a residence in consideration of a rent payable weekly...

He then described s. 2 of the Act of 1962; mentioned the notices required; and read out s. 4 which prescribes the offences and penalties connected with failure to provide a rent book, and continued:

The tenant had been provided with two documents called rent books, one by the landlord's predecessor in title and one by the landlord herself, but it was conceded at once that neither of these complied with the prescribed form. The defence therefore set up this defect as a point of law precluding any order for payment of rent, and the learned judge decided to try this as a preliminary point. He delivered a considered judgment in which he concluded that the point was a good one and he therefore dismissed the landlord's claim. She appeals.

The learned judge followed another decision of a county court, that of his Honour Judge Willis at Shoreditch County Court in *Spitz* v. *Gabriel* ([1968] C.L.Y. 2215). He held that the court could not lend its aid in the recovery by the landlord of a sum which it would be an offence under the 1962 Act for the landlord's agent to ask for or receive on her behalf. Judge Dow differed from Judge Willis in the construction of s. 4 of the 1962 Act, holding that in a landlord's case the offence was the non-provision of the rent book and not the demand for or receipt of rent, which would only be an offence in the case of the agent. This difference is, in my judgment, immaterial. The learned judge relied mainly on *Anderson Ltd* v. *Daniel* ([1924] 1 K.B. 138), which was a decision of the Court of Appeal and certainly at first reading seems directly in point. In that case the court ... held that under the terms of the Fertilizers and Feeding Stuffs Act 1906, where goods to which the Act applied were sold without supplying the invoice there prescribed, the vendor could not recover the price of the goods.

In the headnote I find the following:

'By s. 1, sub-s. 1, of the Fertilizers and Feeding Stuffs Act, 1906: "Every person who sells for use as a fertilizer of the soil any article which has been subjected to any artificial process in the United Kingdom, or which has been imported from abroad, shall give to the purchaser an invoice stating ... what are the respective percentages (if any)" of certain chemical substances contained in the article. By s. 6, sub-s. 1: "If any person who sells any article for use as a fertilizer of the soil ... (*a*) Fails without reasonable excuse to give, on or before or as soon as possible after the delivery of the article, the invoice required by this Act....; he shall, without prejudice to any civil liability, be liable on summary conviction" to a penalty:— *Held*, that, as the object of the state in requiring the vendor to give the statutory invoice and imposing on him a penalty in the event of his default is to protect the purchasers of fertilizers, the effect of non-compliance with the requirement is not merely to render the vendor liable to the penalty, but also to make the sale illegal and preclude the vendor from suing for the price.'

After analysing the judgments of Bankes and Atkin L.JJ., he went on:

In my judgment that case, when looked at carefully, is clearly distinguishable from the present. Here there is nothing illegal in the contract of letting itself and it could be performed in a perfectly legal manner. Moreover the landlord in order to enforce it is not obliged to inform the court of his illegal action in failing to provide a rent book. The existence of the rent book is no part of the contract of letting and is purely collateral to it and this alone distinguishes *Anderson Ltd* v. *Daniel* (above), where the invoice was an essential part of the contract and operated as a warranty under it. The true question is, has the statute impliedly forbidden the contract, and in my judgment it has not. The question whether a statute impliedly prohibits the contract in question is one of public policy, as to which, in his speech to the House in *Vita Food Products Inc.* v. *Unus Shipping Co. Ltd* ([1939] A.C. 277), Lord Wright said this:

'Nor must it be forgotten that the rule by which contracts not expressly forbidden by statute or declared to be void are in proper cases nullified for disobedience to a statute is a rule of public policy only, and public policy

understoood in a wider sense may at times be better served by refusing
to nullify a bargain save on serious and sufficient grounds.'

This is a subject much discussed in the authorities.

HARMAN L.J. then described the case of *Wetherall* v. *Jones* ((1832)
3 B. & D. 221), mentioned *Smith* v. *Mawhood* ((1845) 14 M. & W. 452)
and continued:

This present question came before a Divisional Court consisting of Lord
Darling and Shearman J. on an appeal from the county court in 1923 [in
Narraway v. *Bolster* ((1924) E.G. 83)]. The statutes there in question were the
Housing, Town Planning, Etc, Act 1919, and the Statement of Rates Act
1919, both of which enjoined on a landlord the duty of giving a statement
to a tenant subject to a penalty on failure. The tenant was sued for arrears
of rent and possession, both of which the judge granted; and he appealed
on the ground that no statement, as the statute provided, had been made
to him. The Divisional Court dismissed the appeal. Lord Darling's judgment
is reported in these terms:

'The appeal concerned the construction of section 29 of the Housing and
Town Planning Act of 1919. The tenant occupied the house for 97 weeks
at a rent which he had not paid, and he took the point that he had to
pay nothing because the landlord had not given the name and address of
the medical officer. Mr Nichols argued because of that the landlord could
not recover rent. It was perfectly plain that the landlord was liable to a
400s. fine, but he did not think Mr Nichols' argument was a good one.
To say that because a man let a house to a tenant and the tenant was not
given the name and address of the medical officer – which a man could
perfectly well obtain for himself – that the tenant should live rent free in
the house for years, in that case for 97 weeks, was to argue that the legislature did a wicked injustice. He did not think the legislature intended
any such thing. The appeal should be dismissed.'

Shearman J. agreed. Of course that is not binding on us, but nevertheless
it does seem good sense, and it may well, I think, be good law.

Bankes L.J. in *Anderson Ltd* v. *Daniel* (above) declared that the test was
whether the statute was for the protection of the public. That that is one
test of course we would all agree, but I do not think that can be the only
test. The only test is whether the statute impliedly forbids the provision
to be sued on. In *St John Shipping Corpn* v. *Joseph Rank Ltd* ([1957] 1 Q.B.
267), Devlin J. has a pertinent passage about *Anderson Ltd* v. *Daniel*. The *St
John Shipping Corpn* case was about overloading a ship under the Merchant
Shipping (Safety and Load Line Conventions) Act 1932. The Act provides
a penalty for any infringement of the Plimsoll line enjoined by the statute,
and the defence set up was that the offence precluded the carriers from suing

for the freight. Devlin J. rejected this defence and explained *Anderson Ltd* v. *Daniel*. Dealing with that case, he said: 'I am satisfied that counsel's chief argument is based on a misconception of the principle applied in *Anderson Ltd* v. *Daniel*, which I have already cited'; and then he gave some explanation of that. Then he said:

'The principle enunciated by ATKIN, L.J., and cited previously is an off-shoot of the second principle that a prohibited contract will not be enforced. If the prohibited contract is an express one, it falls directly within the principle. It must likewise fall within it if the contract is implied. If, for example, an unlicensed broker sues for work and labour, it does not matter that no express contract is alleged and that the claim is based solely on the performance of the contract, that is to say, the work and labour done; it is as much unenforceable as an express contract made to fit the work done. The same reasoning must be applied to a contract which, though legal in form, is performed unlawfully. . . .

'Whether it is the terms of the contract or the performance of it that is called in question, the test is just the same: is the contract, as made or as performed, a contract that is prohibited by the statute? Counsel for the defendants' proposition ignores this test. On a superficial reading of *Anderson Ltd* v. *Daniel* and the cases that followed and preceded it, judges may appear to be saying that it does not matter that the contract is itself legal, if something illegal is done under it; but that is an unconsidered interpretation of the cases. When fully considered, it is plain that they do not proceed on the basis that in the course of performing a legal contract an illegality was committed; but on the narrower basis that the way in which the contract was performed turned it into the sort of contract that was prohibited by the statute.'

In this case, in my judgment, it is not an instance in which the manner in which the contract was performed turned it into a contract prohibited by the statute, and consequently *Anderson Ltd* v. *Daniel* is no authority for the proposition which the learned judge drew from it. I therefore would allow the appeal.

SACHS L.J. also allowed the appeal, saying, in part (at pp. 713–14):

The offence created by s. 4(1) of the 1962 Act is as regards landlords an absolute offence. Innocence of mind and inadvertence are no excuse. If it had been intended that the landlord should on committing the offence forfeit sums that can be far greater than the maximum penalty, then the Act would have so stated. The general pattern of the relevant legislation so indicates. It would in any event be contrary to sound policy to hold that such a forfeit was intended unless the Act said so expressly. It would be absurd if such forfeits were incurred should some minor part of the prescribed details not be inserted in the book; yet this was what counsel for the tenant contended was the result.

If in the pool of landlord and tenant legislation to be considered one included, as would seem right, the provisions of the Acts mentioned in relation to *Narraway*'s case, the above conclusions are reinforced. Lord Darling's approach had much in common with that expressed 40 years later by Devlin J. and I consider *Narraway* v. *Bolster* (above) to be correctly decided. It would, of course, not make good sense if offences against the relevant provisions of the 1962 Act and the 1919 Acts had different results on the landlord's entitlement to rent – even if by an exercise of some nicety it were possible so to hold. The essence of the provisions in each case is simply that the landlord must provide the tenant with certain information, is equally simply liable to a stated penalty on failure to provide it, and is not made subject to further forfeitures.

It seems to me appropriate, accordingly, to allow this appeal on the broad basis that, even if the provision of a rent book is an essential act as between landlords and weekly tenants, yet the legislature did not by s. 4 of the 1962 Act intend to preclude the landlord from recovering any rent due or impose any forfeiture on him beyond the prescribed penalty.

Comment

A number of approaches to the law relating to rent books and its enforcement seem possible. Cutting (1979, p. 126) suggests that many complaints of harassment (see below, pp. 448–52) begin with a tenant's request for a rent book: 'a tenant who likes his accommodation and gets on well with his landlord should consider whether he really needs a rent book'. However, if the rules are followed, it has been seen that they would provide tenants with certain information regarding their legal rights. How important is such access to information? Should local authorities be reminded of their powers to prosecute? Or county courts of their powers to call for rent books for rectification? Is the public policy issue as clear-cut as Harman and Sachs L.JJ. suggested in *Shaw* v. *Groom*, or should this decision be reversed (Hoath, 1978–9, p. 13)? Should the obligation to provide rent books be limited to tenancies falling within the Rent Acts (Law Commission, 1975, paras. 71–78)? While the law on rent books may be a less crucial issue than some of the other issues discussed in this book, should it not be regarded as symptomatic of the seriousness, or otherwise, of official attempts to demystify the law by making knowledge of legal rights more accessible to laymen?

6. Creation of leases : informal leases

Although there may be good reasons for requiring written documentation for the creation of legal interests in land – to prevent fraud, define the obligations of the parties, and so on – practical reality shows that there are always people who have tried to create leases but who do not, for one reason or another, comply with the formal rules. Obviously great hardship could be caused if the law were wholly to deny the validity of such informal arrangements. The court of equity developed doctrines which, in effect, gave validity to informal leases by allowing them to be enforced.

A Contract for a lease

When a long-term lease is being negotiated, conveyancing practice is that the parties will usually reach a point where they exchange contracts, before they complete the conveyance of the legal interest in the property. (Any document stated to be 'subject to contract' does not create a contract: *Tiverton Estates* v. *Wearwell* [1975] Ch. 146; cf. *Law* v. *Jones* [1974] Ch. 112.) The courts of equity decided that such exchange of contracts created an equitable interest in the property so that if one of the parties to the agreement broke it, the other party would usually be able to enforce. In order to do this, two essential conditions had to be met:

(*i*) Agreements must conform to the basic law of contract. There must be an offer, which has been accepted, and consideration. In addition, certain essential terms must be agreed: the identification of the parties; the premises to be let; the date of commencement and length of the term; and the rent or other consideration to be paid.

(*ii*) They must usually conform to Law of Property Act 1925, s. 40:

(1) No action may be brought upon any contract for the sale or disposition of land or any interest in land, unless the agreement upon which such action is brought, or some memorandum or note thereof, is in writing, and signed by the party to be charged or by some other person thereunto by him lawfully authorized.

What constitutes a sufficient 'memorandum or note thereof' depends on all the facts of the case (Megarry & Wade, 1975, pp. 549–58). If there is a formal contract the question is easily solved. But the memorandum does not have to be in any particular form nor indeed in a single document, and can be constructed from informal notes or letters. It is important, though, that what written evidence does exist should contain the four essential terms mentioned at (*i*) above. There must also be a signature (*Evans* v. *Hoare* [1892] 1 Q.B. 593; *Pearce* v. *Gardner* [1897] 1 Q.B. 688; *Wragg* v. *Lovett* [1948] 2 All E.R. 968).

If these conditions are satisfied, two remedies are available:

(a) *An action for damages.* Although this is the normal remedy for breach of contract, in the context of land, the potential tenant may not be particularly interested in receiving monetary compensation. He would rather have the actual land for which he was negotiating. Land is immovable; one piece of land in a particular location may have special merits which another piece does not.

(b) *Specific performance.* For these reasons the courts of equity developed the remedy of specific performance to help those who might otherwise be harmed by the breaking of a contract affecting land. This remedy is based on the principle that 'equity looks on that as done which ought to be done' (applied in *Walsh* v. *Lonsdale* (1882) 21 Ch.D. 9). It consists of an order from the court ordering the party in breach of the contract to specifically perform that contract, i.e. in this context, to complete the conveyance.

Nominally it is a discretionary remedy, but this will usually be issued as long as certain conditions are fulfilled. These relate to:

(*i*)   Nature of the contract – it must be complete and definite, and have no terms which are incapable of performance (see *Johnson* v. *Agnew* [1978] 3 All E.R. 314 (C.A.)).

(*ii*) Conduct of the plaintiff – he must come to court 'with clean hands'.

(*iii*) Defective title – no specific performance will be ordered if the lessor has not got good title.

(*iv*) Hardship – specific performance will not be ordered if it would cause serious hardship.

B Part performance

Although the remedies discussed above may be available on breach of the agreement if the requirements of L.P.A., s. 40 are fulfilled, it is also important to note that s. 40(2) specifically states that the law of part performance is not to be affected. This is another doctrine of the courts of equity which provides that if one party to a contract has performed wholly or a substantial part of his half of the bargain, the other party should not be able to evade his obligations merely because there is no written evidence of the contract, as required by L.P.A. s. 40(1).

However, a plaintiff who relies on the doctrine of part performance must show (*per* Romer J. in *Rawlinson* v. *Ames* [1925] 1 Ch. 96):[11]

(a) An act of part performance which is unequivocally referable to the existence of the contract alleged to exist.

(b) That it would be fraudulent for the defendant to rely on a lack of written evidence under s. 40(1).

(c) That the contract is of a kind that the courts will order specific performance.

(d) Other parol evidence of the contract to support the part performance.

Condition (a) has proved difficult to interpret. In *Kingswood Estate Co.* v. *Anderson* [1963] 2 Q.B. 169, a tenant who left a Rent Act protected house and went into alternative accommodation was held to have partly performed an alleged agreement to grant him a tenancy for life of the accommodation. Making expensive alterations to a property has also been held to be part performance (*Wills* v. *Stradling* (1797) 3 Ves. 378). The recent House of Lords' decision in *Steadman* v. *Steadman* [1976] A.C. 536 suggests that the approach of the courts may have relaxed somewhat.

Because of the principles just discussed it is sometimes said that 'a contract for a lease is as good as a lease'. However, whereas between the parties to the agreement this may be more or less true, the owner of an equitable interest (only) in unregistered land will not be able to enforce it against a third party, unless it is registered at the Land Charges Register as an estate contract (Land Charges Act 1972, s. 2, Class C (iv)). For land subject to the system of registered conveyancing, estate contracts should be registered at the Land Registry as minor interests, and protected by notice (Megarry & Wade (1975, pp. 1067–9); Hayton (2nd ed., 1977, pp. 146–53)). If the owner of such an equitable interest is in actual possession of the land, his interest will, in any event, be protected even against third parties as being an 'overriding interest' (Land Registration Act 1925, s. 70(1)(g)).

11. These conditions were based on the House of Lords' decision in *Maddison* v. *Alderson* (1883) 8 App. Cas. 467 and *Fry on Specific Performance* (6th ed.), p. 276.

7. Terms of the lease : covenants

A Examples of tenancy agreements and leases

We have seen when written documentation is required, and when not, and how the courts have developed remedies to cope with failure to conform to the rules. In this section, we look more closely at the content of some of the conditions ('covenants', see above, p. 41) that may be found in written tenancy agreements or leases.

One point, of some sociological importance, should be stressed at the outset. Lawyers may think it quite proper that the terms on which a tenancy is held should be written down. Professor Cullingworth has argued, in his study of landlordism in Lancaster (Cullingworth, 1963), that, particularly where the landlord was an individual or a resident landlord, a legalistic approach to the landlord–tenant relationship was regarded as irrelevant. 'Responsibility for the upkeep of the houses was often shared between the landlord and tenant on the basis of an informal understanding. The legalism of the Rent Act was quite foreign to this loose social situation' (Cullingworth, 1979, p. 64).

However, although this is a useful description of how some parties to a landlord–tenant relationship perceive themselves, by no means all landlords and tenants behave in this way, as the following extract from Rex and Moore's study of housing in Sparkbrook shows (1967, pp. 139–40):

We heard stories of West Indian landlords who frequently 'laid down the law' verbally, giving times for tenants to be in, times for radios and gramophones to be off. West Indian tenants found this very irksome and they felt that the landlord was not treating 'his own kind' in the right way.

However, we encountered one Indian landlord who wrote the rules down and required his tenants to comply with them and signify their compliance by signing the rules over a 2d. stamp. Such a charter could emerge from either side, but the landlord's superior market position and the fact that he is not likely to be divided against himself make it more likely that his will emerge first and be imposed. Here are the rules set out by the landlord, preceded by a list of details required of his tenants.

(1) Name (full) ....
(2) Last address ....
(3) Nationality .... Married .... Children ....
(4) Wife or husband's name and address ....
(5) Employer's address ....
(6) Kind of work ....

  (7) Friend's name and address ....

  (8) Rent one week in advance ....

  (9) Deposit for the articles ....

(10) Furnitures .... How Many? ....

Table	Pillow-cases
Chair	Sheets
Double or single bed	Bedspread
Sofa	Quilt
Cupboard	Carpet
Heater	Curtains

Conditions:

1. The landlord has a right to make any change.
2. Regular payment of rent on Friday evening or Saturday morning to landlord/landlady.
3. Notice of termination of a tenancy on either side.
4. No disturbances at any costs – wireless, radio, television, gramophones etc., very low within the room.
5. No visitors allowed after 8.30 p.m., without the permission of the land-lord or the landlady.
6. Very quiet after 10 p.m.
7. Always co-operation as the landlord-tenant.

    I have received the Rent Book

    Date ....   Stamp   and signature of the tenant.

Although a landlord–tenant relationship that is proceeding smoothly may not need to be finalized, if it begins to break down a written record of the terms of letting may be helpful. The law has only developed a limited number of implied terms for cases where there is no written agreement. (The most important are the landlord's covenant for quiet enjoyment (see below, pp. 452–5) and certain statutory covenants relating to repairing obligations (below, pp. 349–63); and the tenant's covenant to pay the rent and use the premises in a tenant-like manner (below, pp. 243–4 and 346–9).) Furthermore, the existence or otherwise of a written agreement may have important legal consequences, particularly in relation to assignment and sub-letting (see below, pp. 79–91), and security of tenure (see below, p. 424).

Against these points, if the written agreement contains provisions relating to (e.g.) rent, or repairing obligations, or notices to quit, they may, because of the imbalance of bargaining power between land-lords and tenants, be at variance with statutory rules on these topics (see below, respectively pp. 245–75, 350–51 and 412–13) and thus contribute to a weakening of the legal protections theoretically offered by the law.

Whatever the merits of the above arguments, commercial rent books exist which, presumably, are widely used, many of which incorporate a number of written terms. For example *Chirm's Tenant's Rent Book* provides:

This house is let on the following terms (where such terms are not inconsistent with a separate agreement), and the Tenant will be held to be a consenting party to same.

Terms of Tenancy

1. Four weeks' notice to leave must be given and the key delivered to the Collector or his deputy on the day of leaving.
2. The premises shall be carefully used and kept in orderly and clean condition.
3. A TENANT HAVING GARDEN GROUND SHALL PROPERLY CULTIVATE IT.
4. The tenant will be responsible for all damage caused to pavements, floors, steps, etc., by wood chopping, coal breaking etc. Glass cracked or broken during the tenancy shall be immediately replaced by the tenant at his own expense. Notice to quit can in no case be accepted until this, or other damage caused by the tenant, any member of the family, or any other person living with him has been satisfactorily made good.
5. NO PIGEONS OR OTHER LIVESTOCK SHALL BE KEPT ON THE PREMISES without written permission.
6. THE TENANT SHALL NOT ASSIGN, SUB-LET OR OTHERWISE PART WITH POSSESSION OF THE HOUSE OR ANY PART THEREOF, AND SHALL NOT TAKE LODGERS OR PAYING GUESTS.
7. All solid refuse, hair or rags, shall be placed in the ash bin and must not be put or allowed to be put down the w.c. pedestals or basins.
8. The cost of unstopping or repairing w.c. pedestals or basins or drains where resulting from negligence or mis-use by tenants, their children or other persons living with them shall be paid for by the tenant.
9. Arrears of rent are not permitted.
10. The tenants shall not make any alteration in or to the premises, maim or injure in any way the brickwork or woodwork of the premises, and in particular will not erect or install or permit to be erected or installed any wireless pole or aerial on or about the said premises, nor convert any dwellinghouse into a retail shop, without the Owners' or Agent's permission and also the tenants shall not allow any kind of advertise-

ment to be attached to or exhibited on the outside of the premises without the written consent of the Owner or Agent.

11. During the periods of severe frost tenants must protect water pipes by wrappings. Should a burst happen where such precaution has not been adopted, the tenant must immediately inform the Owner or Agent. NO BONFIRES ALLOWED ON THE PROPERTY.

For longer-term leasehold arrangements, the documents are usually somewhat more formal, as can be seen in the following model for a seven-year lease (Lewis & Holland, 1968, Appendix A):

Parties	THIS LEASE made the .... day of .... 1966 BETWEEN JOHN JONES of 1 High Street in the City of Plymouth Schoolteacher (hereinafter called 'the Landlord' which expression shall where the context so admits include his successors in title) of the one part and ANDREW SMITH of 1 Fore Street in the City of Plymouth Gardener (hereinafter called 'the Tenant' which expression shall where the context so admits include his executors administrators and assigns) of the other part
Testatum	WITNESSETH as follows:——
	1. That in consideration of the rent hereinafter reserved and the covenants on the part of the Tenant hereinafter contained the Landlord hereby demises unto the Tenant ALL THAT the messuage or dwelling-house with the outbuildings and garden
Premises demised Habendum	attached thereto and forming part thereof known as Number 57 Ring Road in the City of Plymouth (hereinafter called 'the premises') TO HOLD the premises unto the Tenant from the Twenty-Ninth day of September 1967 for the term of Seven years PAYING THEREFOR yearly during the term hereby granted the rent of £ by equal quarterly payments on the four usual quarter days in every year the first of such payments to be made on the Twenty-Ninth day of September 1967
Tenant's Covenants	2. The Tenant hereby covenants with the Landlord as follows namely:——
	(a) To pay the rent hereby reserved on the days and in the manner aforesaid without any deduction
	(b) To pay all rates taxes assessments and outgoings which now are or may at any time hereafter be imposed assessed or charged upon the premises or the occupier in respect thereof
	(c) To keep the inside of the premises including all garden fences window locks latches and fasteners and all the Landlord's fixtures therein in good and tenantable repair during the said term damage by fire (other than fire due to any default of the Tenant) or tempest or operations of war always excepted

(d) To clear and make good every stoppage of and all damage to the drains caused by the negligence of the Tenant his Agents servants family guests and visitors and to repay to the Landlord on demand all costs incurred by the Landlord in cleaning and making good any stoppage or damage and so that for the purposes of this covenant all stoppages and damage shall be assumed to have been caused by such negligence unless the tenant can prove to the contrary

(e) Not to assign underlet charge or part with the possession of the premises or any part thereof without the previous consent in writing of the Landlord PROVIDED ALWAYS that if the Tenant desires to so assign or underlet the whole or part of the premises he shall first by notice in writing to the Landlord apply to surrender the lease on the next subsequent quarter day or if that be within Twenty-Eight days of the said notice then upon the second subsequent quarter day without any consideration but the Landlord may within Twenty-One days of the service of such notice upon him accept such offer such acceptance to be in writing and without prejudice to the rights and remedies of the Landlord herein in respect of rent or breach of covenant. If the said offer is not accepted by the Landlord or on his behalf within the said Twenty-One days it shall be deemed to have been rejected

(f) Not during the said term to use the premises or any part thereof or permit the same to be used for the purposes of any trade manufacture or business or otherwise than as a private dwelling-house and residence only

(g) Not during the said term without the consent of the Landlord first had and obtained make any alterations or additions in or to the premises or any part thereof

(h) To permit the Landlord or his Agent at any reasonable time after asking permission to enter upon the premises for the purpose of inspecting the state and condition thereof and thereupon the Landlord may serve upon the Tenant a notice in writing specifying any repairs that are necessary to be performed and to request the Tenant forthwith to execute the same and if the Tenant shall not within Twenty-One days after service of such notice execute such repairs then to allow the Landlord to enter upon the premises to execute such repairs and the cost thereof shall be a debt due from the Tenant to the Landlord and forthwith recoverable

(i) In the event of the premises or any part thereof being destroyed or damaged by fire at any time during the term hereof and the insurance money under any policy of insurance effected thereon by the Landlord being by reason of any act or default of the Tenant wholly or partially recoverable forthwith in every such case to rebuild and reinstate fully at his own expense the premises to the satisfaction and under the supervision of the Landlord's surveyor being allowed always at his expense of having done such re-building re-instatement being completed the amount (if any) actually received irrespective of such destruction or damage under any policy of insurance as aforesaid

3. The landlord hereby covenants with the Tenant as follows namely:—

(a) That the Tenant paying the rent hereby reserved and performing and observing the covenants on his part hereinbefore contained shall peaceably and quietly hold and enjoy the premises during the said term without interruption by the Landlord or any person claiming under or in trust for him

(b) That the Landlord will during the said term keep the main walls roof spouts and main timbers of the premises in good tenantable repair and condition

Provisos   4. Provided always and it is hereby agreed as follows:—

(i) that if at any time during the said term the premises or any part thereof shall be rendered unfit for habitation or use by fire then and in such case unless the destruction or damage so caused shall have by the above default of the Tenant or the insurance forfeited for the same reasons the rent hereby reserved or a proportionate part thereof according to the nature and extent of the damage done shall cease and be suspended until the premises are reinstated that any question arising as to the incidence or extent of this proviso shall be referred to a single Arbitrator in accordance with the Arbitration Act 1950 or any statutory modification or re-enactment thereof for the time being in force

(ii) that if the rent hereby reserved or any part thereof shall at any time be in arrear for Twenty-One days after the same shall have become due (whether formally demanded or not) or there shall be any breach of the foregoing covenants on the part of the Tenant or he shall cease to occupy the premises or he shall become bankrupt or have a receiving order made against him or enter into any composition or arrangement for the benefit of his creditors or suffer any committal order to be made against him under the Debtors Act 1869 then the Landlord may (without prejudice to any right in respect of any antecedent breach of covenant by the Tenant) re-enter

upon the premises and determine the tenancy AND whenever
this power of re-entry shall arise (whether the same be exercised or not) the rent for the quarter then current shall immediately become payable

(iii) Any notice under this lease shall be in writing and any notice
to the Tenant shall be sufficiently served if left addressed to
him on the demised premises or sent to him by post or left
at his last known address and any notice to the Landlord shall
be sufficiently served if sent to him by post

IN WITNESS etc.

There will then be attached a seal. Other models are to be found in
books of conveyancing precedents.

Comment

Detailed discussion of particular covenants (e.g. on rent, or repair,
or quiet enjoyment) will follow. Two general points may be raised
here on the content of leases. The first is to ask whether certain of
the clauses incorporated into tenancies or leases are too restrictive of
tenants' activities in their accommodation. This point has recently
been taken up by the National Consumer Council (1976) who, after
a survey of local authority tenancy agreements, were very critical of
the often absurd and detailed rules contained in such agreements. The
new Tenants' Charter has been devised to meet some of these criticisms (Housing Act 1980, ss. 28–44, see below, pp. 512–31). It is
also provided that all council tenants should be given a copy of the
terms of their tenancy (*ibid.*, s. 41). Should private tenants have a
similar charter? (Cf. Law Commission, 1975, para. 78.)

More generally, the Law Commission (1975) has argued that the
law should be reformed so as to increase the number of covenants
implied by law. They propose that there should be two classes of covenants: (a) overriding covenants which will impose mandatory obligations notwithstanding the terms of that lease; and (b) variable covenants, to be varied or excluded by express agreement of the parties
but which will otherwise apply.

Overriding covenants will include: (*i*) by the landlord, to give possession and quiet enjoyment (see p. 452) and to disclose his identity
(see p. 93); (*ii*) by the tenant, to pay the rent, protect the premises
and disclose his identity. This category will also contain, for tenancies
of dwelling-houses, sections 32 and 33 of the Housing Act 1961 (see
pp. 350–53), suitably codified.

Variable covenants will deal with other matters relating to use, repair and maintenance; and also deal with entering and inspection, making good and outgoings.

B Statutory tenancies

The existence of written terms may be important when a statutory tenancy under the Rent Act arises. The circumstances in which this may occur are discussed later (pp. 207–20). Note here Rent Act 1977, s. 3, which deals with the incorporation of existing terms into the statutory tenancy:

3.—(1) So long as he retains possession, a statutory tenant shall observe and be entitled to the benefit of all the terms and conditions of the original contract of tenancy, so far as they are consistent with the provisions of this Act.

(2) It shall be a condition of a statutory tenancy of a dwelling-house that the statutory tenant shall afford to the landlord access to the dwelling-house and all reasonable facilities for executing therein any repairs which the landlord is entitled to execute.

8. Assignment and sub-letting

The distinction between assignment and sub-letting has already been noted (above, p. 40). To be legal, a lawful assignment must be by deed (L.P.A., s. 52, above, p. 57) even where the original lease was created orally. If not, it will be enforced on the equitable principles discussed in relation to informal leases (above, p. 70).

A Lawful and unlawful assignment and sub-letting

The extent to which a tenant may assign lawfully or sub-let depends on the terms of the tenancy or lease, if this exists. There are three possibilities:

(*a*) If the document makes no mention of the issue, then either party has an unrestricted right to assign or sub-let. *A fortiori* will this apply if there is no lease or other document. However, possession proceedings may be taken against tenants protected by the Rent Acts who assign or sub-let the whole of their premises after certain dates, without the consent of the landlord (Rent Act 1977, Schedule 15, Case 6; see below, p. 429). This is so even if the tenancy contained no prohibition against assignment or sub-letting (*Regional Properties* v.

Frankenschwerth [1951] 1 K.B. 631). Statutory tenants cannot assign their premises in any event.

(*b*) More commonly, the lease contains a 'qualified' covenant imposing restrictions on the right to assign. This prohibits the tenant from assigning or sub-letting without the prior consent of the landlord. In this situation, the Landlord and Tenant Act 1927, s. 19(1), provides:

19.—(1) In all leases whether made before or after the commencement of this Act containing a covenant condition or agreement against assigning, underletting, charging or parting with the possession of demised premises or any part thereof without licence or consent, such covenant condition or agreement shall, notwithstanding any express provision to the contrary, be deemed to be subject—

> (*a*) to a proviso to the effect that such licence or consent is not to be unreasonably withheld, but this proviso does not preclude the right of the landlord to require payment of a reasonable sum in respect of any legal or other expenses incurred in connection with such licence or consent; and
>
> (*b*) (if the lease is for more than forty years, and is made in consideration wholly or partially of the erection, or the substantial improvement, addition or alteration of buildings, and the lessor is not a Government department or local or public authority, or a statutory or public utility company) to a proviso to the effect that in the case of any assignment, under-letting, charging or parting with the possession (whether by the holders of the lease or any under-tenant whether immediate or not) effected more than seven years before the end of the term no consent or licence shall be required, if notice in writing of the transaction is given to the lessor within six months after the transaction is effected

The usual form of the covenant can be seen in the lease (above, p. 76, para. 2(e)). In *Marks* v. *Warren* [1979] 1 All E.R. 29, the word 'assign' was omitted. It was argued that this meant assignment without consent was permitted. Browne-Wilkinson J. rejected the argument, stating that the three limbs of the covenant, as usually drawn, were not mutually exclusive; the phrase 'not to part with possession' in effect included 'not to assign'.

The operation of these rules is very important in practice and has been the subject of considerable litigation as to what is or is not unreasonable. (The burden of proof is on the tenant: *Shanly* v. *Ward* (1913) 29 T.L.R. 714.) This is partly because the courts have stated frequently that there are no fixed rules, preferring to deal with each case individually. Megarry & Wade (1975, pp. 695–6, notes omitted) give examples on either side of the line:

Examples of reasonable refusal are –

where the proposed assignee's references were unsatisfactory;

where the tenant had altered and failed to repair the property and proposed to assign before putting matters right;

where the property would be used by the proposed assignee for trade competition detrimental to other property belonging to the landlord;

where a proposed sub-letting was to be at a high premium and a low rent, which would depreciate the landlord's interest in the property;

where the proposed assignee was a development company interested only in development to take place after the end of the lease and conflicting with the landlord's plans;

where consent to the transaction would necessarily preclude the landlord from preventing the premises from being used for purposes prohibited by the lease; and

where the assignee would acquire a statutory protection (*e.g.*, under the Rent Restriction Acts) that the assignor could not claim or did not want.

Examples of unreasonable refusal are –

where the landlord's motive was that he wished to recover the premises for himself;

where the proposed assignee was also his tenant, and would vacate another house which would be difficult to re-let;

where the proposed assignee was a diplomat with diplomatic immunity against legal proceedings; and

where permission was refused unless the proposed sub-tenant covenanted with the head landlord to pay him the rent.

As an example of how the courts deal with such cases consider *West Layton Ltd* v. *Ford* [1979] 2 All E.R. 657 (C.A.):

ROSKILL L.J.: The tenants sought, and indeed obtained from the county court judge, a declaration that the landlords had unreasonably withheld their consent, under a lease dated 22nd June 1971, to the granting of sub-tenancy by the tenants to would be sub-tenants...

Now...the landlords appeal...The gravamen of the argument for the landlords is that the county court judge reached a wrong conclusion and that he ought, instead of declaring that the landlords had unreasonably withheld their consent, to have upheld the landlords' refusal to grant the consent in question.

A few dates are relevant. As I said a moment ago, the term was granted on 22nd June 1971. On 4th March 1974 the benefit of that term was assigned to the respondent tenants, West Layton Ltd, who, we are told, have a number of butchers' shops throughout London. On 5th November 1976 the reversion of the lease passed to the late Mr Joseph as trustee. But between the date of the assignment of the term to the respondent tenants and the acquisition of the reversion by the late Mr Joseph, the Rent Act 1974 had become law, on 14th August 1974.

The lease contained two covenants which are relevant for present purposes. Counsel for the tenants invited us to look particularly at cl 2(9) before we turned to cl 2(18). Clause 2(9) provides that the lessee covenants –

'Not without the previous consent in writing of the Lessor (a) to carry on or suffer to be carried on in or upon the shop portion of the demised premises or any part thereof any trade or business whatsoever other than that of a Butchers and at all times of the year during the usual business hours of the locality to keep the shop portion of the demised premises open as a shop for carrying on the said business and (b) to use the residential portion of the demised premises otherwise than for private residential purposes only.'

Clause 2(18)(a)(i) and (ii) read thus (and this is all-important):

'(i) Not to assign transfer charge underlet or part with the possession of any part of the demised premises except a letting on a service tenancy or occupancy of the living accommodation above the shop to any employee of the Lessee or on a fully furnished tenancy for which furnished tenancy the Landlord's consent in writing shall first be had and obtained and such consent for such a letting shall not be unreasonably withheld and (ii) not to assign transfer underlet or part with the possession of the whole of the demised premises without the previous consent in writing of the Lessor such consent not to be unreasonably withheld in the case of a respectable and responsible person...

It is clear that the intention was that this shop should be used for, and only for, a butcher's shop, and that the tenant should have the right to use upstairs accommodation without let or hindrance from the landlord, the occupant being any employee whom they might let in on a service tenancy or licence for the purpose of the business of butchery that was being carried on underneath, but that if the tenant wanted to use the upstairs accommodation for any other residential purpose dissociated from the butchery two conditions had to be satisfied. One was that the landlord's written consent had to be obtained and such consent was not to be unreasonably withheld, and the other that such tenancy had to be a furnished tenancy.

This lease, as is obvious from the chronology which I have already given, was entered into before the Rent Act 1974 protected furnished tenancies. It is clear, therefore, that the draftsman of this lease thought that, if there were a letting of the type contemplated by cl 2(18)(a), when the term of the lease ran out by effluxion of time, there would be no difficulty in the landlord regaining possession. It is clear that the position has changed since 1974; and it is feared that if [sub-tenants] go into possession now and obtain statutory protection under the Rent Act 1974 there will be difficulty in regaining possession when this lease expires in five or six years' time. That is really what this dispute is all about ...

It seems to me that one has to approach this problem not so much by reference to the authorities, of which there are a great number, as a matter of the construction of the covenant which I have already read. The facts are not in dispute. Against those background facts, which I hope I have outlined sufficiently, can it fairly be said that the tenants have shown that these landlords had unreasonably refused their consent?

I do not find it necessary to refer to more than a few of the cases. The cases suggest that there has grown up a practice of asking the question: is the proposed assignment a 'normal' assignment or an 'abnormal' assignment? If it be the former, then the consent is said to be unreasonably withheld. If, on the other hand, it is the latter, then the consent is said to be not unreasonably withheld. I respectfully question whether, although that phraseology appears to have been used more than once in the cases, it is very helpful phraseology.

Roskill L.J. then discussed *Swanson* v. *Forton* [1949] Ch. 143 and *Norfolk Capital Group Ltd* v. *Kitway* [1977] Q.B. 506, in which the value of this distinction had been questioned. He then turned to Lord Denning M.R.'s judgment in *Bickel* v. *Duke of Westminster* [1977] Q.B. 517, where he said, at 523–4:

'The other proposition is that, where a house is subject to the Rent Acts, the landlord cannot reasonably refuse his consent to a *normal* assignment during the contractual term, even though it means that the assignee will be able to stay on afterwards as a statutory tenant. Such is the result of *Thomas Bookman Ltd v Nathan* [1955] 1 W.L.R. 815. But he can reasonably refuse it in the case of an *abnormal* assignment of the "fag end" of the contractual term, made for the purpose of giving the assignee the benefit of the Acts. Such is said to be the result of *Lee v K. Carter Ltd* [1949] 1 K.B. 85, *Swanson v Forton* (above) and *Dollar v Winston* [1949] Ch. 143. Those decisions are said to be binding on this court. If they are good law, they bear a close analogy to the present case. This is an absolutely normal assignment of the lease for the last seven years of the term. It is not the "fag end" of the lease. There is nothing abnormal about it. The Grosvenor Estates cannot, therefore, reasonably refuse their consent, even though it means that the lady will be able afterwards to enfranchise the premises under the Leasehold Reform Act 1967. If those cases can properly be regarded as laying down propositions of law, I would agree that we ought to hold the landlords' refusal to be unreasonable. But I do not think they do lay down any propositions of law, and for this reason. The words of the contract are perfectly clear English words: "such licence shall not be unreasonably withheld". When those words come to be applied in any particular case, I do not think the court can, or should, determine by strict rules the grounds on which a landlord may, or may not, reasonably refuse his consent. He is not limited by the contract to any particular grounds. Nor should the courts limit him. Not even under the guise of construing the words. The landlord has to exercise his judgment in all sorts of circumstances. It is impossible for him, or for the courts, to envisage them all. When this lease was granted in 1947 no one could have foreseen that 20 years later Parliament would give a tenant a right to buy up the freehold. Seeing that the circumstances are infinitely various, it is impossible to formulate strict rules as to how a landlord should exercise his power of refusal. The utmost that the courts can do is to give guidance to those who have to consider the problem. As one decision follows another, people will get to know the likely result, in any given set of circumstances. But no one decision will be a binding precedent as a strict rule of law. The reasons given by the judges are to be treated as propositions of good sense – in relation to the particular case – rather than propositions of law applicable to all cases.'

Roskill L.J. agreed with this approach and continued:

I think that the right approach, as Lord Denning M.R. suggested in the *Bickel* case, is to look first of all at the covenant and construe that covenant in order to see what its purpose was when the parties entered into it; what each party, one the holder of the reversion, the other the assignee of the benefit of the relevant term, must be taken to have understood when they acquired the relevant interest on either side. It is plain, when one looks at this covenant, that its purpose was that the lessee should have the benefit of the living accommodation for the use of any of his staff linked with the carrying on of the business of butchery; but that if he wished to go beyond that user and to use that accommodation for some purpose disconnected with butchery, he must grant no more than a furnished tenancy for which he must obtain the landlord's written consent, which was not to be unreasonably withheld.

The landlord has not got to consider anybody else's interests except his own. He is the person who has in all the circumstances to decide whether or not he will grant consent. As Lord Denning M.R. said, circumstances may vary endlessly. In the present case one of the matters which has caused a change of circumstance is the passing of the Rent Act 1974, just as, in cases of leases entered into before 1967, the passing of the Leasehold Reform Act 1967 altered the background.

It seems to me that the effect of the request which these landlords have had made to them by the tenants is to invite them to agree to alter the nature of the property which was being let from commercial property, namely a butcher's shop with residential accommodation above, to property which would be let on a multiple tenancy, by which I mean to more tenants or lessees than one, because there will be not only the tenancy of the shop but also the separate sub-tenancy, upstairs of the residential accommodation, which would be a tenancy attracting Rent Act protection. That is indeed conceded ...

With great respect to the county court judge, I feel myself compelled to reach a different conclusion from that which he reached. But even if, contrary to my view, it is still right to ask oneself the question whether this proposed sub-letting is 'normal' or 'abnormal', I would answer the question by saying that it is 'abnormal', in this sense, that it is proposed that there should be a different user of a part of the premises, namely independent residential user, different from and dissociated from the business the letting for which this lease was primarily intended, namely, the carrying on of a butcher's business at these premises.

He therefore allowed the appeal. Lawton L.J. concurred and Megaw L.J. agreed.

In *Greene* v. *Church Commissioners* [1974] 3 All E.R. 609 (C.A.), the lease of a flat contained a 'qualified covenant' against assignment, subject to a proviso that the lessee 'shall first by notice in writing to the lessor ... offer to surrender [the premises] ... without any consideration ...' Lord Denning M.R. suggested, *obiter*, that since the clause meant 'that the lessor can always refuse his consent to an assignment if he thinks he can get a higher rent [and thus] force the tenant to surrender', such a clause might be void as being contrary to s. 19. He doubted the decision of *Adler* v. *Upper Grosvenor Street Investment Ltd* [1957] 1 W.L.R. 227 (Ch. D.) in which Hilbery J. had upheld the validity of such a proviso.

However, the issue was directly tested in *Bocardo S.A.* v. *S.&M. Hotels Ltd* [1979] 3 All E.R. 737 (C.A.), in which the validity of a similar proviso was questioned. Megaw L.J. said (in part):

What was s 19(1) of the 1927 Act intended to achieve? I think, in the end, that it must be taken to have had a very limited objective. Apart from legislation, a landlord and a tenant had freedom of contract, in agreeing the terms of their lease, to permit or to limit or to abrogate the right of either or both of them to assign their respective interests. Section 19(1) did not purport to destroy the freedom of contract of the parties to agree to forbid assignment by the tenant. The proposition is accepted by both parties before us, though counsel were unable to identify any decided case to that effect, such as Hilbery

J appears to have had in mind in his judgment in *Adler's* case (about), when he says: 'It is clear and has been decided...'

The nature of the implied term has in some degree been expounded by decisions of the courts subsequent to the 1927 Act. Such cases as *Re Smith's Lease, Smith v Richards* ([1951] 1 All E.R. 346), a decision of Roxburgh J, hold that as a result of s 19(1) the parties cannot by the terms of their contract abrogate the right and duty of the court, in the event of a dispute as to the reasonableness of the withholding of consent where consent is required by the terms of the lease, to decide by an objective standard whether or not the refusal is reasonable. Thus, if the parties by their contract purport to say that in such and such circumstances the landlord may withhold his consent, that term of the contract is invalid and is to be disregarded. The court itself decides whether in the circumstances which actually existed the refusal of consent is reasonable.

In *Re Smith's Lease* the provision of the contract which Roxburgh J held to be invalid in the light of s 19(1) was a term which provided expressly that a refusal of consent 'shall not be deemed to be an unreasonable withholding of consent...' and then the clause went on to provide, as not being unreasonable, an elaborate formulation of a transaction in which the landlord, when he gave his refusal, offered to the tenant to accept surrender of the tenancy. If that decision be right, the distinction between it and the present case depends, not in any way on the realities of what would be achieved by the respective provisions of the leases, but simply on the fact that a different verbal formula is used. That is not a satisfactory distinction.

He went on to note that after *Re Smith's Lease* a new formula was devised by conveyancers, the validity of which was upheld in *Adler*:

In *Adler's* case, as I have said, Hilbery J upheld the new formula. Thereafter, so far as counsel's researches go, there was no criticism or adverse comment on that decision or its reasoning in any reported, or, so far as is known, any unreported, case until 1974. The decision has been cited by textbook writers, almost without criticism. The *Adler* formula, no doubt with variation, has been set out in widely used books of forms and precedents. It has, we are told, I have no doubt correctly, been used in thousands of leases, agreed between landlords and tenants. So far as is known this present case is one of only two cases in which the *Adler* decision and reasoning have been challenged in the courts of this country. The other challenge was in *Greene v Church Comrs for England* (above) [where] ... there were observations by members of the court, obiter, expressing doubt as to the correctness of *Adler*: see per Lord Denning MR and Sir Eric Sachs.

What does seem clear is that the members of the court who expressed those dicta of doubt as to *Adler* in *Greene's* case did not have the advantage, which we have had, of having had cited the judgments given in the High Court

of Australia in *Creer v P&O Lines of Australia Pty Ltd* (1971) 45 A.L.J.R. 697.
That case involved, directly and indistinguishably, the correctness of Hilbery
J's decision in *Adler*. The case arose on s 133B(1) of the Conveyancing Act
1919–1969 (New South Wales). The statutory terms are identical with s 19(1).
The High Court, with closely reasoned judgments by Barwick C.J., Menzies
and Windeyer JJ., approved and followed *Adler*.

I would do the same. In the balance of conflicting arguments, I reach that
conclusion substantially for three reasons. First, the respect due to the decision
of the High Court of Australia, and to the reasoning of the judgments therein;
secondly (as is, indeed, a ground which clearly strongly influenced Menzies
J in that case), the fact that the *Adler* decision has stood, and has been acted
on, for so many years; and thirdly (a ground which makes me feel able to
place much greater reliance on the second ground than I should otherwise
have done), the fact that I cannot see any good argument of policy for interfering, more than is essentially required by the words of the statute or by binding
authority, with freedom of contract in respect of an agreement between the
parties that the landlord should be entitled to the option of requiring a surrender of the lease, where the tenant desires to be freed from his obligation
under the lease, bearing in mind that the legislature did not in 1927 consider,
and has not since considered, that policy requires infringement of freedom
of contract between a potential landlord and a potential tenant validly and
effectively to agree that there shall be no right of assignment at all, however
reasonable the tenant's subsequent desire to assign might be.

Lawton and Brown L.JJ. delivered concurring judgments.

Comment. What is left of the judgment in *Re Smith*? Do you agree that
parties should in effect be able to avoid the terms of s. 19? Do you
find Megaw's reasoning compelling?

The Housing Act 1957, s. 113(5) used to provide that it should be
a term of all local authority lettings that assignment or sub-letting
was not permitted without consent in writing and such consent would
not be granted unless the authority thought that the rent charged
to the assignee/sub-tenant was reasonable. As part of the Tenants'
Charter, s. 113(5) is now repealed, and under the Housing Act 1980,
s. 35, council tenants are given the right to sub-let their accommodation and to take in lodgers; but again this is subject to consent on
the part of the local authority. If consent is refused, tenants may apply
to the county court. (It remains to be seen how far this new provision
will alter the practice of local authorities.)

If the landlord unreasonably refuses his consent after it has been
sought, the tenant may forthwith assign or sub-let (*Treloar* v. *Bigge*

(1874) L.R. 9 Ex. 151), or he may make application to the court for a declaration that he be allowed to assign or sub-let. The county court has jurisdiction (Landlord and Tenant Act 1954, s. 53(1)) whatever the value of the property. The Law Commission has announced that it will probably be recommending that landlords who unreasonably withhold consent should also be liable in damages (Law Commission, 1978, para. 2.38).

The position of a tenant who assigns or sub-lets without making prior efforts to get the requisite consent may depend on whether it can be said that the landlord has 'waived' the breach of covenant. Waiver will occur in various circumstances (Woodfall, 1978, para. 1–1907), the most common of which is an absolute and unqualified demand for rent made after the breach of covenant. In *Metropolitian Properties Co. Ltd* v. *Cordery* (1979) 251 E.G. 561, an illegal sub-tenant moved into a flat and lived there for some three years openly and to the knowledge of the porters employed by the landlords to look after the block. It was decided that the porters were under a duty to communicate such information to the landlords. Even though this had not been done, the Court of Appeal decided that knowledge of the illegal sub-tenant's presence must be imputed to the landlord company, and the breach was to be regarded as waived. On the other hand in *Creery* v. *Summersell* [1949] Ch. 751, where, after the lessor became aware of the breach, a clerk mistakenly sent out a demand for rent, Harman J. held there was no waiver. This decision is severely criticized by Woodfall (*ibid.*, p. 852, n. 9).

In *Scala House Ltd* v. *Forbes* [1974] Q.B. 575, Russell L.J. held that if the landlord did not waive the breach of covenant, then unlawful sub-letting was a breach of covenant not capable of remedy at all. This was true even if the unlawful sub-letting had come to an end. As unlawful sub-letting was not a breach of covenant capable of remedy, a tenant could not rely on Law of Property Act 1925, s. 146(1) (b)[12] (see below, p. 407) to resist moves by the landlord to forfeit the lease. In this case, the court nevertheless used its discretionary power contained in s. 146(2) to grant relief against forfeiture. However, this would not always happen (see, e.g., *Clifford* v. *Johnson* (1979) 251 E.G. 571 (C.A.)).

Note, also, that under the Rent Acts one of the discretionary

12. Proceedings under s. 146 are to be taken against the unlawful assignee, or (presumably) sub-lessee: *Old Grovebury Manor Farm* v. *W. Seymour Plant Sales & Hire* (*No. 2*) [1979] 3 All E.R. 504 (C.A.).

grounds for possession lies against tenants who assign or sub-let the whole of their protected premises without the landlord's consent (Rent Act 1977, Schedule 15, Case 6, below, p. 429). Failure by a tenant who is protected by the Rent Act 1977 or Rent (Agriculture) Act 1976 to notify the landlord of the details of a sub-letting, within 14 days, is a criminal offence (*ibid.*, s. 139); and over-charging sub-tenants may also be ground for eviction (*ibid.*, Sched. 15, Case 10, below, p. 433).

In cases where such consent is required, it is unlawful for a landlord or any other person to discriminate against a person on grounds of race or sex by withholding the relevant consent for the assignment or sub-letting of the premises to him/her (Race Relations Act 1976, s. 24; Sex Discrimination Act 1975, s. 31). These provisions do not apply in the case of small premises (defined in, respectively, s. 22(2) and s. 32(2)). These provisions apply to tenancies created both before and after the passing of the Acts.

(*c*) A third possibility is that the lease may contain an absolute prohibition against assignment or sub-letting. At present it appears that there is no way around this, unless the landlord consents either expressly, or impliedly, e.g. by accepting rent from an assignee or sub-lessee (*Hyde* v. *Pimley* [1952] 2 Q.B. 506).

As long ago as 1950, the Uthwatt-Jenkins Committee recommended (para. 311) that such absolute covenants be deemed to be qualified covenants and therefore covered by s. 19 of the Act of 1927. This issue was aired more recently by the Law Commission. A special working party was set up to discuss the issue, on whose views the Law Commission commented (1970, para. 10):

It will be seen ... that the views of the' Working Party are substantially different from the recommendations of the Jenkins Committee. This difference of approach may arise in part from the conflict between the contractual and proprietary aspects of the subject. The Working Party attach greater importance to the contractual nature of the landlord and tenant relationship and consider that the terms of the lease should govern ... the tenant's right to deal with his leasehold interest during the term. Another point of view is, however, possible, namely that the landlord's legitimate interest is confined to ensuring that the tenant pays his rent and other tenant's outgoings, does nothing to diminish the value of the demised property ... and at the end of the term, reinstates the property in the condition in which it was before.... Subject to these considerations a tenant should be entitled to exercise all the rights of an absolute owner during term of the lease.

It may be noted that in *Property and Bloodstock Ltd* v. *Emerton* [1968] 1 Ch. 94 at pp. 119–20, Danckwerts L.J. did remark that he wished to reserve his opinion on the question of whether s. 19 should apply to an absolute covenant. However in *Bocardo S.A.* v. *S.&M. Hotels Ltd* (above) Megaw L.J. expressed equally strong doubts as to the correctness of Danckwerts' observation.

The issue is still under consideration: what do you think? Pending resolution of this question, it is clear that tenants who assign or sublet contrary to the terms of the covenant have broken the covenant and may therefore be liable for the breach, unless the courts are prepared to grant relief (see above, p. 88).

B Position of assignees[13]

One consequence of the lawful assignment of a tenancy to a new tenant (or of a reversion to a new landlord) is that the assignee effectively steps into the shoes of the assignor. Thus, even though the assignee was not a party to the original tenancy, the convenient doctrine of 'privity of estate' ensures that those covenants that 'run with the land' (for examples, see p. 42) are directly enforceable by or against the assignee. Theoretically the assignor may also remain liable for any breach of covenant by the assignee; but in any assignment for value a covenant of indemnity by the assignee is implied (L.P.A. 1925, s. 77(1)).

Unlawful assignee-tenants will be trespassers and thus able to be evicted (see below, pp. 455–6) unless the landlord acts unequivocally to legitimate the illegality, e.g. by accepting rent from the assignee in the knowledge that unlawful assignment has occurred. (See above, p. 88).

C Position of sub-tenants

Whether a sub-tenancy is lawful or unlawful, the first point to stress is that the covenants in the tenancy cannot be enforced against the sub-tenant directly by the landlord, for there is not the 'privity of estate' that exists when assignment occurs.

Where the sub-tenancy is lawful, or has been made lawful by the landlord waiving the breach of covenant, the basic common law position was that the sub-tenancy must expire at least some time before the original ('mesne') tenancy (see above, p. 40). Problems could arise however where the original tenancy was brought to an end pre-

13. For further discussion see, e.g., Megarry & Wade (1975, pp. 724–42).

maturely. For example, the original tenant might 'surrender' – give up all claim to – his tenancy (see below, p. 405); in such a case the sub-tenant was not to be dispossessed and was entitled to remain for the full term of his sub-tenancy or until the landlord properly brought the tenancy to an end. (See *Mellor* v. *Watkins* (1874) L.R. 9 Q.B. 400.) In *Solomon* v. *Orwell* [1954] 1 All E.R. 874 (C.A.) it was decided that this principle only applied to the surrender of contractual tenancies, not of statutory tenancies. (It has been argued that this principle applies to any method used by the original lessee to terminate his tenancy, e.g. by issuing a notice to quit (Woodfall, 1978, para. 1– 1769), so that the sub-tenant remains but effectively becomes the direct tenant of the original landlord.) It seems that these common law principles also apply when the sub-tenancy was unlawful, so that the unlawful sub-tenant effectively becomes the lawful tenant of the landlord (*Parker* v. *Jones* [1910] 2 K.B. 32). In addition, if a landlord forfeits the 'mesne' (original) tenancy (see below, p. 406), any sub-tenant, lawful or not, may seek an order under L.P.A. 1925, s. 146(4), which, if granted, may vest the 'mesne tenancy' in the sub-tenant. In *Factors (Sundries) Ltd* v. *Miller* [1952] 2 All E.R. 630 (C.A.), this power was used to protect an unlawful sub-tenant[14] who could not have taken advantage of what is now Rent Act 1977, s. 137 (see below, p. 226). It should be stressed, however, that the court's jurisdiction under L.P.A. s. 146(4) is discretionary; how it is exercised will depend on all the surrounding circumstances.

Despite these exceptions, unlawful sub-tenants are usually in a very weak legal position. Once the mesne tenancy has been brought to an end in any way apart from those mentioned above, they will be trespassers and thus liable to summary eviction under Rules of the Supreme Court Order 113 or County Court Rules Order 26 (*Moore Properties Ltd* v. *McKeon* [1976] 1 W.L.R. 1278 (Ch. D.)).

The protection of lawful sub-tenants under the Rent Acts is discussed further below (pp. 225–7).

Official statistics on the numbers of people accepted as homeless show that in the first half of 1977 some 4% of cases in London were the result of illegal lettings or other unauthorized occupancies; for the rest of England the figure was 2%. This represents a total of some 400 applicants (plus their families) (*Housing and Construction Statistics* No. 25, Supp. Table XXXIX–XLII).

14. The original lease contained a qualified covenant against sub-letting; would the decision have been the same if the covenant had been absolute?

9. Other legal formalities

A Registration of title[15]

There are many areas of the country where the Registration of Title is necessary under the Land Registration Act 1925. Not all leases, however, need be registered. The following extract gives a brief introduction (Hawkins, 1971, pp. 138–9):

> Only the titles to leases for longer than twenty-one years can be registered. The reason why leases for the shorter periods are not either registered or entered on the title is administrative convenience. '. . . In a country like England, where letting, sub-letting and sub-underletting is carried on to a degree unknown in any other part of the world, to note every lease or tenancy would mean that the register of title could become cluttered with a great deal of temporary information that is not usually disclosed in the title deeds or abstracts of unregistered conveyancing'. Leases for less than twenty-one years are nevertheless binding on other persons dealing with the registered estate. The rights of other tenants who occupy under shorter and possibly informal agreements are also binding on third parties dealing with the registered land. In both these cases, the rights of the leaseholder in the first instance and the occupier in the second, are known as overriding interests. It is argued that in addition to administrative difficulties, information about tenancies is not available to persons who deal with unregistered land. Anyone else dealing with the land should make and be able to rely on his inspection of the property and enquiries made of the person who is transferring an interest to him. This view has not passed without trenchant criticism.
>
> It is certainly true that the existence of leases for shorter periods than twenty-one years can give rise to difficulty when dealing with the property. This sometimes happens where there has been a tenancy of part of business premises. The tenant has gone out of possession, but the landlord had done nothing to end the lease. If he sells the premises he may not be mindful of the still outstanding interest of the tenant. When a scheme for development is on foot the old tenant may re-appear, claiming that he still has an interest in the premises. In many cases, his claim may have only a nuisance value. Nevertheless, there is no machinery in the unregistered or registered scheme of conveyancing for noting the existence of such a tenant's interest and his potential claims over the property. Furthermore, the fact that there is so much sub-letting is an argument for, rather than against, the noting of the existence of leases and sub-leases on a register.

B Stamp duty requirements

These are set out in standard text books on tax law (e.g. Monroe &

15. See, generally, Hayton (1977).

Nock, 1976, Ch. 5), and are not repeated here. The estimates above, p. 14, are based on leases sent for stamping, but it may be guessed that many informal tenancy agreements, used for lettings of residential accommodation, never get to the relevant authorities for stamping. Failure to stamp may have important consequences in the rare event that either party wishes to produce the lease in court. However, this defect would not seem to inhibit Rent Tribunals or Assessment Committees.

R. v. *Fulham etc. Rent Tribunal, ex parte Zerek* [1951] 1 All E.R. 482 at 486

> LORD GODDARD C.J.: There is one other matter which ... cannot be passed over without notice. The document produced by the landlord, and on which he relied as a memorandum of agreement, was improperly stamped. It may be that he required the tenant to sign over a stamp with a view to impressing on him that it was a formal document, but the document would in any case have required a sixpenny stamp. Had he attempted to put it in before a court of law, an arbitrator, or a referee, it could not have been looked at without requiring him to pay the proper stamp duty and a penalty of £10. These tribunals cannot be described as courts of law ... nor are its members arbitrators or referees. We could not say, therefore, that they were not entitled to look at the document, and, as we have to consider whether their decision was within their jurisdiction, it is necessary for us to look at the same evidence as was before them. It will be for the Commissioners of Inland Revenue to determine what, if any, action they should take in view of what appears to be a deliberate understamping of the document, and it will be sent to them by the court.

C Disclosure of landlord's identity

Under the Housing Act 1974, s. 121, if a tenant of a dwelling makes a written request for his landlord's name and address to any person who demands the rent, who last received it or who for the time being acts as the landlord's agent in relation to the tenancy, it is a criminal offence for that person to fail without reasonable excuse to supply the name and address in a written statement within twenty-one days. Landlords who refuse to cooperate in the provision of the material also commit an offence. Local authorities are given a specific power to prosecute such offences. Similarly, under s. 122, the assignee of a landlord's interest in a dwelling commits an offence if he fails to notify, in a written notice, the tenant(s) that the assignment has taken place, and supply the name and address of the assignee. Local authorities do not have specific power to prosecute this offence, but may, in any event, act under general powers (Local Government Act 1972, s. 222). The maximum penalty for these offences is a fine of £500.

The Law Commission (1975, paras. 93–104) has proposed an extension of this principle to all tenancies:

We think that every tenant should at all times be able to find out who his landlord is. Almost always he knows to whom he should pay the rent; but he also needs to know the name and address of the person whom he can require to perform the landlord's obligations under the terms of the tenancy or implied by law. The tenant who has a reason to communicate with his landlord should not be left in any doubt after there has been a change of landlord.

Most leases and tenancy agreements include a covenant that makes it necessary for a tenant to obtain the landlord's consent to a change of tenant, or to give notice of a change to the landlord; it is unusual to find any corresponding covenant to tell a tenant of a change of landlord.

The normal practice, when there is a change of landlord, is for the tenant to be told who his new landlord is and to whom the rent should be paid in future; the former landlord's authority for the rent to be paid to the new landlord will usually be produced to the tenant at the same time as he is notified of the change. The new landlord normally gives this notice to the tenant promptly, because it is in his own interest to ensure that he receives the rent. This obviously practical procedure results in tenants being properly informed about almost all changes of landlords. But where the same rent collector or other agent who received rent on behalf of the former landlord continues to do so on behalf of the new landlord the tenant himself may not be told of the change.

The tenant, of course, needs to be protected if, because he has not received any notice of change, he continues to pay rent to his former landlord. He is given that protection by section 151(1) of the Law of Property Act 1925; a tenant, until he actually receives such notice, discharges his liability for rent by paying it to the former landlord.

Under the present law, apart from the recent Housing Act 1974, there is no obligation on an outgoing landlord to notify his tenant of a change of landlord, although there is a statutory obligation in particular circumstances to show a landlord's name and address on a rent book. We think that the practice by which a tenant is told of the change when the landlord, for his own reason, gives notice is inadequate. The cases in which such notices do not reach tenants are likely to include the very ones in which tenants most need to know who their landlords are. If a landlord deliberately conceals his identity from the tenant, the tenant knows no more than the identity of the receiver of the rent and is unable to get in touch with his landlord.

It is not only on the occasion of a change of landlord that a tenant should have a right to be told the true identity of his landlord. A new tenant may not have been given all the information known to his predecessor. When there is a long interval between changes of landlords a tenant may want to verify names and addresses; indeed names or addresses may have changed without any change of landlord. We think that any reasonable written request from a tenant for information about his landlord's name and address ought to be properly answered.

There are nowadays many different reasons for a tenant wanting to know who his landlord is. Two examples are:—

    (*a*) repairs for which the landlord is already responsible may need to be done;

    (*b*) a tenant of a long lease may want to serve a notice under the provisions of the Leasehold Reform Act 1967.

We think that the case for our recommendation is strong and that the code would be incomplete if it did not include a provision that enabled all tenants to identify their landlords.

Thus, they recommended that provision of this information was to be an overriding covenant; they baulked at suggesting that breach of the covenant should become a general criminal offence, though they were happy for the Housing Act provisions to remain.

3
The Lease–Licence Distinction

Introduction

Law in general, and property law in particular, uses many legal concepts – 'conceptual pigeon-holes' – which act as the starting point from which other legal consequences may follow. However, whether any given fact situation falls into one legal pigeon-hole, which leads to one set of consequences, or into another legal pigeon-hole, which leads to another set of consequences, is often hard to determine in advance. Are such decisions taken simply on their merits? Or do they depend on what the judges ate for breakfast? Or the ability of the advocates in the case? Or are such decisions taken in the light of the consequences that are known will follow from the decision – a kind of judicial boot-straps operation? Thinking about these kinds of questions is an essential part of coming to any understanding of the judicial process. All too often, when one begins to ask students of law to think about the underlying reasons why particular decisions are reached by judges, they (students) tend to be seized by a kind of mental paralysis. 'It all depends on policy' is the glib answer that is presented. The materials that follow are designed to encourage students to go beyond that level of analysis. (See, generally, Twining & Miers, 1976, especially ch. 8.)

Besides thinking about the nature of judicial process revealed in these cases, another issue worthy of consideration is the social significance of the power that the judges have when they place particular fact situations into particular legal pigeon-holes. For example, when the parties have entered into an informal relationship which ends in a dispute of some kind, it may be inevitable that the judges need the power to categorize that relationship. But to what extent should this happen when there is some kind of written agreement? Should it be the task of judges to re-write or re-interpret those agreements? Is intervention justified on the grounds of inequality of bargaining power?

It should not be thought, however, that these questions are solely a matter of academic or educational interest. Whether, in the case of examples discussed in this book, fact situations are characterized by judges, on the one hand as 'leases'/'tenancies', or on the other hand as 'licences', can have the most important practical consequences. And this applies to all kinds of tenancy, not just residential tenancies (though see, below, on the decline of the lease–licence distinction, pp. 150–51).

The cases that are reproduced here are only a selection of the cases that could be cited. For reasons of space, choice must be limited. However, what follows is reasonably representative and will permit further discussion of the issues involved.

1. Definition of licence

The familiar definition of a licence is that offered by Vaughan C.J. in *Thomas* v. *Sorrell* (1673) Vaughan 351:

A dispensation or licence properly passeth no interest nor alters or transfers property in any thing, but only makes an action lawful which without it had been unlawful.

In other words, acts that would otherwise be trespass are legitimated. By contrast, a lease or tenancy is said to pass an interest in land to the tenant (Woodfall, 1978, para. 1.0016).

The problem with these definitions is that, although they describe certain of the consequences that flow from the process of characterization, they do not offer any useful clues as to what facts are to be taken into account in order to make the classification in the first place. To explore this question, we have to look in more detail at decided cases.

(i) *Marcroft Wagons* v. *Smith* [1951] 2 K.B. 496 (C.A.)[1]

In 1901 one Sydney Aris was already tenant of 6 Mantle Lane, Coalville, Leicester, where his daughter, the defendant, Mrs. Dorothy May Smith, was

1. The point would not arise in exactly this form today since it is now possible for a statutory tenancy to pass on twice after the death of the original tenant. Rent Act 1977, Sched. 1, Part 1, below, pp. 210–20.

born in that year. Aris continued in occupation of the premises until his death on March 8, 1938. He was survived by his widow, who continued to live in them with the defendant until her death on March 16, 1950. On March 27, 1950, the defendant asked the agent of the plaintiff landlords, Marcroft Wagons Ltd., to transfer the tenancy of 6 Mantle Lane to herself. He refused to do so, because, he said, the landlords would want the premises for one of their employees. However, he accepted from the defendant a sum equal to two weeks' rent, and thereafter she continued to pay weekly to the landlords a weekly sum equal to the rent which had been paid by the widow during her life. In September the landlords, who then wanted the premises, required the defendant to leave, and, on her refusing to do so, brought these proceedings to recover possession.

Evershed M.R. said (in part):

[The defendant's] case must depend (and this has been the main contention put forward to this court) upon the submission that at her meeting with the agent on March 27, and as a result of what took place then and thereafter, the court should infer that a new contractual tenancy between the landlords and the defendant came into existence. I confess that I find this a difficult matter. The court is in a sense hedged around with difficulties, in that whichever way it decides, it is suggested that our decision may lead in other cases to results not entirely satisfactory. I am, however, undeterred by that.

It is a trite saying that each case depends on its own particular facts, and what we decide in this case should, therefore, not be a guide to the proper inference to be drawn from different facts in a different case. The judge, having referred to the evidence given on what transpired on March 27, 1950, and having referred to the arguments put forward by the counsel on both sides, said:

'I think both of the arguments are extremely attractive and at first I was convinced provisionally that anyone who was allowed to live in a house, and deemed to have exclusive occupation of it, must be a tenant, but I have come to the conclusion that upon this branch of the case I ought to hold that the true interpretation of what took place on March 27, 1950, is that the landlords did not agree to grant an estate in land, that is to say, that they did not create a tenancy – that what was done was solely to grant a licence for an undefined time in consideration for her paying a sum equal to that paid by her mother by way of rent. I think it really follows from the decision of Cassels, J., in *Minister of Agriculture and Fisheries* v. *Matthews* ([1950] 1 K.B. 148), where he held that occupants of requisitioned premises were licensees, that persons who inhabit premises with exclusive possession can be mere licensees, and that the proper interpretation is that the defendant was offered and accepted that kind of licence'...

That case illustrates one of the features of modern times, namely, the creation of rights of occupation having in most respects the attributes of a tenancy but lacking the estate in land which is a necessary incident of a tenancy. By illustrating, as it does, that modern conception, it is, of course ... not quite an analogy to the present case, for the case really turned on the circumstance that the Minister could not grant something which he himself did not have to grant.

... I can well understand that a judge trying this case might have come to the conclusion that a tenancy had been created and that that was the right inference as to the intention of the parties ... But ... it is plain that [the judge] having seen the witnesses and heard their evidence and also having referred to the correspondence in September, 1950, came to a conclusion of fact that there was here no intention on the part of either the landlords' representative on the one hand or of the defendant on the other, to create a tenancy ... The most troublesome matter, speaking for myself, has been the length of time that elapsed between March and September before the landlords took any further step. There is no doubt that the intricacies of modern life, as reflected in the Rent Restriction legislation, have made, in many respects, the relationship between landlords and tenants assume an artificial and indeed unfriendly character, which is somewhat to be deplored. In particular, landlords, who may have ordinary human instincts of kindliness and courtesy, may often be afraid to allow to a tenant the benefit of those natural instincts in case it may afterwards turn out that the tenant has thereby acquired a position from which he cannot subsequently be dislodged. In the general interest, it may be necessary that the relationship should have to assume a much more formal character than would otherwise be necessary; nevertheless, I should be extremely sorry if anything which fell from this court were to have the effect that a landlord could never grant to a person in the position of the defendant any kind of indulgence, particularly in cirumstances such as existed in March, 1950, when the defendant lost her mother. It seems to me that it would be quite shocking if, because a landlord allowed a condition of affairs to remain undisturbed for some short period of time, the law would have to infer that a relationship had arisen which made it impossible thereafter for the landlord to recover possession of the property, when, admittedly, by taking proper measures from the start, he could have got possession.

There is another very important matter to be borne in mind in considering what inference should be drawn in cases of this kind. Until, in the present century, the Rent Restriction Act came into play, the law broadly speaking necessarily inferred, when exclusive possession was granted to one of the property of another at a rent payable to that other, that a tenancy had been created. The law did not recognize that those conditions were compatible with any other kind of relationship ... But it is now clear that, to use the formula which I think has been applied, a new 'monstrum horrendum, informe, ingens', has come into our ken – the conception of a statutory tenancy –

the conception that a person may have such a right of exclusive possession of property as will entitle him to bring an action for trespass against the owner of that property but which confers no interest whatever in the land: such a person is unable to dispose of the land by grant or by testamentary disposition. It is, as has been said, a statutory right of irremovability. Many illustrations have been before the court ...

Every owner of property today appreciates that the effect of the Rent Restriction Acts is such that in all human probability, should he claim or desire possession of the property, he will have to go to the county court for an order: in other words, a landlord's right to recover possession is now a right to go to the county court for an order for possession. In judging of the inference to be drawn from such events as those which took place here, it seems to me to be vital to bear in mind that that is the background against which people must now discuss and regulate their affairs.

What, on March 27, 1950, was the defendant's position? She had lived in this house all her life. She was the daughter of a man who undoubtedly had been the contractual tenant and might or might not have become a statutory tenant before he died. She was also the daughter of a woman who, as is now conceded, undoubtedly was the statutory tenant of the premises when she died. If ever there was a case in which it would appear tolerably clear to any thinking person that if possession were required, and the defendant were unwilling voluntarily to vacate, it would be necessary to go to the court for an order, this would clearly be such a case.

It is therefore not surprising that when the defendant went to call on the landlords' agent and asked for the tenancy to be transferred to her, he declined to do so. It is not surprising (if we attribute to the agent the ordinary decencies of human life) that he did not seek, within a few days of her mother's death, to evict the defendant from the house where she had lived all her life – which if Mrs. Frazer were right it was presumably his duty to himself and his employers to do in order to protect their rights.

In other words, it seems to me the natural thing, in such circumstances, and bearing in mind that, according to the agent, the landlords wanted the house for one of their own employees, that he should say, in effect, that he could not put the defendant in the position of being tenant; that he did not want to disturb her immediately; that if he did not want the house for one of the landlords' workmen he might be able to do something better; but that, as at present advised, according to his instructions, he could not do that; but that for the moment the defendant might stay on. If three or four or five or six weeks had elapsed, and then the agent had told the defendant that they had given her a reasonable time, and that now they must ask her to go, it seems to me that the defendant's case would have been almost unarguable. The agent, however, allowed the defendant to remain in possession for six months. That length of time would have been a powerful consideration to any judge considering what, at the end of that period, was the proper inference to be drawn from the evidence. In all the circumstances, I cannot think that six months is necessarily so long a period that we must treat the judge's conclusion that there was no change of intention on the part of either party between March and September, 1950, as wrong. In other words, at the end of that six months, as at the beginning, the real inference was that, the agent and the defendant having met, it was agreed between them that the status quo should be allowed for the time to continue, and it did continue...

Denning L.J. said (in part):

It so happened, however, that after the mother died in 1950 the landlords let the defendant stay on for six months. She paid rent and the landlords accepted it; but they refused to change the rent book into her name, and they refused to let her have the tenancy. What is the result of that?

According to the common law as it stood before the Rent Restriction Acts, when the defendant stayed on with the consent of the landlords, she would become a tenant at will; and when she afterwards paid a weekly rent which was accepted by them, she would become a weekly tenant. That would be the result at common law, notwithstanding the refusal of the landlords to change the rent book into her name. Starting from that position, Mrs. Frazer, in her able argument, contended that, inasmuch as the defendant would at common law be a tenant at a rack rent, she is entitled to the protection of the Rent Restriction Acts ...

In my opinion, however, it is not correct to consider the common law position separately from the new position created by the Rent Restriction Acts...

It must be remembered that at common law the landlords would have had a clear, indisputable right to turn the defendant out; and, even if they did allow her to stay on and accepted rent from her, the consequences would not be serious because the landlords could always get rid of her by giving her a week's notice to quit. In that state of affairs, it was very proper to infer a tenancy at will, or a weekly tenancy, as the case may be, from the acceptance of rent. But it is very different when the rights of the landlords are obscured by the Rent Restriction Acts. Seeing that the house was within the Acts, the landlords had no clear right to turn the defendant out. They could not have done so except by proving to the county court that she was not protected by the Acts. And the consequences of granting her a contractual tenancy would be very far-reaching, because she would then be clothed with the valuable status of irremovability conferred by the Rent Restriction Acts.

In these circumstances, it is no longer proper for the courts to infer a tenancy at will, or a weekly tenancy, as they would previously have done from the mere acceptance of rent. They should only infer a new tenancy when the facts truly warrant it. The test to be applied in Rent Restriction Acts cases is the same test as that laid down by Lord Mansfield in cases of holding over: 'The question therefore is, quo animo the rent was received, and what the real intention of both parties was?': see *Doe* v. *Batten* ((1775) 1 Cowp. 234), followed by this court very recently in *Clarke* v. *Grant* ([1950] 1 K.B. 104). If the acceptance of rent can be explained on some other footing than that a contractual tenancy existed, as, for instance, by reason of an existing or possible statutory right to remain, then a new tenancy should not be inferred.

It may well be asked: if the defendant was not a tenant, what was she? She was, I think, a licensee in this sense, that she did not acquire any interest in the land ... It is used to denote a permissive occupation falling short of a tenancy ... Nothing that I have said must be taken to apply to new occupants let in by a landlord. I confine myself to a person who is in the house and who has some colourable ground for saying that he or she is protected by the Rent Acts. In such cases, I think, the landlord can give such a person permission to occupy and can receive a weekly payment from him without necessarily creating a tenancy; but the longer it goes on, the more likely it is that the court will infer that a new tenancy has been in fact created ...

Roxburgh J. agreed.

(ii) *Errington* v. *Errington* [1952] 1 K.B. 290 (C.A.)

In 1936 the husband of Mrs Mary Elizabeth Errington, the plaintiff, purchased a dwelling-house, No. 27 Milvain Avenue, Newcastle, as a home for his son, who had recently married the first defendant, Mrs Mary Duncan Errington. The purchase was financed through a building society, the father paying a lump sum of £250, leaving the balance of £500 on mortgage. The father, who was on terms of affection with his daughter-in-law, handed her the building society's book, told her not to part with it, and promised that the property would be hers and her husband's when they had paid the last instalment on the mortgage. He had, however, retained the conveyance in his own name and paid the rates.

The father died in July, 1945, and by his will left all his property, including the house in question, to his widow. Up to that time the first defendant and her husband had occupied 27 Milvain Avenue and had duly, in accordance with the arrangement with the father, paid the instalments on the mortgage. After the death of his father the son left his wife and went to live with his mother, who now claimed possession of the house from her daughter-in-law, who had remained in the house with her sister, the second defendant, and continued to pay the instalments.

The county court judge dismissed the action. He held that the first defendant and her husband were tenants at will and therefore the claim was barred by the Limitation Act, 1939.

The plaintiff appealed.

Denning L.J. said (in part):

The classic definition of a licence was propounded by Vaughan C.J. in the seventeenth century in *Thomas* v. *Sorrell* (above) ... The difference between a tenancy and a licence is, therefore, that, in a tenancy, an interest passes in the land, whereas, in a licence, it does not. In distinguishing between them, a crucial test has sometimes been supposed to be whether the occupier has exclusive possession or not. If he was let into exclusive possession, he was said to be a tenant, albeit only a tenant at will (see *Doe* v. *Chamberlaine* ([1839] 5 M. & W. 14) and *Lynes* v. *Snaith* ([1899] 1 Q.B. 486)), whereas if he had not exclusive possession he was only a licensee: *Peakin* v. *Peakin* ([1825] 2 I.R. 359). This test has, however, often given rise to misgivings because it may not correspond to realities. A good instance is *Howard* v. *Shaw* (1841) 8 M. & W. 118), where a person was let into exclusive possession under a contract for purchase. Alderson B. said that he was a tenant at will; and Parke B., with some difficulty, agreed with him, but Lord Abinger said that 'while the defendant occupied under a valid contract for the sale of the property to him, he could not be considered as a tenant.' Now, after the lapse of a hundred years, it has become clear that the view of Lord Abinger was right. The test of exclusive possession is by no means decisive.

The first case to show this was *Booker* v. *Palmer* ([1942] 2 All E.R. 674), where an owner gave some evacuees permission to stay in a cottage for the duration of the war, rent free. This court held that the evacuees were not tenants, but only licensees. Lord Greene M.R. said: 'To suggest there is an intention there to create a relationship of landlord and tenant appears to me to be quite impossible. There is one golden rule which is of very general application, namely, that the law does not impute intention to enter into legal relationships where the circumstances and the conduct of the parties negative any intention of the kind.' Those emphatic words have had their effect. We have had many instances lately of occupiers in exclusive possession who have been held to be not tenants, but only licensees. When a requisitioning authority allowed people into possession at a weekly rent: *Minister of Health* v. *Bellotti* ([1944] K.B. 298), *Southgate Borough Council* v. *Watson* ([1944] K.B. 541), *Ministry of Agriculture* v. *Matthews* ([1950] 1 K.B. 148); when a landlord told a tenant on his retirement that he could live in a cottage rent free for the rest of his days: *Foster* v. *Robinson* ([1951] 1 K.B. 149); when a landlord, on the death of the widow of a statutory tenant, allowed her daughter to remain in possession, paying rent for six months: *Marcroft Wagons Ltd* v. *Smith* ([1951] 2 K.B. 490); when the owner of a shop allowed the manager to live in a flat above the shop, but did not require him to do so, and the value of the flat was taken into account at £1 a week in fixing his wages: *Webb Ltd* v. *Webb* (Unreported, 24 Oct. 1951); in each of those cases the occupier was held to be a licensee and not a tenant. Likewise there are numerous cases where a wife, who has been deserted by her husband and left by him in the matrimonial home, has been held to be, not a tenant of the husband owner (*Bramwell* v. *Bramwell* ([1942] 1 K.B. 370), *Pargeter* v. *Pargeter* ([1946] 1 All E.R. 570)), nor a bare licensee (*Old Gate Estates* v. *Alexander* ([1950] 1 K.B. 311)), but to be in a special position – a licensee with a special right – under which the husband cannot turn her out except by an order of the court: *Middleton* v. *Baldock* ([1950] 1 K.B. 657).

The result of all these cases is that, although a person who is let into exclusive possession is prima facie to be considered to be a tenant, nevertheless he will not be held to be so if the circumstances negative any intention to create a tenancy. Words alone may not suffice. Parties cannot turn a tenancy into a licence merely by calling it one. But if the circumstances and the conduct of the parties show that all that was intended was that the occupier should be granted a personal privilege, with no interest in the land, he will be held to be a licensee only. In view of these recent cases I doubt whether *Lynes* v. *Snaith*, and the case of the gamekeeper referred to therein, would be decided the same way today.

Applying the foregoing principles to the present case, it seems to me that, although the couple had exclusive possession of the house, there was clearly no relationship of landlord and tenant. They were not tenants at will but licensees. They had a mere personal privilege to remain there, with no right to assign or sub-let. They were, however, not bare licensees. They were licensees with a contractual right to remain. As such they have no right at law to remain, but only in equity, and equitable rights now prevail ...

(iii) *Addiscombe Garden Estates* v. *Crabbe* [1958] 1 Q.B. 513 (C.A.)

JENKINS L.J.: As to the first question – whether the so-called licence of 12 April 1954, in fact amounted to a tenancy agreement under which the premises were let to the trustees – the principles applicable in resolving a question of this sort are, I apprehend, these. It does not necessarily follow that a document described as a licence is, merely on that account, to be regarded as amounting only to a licence in law. The whole of the document must be looked at; and if, after it has been examined the right conclusion appears to be that, whatever label may have been attached to it, it in fact conferred and imposed on the grantee in substance the rights and obligations of a tenant, and on the grantor in substance the rights and obligations of a landlord, then it must be given the appropriate effect that is to say, it must be treated as a tenancy agreement as distinct from a mere licence.

His Lordship read the agreement of 12 April 1954, and continued:

First, one must observe that the document is described by the parties as a licence. Secondly, one must observe that the draftsman has studiously and successfully avoided the use either of the word 'landlord' or the word 'tenant' throughout the document. The nearest to the use of the word 'tenant' is the reference to 'tenantable repair' in clause 4, subclause (iii); so that if the question depended on the label attached to the document, one would be constrained to say that this, in accordance with its label, was a licence. But if it is right (as I have no doubt it is) to look at the substance of the matter, I think that a different conclusion inevitably ensues ...

Looking at the substance of the matter, what do the grantees get? By clause 1 they are licensed and authorized 'to enter upon use and enjoy' the items mentioned; and it seems to me that those words, taken together, are apt to give to the tenant something in the nature of an interest in the land. I would next observe that in clause 2 provision is made for the licence, as it is called, extending for the fixed period of two years from 1 May 1954. There is thus a term certain which would be appropriate to the grant of a tenancy. Then in clause 3 it is provided that 'The grantees shall have the use and enjoyment of the premises in consideration' of a payment. The payment is described as a payment of 'court fees'; it is fixed at the sum of £37 10s. per month, and it has to be paid in advance on the first day of each month. In all but name, that appears to me to be a rent or reddendum in consideration of the right to 'enter upon, use and enjoy' the premises which is granted by clause 1 ...

Then there are the various agreements by the grantees with the grantors in clause 4, beginning with the agreement to make the monthly payment of the court fees very much like the agreement to pay the rent which is always to be found in a tenancy agreement. There is a significant provision in subclause (iii) under which the grantees agree 'to repair and maintain the club house'. It seems inappropriate that a mere licensee should be saddled with an obligation to repair. Then one finds as to repairs that the items mentioned are to be maintained 'in good tenantable repair', an expression to which I have already called attention. That, one cannot help thinking, to some extent supports the view that the grantees are tenants ...

Then under subclause (iv) there is the obligation to maintain the tennis courts. In subclause (v) there is a provision which, I think, is not without significance. That is the provision under which the grantees shall not 'without the grantors' previously written consent cut down or injure any plants trees bushes or hedges or remove from the said property any soil clay sand or other materials and not make any excavations thereon except for the purpose of maintaining the [tennis courts] in accordance with the agreement and conditions hereinbefore contained.' The significance of that is that it should have been thought necessary expressly to prohibit the grantees from doing certain things which quite plainly, if they were mere licensees, they would have no right or power to do ... In a similar sense one may note the provision in subclause (vi): 'not to erect any building or other structures upon the said property except such as shall be approved by the grantors.'

Then there is the provision which Mr Blundell called in aid, which is the restrictive provision in subclause (vii): 'to use the said premises as a private lawn tennis club and club house for the convenience of members of the club their guests and their staff only', and so on; and in subclause (viii): 'not to allow any persons except members guests and servants of the club to use the said premises for any purpose but this clause shall not prevent the club inviting or allowing a reasonable number of members of the general public to enter thereon for the purpose of attending functions specially organized for those interested in the game of lawn tennis'. In my view, those provisions afford no real assistance to Mr Blundell, for they are just what one would expect to find in a tenancy agreement of premises intended for use as a lawn tennis club ...

The next provision of importance is the agreement to permit 'the grantors and their agents at all reasonable times to enter the said premises to inspect the condition thereof and for all other reasonable purposes.' The importance of that is that it shows that the right to occupy the premises conferred on the grantees was intended as an exclusive right of occupation, in that it was thought necessary to give a special and express power to the grantors to enter. The exclusive character of the occupation granted by a document such as this has always been regarded, if not as a decisive indication, at all events as a very important indication to the effect that a tenancy, as distinct from a licence, is the real subject-matter of a document such as this.

In subclause (xii) there is provision 'to deliver up the said premises at the termination of this licence in a condition consistent with the foregoing provisions.' 'To deliver up' seems to me to be an expression more appropriate to a tenant with an interest in the land than to a person who has a mere contractual right to be on the land; it is an expression universally used, I think, in all tenancy agreements and leases. The provision as to insurance points in the same direction; it would, I think, be curious if a mere licensee, with no interest in the premises, was made liable for insurance. Then in clause 5, subclause (ii), there is what is practically a common form covenant for quiet enjoyment such as is found in every tenancy agreement or lease; and it seems to me that this clause points strongly in the direction of a tenancy agreement here. In clause 6, subclause (i), there is the provision: 'that the grantors may re-enter and determine the licence in the event of non-payment of any of the said payments of court fees for fourteen days (whether formally demanded or not) or on breach of any of the grantees' stipulations.' Those references to re-entry and 'non-payment of any of the said payments of court fees for fourteen days (whether formally demanded or not)' are provisions wholly appropriate to a tenancy agreement; and I should have thought that a reference to re-entry was really inappropriate to the case of a licence; the conception of re-entry is the resumption of possession by the landlord, and the determination of the interest of the tenant.

Taking all those considerations together, I am of opinion that the judge was perfectly right in holding, as he did, that this was a tenancy ...

The judge cited a useful authority in the shape of the decision of this court in *Facchini* v. *Bryson* [1952] 1 T.L.R. 1368). The headnote reads:

'Where an employer lets his employee into occupation of a house, in consequence of his employment, at a weekly sum payable by him and the occupation had all the features of a service tenancy, the agreement was so construed, notwithstanding a clause that "nothing in this agreement shall be construed to create a tenancy"; the agreement must be construed as a whole, and their relationship was determined by the law and not by the label which they chose to put on it. The agreement accordingly operated as a tenancy agreement, not a mere licence to occupy, and the employer was not entitled to an order for possession except in accordance with the provisions of the Rent Restriction Acts.'

At the beginning of his judgment Somervell L.J. said:

'This appeal turns on the construction of an agreement, and it involves one of those problems which parties sometimes set the court when they use words in some of the paragraphs of an agreement indicating one relationship, and use words in other paragraphs of the agreement which would indicate another. The court has to construe the agreement as a whole. The question is whether the document here is a lease or a licence to occupy the premises.'

The Lord Justice then referred to the decision in *Three D's Co. Ltd* v. *Barrow* ((1949) 99 L.J. 564) and said:

'I agree with Mr Megarry that that agreement was not this agreement, and that there are material differences between the two, but what I said about the similar clause in that agreement is, I think, applicable here. I said: "That provision is one which is only appropriate and relevant if the document is giving to the party who is going to live in the house exclusive possession. I should have thought that it was quite unnecessary if a servant was merely occupying the house that the landlord should stipulate that he should be allowed to go in and see the condition of it" – the reference there being to a provision comparable to the provision in the present case in clause 4, subclause (xi), as to permitting the grantors to enter for certain purposes.'

Then continuing his reference to *Three D's Co. Ltd* v. *Barrow* he went on:

'I think that that is equally applicable in the present dispute whether this was a lease or a licence. Mr Megarry asked us to treat it like a declaratory section in an Act of Parliament, that is to say, merely declaring a right and not giving one. I do not think that the words are apt to be considered in that way, but are apt in the sense in which I thought that they were apt in the other case, namely, they assume a right to keep the landlord out, if I may so put it, and state the circumstances and conditions on which he may enter.'

Then, after referring to a prohibition of underletting, which has no counterpart here, Somervell L.J. proceeded:

'Those seem to me to be the main and operative clauses in which one would seek to find what the rights as between the two parties are. It is true that the clause with reference to the payment does not use the word "rent", and that the earlier part of clause 2 refers to occupation and use. But, taking the agreement as a whole for a moment, apart from the last two lines of clause 2, I would have come to the conclusion that this was a lease.'

Denning L.J. agreed, and said:

'We have had many cases lately where an occupier has been held to be a licensee and not a tenant. In addition to those which I mentioned in *Errington* v. *Errington* we have recently had three more, *Gorham (Contractors) Ltd* v. *Field* ([1952] C.P.L. 266), *Forman* v. *Rudd* (Unreported), and *Cobb* v. *Lane* ([1952] 1 All E.R. 1199). In all the cases where an occupier has been held to be a licensee there has been something in the circumstances, such as a family arrangement, an act of friendship or generosity, or suchlike, to negative any intention to create a tenancy. In such circumstances it would be obviously unjust to saddle the owner with a tenancy, with all the momentous consequences that that entails nowadays, when there was no intention to create a tenancy at all. In the present case, however, there are no special circumstances. It is a simple case where the employer let a man into occupation of a house in consequence of his employment at a weekly sum payable by him. The occupation has all the features of a service tenancy, and the parties cannot by the mere words of their contract turn it into something else. Their relationship is determined by the law and not by the label which they chose to put on it ... It is not necessary to go so far as to find the document a sham. It is simply a matter of finding the true relationship of the parties. It is most important that we should adhere to this principle, or else we might find all landlords granting licences and not tenancies, and we should make a hole in the Rent Acts through which could be driven – I will not in these days say a coach and four, but an articulated vehicle.'

The present case, of course, has nothing to do with the Rent Acts, but the important statement of principle is that the relationship is determined by the law, and not by the label which parties choose to put on, and that it is not necessary to go so far as to find the document a sham. It is simply a matter of ascertaining the true relationship of the parties.

We were also referred by Mr Blundell to *Errington* v. *Errington* ...

[In] the course of his judgment, Denning L.J. said: 'The test of exclusive possession is by no means decisive.' I think that wide statement must be treated as qualified by his observations in *Facchini* v. *Bryson*; and it seems to me that, save in exceptional cases of the kind mentioned by Denning L.J. in that case, the law remains that the fact of exclusive possession, if not decisive against the view that there is a mere licence, as distinct from a tenancy, is at all events a consideration of the first importance. In the present case there is not only the indication afforded by the provision which shows that exclusive occupation was intended, but there are all the various other matters which I have mentioned, which appear to me to show that the actual interest taken by the grantees under the document was the interest of tenants, and not the interest of mere licensees.

For these reasons, I hold that the judge came to a perfectly right conclusion when he decided that this must be treated as a tenancy agreement.

(iv) *Shell-Mex* v. *Manchester Garages* [1971] 1 W.L.R. 612 (C.A.)

LORD DENNING M.R.: Shell-Mex and BP Ltd, the plaintiffs, own the Grey-hound Filling Station at Kirkmanshulme Lane, Manchester. In 1966 they allowed a company called Manchester Garages Ltd, the defendants, to go into occupation. There are two documents for two different parts of the premises. The front land is covered by a document called a licence. It consists of the site of the filling station itself, where there are three petrol pumps, a kiosk, car sales display canopy and offices. The defendants supply petrol on this site to customers ...

The latest licence of the front land was for one year, from 1st August 1969, expiring on 31st July 1970. Difference arose between the parties. The plaintiffs decided not to continue the licence. On 30th July 1970, their solicitors wrote to the defendants:

'This Licence expires on 31st July, 1970, and [the plaintiffs] will expect and require [the defendants] to cease all use of the Filling Station under the said Licence after that date.'

The defendants did not comply. They continued to use the filling station. So on 7th August 1970, the plaintiffs issued a writ claiming an injunction to restrain the defendants from entering on the premises and from trespassing thereon. If this licence were truly a licence, then the defendants have no defence. But they say that the word 'licence' was only a label put on it. It was, in truth, they say, a tenancy. It was a tenancy of business premises, and, accordingly, they are entitled to the benefit of the Landlord and Tenant Act 1954. By Part II of that Act a tenancy of business premises does not come to an end unless terminated in accordance with the Act, and the parties cannot contract out of it. So, if it is a tenancy, and not a licence, the defendants are entitled to stay in the filling station ...

I turn, therefore, to the point: was this transaction a licence or a tenancy? This does not depend on the label which is put on it. It depends on the nature of the transaction itself: see *Addiscombe Garden Estates Ltd v Crabb* (above).

Broadly speaking, we have to see whether it is a personal privilege given to a person, in which case it is a licence, or whether it grants an interest in land, in which case it is a tenancy. At one time it used to be thought that exclusive possession was a decisive factor, but that is not so. It depends on broader considerations altogether. Primarily on whether it is personal in its nature or not: see *Errington v Errington and Woods* (above). Applying this principle, I turn first to the document itself. It is called a licence. By its terms the plaintiffs:

'1. ... [grant] to the [defendants] licence and permission to use upon the terms and conditions and solely for the purpose hereinafter specified the land and buildings situate at and known as Greyhound Filling Station ...
'2. The purposes for which this licence is granted are to enable the [defendant] to carry on upon the premises: (i) The business of selling ... such grades of the brand or brands of motor fuel as the [plaintiffs] may from time to time nominate ...'

and also rendering such services as are commonly supplied at service stations. By the conditions the defendants agree:

'To use every endeavour and due diligence to sell and foster the sale of the [plaintiffs'] motor fuel ... and other petroleum products in such manner as the [plaintiffs] may from time to time direct.'

And the plaintiffs agree:

'... to supply or cause to be supplied to the [defendants] at the premises such quantities of the [plaintiffs'] motor fuel ... and other petroleum products as the [defendants] may from time to time reasonably require and order from the [plaintiffs] at the wholesale price ruling at the date and place of delivery for such supply...'

The provisions seem to me to be personal in their nature. There is a personal tie between the parties whereby the defendants are to deal in Shell petrol only and are to take all their supplies from the plaintiffs, who are to supply them. It is noticed also that there is no proviso for a right to re-enter. There is a special stipulation which seems to me to connote that the plaintiffs remain in possession themselves. It is cl 19 of Sch 1 under which the defendants agree:

'Not to impede in any way the officers servants or agents of the [plaintiffs] in the exercise by them of the [plaintiffs'] rights of possession and control of the premises and in particular to give all reasonable assistance and facilities to such officers servants or agents for the alteration at any time of the layout decorations or equipment of the premises.'

That shows that the plaintiffs' men can go and visit the premises whenever they like. The defendants are not to impede them in any way, but are to give them assistance. Those provisions point to a licence and not a tenancy. But counsel for the defendants says that the defendants have exclusive possession, and that that carries with it a tenancy. That is old law which is now gone. As I have said many times, exclusive possession is no longer decisive. We have to look at the nature of the transaction to see whether it is a personal privilege, or not. Next counsel for the defendants says that all these clauses are just what one would find in an ordinary tenancy of a filling station. He suggests that, if this case were to go for trial and he was to have discovery, he would find many a tenancy agreement of a filling station in which there were parallel clauses. He refers to *Little Park Service Station Ltd v Regent Oil Co Ltd* ([1967] 2 Q.B. 655), where there was a tenancy of a filling station and not a licence.

It seems to me that when the parties are making arrangements for a filling station, they can agree either on a licence or a tenancy. If they agree on a licence, it is easy enough for their agreement to be put into writing, in which case the licensee has no protection under the Landlord and Tenant Act 1954. But, if they agree on a tenancy, and so express it, he is protected. I realise that this means that the parties can, by agreeing on a licence, get out of the Act; but so be it; it may be no bad thing. Especially as I see that the parties can now, with the authority of the court, contract out of the Act, even in regard to tenancies: see s. 5 of the Law of Property Act 1969. I think it plain that in this case there was a licence for one year, and not a tenancy. When the licence came to an end, the defendants had no right to be there. There is no defence to this case. The judge was quite right to give summary judgment for an injunction. I think that we should dismiss the appeal.

Sachs and Buckley L.JJ. delivered concurring judgments.

(v) *Heslop* v. *Burns* [1974] 3 All E.R. 406 (C.A.)

STAMP L.J.: The deceased owned certain properties in the King's College area of Lambeth. In about 1951 the defendants, Mr and Mrs Burns, who had recently come to London, were living in an attic. Mr Burns was a bus conductor. Mrs Burns was expecting a child. She was also looking for light employment. She was put in touch with the deceased. There was a business in which the deceased was concerned at another address in Warner Road, and Mrs Burns was engaged to do some light work in the nature of cleaning in the office. She was there only six weeks, but during that period the deceased appears to have formed a romantic attraction for her. He visited the defendants, and expressed concern at the conditions in which they were living and, either shortly before or shortly after their baby (who was a girl) was born in April 1951 he bought a cottage in Fowler Street, which was in the neighbourhood, for the family to live in. He became godfather to the child. To anticipate for a moment, he subsequently paid for the girl's education and gave her presents.

From the time of the purchase of the cottage in Fowler Street until his death, the deceased provided the family with a residence, at first at the cottage in Fowler Street, then at an address in Love Walk, and, from 1954 onwards, at 116 Warner Road. All these properties were in the near neighbourhood.

There never was any question of either of the defendants doing any work for the deceased in return for their accommodation. Mrs Burns worked for the deceased for a short time while they were living at Fowler Street, but she was paid for her services. Similarly, when Mr Burns did jobs for the deceased, as he did, he was paid for what he did. Any suggestion that there was a service tenancy was not, and is not, pursued. In 1953 the family moved into the residence at Love Walk, which the deceased purchased for the purpose, and, in 1954, into 116 Warner Road, the subject of this action.

The deceased was from the outset very friendly with the family. During the whole period from the time when the defendants entered into occupation of the Fowler Street cottage, down to 1968, when the deceased became ill, he was in the habit of visiting the defendants regularly, sometimes twice a day. He gave money to the daughter to whom he became godfather; and in a word he was extremely generous to the defendants. He paid the rates on the several properties which he had obtained for them, and he never required any payment whatsoever in respect of their occupation. Frequently on his daily visits to whichever house the defendants were living in he had supper with them, and according to the evidence he visited them every day, except at weekends. There were visits together to the seaside in the summer.

The learned county court judge found as a fact that the deceased meant to provide a home for the defendants and intended them to go on living there. It was the evidence of Mr Burns that the deceased said about each of the three dwelling-houses when the defendants were in them that 'if anything happened to him the premises would be left to us'. As I have said, the deceased paid the rates. Asked, towards the end of her cross-examination: 'If the property was regarded as being yours, did it occur to you that Mr Timms was being more than usually generous by paying all rates etc?', Mrs Burns answered: 'No, he had our company. He could come into the house any time he wanted.' Mrs Burns in the course of her examination said that in 1959 (there must be an error in the transcript there) the deceased said he was buying 116 Warner Road 'for me', and that he told a Salvation Army welfare officer that he had bought the house for her; and at one time he said 'Don't worry about the house: it's yours'. She was shocked when, following the death of the deceased, she found that this property had not been left to her; and I am bound to say that I have the greatest possible sympathy for her in that regard. Of course, the property was not at the outset the property of the defendants, and it never became so, unless it be by the effect of the 1939 [Limitation] Act . . .

On the facts of this case it is, in my judgment, abundantly clear that the parties did not enter into any arrangement, far less any arrangement intended to create a legal relationship, as to the terms on which the defendants should occupy the property. There was no contract, no arrangement, no statement by the deceased. The defendants, as I see it, were allowed to move into the property and occupy it simply as a result of the bounty of the deceased and without any arrangements as to the terms on which they should do so. There was no evidence of any discussion whatsoever taking place as to the terms of the occupation. It was by the effect of the bounty of the deceased or, if you will, because of his feelings of affection for Mrs Burns, that the home was provided, and it was, I think, for those reasons that the defendants remained there.

The fact, which was relied on by counsel for the defendants, that the deceased had already said, in relation to each of the properties in Fowler Street and Love Walk, that he would leave it to the defendants, is no evidence that it was the intention of the deceased that the defendants should in the meantime be tenants at will rather than licensees. Counsel for the defendants submitted that, since the deceased intended to provide the defendants with a home, he must have intended to give them an interest in the property. But a tenancy at will was no more apt to achieve that purpose than a revocable personal licence to occupy the property; and if one asks the question what interest he intended them to have, it could only, consistently with counsel's submission, be an interest during the rest of the life of the deceased of such a nature as would exclude him from any right to turn them out. No such interest was created and I find it impossible to infer an intention on the part of the deceased to create such a situation. In my judgment the proper inference is that the defendants at the outset entered into occupation of the premises as licensees and not as tenants at will; not with a right to exclude the deceased from possession.

In the course of the debate we were referred to a number of passages in judgments where the effect of exclusive possession in the determination of the question 'tenancy or licence?' has been discussed. As Somervell L.J. indicated in *Cobb* v. *Lane* ([1952] 1 All E.R. 1199), the expression 'exclusive possession' in relation to the occupier of a property may be used in more than one sense. It may, as I see it, be used to mean that, as a factual matter, the occupant, alone or together with his family, occupies the premises and does not share them with any other person. Such a situation is not inconsistent with the occupation being enjoyed under a mere licence. Or the expression may be used to mean that the occupant has a right to exclude the owner from the premises. I think it must have been in the former sense that Denning L.J. used the expression in *Shell-Mex and BP Ltd* v. *Manchester Garages Ltd* ([1971] 1 All E.R. 841), in dealing with the argument of counsel for the defendants there: for there the occupant had by the very terms of the contract no right to exclude the owner; and possibly he used it in that same sense in the earlier case of *Errington* v. *Errington* (above). Where the expression is used in the latter sense as describing a situation where the occupier has the right to exclude the owner it is clearly more difficult to reconcile it with the existence of a mere licence to occupy. But rights do not arise in vacuo and before concluding that an occupant was intended to be in a position to exclude the owner from the premises, one must, as I see it, ask the question: did the parties intend that the occupant should have such a right? It may, I think, be that, coming to the conclusion that that indeed was the intention of the parties, the court may usually be constrained to hold that what was intended was a tenancy at will and not a mere licence to occupy. It is, however, not in my judgment necessary to express any concluded view on this aspect of the matter. The deceased here could, as Mrs Burns remarked, 'come into the house any time he wanted'; and in a conversation (to which I have not hitherto referred) with the plaintiffs' representative when he came to value the property for the purposes of probate after the death of the deceased, she told him that the deceased regarded the house as 'his second home'. The home was not to be the defendants' castle but the house in which he allowed them to live.

In the circumstances in which the deceased let the defendants into occupation, I find it impossible to infer that he intended them to have the right to exclude him; for in my judgment the circumstances and the relationship between the parties were wholly inconsistent with such a view of his intentions...

If it was the defendants' case that they held 116 Warner Road under a periodic tenancy at a rent, the income tax returns and the entries made by the deceased in the books to which I have referred, and the rent book, would no doubt be corroboration of that case. But, since the defendants deny the existence of a tenancy at a rent and it is common ground that they never paid or agreed to pay rent, and indeed the payment of rent was never mentioned, I do not think that one is led to the conclusion, as a result of these entries and the payment of tax, that they were intended to be tenants at will. Whatever motive the deceased may have had in treating the defendants in his books, for the purposes of tax, as tenants – and guessing at the motive one would have to remember that the relationship between him and the defendants was perhaps a somewhat delicate one – it cannot, in my judgment, support the inference that they occupied the premises as tenants at will and not as bare licensees.

I would allow the appeal.

SCARMAN L.J.: Had counsel for the defendants been addressing this court a hundred years ago ... I think that *Lynes* v. *Snaith* ([1899] 1 Q.B. 486) indicates how the law then stood. Lawrance J. said: 'As to the first question, I think it is clear that she was a tenant at will and not a licensee; for the admissions state that she was in exclusive possession – a fact which is wholly inconsistent with her having been a mere licensee.' Today, however, a very different approach appears to be adopted by the courts; and one can see it in the first sentence of the headnote in *Cobb* v. *Lane* ([1952] 1 All E.R. 1199) ... 'The fact of the exclusive occupation of property for an indefinite period is no longer inconsistent with the occupier being a licensee and not a tenant at will.' What on earth had happened between 1899 and 1952? Are we witnessing judicial legislation without the assistance of Parliament? The answer is No. The law as I understand it is precisely the same today as it was then. The legal question is a question as to the intention of the parties. The legal balance still shows a tilt in favour of a tenancy at will; for, once an exclusive occupation had been established, a tenancy at will is presumed unless there are circumstances which negative it. What has happened, of course, is not that the law has changed but that society has. To deal with changed social conditions, the Rent Restrictions Acts since 1914–15 have introduced a new dimension to the law of landlord and tenant, and there has also emerged into prominence the licence to occupy. This concept has been developed by the courts so that now it is present as a possible mode of land-holding—a mode which had certainly not been developed into anything like its current maturity in the nineteenth century. Indeed, *Errington* v. *Errington* (above) is now an authority binding on this court, to the effect that a contractual licence may confer on a licensee an exclusive right to the occupation of land in the sense that during the currency of the contract the licensee may keep out the licensor.

What has happened, therefore, is that the facts of society have changed and a more subtle investigation of the facts has to be undertaken in answering the two questions: 'What is the intention of the parties?' and 'Are there circumstances negativing the inference of a tenancy at will?' It seems to me, with respect, that Denning L.J. in *Facchini* v. *Bryson* ([1952] 1 T.L.R. 1368) gives some helpful guidance as to the sort of circumstances that now have to be examined and assessed in determining whether or not a tenancy has been created. In the course of his judgment he used these words: 'In all the cases where an occupier has been held to be a licensee there has been something in the circumstances, such as a family arrangement, an act of friendship or generosity, or such like, to negative any intention to create a tenancy.' In the present case I think that one can find something very akin to a family arrangement. After all, we are considering the occupation of a house which is described by the lady most concerned as the 'second home' of Mr Timms. We are certainly considering a whole course of dealing within the realm of friendship, and we are certainly faced with very great generosity shown over a long number of years by Mr Timms to the Burns family. When one considers the peculiar circumstances of this case and considers them sympathetically, as one is bound to do, it becomes very difficult to see how in principle this case can be distinguished from *Cobb* v. *Lane* ([1952] 1 All E.R. 1199), and very difficult to see how, even on the two assumptions that I have made in favour of counsel for the defendants, there is here any evidence on which it is possible to infer a tenancy at will.

In the books (and we were referred to a passage in Woodfall) one finds still the assertion that an exclusive occupation of indefinite duration can create a tenancy at will. The social changes to which I have alluded seem to show that less and less will the courts be inclined to infer a tenancy at will from an exclusive occupation of indefinite duration. It may be that the tenancy at will can now serve only one legal purpose, and that is to protect the interests of an occupier during a period of transition. If one looks to the classic cases in which tenancies at will continue to be inferred, namely, the case of someone who goes into possession prior to a contract of purchase, or of someone who, with the consent of the landlord, holds over after the expiry of his lease, one sees that in each there is a transitional period during which negotiations are being conducted touching the estate or interest in the land that has to be protected, and the tenancy at will is an apt legal mechanism to protect the occupier during such a period of transition; he is there and can keep out trespassers; he is there with the consent of the landlord and can keep out the landlord as long as that consent is maintained. It may be, therefore, that, not under any change in the law, but under the impact of changing social circumstances, the tenancy at will has suffered a certain change, at any rate in its purpose and function.

(vi) *Marchant* v. *Charters* [1977] 3 All E.R. 918 (C.A.)

LORD DENNING M.R.: 131 Clapton Common is an ordinary sort of house. It is owned by the plaintiff, Mrs Marchant. It was at one time a private dwelling-house, but for the last 23 years she has let it off in single rooms to men only. She has regularly put the same advertisement in the local newspaper:

'Attractive Batchelor Service Apartments. Superior House. Resident Housekeeper, Every convenience.'

There are seven bed-sittingrooms. Each room is simply but nicely furnished with a bed, table, a couple of chairs and so forth. Each room has, of course, its gas ring and grill, so that the residents can do a little cooking on their own, as meals are not included. The bathroom and lavatory are shared. The housekeeper cleans the rooms every day and provides clean linen every week. It is a very usual sort of arrangement. Many young people live in bed-sittingrooms like this.

The question is whether the occupier of such a bed-sittingroom has security of tenure.

In order to describe the facts, I will now read Mrs Marchant's evidence:

'I go to [the house] practically every day. I occasionally sleep there. [It] is a fine old house: a self-catering residential hotel for single men. Been running like this for 25 years. Each resident has a room of his own. They are completely furnished, wall to wall carpeting, curtains, bed, blankets, sheets, pillow, pillow case, towels, even tea towels, one arm chair and two wooden chairs, wardrobe, occasional tables, cooker, sink, with gas water heater, gas fire for heating, points for power. Each room has own meter for gas and electricity. Every resident gets daily cleaning of room, clean linen weekly, bathrooms are common. They can get an evening meal by arrangement with housekeeper, they pay her. She is engaged on basis that she will provide food if required. All rooms are provided with cutlery, crockery, and cooking utensils, all that is necessary. They can also get breakfast and lunch. Through the years, I find more and more people are providing their own meals. The housekeeper keeps the money for the food she provides.'

On that evidence the final question is, was Mr Charters a tenant or only a licensee? The law on this subject has been developed greatly in the last 25 years. I might almost say revolutionised. In 1952 I collected several of the cases in *Errington v Errington* (above) and since that time there have been many more. The difference is very important under the Rent Acts (including the 1974 Act) because a 'tenant' is given complete security of tenure, but a licensee is not. There are four or five cases, somewhat like the present, to which we have been referred. The first is *Appah v Parncliffe Investments Ltd* ([1964] 1 W.L.R. 1064). A house had been split up into 17 different rooms, each with its own Yale lock and key. The rooms were furnished. No meals were provided, but the rooms were cleaned daily and beds made. Fresh linen was provided. A lady took one of the rooms but, owing to the negligence of the owners, someone was able to break into her room and steal her belongings. It was held that she she was not a tenant but a licensee for reward; and so able to sue the owner for negligence.

The next case is *Abbeyfield (Harpenden) Society Ltd v Woods* ([1968] 1 W.L.R. 374). A charitable society had converted a big house into an old people's home with 12 rooms. They let one of the rooms unfurnished to an old man of 85. He furnished it himself. The society provided food in a common dining room and so forth. There was a resident housekeeper. It was held that the old man was only a licensee and not a tenant. So he was not protected by the Rent Acts and had to go.

The nearest case to the present case is *Luganda v Service Hotels Ltd* ([1969] 2 Ch. 209). A student was reading for the bar. He took a furnished room in a building called the Queensborough Court Hotel. There were 88 rooms. They were said to be 'let' out to tenants. Every student had a Yale key for his room. It was a bed-sittingroom with a double gas ring. He got his own meals and provided his own towels and soap. The chambermaids came in every day and made the bed and cleaned the room. Every week they changed the linen. It was held that he was a contractual licensee and not a tenant. But as he had applied to the rent tribunal he was protected for a limited period from being evicted.

The next case arose under the planning Acts. *Mayflower Cambridge Ltd v Secretary of State for the Environment* (1975) 30 P.&C.R. 28. A building in Cambridge had been erected for students to stay in, but it was not needed for them. So it was used for visitors who wanted to come to Cambridge. The question was whether the change of use was to a 'hotel' Lord Widgery CJ said: 'The essence of a hotel is that it takes transient passengers.' That may well be a test under the planning Acts but it is not a test for seeing whether there is a tenancy or a licence.

The last case is *R v South Middlesex Rent Tribunal, ex parte Beswick* ((1976) 32 P.& C.R. 67). A young lady lived in a single room at a YMCA hostel. It was a furnished room. It was her sole home. She was permanent, not temporary. In common with other residents, she had the use of a kitchen, dining-room, livingroom, laundry room, bathroom and toilet. It was held that she was not a tenant but a licensee. So the fair rent was to be fixed, not by the rent officer, but by the rent tribunal.

Gathering the cases together, what does it come to? What is the test to see whether the occupier of one room in a house is a tenant or a licensee? It does not depend on whether he or she has exclusive possession or not. It does not depend on whether the room is furnished or not. It does not depend on whether the occupation is permanent or temporary. It does not depend on the label which the parties put on it. All these are factors which may influence the decision but none of them is conclusive. All the circumstances have to be worked out. Eventually the answer depends on the nature and quality of the occupancy. Was it intended that the occupier should have a stake in the room or did he have only permission for himself personally to occupy the room, whether under a contract or not, in which case he is a licensee?

Looking at the position in this case, in my opinion Mr Charters was not a tenant of this one room. He was only a licensee. A contractual licensee, no doubt, but still only a licensee. So he does not have security of tenure under the Rent Acts. He is not protected against eviction. On this point I differ from the judge. It is sufficient for the deciding of this case. Mr Charters has no right to stay ...

Orr and Waller L.JJ. agreed.

Comment. How important is the existence of a written agreement? Is it possible to summarize the criteria for the finding of a licence revealed by the above cases? How important is 'exclusive possession' as a badge of tenancy? What does Scarman L.J.'s judgment in *Heslop* reveal about the approach of the courts to such cases? Does this differ from Denning L.J. in *Marcroft*? To what extent will commercial transactions be classified as licences? Is equality of bargaining power a factor that has been taken into consideration? Is it 'simply a matter of finding the true relationship between the parties'? How do the courts ascertain 'intention'? Is it a subjective or objective test? What do you learn from these cases about the attitudes of judges to the Rent Acts (and see Arden (1976))? Note that, very occasionally, it may be advantageous to the occupier to be classified as a licensee rather than a tenant (*Moss* v. *Brown* [1946] 2 All E.R. 557 (C.A.)).

2. Non-exclusive occupation agreements

One principle of the common law relating to the definition of leases is that the right to exclusive possession must be granted (above, p. 52). Indeed one of the main questions discussed in the cases in the last section is whether a licence can be created when the right to exclusive possession/occupation (the terms get fudged) appears to have been granted.

Given the uncertainty that surrounds this area of law, there has recently emerged the 'non-exclusive occupation agreement' which purports to deny occupiers the right to exclusive occupation and thus, it is argued, by definition creates a licence only. The way the courts have dealt with this is illustrated in the following reported cases.

(i) *Walsh* v. *Griffiths-Jones* [1978] 2 All E.R. 1002 (County Court)

HIS HONOUR JUDGE MCDONNELL: The plaintiffs are the owners of a house at 34 Brailsford Road, London SW2, which is divided into three flats. They had lived in the house themselves but had from time to time let each of the flats. In 1976 they were very anxious to sell the property, and thought that they might be able to sell it to the Lambeth Borough Council. They knew that they would obtain a better price if they could sell the whole house with vacant possession on completion. In December 1975 they had been warned by their mortgagees that the creation of lettings of any part of the house would be in breach of the conditions of their mortgage. In the spring of 1976 Mrs Walsh saw an advertisement in the Evening Standard newspaper by a firm of estate agents called David Dixon & Co which read: 'ANSWERS to the Rent Act. Complete control over your property.' She got in touch with a member of the firm, a Mr Rickard, and thereafter employed David Dixon & Co as agents to deal with properties of the plaintiffs which had been let . . .

The defendants, who had shared rooms at Cambridge, came to London during 1976. After living with friends for a time they urgently required furnished accommodation. The first defendant applied to the West End Flats Agency, who relieved him of a fee of £40 and referred him to David Dixon & Co. On 4th October the first defendant saw Mr Rickard and completed an application form in respect of flat 3 at 34 Brailsford Road [but this turned out not to be available] . . .

On 18th October the defendants visited flat 1 and found that Mrs Walsh was there. There had been some damage to the roof of the back room which had necessitated repairs to the ceiling and some replastering and she was re-decorating that room, lining the ceiling and painting the new plaster. The defendants looked around the flat and decided that it would suit their needs and asked whether they could move in straight away. Mrs Walsh said that the flat was not ready because she had not finished the redecoration. The defendants offered to complete that work themselves...

She telephoned David Dixon & Co and arranged to send the defendants round to their office to complete the transaction ... She said in evidence that she explained to the defendants that it was hoped that the property would shortly be included in a housing action area and that therefore she only wanted to let it on a short term basis. She made it clear to them that this was because she was hoping to sell the property. Neither defendant recalls hearing anything about a housing action area but they only wanted the premises for a period of six months to one year. I find that they were told that Mrs Walsh wanted to sell the property but that this was not a matter of great importance in view of the fact that they did not require it for more than a year. The defendants returned to the office of David Dixon & Co where they saw Mr Rickard who proceeded to conclude an agreement with them. He said that he was prepared to grant them an agreement for three months but they wanted an agreement for not less than six months. He was not pre-pared to grant more than three months but said that it would be 'renewable' and the defendants agreed to that without any closer definition of what was meant by 'renewable'. A calculation was made that £28 per week was equiv-alent to £364 for three months. Two printed forms of agreement were pro-duced and details were inserted in typescript; there was one agreement for each defendant under which he undertook to pay £182 by monthly in-stalments. The agreements were identical save that one was in the name of the first defendant and the other in the name of the second defendant.

Each agreement started with the words 'THIS LICENCE' and stated that it was made between –

'Mrs Walsh c/o David Dixon & Co. 1 North End Road, London W14 (hereinafter referred to as "the Licensor") of the one part and [the defendant in question] (all hereinafter referred to as "the Licensee") of the other part.'

It then continued:

'WHEREAS the Licensor is not willing to grant the Licensee exclusive possession of any part of the rooms hereinafter referred to AND WHEREAS the Licensee is anxious to secure the use of the rooms notwithstanding that such use be in common with the Licensor and such other Licensees or invitees as the Licensor may permit from time to time to use the said rooms, AND WHEREAS this Licence is entered into by the Licensor and the Licensee solely upon the above basis. By this Licence the Licensor licenses the Licensee to use (but not exclusively) all those rooms (hereinafter referred to as "the Rooms") on the ground floor of the building...'

Condition 2 provided that the licensee should –

'be responsible for the payment of all gas, electric light and power which shall be consumed or supplied in or to the Rooms during the Licensee's occupation thereof...'

Condition 3 provided that the licensee should –

'use his best endeavours amicably and peaceably to share the use of the Rooms with the Licensor and such other Licensees or invitees whom the Licensor shall from time to time permit to use the Rooms and shall not interfere with or otherwise obstruct such shared occupation in any way whatsoever.'

Condition 4 provided that the licensee should –

'keep the interior of the Rooms and all furniture, furnishings, fixtures and fittings therein in good and clean condition and complete repair (fair wear and tear and damage by accidental fires only excepted) and immediately replace all broken glass.'

Condition 8 provided:

'ON notice in writing being given to the Licensee by the Licensor or his/her agent of all wants of repair, cleansings, amendments and restorations to the interior of the Rooms and of all such destruction, loss, breakage or damage of or to the furniture and effects as Licensee shall be bound to make good found therein the Licensee shall repair, amend and restore or make good the same within two weeks of the giving of such notice.'

Condition 16 provided that the licensee should 'not cause or permit any waste, spoil or destruction to the Rooms or to the building'. Condition 19 provided that the 'Licensor shall not at any time permit more than three other persons to use the Rooms together with the Licensor and Licensee'. Condition 22 provided: 'THE Licensee shall at all reasonable times allow the Licensor or the Licensor's Agents or workmen to gain access to the Rooms occupied by the Licensee.' Condition 32 provided:

'UPON the Licensee being in breach of any of the conditions referred to above this Licence shall immediately determine without prejudice to any other remedies of the Licensor and the Licensee shall immediately cease his use of the Rooms and the Building as permitted hereunder.'

Immediately under each defendant's signature appeared the words 'Licensee hereby states having received a copy of this contract....'

Each defendant did read the printed agreement and they expressed some surprise at the recitals which said they were not granted exclusive possession and that the use was to be in common with the licensor and other persons.

They said that there had been no discussion of the terms of the agreements until the printed documents had been completed in typescript and placed before them for signature. The defendants said that when Mr Rickard presented the agreements for signature he used some such words as 'This is just the legal side of it, just a legal formality'. Mr Rickard said that it was his normal practice to explain that a licence does not grant the licensee an exclusive right of occupation and that if he chose to do so a grantor could either claim his own rights of occupancy or issue further licences to another party. He said that he had a conversation of that nature with the defendants but could not remember precisely what was said. The defendants said that when they raised the question of an obligation to share with Mrs Walsh or other persons Mr Rickard assured them that there was no danger whatsoever of Mrs Walsh or any other person seeking to enter into occupation of the flat. Both defendants accepted in evidence that they had ample opportunity to read the documents and that they signed them intending to enter into a legal relationship and to be bound by them. I prefer the evidence of the defendants and am satisfied that before they signed the agreements they were assured by Mr Rickard that the terms about use in common with the licensor and other persons were just a legal formality and there was no danger whatsoever of anybody else being put in. As the first defendant put it in evidence they were firmly of the impression that they were paying the full rent of £28 per week for the security of occupying the flat to the exclusion of anybody else.

On the same day the defendants obtained the keys of the flat from Mrs Walsh and went into occupation.

It has been held on many occasions that agreements described as 'licences' have effectively granted tenancies: *Foster v Robinson* ([1951] 1 K.B. 149), *Marcroft Wagons Ltd v Smith* (above), *Addiscombe Garden Estates Ltd v Crabbe* (above). As Viscount Simonds said in *Elmdene Estates Ltd v White* ([1960] A.C. 528 at 538).

'... it has been said before and it must be said again that in the consideration of questions arising out of the Rent Acts the court must look at the substance and the reality of the transaction and not its form.'

See also *Woods v Wise* ([1955] 2 Q.B. 29). Such a question was exhaustively considered in *Addiscombe Garden Estates Ltd v Crabbe* (above)...

The grant of exclusive possession of the property is no longer decisive but it is a very important consideration: see *Errington v Errington and Wood* (above). Although the grant of the right of exclusive possession may create a licence and not a tenancy, there is no authority for the proposition that there can be a tenancy where the tenant is not granted the right of exclusive possession and I hold that there cannot be the estate in land known as a tenancy without a grant of exclusive possession. Reservation to a grantor of a right of access 'at all times' does not of itself destroy the right granted by contract to exclusive possession of rooms as a residence since the grantor has no right to occupy the rooms as a residence or to put anyone else in them: see *R v Battersea, Wandsworth, Mitcham and Wimbledon Rent Tribunal, ex parte Parikh* ([1957] 1 W.L.R. 410)...

Looking at the terms of the written agreements in the present case the recitals and the words of grant, together with conditions 3 and 19, point very strongly in the direction of a licence. On the other hand condition 2, conditions 4 and 8, which impose obligations on the grantee to carry out repairs wider than remedying damage caused by his own act or default, and the provision in condition 22 requiring him to allow the grantor and his agents or workmen to gain access are much more consistent with the grant of a tenancy...

The circumstances before the documents were produced for signature by the defendants were: (a) The defendants came to Mr Rickard looking for a tenancy of a flat to be let to them jointly. (b) The flat was said to be suitable for four persons and was offered for £28 per week and the amount payable by each defendant was calculated so that between them they paid the whole of this sum. (c) It was argued that Mrs Walsh made it clear that the flat was only available for occupation for a short term and that this was more consistent with a licence than with a tenancy. The defendants were not contemplating occupying the premises for more than a year and as many tenancies are granted for periods of three or six months I think that little weight can be attached to this consideration.

The following circumstances in which the agreements came to be signed seem to me to be relevant, namely: (a) Each defendant was required to sign a separate agreement on the face of which he made himself liable only for half the total consideration. At first sight this points to licences rather than a joint tenancy, but the fact of the matter was that it was never contemplated that one defendant alone would enter into an agreement. The essence of the arrangement was that both or neither would sign an agreement. (b) Having read the agreements the defendants did express some surprise that their use of the flat was to be in common with Mrs Walsh and other licensees. I am perfectly satisfied that Mr Rickard told them unequivocally that there was no danger whatsoever of anyone else being introduced into the flat. I am quite satisfied that neither would have dreamt of sharing the self-contained flat with Mrs Walsh or with other strangers. (c) The defendants were conscious of the provisions of condition 19 which contemplated that there might be up to four occupants in the flat at any time in addition to Mrs Walsh. The first defendant construed the agreement as not giving him exclusive possession of the whole flat because he was required to share with the second defendant just as the second defendant had agreed to share with him. He thought, however, that exclusive possession was being given to them both jointly, and this was not unreasonable in the view of what they had been told by Mr Rickard.

Bearing all these considerations in mind I am driven to the conclusion that the documents signed by the defendants were no more than shams designed to conceal the true nature of the transaction.

(ii) *Somma* v. *Hazlehurst* [1978] 2 All E.R. 1011 (C.A.)

CUMMING-BRUCE L.J.: In February 1976 two young people, Mr Martin Hazlehurst and Miss Savelli (herein called H and S), were looking for accommodation in which to live together in London. He was an educated man employed as a computer programmer, a job involving some mathematical qualifications. She also had a job. They were not married. On Wednesday, 18th February, they saw an advertisement in the Evening Standard in the column headed 'Flats and Maisonettes to Let' which read: 'ACTON/HAMMERSMITH West Kensington. Double bedsits & flatlets. All amenities. Near Tubes. £13 to £19 per week 602 5464.' They telephoned the number given and by appointment visited a house at 4 Cornwall Mansions, W 14, which belongs to Miss Somma. The house is divided into four flats, subdivided into four rooms and two maisonettes. There they met Mr Ritter, resident managing agent for Miss Somma. Mr Ritter showed them a room 22 feet by 18 feet on the third floor, with two beds in it which he described as a double room. They looked at it and went away. On Friday, 20th February, they returned, saw Mr Ritter again and said they wanted to take the room and to move in next day. Mr Ritter gave each of them a printed form of agreement into which he wrote the appropriate detail in the blank spaces. They each read the form they were given. He asked a few questions including a query about the clauses which indicated that they would have to share with a third person described as the licensor. They each signed their agreement before they moved in, and though they had not thought out the legal implications of the contracts they urgently wanted accommodation and, in the judge's phrase, understood what they were letting themselves in for. The agreements were identical save the name of the licensee...

He read out the licence. It was not as long as the one in *Walsh* v. *Griffiths-Jones* (above) but contained many conditions that were identical to the ones found in the earlier case. The County Court having been asked to make a declaration as to the status of Hazlehurst and Savelli held they were tenants. Cumming-Bruce L.J. continued:

On the issue whether the transaction fell within the protection of the Rent Acts counsel for the respondents submitted: (1) In consideration of questions arising under the Rent Acts the court must look at the substance and reality of the transaction. (2) In ascertaining the substance and reality of the transaction the court is entitled to look both at the documents and at the surrounding circumstances. (3) Documents which purport to grant licences will be held to grant tenancies if either one of two sets of circumstances apply: (a) if on examining the documents in the light of the surrounding circumstances they are found to be in substance documents granting a tenancy, which he called 'the construction route'; and (b) if on examining the surrounding circumstances the court finds that the documents are a disguise which cloaks the reality of the transaction, which he calls 'the disguise route', for such a transaction may disguise the reality of the rights and obligations granted and assumed by the parties without necessarily being fraudulent or attracting the label of a mere sham. (4) Residential licences should only be upheld as such by the courts in three special classes of case with which we deal hereafter. (5) The courts must have regard to the policy of the Rent Acts and be astute to prevent their evasion.

In applying those principles to the instant case, counsel for the respondents submitted that the judge did address himself to the right question, and sought for and found the reality of the transaction in the surrounding circumstances which he admitted in evidence and took into account. Pursuing the construction route, the written contracts are to be construed as parts of a single transaction, granting joint rights and giving rise to joint obligations such as to transfer to the grantees a joint tenancy. Alternatively, pursuing the disguise route, he submitted the true nature of the transaction was, and that the judge's findings can and should be read as finding, that the reality and substance of the transaction was that H and S were granted a joint tenancy disguised by the cloak of the documents drafted for Miss Somma, and that that finding of fact was amply supported by the evidence.

Alternatively, counsel for the respondents sought leave to amend his respondents' notice to seek a new trial on the ground that the judge failed to appreciate the relevance of the circumstances surrounding the written agreements, stopped the solicitor who appeared for the respondents from investigating them in cross-examination, and so decided the case without making findings of fact on relevant matters which should have been explored ...

We are confronted with one more attempt by an owner of housing accommodation to provide it at a profit for those in great need of it without the restrictions imposed by Parliament on his or her contractual rights to charge for it and regain possession of it. The attempt which has led to this appeal is made by a document drawn up by one, or a combination, of those who seem to have studied all the efforts, recorded in a welter of cases decided in every court from the county courts to the House of Lords, to avoid letting a dwelling-house or part of it by arranging to licence or to share the occupation of it. On the particular facts of this case has this attempt failed as the judge held?

Each document which we have to consider is on its face a licence to each respondent to share occupation – of one double bed-sitting room for 12 weeks. But the obligation which the document imposes on each respondent is an obligation to share with (1) the owner (described as the licensor), (2) the

other respondent (described as a person permitted by the licensor but identified, by reading the respondents' documents with each other, as the other
respondent). And the document so repeatedly proclaims itself a licence, and
the relationship it creates between the applicant and each respondent as being
that of licensor and licensee, that it raises the question why it should be necessary to protest so much and whether so many labels so clearly written all
over it give a true or a false description of its real contents.

Our first task is to examine closely the course of the proceedings in the
county court. The next to observe and analyse findings made by the judge.

Sidney Ritter, resident manager of Miss Somma, gave evidence of the circumstances preceding the signature of the agreements. However, the judge
observed that he did not think it necessary to go into the background of the
agreement because it could not affect the agreements subsequently entered
into. But he did not in fact stop counsel for the applicant in his examination
in chief eliciting from the witness the facts that we set forth at the beginning
of this judgment.

During cross-examination, the judge again said that he was not concerned
with the surrounding circumstances of the agreement and asked to what issue
the cross-examination was relevant. The solicitor for the respondents said that
he was endeavouring to show that an agreement was entered into before the
forms of licence were signed and suggested that H and S had paid a deposit
and moved in before they signed the agreements. The judge then observed
that unless there was fraud or mutual mistake the parties were bound by what
they signed. The witness gave evidence that H and S signed the agreements
before they moved in; there was no evidence of a deposit being paid before
the agreements were signed, and it appears from the judgment that the solicitor for the respondents did not pursue the allegation of any agreement or
bargain antecedent to the written agreements. And indeed he could not do
so, because when H gave evidence he did not suggest any such antecedent
bargain. Miss Somma gave evidence. She said that she had used the licence
agreement for about three years, and that she did not think that she introduced the form of licence because of the Rent Acts. She said that normally
if one licensee went, then a friend of the remaining licensee would move in
with her approval, and that if another licensee did not move in then she would
lose the money and would not be able to recover it from the remaining
licensee ...

H in evidence said that he was not shown the licence agreement on the
first visit to Mr Ritter whereupon the judge observed that there was no point
in pursuing that line of questioning as H was an intelligent man and he
entered into the agreement and was therefore bound by it, and that he, the
judge, had to construe the documents. H said he read the document for five
or ten minutes at the most, and queried it slightly but was told it was a standard document for letting. He asked about cl 19, as it looked as if three people
could share, but Mr Ritter 'brushed it off'. He said he had moved his posses-

sions into the flat, and that it did not seem a good thing to quarrel with the licence. In cross-examination he said that he and S signed separate agreements and made payments under the licences separately. He said he did not know if he would be responsible for paying both licence fees if S left; that he did not take legal advice because it would have been too expensive; and that he preferred to have the accommodation on the terms offered to him than not to have the accommodation at all. That concluded the evidence. The judge did not call on the solicitor for the respondents until after he had heard counsel for the applicant. Counsel for the applicant invited the judge to construe the documents, and in the course of argument the judge said that everything in the documents was utterly artificial from start to finish. The document was not a licence at all but a joint tenancy, and the landlord could not wrap it up with extraordinary expressions. Counsel for the applicant said that was at variance with what the judge had said earlier when he said that he had to construe the documents, and asked to pursue further cross-examination of H. The judge refused to hear further evidence. At the end of counsel for the applicant's speech, the solicitor for the respondents was called on, and reminded the judge of the relevance of surrounding circumstances. Against that background we come to the judgment.

It is clear from the terms of his judgment, from the note to his judgment which he has supplied, and from what he is reported to have said in the course of argument, that he was seeking to ascertain the nature of the agreement solely from the terms of the written documents. Thus, despite the fact that a fair body of evidence was called before him as to the surrounding circumstances, it seems from what the judge himself says in his judgment, that the solicitor for the respondents did not press or at least did not press very strongly that the judge should consider anything outside the terms of the documents . . .

It is clear . . . that the judge rejected, inferentially at least, that there was any oral agreement outside the two documents which would be capable of affecting their meaning. Thus we start from the basis that it is to the documents that we must look and to the documents alone. This has an important bearing on the whole of the case.

The next matter is to discover what was the ground of the agreement for a joint tenancy vested in H and S. The judge in his judgment says: 'They understood what they were letting themselves in for. On 21st February 1976 there was really a joint licence relating to the flat albeit cloaked around by the documents'. There he is saying it is a joint licence. Does he mean joint 'interest' of some sort? That is probably the case although it is difficult to say. Then he goes on to say:

> 'There is no sign here of the incidents which one finds for a landlord
> and tenant relationship but heaps of indications which show that the parties
> if they applied their minds to it conferred on these people a joint tenancy

or the rights of joint tenants or the equivalent rights on them. It is not an elaborate matter of this sort. It is trite law that one does not now look for exclusive possession. We are warned off placing too much emphasis on exclusive possession. The relationship between the landlord and these two young people was one of joint tenants I have no doubt about that whatever.'

He then goes on to deal with cl 19 of the documents which permits or purports to permit the landlord to impose another occupant on a remaining grantee whether it be H or S and to say that such a clause must be illegal and is therefore not binding on the grantees.

It seems to us that the reasoning behind the judge's ultimate conclusion is this: (1) Although there are on the face of it two documents here which if taken separately would give neither grantee exclusive possession, this is not fatal to the claim of the occupants that this was a tenancy, because the two documents must be construed together and if that is done they are apt to confer on the couple a joint interest of some sort in the room. (2) The other clauses which appear to make the occupation non-exclusive are illegal, possibly on the grounds of public policy, and therefore are not binding on the grantees. (3) Consequently, one is left with a joint and exclusive occupation. (4) The nature of the occupation is a tenancy because there are 'heaps of indications' which show that the parties if they applied their minds to it conferred on these people a joint tenancy or the equivalent rights. He does not say what these indications may be.

We find ourselves unable to come to the same conclusion as the judge. Counsel for the respondents, basing himself on the judgment of Denning LJ in *Facchini v Bryson* ([1952] 1 T.L.R. 1386) and the reasoning in *Merchant v Charters* (above), submits that in a 'Rent Act' situation any permission to occupy residential premises exclusively must be a tenancy and not a licence, unless it comes into the category of hotels, hostels, family arrangements or service occupancy or a similar undefined special category. We can see no reason why an ordinary landlord not in any of these special categories should not be able to grant a licence to occupy an ordinary house. If that is what both he and the licensee intend and if they can frame any written agreement in such a way as to demonstrate that it is not really an agreement for a lease masquerading as a licence, we can see no reason in law or justice why they should be prevented from achieving that object. Nor can we see why their common intentions should be categorised as bogus or unreal or as sham merely on the grounds that the court disapproves of the bargain. This matter was expressed most happily by Buckley LJ in *Shell-Mex and BP Ltd v Manchester Garages Ltd* (above) as follows:

'It may be that this is a device which has been adopted by the plaintiffs to avoid possible consequences of the Landlord and Tenant Act 1954, which would have affected a transaction being one of landlord and tenant, but in my judgment one cannot take that into account in the process of construing such a document to find out what the true nature of the transaction is. One has first to find out what is the true nature of the transaction and then see how the Act operates on that state of affairs if it bites at all. One should not approach the problem with a tendency to attempt to find a tenancy because unless there is a tenancy the case will escape the effects of the statute ...'

There seem to us to be two questions which we have to answer. (1) Did the parties intend to be bound by the written agreement? (2) Can it be said from the words which they used in those agreements that they intended to create a tenancy rather than a licence? As to the first question there is a clear finding of the judge that H and S 'knew what they were letting themselves in for'; also that they were both educated and that they both signed the document ... The second question is really the nub of the whole case, namely, do the terms of the two documents show an agreement for a licence rather than an agreement for a tenancy. Immediately one faces the problem of the two separate agreements, one with H and the other with S. If they are truly separate then it must follow that neither H nor S has the necessary exclusive occupation ... The judge, while saying that he is confined to interpreting the documents themselves says simply, in the passage already quoted, 'on 21st February 1976 there was really a joint licence relating to the flat albeit cloaked around by the documents'. If indeed he was confining himself to the documents, there was no basis for saying that they were joint agreements at all. However, if that is too legalistic a way of looking at the situation, as counsel for the respondents submits, it is impossible to reconstruct the separate obligations into one joint obligation without doing violence to the obvious intentions of the parties, particularly of the two grantees, H and S. For example, if one takes cl 1[2] which deals with the consideration which the grantees are bound to pay, it would be necessary as we see it, either to have a joint interest coupled with a several liability for half the weekly amounts, which is something of a logical inconsistency, or else to redraw the terms of the agreements to make each grantee jointly and severally liable for the full four-weekly instalment of £77.60, as against the contractual liability resting on each under the agreement of £38.80. This is not construing the agreement between the parties: it is rewriting it in the absence of any claim for rectification or any allegation of fraud. Counsel for the respondents was unable to provide any answer to this problem which came near to satisfying us on this point. We find it impossible to say that on the contents of these two documents, even adding the fact that the two grantees made their bid for the room together, a joint interest was created in their favour. That is really the end of the matter, because

---

2. Clause 1 reads as follows: '1. THE Licensee agrees to pay the said sum of £116.40 by 4 weekly instalments of £38.80 commencing on the 21st day of Feb. 1976 next and thereafter on Saturday of each 4th week until 15.5.76.'.

if the rights of the parties are several as opposed to joint, it is impossible to say that either has the necessary exclusive possession to found a tenancy.

However, assuming that that conclusion is wrong and that the interest is indeed joint, one must next examine the other clauses to see whether any of them prevents the joint occupation from being exclusive.

The recitals and conditions 3, 19 and 21 point very strongly to a licence. Condition 2 imposes an obligation on the grantee 'for the payment of all gas, electric light and power which shall be consumed or supplied in or to the Rooms during the Licensee's occupation thereof' which is a wider obligation than payment for his own proportion of a consumption or supply required or enjoyed also by a second licensee. This points in the direction of a lease rather than a personal licence. Likewise the obligations to repair and replace in conditions 4 and 5 are wider than an obligation to remedy damage caused by his own default and are more consistent with a lease than a licence. Condition 8 is the kind of clause which is more appropriate for a lease than a licence for a short term. Conditions 9 and 10 are neutral. Condition 11 by its reference to a duty to other occupiers or users of the rooms is more suitable in a licence than in a lease. Clause 14 is to be read in the knowledge that if another licensee fulfils his obligation the windows will be cleaned twice a month. On balance, though it is not particularly strong, this suggests a joint obligation to clean once a month. Condition 16 prohibits 'waste spoil destruction to the Rooms or to the Building'. Waste is a familiar term of art in the law of real property and carries the meaning of damage or prejudice to the reversion. In a document such as this which is obviously carefully drafted by a hand skilled in property law the condition points to a lease rather than a licence. Condition 17 prohibits alteration or interference with the construction or arrangements of the rooms. It contemplates a continuing control by the licensor and is more consistent with a licence than a lease.

So some of these obligations are more consistent with a licence than a lease, and some lead to a contrary inference. The balance comes down in favour of a licence because the document cannot be construed as a lease without substantial rewriting. The recitals, conditions 1, 3, 19, 21 and 22 would all have to be written in substantially different terms or disregarded altogether. But cl 1 cannot be either rewritten or disregarded, and if it is to the documents that one looks for the terms of the contract the conclusion is that the document as drafted gives rise to personal obligations. The conditions which point to a joint obligation can without violence be explained as a protection required by the licensor who assumes that the licencees who share the use of the rooms from time to time will come to some arrangement of work or financial contribution between themselves in respect of the obligations which each has severally undertaken.

When the agreements were entered into the unidentified one person in cl 19 was clearly identified as the grantee who signed the other agreement. But if at any time during the currency of the agreement either H or S decided to leave, either by agreement with Miss Somma on surrender of the unexpired portion of the 12 week term, or by one of them repudiating the agreement by leaving without paying the balance of instalments as they fell due, Miss Somma has reserved the right to introduce a second licensee. She explained in evidence how she set about it, and was not cross-examined to suggest that the rights reserved of replacing the second sharing licencees were unworkable or other than of reasonable business effacacy. Such a right to introduce a new licensee as a replacement is wholly inconsistent with a grant of exclusive occupation, much less exclusive possession.

Clauses 3 and 19 also impose on the licensee the obligation to share the room with the licensor as well as with another licensee. The room was that described as being 22 feet by 18 feet, with two beds in it. The question of construction is what are the rights and obligations to be ascertained from the agreement ... Miss Somma has a house. She grants to H and to S the right to use one room, but expressly reserves the right to use that room in common with them. On no construction of such a contract can H and S claim that they have been granted exclusive occupation of the room.

In the second part of his judgment the judge considered cll 3 and 19 ... In our view the illustrations given by the judge of the kind of uncongenial persons who might be imposed on H and S by Miss Somma if either of them left only illustrate the risk inherent in the bargain that they made and are no ground for invoking public policy to render unenforceable the right retained by the licensor. The judge did not like the bargain, but the agreements were the agreements of the parties and the fact that the judge envisaged circumstances in which the exercise of Miss Somma's rights would be uncongenial to the remaining licensee does not entitle the court to rewrite the agreement. The judge was deeply offended by the thought that the grantor could introduce a person of a different sex to succeed to the vacancy left after H or S had left. But we can find nothing to indicate that there was such an intention. If S were to depart, and the licensor permitted another lady congenial to H to take her place, a moralist might regard the new sharing arrangements with regret or indignation, but the court would be reluctant to intervene as it is in the case of the sharing arrangements of H and S. Nor can we construe the clause to find an intention on the part of the licensor to impose on one licensee the company of another licensee of the opposite sex against the wishes of either of them. For those reasons we cannot uphold the learned judge's decision that cll 3 and 19 are contrary to public policy ...

So we arrive at the decision that on an analysis of the judgment the result in law is that H and S entered into separate contracts; those contracts were personal licences and not leases or a lease; and by those contracts neither H and S was given a right of exclusive occupation of the room that they shared. That brings us to the respondents' application for a new trial, leave for which we granted as an amendment to the respondent's notice. Counsel for the respondents submits that the judge approached the case in the wrong way. He confined himself to a construction of the documents when it was his duty, on the authority of the cases which have been concerned with different but in some ways similar problems under the Rent Acts, to admit extrinsic evidence and to consider whether the surrounding circumstances establish that the documents do not record the real intention of the parties at the time when the grantor agreed to let the grantees live in the room. The onus was on the respondents to establish that the contract was other than that recorded in the documents that they signed ...

Counsel for the respondents submits that they failed to do so because the judge made it clear that he was not interested in hearing evidence of the surrounding circumstances and so either closed his mind to the correct approach or alternatively made it impracticable for the respondents' solicitor to present their case adequately.

It was noted that in, *inter alia*, *Walsh* v. *Griffith-Jones* (above), such evidence had been admitted.

We say with respect that Judge McDonnell's judgment is a model of the approach to and analysis of an alleged agreement to grant licences to two persons to share residential accommodation, and it deserves wider publicity. Counsel for the respondents contrasted the hearing before Judge McDonnell with the proceedings in the county court with which we are concerned. He pointed to the observations of the judge calculated to discourage the advocates for both sides from leading evidence of the surrounding circumstances or from cross-examining in relation thereto. In our view there is great force in his submission that the hearing had unsatisfactory features as the judge's interventions point to an inference that he was confused as to the relevance of extrinsic evidence. But with some hesitation we have decided that though there was confusion in the judge's mind while the evidence was being given, in fact his interventions did not have the effect of shutting up the evidence of surrounding circumstances which was relevant to the transaction. In spite of the judge's comments Mr Ritter, Miss Somma and H appear to have been permitted to give the evidence that they wanted to present of the relevant surrounding circumstances. The solicitor for the respondents did not persist in his contention that H had paid a deposit and moved in before he signed the agreement, and H's evidence was not consistent with the payment of any deposits save the deposits of £38·60 that each paid after the agreements had been signed. Where parties are professionally represented, our forensic system requires that parties must persist in examining or cross-examining on facts, and must seek a ruling from the court if the court indicates an intention to exclude material which the advocate regards as relevant. We do not underestimate the difficulties of the solicitor appearing for the respondents, but he did not persist in his cross-examination of Mr Ritter or his examination-in-chief of H about the events of the first occasion when he met Mr Ritter when the judge intervened. We conclude that in this court the case must be scrutinised on the evidence that was given, and that in spite of the criticisms that we have made of the judge's interventions and approach to the case before he came to deliver judgment, it is not a proper case for a new trial in order to enable parties to canvass again the evidence of the circumstances in February 1976 which surrounded the signature of the two agreements in writing. Further, having regard to the uncontroverted facts in evidence at the trial it seems unlikely that a second trial would enable H or S to discharge the onus of establishing that the intentions of the parties are not to be collected from the written documents that they signed, particularly having regard to H's candid evidence that after he had read the document it did not seem a good thing to quarrel with the licence and that he preferred to have the accommodation on the terms offered to him rather than not to have accommodation at all. This court has today construed those arrangements. The respondents' application for a new trial is therefore refused.

The appeal is allowed.

(iii) *Aldrington Garages* v. *Fielder* (1978) 247 E.G. 557 (C.A.)

GEOFFREY LANE L.J.: said that the agreement entered into by the defendant with the plaintiffs recited that the agreement was entered into to avoid the situation where a tenancy was created, that the occupier should not part with possession to persons not approved by the owners, and that he should have no right to grant a licence or to control the owners' choice of person 'to whom we may grant a licence to share with you.' Miss Maxwell, who also occupied the flat, had signed an agreement in identical terms.

It was also plain from the agreements that each could independently determine his or her respective agreement within seven days, and it was also clear that there was no clause which on the face of it was inconsistent with the grant of a licence rather than a tenancy. There was no doubt that Mr Fielder, and possibly to a lesser extent Miss Maxwell, were somewhat reluctant to sign. Mr Fielder said he knew that the flat had previously been allocated at a registered rent, and, though he was obviously somewhat confused as to its precise legal effect, he seemed to have assumed that that entitled him to be what he himself called a registered rent tenant.

The owners' agent with whom he was dealing made it plain that ... the agreement which he (the agent) was proffering was not caught by the Rent Act in his view, and that the registered rent was irrelevant to the considerations then facing the parties. In the end, as a concession, he added clause 6 to enable the occupier to determine the agreement at any time on seven days' prior written notice. Mr Fielder and Miss Maxwell stayed in flat 3 until on June 1 1977 Miss Maxwell, having duly terminated her agreement by written notice under clause 6, departed, having had her £30 deposit returned to her pursuant to the agreement. Thereafter Mr Fielder remained in occupation, paying £54.17p a month in respect of the months of June and July 1977.

The learned judge, in a detailed and well-thought-out judgment, weighed the pros and cons of the 'tenancy' view and the pros and cons of the 'licence' view, and then stated his conclusion. If, on a proper view of the agreements, neither Mr Fielder nor Miss Maxwell had exclusive possession, neither could be a tenant; their liability would be several and not joint. The learned judge concluded that the joint signing of document P3 (a letter) in the presence of a director of the plaintiff company, and the simultaneous signing of documents P1 and P2 in such presence, meant that P1 and P2 constituted in substance and in fact one single agreement made between the plaintiffs on the one hand, and the defendant and Miss Maxwell jointly on the other.

Mr Rich agreed that it was true that neither agreement would have been signed without the other, and the joint signature of the letter reinforced that point, but in his submission that did not make them one single agreement, nor did it make them a joint agreement, if there was any difference between those two concepts. In his submission what happened afterwards did not help in construing the nature of the agreement, and the learned judge reached his conclusion – that this amounted to a joint tenancy, and not to separate licences – only by looking at extraneous matter. Was that a right conclusion? Lord Gifford wished to repeat the arguments he advanced in *Somma v Hazelhurst* (above) that, in considering questions arising under the Rent Acts, the court must look to the substance and reality of the transaction rather than merely to the form. The court was entitled, indeed bound, to look back at the documents and the surrounding circumstances. One could not alter the nature of a document by giving it a wrong label. Apart possibly from matters of emphasis, his Lordship would find little to quarrel with in that submission. But Lord Gifford finally submitted that the court must have regard to the policy of the Rent Acts and should be astute to prevent their evasion. With that his Lordship did not go – at least, not to the extent that Lord Gifford would wish ... The mere fact that an agreement which did not fall within the Rent Act might result in large profits for the owners did not necessarily mean that agreement should be construed as a tenancy and not as a licence.

Lord Gifford cited *Samrose Properties Ltd v Gibbard* [1958] 1 WLR 235, a case where a sum paid by the occupier was held to be commuted rent; *Elmdene Estates Ltd v White* [1960] AC 528, where a premium was masquerading as a sale at an undervalue; and *Regor Estates Ltd v Wright* [1951] 1 KB 689, another premium case. As his Lordship saw it, the most one could derive from those decisions was that in Rent Act cases the court had to be specially wary, and specially careful to see that the wool was not pulled over its eyes, and specially careful to see that things like premiums were not being used to conceal payment of rent, and so on; but in the present case there seemed to his Lordship to be nothing disguised as a licence, no one was disguising exclusive possession to make it look like something else ...

There was a temptation to strain the facts or the law in favour of the occupier because the owner was obviously trying to avoid the provisions of the Rent Act, in order, *inter alia*, to increase his profits. But there seemed to be nothing wrong in trying to escape onerous provisions, or increase one's profits, if one could legitimately do so. If there was here truly a licence, and not a tenancy dressed up in the verbiage or trappings of a licence, the landlord was entitled to succeed. It was not a situation where the court should allow itself to be influenced one way or the other by its sympathies ... Mr Fielder must show that the two agreements must be read together and, being so read, were effective to create a joint tenancy between himself and Miss Maxwell on the one hand, and the owners on the other. It was here that his case faltered. If the two agreements were separate, there was no exclusive possession and no tenancy. If joint, how was the obligation upon each occupier to pay his consideration of £54.17 per month to be construed? In order to find the intention of the parties to be to create a joint tenancy, it would be necessary to read the agreement as making Mr Fielder and Miss Maxwell jointly and severally liable for the total consideration of £108.34 per month, as opposed to the several liability under the agreement of £54.17 each. As Cumming-Bruce LJ said in *Somma*, this would not be construing the agreement between the parties, but re-writing it in the absence of any claim for rectification or any allegation of fraud. That passage was one of the *rationes decidendi* in the *Somma* case, and their Lordships were accordingly bound by it.

Roskill and Stephenson L.JJ. agreed.

(iv) *O'Malley* v. *Seymour* (1979) 250 E.G. 1083 (C.A.)
STEPHENSON L.J. said (in part):

The questions which arise are, it seems to me: first, what on its true construction is the nature of the written agreement on which the plaintiff relied and relies in his claim for possession, against the background of the evidence? Secondly, does the evidence prove and entitle the judge to hold that the document, on its proper construction, does not truly represent or reproduce the real transaction between the parties? Those are the questions which arise in all these cases. In this case the learned judge has, I think, construed the document as a tenancy rather than a licence because he said that 'it in fact created a tenancy' (according to the note); but even if the document is at any rate capable of being construed as a licence, the judge has clearly found that it was a sham and did not embody the real transaction between the parties.

He approached the document in this way:

'I remind myself of the warnings issued over the years in cases dealing with the Rent Act legislation that courts must be astute to see that a coach and horses are not driven through the Rent Acts or, as Lord Denning has put it, that an "articulated vehicle" is not driven through them. Unless I am persuaded to construe the agreement in this case as a licence, it is quite plain that it is otherwise a tenancy and that on the expiry of the six months specified in the agreement'

which is exhibited

'Mr Seymour could hold over as a protected tenant. If, on the other hand, it is a licence, then the period has expired and the plaintiff is entitled to the order which he seeks.'

In my judgment, that passage, if it accurately records the learned judge's concluded opinion, does indicate an approach too favourable to the defendant; but, for the reasons which I shall try to give, I do not think that the judge would have reached any different conclusion had he modified that language...

He went on to say that it was 'essential to look at the background to this matter.' He stated that the plaintiff had 'his main home in Eire, where he has his family and farm. He has become the owner of more than one property in or around London, and he makes periodic trips to this country to look after the property he owns and to see if the necessary "moneys" payable by the occupants has been received.'

Then he called attention to other facts which were common ground. First of all, among the properties which the plaintiff owned was a property at 88 Cecile Park. Part of that property he advertised in, I think, the *Evening Standard* as to let – 'a flat to let' in that property – and it was that advertisement which the defendant, Mr Seymour saw; ... it was as a result of answering that advertisement that he met the plaintiff ... Now that property was let off in five or six bed-sitting rooms, and there was evidence before the learned judge of rent books in respect of two of those; rent books held by occupants who were not occupants under licence but were tenants. The learned judge found that the plaintiff was not a resident landlord and quite clearly knew very well that he was, as the learned judge put it, 'saddled with the people in those bedsitters.' He rejected the plaintiff's evidence that he did not know that ...

At the defendant's meeting with the plaintiff the plaintiff told the defendant that he did have another flat which might be suitable for the defendant. So both went off to that other flat, which was the ground-floor flat at 13 Ribblesdale Road of which the plaintiff has been refused possession. The defendant was told – and this is all common ground – that he would have to pay a deposit in relation to the condition of the flat and a month's rent in advance, and he would be allowed into occupation for a period of six months. So far, the background is one of negotiating for a suitable flat to let.

The learned judge then went on to deal with the written agreement which the plaintiff told him he got hold of from another property owner; an agreement which was clearly devised ... to avoid the consequences of the 1974

Rent Act. That agreement ... was presented to the defendant for signature on September 11 1976. But before that agreement was presented to him or signed, the evidence showed an oral agreement which is not in terms, as Miss Catterson rightly pointed out, referred to or found as an agreement by the learned judge. It is, however, in my judgment, the basis of his finding that the written agreement signed on September 11 1976 was a sham, and it emerges clearly from the evidence of the plaintiff in cross-examination. The judge's note of the plaintiff's evidence (which we have got) reads in this way:

'I told him I would want a month's rent in advance. He did pay this sum. He said he would return next day to give me the deposit money and a month's rent. He said he wanted to move in that week-end. It was a firm verbal agreement made on the evening. I took him to no 13. I expressed in no uncertain terms that the tenancy was for six months only.' The agreement itself is in these terms:

'This agreement is made the 11th day of September 1976 between John O'Malley (hereinafter called "the owner") of the one part and Colin Michael Seymour (hereinafter called "the licensee") of the other part ... Whereby it is agreed as follows: (1) In consideration of the sum of £520 payable by the licensee to the owner as hereinafter mentioned, the owner grants to the licensee the right to use in common with others who have been granted or will be granted the like right the premises known as ... ground-floor back flat, 13 Ribblesdale Road, Crouch End, London N8, together with the fixtures furniture furnishings and effects now in the said premises for six months from the date hereof.

'(2) The licensee agrees with the owner as follows: (i) to pay the said sum of £520 by equal instalments of £86.66 per month on the first day of each month, the first of such payments to be made on the signing hereof; (ii) not to damage or cause any damage to the walls or floors of the said premises or any part thereof and to preserve the fixtures furniture and furnishings and effects from being destroyed or damaged in any way and to replace all broken glass; (iii) upon the termination of this licence (whether by effluxion of time or otherwise) to pay to the owner a sum equal to £7.50 of the cost of washing and cleaning all counterpanes, blankets and curtains soiled, whether or not by the licensee, during the period of this licence; (iv) not to impede the use of the said premises or any part of it not nor [*sic*] upon the terms that each shares the cost of gas electricity and telephone services to impede the use of any services supplied to the said premises or any part of it by such other persons not exceeding three in number to whom the owner shall grant licence ...

(v) not to assign this agreement nor to permit any other person, except as licensed by the owner, to sleep reside in or share occupation of the said premises or any part of it at any time: (vi) not to do or suffer to be done in or upon the said premises any act or thing which may be a nuisance damage or annoyance to the owner or to the occupiers of any adjoining property or which may vitiate any insurance on the premises against fire or otherwise or increase the ordinary premium thereon;

'(3) Provided as follows: (i) if the said instalments or any of them or any part thereof shall be in arrear or unpaid for at least seven days after the same shall have become due, or (ii) in the event of any breach by the licensee of the agreements herein contained, then the owner may terminate this agreement and the licensee's rights hereunder shall absolutely determine but without prejudice to any other remedies of the owner hereunder.

'(4) The owner agrees with the licensee to pay all general and water rates payable in respect of the premises but not any charges for the supply of gas or electricity or for the use of the telephone.

'(5) The licensee shall pay the sum of'

and that is left blank.

'which shall be retained by the owner until the termination of this agreement as a deposit to secure to the owner the performance by the licensee of the agreements on the part of the licensee here contained, but without prejudice to the owner's rights under and in respect of this agreement. At the termination of this agreement and on the licensee vacating the said premises and subject to the proper performance by the licensee of his obligations herein contained, the owner will refund the said deposit to the licensee.

'(6) It is hereby agreed and declared that possession of the premises vests in and is retained by the owner subject to the right of the licensee to use of the premises given by this licence.'

In fact a deposit was paid by the defendant by cheque dated September 9 for £50, and the learned judge also saw a receipt undated for £86, which it was accepted was paid before the defendant went into occupation ...

The learned judge said of the defendant: 'I am not dealing with an illiterate or an unsophisticated person. Mr Seymour has a good job and I found him an honest and straightforward witness.' The defendant conceded that he had read through the agreement which I have read before he signed it, so there was no doubt about that; this agreement was signed by a sophisticated and literate person. The learned judge added that he did 'not think for a moment that he' (the defendant) 'appreciated the legal effect of the term "licensee."' He was bothered about the limitation of the period to six months because he was reluctant to take the place with that limitation, but in the event he was so anxious for accommodation that he accepted it.'

The learned judge then went on to consider the written agreement. He referred to the opening provision for the payment of £520 by instalments and said 'the crux of the case is to be found immediately in clause 1 of the agreement ...' that is in the opening words which stamp the agreement with the attempt, at any rate, to make the grant a grant of a right to use in common with others, a grant to a licensee to share with others, not a right of exclusive possession granted to a tenant. Of that the learned judge said: 'I am convinced that that wording was designed to try and defeat one of the tests used to distinguish between a licence and a tenancy, that is to say whether there is exclusive possession. Mr O'Malley' (the plaintiff) 'was honest enough to admit that he never contemplated for a moment foisting any other persons on the defendant. He knew that Mr Seymour wanted exclusive occupation for his own purposes. There was no suggestion ever made in the six months that Mr Seymour should accept any other person.'

The learned judge went on: 'Because he,' that is the defendant, 'signed a document referring to him as a licensee, the court is asked to infer that he does not have a tenancy under the Rent Act and that the plaintiff is entitled to the order he seeks.' That might be criticised as an over-simplification of the plaintiff's case, but the judge went on: 'The defendant says that this is not a genuine licence agreement but in effect a sham to avoid the Rent Acts, and that he is therefore entitled to remain.' ... He came 'unhesitatingly to the conclusion' – and I quote from the note – 'that this is an attempt by the plaintiff to avoid the provisions of the Rent Acts. To set up this agreement as a licence is a sham: it in fact created a tenancy and I find that Mr Seymour is holding over as a protected tenant' and so he gave judgment for the defendant.

Miss Catterson, in what, in my judgment, was a model argument, has challenged that conclusion of the learned judge. She submits that the written agreement is appropriate to, indeed is, a licence, not a tenancy. She accepts that the learned judge was fully entitled to look at the background in order to see what the real transaction between the parties was. She does not challenge the right, and the duty, of the judge to find that the written agreement was a sham if that finding is justified on the primary facts which he finds, but she submits that his conclusion that this agreement was a sham is an inference which he ought not to have drawn from the facts he found ... She relies strongly on the fact found by the learned judge, and indeed admitted by the defendant, that he had read this agreement before he signed it, and the finding of the judge that he was not illiterate or unsophisticated. Though she cannot challenge the judge's finding that the defendant did not understand the legal consequences of the label 'licence' and 'licensee' the only part of the agreement which he was really interested in was the limitation of his occupation to six months. She said it was clear from his evidence that he did not regard himself as entitled under the agreement to stay on beyond the six months' period, and that evidence is quite inconsistent with his believing that he had a right to stay on given him by the law: he knew that that right was entirely dependent upon the will of the plaintiff, and that could only be true of a licence and not of a protected or regulated tenancy ...

Miss Catterson correctly submits that if there is no exclusive possession there cannot be a tenancy, although the converse is not true, and here, she says, are provisions in this agreement which show that possession is not to be exclusive; there is a right in the owner, the plaintiff, to share it with the defendant, and there is provision for others, not more than three, to share it. She submits that not only is that the position demonstrated by the written agreement, but that is what the judge should have found the oral agreement between the parties to have been ... She submits that the statement of both parties that there was no intention of sharing at the time the agreement was entered into is not really relevant, because an agreement may give you a right to share even if you do not intend to exercise it.

The great difficulty in the way of her submissions is the finding of the learned judge that all these so-called rights to share, or references to sharing, were bogus, they were all part of the sham. If the 'rights' really existed, if they were really agreed upon between the parties, they would take this groundfloor flat out of the Rent Act ... But the learned judge has found that that was not the agreement between the parties. The real transaction between the parties was the grant of a six months' tenancy ...

Miss Catterson summarised her contentions as well as she had made them. She said that the learned judge was wrong to give the weight he did to the evasion of the Rent Act. I have already indicated the extent of my agreement with that submission, but my opinion is that it did not alter the judgment which he would have come to had he had later decisions of this court before him ...

It is relevant to point out, as was pointed out by my Lord Geoffrey Lane L.J. in the course of the argument, that this case differs very materially from the two other cases, the *Somma* case and the *Aldrington Garages* case, not only that in one of those cases there was evidence about the possible use of that right which would have entitled the court to regard the provision of it as genuinely agreed and not a dead letter or a sham, but in each of those cases there was a contemporaneous agreement signed by a person wishing to share the same accommodation and granting exactly the same rights on the same terms, and those two agreements had to be read together. So there was absent from those cases the striking feature of this case that there was, in fact, no one to share this flat with the defendant and no intention of there being anyone to share this flat with the defendant during the period of his occupation.

Finally, Miss Catterson submitted that the defendant having read this agreement before he signed it, the court can look at the agreement and discern in it the true nature of the relationship between the parties. Of course it must look at the agreement, but the question whether it discerns there the true relationship between the parties has, in my judgment, already been decided for us by the learned county court judge. There was, in my opinion, clearly evidence on which he could have found that this agreement was a sham. I would go further and say on the evidence that was before him, if I had taken the same view of the witnesses as he did – as no doubt I should – I should have reached the same conclusion as he did, that it was a sham.

For those reasons, in spite of the excellent argument of Miss Catterson, I would affirm the judgment of the learned judge and dismiss the appeal.

Lawton and Geoffrey Lane L.JJ. agreed, the latter emphasizing that 'each case must depend upon its own particular facts'.

(v) *Demuren* v. *Seal Estates* (1979) 249 E.G. 440 (decided *after O'Malley*, above)

MEGAW L.J. said (in part):

The two applicants are both post-graduate students who had come from Nigeria to this country to pursue their studies. They were anxious to obtain accommodation together in London, They saw an advertisement which appeared in the *Evening Standard* on September 13 1976, which said: 'Flats and Maisonettes to Let. Sharers: Available now or Oct 1st super s/c' – which means 'self-contained' – 'Flats and Houses. North, South, East and West London for 2, 4 or 6 single sharers. £7.50 per week to £12.50 per week each. Crawfords': and then a telephone number.

The applicants telephoned the telephone number given as being 'Crawfords.' Crawfords, it would appear, are estate agents, who act for, among others, Seal Estates Ltd, or at any rate have some connection with them. There was really no evidence as to their status. Their precise position in this transaction is obscure; but it seems to me that they have got to be treated for present purposes as agents for Seal Estates Ltd who appear to be the owners of Spencer Park Court. The vagueness about all these matters will perhaps be less surprising when I mention that at the hearing no evidence was offered on behalf of Seal Estates Ltd. The applicants, having telephoned, arranged to see the flats at Spencer Park Court, of which they had no doubt been told by whoever, representing Messrs Crawfords, had answered the telephone. They went and saw the flats. They were taken round them by a lady, Mrs Ainsworth, who lived in no 7. The flats which they saw, including no 6, had three rooms as well as a kitchen and bathroom. They liked flat no 6. . . . They were told by Mrs Ainsworth, to get in touch with Mr Charles who, it appears, was a caretaker. Mr Charles in his turn told them to go to an address which he gave them, in Addison Gardens in West London, with their cheque books, and to see somebody whose name, it would appear, was Mr Keating.

The two applicants went on that same day, September 13 1976, to the address in Addison Gardens and they saw there a young man, unidentified, who apparently said that he was Mr Keating's assistant. The applicants, according to the findings made by the judge on the evidence, told Mr Keating's assistant that they were interested in a flat. They were told that no 6 alone was available; and they said that they would take no 6. They were then given certain documents to read over, which they read; and after Mr Keating's assistant had dealt with other persons he turned his attention to the applicants and, it would seem, invited them to sign, each of them separately, forms called 'Applications,' and also, having signed them, to sign and initial what purported to be licence agreements, each of them being invited to initial and sign a separate such agreement. Having done that, they were asked to give cheques for their proportion of the rent.... So they gave post-dated cheques for the rent month by month, to be used monthly in advance for the payment of rent ... In addition, the applicants gave cheques for a 'deposit,' against, presumably, the possibility of non-payment of the other cheques, or damage, or suchlike. They also, curiously, were asked to give, and did give, cheques each in the sum of £25 to whoever was the person dealing with them, apparently as being commission for the aid and assistance that that person, or Messrs Crawfords, gave in the transaction. If Messrs Crawfords were the owners' agents, it gives rise to certain queries that they should be taking commission from the applicants. If they were the applicants' agents other queries would arise. We need not seek to answer them.

The applicants asked when they could move in. They were told they could move into the flat at any time. In fact they did not move in until the following Saturday, September 18. They asked if it was possible for them to stay beyond a year – again dealing with this on the collective basis of the two seeking occupation together. They were told by Mr Keating's assistant that if they wanted to stay beyond a year they would have to sign a fresh agreement and give fresh cheques.

Mr Adefope said in evidence that he thought he was signing to rent a flat. It is clear that they did read the documents – whether in whole or in part is not clear; and it is said that they ought to have understood that what they were signing were separate licences and not tenancy agreements. Neither of the gentlemen, so far as appears, was a lawyer or had any experience in law; and they were not asked any questions as to what they knew about the technical difference between a tenancy and a licence or its possible effects ...

The question that arose in the proceedings in the county court was whether in the circumstances the agreement which existed in law between the applicants, either jointly or severally, and Seal Estates Ltd were licences or were tenancies. The learned judge held that they were tenancies and that accordingly these two applicants were entitled to the protection of the Rent Act. It is against that decision that the respondents in the county court, the appellants in this court, Messrs Seal Estates Ltd, appeal...

I would be content to say that I agree in its entirety with the judgment of Judge Figgis in the court below; that his findings of fact are findings which are justified, on the notes of evidence which we have seen, and that his conclusions of law drawn therefrom are unexceptionable. However, in this court we had cited to us two authorities, cases decided in this court since the decision of Judge Figgis in the present case, and of which, therefore, obviously, he could not be aware because they were not in existence when he delivered judgment. Those two cases are *Somma v Hazlehurst* (above) and ... *Aldrington Garages v Fielder* (above). Mr Stevens'[3] real point is that the present case is indistinguishable on its facts from those two cases, in which it was held that agreements that in some respects were similar to the agreements with which we are concerned in the present case created licences and not tenancies.

In the second of the two cases, *Aldrington Garages v Fielder*, my lord, Roskill L.J. made it quite clear that in his view that case was a case which depended upon its own particular facts and that neither it nor *Somma v Hazlehurst* was to be treated as laying down principles which could necessarily be applied in any case where there were similar but not identical agreements, or where there were relevant facts which were different from the facts in those two cases. In my judgment the facts in the present case distinguish it from each of those two authorities, so that neither of them affects the decision of Judge Figgis.

I do not propose to go in detail into the terms of the purported licence agreements here. But there are certain points which I should mention. First, there were two separate agreements, signed separately by Mr Demuren and Mr Adefope. Second, in each of them there was a clause 9 which said 'Nothing herein contained shall create the relationship of Landlord and Tenant between the parties hereto and the benefit of this Licence shall be personal to the Licensee.' Beyond that there are certain curious provisions in the earlier clauses of the 'licence' agreements. I am using the word 'licence' in inverted commas. The agreement itself is described at the beginning as being 'This Licence made the 13th September 1976.'

By clause 1 it is provided: 'The Owner' – that is Seal Estates Ltd – 'gives the Licensee permission to reside in common with such other person as shall from time to time be nominated by the Owner in the room numbered One (hereinafter called the room) forming part of the Flat known as Number Six (hereinafter called the Flat) in the building known as Spencer Park Court, Spencer Park, SW18.'

Mr Adefope signed one such agreement referring to 'the room numbered One.' Mr Demuren signed another agreement, in identical terms except for the name of the so-called 'licensee'; and in his agreement also there was a reference to 'the room numbered One.' Although these were separate agreements, they both applied to the same flat; and both Mr Adefope and Mr Demuren were to 'reside' (whatever that means) in 'the room numbered One' ...

Although the agreements purported to say that these two gentlemen would, under their separate agreements, 'reside' in that supposedly identified room, clause 2 provided that 'The Licensee shall be entitled to use the lounge dining room bathroom toilet kitchen (hereinafter called the common parts) in the

3. Counsel for Seal Estates (ed.).

Flat in common with all other occupants of any part of the Flat for the time being.' It is 'all other occupants,' in the plural, as distinguished from 'such other person as shall from time to time be nominated,' which is in the singular, as provided in clause 1. The explanation which Mr Stevens offers ... is that this was what he described as being a common form agreement which might be used by the owners, Seal Estates Ltd, for flats which had more than one bedroom (not being the case in relation to the flat with which we are concerned). In those circumstances it is said that the owners might wish to provide that there should be two or more people residing in common in one bedroom and two or more people residing in common in another bedroom and that they should each be limited, so far as their exclusive residence is concerned – when I say 'exclusive' I mean exclusive to the two or more people in a bedroom – to their particular, defined, bedroom; but that they all should be entitled to use the lounge, dining room, bathroom, toilet and kitchen as being in common for all the occupants of all the bedrooms. It may be that that is the purpose of using the phrase 'in common with all other occupants of any part of the flat.' If so, it is an agreement which was not appropriate to the present case.

The so-called 'licence' agreement, then sets out an even more curious provision. Clause 3 says: 'The permission hereby granted shall continue until the 30th day of September 1977 unless previously determined by the Owner giving to the Licensee not less than one week's previous notice in writing.' So far, so good – until one realises that under this agreement, there is no corresponding provision for the 'licensee,' so called, to give one week's notice, or any other notice, in writing. So far as he is concerned the obligation which this agreement purports to put upon him, so far as it is capable of being reconciled with other clauses in the agreement, is that he is under an obligation, not, of course, to remain physically living in the nominated 'room numbered One' up to September 30 1977, but, whether he continues to reside there or not and to make use of the common part, to continue to pay for his right to 'reside' in room number one during the whole of the time up to September 30 1977. One provision, for the owner, that he can give one week's notice: another, and very different, provision, for the 'licencees,' under which they have no corresponding provision for bringing the so-called 'licence' to an end.

But it becomes even more curious when one comes to clause 4. I have said that when the agreement was made in the offices of Messrs Crawfords on September 13 1977 – which stage was reached, as the judge has found, before these documents were signed – the applicants were both required to give cheques over the period of a year, post-dated month by month, in the sum of £54.17 each, as well as a cheque for 'deposit.' Clause 4 provides: 'The consideration for such permission' – that is, the 'permission to reside in common with such other person' as should be nominated 'in the room numbered One' – shall be the sum of £54.17 per calendar month payable by the Licensee to the Owner in advance on the 1st day of each month the first payment being the appropriate proportion from the 17th September 1976 to the 30th September 1976 next being made on the signing hereof.'

So, here are these applicants, who have given post-dated cheques covering the future, month by month, for a year, under an agreement in which their occupation as 'licensees,' so it is said, can be terminated by the owner at a week's notice at any time: and they themselves have no corresponding right. So what would happen if the owner exercised his right under this agreement, if it be a right, to give a week's notice after one of the post-dated cheques had been paid? Would the position be that the owner would be in possession of payment for the ensuing month and the 'licensee' (so called) would be turned out, possibly within a week of that payment having been made? It is said by Mr Stevens, on the basis of some propositions which I am afraid I am wholly unable to follow, that in those circumstances the 'licensee' would be able to get back the proportionate balance of his month's payment by some action on the basis of a consideration which had partly failed.

To my mind the provisions of those two clauses are irreconcilable. There is something which is so badly wrong with this agreement that one is bound to look at it with the gravest suspicion.

The real argument put forward on behalf of Seal Estates Ltd in this court to suggest that the learned judge was wrong was the fact that under these two 'licence' agreements each of the 'licensees' separately is obliged to pay month by month £54.17 for his shared accommodation. It is said that that is inconsistent with its being a joint tenancy agreement because, if it were a joint tenancy agreement, each of the two joint tenants would be under a liability to pay the whole of the rent, subject, of course, to the right to reimburse himself, if he did pay the whole of the rent, from the other joint tenant. Judge Figgis was impressed with that point. In his judgment, having come to the conclusion, as I think for wholly unexceptionable reasons, that in all other respects the indications were that the true nature of these arrangements was a tenancy and not a licence, he went on:

> 'That does not necessarily mean that a tenancy and not a licence was created. There is still the question raised by the fact that I am satisfied that it was a term that each applicant should be liable for one half of the money payment. It seems to me to be a matter of some difficulty which side of the line that may make the arrangement taken as a whole. My conclusion is that it is not necessarily inconsistent with a tenancy for a landlord to agree not to look to each of two joint tenants for more than one half of the rent.'

He then discussed the passage from Cumming-Bruce L.J. in *Somma* v. *Hazlehurst* (above, p. 129) where he refused to re-write clause 1 of the contract; and Geoffrey Lane L.J.'s statement in *Aldrington*

Garages that that passage was one of the *rationes decidendi* of the case (above, p. 135). Then Megaw L.J. continued:

In the present case, in contrast, the learned judge did make findings of fact as to what had been the agreement between these two applicants and Mr Keating's assistant at Crawford's office on September 13 1976. The judge said this:

'There was no evidence as to what the landlords really intended, apart from inferences which may be drawn. Counsel for the respondents elected, as he was entitled to do, to call no evidence. I find that when the parties went to see the person who told them to fill-in these documents, they said they wanted to take one of the flats. They were told only Flat 6 was available and said they would like to take it. In so far as the documents provide that they should reside in common in room no 1, they do not represent what anyone contemplated, including the landlord. If anyone had gone into the witness-box on their behalf to say that they expected two applicants to occupy one bedroom and the rest of the flat as a lounge and dining room, I would not have believed him. In my judgment there was a mutual, concurrent intention of all the parties that the applicants should together have and enjoy exclusive occupation of the whole of the flat. Indeed that seems to be borne out by the fact that the advertisement refers to a self-contained flat.'

In my opinion there was ample evidence to justify the learned judge in reaching the conclusion that there was such an oral agreement which had been made between the parties before the so-called 'licence' agreement came to be signed on that day by the two applicants and, on some unknown date thereafter, before September 21, by somebody representing Seal Estates Ltd.

There would, therefore, have been, on that basis, strong ground for thinking that there could have been a claim for rectification of those written agreements as not giving effect to what was the express intention of the parties in arriving at their oral agreement. But, however that may be, there would still remain the question about the joint tenancy, having regard to the provision for separate payment of rent by the two licensees or joint tenants, as the case may be. I find it unnecessary to go further into that matter, having regard to the particular facts of this case as they were, which in my judgment distinguish them from both of the cases which I have cited, *Somma v Hazlehurst* and *Aldrington Garages v Fielder*.

A joint tenancy with each of the two tenants paying only one half of the total amount of the rent due for the joint tenancy could indeed, in certain circumstances, be regarded as creating a logical inconsistency. It would particularly be so, perhaps, if the position were that the landlord, if one of the two joint licensees or tenants walked out, would be left without having any recourse in respect of the rent that was due under the agreement from that person other than the personal action against him. In this case one would have perhaps less sympathy for the owners than might otherwise have been the case because under clause 1 of their own agreement, assuming that it is valid and effective, they would have the right to nominate some other person to occupy the room numbered '1,' charging such payment as might be appropriate to that person thereafter. Moreover, they would have their remedy against the outgoing licensee, if this licence agreement is capable of being given any meaning at all, because as I have said, there is no provision in that agreement for the licensee to cease to be liable for payment up to September 30 1977 merely because he chooses to leave his residence in room no 1. There might indeed be a problem after September 30 1977 in relation to a continuing rent-restricted tenancy; but, again, the provisions of clause 1 would seem to be of some avail there.

However, in the circumstances of the present case there are facts which in my view make it not 'logically inconsistent' at all, as it was thought to be logically inconsistent in the two earlier cases. There is here the provision of the post-dated cheques, the effect of which is that the landlord has got his payment in advance up to September 30 1977 from each of the two applicants. He has secured for himself the whole amount due from the two joint tenants (if that is what they are) for the whole period. It seems to me that here there is no logical inconsistency in the conclusion at which the judge arrived, namely, that the agreement was one which involved that, though it was a joint tenancy, nevertheless, unusually, each of the two should be personally liable for, and only for, his share of the total rent of the flat. That is something which may be unusual but is not, as I see it, such as to prevent it from being a joint tenancy, at any rate in the circumstances of this case. It represents, as I see it, the oral agreement between the parties in this case.

In so far as this curious, and in some respects unintelligible, 'licence' agreement purports to provide otherwise, it is not consistent with the reality of the agreement which was made for the letting of a shared flat, particularly because of the advance payments for a year (inconsistent with the purported contractual right to determine on a week's notice) and because of the absence of any provision which could properly or sensibly be said to preclude exclusive possession of the flat by the two sharing tenants. The reference to 'all other occupants,' when there could be none such in the intention of the parties, is a strong indication that the 'licence' agreement does not reflect the real agreement.

I would, accordingly, dismiss this appeal.

Browne and Roskill L.JJ. agreed, the latter again emphasizing the importance of looking at each case individually. (They also both praised the work of the Garratt Lane Law Centre in the preparation of these cases.)

Comment

Not surprisingly, perhaps, these cases have been subject to critical analyses (e.g. Finnis (1978b); Arden (1978b) and (1979b); Garratt Lane Law Centre (1978); Partington (1979)). There can be no doubt that they raise difficult and important questions. For example:

Is the insistence of the court in treating each case individually justifiable? Will this not encourage increased litigation? Should not the courts be attempting to lay down more general principles? Can you say in the light of these cases when the courts will re-write the contract and when they will not? What sort of evidence is thought to be relevant? Is there a case for allowing in more general evidence (e.g. relating to shortages of housing, the problems of homelessness etc.) so that judges have a better idea of the social background to the cases they are having to decide? Why have the courts relied so heavily on the proposition that they will only strike down 'sham' arrangements? What alternative approaches might they have adopted? Do these cases reveal a conflict between the legal principle of sanctity of contract and the social consequences which can arise from the principle? (For further discussion of 'sham' arrangements see *Buchmann* v. *May* (below, pp. 198–201); *Conqueror Property Trust* v. *Barnes Corporation* [1944] 1 K.B. 96 (C.A.); and *Snook* v. *London and West Riding* [1967] 1 All E.R. 518 (C.A.).)

It seems clear that estate agents are still using non-exclusive licence agreements extensively. In one agreement which has come to the attention of the author, the 'licensee' is required to answer, in writing, nine questions relating to his/her understanding that the agreement is a licence. It will be interesting to see if this agreement is litigated and, if so, what the approach of the courts would be.

3. Consequences of finding that a licence exists

In the last two sections we have been discussing the circumstances in which a licence may or may not be held to exist. One consequence of a finding of licence has already been noted; the arrangement will be outside the scope of protective legislation such as the Rent Acts and the Landlord and Tenant Act 1954, Part II. However there are other consequences that flow from a ruling that a licence exists which will be discussed under the following two heads:

A Relationship between licensee and licensor

The problem here is to know when a licence may be validly terminated. The law recognizes various kinds of licence.

(a) a 'gratuitous' or 'bare' licence may be revoked, at any time, at the will of the licensor, subject to his giving the licensee a reasonable time in which to leave the premises (*Minister of Health* v. *Bellotti* [1944] K.B. 298);

(b) a 'licence coupled with a grant or interest' in land is, however, irrevocable: e.g. the right to enter another's property to cut down a tree and take it away involves a licence to enter the land together with the interest in land (the right to take the tree – which is a *profit a prendre*) (see *James Jones & Sons Ltd* v. *Earl of Tankerville* [1909] 2 Ch. 440);

(c) a 'contractual' licence can only be brought to an end in accordance with the terms of the contract. If there is no right of revocation, express or implied, revocation will be a breach of contract (*Winter Garden Theatre* (*London*) *Ltd* v. *Millennium Productions Ltd* [1948] A.C. 173);

(d) licences by 'estoppel' (i.e. where a licensee has been permitted or encouraged by the licensor to act to his detriment for example by the expenditure of money on land) are more complex. Here, in a suitable case, equitable doctrines may be invoked so that an injunction may be granted to prevent revocation in circumstances which have raised a reasonable expectation in the mind of the licensee that the licence will not be revoked. In some cases a constructive trust has been imposed (Megarry & Wade, 1975, pp. 778–9; Maudsley & Burn, 1975, pp. 451–61).

B Effect of licences on third parties

It was stressed in a number of cases cited above that the licence was essentially a 'personal' right. In principle, therefore, it might be thought that they should only be effective as against the licensor and licensee and not operate as against third parties. To permit this, property lawyers would argue, would be to turn an essentially personal interest into something akin to a proprietary interest. There have, however, been a number of important developments which raise the interesting question as to whether a new proprietary interest may be in the process of judicial development.

In *Errington* v. *Errington* (above, pp. 102–4) the Court of Appeal held that the licence that the father originally gave the children to last while they paid the mortgage instalments was binding on the mother who became the owner of the house after the father died. In *National Provincial Bank* v. *Ainsworth* [1965] A.C. 1175, judges in the House of Lords were extremely critical of this development. '[Their] comments are damaging to *Errington* v. *Errington* as an authority for any new principle that contractual licences, merely as such, may be interests in land' (Megarry & Wade, 1975, p. 783). Despite this, a number of more recent cases in the Court of Appeal indicate that the issssue is far from dead. (See, e.g., *Williams* v. *Staite*; *Hardwick* v. *Johnson*; *Chandler* v. *Kirby* [1978] 2 All E.R. 928, 935, 942; Anderson (1979).) Another strategy that has been used by the courts in a number of cases has been the imposition of a constructive trust (e.g. *Bannister* v. *Bannister* [1948] 2 All E.R. 133; *Binions* v. *Evans* [1972] Ch. 359).

The nature of the new interest that is, or may be, in the process of development is extremely controversial and must be beyond the scope of this book. However, two comments may be made. First, the judges have clearly become uneasy about the limits of the traditional legal concept of the licence and are looking for ways of extending that concept. It is interesting to consider why this development should be occurring now. Second, a more general comment, which it is important to emphasize, is that the rights of a licensee can be quite extensive. Sections 1 and 2 of this chapter may have given the impression that all that licensees would be interested in is demonstrating that they were tenants, in order to obtain various statutory protections. If they fail in that, however, all may not be lost. As the discussion in this section indicates, much will depend on the type of licence they have, and the circumstances that surrounded its creation. (For further discussion of this question, see Dawson & Pearce (1979).)

4. The death of the occupational licence?

Because of the difficulties surrounding the use of the traditional legal concepts of lease and licence, and the uncertainties that they cause in deciding the extent of the operation of statutory protection, it has been suggested that the basis on which the statute law operates should shift from the technical concept of the lease to the fact of occupation. In that way, it has been suggested, complex (and expensive) arguments over occupational status could be avoided (e.g. LAG (1977)

p. 13). This is clearly a difficult question which, if it comes up for public debate, is likely to generate much controversy.

It is worth noting, however, that government lawyers in the Department of the Environment and elsewhere do seem to have implicitly taken the point; for a number of Acts of Parliament have been passed in recent years in which it is made clear that the legislation is to apply both to tenants, strictly so called, and other licensees. (See, e.g., Rent (Agriculture) Act 1976, Sched. 2; Housing (Homeless Persons) Act 1977, s. 1(1)(a) (ii); Housing Act 1980, s. 48; Protection from Eviction Act 1977, s. 3 (as amended).) Consider the arguments for and against the effective abolition of the lease/licence distinction in cases of residential occupation.

4
The Scope of Rent Act Protection

Introduction

The series of Rent Acts that have been passed since 1915 has been the cornerstone of legislative attempts to regulate by law the landlord–tenant relationship in the private sector of the housing market. The substance of the protections contained in the legislation – rent regulation, security of tenure and control of premiums – will be dealt with in individual chapters below. In this chapter we look at the difficult questions that must be explored before any substantive issue can be dealt with relating to what categories of tenancy fall within the Rent Act.

The structure of this chapter is as follows: after a look at the history of rent control there is a brief discussion of the different categories of occupational status known to the law. The definition of a protected tenancy is then examined, followed by a discussion of the exemptions to protection. Certain difficult cases are then mentioned. Finally there is a description of the principles relating to the question of who has jurisdiction to resolve difficult issues.

1. An outline of the history of Rent Act protection, 1915–80

Rent control was first introduced into this country in 1915.[1] It is clear that the Increase of Rent and Mortgage Interest (War Restrictions) Bill was seen essentially as a temporary measure, introduced as the

1. There are many accounts of this. See, e.g., Gallacher (1936); Barnett (1969, ch. 3); Bierne (1977, ch. 2); and Watchman (1980).

result of agitation by munition workers who were extremely angry at proposals to raise their rents (Hunter/Scott, 1915). Evidence of this anger appears, for example, in the words of Mr Andrew Hood (Hunter/Scott, *Evidence*, 1916, p. 41):

1041. Was your feeling about that, that these were more than was necessary; or was it that some people found it impossible to pay? – Our feeling was that the increases that they are seeking to impose are far more than is necessary.

1042. Would you be dissatisfied with an increase if you were convinced that it was necessary through war conditions? – No, I would not even be satisfied with that, because we as workers have been called upon to make certain sacrifices, and we think it is the least that the factors and landlords should do to endeavour to share the sacrifices with us and not to extort what they are expected to pay from us every time.

1043. Your view is that during a state of war you are not prepared to pay any increase of rent in any circumstances whatsoever? – My feeling is that the Government should do something, whatever it may be, to make it impossible for the factor and the landlord to exercise his characteristic greed at this particular time and to jeopardize the chances of maintaining national unity. I have had statements from quite a number of tradesmen in Partick district who declare that, while it may be costing the landlords and factors more to carry out repairs, the factors and landlords in the bulk are not spending anything like so much on repairs and material as they were doing prior to the war.

1044. (*By Lord Hunter.*) You have not got any detailed information which you could put before us upon that point, have you? – No, further than those statements from particular tradesmen whom I have interviewed on the question. In one case a man told me that his account for a Govan property during the war was not anything like what it had been for the corresponding period before the war. The statement that factors are paying increased rates for repairs and that their outlays are considerably increased on that account appears to us, as a Committee, to be an absolute fallacy. We cannot get repairs in Partick in some cases without having to notify the sanitary authorities.

The categories of properties whose rents were controlled by the Increase of Rent and Mortgage Interest (War Restrictions) Act 1915 were those whose net rateable value was £35 or below in London, and £26 in the rest of England and Wales. The Second Reading debate clearly indicates that this protection was intended for 'comparatively poor people'.

In 1918, the Hunter Committee reported (Hunter, 1918). This report summarized the main themes in the continuing debate about rent controls. The majority felt control had to end if free enterprise was ever to provide accommodation again (while conceding that ending controls could not happen at once). The minority, however, said they saw no end to control as long as accommodation was scarce. The result of the report was that in 1919 a new Increase of Rent and Mortgage Interest (War Restrictions) Act permitted increases of 10% in rent levels, at the same time doubling the rateable value limits. However, these controls, and their subsequent amendments up to 1939, only applied to houses already in existence in April 1919, not to new building.

In 1920, following the report of the Salisbury Committee (Salisbury, 1920) the legislation was put on a slightly more permanent footing. The rateable value limits were raised again to £105 in London and £78 elsewhere in England and Wales. 'Thus, all except the largest houses were made subject to control' (Paish, 1950, p. 46). The Act also authorized a further 15% rise in rents, being an estimate of the increase in return to be expected on an investment since 1914, and yet another 25% if the landlord was responsible for all repairs.

In 1923 the Onslow report (Onslow, 1923) suggested decontrol on vacant possession. This was condemned by Labour MPs. Nevertheless, 'after the short but violent depression which ended the post-war boom, the first steps were taken towards the withdrawal of rent control' (Paish, 1950). Under the Rent and Mortgage Interest Restriction Act 1923, premises were decontrolled but only when the landlord obtained vacant possession. However, this Act had a disastrous effect on landlords for it coincided with a further economic recession and tenants were able to use a number of devices to avoid paying rent increases. The tensions that this situation caused were examined, first by the Constable Committee (1925) and later by the Marley Committee (1931).

The latter Committee felt that decontrol of the smaller houses had been too fast while that of the larger houses had been too slow. At the same time the Committee emphasized that the shortage of working-class housing had since World War I been mitigated solely by the endeavours of local authorities.

Thus, by the Rent and Mortgage Interest Restrictions (Amendment) Act 1933, controlled houses were divided into three groups: (i) Class A, where both the recoverable rent and the net rateable value (NRV) was above £45 in London and £35 elsewhere in England and Wales, were decontrolled at once. (ii) Class B, where the NRV was between £20 and £45 in London and £13 and £35 in the rest of England and Wales, continued to be decontrolled on vacant possession. (iii) Class C houses whose NRVs were below those of Class B ceased to be decontrollable.

In 1938, Class B was divided so that houses with NRVs of £35 and above in London and £20 elsewhere were decontrolled at once; all those with lower rateable values became permanently controlled.

The situation in August 1939 was thus quite different from 1923 in that:

all pre-1914 houses with net rateable values above £35 in London and £20 elsewhere had been excluded from control, together with a substantial though unknown number of smaller houses. The number of those decontrolled houses was estimated by the Ridley Committee in 1945 at 4.5 million. Also outside the control were some 4.5 million houses built since 1919 ... Thus, out of a total of about 13 million houses and flats, only about 4 million, all with net rateable values not exceeding £35 in London and £20 elsewhere and almost entirely owned by private landlords, were still subject to control (Paish, 1950).

On the outbreak of World War II, however, a new system of control was introduced. On 1 September 1939 all dwelling-houses not subject to the old control and with net rateable values of not more than £100 in London and £75 elsewhere were made subject to this. The result was that in 1953 the government stated that: 'Over 90% of the dwelling-houses in England and Wales are within the limits of rateable value ... and generally speaking all unfurnished tenancies are protected by the Act...' (*UK Government*, 1953, para. 34).

The same report also took up a suggestion originally made by the Leasehold Committee (Uthwatt-Jenkins, 1950) and recommended that some measure of protection be given to long leaseholders on the expiry of their leases. Their proposals, subsequently modified (see below, pp. 188–9), were incorporated in the Landlord and Tenant Act 1954, Part 1.

Also in 1954, the Housing Repairs and Rents Act, which was concerned with the encouragement of house repairs and slum clearance, provided that all new housing built for letting should be outside Rent Act control, as should houses which had been converted in order to be let. This Act was the first major effort after World War II to encourage private enterprise to provide accommodation for letting.

This policy was extended dramatically in 1957, when the Rent Act of that year proposed to decontrol all houses with rateable values above £40 in London and £30 elsewhere. Other properties would be decontrolled when the landlord obtained vacant possession. The Act was not fully implemented at once because the Landlord and Tenant (Temporary Provisions) Act 1958 (which provided that decontrolled houses could not be repossessed without court order (s. 1) and gave the court power to postpone the operation of an order for possession (s. 3)) effectively postponed the full operation of the 1957 Act until 1 August 1960. (See generally, Barnett, 1969.)

However, creeping decontrol (when the property became vacant) did continue. Problems thrown up by the effects of this process were revealed by the Milner-Holland Report (Milner-Holland, 1965). The result was the introduction, first of a new Protection from Eviction Act 1964 (see too Harvey (1964)); and, second, the introduction of the 'fair rent' scheme by the Rent Act 1965 (Crossman, 1975). Initially the rateable value limits for this protection were set at £400 in Greater London and £200 elsewhere. They have now been substantially increased (see below, p. 175) partly to take account of the revaluation of property in 1973, partly as a consequence of counter-inflation measures taken in 1973.

In 1974, the Labour Government extended Rent Act protection to furnished accommodation, hitherto excluded from the full range of statutory protection, but at the same time created a new category of what are now called 'restricted contracts' (basically tenancies created by resident landlords). (See below, pp. 202, 221.) A number of other exemptions from protection were created at the same time. In 1980, the Conservative Government created two further special categories of tenancy: the 'shorthold' tenancy (see below, p. 205); and the 'assured' tenancy (see below, p. 204).

Two particular lessons may be drawn from this brief historical account. The first is that although Rent Act protection was initially designed to concentrate on housing occupied by the poorest tenant only, there has been a gradual, if haphazard, extension to more and more types of property. Today, very few properties are excluded on the rateable value ground though they may be excluded for other reasons. The numbers of people potentially affected by this legislation makes it most desirable that its provisions are as widely known and understood as possible.

The second point is that the creation of and subsequent developments in this area of the law must not be seen from a purely legal point of view. It must be understood that housing policy, and the law that purports to give effect to that policy, has long been a matter of acute political controversy. Suggestions that 'politics should be taken out of housing' are inevitably misguided. The history of the Rent Acts is just one manifestation of a much wider debate about the extent to which the social need for housing can be met by the operation of the private sector of the economy. The social function of the Rent Acts cannot be understood without some awareness of the underlying political issues.

2. A word on the status of residential occupiers

Apart from owner-occupiers, occupiers of property belonging to another may be characterized in legal terms in three ways, depending on the facts of the occupation:

(*a*) *Trespassers:* Those on the property of another without permission will be trespassers (see further, e.g. Clerk & Lindsell, 1975, ch. 17).

(*b*) *Licensees:* As discussed in the last chapter they have, broadly speaking, personal rights to land which fall short of the full interest in land necessary to comprise a tenancy.

(*c*) *Tenants:* The main points relating to the creation of tenancies have been discussed in chapter 2.

The point to stress here is that whether a particular individual may take advantage of Rent Act protections or not may depend on the occupational status of that individual. This is a result of the principle that the Rent Acts usually only operate where accommodation is 'let' (see below, p. 158). Thus, problems relating to the scope of Rent Act protection do not simply depend on analysis of the statutory provisions themselves, but may also have to be considered in the light of the common law principles analysed in chapters 2 and 3.

3. Protected tenancies

Section 1 of the 1977 Rent Act provides:

Subject to this Part of this Act, a tenancy under which a dwelling-house (which may be a house or part of a house) is let as a separate dwelling is a protected tenancy for the purposes of this Act.

Any reference to this Act to a protected tenant shall be construed accordingly.

This section involves two problems of interpretation: (i) what is implied by the phrase 'subject to this Part of this Act'. The main exceptions to protection will be discussed in the next section; and (ii) what is the meaning of the rest of the words used in section 1. This will be discussed here.

A 'Tenancy'/'let'

As has already been noted, for section 1 to operate there must be in existence a tenancy valid according to ordinary common law principles. (*Oakley* v. *Wilson* [1927] 2 K.B. 279 at 289. See above, chapters 2 and 3.) 'Let' includes 'sub-let' (Rent Act 1977, s. 152).

B 'Dwelling-house'

This term is not defined in the legislation. However it would appear to exclude moveable structures such as caravans, and structures which though not permanent are not suitable for living in (Woodfall, 28th ed., 1978, para. 3-0039; see also below, p. 449).

In *Metropolitan Properties* v. *Barder* [1968] 1 All E.R. 536, the tenant of a flat subsequently negotiated another tenancy for a single 'servant's room' which he apparently needed for an *au pair* girl. The Court of Appeal held that this second tenancy could not be regarded as a 'dwelling' and was thus not protected by the Rent Acts. Edmund Davies L.J. noted:

The size of the room, its furnishing and the use to which it was being put (i.e. as the *au pair* girl's bedroom) establish that its user was an annexe or overflow of the flat, and its entirely distinct letting on a quarterly basis was not the letting of a dwelling-house.

I would stress that the present decision has no application to a case where a single room is let as the occupier's place of habitation for all purposes; to adopt the words of Lord Greene M.R. in *Curl* v. *Angelo* ([1948] 2 All E.R. 189) the present case is totally different:

. . . from the case where the only premises demised consist of one room and that is the only place where the tenant moves and has his being . . .

(See, too, *Wright* v. *Howell* (1947) 204 L.T. 299.)

Special provisions relate to

(i) Agricultural holdings (Rent Act 1977, s. 10):

A tenancy is not a protected tenancy if the dwelling-house is comprised in an agricultural holding (within the meaning of the Agricultural Holdings Act 1948) and is occupied by the person responsible for the control (whether as tenant or as servant or agent of the tenant) of the farming of the holding.

(ii) Pubs (*ibid.*, s. 11):

A tenancy of a dwelling-house which consists of or comprises premises licensed for the sale of intoxicating liquors for consumption on the premises shall not be a protected tenancy, nor shall such a dwelling-house be the subject of a statutory tenancy.

(The meaning of 'statutory tenancy' is discussed below, p. 207.)

(iii) Dwellings let with other land (*ibid.*, ss. 6 and 26):

Subject to section 26 of this Act, a tenancy is not a protected tenancy if the dwelling-house which is subject to the tenancy is let together with land other than the site of the dwelling-house. [s. 6]

For the purposes of this Act, any land or premises let together with a dwelling-house shall, unless it consists of agricultural land exceeding 2 acres in extent, be treated as part of the dwelling-house ... [s. 26]

Question. What *do* these two sections mean? In *Feyereisel* v. *Parry* [1952] 2 Q.B. 29 (C.A.), Denning L.J. said that the court would have to look at the 'dominant purpose' of the letting. If the dwelling was a mere 'adjunct' to, say, a camping-site or a factory, no protected tenancy; if the land was a garden or garage let as an 'adjunct' to a dwelling-house, the whole would be protected. In *Jelley* v. *Buckman* [1974] 2 Q.B. 488 (C.A.), a strip of land used as a vegetable garden was held to be part of the dwelling and thus could not be severed by a purported conveyance by the landlord to a third party.

(iv) Business tenancies (Rent Act 1977, s. 24 (as amended by Housing Act 1980, which leaves only sub-section (3) in force)):

A tenancy shall not be a regulated tenancy if it is a tenancy to which Part II of the Landlord and Tenant Act 1954 applies (but this provision is without prejudice to the application of any other provision of this Act to a sub-tenancy of any part of the premises comprised in such a tenancy).

Deciding whether a tenancy is for a dwelling or for a business tenancy has not always been easy to determine. In *Ponder* v. *Hillman* [1969] 1 W.L.R. 1261, Goff J. said (in part):

... This is a case in which the plaintiffs claim against their tenant and a person who alleges that he has a valid subtenancy possession of the demised premises ...

The demised premises consist of a shop and other premises which can be, and are in fact being used by the second defendant as dwelling accommodation...

[The plaintiffs] say, and I accept, that I am entitled to look at the lease referred to in the statement of claim, and they have produced the counterpart to me. The submission is that it is plain, both from the description of the property in the parcels and from the covenants in the lease – the user covenants, a covenant about advertising and a proviso in the covenant whereby the tenant agrees to permit the lessors to advertise the premises during the last three months of the term – that the contemplation of the parties at the time was a letting as a shop and not as a dwelling-house.

In my judgment, that is a fair conclusion from the terms of the lease and, at all events in the absence of any evidence to the contrary by the first defendant, it is sufficient to take the case out of the Act and entitle the plaintiffs to leave to sign judgment. I think that clearly appears from the decision of the Court of Appeal in *Wolfe* v. *Hogan* ([1949] 2 K.B. 194) ... and in particular the judgment of Evershed L.J. ... where he approved the following passage in *Megarry* on *The Rent Acts* (1967), 10th edn., p. 19:

'Where the terms of the tenancy provide for or contemplate the use of the premises for some particular purpose, that purpose is the essential factor, not the nature of the premises or the actual use made of them. Thus, if premises are let for business purposes, the tenant cannot claim that they have been converted into a dwelling-house merely because somebody lives on the premises...'

If, of course, the plaintiffs had consented or not objected to the occupation by the second defendant, different considerations would apply. However, their case is to the contrary and is not disputed by the first defendant.

In *Lewis* v. *Weldcrest Ltd* [1978] 1 W.L.R. 1107, the Court of Appeal had to consider whether the tenant of a five-roomed dwelling house, who took in lodgers, was a business tenant. Although the tenant appeared to have had a lease, its terms were not discussed by the court. Instead Stephenson L.J. (at 343) concentrated on the purpose of the Landlord and Tenant Act 1954, which, he said:

... was primarily to give security of tenure to people who would be said, in the ordinary use of language, to be using the premises for a business, even if they were living there as well, using part as a dwelling and part as a business. When I look at the words of the definition in section 23 (2), I see nothing that extends that purpose to cover such activity in providing accommodation for boarders as the applicant in the present case provided in this house.

It seems to me that there is nothing in the Act, in its wording or in my understanding of its purpose, to put this lady in the category of a trader or of a person carrying on business at these premises. It is no one factor; it is all the factors – the number of lodgers, the size of the place, the sort of sums and services that were involved. I am unconvinced by Mr. Lewis's attempts, without having challenged her evidence, to show that this lady was really reaping any commercial advantage out of this activity in taking in lodgers. She was, it seems to me, doing it probably because she liked it and because the lodgers helped her to pay her way. As Mr. Lewis says, it was her only occupation. I have no doubt that she was good at it. She was rendering a service to the lodgers, and, indeed, to the public and sometimes to the welfare authorities, and she was rendering a service to the taxpayer in reducing the amount of social security that had to be paid to her. The one thing that she was not doing, however, in my judgment, was carrying on a business or trade, whether 'business' is limited to trade or whether it can have any wider connotation . . .

Ormrod and Walker L.JJ. agreed.

In *Cheryl Investments* v. *Saldanha* and *Royal Life Saving Society* v. *Page* [1979] 1 All E.R. 5 a pair of contrasting cases were considered simultaneously by the Court of Appeal. Lord Denning M.R. said (in part):

Royal Life Saving Society v. *Page.*

No. 14, Devonshire Street, is a house with four floors. It is owned by the Howard de Walden Marylebone Estate. In 1945, they let it on a long lease to the Royal Life Saving Society for 64-and-a-half years. That society occupy most of the house themselves, but in 1960 they let the top two floors as a maisonette to a Mr. Gut for 14 years at a rent of £600 a year. There was a covenant prohibiting assignment without the landlords' consent. There was no restriction on the use that the tenant made of the premises. It would appear, however, that the maisonette was constructed for use as a separate dwelling and that the letting was 'as a separate dwelling' within the tests laid down in *Wolfe* v. *Hogan* ([1949] 2 K.B. 194, at 204–5).

In 1963, Mr. Gut made arrangements to assign the lease to the present tenant, Dr. Page. He was a medical practitioner who had his consulting rooms at 52, Harley Street. His major appointment was as medical adviser to Selfridges, and he held clinics there five days a week. Dr. Page took the maisonette in Devonshire Street so that he could live there as his home, but he thought that, in the future, he might possibly want to use it occasionally to see patients there. So, when he took the assignment, he asked for consent to do so. Such consent was readily given by the Royal Life Saving Society (his immediate landlords) and the Howard de Walden Marylebone Estate (the head landlords). It was a consent for Dr. Page to carry on his profession in the maisonette. After the assignment, he moved in and occupied it as his home. He put both addresses (Harley Street and Devonshire Street) in the medical directory. He had separate notepaper for each address and put both telephone numbers on each. That was, of course, so that anyone who wished to telephone him could get him at one or other place. He did, however, very little professional work at the maisonette. Over the whole period of the tenancy, he had only seen about one patient a year there. The last patient had been in distress 18 months before. He summarised the position in one sentence: 'Harley Street is my professional address and the other is my home.'

On those facts it is quite clear that 14, Devonshire Street, was let as a separate dwelling and occupied by Dr. Page as a separate dwelling. There was only one significant purpose for which he occupied it. It was as his home. He carried on his profession elsewhere, in Harley Street. His purpose is evidenced by his actual use of it. Such user as he made of 14, Devonshire Street, for his profession was not a significant user. It was only incidental to his use of it as his home. He comes within my first illustration. He is, therefore, protected by the Rent Acts under a regulated tenancy.

The landlords later alleged that he was a business tenant and gave him notice to terminate under the Act of 1954. He was quite right to ignore it. He is entitled to stay on as a statutory tenant under the Rent Acts. I agree with the judge and would dismiss the appeal.

Cheryl Investments Ltd v. Saldanha.

Beaufort Gardens is a fine London square, in which there were in former times large houses occupied by well-to-do families and their servants. These houses have long since been converted into apartment houses. In particular, nos 46/47, Beaufort Gardens, have been turned into 25 separate apartments. These are owned by a property company called Cheryl Investments Ltd., which is run by a Mr. Welcoop. In December 1975, the company advertised the apartments in the 'Evening Standard' in these words: 'Knightsbridge. Essex House, near Harrods, serviced flat and flatlets. Doubles from 20 guineas, Flats from 27 guineas. Short-long lets.'

Mr. Roland Saldanha answered the advertisement. He had been living in Weybridge, but he wanted a permanent residence in the centre of London. He was shown one of the flats, which he liked. It had a large double room with twin beds in it, a bathroom and a toilet. It had no separate kitchen, but there was an entrance hall with a cooker in it that could be used as a kitchen. The landlords provided the furniture and service in the shape of a maid to clean it and change the towels, etc. It took her half an hour a day. The charge was £36.75 a week, plus five per cent surcharge.

Mr. Saldanha's stay there turned out to be very unhappy, with quarrels between him and the landlords. Eventually, on February 9, 1977, the landlords gave him notice to quit on March 26, 1977. He claimed the protection of the Rent Acts ... [The landlords claimed] that Mr. Saldanha occupied the flat for business purposes and was, therefore, not entitled to the protection of the Rent Acts, and they sought a declaration accordingly. The judge rejected that claim. It is from that decision that the landlords appeal to this court.

On this point, the evidence was that Mr. Saldanha was an accountant by profession and a partner in a firm called Best Marine Enterprises. They carry on the business of importing sea foods from India and processing them in Scotland. The firm has no trade premises. The two partners carry on the business from their own homes. The other partner works at his home in Basildon. Mr. Saldanha works at the flat in Beaufort Gardens, and goes from there out to visit clients. When he went into the flat, he had a telephone specially installed for his own use, with the number 589 0232. He put a table in the hall. He had a typewriter there, files and lots of paper – 'the usual office equipment,' said the manageress. He had frequent visitors carrying brief-cases. He had notepaper printed: 'Best Marine Enterprises. Importers of Quality Sea-foods. Telephone 589 0232' – that is the number that I have just mentioned – 'P.O. Box 211, Knightsbridge, London, S.W.3.'

He issued business statements on that very notepaper. A copy of one was found by the maid in a wastepaper basket showing that the firm had imported goods at a total cost of £49,903.30 and sold them for £58,152.35. The maid (whose evidence the judge explicitly accepted in preference to Mr. Saldanha's) said: 'I presumed Mr. Saldanha conducted business there.'

On that evidence, I should have thought it plain that Mr. Saldanha was occupying the flat not only as his dwelling but also for the purposes of a business carried on by him in partnership with another. When he took the flat, it was, no doubt, let to him as a separate dwelling. It was obviously a residential flat with just one large room with twin beds in it. No one can doubt that it was constructed for use as a dwelling and let to him as such within the test in *Wolfe* v. *Hogan* (above). As soon, however, as he equipped it for the purposes of his business of importing sea foods – with telephone, table and printed notepaper – and afterwards used it by receiving business calls there, seeing customers there and issuing business statements from there, it is plain that he was occupying it 'for the purposes of a business carried on by him.' That was a significant purpose for which he was occupying the flat, as well as a dwelling. The flat was his only home, and he was carrying on his business from it.

He did it all surreptitiously. He tried to keep all knowledge of it from the landlord, but that does not alter the fact that, once discovered, his was a 'business tenancy' within section 23 of the Landlord and Tenant Act 1954. Some may say: 'This is a very strange result. It means that he can alter the nature of his tenancy surreptitiously without the consent of his landlord and thus get a statutory continuation of it, with all the consequences that this entails for the landlord.' This is true, but I see no escape from the words of the Acts...

The judge took a different view. He said: 'I think [Mr. Saldanha] is carrying on some business on the premises, but of a nominal kind, and not worth even considering. It is, in my view, *de minimis*. It amounts to having a few files at home and making a few telephone calls at home.' It is to be noticed that the judge was there speaking of the actual 'use' made of the premises, whereas the Act requires us to look at 'the purpose' for which he is occupying it. A professional man may occupy premises for the 'purpose' of seeing clients, but he may make little 'use' of them because no clients come to see him. On the evidence, it seems to me that Mr. Saldanha ... is occupying [the flat] not only for the purpose of his home but also for the purpose of a business carried on by him, and this is a significant purpose. It cannot be dismissed by invoking the maxim *de minimis non curat lex*. This maxim must not be too easily invoked.

Geoffrey Lane and Eveleigh L.JJ. agreed.

Comment. How far are the judicial approaches to the problem, revealed in the above cases, consistent?

C 'A'

Whitty v. *Scott-Russell* [1950] 2 K.B. 32

In 1937 premises consisting of a house known as Tower House, Wadhurst, and a cottage and the garden, were let by the predecessor in title of the present landlords to the defendant for three years at a rent of 75*l.* a year, payable quarterly. The house and cottage were semi-detached, but there was no internal communication between them. The garden and land extended considerably beyond the site of the house. The lease described the demised premises as 'the dwelling-house and cottage with the garden and land thereto belonging,' and the tenant covenanted 'to use the premises as and for a private dwelling-house only.' The tenant did not require the cottage for use as part of his own home, and, with the assent of the original landlord, sub-let it. At the end of the three years the tenant held over as a yearly tenant. On December 22, 1948, the original lessor having died, his executors, the present landlords, gave the tenant notice to quit expiring on June 24, 1949. The tenant failed to vacate the premises, and the landlords brought the present action, claiming possession of the house and cottage. On December 15 the judge dismissed the action, holding that the house and cottage were let as one dwelling-house within the meaning of the Rent Restriction Acts, and that the tenant was protected.

The landlords appealed.

Asquith l.j. said (in part):

[Was] the 'complex' let a 'dwelling-house'? ...

The main authority relied on by the tenant on this issue is *Langford Property Co., Ld* v. *Goldrich* ([1949] 1 K.B. 511). That was a case in which two flats, not contiguous but forming part of the same block of flats under a single roof, were held to be a 'dwelling-house' within the definition. Somervell LJ, in a judgment with which the other two members of the court concurred, says: 'In my opinion, if the facts justify such a finding, two flats, or indeed so far as I can see two houses could be a separate dwelling-house within the meaning of the definition.' . . .

He appears to base this conclusion partly on the terms of the lease, under which the subject-matter let is expressed to be two flats; partly on the Interpretation Act, whereby the singular prima facie includes the plural, hence 'house' in the definition includes houses; but partly also (in relation to the part of the definition which reads 'let as a separate dwelling') on the fact that the tenant in that case wanted the two flats as a home for his family or its overflow, which one flat would have been unable to accommodate.

If the Interpretation Act alone were concerned, this reasoning would be open to the comment that, if the inclusion of the plural in the singular permitted us to read 'house' as including houses, it would equally permit (or perhaps require) us to read 'let as a separate dwelling' as including 'let as two separate dwellings.' An impartial application of the Interpretation Act might lead to odd results.

It is unnecessary, however, to speculate on this, since we are bound by the decision in *Langford Property Co., Ld* v. *Goldrich*, of which this was part of the ratio decidendi. It enables us to read 'house' as covering two houses. But is this (composite) 'house' in the present case 'let as a separate dwelling'? In *Langford Property Co., Ld* v. *Goldrich*, the tenant's purpose in taking two flats was that his family should occupy both, as in fact they did. 'What happened here,' says Somervell LJ, 'was that the tenant wished to accommodate in his home these relatives to whom I have referred, and he wanted more accommodation than could be found or conveniently found in one flat. He . . . thereupon took the two flats and made those two flats his home.' It would seem that the circumstance that the tenant intended to make the two flats – the totality of the parcels let – his home, was thought material, and indeed necessary, by Somervell LJ, to his decision that the flats were let 'as a separate dwelling.' If the flats had been let to the tenant, one to be dwelt in by him and his family, the other not to be so dwelt in, the decision might, it appears, have been different. In the present case the tenant only took the cottage along with the house because the lessor refused to let the one without the other. He never lived in, and never from the start intended to live in, the cottage.

In these circumstances, we are of opinion that the complex 'let' in this case was a dwelling-house within the definition, and we are fortified in that opinion by the concession, in argument, that if X took a tenancy of a house consisting of, say, three floors, and sub-let one floor at once and permanently, the fact of the sublease would not deprive the subject-matter of the head lease of its character as a dwelling-house, provided that in other respects it possessed that character. It cannot in our view make a crucial difference that in the case supposed the part sub-let and the part not sub-let possess internal inter-communication through the common stair, whereas in this case the two units, one of which is sub-let, are two houses clamped together and without such internal inter-communication.

In *Horford Investments Ltd* v. *Lambert* ([1976] Ch. 39), SCARMAN L.J. said, in part:

These two appeals arise from two possession actions, in each of which Horford Investments Ltd, the landlords, sued Norman Alfred Lambert, the tenant, alleging a forfeiture for non-payment of rent. The defence in each case was that the tenancy was protected by the Rent Act 1968 and that the tenant had paid the fair rent assessed in accordance with the provisions of the Act. But the landlords claimed they were entitled to be paid the contract rent, which was substantially higher than the assessed fair rent, alleging that the tenancy was outside the protection of the Act...

The first case concerned 35 Addison Gardens, Hammersmith. The tenancy was created by a lease dated 13th July 1964 between the landlords' predecessor in title and the tenant for a term of 21 years expiring on 29th September 1984, at a rent of £1,298 per annum for the first seven years, £1,550 per annum for the second seven years and £1,930 per annum thereafter until expiry of the term. In December 1970, a rent assessment committee, on appeal from a rent officer to whom the defendant had applied to register a fair rent, assessed a fair rent at £700 per annum. No 35 is a 19th century dwelling-house which, when the tenancy was granted, was used as to the ground and upper floors for letting off in rooms and as to the basement as a separate and self-contained flat. It has continued to be so used and in 1970 was yielding the tenant £3,000 per annum. The user clause of the lease is in these terms:

'The Lessee will not use ... the ... premises or any part thereof for the purpose of any trade or business nor for any purpose other than residential in multiple occupation.'

There is also a covenant against assignment without consent, which contains a specific provision, the effect of which is that the tenant may underlet a part (but not the whole) of the premises for a term not exceeding six months without consent. Finally, it was agreed that the tenant had never resided in the premises or any part of them ... Counsel for the landlords conceded in this court, as on the state of the authorities he was bound in my opinion to do, that, if there be a letting of a house as a separate dwelling, the tenancy is protected notwithstanding that: (1) the tenant never dwells in the house or any part of it, (2) the tenancy includes land or buildings not used as a dwelling as well as premises used as a dwelling (subject to exceptions specifically provided for in the [1977 Act: e.g. ss. 10 and 24]); (3) the premises are used for business purposes as well as for a dwelling (again subject to the statutory exception to be found in [s. 24] of the [1977] Act).

In my opinion only two questions call for decision by this court: (1) whether, on the true construction of s. 1(1) of the [1977] Act, the tenancy of a house let as several dwellings is within its terms; and (2) if it is, whether it loses protection as being a business tenancy excluded from protection by [s. 24] of the Act...

In the absence of direct authority on the point of construction, I prefer first to consider the terms of the section in its statutory context and then to see whether there is any case law which should lead one to modify one's view as to its meaning... The section is concerned with the tenancy of a dwelling-house (or part of one). It must be a question of fact whether premises are a house or not: as Bankes L.J. said in *Epsom Grandstand Association Ltd* v. *Clarke* ([1919] W.N. 170), if the agreement is to let a barn, the tenant even though he lives there, cannot be heard to say it is let as a dwelling-house. The agreed statement of facts describes no 35 as [a] dwelling-house and I therefore hold that the tenancy ... is the tenancy of a dwelling-house.

The section affords protection to the tenancy of a house only if the house is let as a separate dwelling. The section directs attention to the letting, that is to say, the terms of the tenancy. The courts have proceeded on the basis that the terms of the tenancy are the primary consideration: see *Wolfe* v. *Hogan* ([1949] 2 K.B. 194). In my opinion there is here a principle of cardinal importance; whether a tenancy of a house (or a part of a house) is protected depends on the terms of the tenancy, not on subsequent events. If, as may happen, subsequent events modify or alter the terms of the tenancy, they are relevant: otherwise, not. In the present two cases no such events have occurred: the question of protection under the Act therefore depends on the terms of the tenancy that is to say, the letting.

The letting ... was of a house comprising more dwellings than one. Was it the letting of a house as a dwelling (both parties agree that the word 'separate' is of no importance in this connection)? If counsel for the tenant is right that the Interpretation Act 1889 requires us to construe the subsection's phrase 'a dwelling' so that it includes 'dwellings', *cadit quaestio*: each tenancy is protected. But I agree with the county court judge in thinking that Parliament when it enacted s. 1(1) used the singular deliberately, and in this instance did not intend the singular to include the plural. The policy of the Rent Acts was and is to protect the tenant in his home, whether the threat be to extort a premium for the grant or renewal of his tenancy, to increase his rent, or to evict him. It is not a policy for the protection of an entrepreneur such as the tenant in this case whose interest is exclusively commercial, that is to say, to obtain from his tenants a greater rental income than the rent he has contracted to pay his landlord. The Rent Acts have throughout their history constituted an interference with contract and property rights for a specific purpose – the redress of the balance of advantage enjoyed in a world of housing shortage by the landlord over those who have to rent their homes. To extend the protection of the Acts to tenancies such as these in this case would be to interfere with contract and property rights beyond the requirements of that purpose.

I, therefore, think that the context requires that the words of the subsection 'let as a dwelling' be confined to the singular: they mean what they literally say ... The court must construe these words in the light of the policy of the [1977] Act and of the earlier legislation which it replaces. This policy has been recognized more than once by the courts and does not require the very substantial interference with property and contract rights implicit in counsel for the tenant's submission.

Accordingly, I agree with the county court judge. A house (or part of a house) must be let as *a* dwelling, that is to say, as a single dwelling, for the tenancy to be protected for the purposes of the Act. If it is let as a single dwelling, the fact that the tenant does not himself live there, or that he carries on a business as well as living there, or that he sub-lets part or the whole, or that he uses only part of the premises for habitation does not put the letting outside the Act – unless what is done either modifies the terms of the letting or brings the house within some specific exclusion stated in the Act...

RUSSELL L.J. also came to this conclusion, though he noted:

It appears to me somewhat anomalous that there should be this radical distinction between a case where at the time of the letting there are comprised more than one unit of habitation (save in exceptional cases such as *Langford Property Co., Ltd* v. *Goldrich* ([1949] 1 K.B. 511) and *Whitty*'s case (above, p. 164)) and a case where there is at the outset only one, though immediately to be converted into two or more. Similarly it seems somewhat anomalous to find that a letting of premises comprising a shop and one unit of habitation is within protection (see e.g. *British Land Co. Ltd* v. *Herbert Silver* (*Menswear*) *Ltd* ([1958] 1 Q.B. 531)), while a letting of premises comprising two units of habitation is not. But it appears to me that the weight of authority makes it necessary to accept these anomalies.

PLOWMAN J. concurred.

See also *St Catherine's College* v. *Dorling* (below, pp. 194–5).

D 'Separate'

The requirement for the 'separateness' of the dwelling causes some difficulty. A number of propositions may be advanced.

(*i*) If the tenancy had been created jointly with a number of joint tenants (e.g. a husband and wife, or a close-knit group of friends) all of whose names appear on the lease, or, if oral, the circumstances of creation are unequivocal, it appears these tenants will jointly be Rent Act protected and be deemed to live as a unit in the separate accommodation. (Farrand, 1978, notes to section 1; Pettit, 1978, p. 27; see also *Lloyd* v. *Sadler* below, pp. 230–34.)

(*ii*) If a tenant has rented accommodation on terms that he shares it with another, it has been argued that if the sharing is total there is no 'exclusive occupation' so that no tenancy will be created; *a fortiori* there would be no 'separate' dwelling. However, the discussion of 'non-exclusive occupation agreements' reveals a considerable confusion amongst the judges as to how they should be interpreted (above, pp. 119–48).

(*iii*) If the sharing of the accommodation is partial, the position of the tenant will be governed by the following principles:

(*a*) *Marsh* v. *Cooper* [1969] 2 All E.R. 498 (C.A.)
DANCKWERTS L.J. said (in part):

We are concerned with a flat, No. 92, Finchley Court in Finchley, which consists of four rooms and a bathroom. It appears there are two rooms which were let eventually to the tenant when one Mrs Samuel was the landlady. There is also a kitchen and next to it a bathroom with lavatory and washbasin. Then there is also one room which was retained by the landlady and used for some time as a letting office.

Now I turn to the terms of the agreement between the parties dated 17 September 1964, expressed to be made between –

'Mrs. Ada Samuel of 49 Finchley Court Ballards Lane Finchley London N.3 (hereinafter called "the Landlord" which expression shall where the context so admits include the persons deriving title under her) of the one part and Mrs Mabel Irene Cooper [giving her address] (hereinafter called "the Tenant" which expression shall where the context so admits include the persons deriving title under her) of the other part...'

The present landlords became the landlords in 1966 and the defendant is still the tenant. Turning to the body of the agreement, cl. 1 provides as follows:

'The Landlord agrees to let and the Tenant agrees to take ALL THAT part of flat or rooms (hereinafter called 'the Flat') numbered 92 and situate on the ground floor of the building known as Finchley Court Ballards Lane Finchley London N.3, together with...'

certain landlord's fixtures, and so on. Before the word 'together' there is an asterisk which introduces the words 'more particularly defined in the Schedule hereof'. The schedule appears on the back of the document and is as follows:

'The small front room and the small room with windows facing the side and back together with the use of the kitchen and the bathroom together with the employees of the Landlord.'

Now a good deal of case law has accumulated on the subject and the point is this: it is alleged on behalf of the landlords that the tenant not having included in the letting to her the kitchen and the bathroom but only being given the use of them is burdened with sharing those portions of the flat with the employees of the landlords and, therefore, under the numerous cases which deal with the sharing by parties in regard to a letting the tenant has not got the protection of the Acts because she has not what is 'a dwelling-house or part of a dwelling-house'.

The matter has given rise to a great deal of judicial discussion. Various cases have dealt with what is a living room and in particular it has been said that a kitchen is a living room. In the present case the kitchen is so small that it is only possible to use it for cooking. There is no furniture in it, I understand, and I myself think that it does not constitute a living room in the proper meaning of that term, which conclusion would of course put it outside the application of those cases, which depend on the tenant not having one of the essential living rooms for the purposes of the letting. Furthermore, there have been great discussions about the various cases which have arisen, the facts of those cases and so on. I should like to read now the observations of LORD RADCLIFFE in *Goodrich* v. *Paisner* ([1957] A.C. 65):

'Secondly, it cannot always be clear what ought to be treated as a "living room" for this purpose. The complexities of individual situations and requirements are infinitely various, since patterns of living themselves vary so much, and what is important or even essential for one occupant of rooms separately let may be unimportant or unnecessary for another. I cannot, myself, frame any formula which, in this context, necessarily embraces a kitchen but necessarily excludes a bathroom. The difficulty has led to attempts to speak of "essential living rooms" or "essential manifestations of living"; but I am bound to say that these glosses seem to me either to beg the question or to confuse the issue. And I am afraid that I cannot see anything more satisfying in the definition offered during the course of argument in this case: "a living room is a room wherein you cook, eat, sleep, and put your feet on the fender". Why ever should courts of law tie themselves down in this way?'

Of course, if one applies that definition to the present case one could not, I should have thought, live in the kitchen, one could not sleep there and one could not put one's feet on the fender.

Anyhow, the point I am trying to make is this: that the courts have got so much into discussion of the language used in other cases (as so often happens with regard to authorities) that they have lost sight of the origin that they had to deal with in the course of the various cases which had put glosses and interpretations on various points. The matter still remains as it is in the statute and it is the words in the statute which have to be applied. Referring back to s. 12(2) of the Act of 1920, that provides: 'This Act shall apply to a house or a part of a house let as a separate dwelling.' The sole point, and the point the courts have to make up their minds about, is whether the premises are 'a house or a part of a house let as a separate dwelling'.

In this case there is a further matter which arises in my view. It seems to me that the description in the schedule is far from clear. It is vague and until one considers the circumstances it is quite impossible to understand what is meant by 'the use of the kitchen and the bathroom together with the employees of the Landlord'. It might have been that they are all having baths together or cooking together. But in fact the circumstances of this case from the evidence show that the situation was very different from that. It appears that all the use which the employees were allowed to have in respect of the kitchen was they could go there to get fresh water for drinking or cooking purposes. There was a gas ring in the letting office and the cooking, so far as any was done in the letting office for the benefit of the employees of the landlords, was done there and not in the kitchen and they merely got water for any purpose they required. As regards the use of the bathroom they used it for the purpose of using the lavatory or for washing their hands or for wash- ing up apparently. That very minor use was the whole of the use which they were entitled to have in regard to the property of which the tenant was given practically the entire use.

Now those circumstances were told to the tenant before she took the premises, for she was told there was some sharing to be done and she asked what was the extent of the sharing and was told the facts I have mentioned.

The fact (which is merely history) is that after the acquisition by the present landlords of the premises they ceased to use the room as a letting office and for a year or so no use was made of it at all, but eventually the porter was told by them he must make some use of it and he used it for the purpose of storing bits of carpets which could be used to show to tenants who might want to order carpets for the purpose of their flats.

In those circumstances it seems to me the facts of this case differ immensely from the facts of the various decisions which have been quoted to us. Indeed in *Goodrich* v. *Paisner* (above) the House of Lords in their speeches said that the question was really a matter of fact and a matter of degree. In this case it seems to me that the degree of use by the employees of the landlords was so small as to be almost negligible and cannot, in my opinion, amount to sharing the use of the bathroom and the kitchen. Consequently, in my view, all those cases are different cases on different facts and do not compel us to reach a conclusion which, to my mind, would be devoid of common sense. In my view there was a definite letting of two rooms and the provision of cooking facilities in a small kitchen that was not really properly called a living room at all and therefore the provisions of the Act apply to the letting to the tenant and she is entitled to the protection of the Acts. In my view, there- fore, the learned judge reached the wrong conclusion and the appeal should be allowed.

PHILLIMORE L.J. agreed.

(b) *Sharing with Landlord :* Rent Act 1977, s. 21

Where under any contract –

(a) a tenant has the exclusive occupation of any accommodation, and

(b) the terms on which he holds the accommodation include the use of other accommodation in common with his landlord and other persons, and

(c) by reason only of the circumstances mentioned in paragraph (b) above, or by reason of those circumstances and the operation of section 12 of this Act, the accommodation referred to in paragraph (a) above is not a dwelling-house let on a protected tenancy,

the contract is a restricted contract notwithstanding that the rent does not include payment for the use of furniture or for services.

(Restricted contracts are discussed below, p. 221.)

According to the cases discussed in *Marsh* v. *Cooper* (above, p. 170), the 'accommodation' must be living accommodation.

(c) *Sharing with persons other than landlord :* Rent Act 1977, s. 22

(1) Where a tenant has the exclusive occupation of any accommodation ('the separate accommodation') and –

(a) the terms as between the tenant and his landlord on which he holds the separate accommodation include the use of other accommodation ('the shared accommodation') in common with another person or other persons, not being or including the landlord, and

(b) by reason only of the circumstances mentioned in paragraph (a) above, the separate accommodation would not, apart from this section, be a dwelling-house let on or subject to a protected or statutory tenancy,

the separate accommodation shall be deemed to be a dwelling-house let on a protected tenancy or, as the case may be, subject to a statutory tenancy and the following provisions of this section shall have effect.

(2) For the avoidance of doubt it is hereby declared that where, for the purpose of determining the rateable value of the separate accommodation, it is necessary to make an apportionment under this Act, regard is to be had to the circumstances mentioned in subsection (1)(a) above.

(3) While the tenant is in possession of the separate accommodation (whether as a protected or statutory tenant), any term or condition of the contract of tenancy terminating or modifying, or providing for the termination or modification of, his right to the use of any of the shared accommodation which is living accommodation shall be of no effect.

(4) Where the terms and conditions of the contract of tenancy are such that at any time during the tenancy the persons in common with whom the tenant is entitled to the use of the shared accommodation could be varied, or their number could be increased, nothing in subsection (3) above shall prevent those terms and conditions from having effect so far as they relate to any such variation or increase.

(5) Without prejudice to the enforcement of any order made under subsection (6) below, while the tenant is in possession of the separate accommodation, no order shall be made for possession of any of the shared accommodation, whether on the application of the immediate landlord of the tenant or on the application of any person under whom that landlord derives title, unless a like order has been made, or is made at the same time, in respect of the separate accommodation; and the provisions of section 98(1) of this Act shall apply accordingly.

(6) On the application of the landlord, the county court may make such order either –

> (a) terminating the right of the tenant to use the whole or any part of the shared accommodation other than living accommodation, or
> (b) modifying his right to use the whole or any part of the shared accommodation, whether by varying the persons or increasing the number of persons entitled to the use of that accommodation, or otherwise,

as the court thinks just.

(7) No order shall be made under subsection (6) above so as to effect any termination or modification of the rights of the tenant which, apart from subsection (3) above, could not be effected by or under the terms of the contract of tenancy.

(8) In this section 'living accommodation' means accommodation of such a nature that the fact that it constitutes or is included in the shared accommodation is (or, if the tenancy has ended, was) sufficient, apart from this section, to prevent the tenancy from constituting a protected tenancy of a dwelling-house.

(d) *Creation of sub-lettings:* Rent Act 1977, s. 23

(1) Where the tenant of any premises, consisting of a house or part of a house, has sublet a part but not the whole of the premises, then, as against his landlord or any superior landlord, no part of the premises shall be treated as not being a dwelling-house let on or subject to a protected or statutory tenancy by reason only that –

> (a) the terms on which any person claiming under the tenant holds any part of the premises include the use of accommodation in common with other persons; or

(*b*) part of the premises is let to any such person at a rent which includes payments in respect of board or attendance.

(2) Nothing in this section shall affect the rights against, and liabilities to, each other of the tenant and any person claiming under him, or of any 2 such persons.

E A note on furnished tenancies

Before 14 August 1974 furnished tenancies were outside the full protection of the Rent Act, though they fell within the jurisdiction of the Rent Tribunal. However, Rent Act 1974, s. 1 (1) (which, absurdly, was not incorporated in the consolidation of the Rent Act 1977), provided

1.—(1) On and after the commencement date, –

(*a*) a tenancy of a dwelling-house shall no longer be prevented from being a protected tenancy for the purposes of the Rent Act by reason only that, under the tenancy, the dwelling-house is bona fide let at a rent which includes payments in respect of the use of furniture; and

(*b*) subject to the following provisions of this Act, references in the Rent Act (and in any other enactment or instrument in which those expressions have the same meaning as in that Act) to a protected tenancy, a statutory tenancy or a regulated tenancy shall be construed accordingly...

Lettings created before the commencement date, 14 August 1974, remain subject to the old law; thus whether they were furnished or not is still to be determined according to the principles advanced by the House of Lords in *Palser* v. *Grinling* [1948] A.C. 291, and more recently by the Court of Appeal in *Woodward* v. *Docherty* [1974] 1 W.L.R. 966 (Partington, 1974). Also *Christophides* v. *Cumming* (1976) *Times*, 14 February (C.A.), *Mann* v. *Cornella* (1980) 254 E.G. 403.

4. Exemptions from protection

Even if the tests in section 1 of the Rent Act (above) are satisfied, the tenancy will still not be protected if it falls within one of the categories of exemption specified in the legislation.

A Rateable value limits : Rent Act 1977, s. 4

(1) A tenancy is not a protected tenancy if the dwelling-house falls within one of the Classes set out in subsection (2) below.

(2) Where alternative rateable values are mentioned in this subsection, the higher applies if the dwelling-house is in Greater London and the lower applies if it is elsewhere.

Class A

The appropriate day in relation to the dwelling-house falls or fell on or after 1st April 1973 and the dwelling-house on the appropriate day has or had a rateable value exceeding £1,500 or £750.

Class B

The appropriate day in relation to the dwelling-house fell on or after 22nd March 1973, but before 1st April 1973, and the dwelling-house –

(a) on the appropriate day had a rateable value exceeding £600 or £300, and

(b) on 1st April 1973 had a rateable value exceeding £1,500 or £750.

Class C

The appropriate day in relation to the dwelling-house fell before 22nd March 1973 and the dwelling-house –

(a) on the appropriate day had a rateable value exceeding £400 or £200, and

(b) on 22nd March 1973 had a rateable value exceeding £600 or £300, and

(c) on 1st April 1973 had a rateable value exceeding £1,500 or £750.

(3) If any question arises in any proceedings whether a dwelling-house falls within a Class in subsection (2) above, by virtue of its rateable value at any time, it shall be deemed not to fall within that Class unless the contrary is shown.

'Appropriate day' is defined in Rent Act 1977, s. 25 (3):

(a) in relation to any dwelling-house which, on 23rd March 1965, was or formed part of a hereditament for which a rateable value was shown in the valuation list then in force, or consisted or formed part of more than one such hereditament, means that date, and

(b) in relation to any other dwelling-house, means the date on which such a value is or was first shown in the valuation list.

The effect of a retrospective alteration in rateable value was discussed by the House of Lords in *Rodwell* v. *Gwynne Trusts* [1970] 1 W.L.R. 327.

In cases where a dwelling-house forms part only of a building ('hereditament'), apportionment is permitted (Rent Act 1977, s. 25(1) and (2)).

B Tenancies at no rent, or low rent : Rent Act 1977, s. 5

5.—(1) A tenancy is not a protected tenancy if under the tenancy either no rent is payable or, subject to section 17(2) of this Act, the rent payable is less than two-thirds of the rateable value which is or was the rateable value of the dwelling-house on the appropriate day.

(2) Where –

(a) the appropriate day in relation to a dwelling-house fell before 22nd March 1973, and

(b) the dwelling-house had on the appropriate day a rateable value exceeding, if it is in Greater London, £400 or, if it is elsewhere, £200,

subsection (1) above shall apply in relation to the dwelling-house as if the reference to the appropriate day were a reference to 22nd March 1973.

(3) In this Act a tenancy falling within subsection (1) above is referred to as a 'tenancy at a low rent'.

(4) In determining whether a long tenancy is a tenancy at a low rent, there shall be disregarded such part (if any) of the sums payable by the tenant as is expressed (in whatever terms) to be payable in respect of rates, services, repairs, maintenance, or insurance, unless it could not have been regarded by the parties as a part so payable.

(5) In subsection (4) above 'long tenancy' means a tenancy granted for a term certain exceeding 21 years, other than a tenancy which is, or may become, terminable before the end of that term by notice given to the tenant.

Interpretation of this section has caused a number of problems:

(i) THE MEANING OF 'RENT'

The following cases discuss, *inter alia*, the meaning of 'rent'. The contrast between the definitions adopted for the purposes of the Rent Act and common law definitions (see below, p. 242) should be noted.

Hornsby v. *Maynard* [1925] 1 K.B. at 521

SHEARMAN J.: In my opinion this appeal should be dismissed. The facts of the case may be shortly stated. The plaintiff, who is the owner of the dwelling-house in question, had let it on a lease, which was in existence in August, 1914, at a rent of 46*l*. 16*s*., that being accordingly its standard rent, the rates being paid by the plaintiff. In 1917 the plaintiff let the house to the defendant on the agreement which forms the subject of the present dispute. [His Lordship read the agreement so far as material and continued:] Thus, by that agreement the plaintiff let to the defendant 'all that messuage, tenement and premises situate and being No. 33 Ranelagh Road,' the defendant agreed to pay the rates, and the defendant further agreed to give to the plaintiff in consideration of the rent payable the use of the dining-room and bedroom on the same floor for her own occupation rent free. The rent reserved by that agreement was less by 10*l.* 16*s.* than the standard rent of the house. Disputes arose between the parties, and in November, 1923, the plaintiff brought this action against the defendant in the county court for alleged arrears of rent, and the defendant counterclaimed for rent alleged to have been overpaid. The county court judge found that the exchange of the rates from the plaintiff to the defendant was an advantage to the former and a disadvantage to the latter, the value of which he assessed at 10*l.* 16*s.* a year, and that that should be treated as rent, thus bringing the new rent exactly up to the standard rent. He found that the right given by the defendant to the plaintiff to use the two rooms was an advantage to the plaintiff, and he assessed the value of that also at 10*l.* 16*s.* He gave judgment for the plaintiff for a certain sum, and the defendant now appeals.

It is contended on behalf of the defendant in support of the appeal that the value of the grant by the defendant to the plaintiff of the use of the two rooms was 'rent' within the meaning of the Increase of Rent, &c., Restrictions Act, 1920, that under s. 1 of that Act the rent of the house had been thereby increased, and that the increased rent exceeded the standard rent by more than the permitted amount...

The remaining point taken on behalf of the defendant is that the value of the right given by the defendant to the plaintiff to use the two rooms is 'rent' within the meaning of the Act of 1920, and that under s. 1 of that Act the rent of the house has thereby been unduly increased above the standard rent. It is said that there may be rent or an increase of rent in things other than money which are capable of being assessed in money. On the true construction of the provisions of the Act it seems to me that the term 'rent' in s. 1 and the other sections in which it occurs means rent payable in money and in money alone. It is urged that, if this be so, the Act has left it open to the parties to an agreement of tenancy successfully to evade its provisions by arranging that the landlord shall have some privilege, the value of which, added to the pecuniary rent, will increase the total actual rent beyond the statutory limit. It is not for me to criticize the policy of the Act and I do not presume to do so. I take the Act as I find it. So taking it I think it is restricted to pecuniary rent. The only way in which persons can be prevented from evading it by substituting some other consideration for rent in money, is by showing that the giving of that other consideration comes under s. 2, sub-s. 3, relating to the transfer of a burden or liability previously borne by the landlord, or under s. 8, which prohibits a person from requiring a fine or premium as the condition of the grant of a tenancy. The third point taken on behalf of the defendant also fails.

In my opinion the appeal should be dismissed.

Salter J. was of the same opinion. He noted, *inter alia*:

At common law the term 'rent' was not restricted to pecuniary rent. Tenancies under which the rent was payable by way of services were formerly very common, and such tenancies are still to be met with. In this Act, however, having regard to its own provisions and to the authorities decided upon it to which our attention has been called, I think that the term 'rent' applies only to pecuniary rent. I regret to have to come to this conclusion, because it follows that the Act can be in some respects evaded.

Montague v. *Browning* [1954] 1 W.L.R. 1039

SINGLETON L.J.: In 1941 there was created a tenancy of the house between the trustees and Mr Browning; and it is not disputed that at that time there was created a tenancy to which the Rent Acts applied.

In 1946 the trustees realized that much more work had to be done in the way of cleaning the synagogue and that the duties of Mr and Mrs Browning, the caretakers, were much heavier than they had been during war-time, and so they passed a resolution dated 18 February 1946, in these terms: 'Mr P. Milstone proposed and Mr S. Schonfeld seconded that the wages of the caretaker be increased by £26 per annum, making a total of £66 per annum.' That increase was 10s. a week, and it meant that the wages to be paid to the caretaker, or caretakers, were precisely the same as the yearly value which had been placed on the house. The minister called to see Mrs Browning, and said to her: 'I have some good news for you; you won't have to pay 10s. a week any more; we are raising your wages.' 'Thank you very much,' said Mrs Browning.

It is said on behalf of the trustees that that constituted an entirely new agreement, and that from that moment – I suppose from the moment of communication to Mrs Browning – there was no tenancy which was protected by the Rent Acts, but that there came about an arrangement which was not the letting of a house for rent, but an arrangement that the Brownings should have the house in return for services rendered. I do not think that that was the agreement. Mr Browning said that 'there was no suggestion of a new agreement of tenancy when the plaintiffs agreed to pay me or my wife an extra 10s. a week.' Mrs Browning, in response to the news from the minister, had said: 'Thank you very much.' There was nothing to alter the nature of the tenancy between the parties; indeed, the minutes of the trustees showed that the trustees had agreed to pay the caretaker an extra 10s. a week in wages, which would put up the total payment to £66 a year. If there was (as I think it is clear there was) a tenancy which was covered by the Rent Acts between 1941 and 1946, I cannot see that any change was made by that which took place in 1946.

There remains, however, in force section 12 (7) of the Act of 1920, which is in [terms similar to Rent Act 1977, s. 5(1)] ... Before the Rent Acts come into operation there must, of course, be a tenancy; and if there is a tenancy there is usually a rent. When this house was first let to Mr or to Mrs Browning there was a rent; no one disputes that; but it was submitted to the county court judge that the change which took place in 1946 took the case out of the Rent Acts altogether, and the county court judge acceded to that submission, and said: 'On the evidence called before me I found as a fact (as counsel for the plaintiffs submitted I should find) (1) that from June, 1941, until February, 1946, the first defendant was a tenant of the plaintiffs paying a rent partly in money, viz., 10s. per week, and partly in services, the value of those services being agreed between the parties as £40 per annum; (2) that from February, 1946, no rent in money was paid, credited, offered or demanded and that from that time the first defendant was a tenant of the plaintiffs paying his rent entirely in services, which were agreed between the parties as being worth £66 per annum.'

I do not think that that last finding is warranted on the evidence. The minutes show that there was an increase of wages. The wages had to be paid in some way, and it was probably a saving to the officials of the synagogue not to have to make cross-entries. I cannot see that there was an agreement between the parties under which the tenancy of the house which had existed prior to that time was altered or changed. There was a tenancy to which the Rent Acts applied from the years 1941 to 1946: that is common ground. There was no change in the character of that merely by the increase of wages or merely by the remarks made by the minister to Mrs Browning: 'We are putting up your wages, so you need not pay the 10s.'

The county court judge would have been inclined to decide the case in favour of the defendants but for the citation to him of *Hornsby* v. *Maynard* (above, p. 176), decided the Divisional Court in 1924. There are passages in the judgment of Shearman J. and in the judgment of Salter J. on which reliance was placed by counsel for the trustees, and which impressed the county court judge...

I think that it may be necessary at some time for those words of Salter J. and some words of Shearman J. to the like effect to be reconsidered. I do not think that the decision of the Divisional Court in *Hornsby* v. *Maynard* affects the present case in any degree. There was a protected tenancy from 1941 to 1946, and the same class of tenancy remains notwithstanding the increase of 10s. in the wages, and notwithstanding the fact that the one was written off against the other. There was no new agreement which put an end to the old tenancy or which changed its character.

DENNING L.J. also said, in part:

I cannot agree with that restricted meaning of the word 'rent'. It seems to me that even under the Rent Acts, in cases when rent is not payable in money but in kind, as in goods or services, then, so long as the parties have by agreement quantified the value in terms of money, the sum so quantified is the rent of the house within the meaning of the Rent Restriction Acts; and, if it exceeds two thirds of the rateable value, the house is within the Acts.

If the tenancy is determined and the landlord has no further use for the services the landlord can recover the standard rent in lieu of the services. I say nothing about the position where the services are not quantified in money, which was the case in *Hornsby* v. *Maynard*, except to say that even on that point some of the observations in that case may need reconsideration. Suffice it to say in the present case that, accepting the findings of fact of the county court judge, nevertheless the tenant was protected because there was the quantified sum which the services were worth, £66 a year. The house was, no doubt, let to him in consequence of his employment, but the landlords do not suggest that they can bring the case within the provisions of the Act so as to recover possession on that score. I agree, therefore, that the appeal should be allowed accordingly.

Barnes v. *Barratt* [1970] 2 Q.B. 657

SACHS L.J.: The action was brought by the plaintiffs for the possession of that part of a house, known as 7 Amesbury Road, Bromley, which was in occupation of the defendants, Mr and Mrs Barratt ... In 1951, when he was a widower, Mr Constable had found the house larger than was needed for his personal occupation. In that year he made an arrangement with the defendants which has been the subject of conflicting submissions in this court. In effect, the defendants were to come into the house and occupy part of it and, in return, were to look after Mr Constable.

According to the findings of the county court judge the defendants were to have exclusive use of three rooms and the kitchen; Mr Constable was to have similar use of two rooms; the bathroom was to be shared. In return for their use of the above accommodation the defendants were to clean Mr Constable's part of the house; the second defendant was to shop for him and cook for him; and they were to provide him with light and warmth, paying the electricity, gas and fuel bills for the house as a whole. It was clear that the second defendant was not to become, and did not become, an employee of Mr Constable; nor did the first defendant. It is material to note that both the defendants, in their evidence, each emphasized that they had exclusive occupation of the kitchen. The learned county court judge so found when he stated:

'They were to come and live there ... with the exclusive occupation and Interest in the whole of the house except for 2 rooms, which were to remain Mr Constable's. They had joint use of the Bathroom with Mr Constable ...'

It is his finding that they went there as his sub-tenants which is now in issue.

There was no question of there being a rent book nor was any monetary rent agreed. The services of the defendants were to suffice in return for the accommodation they were to get. The parties, according to the defendants' evidence, which was accepted by the county court judge, spoke in terms of a tenancy using words such as 'rent' and 'sub-tenant'. On the other hand, Mr Constable on more than one occasion refused to accept any payment of rent. In those circumstances the defendants' case was put by the second defendant as 'my services constituted rent'. That arrangement was put into effect. All three concerned were, for a considerable number of years, in happy co-occupation of this house as a result. This, indeed, continued until Mr Constable died. Then the interest in the house, previously held by Mr Constable, was in due course surrendered to the plaintiffs who have brought these proceedings. It is convenient first of all to deal with the issue whether, assuming there was a tenancy, the defendants did pay rent within the meaning of that word in the Rent Acts. The county court judge held that the services rendered by the defendants in caring for Mr Constable, cooking for him and providing him with warmth and light did constitute such rent. That the rendering of services can constitute rent at common law is well settled but whether it can, when there has been no quantification of their value, constitute rent under the Rent Acts is a different question. It was answered 45 years ago in *Hornsby* v. *Maynard* (above, p. 176) by a Divisional Court particularly experienced in dealing with the manifold problems then regularly being raised by the Increase of Rent and Mortgage Interest (Restrictions) Act 1920, the Act from which so much of the later rent legislation is derived. In that case, a tenant allowed his landlord the use of two rooms and the unquantified value of that user was alleged to constitute rent ...

The court, as we have seen, rejected this argument.

In the decades that immediately followed this clear decision, and indeed the decades which subsequently transpired, there were passed a whole series of Acts which adopted the 1920 Act as the principal Act and brought into operation extensive amending provisions, using, in every case the same phraseology so far as was relevant to the meaning of the word 'rent'. In none of those Acts was that word given a fresh definition, nor has it been given any fresh definition in the Rent Act 1968. In such circumstances it is axiomatic that the legislature must normally be taken to have been aware of the courts' well-established view of the meaning of a specific word and to have embodied that meaning in the succeeding Acts. That, in itself, would be a good ground for holding that the *Hornsby* v. *Maynard* interpretation of the word 'rent' continues in force in essence. However, if one turns to look at the structure of the Rent Acts as a whole, it is equally clear that their provisions with regard to rent restriction can only, in practice, be operated if that interpretation is correct. The effective basis of the restrictions turns on there being quantified sums to which the provisions of the Acts can apply. It is not necessary to proceed in detail through those provisions, though we were most helpfully guided by counsel amongst them from s. 1 of the 1920 Act onwards. It is sufficient to refer to two of them. The first relates to the sole permissible method of increasing rents. This was laid down in the 1920 Act by s. 3 (2); in the 1968 Act by s. 26. In each and every Rent Act from 1920 onwards the same pattern has been adopted as regards the increasing of rents. It has always been made mandatory to use forms of notice of increase which are prescribed by the statutes. The first of these forms is to be found in Sch. 1 to the 1920 Act. Each form in turn is based on the existence of a quantified rent at the time when the notice is served. Moreover, one glance at it is sufficient to show how ill-adapted it would be to the present case if, for instance, the defendants and Mr Constable had, in the middle of their occupation, agreed that the second defendant should also wash Mr Constable's linen or that the first defendant should clean his car.

The second set of provisions to be noted are those which are to be found in s. 14 of the 1920 Act, of which the lineal successor is s. 33 of the 1968 Act. Section 14 provides for the recovery by the tenant of 'any sum' – and it is to be observed that the word 'sum' is used – 'paid on account of any rent' to the landlord which was 'irrecoverable by the landlord', i.e. the amount by which the payment exceeded the permitted rents whether that rent was permitted in the original tenancy or in a later supervening statutory tenancy. So if, as seems probable, the value of the defendants' services at times exceeded the permitted rent, how, in this case, could the provisions of those sections in practice be operated? The answer, to my mind, is that they could not. Moreover, what would be the position as regards the 'irrecoverable' part of the services when once the parties had come to arm's length on such matter? Could the second defendant be held, as from the date when the point was raised, to be liable only to do the cooking on three days out of every seven and, if so, on which days? It suffices to say that the good sense of the decision in *Hornsby* v. *Maynard* is patent; it was correctly decided. Moreover, counsel was unable to point to any case which has come before the courts over the last 50 years in which unquantified services of this type have been held to produce a tenancy within the ambit of the Acts.

From there it is right to turn to the case of *Montague* v. *Browning* (above, p. 178), a case decided in this court on somewhat special facts. There it had been agreed, between a caretaker and his employers, that the appropriate rent for premises which they let to him was £66 per annum and that as regards payment, he could set against that sum his wages which were at the same time agreed at £40 a year. Thus he actually only needed to pay the balance of £26 a year. (Some complications, which are irrelevant, arose when his wages were raised by 10s. a week). The Court of Appeal in that case, reversing the county court judge, held that the tenancy fell within the Rent Acts. That was a case of an agreed monetary rent with a set-off. On those facts it was, of course, unnecessary for the appellant tenant to argue in this court that *Hornsby* v. *Maynard* had been wrongly decided. Incidentally, counsel for the plaintiffs, who on that occasion appeared for the appellant tenant, has informed us that no such submission was made. Singleton LJ, when giving the leading judgment, said: 'I do not think that the decision of the Divisional Court in *Hornsby* v. *Maynard* affects the case before this court in any degree'. Denning LJ carefully restricted his judgment to cases where the parties had, by agreement, quantified the rents in terms of money and both he and Morris LJ refrained expressly from giving any general or final opinion on *Hornsby* v. *Maynard*. It is true that each of the members of the court, not having heard full argument on the matter, did obiter express the view that *Hornsby* v. *Maynard* might have to be further considered but plainly, when one looks at their judgments as a whole, they neither purported to overrule that case, nor did they overrule it. It is indeed not entirely easy to see how the learned county court judge misled himself into saying that he thought it had inferentially been overruled. Accordingly, in the present case, even if there was a tenancy, the Rent Acts could not apply to it. At no time was there any agreed monetary quantification of the rent, nor was there any agreed method of quantification, nor was there any Act which provided a substitute for an agreed method of quantification. There is thus no need to discuss difficulties such as those which could occur if, for instance, an agreed valuation was found to be well below the manifestly true value of the services. Nor is this a case where there was a master and servant relationship agreement, in other words, what is normally referred to as a service tenancy.

Comment. In what circumstances, today, might non-monetary rent be regarded as rent for the purpose of the Rent Act? Are the above cases reconcilable?

(ii) 'COMMUTED RENT' V. 'PREMIUM'
Samrose Properties v. *Gibbard* [1958] 1 W.L.R. 235

LORD EVERSHED M.R.: The sole question raised in this appeal is whether the rent payable in respect of certain premises (which were the subject of a tenancy made in August, 1955), was less than two-thirds of the rateable value of the premises. It is not in doubt for the purposes of this appeal that the rateable value of the premises is or was at all relevant dates £7 per annum; so that if the rent payable in respect of the tenancy was less than two-thirds of £7, then the tenant cannot claim, as he has sought to do, the protection of the Rent Acts...

The premises consist of a flat known at 117, Waterloo Square, Lomond Grove, Camberwell; but even that description might be thought to be in some degree euphemistic, for the subject-matter of the tenancy was two rooms, the tenant having the right to share with other occupants the kitchen and the lavatory. The subject-matter being of this somewhat meagre character, the tenant must, if he reflected upon it, have been somewhat surprised by the extraordinary elaboration of the arrangements for the letting with which he was presented. The documents which we have to look at were three in number, and a period of a week separated the second from the first and the third from the second. Anticipating for a moment the oral evidence which was given before the judge, this elaboration was the declared policy of the landlords and, as the second of the three documents plainly and quite properly declares, their object was to avoid the impact upon the premises in question of the rent restriction legislation. But it is plainly a matter to which this court must properly address itself in matters where the Rent Restrictions Acts might be said to apply, whether the transaction, viewed as a whole and according to the substance of it, is in truth one which, to use Mr Megarry's phrase, is on that side of the line which frees the premises from the impact of the Act, or whether, so regarded, the transaction is one which is of the mischief which the Acts were designed to avoid . . .

I may perhaps venture to refer to my own language rather later in *Woods* v. *Wise* ([1955] 2 Q.B. 29), which the county court judge in the present case also invoked. 'In cases', I said, 'under the ordinary law, unaffected by the Rent Acts, the question, how much rent should be payable under, and what other considerations there should be for, a demise were matters for free bargaining. A landlord might charge any sum that he could get for rent. If he preferred, he could charge a low rent and demand a "premium" or lump-sum payment. There was no such purpose as now exists in any attempt to disguise the one in the shape of the other. In these circumstances, the word "rent", even though not confined to the old common law meaning of that for which distress might be levied, would naturally and ordinarily be used to signify the periodic payments under a demise in contrast to lump-sum or other kinds of consideration.' And then a little later, after considering whether a lump-sum payment called a 'premium' might none the less be rent, I said: 'I cannot, for my part, think that the arm of the law would be so short as to disable it from dealing appropriately with such a case as that last suggested, if it appeared that the so-called premium was, in truth and substance, nothing more or other than the rent quantified and provided for in "an abnormal form".'

I therefore approach the present case with that matter of principle to guide me. I, of course, fully accept the proposition which Mr Megarry made the foundation of his case, that a landlord is entitled so to arrange his affairs that the legal result will bring him outside the statutory provisions; but, on the other hand, merely giving a label to a particular type of payment will not by any means necessarily have the effect indicated by the label; for the truth and substance, in cases of this kind, must be examined. There are, I think, three circumstances which convince me that the judge here was well entitled to reach the conclusion he did: The first is the disproportion which the arrangements made appear to me to bear to the subject-matter of that arrangement. I am dealing here with two rooms, and for a term, a period of occupation, which was limited to 12 months. This is not a case of a lease of some piece of land or a house for 14 years or some other long period at a ground rent upon payment of a sum designed to produce the effect that the periodic rent will be small; we are not dealing with that kind of case; and, tempting though Mr Megarry's arguments always are, I do not find it necessary to indicate where any line should be drawn. We are here dealing with a period of one year – no more – and with two rooms, but with the right to share the kitchen and the lavatory. That is the first point.

The second point is that, when you examine it, the vital document upon its face seems to have not only indeed the declared object which it is intended to serve, but also an important inconsistency in itself. And, thirdly, I think that on further examination it is seen that this vital second document in truth is very largely, if not altogether, unnecessary. The cumulative effect of those reasons is, as I think, to justify the judge's conclusion. Let me, however, repeat that I am not for a moment suggesting that there is any deception or impropriety on the part of these landlords. They acquired these premises (it appears) in 1952, and they adopted this method of procedure which they instructed their agents to require from all proposed tenants, in the hope, belief and expectation, if you will, that thereby they would not be within the scope and restrictive effect of the Rent Restriction Acts. If they fail, that does not therefore reflect upon the ethics of their business methods.

In order to make clear those grounds which I have indicated, I can do no better than refer in such detail as is necessary to the three documents which were executed and which form the three stages of this elaborate superstructure for the letting ... The first was a document called 'Application for tenancy', signed by the tenant and bearing the date August 16, 1955. It is addressed to the landlords' agents: 'I hereby apply for a tenancy of a flat at Waterloo Square, Lomond Grove, Camberwell.' He gave his name in full and his present address. He stated how long he had been where he was; that he was married and had one son aged five years living with him. He stated that he required two rooms; that his occupation was that of a lorry driver; he gave the name and address of his employer, his weekly wages, the income of his wife, and the name and address of his present landlord. Finally, he stated the rent which he was then paying and gave two references. It will be observed that the questions which were asked enabled the landlords to obtain quite a lot of information about the proposed tenant's status and circumstances; but, most important of all, the proposed tenant gave names and addresses of two referees. A week then passed, and on August 23 the document, which is the real foundation of the landlords' case, was executed. [His Lordship read clauses 1–4 of the agreement and continued:] Then there were two features which might have been regarded by the tenant as 'stings in the tail'.

Paragraph 5: 'On completion the applicant shall pay to the company the sum of £5 5s as a contribution towards the company's costs in respect of this agreement and the said lease.' And, finally, it was part of the arrangement that, in addition to paying those sums for legal costs, the tenant should himself consult a solicitor, who was required to sign the following certificate at the foot of this agreement: 'I' – then the name of the solicitor appears – 'hereby certify that I have explained the above proposed agreement to the applicant therein named and that he appeared fully to understand the same. I further certify that he has instructed me that he is entering into such agreement in reliance only on its contents and he acknowledges that there is no verbal agreement or representation relating to the subject-matter thereof.'

That was on August 23, and on August 30, one week later, there is executed the lease bearing the date. It is a lease of the same flat at the rent of £1 per quarter. There is no reference in it in fact to the previous agreement. There are certain covenants in common form, though not commonly found in tenancies for one year only for two rooms in a building of this kind; but they included a covenant: 'On the expiration or sooner determination of the said term' – that is one year – 'to deliver up the said premises.'

Those are the three documents, and upon the first of the three points I mentioned I think I need add little, if anything. When the subject-matter is borne in mind, this superstructure is clearly disproportionate. But, secondly, I draw attention particularly to this, as I think, very important circumstance: by the second recital in this agreement the landlords stated that they were not willing to grant a lease such that the Rent and Mortgage Interest Acts would apply. The landlords were saying – perfectly properly, of course: 'What we are doing is asking you to embark upon this elaborate arrangement because we are not willing, if we can help it, to grant such a lease as will bring the Rent Restriction Acts into force as regards the premises.' Having, therefore, declared that that was what they were about, it is interesting to see how they proceeded to achieve it; for the consideration for the £35 was stated to be the landlords' agreement to grant the lease. But it will not be forgotten that two clauses later there is a provision that the agreement to grant the lease was not, as might here be supposed, a positive agreement so to do; for the whole instrument was expressed to be conditional on the landlords being satisfied, in their absolute discretion, that the tenant will be a suitable tenant; and presumably so long as the landlords acted bona fide, they could, for any reason at all, say that they were not satisfied that the proposed tenant would be a suitable tenant. So that it manifestly is not really true to say that the £35 was paid as consideration for a promise, in any real sense of the term, on the landlords' part to grant a lease. And then it will be observed that this clause went on to say that 'the applicant shall accordingly furnish references forthwith'.

That brings me to the third of my grounds, for it will not be forgotten that the tenant a week before had already produced the references. Whether a week would have been sufficient in order that those referees might be con-sulted is a question on which I think some light is thrown by the fact that the completion date of the lease in this document was stated to be a week – no more – from the date when the document was executed. As here earlier stated, in truth this agreement practically serves no useful purpose at all. It was stated (and I have no doubt it was the fact) that the form of the lease was already agreed; it was to be prepared by the landlords. No real purpose then was served by making these intermediate arrangements, the landlords already being in possession of all the information they required about the tenant, including the names of his referees.

As I have said, I think these considerations amply justify the conclusion to which the judge arrived; but before I make a brief reference to the way in which he expressed that conclusion, I should say that two witnesses were called for the landlords. It is a point made and made with force by Mr Megarry that though the tenant said in his defence that the vital agreement or the general substance of it was a sham, he did not come forward to say so; nor did he call any evidence himself; and if by the use of the word 'sham' he was suggesting that there was some deception on the part of the landlords, I of course entirely disagree with him: the matter was entirely above board in that sense. It was made plain to the tenant that this was the means whereby the landlords were openly saying that they were proposing to keep outside the scope of the Rent Acts. But the witnesses showed, I think, two things: first, that the scheme of operations, which resulted in these three documents, was part of the deliberate policy of the landlords, designed, as was freely admitted, for the purpose expressed in the recital. But there was one other matter also, appearing in an answer to cross-examination of the first witness, the agent of the landlords, which I think is of some significance. The evidence as recorded by the judge in this: 'We have made lettings of other flats in block at about 13s a week. On expiration of term of lease the tenant can apply for a new lease. The terms of the new lease "might not be the same".' I ask myself what is really the effect of that? If the landlords are right, what will happen at the end of the year in what I take as a hypothetical case, where the tenant says: 'Can I please have another year'? This performance will have to be gone through again. Will it be found that there will be a series of arrangements whereby for a payment of £X down and the promise to pay a periodic rent of say £1 a quarter, these tenants will on such occasion get the right to occupy for a year – no more – their respective premises? Looked at over a period of time, I think it would be impossible to avoid the conclusion that the whole 12-monthly consideration in each succeeding case formed in truth the compensation, the money payment, for the use of the flat; that is to say, was the rent. I think that consideration clearly entered into the con-clusions of the judge, for he referred to the evidence which had been given before him. His conclusion is summarized in these terms: 'Whilst giving every consideration to the argument, that the landlords are entitled to evade the

Acts, I feel it is my duty to scrutinize very carefully the scheme proposed for this purpose. In my view the scheme fails. In my judgment, if the agreement and the lease are viewed together, it becomes clear that the real substance of the transaction is the landlords' demand of £39 for a year's occupancy, and that this is simply divided into an immediate payment of £35, and the balance by quarterly instalments of £1 each. I regard the £35 as commuted rent, which, in my view, together with the quarterly rent, is the true consideration for the letting. If I am right, this tenancy is one protected by the Acts.'

I think on consideration of all the evidence – the intrinsic evidence of the documents and the evidence of the witnesses – the judge was well entitled to reach the conclusion that he did. And, I, independently agree with it. It is perhaps to be noted – and this is my last point – that £39 a year happens to be 15s a week. I am not saying that that was at all an excessive rent, but that may have a bearing upon the way in which this sum was calculated. However that may be, I think the judge was entitled to reach the conclusion he did, that he rightly reached it, and I would therefore dismiss the appeal . . .

Comment. This case in interesting not only for the discussion on the definition of rent, but more generally on the approach of Lord Evershed M.R. to this particular attempt at Rent Act evasion.

(iii) TENANCIES AT A LOW RENT

The owners of property on long-term leases are the typical example of tenants at a low rent. They will have paid a substantial capital sum for the property, plus a small ground rent of, say, £25 or £50 a year. Originally they were wholly excluded from statutory protection; and they remain outside the Rent Acts. However, in 1954, the Landlord and Tenant Act, Part I gave rights of security to *long* leaseholders at low rent, i.e. where the tenancy was for 21 years or more. The Rent Act 1957 put all long tenancies, whatever the rent, under the Landlord and Tenant Act 1954, Part I, thereby excluding them from the Rent Act 1957. The basic scheme of the 1954 Act was to confer a right to a 'statutory tenancy' (basically similar to that provided under the Rent Acts) upon a tenant under a 'long tenancy' who satisfies the 'qualifying condition' at the 'term date'. Alternatively, the landlord could seek repossession on two broad grounds: (i) that the circumstances set out in Schedule 3 of the Act were satisfied (these are very similar to the grounds for seeking repossession in Rent Act cases (see below, pp. 419–39)); or (ii) that he could demonstrate to the court that he needed the property for redevelopment.

The Leasehold Reform Act 1967 altered the position still further. As regards *houses* (s. 2), tenants under long leaseholds at low rent are given either a right to enfranchisement, i.e. to buy the landlord's reversionary interest (s. 8) or the right to demand an extension of the tenancy for a period of up to 50 years (s. 14). 'Long lease' here includes leases granted for a shorter period than 21 years with an option or obligation to renew which has been exercised so as to make the period longer than 21 years in fact (s. 3(4)). If the tenant exercises neither of these, the Landlord and Tenant Act 1954, Part I still applies.

Tenants of *other residential accommodation* under leases (of any length) at low rents are excluded from the Rent Act 1977. Where the lease is a *long* lease (see Rent Act 1977, s. 5(5) above) at low rent, then the Landlord and Tenant Act 1954, Part I is still operative. However, the grounds under which the landlord may repossess in order to redevelop have been cut down. It is only available where the landlord is a body to which s. 28 of the Leasehold Reform Act 1967 applies and the property is required for redevelopment within the meaning of that section.[2]

Note carefully the special definition of 'rent' (Rent Act 1977, s. 5(4) above) which may have the effect of excluding a number of long tenancies from Rent Act protections, including, most importantly, the prohibitions on illegal premiums (see below, p. 312).

C Board and attendance: Rent Act 1977, s. 7

7.—(1) A tenancy is not a protected tenancy if under the tenancy the dwelling-house is bona fide let at a rent which includes payments in respect of board or attendance.

(2) For the purposes of subsection (1) above, a dwelling-house shall not be taken to be bona fide let at a rent which includes payments in respect of attendance unless the amount of rent which is fairly attributable to attendance, having regard to the value of the attendance to the tenant, forms a substantial part of the whole rent.

(i) 'BONA FIDE'

In *Palser* v. *Grinling* [1948] A.C. 291 Viscount Simon said:

In my opinion '*bona fide*' in this phrase governs the whole of the words which follow. The words amount to a stipulation that the rent to be paid genuinely

2. Section 28 broadly applies to public bodies such as local authorities, universities, nationalized industries etc., and for these bodies to be exempt from the Landlord and Tenant Act 1954 a Minister of the Crown must certify that the relevant body will need the relevant land for redevelopment within the next ten years.

includes payments in respect of board [or] attendance: ... the Act is not to be evaded ... by a merely colourable use of words which do not correspond with what is really provided.

See also *Maclay* v. *Dixon* [1944] 1 All E.R. 22 (C.A.).

(ii) 'BOARD'

This has not been defined in the Rent Act or in case-law. Some observations by Younger L.J. in *Wilkes* v. *Goodwin* [1923] 2 K.B. at 110 may, however, be of assistance.

'Board,' however, is a different word altogether. It is defined, I see, in the Oxford Dictionary as 'daily meals provided in a lodging or boarding house according to stipulation; the supply of daily provisions.' The word without suffix or affix suggests to my mind sufficiency. It could never, I think, be satisfied by the provision, say, of an early morning cup of tea. If you wish to accentuate its abundance you may call it 'full board,' but if you would convey that it is limited then you must call it 'partial' or qualify it by the use of some other adjective of limitation. It appears to me that the natural interpretation of the word as we find it in this exception involves the conception of a provision by the landlord of such food as in the case of any particular tenancy would ordinarily be consumed at daily meals and would be obtained and prepared by the tenant for himself, it it were not provided by somebody else.

However, other *obiter dicta* in the same case do not go so far. Bankes L.J. (at 93) thought 'any amount of board [would suffice] which is not ruled out of consideration by the application of the rule *de minimis non curat lex* ...'. And Scrutton L.J. (at 96) observed 'Partial board will suffice to bring the proviso into operation.'

Comment. What is the purpose of this provision? Would the practice of some landlords leaving supplies of provisions outside their tenants' doors constitute 'board'? In *Holiday Flat Co.* v. *Kuczera* (1978) S.L.T. 47, the Sheriff of the Court of Lothian and Borders at Edinburgh thought that a 'continental breakfast' constituted board 'particularly since the British entry into the European Economic Community'. Note also the interaction of this section with Rent Act 1977, s. 19(5)(*c*) (below, p. 221).

(iii) 'ATTENDANCE'

Viscount Simon in *Palser* v. *Grinling* [1948] A.C. 291 at 310–31 said:

It means service personal to the tenant performed by an attendant provided by the landlord in accordance with his covenant for the benefit or convenience of the individual tenant in his use or enjoyment of the demised premises. 'Service' is a wider word than attendance. Attendance, being personal in its nature, may be dispensed with by an individual tenant at his pleasure, though it is not on that account excluded from what the tenant pays for when the landlord has covenanted to supply it. But services common to others (e.g., the heating of a communal water supply, or the cleaning of passages, halls, etc., outside the demised premises) will not constitute attendance. It follows from the above that a landlord's covenant to supply someone to carry up coals to a flat or to carry down refuse from the flat is a covenant to provide attendance.[3] Similarly, the provision of a house-maid or valet to discharge duties in connection with the flat would be the provision of attendance, but a covenant by the landlord to provide a resident porter or housekeeper for a block of flats would not. In this last connection it might be well to point out that in the English language 'porter' is not one word, but two distinct words – two words of the same sound and spelling, but of different meaning and derivation, which may be confused. Sometimes 'porter' means a door-keeper or janitor, and is derived through medieval French from the Latin noun *porta*. The Porter in Macbeth, or Cerberus as the Porter of Hades, was a porter in this sense. The second word means someone who carries things (e.g. a railway porter) and is derived from the Latin verb *portare*. There can be no doubt that the 'porter' often to be found at the entrance of a block of flats is a porter within the first meaning, in the absence of a special covenant by the landlord that the porter shall carry things. It may be that on occasion he does some carrying for tenants, but unless this is provided in the lease, he does this, not because the landlord has covenanted to provide a person to carry, but as a private service for which he may reasonably expect from time to time some private remuneration.

In *Mischeff*'s case, the position of the porter when rendering services to the lessee is put beyond doubt by the second schedule of the lease quoted above, for this provides that the porter shall be under no obligation to furnish attendance or other use of his service to occupiers for their private convenience, and that service rendered to the lessee by the porter shall be considered as rendered by him as the servant of the lessee. The porter of a block of flats, therefore, does not provide 'attendance' in respect of which payment is included in the rent unless the landlord covenants that he shall render personal service to the tenant involving attendance at the individual flat.

The above view of the meaning of the word 'attendance' in the statute is in accord with what was said by Lord Greene M.R., in *Engvall* v. *Ideal Flats, Ltd* ((1945) 172 L.T. 134) ...

---

3. This was the example given by Horridge J. in *Nye* v. *Davis* [1922] 2 K.B. at 59; cf. *King* v. *Millen* (*ibid.*), at 647, and *Wood* v. *Carwardine* [1923] 2 K.B. 185.

(iv) 'SUBSTANTIAL PART'

Viscount Simon in *Palser* v. *Grinling* [1948] A.C. 291 at 34–5 said:

It is convenient first to observe that the 'amount of rent' is equivalent to 'the portion of the whole rent' ... A question of some difficulty arises as to the meaning of the 'tenant' – does the expression refer to the particular individual whose lease is in question, or does it refer to the average or normal tenant of that class of property? I think the phrase refers to the actual tenant whose lease is under examination. It is the analysis of the particular transaction to which he is a party that is the subject matter of the inquiry. It is the value to him (and included in that value is the fact that he may assign or sublet) which must be taken into account. But in taking this view, it is of the utmost importance to observe that the section directs that 'regard shall be had' to the value to the tenant, and not that the value to such tenant is to govern the calculation absolutely. In the recent case of *Newport Borough Council* v. *Monmouthshire County Council* ([1947] A.C. 520) ... I pointed out that such a direction called for the exercise of a broad judgment, and that any arithmetical conclusion was qualified by what is deemed to be fair and reasonable. In the present case the direction that regard is to be had to the value to the tenant, i.e. that such value must not be overlooked but must be suitably allowed for, is made clear by the main direction that the amount of rent is to be such as 'is fairly attributable to' the item in question. Other factors have to be duly weighed and allowed for. In some cases the parties to the lease may themselves have placed a value upon various elements which enter into the total rent. Even so, the statement of these respective values in the lease is not a conclusive distribution, though it may be strong evidence of what a proper distribution would be. Nevertheless, the amount to be arrived at is the amount which is 'fairly attributable' to the item, not the amount which is actually attributed to it in the lease ...

A number of factors may be relevant in arriving at the proper figure. The governing consideration is the word 'fairly'. The questions involved are to be answered by common-sense considerations rather than by any formula which can be laid down by this House ... The words of the section have to be applied according to their proper meaning and an agreement between the parties as to their application in a particular case is not conclusive, though it may be some evidence of the fact.

What does 'substantial portion' mean? It is plain that the phrase requires a comparison with the *whole rent*, and the whole rent means the entire contractual rent payable by the tenant in return for the occupation of the premises together with all the other covenants of the landlord. 'Substantial' in this connection is not the same as 'not unsubstantial', i.e. just enough to avoid the 'de minimis' principle. One of the primary meanings of the word is equivalent to considerable, solid, or big. It is in this sense that we speak of a substantial fortune, a substantial meal, a substantial man, a substantial argument or grounds of defence. Applying the word in this sense, it must be left to the discretion of the judge of fact to decide as best he can according to the circumstances in each case, the onus being on the landlord. If the judgment of the Court of Appeal in *Palser*'s case were to be understood as fixing percentages as a legal measure, that would be going beyond the powers of the judiciary. To say that everything over 20 per cent of the whole rent should be regarded as a substantial portion of that rent would be to play the part of a legislator: if Parliament thinks fit to amend the statute by fixing percentages, Parliament will do so. Aristotle long ago pointed out that the degree of precision that is attainable depends on the subject matter. There is no reason for the House to differ from the conclusions reached in these two cases that the portion was not substantial, but this conclusion is justified by the view taken on the facts, not by laying down percentages of general application.

What is the 'whole rent'? As already indicated, it is the entire contractual rent payable by the tenant to his landlord. In cases where the landlord covenants to pay rates, it would be an error to deduct the rates from the contractual rent in order to arrive at the whole rent. Whether the landlord pays the rates or not is immaterial in arriving at the whole rent. In *Palser* v. *Grinling*, Lord Goddard CJ deducted the rates (which the landlord had to pay) from the contractual rent of £175, but the Court of Appeal rightly corrected this. Morton LJ said: 'It is wrong for the judge to deduct the rates from the rent – in cases where the rates are paid by the landlord – and then to compare the amount of rent fairly attributable to the attendance with the figure so arrived at. The section refers to the *whole* rent, and I think there is clear authority for the proposition that in ascertaining the whole rent it is not legitimate to make any deduction on account of rates ...' Inasmuch as a sum may be a substantial portion of a given figure, though it would not be regarded as a substantial portion of a larger figure, this distinction may be important in some cases, though it does not seem to make any practical difference in the two cases now before the House ...

Consider too this extract from *Woodward* v. *Docherty* [1974] 1 W.L.R. 966. Scarman L.J.:

Common sense considerations require the court to exercise its knowledge of the world. Today there is, as there has been since 1914, a shortage of dwelling-houses; a landlord who can on the expiry of a contractual tenancy evict his tenant has an asset incomparably more valuable than has the landlord who cannot; a man with a wife, or wife and family, who is seeking a home will accept [attendance] he does not really want in order to obtain accommodation he desperately needs, even though by accepting it he loses security of tenure which he would dearly like to have. In applying the subsection, county court judges must bear in mind general considerations such as these

– considerations which can and will change with social and economic changes in our society.

D Lettings to students: Rent Act 1977, s. 8

8.—(1) A tenancy is not a protected tenancy if it is granted to a person who is pursuing, or intends to pursue, a course of study provided by a specified educational institution and is so granted either by that institution or by another specified institution or body of persons ...

The specified list of institutions is to be found in the Protected Tenancies (Exceptions) Regulations, 1974 (S.I. 1974 No. 1366) and the Protected Tenancies (Further Exceptions) Regulations, 1976 (S.I. 1976 No. 905). For general discussion of the use of this section, see Finnis (1978a).

An interesting case in which use was made of this section, and in which the further consideration was given to the *Horford Investments* case (above, pp. 166–8) is *St Catherine's College* v. *Dorling* [1979] 3 All E.R. 250. Eveleigh L.J.:

[As a result of the passing of Rent Act 1977, s. 8] a firm of estate agents in Oxford, Messrs Runyards, with the co-operation of a large number of Oxford colleges, introduced a scheme by which it was envisaged that accommodation would more readily be made available to undergraduates. They published a booklet giving details of that scheme. The general idea was that the owner of the house would let premises to the college, who would then make the accommodation available to undergraduates. A £50 deposit was taken from undergraduates who had made an application for the accommodation, and that deposit was treated as an application fee, unless the arrangements were finally completed, when it was treated as part-payment of rent. Runyards orally guaranteed to the colleges concerned that every undergraduate would have a separate room.

In so far as 208 Headington Road is concerned, there were four undergraduates of the college who applied to Messrs Runyards for accommodation. They found a suitable house, namely, 208 Headington Road. The college was willing to take those premises under a lease.

On 12th June 1978 the undergraduates signed a document entitled 'Agreement and Indemnity', which stated:

'In consideration of the College, through the Domestic Bursar, entering on my behalf into a Lease of 208 Headington Road, Oxford, from 8th July 1978 for one year less 7 days at a rent of £224.25 per month ... I hereby agree with the College to fulfil and observe all conditions and covenants contained in their lease and to indemnify the College against all liabilities which it may incur there under.'

The question in this case is whether the premises were let as a separate dwelling within the meaning of s. 1. The important point in answering that question is to determine the contemplated use of the premises.

He quoted the extract from *Ponder* v. *Hillman* (above, pp. 159–60) and continued:

So it follows that one has to consider the terms of the lease and the surrounding circumstances at the time that the lease was granted. It may be that in some cases that assistance can be obtained from the subsequent user of the premises. But in my opinion generally speaking such assistance will be found to be a matter of last resort.

I turn to consider the terms of the tenancy agreement in this case. There is the usual habendum and reddendum, and then I turn to cl 2 (l) (i), in which the tenant covenants:

'Not to use the demised premises otherwise than for occupation by a person or persons who are as specified by Section 8 of the Rent Act 1977 pursuing or intending to pursue a course of study provided by the Tenant whether the said person or persons occupy the demised premises as sub-tenants or licensees.'

Sub-clause (l) (ii) reads:

'Not to assign sub-let part with possession or share possession or occupa-tion of all or part of the demised premises furniture fittings or effects or any part thereof provided that there shall be no breach of this clause if the Tenant shall be a specified educational institution as defined by Section 8 of the Rent Act 1977 and either the Tenant sub-lets only to a person who is pursuing or intending to pursue a course of study provided by the Tenant or the Tenant grants a licence for the use of the demised premises to such person.'

Then sub-cl. (m), the user clause, reads as follows:

'Not to carry on or permit to be carried on upon the demised premises any profession trade or business whatsoever or let apartments or receive paying guests in the demised premises but to use or permit the same to be used as private residence only in occupation of one person per room and not in any way to contravene the Town and Country Planning Acts and not to exhibit any notice or poster on any portion of the demised premises.'

Counsel for the college has submitted that here a group of students, or undergraduates, intended to occupy the premises as joint occupants of the whole, and that this was the object and purport of the tenancy granted to the college. He particularly relied on sub-cl (m) and invited the court to say that the words 'to be used as private residence only' should be read to include the indefinite article: that is to say, 'to be used as *a* private residence only' ...

Counsel for the college has argued that if these premises were to be used as *a* private residence, the emphasis being on the indefinite article, it meant that they were not to be used as a number of different private residences, therefore they were let as a whole, with the object of their being inhabited jointly by the students. He also placed some reliance on the words of sub-cl (l) (ii), where it reads 'either the tenant sublets only to a person who is pursuing' etc. He said it was therefore contemplated that no more than one person would take, or that person could take jointly being responsible for the whole.

On the other hand, counsel for the respondent landlord has contended that cl 2(m) comes to his aid. He has invited the court to construe the phrase 'as private residence' as meaning for residential purposes. I would myself accept that submission. One cannot read the words 'as private residence' without reading the words that follow, namely, 'in the occupation of one person per room'. In my opinion it is no accidental omission of the indefinite article. There is an intentional omission; and the phrase 'as private residence' is used similarly to the expression 'as business premises'. It is descriptive of the user and not of the premises themselves.

When one then sees that what is envisaged is the occupation of one person per room, using that for private purposes, and then turns to the other provision in sub-cl (l) which I have read, one sees that subletting or a licence to use is contemplated, and the words used are 'sublet only to a person'. The importance, to my mind, of the words in that sub-clause is that they show that a subletting is envisaged. That envisages as I see it (for one must read this as a whole) that the college is permitted to sublet to a person who is to occupy a single room as a private residence. If the college is to be allowed to 'sublet to a person' (to use the words of the sub-clause) any part of the building, it would follow that it should be allowed to let to more than one person, or the building would otherwise have another part unused. Quite clearly it was never contemplated that the college itself should occupy or make any particular use of the premises, other, that is to say, than as accommodation for undergraduates. Furthermore, of course, the plural is used in sub-cl (l) (i), where we see the words 'for occupation by a person or persons'.

I therefore read these two sub-clauses as saying that the college shall be in a position to sublet, and shall be in a position to sublet to 'persons'; but they must be persons 'pursuing or intending to pursue a course of study'. The use of the singular in para (ii) is simply because it is describing the type of person who may be a sub-tenant; and, as the college may sublet to a particular type of sub-tenant and must do so only for occupation of one person per room, it follows, in my opinion, that the purpose of this letting was that the college should be in a position to do just that. In other words, what was being granted to the college here was a tenancy of a building which contained a number of units of habitation, as they have been called. From that interpretation of this lease I would conclude that the premises were not let as separate dwellings...

Megaw L.J. also commented:

The agreement in this case was made on 8th July 1978. On the face of it, it was agreed on that day by St Catherine's College that a certain rent should be payable. Five days later, on 13th July 1978, St Catherine's College, being a party to that agreement, applied to the rent officer for registration of a fair rent. That is to say, the college sought to challenge that the rent which they appeared to have agreed five days earlier was a fair rent, or the rent which in law could be insisted on. There is no doubt that the other party to that agreement of 8th July 1978, Mr Dorling, through his authorised agents, was firmly of the opinion that the form of the agreement was such as to take it outside the scope of the provisions of law which would have enabled the rent to be referred for an assessment of any rent different from the rent which had been, apparently, agreed. It is difficult to think that the college, in entering into the agreement on 8th July 1978, was not aware that that was the view held by the other party to the agreement. But, as counsel for the college, in my opinion rightly, submits, whatever view might be taken of that in other respects, no such view can properly influence the decision as to the legal effect of the agreement. All that I would say about it, then, is this: it seems to me that the decision at which this court has arrived is more likely to help the continuance of schemes of this sort, if schemes of this sort are desirable, than would have been the result if we had arrived at the contrary conclusion. But, once again, that is not a matter that can rightly affect our judgment in this matter. If indeed it was the view of St Catherine's College, when it made this agreement on 8th July 1978, that the figure of rent contained in that agreement was higher than a fair rent and that therefore the rent which it itself thereafter required the five undergraduates to pay was higher than the college thought to be a fair rent, it might be a matter of hope, and expectation, that the college, now that it has been established that its view of the legal effect of that agreement is not justified, would feel that it would not be appropriate that the undergraduates should bear the consequences of the college having seen fit to agree a rent which it believed (if indeed it did so believe) was a rent higher than a fair rent.

E Holiday lettings: Rent Act 1977, s. 9

9. A tenancy is not a protected tenancy if the purpose of the tenancy is to confer on the tenant the right to occupy the dwelling-house for a holiday.

It seems likely that it is this exception that has been used most frequently by landlords anxious to evade the Rent Acts. Surprisingly, perhaps, what is or is not a genuine holiday letting has not received much judicial attention. The main case to date is *Buchmann* v. *May* [1978] 2 All E.R. 993 (C.A.). Sir John Pennycuick said:

Mr Buchmann is the owner of 24 Avenue Road, which had been his own home until 1972. He or his company own a number of other properties in the district which that company lets. The defendant, Mrs Colleen May, is an Australian national. Her husband, Richard Ernest May, is a New Zealand national. He is by profession an entertainer; and Mrs May herself was until recently a professional dancer. They have a child, Shari, aged 7 or 8. They worked in England from time to time between 1972 and 1974 on a series of temporary residence permits but had not, at any rate at the date of the hearing been successful in obtaining full residence permits.

In or about May 1972, Mr Buchmann let 24 Avenue Road to Mr May, the defendant's husband, on a six month furnished tenancy at £20 a week. There followed a succession of short furnished tenancies, at the same rent, up to and including a three month tenancy expiring on 31st July 1974. These were ordinary residential tenancies.

In or about March 1974, Mr and Mrs May left England on business. They allowed some friends, Mr and Mrs Kent, to occupy 24 Avenue Road in their absence; and Mr and Mrs Kent remained in occupation until about the middle of October 1974.

There was a conflict of evidence as to whether Mr and Mrs May left various chattels of their own in 24 Avenue Road at the expiration of the last tenancy on 31st July 1974. The judge found that they did leave certain chattels in the house.

In the absence abroad of Mr and Mrs May, Mr Buchmann then granted a two-months tenancy, at the same rent, to a Mrs Blackshaw, who was a neighbour and friend of Mr and Mrs May, that tenancy running from 1st August 1974 and ending on 30th September. The judge found that this tenancy was granted to Mrs Blackshaw as agent for Mr May.

In the middle of October 1974, Mrs May returned to England, to be followed shortly afterwards by Mr May. Before Mr May's return, Mrs May rang up Mr Garlant, an employee of Mr Buchmann, and enquired as to the possibility of a further short tenancy. Mrs May told Mr Garlant that she would be leaving England before Christmas, and in any event she had in fact only a six month residence permit, which would expire before then. On 16th October Mr Buchmann, accompanied by a Mr Von Conrat, went to see Mrs May at 24 Avenue Road, where she was already installed. They then agreed in principle on the grant of a tenancy to run until 31st December 1974.

The next day, 17th October, Mr Buchmann and Mr Von Conrat again called on Mrs May. Mr Buchmann then produced two documents, namely a tenancy agreement and a counterpart. This agreement bears date 1st October 1972. The counterpart was in evidence. Mr Buchmann and Mrs

May signed the respective documents. The agreement is made between Mr Buchmann, called 'the landlord', and Mrs May, called 'the tenant'. Clause 1 provides that the landlord shall let and the tenant shall take 24 Avenue Road (describing it) 'for the term of three months from the first day of October, 1974, at the rent of £80 ... for every four weeks of the said term ...' Clause 2 contains various terms agreed on behalf of the tenant, including (in case it is material) para (13): '... to use the same as a private residence in the occupation of one family comprising of the tenant and one child only.' I need not read cll 3, 4 and 5. Clause 6 is of critical importance:

'It is mutually agreed and declared that the letting hereby made is solely for the purpose of the tenant's holiday in the London area.'

There was a conflict of evidence as to how far Mrs May studied this agreement before signature. She deposed as follows:

'He [i.e. Mr Buchmann] said how would I like to sign for three or six months. I said "It does not matter". I said this because Rick [i.e. her husband] would be back by Christmas. He said "I will make it three months". I said "O.K." He said it was the usual type of agreement. He asked me to sign the agreement and inventory and said he would send me a copy in a couple of days. He did not draw my attention to cl 6. He said nothing about a holiday letting that I can remember. He did not send me the lease. I first knew it was a holiday letting after I received a letter in December or January from the plaintiff's office.'

Then, in cross-examination:

'I agree I did have opportunity to read the agreement but I did not read it ... Re cl 6, I did not read the agreement. I thought it was the same lease as I had signed before I did not intend it to be a holiday letting. When I arrived in the United Kingdom I mostly say "I'm holidaying here".'

It may well be that that is what she said to the immigration officer.

Mr Buchmann and Mr Von Conrat gave a rather different account, but I think it is right to say that neither of them said that he in terms said to Mrs May that this was an agreement for a holiday. True, Mr Buchmann, said it was a holiday letting. He said 'I quite understand she wanted a holiday letting for six to eight weeks', but he does not say that he so informed Mrs May. Mr Von Conrat is rather more positive as to her reading the agreement. He said: 'She held the agreement some time. I thought she was looking at it ... She spent some twenty minutes looking at the agreement.' There is no suggestion of any misrepresentation on the part of Mr Buchmann as to the terms of this agreement.

Mr May returned to England, and Mr and Mrs May remained in residence at 24 Avenue Road with the child Shari until after the expiration of the three month tenancy on 31st December. Apparently an expected engagement abroad for Mr May before Christmas had fallen through. Mrs May now maintains that the tenancy was not for a holiday at all and that she has an ordinary protected tenancy. If the tenancy was not for a holiday, it appears clear that the tenancy would indeed be protected ...

[The County Court] judge said this:

'The defendant claims the protection of the Rent Act, because she says that it was not a holiday letting. Really, that is the issue I have to decide. As counsel rightly said, one is not tied down to the terms of the agreement; one must look at the reality of the situation. Were the premises let conferring a right to use for the purposes of a holiday?'

That is an extremely important statement, and, with all respect to the learned judge, it very considerably distorts the proper approach to this question ...

It seems to me that that judgment contains a fundamental misdirection in that the judge treats the purpose of the tenancy as something to be determined at large on the evidence of the various parties concerned, altogether, or at any rate in great part, without regard to cl 6 of the agreement, to which he does not expressly refer at all in his judgment. Where parties to an instrument express their purpose in entering into the transaction effected by it, or the purposes for which, in the case of a tenancy agreement, the demised property is to be used, this expression of purpose is at least prima facie evidence of their true purpose and as such can only be displaced by evidence that the express purpose does not represent the true purpose. There is no claim here based on misrepresentation, and no claim for rectification. When I say the express purpose does not represent the true purpose, I mean that the express purpose does not correspond to the true purpose, whether the express purpose is a deliberate sham or merely a false label in the sense of a mistake in expression of intention ...

He then discussed *Wolfe* v. *Hogan* [1949] 2 K.B. 194; *British Land Co. Ltd* v. *Herbert Silver* (*Menswear*) *Ltd* [1958] 1 Q.B. 530; and *Horford Investments Ltd* v. *Lambert* (above, pp. 166–8), and continued:

In all those cases this court laid down the principle that, in considering whether a house is let as a separate dwelling, where there is a written lease you ascertain the purpose of the parties from the terms of the lease and you do not go beyond the terms of the lease to ascertain what is the purpose of the parties. That is always so apart from the case where the terms of the lease do not correspond to the true intention of the parties.

It seems to me that on that fundamental ground the learned judge was in error in treating this as a question to be determined by reference to the oral evidence of the parties and without regard to the terms of cl 6, which would stand unless it is shown to be something in the nature of a sham or of a false label, and that on that ground his judgment cannot be supported.

What, then, is to be done? It seems to me that there was no evidence before the judge on which he could have held that cl 6 did not truly represent the common intention of the parties. Mrs May is a Dominion national not resident in England except on a series of short residence permits, the current one of which was due to expire in December 1974. She had been out of England since the spring of 1974, leaving only some personal chattels in 24 Avenue Road. She informed Mr Buchmann that she wished to stay in England for two months only before going abroad with her husband, who was taking up an engagement abroad. Mr Buchmann had no reason to suspect that this was untrue. It seems to me that a stay of less than three months in such circumstances would constitute a 'holiday' within the ordinary meaning of that word; and I can find no ground on which it could be properly said that the statement of purpose in cl 6 was a sham or was, without intention to deceive, an untrue statement of the purpose of the letting.

Counsel for the defendant, who has said all there was to be said on her behalf, contended, truly, that one must look at the true relation contemplated by the parties and not merely at the label. In other words, if it can be shown that the terms of this agreement do not correspond with some label in the agreement, then one can look behind the label. Then he says that here the evidence as accepted by the judge established that a holiday was not the true relation, in other words, not the true purpose for which 24 Avenue Road was being let. He said that Mrs May's motive was to protect her right of occupation, in other words, to continue it for the benefit of Mrs May and Mr May together; and he said that Mrs May did not know her rights and thought it was just one of the usual agreements. There is no evidence that Mr Buchmann thought that was the motive of the provision as to a holiday; indeed it plainly was not his motive. Whatever Mrs May may or may not have had in mind when she signed the agreement cannot of itself displace the effect of the express provision within the agreement. Her mere ignorance of her rights certainly could not do so.

I conclude that there is nothing in the evidence which could displace the effect of cl 6 of the agreement, and so one is left with a tenancy for a holiday.

Comment. Would the judge have decided differently if the tenants had been permanently resident in the UK? How does the judge's approach to this case compare with the 'non-exclusive occupation agreement' cases (above, pp. 119–48)?

Note. In the county court case *McHale* v. *Daneham* (1979) 249 E.G. 969 Judge Edwards 'could see no reason why a working holiday should not fall within the provisions of section 9 of the Rent Act'.

F Resident landlord cases: Rent Act 1977, s. 12

(as amended Housing Act 1980, s. 65)

12.—(1) Subject to subsection (2) below, a tenancy of a dwelling-house granted on or after 14th August 1974 shall not be a protected tenancy at any time if –

(a) the dwelling-house forms part only of a building and, except in a case where the dwelling-house also forms part of a flat, the building is not a purpose-built block of flats; and

(b) the tenancy was granted by a person who, at the time when he granted it, occupied as his residence another dwelling-house which—

(i) in the case mentioned in paragraph (a) above, also forms part of the flat; or

(ii) in any other case, also forms part of the building; and

(c) subject to paragraph 1 of Schedule 2 to this Act, at all times since the tenancy was granted the interest of the landlord under the tenancy has belonged to a person who, at the time he owned that interest, occupied as his residence another dwelling-house which—

(i) in the case mentioned in paragraph (a) above, also formed part of the flat; or

(ii) in any other case, also formed part of the building.

(2) This section does not apply to a tenancy of a dwelling-house which forms part of a building if the tenancy is granted to a person who, immediately before it was granted, was a protected or statutory tenant of that dwelling-house or of any other dwelling-house in that building.

Part I of Schedule 2 provides:

1. In determining whether the condition in section 12(1)(c) of this Act is at any time fulfilled with respect to a tenancy, there shall be disregarded –

(a) any period of not more than 28 days beginning with the date on which the interest of the landlord under the tenancy becomes vested at law and in equity in an individual who, during that period, does not occupy as his residence another dwelling-house which forms part of the building or, as the case may be, flat, concerned;

(b) if, within a period falling within paragraph (a) above, the individual concerned notifies the tenant in writing of his intention to occupy as his residence another dwelling-house in the building or, as the case may be, flat, concerned, the period beginning with the date on which the interest of the landlord under the tenancy becomes vested in that individual as mentioned in that paragraph and ending

(i) at the expiry of the period of 6 months beginning on that date, or

(ii) on the date on which that interest ceases to be so vested, or

(iii) on the date on which the condition in section 12(1)(c) again applies,

whichever is the earlier; and

(c) any period of not more than 2 years beginning with the date on which the interest of the landlord under the tenancy becomes, and during which it remains, vested –

(ii) in trustees as such; or

(iii) by virtue of section 9 of the Administration of Estates Act 1925, in the Probate Judge, within the meaning of that Act.

2. During any period when –

(a) the interest of the landlord under the tenancy referred to in section 12(1) is vested in trustees as such, and

(b) that interest is or, if it is held on trust for sale, the proceeds of its sale are held on trust for any person who occupies as his residence a dwelling-house which forms part of the building or, as the case may be, flat, referred to in section 12(1)(a),

the condition in section 12(1)(c) shall be deemed to be fulfilled and, accordingly, no part of that period shall be disregarded by virtue of paragraph 1 above.

2A.—(1) The tenancy referred to in section 12(1) falls within this paragraph if the interest of the landlord under the tenancy becomes vested in the personal representatives of a deceased person acting in that capacity.

(2) If the tenancy falls within this paragraph, the condition in section 12(1)(c) shall be deemed to be fulfilled for any period, beginning with the date on which the interest becomes vested in the personal representatives and not exceeding two years, during which the interest of the landlord remains so vested.

3. Throughout any period which, by virtue of paragraph 1 above, falls to be disregarded for the purpose of determining whether the condition in section 12(1)(c) is fulfilled with respect to a tenancy, no order shall be made for possession of the dwelling-house subject to that tenancy, other than an order which might be made if that tenancy were or, as the case may be, had been a regulated tenancy.

4. For the purposes of section 12, a building is a purpose-built block of flats if as constructed it contained, and it contains, 2 or more flats; and for this purpose 'flat' means a dwelling-house which –

(a) forms part only of a building; and

(b) is separated horizontally from another dwelling-house which forms part of the same building.

5. For the purposes of section 12, a person shall be treated as occupying

a dwelling-house as his residence if, so far as the nature of the case allows, he fulfills the same conditions as, by virtue of section 2(3) of this Act, are required to be fulfilled by a statutory tenant of a dwelling-house ...

Note. (*a*) The landlord must occupy the dwelling as his residence. Schedule 2, para. 5 rather unhelpfully defines when this test is satisfied (and see below, pp. 207–10). Can a landlord be resident in more than one dwelling?

(*b*) Generally on resident landlords, see Whitehead, 1979a.

G Public sector tenancies (Rent Act 1977, ss. 13 and 14)

(As amended Housing Act 1980, s. 73 and Sched. 8.)
Certain properties belonging to the Crown are exempt. Properties belonging to local authorities are now subject to Housing Act 1980, Part 1, Chapter II (see below, pp. 510–53).

H Housing association tenancies (Rent Act 1977, s. 15)

(As amended Housing Act 1980, s. 74 and Schedule 9; see below, pp. 506–7.)

I Housing co-operatives (Rent Act 1977, s. 16)
J 'Assured tenancies' (Rent Act 1977, s. 16A)

(Introduced by Housing Act 1980, s. 56(5).) Housing Act 1980, s. 56 gives some further details of 'assured tenancies':

56.—(1) A tenancy under which a dwelling-house is let as a separate dwelling is an assured tenancy and not a housing association tenancy (within the meaning of section 86 of the 1977 Act) or a protected tenancy if –

(*a*) it would, when created, have been a protected tenancy or, as the case may be, housing association tenancy but for this section; and
(*b*) the conditions described in subsection (3) below are satisfied ...

(3) The conditions are that –

(*a*) the interest of the landlord has, since the creation of the tenancy, belonged to an approved body;
(*b*) the dwelling-house is, or forms part of, a building which was erected (and on which construction work first began) after the passing of this Act; and
(*c*) before the tenant first occupied the dwelling-house under the tenancy, no part of it had been occupied by any person as his residence except under an assured tenancy.

(4) In this Part of this Act 'approved body' means a body, or one of a

description of bodies, for the time being specified for the purposes of this Part of this Act in an order made by the Secretary of State ...

The list of 'approved bodies' has not at the time of writing been published. It is likely to include such institutions as building societies.

5. Shorthold tenancies

These are created by Housing Act 1980:

52.—(1) A protected shorthold tenancy is a protected tenancy granted after the commencement of this section which is granted for a term certain of not less than one year nor more than five years and satisfies the following conditions, that is to say, –

(a) it cannot be brought to an end by the landlord before the expiry of the term, except in pursuance of a provision for re-entry or forfeiture for non-payment of rent or breach of any other obligation of the tenancy; and

(b) not later than the beginning of the term the landlord has given the tenant a valid notice stating that the tenancy is to be a protected shorthold tenancy; and

(c) either a rent for the dwelling-house is registered at the time the tenancy is granted or (i) a certificate of fair rent has, before the grant, been issued under section 69 of the 1977 Act in respect of the dwelling-house and the rent payable under the tenancy, for any period before a rent is registered for the dwelling-house, does not exceed the rent specified in the certificate; and (ii) an application for the registration of a rent for the dwelling-house is made not later than 28 days after the beginning of the term and is not withdrawn.

(2) A tenancy of a dwelling-house is not a protected shorthold tenancy if it is granted to a person who immediately before it was granted, was a protected or statutory tenant of that dwelling-house.

(3) A notice is not valid for the purposes of subsection (1)(b) above unless it complies with the requirements of regulations made by the Secretary of State.

(4) The Secretary of State may by order direct that subsection (1) above shall have effect, either generally or in relation to any registration area specified in the order, as if paragraph (c) were omitted.

(5) If a protected tenancy is granted after the commencement of this section –

(a) for such a term certain as is mentioned in subsection (1) above, to be followed, at the option of the tenant, by a further term; or

(b) for such a term certain and thereafter from year to year or some other period;

and satisfies the conditions stated in that subsection, the tenancy is a protected shorthold tenancy until the end of the term certain.

There are also specific provisions relating to sub-letting and assignment:

54.—(1) Where the whole or part of a dwelling-house let under a protected shorthold tenancy has been sublet at any time during the continuous period specified in subsection (3) below, and, during that period, the landlord becomes entitled, as against the tenant, to possession of the dwelling-house, he shall also be entitled to possession against the sub-tenant and section 137 of the 1977 Act shall not apply.

(2) A protected shorthold tenancy of a dwelling-house and any protected tenancy of the same dwelling-house granted during the continuous period specified in subsection (3) below shall not be capable of being assigned, except in pursuance of an order under section 24 of the Matrimonial Causes Act 1973.

(3) The continuous period mentioned in subsections (1) and (2) above is the period beginning with the grant of the protected shorthold tenancy and continuing until either –

(*a*) no person is in possession of the dwelling-house as a protected or statutory tenant; or

(*b*) a protected tenancy of the dwelling-house is granted to a person who is not, immediately before the grant, in possession of the dwelling-house as a protected or statutory tenant.

The creation of this new category of tenancy has long been a feature of Conservative party policy. The argument is that a primary reason for the decline in the availability of privately rented accommodation is the security of tenure which tenants are said to enjoy under the Rent Acts (see below, ch. 8). Shorthold tenants will have no such security (see below, p. 439). It is at present a matter of speculation whether this change in the law will result in an upsurge of new tenancies. Certainly the last 'liberalization' of Rent Act principles – the Rent Act 1957 – was not accompanied by any increased investment in accommodation for renting. Consider the following questions: what problems are likely to be caused by removal of security of tenure? How will this affect local authorities' duties regarding the homeless (below, pp. 482–96)? Can shorthold tenancies operate in a socially desirable way if there is little or no increased investment in public sector housing? Are the conditions contained in s. 52 adequate? (Cf. Sir Brandon Rhys Williams' Private Member's Bill of 1979; SHAC (1979).) Should shortholds have been introduced only in those parts of the country where there is no housing stress?

6. Statutory tenancies

It will be realized from the above that whether a tenancy is or is not Rent Act protected depends on considering both the definition of protected tenancy and the exemptions to that definition. Whether or not a protected tenancy exists is crucial to answering the further question: when does a statutory tenancy exist?

Rent Act 1977, s. 2, states:

2.—(1) Subject to this Part of this Act –

> (*a*) after the termination of a protected tenancy of a dwelling-house the person who, immediately before that termination, was the protected tenant of the dwelling-house shall, if and so long as he occupies the dwelling-house as his residence, be the statutory tenant of it; and

> (*b*) Part I of Schedule 1 to this Act shall have effect for determining what person (if any) is the statutory tenant of a dwelling-house at any time after the death of a person who, immediately before his death, was either a protected tenant of the dwelling-house or the statutory tenant of it by virtue of paragraph (*a*) above.

(2) In this Act a dwelling-house is referred to as subject to a statutory tenancy when there is a statutory tenant of it.

(3) In subsection (1)(*a*) above and in Part I of Schedule 1, the phrase 'if and so long as he occupies the dwelling-house as his residence' shall be construed as it was immediately before the commencement of this Act (that is to say, in accordance with section 3(2) of the Rent Act 1968).

(4) A person who becomes a statutory tenant of a dwelling-house as mentioned in subsection (1)(*a*) above is, in this Act, referred to as a statutory tenant by virtue of his previous protected tenancy.

(5) A person who becomes a statutory tenant as mentioned in subsection 1(*b*) above is, in this Act, referred to as a statutory tenant by succession.

Note

(*a*) For s. 2 to operate, the tenant must have been Rent Act protected, immediately before termination of the tenancy (*Smalley* v. *Quarrier* [1975] 1 W.L.R. 938 (C.A.)); and the tenant must have been occupying the dwelling as a residence (*Cove* v. *Flick* [1954] 2 Q.B. 326n; *Dando* v. *Hitchcock* [1954] 2 Q.B. 317 (C.A.)).

(*b*) The test in s. 2(3) in fact derives from case-law, not Rent Act 1968, s. 3(2). A leading case is *Skinner* v. *Geary* [1931] 2 K.B. 546 (C.A.).

The plaintiff Mrs Alice Mary Skinner, claimed from the defendant,

Edward Geary, possession of a dwelling-house and premises known as 26 Oxford Road, Upper Norwood, London, of which premises the defendant was weekly tenant at 10s a week. It was admitted that the premises came within the scope of the Rent Restriction Acts, and that on May 6, 1930, due notice to quit had been served on the defendant, who had thereby become a statutory tenant. The defendant denied that the plaintiff was entitled to possession of the premises.

For a considerable period before 1919 the defendant had been the tenant and occupier of the premises. In 1919 he went to live at a house at Tatsfield, Surrey, of which his wife was the tenant. A married sister of the defendant's wife with her husband then resided at 26 Oxford Road until June, 1930, when she left, and a sister of the defendant went to live in the house. She was residing there when proceedings were begun in the county court.

The county court judge found that the defendant was not in actual possession of the premises at the material time – namely, at the time the notice to quit was given – and that he did not retain possession within the meaning of the Rent Restriction Acts by the occupation of his wife's or his own relatives, since the purpose of that occupation was not to preserve the house as a residence for the defendant. The county court judge accordingly made an order for possession of the premises.

The defendant appealed ...

The Divisional Court affirmed the order. In the Court of Appeal, Scrutton L.J. said:

The history of the Rent Restriction Acts shows that there has been a very gradual feeling of its way by the Court with regard to the principles upon which these Acts are to be worked. When they were drawn there is no evidence that Parliament or the draftsman ever thought out what rights they were giving to the tenant of a house to which the Acts applied. They never considered whether they were giving him something which the tenant could assign or could leave by will, or a property which on his death intestate would pass to his administrator, or which on his bankruptcy would pass to his trustee. Consequently the Courts have had to proceed slowly and with extreme caution ...

Parliament ... [in] my opinion ... never contemplated the possibility of the tenant living somewhere else. A non-occupying tenant was in my opinion never within the precincts of the Acts, which were dealing only with an occupying tenant who had a right to stay in and not be turned out. This case is to be decided on the principle that the Acts do not apply to a person who is not personally occupying the house and who has no intention of returning to it. I except, of course, such a case as that to which I have already referred – namely, of temporary absence, the best instance of which is that of a sea captain who may be away for months but who intends to return, and whose wife and family occupy the house during his absence ...

For the reasons I have given the Act does not in my opinion apply to protect a tenant who is not in occupation of a house in the sense that the house is his home and to which, although he may be absent for a time, he intends to return. If it were to be held otherwise odd consequences would follow. The appellant in this case has contented himself with living in one house and claiming another. Suppose he had a number of houses. One object of the Acts was to provide as many houses as possible at a moderate rent. A man who does not live in a house and never intends to do so, is, if I may use the expression, withdrawing from circulation that house which was intended for occupation by other people. To treat a man in the position of the appellant as a person entitled to be protected, is completely to misunderstand and misapply the policy of the Acts. The appeal must be dismissed.

Slesser L.J. agreed; Greer L.J. also found for the plaintiff but on different grounds.

The most difficult question is to decide whether a tenant with two homes can have Rent Act protection, and if so how much. Megarry writes (1967, pp. 186–7):

There is nothing in the Rent Restriction Acts to prevent a man having more than one home, provided that there is evidence on which it can properly be said that the second one was a home and not merely a place used when convenient, and rarely. Thus a tenant may be protected even if he has another home and only uses the premises in question as a home to the extent that for business reasons he sleeps there on an average twice a week. Again, a railway guard who spends three nights a week in Edinburgh and four in London may be protected in respect of both homes, and so may a schoolmaster who retains a bedroom at the school he runs, even if he sleeps there infrequently. If the statutory tenant of one house also becomes tenant of another house, and members of his family occupy both houses, his statutory tenancy will continue unaffected if he remains in the first house, but will terminate if he moves to the second house; and if a statutory tenant uses the house as a home with her sons, her tenancy is not destroyed merely because she sleeps in a house nearby, e.g., on account of dampness. It has also been said that a week-end cottage may be capable of supporting a statutory tenancy, and it has been so held where in addition a member of the tenant's family resided there continuously. A tenant in the course of moving from one house to another may be protected in each.

Nevertheless, attempts to extend the doctrine of the 'two-home man ...' should be regarded with some reserve ...

On this last point see now *Bevington* v. *Crawford* (1974) 232 E.G. 191

(C.A.). There it was said that use as *a* residence, not *the* residence was the test to be applied. Thus, even though the tenant had more than one home and was absent for long periods, the tenant remained statutory because he retained the intention to return. (Cf. *Walker* v. *Ogilvy* (1974) 28 P.& C.R. 288 (C.A.).)

In *Colin Smith Music* v. *Ridge* [1975] 1 W.L.R. 463 (C.A.), a statutory tenant left his mistress and children in occupation. However, since he himself had no intention to return, it was held that the statutory tenancy had come to an end. Deserted wives acquire a right to a statutory tenancy by virtue of their own occupation because the Matrimonial Homes Act 1967, s. 1(5) and s. 7(3) specifically provides for this. By contrast in *Atyeo* v. *Fardoe* (1979) 39 P.&C.R. 494 (C.A.) an elderly statutory tenant, who moved out of his bungalow during the winter while his son renovated the premises, was held not to have lost the *corpus possessionis*; he therefore retained possession and remained a statutory tenant. See also Rent Act 1977, Schedule 1, Part II for special provisions regarding the giving up of statutory tenancies and changing statutory tenants by agreement.

In *Roland House Gardens Ltd* v. *Cravitz* (1974) 29 P.&C.R. 432, the Court of Appeal held that the burden of proof is primarily on the landlord to show that the tenant has gone out of occupation.

(c) Statutory tenants by succession. Rent Act 1977, Schedule 1 (as amended by Housing Act 1980, s. 76) provides for a statutory tenancy by succession to arise on two occasions:

1. The provisions of paragraph 2 or, as the case may be paragraph 3 of this Schedule shall have effect, subject to section 2(3) of this Act, for the purpose of determining who is the statutory tenant of a dwelling-house by succession after the death of the person (in this Schedule referred to as 'the original tenant') who, immediately before his death, was a protected tenant of the dwelling-house or the statutory tenant of it by virtue of his previous protected tenancy.

2. The surviving spouse (if any) of the original tenant, if residing in the dwelling-house immediately before the death of the original tenant, shall after the death be the statutory tenant if and so long as he or she occupies the dwelling-house as his or her residence.

3. Where paragraph 2 above does not apply, but a person who was a member of the original tenant's family was residing with him at the time of and for the period of six months immediately before his death then, after his death, that person or if there is more than one such person such one of them as may be decided by agreement, or in default of agreement by the

county court, shall be the statutory tenant if and so long as he occupies the dwelling-house as his residence.

4. A person who becomes the statutory tenant of a dwelling-house by virtue of paragraph 2 or paragraph 3 above is in this Schedule referred to as 'the first successor'.

(**Paras. 5–8 deal with the second right of succession in similar terms.**)

The meaning of 'family' in para. (3) has been considered in a number of recent cases.

(*i*) *Dyson Holdings Ltd* v. *Fox* [1975] 3 All E.R. 1030 (C.A.)

LORD DENNING M.R.: So far as we know, Jack Wright was a bachelor and Olive Agnes Fox was a spinster, who met 40 years ago and lived happily ever after. They lived together as man and wife. She took his name and was known as Mrs Wright. In 1940 they were bombed out and went to live at 3 Old Road, Lewisham. The rent book was in the name of Mr J Wright. They both went out to work and used their earnings to run the house. In every respect they were man and wife save that they had not gone through a ceremony of marriage.

After 21 years in the house, on 28th August 1961 Mr Jack Wright died. She remained on in the house and paid the rent, using the name Mrs Wright. The rent book remained in the name of 'J Wright' and the records of the landlord still showed the tenant as 'J Wright'.

I expect that the ownership changed hands from time to time, but in March 1973 the owners were a property company, Dyson Holdings Ltd. By this time Mrs Wright (as she was known) was herself getting on in years. She was 73. She wrote to the landlords asking for a statement of the weekly rent. She signed herself 'O A Wright'. This put the property company on enquiry. They asked their agents to call at the house. She told them that Mr Jack Wright died on 28th August 1961 and that she was his widow. The property company asked their agents to check up on the electoral roll. They did so. They found that she had given her name there as 'Olive Fox'. The property company inferred that she was not really his widow. If she had been his widow, she could, of course, have had protection under the Rent Acts. But, if she was not his widow, they thought they were entitled in law to get her out. So on 27th March 1973 they wrote to her:

> 'We are addressing you as Mrs. O. Wright although we understand from the Electoral Register that the person in occupation is Olive Fox and perhaps you would explain this in your reply. Until this matter is clarified, we are unable to accept any rent ...'

So after all those years, the truth was out. She was not his widow. She was only a woman who had lived with him as his wife for 21 years. The property company refused to receive any rent from her and brought proceedings against her for possession on the ground that she was not protected by the Rent Act [1977]. She had, they said, no tenancy and was a trespasser. They had accepted the rent from her, not knowing that the tenant had died. As soon as they discovered it, and that she was not his widow, they were entitled to possession. The judge accepted their argument. He held that he was bound by the decision of this court in *Gammans v Ekins* ([1950] 2 K.B. 328). It was sad, he said, to have to turn this lady of 74 out; but felt he had no alternative. He ordered her out in 28 days. She appeals to this court.

Ever since 1920 the Rent Acts have protected a 'member of the tenant's family' ...

So in the present case the lady is protected if she was a 'member of the tenant's family'; but not otherwise. Those words have often been considered by the courts. The cases are collected in Megarry on the Rent Acts (1967, pp. 214–16). The word 'family' in the [1977] Act is not used in any technical sense, but in a popular sense. It is not used in the sense in which it would be used by a studious and unworldly lawyer, but in the sense in which it would be used by a man who is 'base, common and popular' ... or, in modern words, by the ordinary man in the street ...

Applying this test, there are two cases in this court which are near to the present. The first is *Gammans v Ekins*. A dwelling-house was let to a Mrs Smith. A man named Ekins went to live in the house. He lived for a very long time, 20 years or so, in close but unmarried association with Mrs Smith. He adopted her name and posed as her husband. In 1949 she died. Mr Ekins claimed that he was a member of her 'family'. The county court judge held that he was. This court held that he was not. Asquith L.J. said:

> 'To say of two people masquerading, as these two were, as husband and wife – there being no children to complicate the picture – that they were members of the same family, seems to me an abuse of the English language ...'

The other case is *Hawes v Evenden* ([1953] 1 W.L.R. 1169). A dwelling-house was let to a Mr Randall. He lived there with a Miss Evenden. For 12 years they occupied the same house as man and wife, though they were not married, and two children had been born of the association. She kept her own name – Evenden – but the children used the name Randall. He died. She claimed to be a member of the tenant's family. The county court judge held that she was. This court upheld his decision. Somervell L.J. said: '... there the evidence justifies a finding that they all lived together as a family, and so ... I think that the [mother] is a member of the family ...'

If both those cases were rightly decided, it seems to follow that an unmarried woman (who has lived with a man as his wife for many years) is a 'member of the tenant's family' if she has children by him; but she is not a member of his family if she has no children. That means this: if the couple had a baby 19 years ago which died when a few days old, or as a young child, the woman would be a 'member of the tenant's family'; but if the baby had been still-born, or if the woman had had a miscarriage 19 years ago, she would not be a member of his family. Yet for the last 19 years they had lived together as man and wife. That seems to me a ridiculous distinction. So ridiculous, indeed, that it should be rejected by this court; and that we should hold that a couple who live together as man and wife for 20 years are members of the same family, whether they have children or not.

But, is this court at liberty to reject the distinction? Are we bound by *Gammans v Ekins*? That case can be distinguished on narrow grounds, such as that the woman was the tenant and not the man, or that their relationship might perhaps have been platonic. But I dislike the device of distinguishing a case on narrow grounds. I prefer to say, as I have often said, that this court is not absolutely bound by a previous decision when it is seen that it can no longer be supported. At any rate, it is not so bound when, owing to the lapse of time, and the change in social conditions, the previous decision is not in accord with modern thinking ... I can [also] put the case on a conventional ground. It has been decided by the House of Lords that, when an Act uses an ordinary English word in its popular meaning as distinct from its legal meaning, it is for the tribunal of fact to decide whether or no that popular meaning covers the case in hand. The tribunal of fact must use its own understanding of the word and apply it to the facts which have been proved. A Court of Appeal should not interfere with its decision unless it was unreasonable in the sense that no tribunal acquainted with the ordinary use of language could reasonably reach that decision. That was the very ground of the decision of the House of Lords in *Brutus v Cozens* [1973] A.C. 854. In the light of that decision, it appears to me that *Gammans v Ekins* was wrongly decided. In that case, the tribunal of fact – the county court judge – gave judgment for the man, finding him to be a 'member of the tenant's family'. The Court of Appeal recognised that the words were to be given their ordinary and popular meaning, but nevertheless they reversed the county court judge. I do not think they should have done. To my mind the decision of the county court judge in that case was a perfectly reasonable decision, as Evershed MR recognised. And, on the authority of *Brutus v Cozens*, the Court of Appeal ought not to have interfered with it ...

Bridge L.J. (in part):

Can we give effect to this change in social attitude and consequent change in the scope of a common English word without doing violence to the doctrine of judicial precedent and notwithstanding that in this case the appellant's status must be considered at the date of the original tenant's death in 1961? I have felt some hesitation on both these points, but in the end have concluded that it would be unduly legalistic to allow either consideration to defeat the appellant's claim. On the first point, if language can change its meaning to accord with changing social attitudes, then a decision on the meaning of a word in a statute before such a change should not continue to bind thereafter, at all events in a case where the courts have consistently affirmed that the word is to be understood in its ordinary accepted meaning. On the second point, where the modern meaning is plain, we should, I think, be prepared to apply it retrospectively to any date, unless plainly satisfied that at that date the modern meaning would have been unacceptable.

James L.J. agreed.

(ii) Helby v. Rafferty [1978] 3 All ER 1016 (C.A.)

STAMP L.J. This is an action by a plaintiff landlady for possession of premises known as Flat 1, 8 Abercorn Place, London NW6. The appeal is by the defendant, Mr Charles Rafferty, who appeals against an order of his Honour Judge Curtis-Raleigh made on 7th November 1977 in Bloomsbury and Marylebone County Court, whereby Mr Rafferty was ordered to deliver up possession of the premises.

The late Miss Barbara Taylor at the date of her death was tenant of the flat. She had been there since about 1966 as tenant and in 1969 the term of her lease expired and she thereupon became a statutory tenant. She died on 15th March 1977. From about June 1972 (that is to say for about five years) Mr Rafferty had been living in the flat. He had known Miss Taylor for some time before he took up residence there, and when he did take up residence there he had become her lover, and there they lived together until the date of her death sharing board and bed.

Mr Rafferty claims that on Miss Taylor's death he became the statutory tenant ... The question accordingly turns on whether Mr Rafferty was at the date of Miss Taylor's death a member of Miss Taylor's family within the meaning of Sch 1, para 3.

Had the case fallen to be decided prior to Dyson Holdings Ltd v Fox (above), we would have been constrained to dismiss the appeal on the authority of Gammans v Ekins ([1950] 2 K.B. 328), a decision of this court which was subsequently applied by this court in Ross v Collins ([1964] 1 W.L.R. 425).

The ordinary or natural meaning of the expression 'member of a family' would not, in my judgment, apply to a person in the position of Mr Rafferty ... I confess that, apart from authority, I would have taken the view that the language of a statute by whatever process you apply to its construction, whether you construe it in its natural and ordinary meaning or whether you construe it in a popular way or whether you construe it in what has sometimes been called 'a legal way' (and I am not sure I understand what the difference is) cannot alter its meaning from time to time and that, in order to find out what Parliament intended by the statute, you must ascertain what the words of the statute meant when Parliament used those words. There is the further difficulty, as I see it, that the language of the relevant statutory provision has been repeated in successive Rent Acts with only a very slightly different arrangement of the words. As I rather indicated, I think, it appears to me that the difficulty of determining whether a particular meaning of the words in an Act of Parliament would be given to those words by popular vote or not would be of a different kind. Do you listen to the vociferous minority or do you imagine what the silent majority might have said at a particular time?

He then discussed *Dyson Holdings* v. *Fox* and continued:

I conclude that *Dyson Holdings Ltd v Fox* established two propositions: first, that, notwithstanding *Gammans v Ekins*, a relationship between an unmarried man and an unmarried woman living together over a very long period can constitute the family relationship which is necessary in order to satisfy the section, and second, that on the facts in *Dyson Holdings Ltd v Fox* such a relationship was established. One has to ask: has the union such a degree of apparent permanence and stability that the ordinary man would say that the parties were, in the words of Bridge L.J., 'members of a single family'? ...

The relevant facts in the instant case are these. Mr Rafferty, as I have said, took up residence about five years before Miss Taylor's death. They lived together, sharing a bed. They shared expenses, the life of each being bound up very closely with the life of the other. They went out together. They went about together. They went to shows together. They did shopping together. They went, I think, to the cinema together. As she got more ill, as unhappily she did, Mr Rafferty did all the things for her that a loving husband might be expected to do. He nursed her as a husband would have done. If it stopped there you might conclude that the situation was just such a one as the Court of Appeal in *Dyson Holdings Ltd v Fox* held satisfied the definition. But there was another side of the picture. In the first place, there was no charade. Miss Taylor did not call herself Mrs Rafferty. Nor was any attempt made, as I understand it, to throw dust in the eyes of friends as to the true nature of the relationship. Far from passing themselves off as husband and wife, when the time came for the mother to visit the flat, the parties did put up something in the nature of a charade in pretending that they were less intimate than was in fact the case.

Then there is a letter which throws light on the situation, written by the brother of Miss Taylor, dated 31st July 1977, to Messrs Keene Marsland & Co in reply to a letter of theirs dated 28th June. In the latter letter the writer said this:

'Further to our telephone conversations of yesterday and 20th May, as you know we have been advised by Counsel to approach you for a statement in this matter. We appreciate of course that your loyalties are mostly with Mr Rafferty and that you may require to take independent advice before you decide to make such a statement or not. If you feel prepared to make such a statement, we should be grateful of your confirmation that your sister refused to marry Mr Rafferty and furthermore that as far as you are aware, although they may have been living together under the same roof, they did not represent themselves to the outside world as being married.'

The reply, as I have said, was dated 31st July. I am finding it somewhat difficult to read, but I think it reads as follows:

'Dear Sirs, I would refer to your letter dated 28 June 77 relating to the situation regarding Mr Charles Rafferty and my sister. Firstly I would dispute your use of the word "refused" which I think by definition and in isolation gives a wrong impression of the actual situation. My sister was a well known writer having written for the Daily Express and Evening Standard on a regular basis and having also written for many other papers/ mags as a freelance. She had also appeared on television and been heard on radio all these activities under her own name of Barbara Anne Taylor. Furthermore she had a very strong streak of independence. (She left home to start her career before she was 18). All of which I mention in order to explain that she did not 'REFUSE' to marry Mr Rafferty. She simply preferred an arrangement which left her fully independent but with the security etc that marriage gives. In the casual society enjoyed by many people today, particularly in areas similar to St John's Wood, my sister and Mr Rafferty were regarded by local tradesmen, innkeepers etc as being "man and wife".'

The writer of that letter, Miss Taylor's brother, did not give evidence at the trial because he was going abroad, but he did make an affidavit which was, I assume, accepted.

I have read and reread the judge's judgment in the court below and, because it so clearly sets out the problem and deals with it so fairly, I am constrained to read the greater part of it because he expresses the matter far better than I could myself. After referring to the fact that Miss Taylor was a newspaper journalist and so on, he says:

'She was an alcoholic and it is clear that towards the end of her life, her health and working ability had seriously deteriorated as a result of that fact, although it is not clear from the evidence at what rate the deterioration took place. She died eventually by taking an overdose of tablets, either accidentally or deliberately. An affidavit which Mr William Taylor, her brother, swore was admitted in evidence. Mr Taylor states that in the last three years of her life his sister became increasingly ill, suffering symptoms of alcoholism, liver damage and depression and she became increasingly dependent on Mr Rafferty. Mr Rafferty is a geologist who has worked for construction companies. He met her and had intercourse with her about a year before they started to live together. He moved into her flat about five years ago and thereafter they lived together, he sharing her bed. She mainteained as long as possible her working capacity but as her health deteriorated he assumed more and more responsibility for looking after her; he paid the electricity account which was in his own name; and they shared the expenses of her flat; he did the shopping and arranged the cleaning of the flat. Save in one small respect, I accept his evidence; he was straight-forward. The only piece of evidence which he gave which I was not prepared to accept was that on being asked about the question of their marriage he said, "We discussed the question of marriage and concluded that we would get married". He did not give a date and it appears to be in conflict with Mr Taylor's affidavit and with probability. These are briefly the circum-stances of the case and I have to decide whether he was a member of the tenant's family. He did of course satisfy the other requirements of the Rent Act in relation to residing there. This question is by no means an easy one and the argument in the case in a large measure turned on the application to the facts of this case of the case of *Dyson Holdings Ltd v Fox* ... It is well to bear in mind that the facts in that case relate to a woman who was anxious to give to the outside world every appearance of being the wife of the de-ceased man ... Lord Denning M R is saying first of all that the facts in that case are that the parties had been living for many years as man and wife. In applying that principle, one has to decide what "for many years as man and wife" means ... [Even] a short period of cohabitation combined with children would make the court much more ready to say, "These two adults are members of the family". That is one characteristic of a family. The second characteristic is the adoption by the woman of the name of the husband and/or the encouragement of people to regard them as being members of a family. So far as that aspect is concerned Mr Rafferty said, "She may have called herself Mrs Rafferty, but I cannot recall her having done so". Certainly so far as Miss Taylor's own mother is concerned, they went out of their way to pretend not to be living together in an unmarried state, since Mr Taylor says in his affidavit: "My late sister explained to me and I verily believe that the said Mr Rafferty had been living with her for some time prior to this, but that Mr Rafferty arranged to be away from the flat when our mother visited there, in the event that our mother might disapprove of my sister living with a man out of wedlock." Of course this is only one comparatively small fact; it was due to the sensitivity of the mother, and the couple might appear to all the rest of the world as man and wife: but there was no evidence that they were so regarded or sought to be. Marriage is essentially a public status, which can however be assumed by a couple without the formalities, by "living as man and wife". In the present case there is no evidence that such status enjoyed any public recognition, and the woman's mother was deliberately led to believe that such a status did not exist. For the law to recognise such status in these circumstances seems to me to be unjustified ... [Couples] live together now much more freely for a variety of reasons. But because cohabitation carries little if any social stigma, people do make the distinction between a family relationship and non-family relationship from which they can easily withdraw. In Mr Taylor's affidavit, he says that, "My sister made it clear to me that she did not marry Mr Rafferty because she wished to retain a certain amount of independence and freedom." In saying that his sister wanted to keep her freedom it appears to me to follow inevitably that she was deliberately choosing to avoid permanence in the relationship. Freedom to do what? Among other things, freedom to withdraw from the relationship with the minimum of disruption and without legal or other formalities. This is a different relationship from that of the woman in *Dyson Holdings Ltd v Fox*.'

On these grounds the Court of Appeal unanimously held that Mr Rafferty was not a member of the tenant's family.

(*iii*) *Carega Properties S.A.* v. *Sharratt* [1979] 2 All E.R. 1084 (H.L.)

LORD DIPLOCK : The facts of the instant case, if they are not unique, are certainly most unusual, and for that reason they do not, in my opinion, provide a suitable occasion for this House to undertake a general consideration of what persons may be included in the expression 'a member of the original tenant's family' where at the time of the tenant's death there did exist between him and the claimant to a statutory tenancy by succession a relationship of one or other of the various kinds to which I have referred above. In particular, the difficult question posed by *Dyson Holdings Ltd v Fox* ([1976] Q.B. 503) as to the extent, if any, to which changed social attitudes towards co-habitation between unmarried couples and the offspring of such liaisons may have enlarged the meaning of the expression 'family' in the Rent Act 1977 does not arise in the instant case and is best left for consideration in the light of the actual facts of a case in which it does arise.

The deceased statutory tenant of Flat 48, Coleherne Court, London SW5, of which the respondents claim possession, was Lady Salter, the widow of a High Court judge, who had died as long ago as 1929. In 1957, when she was aged 75, she first met the appellant, Mr Sharratt, who was then aged 24. They shared a mutual interest in politics and the theatre and a close friendship grew up between them. In the following year, Lady Salter suggested that Mr Sharratt should come to live in her flat at Coleherne Court. He fell in with this suggestion and for the first three years that he resided there he paid her £4 a week for bed and breakfast. After that the payments ceased. Lady Salter at all times paid the rent of the flat, but the other expenses were shared between them. This continued until her death at the age of 94 in April 1976.

The relationship between them throughout was platonic and filial. He behaved towards her as a dutiful and affectionate son and looked after her during her declining years. She would have liked to speak of him as her son, but this was not acceptable to Mr Sharratt, whose mother was still alive; so they decided that he would call her Aunt Norah and she addressed him by an affectionate nickname. There was throughout no question of his being financially dependent on her. All that he did for her over the 18 years that he resided with her in the flat had no other motive than kindness and affection.

My lords, the bare recital of these facts makes one desirous, if one can, to gratify Mr Sharratt's wish to continue to reside in the flat where he had lived for so long before Lady Salter's death. Judge Solomon in the West London County Court, where the action by the landlords for possession of the flat was brought, felt himself able to do so. He said:

'I have come to the conclusion that Lady Salter and this defendant achieved through their relationship what must surely be regarded in a popular sense, and in common sense, as familial nexus. That is to say, a nexus as one would find only within a family. I am sure Shakespeare's man would say: "Yes, it is stranger than fiction, but they established a familial tie. Everyone linked to her through the blood was remote by comparison with the defendant".'

The reference to Shakespeare's man is an allusion to the description 'base, common and popular' which in *Langdon v Horton* ([1951] 1 K.B. 666), Evershed M.R. borrowed from Henry V, to describe the ordinary man mentioned by Cohen L.J. in *Brock v Wollams* ([1949] 2 K.B. 388), where he said:

'The question the learned county court judge should have asked himself was: Would an ordinary man, addressing his mind to the question whether Mrs Wollams was a member of the family or not, have answered "Yes" or "No".'

This test, which does no more than say that 'family' where it is used in the Rent Acts is not a term of art but is used in its ordinary popular meaning, has been repeatedly referred to and applied in subsequent cases.

The Court of Appeal (Megaw, Lawton and Browne L.J.) unanimously reversed the judgment of Judge Solomon. Megaw L.J. after quoting the 'Cohen question' went on to say, in my view, quite correctly:

'... it is for this court to decide, where such an issue arises, whether, assuming all the facts found by the judge to be correct, the question may, as a matter of law, within the permissible limits of the meaning of the phrase "a member of the tenant's family", be answered "Yes".'

Megaw L.J. and Lawton L.J. both answered the question with a confident 'No'; and so would I. Browne L.J. agreed, but rather more hesitantly.

However, he also thought that the Court of Appeal was bound to allow the appeal because of two previous decisions of its own, *Gammans v Ekins* ([1950] 2 K.B. 328) and *Ross v Collins* ([1964] 1 W.L.R. 425).

Gammans v Ekins was a case of co-habitation by an unmarried couple, a relationship which rasises questions on which I find it unnecessary and inappropriate to enter for the purpose of disposing of the instant appeal. *Ross v Collins*, on the other hand, was much like the instant case, save that the sexes of the older party, who was devotedly cared for, and the younger party who did the caring, were reversed. As my reason for dismissing the instant appeal, I would not seek to improve on what was said there by Russell L.J.:

'Granted that "family" is not limited to cases of a strict legal familial nexus, I cannot agree that it extends to a case such as this. It still requires, it seems to me, at least a broadly recognisable de facto familial nexus. This may be capable of being found and recognised as such by the ordinary man – where the link would be strictly familial had there been a marriage, or where the link is through adoption of a minor, de jure or de facto, or where the link is "step-", or where the link is "in-law" or by marriage. But two strangers cannot, it seems to me, ever establish artificially for the purposes of this section a familial nexus by acting as brothers or as sisters, even if they call each other such and consider their relationship to be tantamount to that. Nor, in my view, can an adult man and woman who establish a platonic relationship establish a familial nexus by acting as a devoted brother and sister or father and daugher would act, even if they address each other as such and even if they refer to each other as such and regard their association as tantamount to such. Nor, in my view, would they indeed be recognised as familial links by the ordinary man.'

I would accordingly dismiss this appeal.

Viscount Dilhorne and Lords Elwyn-Jones, Fraser of Tullybelton and Russell of Killowen agreed. (See Sherrin, 1980.) In *Watson* v. *Lucas* (*The Times*, 8 July 1980 (C.A.)) it was held, 2–1, that a married man, who had not married his mistress because of her religious objections, could nonetheless be a member of her family.

The word 'reside' was considered in *Morgan* v. *Murch* [1970] 2 All E.R. 100 where the court held that it must be given its ordinary, natural, common language meaning. Thus a man who was living in his mother's house – the mother being a statutory tenant who had just died – was held entitled to succeed to the statutory tenancy, even though he was also notionally the tenant of a council house in which his wife and children lived. He had made no moves to become reconciled with his wife and there was no immediate prospect of his returning to the matrimonial home.

7. **Restricted contracts**

Rent Act 1977, ss. 19–20: (as amended) (also s. 21, above, p. 172)

19.—(1) A contract to which this section applies is, in this Act, referred to as a 'restricted contract'.

(2) Subject to section 144 of this Act, this section applies to a contract whether entered into before or after the commencement of this Act, whereby one person grants to another person, in consideration of a rent which includes payment for the use of furniture or for services, the right to occupy a dwelling as a residence.

(3) A contract is not a restricted contract if the dwelling falls within one of the Classes set out in subsection (4) below.

(4) Where alternative rateable values are mentioned in this subsection, the higher applies if the dwelling is in Greater London and the lower applies if it is elsewhere.

Class D

The appropriate day in relation to the dwelling falls or fell on or after 1st April 1973 and the dwelling on the appropriate day has or had a rateable value exceeding £1,500 or £750.

Class E

The appropriate day in relation to the dwelling fell before 1st April 1973 and the dwelling –

(a) on the appropriate day had a rateable value exceeding £400 or £200, and

(b) on 1st April 1973 had a rateable value exceeding £1,500 or £750.

(5) A contract is not a restricted contract if –

(a) it creates a regulated tenancy; or

(aa) under the contract the interest of the lessor belongs to a body mentioned in section 14 of this Act;

(b) under the contract the interest of the lessor belongs to Her Majesty in right of the Crown or to a government department, or is held in trust for Her Majesty for the purposes of a government department except that an interest belonging to Her Majesty in right of the Crown does not prevent a contract from being a restricted contract if the interest is under the management of the Crown Estate Commissioners; or

(c) it is a contract for the letting of any premises at a rent which includes payment in respect of board if the value of the board to the lessee forms a substantial proportion of the whole rent;

(d) it is a protected occupancy as defined in the Rent (Agriculture) Act 1976; or

(e) it creates a tenancy to which Part VI of this Act applies.

(6) Subject to subsections (3) to (5) above, and to paragraph 17 of Schedule 24 to this Act, a contract falling within subsection (2) above and relating to a dwelling which consists of only part of a house is a restricted contract whether or not the lessee is entitled, in addition to exclusive occupation of that part, to the use in common with any other person of other rooms or accommodation in the house.

(7) No right to occupy a dwelling for a holiday shall be treated for the purposes of this section as a right to occupy it as a residence.

(8) In this section –

'dwelling' means a house or part of a house;

'lessee' means the person to whom is granted, under a restricted contract, the right to occupy the dwelling in question as a residence and any person directly or indirectly deriving title from the grantee; and

'lessor' means the person who, under a restricted contract, grants to another the right to occupy the dwelling in question as a residence and any person directly or indirectly deriving title from the grantor; and

'services' includes attendance, the provision of heating or lighting, the supply of hot water and any other privilege or facility connected with the occupancy of a dwelling, other than a privilege or facility requisite for the purposes of access, cold water supply or sanitary accommodation.

20. If and so long as a tenancy is, by virtue only of section 12 of this Act, precluded from being a protected tenancy it shall be treated as a restricted contract notwithstanding that the rent may not include payment for the use of furniture or for services.

Notes: (a) Section 12 is set out above, p. 202.

(b) S. 19(5)(aa) effectively overrules *Lambeth* v. *Udechuka* (1980) *The Times*, 30 April (C.A.).

(c) Despite the wording of s. 19(2), remember that Rent Act 1974, s. 1(1) (above, p. 174) is still in force. Thus, furnished tenancies created after 14 August 1974 are now protected tenancies. However, furnished contractual licences may still fall within s. 19, as well as tenancies created before 14 August 1974.

Luganda v. *Service Hotels* [1969] 2 Ch. 209

LORD DENNING M.R.: The plaintiff, Mr Kasozi Luganda, came to this country from Uganda in 1958. He is employed as a clerk in a company in London, but he is also a student. He is reading for the Bar and is going to take his final examinations in May 1969. Nearly three years ago he took a furnished room in a building which is known as Queensborough Court Hotel, Queensborough Terrace, W.2. It is called a hotel, but it is very different from an ordinary hotel. It has 88 rooms which are 'let' out to 'tenants'. But they are not strictly 'let', and they are not strictly 'tenants'. Each 'tenant' is really a contractual licensee who has the right to occupy a room in return for a weekly payment. The plaintiff has a Yale key for his room. It is a bed-sitting room with a double-ring gas ring. He gets his own meals. He provides his own towel and soap; but the defendants provide the bedding. The chambermaids come in every day and make his bed and clean the room; and every week they change the linen. Along the corridor there are lavatories and bathrooms which are used by all the occupants. There is, of course, a lift. There is a porter on duty down below; and there is a receptionist who puts telephone messages through to a common telephone on each floor.

The plaintiff has been in the same room, no. 53, for nearly three years. When he went there in April 1966, he paid £4 14s. 6d. a week. In September 1967, it was raised to £4 18s. a week. In January 1969, the defendants wanted to decorate his room, no. 53. So he went out of no. 53 into no. 4 for a fortnight whilst they redecorated the room. He went back into no. 53 on 31st January, a Friday. On the next morning, Saturday, 1st February, he received a letter from the manager telling him that his rent was to be increased by a guinea a week. It was in future to be £5 19s. a week. He did not like this increase in rent. So he went to the rent tribunal and told them about it. They gave him some advice; and, in consequence, on Monday, 3rd February, the plaintiff wrote to the defendant saying: 'I note that you have put up the rent by £1 1s. 0d. a week! I am taking legal advice on this matter, but in the meantime I will continue to pay £4 18s. 0d. as in the past.'

The defendants did not like this. They went to their solicitors who wrote a letter which the plaintiff got on the Wednesday, 5th February. They told him that he had to vacate his room by 10.00 a.m. on the Friday, 7th February. That was only two days' notice. The plaintiff did not obey their notice. He did not vacate the premises on the Friday morning. He went to work as usual. When he got back on the Friday evening, he found that the defendants had changed the lock. He could not get in. He could not even get his belongings. He had to go and spend the night with a friend nearby. Meanwhile the rent tribunal wrote to him saying that his application to them had been received and would be dealt with as early as possible. They told the defendants also. The defendants did not leave room 53 empty for very long. They soon let it to a Turkish lady; and they told the plaintiff that he could not come back. The plaintiff applied for an injunction. CROSS, J., held that the plaintiff had a prima facie right to remain in possession. He was within the statute which affords protection to the tenants of furnished rooms. The judge granted an injunction so as to enable him to go back to room 53; and an injunction to prevent the defendants from stopping him having access. Now the defendants appeal to this court.

The statutory provisions about furnished lettings ... were especially designed to cover a letting of furnished rooms, either under a tenancy or a contractual licence, and thus to cover such a case as the present. But counsel for the defendants has submitted that they do not cover it. I will take his points in order. First, the Act only applies to a contract relating to a 'dwelling' ... and 'dwelling' is defined ... as 'a house or part of a house'. Counsel for the defendants submitted that this hotel was not a 'house'. He referred us to a passage in *Megarry on the Rent Acts* (10th edn), p. 50, where it is stated that 'premises used as a hotel may be protected if they were constructed as a dwelling-house, but perhaps not if constructed as a hotel'. I do not accept this submission. I am quite clear that a building which is used as a hotel is a 'house', no matter whether it was purpose built or not. As it happens, the Queensborough Court Hotel was constructed as four houses, but they have been knocked into one so as to form the hotel. It is clearly a 'house'; and room 53 is 'part of a house'.

Secondly, the Act only applies to a contract which gives to the lessee 'the right to occupy as a residence' a dwelling ... Counsel for the defendants submitted that the contract here did not give the plaintiff the right to occupy room 53 'as a residence'. He referred us again to a passage in Megarry at p. 505, where it is stated: 'The words "as a residence" have a limiting effect. Thus the Act does not apply to temporary accommodation of the normal hotel type, whether the Ritz or Rowton House, presumably because there is no occupation "as a residence".' I agree about the Ritz or Rowton House. A person taking a room there on a short visit does not have the right to occupy it 'as a residence'. Counsel for the defendants submitted that the contract, to come within the Act, must give to the lessee, in express words, the right to occupy as a residence. But I do not think so. It is sufficient if 'the lessee is within his rights in occupying the premises as a residence', even though the contract says nothing about it; see *R.* v. *York, Harrogate, Ripon and Northallerton Areas Rent Tribunal, Ex p. Ingle*, per PARKER, J. ([1954] 1 Q.B. 456). It is plain here that the plaintiff was occupying room 53 as a residence. He had been there nearly three years; and he was within his rights in so occupying it. So that requirement is satisfied.

Thirdly, in a case like the present when the lessee occupies only a part of a house (namely, one room) the contract must entitle the lessee to 'exclusive occupation' of that part ... Counsel for the defendants submitted that the Act only protected a tenant, properly so called, and did not protect a contractual licensee or lodger who took a furnished room. The plaintiff was, of course, only a contractual licensee; and not a tenant. Counsel sought to support his submission by taking us through many provisions of earlier Rent Acts. But I do not propose to go through them now. I am quite satisfied that 'exclusive occupation' in [s. 19(6)] does not mean 'exclusive possession' in the technical sense in which it is sometimes used in landlord and tenant cases. A lodger who takes a furnished room in a house is in exclusive occupation of it; notwithstanding that the landlady has a right to access at all times. It was so held twelve years ago in *R.* v. *Battersea, Wandsworth, Mitcham and Wimbledon Rent-Tribunal, Ex p. Parikh* ([1957] 1 All E.R. 352). LORD GODDARD C.J., said that, although the landlady had a right of access, she had not the right 'to come in and occupy it herself, nor had she the right to put somebody else into the room'. Counsel for the defendants submitted that that case was wrongly decided and should be overruled. But I think that it was rightly decided. A person has a right to 'exclusive occupation' of a room when he is entitled to occupy it himself, and no one else is entitled to occupy it. Even though, as here, the chambermaids come in daily to make the bed and clean the room, and change the linen each week, nevertheless, the plaintiff had exclusive occupation of the room, that is, the right to occupy it to the exclusion of anyone else occupying it. He has the right under the contract. This requirement, too, is satisfied ...

It seems to me, therefore, that prima facie at least the plaintiff is entitled to the protection of the Act, that is, the protection which is afforded to lessees of furnished lettings. He was entitled to refer the contract, as he did, to the rent tribunal ...

Counsel for the defendants submitted that, as the plaintiff was not now in occupation, no mandatory order should be made to put him back. He suggested that such an order would require the constant superintendence of the court, which the court would not do. He cited *Ryan* v. *Mutual Tontine Westminster Chambers Association* ([1893] 1 Ch. 116). I look on the case quite differently. The plaintiff is prima facie entitled by statute to security of tenure of this room. It was unlawful for the defendants to lock him out of it ... If the defendants had not changed the lock – and the plaintiff was still in occupation – I am sure that the court would have granted an injunction to prevent the defendants from locking him out. They should not be in a better position by wrongfully locking him out. We must see that the law is observed. To do this, we should, I think, order that the plaintiff should be restored to his room. There is no difficulty about the Turkish lady. Rooms often become vacant. She can go into another room.

In my opinion, the judge was quite right. An injunction should be made pending trial.

Edmund Davies and Phillimore L.JJ. agreed.

See also *Marchant* v. *Charters* (above, pp. 116–18); and *R.* v. *South Middlesex Rent Tribunal, ex parte Beswick* (1976) 32 P.&C.R. 67.

8. Difficult cases

A Sub-tenants

The common law relating to the limited rights of sub-tenants to remain in premises after the 'mesne' tenancy has ended has been discussed above (pp. 90–91). The Rent Act 1977, s. 137, provides a very limited additional protection, whereby certain sub-tenants may become protected tenants.

137.—(1) If a court makes an order for possession of a dwelling-house from –

(a) a protected or statutory tenant, or

(b) a protected occupier or statutory tenant as defined in the Rent (Agriculture) Act 1976,

and the order is made by virtue of section 98(1) or 99(2) of this Act or, as the case may be, under Part I of Schedule 4 to that Act, nothing in the order shall affect the right of any sub-tenant to whom the dwelling-house or any part of it has been lawfully sublet before the commencement of the proceedings to retain possession by virtue of this Part of this Act, nor shall the order operate to give a right to possession against any such sub-tenant.

(2) Where a statutorily protected tenancy of a dwelling-house is determined, either as a result of an order for possession or for any other reason, any sub-tenant to whom the dwelling-house or any part of it has been lawfully sublet shall, subject to this Act, be deemed to become the tenant of the landlord on the same terms as if the tenant's statutorily protected tenancy had continued.

(3) Where a dwelling-house –

(a) forms part of premises which have been let as a whole on a superior tenancy but do not constitute a dwelling-house let on a statutorily protected tenancy; and

(b) is itself subject to a protected or statutory tenancy,

then, from the coming to an end of the superior tenancy, this Act shall apply in relation to the dwelling-house as if, in lieu of the superior tenancy, there had been separate tenancies of the dwelling-house and of the remainder of the premises, for the like purposes as under the superior tenancy, and at rents equal to the just proportion of the rent under the superior tenancy.

In this subsection 'premises' includes, if the sub-tenancy in question is a protected or statutory tenancy to which section 99 of this Act applies, an agricultural holding within the meaning of the Agricultural Holdings Act 1948.

(4) In subsections (2) and (3) above 'statutorily protected tenancy' means –

(a) a protected or statutory tenancy;

(b) a protected occupancy or statutory tenancy as defined in the Rent (Agriculture) Act 1976; or

(c) if the sub-tenancy in question is a protected or statutory tenancy to which section 99 of this Act applies, a tenancy of an agricultural holding with the meaning of the Agricultural Holdings Act 1948.

Note. (a) The sub-letting must be lawful, though it may have been made lawful by 'waiver' (see above, p. 88; and *Maley* v. *Fearn* [1946] 2 All E.R. 583 (C.A.); cf. *Oak Property Co. Ltd* v. *Chapman* [1947] 1 K.B. 886 (C.A.)).

(*b*) Although sub-s. (2) does not so require, it has been interpreted judicially as meaning that the sub-letting must also be Rent Act protected (*Stanley* v. *Compton* [1951] 1 All E.R. 859). Thus s. 137 will not operate where the sub-letting creates only a 'restricted contract'. Given the new law relating to resident landlords, this means that the scope of s. 137 has been (inadvertently perhaps?) substantially reduced.

(*c*) The meaning of the word 'premises' in s. 137(3) was discussed by the House of Lords in *Maunsell* v. *Olins* [1975] A.C. 373. By a majority, their Lordships held that premises meant 'dwelling-houses' (*per* Lords Reid, Wilberforce and Viscount Dilhorne) and could not be used to include all premises (which Lord Diplock and Simon thought was correct). Thus a sub-letting of a farm cottage carved out of an agricultural tenancy was not brought within the Rent Act by s. 137(3).

(*d*) If the sub-tenancy was furnished and the sub-tenant becomes the tenant of the head landlord by the operation of s. 137, the head landlord is not to be landed with obligations to provide furniture or services if certain conditions are met. (For details, see Rent Act, 1977, s. 138.)

B Tenants of mortgagors

Most mortgage deeds contain a prohibition against the creation of tenancies. If a tenancy is granted in contravention of such a term (which will not affect the validity of tenancies created before the mortgage was entered into), the tenancy will not usually bind the mortgage company (mortgagee) if it has to foreclose or repossess the property from the landlord. It also appears that the doctrine of 'waiver' does not apply, so that the mortgage company is still not bound by the tenancy even if it knew of the illegal letting and went on accepting mortgage repayments. (See, e.g., *Bolton Building Society* v. *Cobb* [1966] 1 W.L.R. 1; *Dudley and District Benefit Building Society* v. *Emerson* [1949] Ch. 707.)

These principles may, however, be replaced if there are special circumstances surrounding the creation of the mortage. See *Quennell* v. *Maltby* [1979] 1 All E.R. 568.

LORD DENNING M.R.: Mr Quennell is a gentleman who lives in Cheyne Row in London. But he is the owner of a large house in Lewes. It is No 6 Wallands Crescent, Lewes, with about nine bedrooms. He has an agent in

Lewes who looks after it for him. The house is very suitable for students. In 1973 the agent let it to some students of the University of Sussex. Two of them became the tenants. They were Mr Maltby and Mr Jack. They were let into possession for a term of one year at a rent of £90 a month, expiring on 31st December 1974. They had other students there with them, about nine students in the house.

Whilst Mr Maltby and Mr Jack were tenants, Mr Quennell borrowed money from Barclays Bank and mortgaged this house to secure the loan. It was only for the sum of £2,500. He executed a legal charge on 13th August 1974 in favour of Barclays Bank to cover any moneys which might from time to time be owing to the bank. In that legal charge there was this clause, cl 4, which is in common form:

'During the continuance of this security no statutory or other power of granting of agreeing to grant or of accepting or agreeing to accept surrenders of leases or tenancies of the Mortgaged Property or any part thereof shall be capable of being exercised by the Mortgagor without the previous consent in writing of the Bank ...'

That meant thereafter from 13th August 1974 so long as this legal charge subsisted to the bank, Mr Quennell could not let the premises or accept surrenders without the consent in writing of the bank.

The tenancy of Mr Maltby and Mr Jack came to an end at the end of December 1974. The house was then relet to two other students, a Mr Quilter and Mr Lyth, again for a year. It was not relet to Mr Maltby because it was thought he was going to the United States. As it happened Mr Maltby did not go to the United States. In fact he stayed on living in the house. So did several other students.

At all events, the important thing to note is that the bank did not give its consent to this letting to Mr Quilter and Mr Lyth. No one asked the bank for its consent. No one realised it was necessary. No one interfered and nothing happened. That year 1975 passed. Then at the end of that year there was a fresh letting. This was between Mr Quennell as landlord and Mr Maltby and a Mr Lupton as tenants. That tenancy lasted until December 1976. Again no one asked the bank for consent. No one realised it was necessary. And from January 1977 onwards the tenants remained as statutory tenants, paying the rent to the agents.

The position then arose that Mr Quennell wanted to get possession of the house. If he could get vacant possession, he could sell it at a high price. It might be worth £30,000 to £40,000 with vacant possession. Mr Quennell started proceedings for nuisance and annoyance, but he dropped them. Then he went to lawyers for advice. After consulting them, in October 1977 Mr Quennell went to the bank and told them about the tenants in the house. The bank had not heard before about the various changes in the tenancies. Even when they were told the bank made it clear that they had no intention of taking any proceedings to enter the property or to turn the tenants out or anything of that kind. The bank were not concerned to get possession.

Then Mr Quennell's lawyers in London advised him that there was a good way in which possession could be achieved. This is what it was: Mr Quennell's wife, Mrs Quennell, paid off the bank. She paid the £2,500 which was owing to the bank and took a transfer of the charge. The bank transferred it to her by a transfer dated 17th January 1978.

Then Mrs Quennell brought proceedings against the tenants Mr Maltby and Mr Lupton seeking possession. She said that she stood in the shoes of the bank; and, seeing that the tenancy was granted without the consent of the bank, it was void. So she could recover possession.

Now it has been held that, when the bank holds a charge and there is a clause in it whereby there are to be no tenancies granted or surrendered except with the consent of the bank in writing, then in those circumstances, if the mortgagor does thereafter grant tenancies without the consent of the bank, then those tenancies are not binding on the bank and the tenants are not entitled to the protection of the Rent Acts. This was held in *Dudley and District Benefit Building Society v Emerson* (above). Mrs Quennell relies on that case. She says that, as transferee of the legal charge, she stands in the shoes of the bank and can obtain possession. [Her objective was plain] ... It was not to enforce the security or to obtain repayment or anything of that kind. It was in order to get possession of the house and to overcome the protection of the Rent Acts.

Is that permissible? It seems to me that this is one of those cases where equity steps in to mitigate the rigour of the law. Long years ago it did the same when it invented the equity of redemption. As is said in Snell's Principles of Equity:

> 'The courts of equity left the legal effect of the transaction unaltered but declared it to be unreasonable and against conscience that the mortgagee should retain as owner for his own benefit what was intended as a mere security.'

So here in modern times equity can step in so as to prevent a mortgagee, or a transferee from him, from getting possession of a house contrary to the justice of the case. A mortgagee will be restrained from getting possession except when it is sought bona fide and reasonably for the purpose of enforcing the security and then only subject to such conditions as the court thinks fit to impose. When the bank itself or a building society lends the money, then it may well be right to allow the mortgagee to obtain possession when the borrower is in default. But so long as the interest is paid and there is nothing outstanding, equity has ample power to restrain any unjust use of the right to possession.

It is plain that in this transaction Mr and Mrs Quennell had an ulterior motive. It was not done to enforce the security or due payment of the principal or interest. It was done for the purpose of getting possession of the house in order to resell it at a profit. It was done so as to avoid the protection which the Rent Acts afford to tenants in their occupation. If Mr Quennell himself had sought to evict the tenants, he would not be allowed to do so. He could not say the tenancies were void. He would be estopped from saying so. They certainly would be protected against him. Are they protected against his wife now that she is the transferee of the charge? In my opinion they are protected, for this simple reason : she is not seeking possession for the purpose of enforcing the loan or the interest of anything of that kind. She is doing it simply for an ulterior purpose of getting possession of the house, contrary to the intention of Parliament as expressed in the Rent Acts.

On that simple ground it seems to me that this action fails and it should be dismissed. The legal right to possession is not to be enforced when it is sought for an ulterior motive. I would on this account allow the appeal and dismiss the action for possession.

Bridge and Templeman L.JJ. agreed.

C Joint tenants/flatsharers

The Rent Acts were conceived with lettings to families principally in mind. However, many people live in privately rented accommodation, sharing that accommodation with others. It has often been difficult to determine the legal status of flatsharers for the purposes of the Rent Acts. Much will depend on the circumstances surrounding the creation of the tenancy. A number of possible classifications may be suggested.[4]

(a) They are all classified as joint tenants. See *Lloyd* v. *Sadler* [1978] 2 All E.R. 529 (C.A.).

MEGAW L.J. : By an agreement in writing a tenancy of the top floor flat, 22 Cottesmore Gardens, London W8, was granted by the landlord to Miss G Sadler and Miss M Lunt from 27th December 1975 to 25th December 1976. The tenancy was a protected tenancy under the Rent Act 1968. On about 28th October 1976 Miss Lunt left the flat in order to get married. She did not intend to resume, and she did not in fact resume, occupation of the flat. Miss Sadler remained in occupation of the flat during the remainder of the contractual tenancy, and she continued in occupation after 25th December 1976 when the contractual tenancy ended. In January 1977 the landlord started proceedings in the West London County Court, claiming possession of the flat. The defendants were Miss Sadler and three other ladies whom Miss Sadler had brought in to live in the flat as her licensees. No separ-

---

4. For further discussion see Aldridge (1974); Adams (1976); Martin (1978).

ate question arises as to them. Their right to stay in occupation stands or falls with that of Miss Sadler. So much for the relevant facts.

The question of law also can be simply stated. Was Miss Sadler a statutory tenant and thus entitled to the security of tenure given to statutory tenants by the Rent Acts, despite the fact that Miss Lunt, before the contractual tenancy had ended, had ceased, permanently, to occupy the flat?

The contractual tenancy was a joint tenancy of Miss Sadler and Miss Lunt. The contractual tenancy ended on 25th December 1976. The right of Miss Sadler to remain in possession thereafter, if it existed at all, could exist only because she had become the statutory tenant ... The landlord contended that the contractual, admittedly protected, tenancy was a joint tenancy; and that, as a result of the doctrine of joint tenancy in the law of property, anything that had to be done in connection with the joint tenancy, to have any legal effect, had to be done by the joint tenants; that is, by all the individuals acting collectively. One of the joint tenants, it was submitted (otherwise than when in law one joint tenant could be treated as acting as agent for them all), could not achieve any result recognised by law, he could not act validly, by anything which he himself did as an individual. Hence Miss Sadler's continuance in occupation of the flat after the end of the contractual tenancy did not, in law, produce the result that 'the protected tenant ... occupies the dwelling-house as his residence'. Hence there was no statutory tenant. Miss Sadler did not achieve that status in law. That submission by the landlord was rejected by Judge McIntyre in his judgment delivered on 23rd March 1977. The landlord appeals to this court.

This case has brought to light two remarkable facts. First, the Rent Acts through all their long history have never made any relevant express provision relating to joint tenants or joint tenancies, whether protected or statutory. Secondly, and perhaps even more strangely, there seems to have been no previous case decided by any court, or at least no reported case, in which a question such as falls to be decided in the present case has been raised for consideration ... Yet there must have been, over the years, thousands of instances in which one of two joint tenants has ceased to occupy the dwelling-house before the end of the contractual tenancy, and the other original joint tenant has continued to live there, on the assumption that he has become the statutory tenant. If the landlord's submission is right, that assumption has been wrong. Similar instances must have arisen thousands of times where two or more persons have duly become 'the statutory tenant', and thereafter one or more of them has, or have, died or ceased to occupy the house as his, or their, residence. What is the effect on the legal status of the person, or persons, remaining in occupation? Does the statutory security of tenure cease?

I do not think that the absence of previous litigation helps one way or the other towards a decision of the issue. But the fact that there are likely to be very many cases with facts similar to those of the present case shows the practical importance of this issue. Whatever the answer be, it must affect many people, landlords and tenants, in a matter of great importance to them. If the landlord's submissions in the present case are wrong, the result may be a measure of prejudice to landlords. It would mean that a landlord who looked to two persons as both being liable to him for the rent might find that when the contractual tenancy ended there was only one person who was liable to him for the rent. On the other hand, if the landlord's submissions are right, the potential prejudice to joint tenants would be very much more serious; that is, the value of their legal rights as compared with what those legal rights would be if the landlord's submissions are wrong.

In view of the importance of the issue, it may be helpful to set out the landlord's submissions as they were conveniently summarised by his counsel in nine propositions, in the course of his very clear and careful argument: (1) The grant to Miss Sadler and Miss Lunt of a contractual tenancy resulted in Miss Sadler and Miss Lunt being joint tenants. (2) Therefore 'the tenant' under the contractual tenancy was Miss Sadler and Miss Lunt. (3) The contractual tenancy was a protected tenancy. (4) Therefore 'the protected tenant' was Miss Sadler and Miss Lunt. (5) On the determination of a protected tenancy a statutory tenancy can only arise 'if . . . he occupies the dwelling-house as his residence'. (6) The 'he' in the above quotation clearly refers to 'the person who . . . was the protected tenant'. (7) On the determination of the protected tenancy in this case it cannot be said that Miss Sadler and Miss Lunt were occupying the dwelling-house as *their* residence. (8) Therefore the protected tenant was not occupying the premises in question on the determination of the protected tenancy in this case. (9) Therefore no statutory tenancy can arise.

If the ordinary law as to joint tenancy, as it affects rights of property, is to be treated as applicable in all its strictness to s [2](1)(a) of the [1977] Act, the logic of counsel for the landlord's propositions appears to me to be unassailable. I agree with the view expressed by Judge McIntyre that s 1(1)(b) of the Interpretation Act 1889 is not of assistance one way or the other.

I have come to the conclusion that, on the true construction of s [2](1)(a) of the [1977] Act, the ordinary law as to joint tenancy does not have to be, and ought not to be, applied in all its strictness. I base that opinion, primarily at least, on the judgment of Scrutton LJ in *Howson v Buxton* ((1928) 97 L.J.K.B. 749). It is not a direct authority. There is no direct authority. There are various decided cases to which we were properly referred as providing guidance by analogy, or as illustrating the general rule as to a joint tenancy. Some of them, or dicta in them, certainly lend support to the submissions on behalf of the landlord; but I find the most helpful guidance in *Howson v Buxton*. It appears to me to decide that, where an Act of Parliament refers to 'the tenant', and the letting is to two or more persons jointly, it is permissible for the court to hold, if so to do makes better sense of the relevant statutory provision in its particular context, that one of those persons, by himself, may for certain purposes be treated as being 'the tenant'. So here Miss Sadler can be treated, and should on the facts be treated, as having been 'the protected tenant' immediately before the términation of the contractual tenancy, and as being 'the statutory tenant' thereafter. Hence she has security of tenure under the Act.

He discussed *T. M. Fairclough* v. *Berliner* [1931] 1 Ch. 60; *Re Lower Onibury Farm* [1955] 2 Q.B. 298; *McIntyre* v. *Hardcastle* [1948] 2 K.B. 82; *Baker* v. *Lewis* [1947] K.B. 186; *Turley* v. *Panton* (1975) 29 P.&C.R. 397; and *Jacobs* v. *Chaudhuri* [1968] 2 Q.B. 470, all of which, he conceded, pointed in the landlord's favour. He continued:

In *Howson v Buxton* it was held by Scrutton L.J., with the concurrence of Sankey L.J., who expressly agreed 'for the reasons given by Scrutton, L.J.', that it was permissible for the court to hold that the statutory requirements which had to be fulfilled by 'the tenant' could validly and effectively be fulfilled by the individual act of one of the joint tenants. Thus, one of the two joint tenants could, acting by and for himself alone, give the requisite statutory notice. He could, without the concurrence or co-operation of the other participant in the joint tenancy, become entitled to the compensation which under the statute was payable to 'the tenant'. Even though it was a joint tenancy, 'his goods' could be construed to mean 'the goods which belong exclusively to one of the two joint tenants'. It did not have to be read as though, whether by the operation of the Interpretation Act 1889 or otherwise, it said 'their goods'. It will be remembered that in proposition 7 of counsel for the landlord's propositions, set out above, it was asserted as a step in his argument that the statutory tenancy could arise only if the dwelling-house could be said to be '*their* dwelling-house', that is, the dwelling-house occupied by Miss Sadler *and* Miss Lunt. Yet in *Howson v Buxton* 'his goods' (the goods of 'the tenant') applied to goods in respect of which the other joint tenant had no right of ownership.

In my opinion, the judgment of Scrutton LJ in *Howson v Buxton* shows that, where the strict application of the doctrine of joint tenancy would lead to unreasonable results, or results which the legislature is unlikely to have intended, it is permissible for the court to conclude that the legislature did not so intend; but that, instead, in such a case, the phrase 'the tenant', where there is a joint tenancy, is to be read as meaning 'the joint tenants or any one or more of them'. There is thus authority that the doctrine of joint participation by joint tenants is not a sacrosanct or immutable doctrine of statutory interpretation, where such phrases as 'the tenant' and 'the tenancy' are used. Where, then, is the line to be drawn? When does a suggested exception become a heresy? In the present case I believe that, for the purposes of s [2](1)(a) of the [1977] Act, the freedom from strict doctrinal restraint should, as in *Howson v Buxton*, be held to apply.

I would therefore hold that Miss Sadler became a statutory tenant on the expiration of the contractual tenancy on 25th December 1976, and that she so remains. I would dismiss the appeal.

Lawton and Shaw L.JJ. delivered concurring judgments.

The importance of the landlord knowing the identity of all the joint tenants was stressed in *Hanstown Properties Ltd* v. *Green* (1978) 246 E.G. 917 (C.A.).

(*b*) There are a number of individual tenants sharing the accommodation. In such cases it is necessary that each has some element of 'exclusive occupation' (see Rent Act 1977, s. 22, above, p. 172).

(*c*) There is a single tenant, and the sharers are either sub-tenants (see above, pp. 40, 90 and 225–7) or mere licensees (see above, pp. 97–119). If the original tenant leaves, the remaining sub-tenants/licensees will only have such statutory protections as are afforded to persons falling within those legal statutes.

(*d*) None of the occupiers is a tenant because they occupy under a 'valid' non-exclusive occupation agreement (above, pp. 119–48). In such case they will all be licensees. If the accommodation is furnished, and each has some right of exclusive occupation, they may have 'restricted contracts' (above, pp. 221–5).

D Rental purchase

'Rental purchase' is described by Francis (1971, pp. 112–13) thus:

Rental purchase is a mode of house purchase – unevenly spread about the country and commoner in the north than the south – used chiefly for the sale of the sort of house that would be unlikely to qualify for a mortgage to the sort of purchaser of whom the same is true (though local authorities occasionally employ it). It is really the purchase of houses on the instalment system. Though arrangements vary, the commonest pattern is that A agrees to sell B a house for, say, £500, to be paid by instalments of, say, £3 a week, B meanwhile being given the right to occupy as licensee and becoming liable to discharge all outgoings: when B's £3s have amounted to £500 the house is transferred often merely by the handing over of title deeds, the As and Bs not being the sort of people to whom the employment of (or the spending of money on) solicitor's services come naturally. The true rental purchase involves no mortgage, and should not be confused with the 'mortgage back' system in which sales takes place at the outset and the dwelling is then mortgaged to the vendor.

We were informed that about three years ago, it having been alleged that 'rental purchase' was simply a means of evading the Rent Act, the Department made a study of the system. The conclusion reached was that it did represent a genuine form of house purchase and did serve a useful purpose in that for some people it was probably their only hope of home ownership; it was held therefore that the system should not be prohibited or burdened with restrictions that would kill it. The study concluded that further consideration should be given to the question whether the purchaser under this system should be given certain protections *as* a purchaser, such as by empowering county courts, when making orders for possession of dwellings subject to rental purchase agreements where the purchaser had fallen into arrears with his instalments, to suspend the orders on conditions varying the terms for recovery of payments by instalments.

The study took in the possibility that the system might be used to evade the Rent Act by the disguising of tenancies as rental purchase agreements, but concluded, in the light of the dictum in *Hopwood* v. *Hough* ([1944] L.J.N.C.C.R. 80) that the Rent Acts would apply to an occupancy under an alleged contract to purchase which could not be regarded as a bona fide contract, that the courts could be relied on to frustrate any such attempts that might reach them.

The legal problems arising from such transactions have been discussed on a number of occasions (see, e.g., Tyler (1971), Hoggett (1972) and (1975)). Are payments under a rental purchase scheme 'rent' for the purposes of the Rent Act? Can it be said that the transactions are a 'sham' designed to evade the Acts? (See *Martin* v. *Davies* (1952) 42 T.C. 114; *Dunthorne and Shore* v. *Wiggins* [1943] 2 All E.R. 678.) Is the purchaser a 'residential occupier' for the purposes of the Protection from Eviction Act 1977 (below, p. 448)? Can a purchaser claim equitable relief against 'forfeiture' (i.e. re-possession) if he fails to keep up the payments? (See now the special jurisdiction given to the Court in Housing Act 1980, s. 88.) What is the effect of the Consumer Credit Act 1974 on such arrangements? These issues will not be pursued here; but changes in the law contained in Housing Act 1980, Supplementary Benefit Regulations, 1980, and Protection From Eviction Act 1977 should be noted.

An interesting discussion of the social consequences arising from rental purchase schemes in a poor area of Birmingham is in Shutt and Stewart (1976). A recent account of rental purchase in East London is in *The Economist* (5 May 1979).

9. Problems of jurisdiction

Given the complexity of the law discussed above, it may on occasion be hard to determine which legal category a particular fact situation falls into. This raises the question of who has jurisdiction to decide such questions. There are a number of possibilities (see Pettit (1977)).

A The rent-fixing agencies

Those whose task it is to fix rents – rent officers, rent assessment committees and rent tribunals (see generally, below, chapter 5) – are said to have an inherent jurisdiction to determine questions relating to their jurisdiction.

In *R. v. Fulham, Hammersmith and Kensington Rent Tribunal ex parte Zerek* [1951] 2 K.B. 1, Devlin J. stated:

> When, at the inception of an inquiry by a tribunal of limited jurisdiction, a challenge is made to their jurisdiction, the tribunal have to make up their minds whether they will act or not, and for that purpose to arrive at some decision on whether they have jurisdiction or not.

In *R. v. Brent London Borough Rent Officer, ex parte Ganatra* [1976] 1 Q.B. 576, the Divisional Court considered the extent to which the above dictum applied to the work of Rent Assessment Committees. Park J. thought that the primary task of these committees was to review the rent already fixed by a rent officer, not to act as an appeal body on questions of jurisdiction. Thus he concluded that Rent Assessment Committees could only consider questions relating to their jurisdiction if new facts came to light which had not been presented to the Rent Officer.

In *R. v. Croydon and South West London Rent Tribunal, ex parte Ryzewska* [1977] 1 All E.R. 312, any suggestion that the decision in *Ganatra* had undermined the generality of the principle in *Zerek* was rejected by Caulfield J., giving the principal judgment of the Divisional Court. He said, in part:

> So when the question of jurisdiction is raised before a rent tribunal, the rent tribunal should look at all the circumstances. Plainly the tribunal would not deny the wishes of a party before it to test the question of jurisdiction under s [141], but of course it all depends on the circumstances of the particular case. In this particular case, on its facts, what the tribunal did before proceeding to determine the question of jurisdiction was to give the parties the opportunity, if they so wished, to test the quality of the letting by going to the county court – an invitation that was not accepted.
>
> In my judgment the rent tribunal proceeded strictly according to the principles which should be observed by a tribunal in a situation such as this. What a tribunal will do in future on certain given facts remains to be seen. But

what the tribunal should do where there is an alternative forum (as there is here under s [141]) is to listen to the contentions of the parties and make up their own minds there and then whether it is better for them to proceed with the determination, having first of all decided the preliminary point of jurisdiction. Even if they decide the preliminary point of jurisdiction wrongly, it would mean that the person who has been aggrieved by that particular determination is not precluded from testing henceforth in the county court on the particular facts of his case his rights under s [141].

This passage suggests there may be particularly complex fact situations in which it would be improper for a rent tribunal to proceed; but this will not be the usual case. In any event, the parties can always go to the county court after the rent tribunal has finished its work.

Further, in *R*. v. *Rent Officer for Kensington and Chelsea, ex parte Noel* [1977] 1 All E.R. 356, Slynn J. said, in part:

Accordingly in my judgment *R v Brent London Borough Rent Officer, ex parte Ganatra* [above] is not to be construed as meaning, and was not intended to mean, that whenever a question falling within s [141] arises the rent officer must automatically leave the disputed issue to be decided ... In the present case in my judgment the rent officer was entitled to conclude on the material before him that it was proper for him to proceed to a decision on the jurisdictional fact as to whether there was a tenancy at all. This is a matter which must frequently arise in cases of this sort and it is clearly Parliament's intention that decisions under the Rent Act 1968 shall be dealt with expeditiously and cheaply by rent officers. I would therefore not myself intefere with his decision simply because he went ahead.

(Notwithstanding these observations, the Divisional Court quashed the rent officer's decision on the grounds that he had decided a difficult question of jurisdiction solely on the basis of submissions made and arguments put before him by solicitors to the parties. What he should have done was to hear oral evidence on the issues and have permitted, if necessary, cross-examination.)

B The county court

The county court has an extensive jurisdiction to determine questions that might arise in Rent Act cases and issue a declaration (Rent Act 1977, s. 141). It may be noted that, in a number of the cases just cited, the Divisional Court emphasized that the county court was the best place for the resolution of such matters. Lord Widgery C.J. was clearly anxious that his court, already very busy, should not become overburdened with Rent Act cases.

It is usually assumed that only the parties to the dispute are able to seek a declaration before the county court. Could the rent-fixing agencies themselves take a complex case to the court? Should they be given the power so to do? (See Partington, 1975b.)

C The High Court

Under the Tribunals and Enquiries Act 1971, s. 13, any party to proceedings before either a rent tribunal or a rent assessment committee (but *not* a rent officer) may, if dissatisfied on a point of law with a decision of that tribunal, 'either appeal therefrom to the High Court, or require the tribunal to state and sign a case for the opinion of the High Court'.

More generally there is, under R.S.C. Order 53, the possibility of seeking judicial review. The full range of circumstances in which judicial review may be sought is beyond the scope of this book (see generally, de Smith, 1980); however, one of the grounds for seeking review is that the original decision-taker lacked the jurisdiction to decide the case.

Despite Lord Widgery's pleas that the county court should be regarded as the normal place for discussion of such questions, it may be noted that there may be occasions on which an application to the High Court is essential (Arden, 1978a, p. 116).

5
Rent and Rent Regulation

Introduction

The bulk of this chapter will be devoted to an analysis of the various systems of rent regulation that exist in Britain with, as usual, particular emphasis on housing rents. Before that, I wish to introduce a brief discussion of the theories of rent, and also to look at the common law on the obligation of tenants to pay rent.

1. Theories of rent

Lawyers tend to regard rent in positivistic terms. Rent is 'a retribution or compensation for the land demised. It is defined to be a certain profit issuing yearly out of lands and tenements corporeal' (Woodfall, 1978, para. 1-0679; *C.H. Bailey* v. *Memorial Enterprises* [1974] 1 All E.R. 1003). Such a definition, however meaningful for lawyers, tells us very little about the social and economic functions of rent. This is an extremely complex and controversial issue which is beyond the scope of this book and its author to explore in detail. However, it is important to realize that different analyses of the functions of rent are possible.

For example, Wallace F. Smith (1970, pp. 18–21) argues:

> The term *rent* . . . is, of course, a very familiar word . . . in its ordinary sense – the payment made by a tenant for the right to live in a dwelling which belongs to another. To the economist, however, the word 'rent' conveys something more than this . . .
>
> To begin with, economists have traditionally given the name 'rent' to the price of a commodity which is fixed in supply. Land, whether agricultural or urban, fits in this category. Housing or other buildings are relatively fixed

in supply, because they are so durable that the size of the stock changes very slowly...

The problem with rent is to understand why it should be paid at all. The equilibrium price of something which is absolutely fixed in supply is determined entirely by demand. If I own an acre of land in the wilderness, the demand for it will be very limited and my rental income will be very modest. If this acre of land is located at the centre of a large, prosperous city, however, the demand will be so great that rent from this land will provide me with a handsome income. The land is a free gift of nature, however, wherever it is located. It cost nothing to produce and the supply cannot be expanded at any price. If nothing at all is paid as rent for the land, this acre continues to exist and to be useful. Why should I receive a handsome income from rent-payers if I happen to own some city land? Why should the city landowner receive more than the owner of wilderness land? The existence of rent raises questions of equity or fairness. Why should one owner receive more rent than another owner receives? Why should tenants pay for something which is essentially 'costless'?

The issue of equity is obscured somewhat by two notions about 'cost'. The owner of a building may feel that the rents he collects are only a fair return on the price he paid for the building, that is, on his cost of acquiring the property. This investment cost, however, did not represent a use of physical resources and so it is not a 'cost' in the economist's sense. The price of an existing building may be said to represent the capitalized value of the rents expected from that building, using 'rents' in our specialized sense of a payment in excess of resource cost. The present owner of a building has simply paid the previous owner in advance much or all of the expected future economic rent from the property. A transfer in ownership seems to disguise, but does not really change, the 'unnecessary' nature of rental payments because financial investment costs are transfers of wealth rather than sacrifices of physical resources.

Suppose, however, that the present owner of a building was responsible for having it constructed in the first place. Certainly, buildings, unlike land, can be created out of other resources and these resources have real economic cost. Are not rent payments necessary to recover these real costs? The property owner would certainly argue that they are.

Unfortunately for his argument, the real costs incurred in constructing a building must be considered 'sunk' for business and economic purposes. If the building does not earn rent, the costs cannot be withdrawn. There is no alternative, once the building has been completed, but to let it be used for whatever rent it will bring. The level of rents has no necessary relation to the historical costs incurred. An extravagantly constructed building may represent costs far greater than the capitalized value of market-determined rents, and a building constructed just before an inflation may produce rents greatly in excess of its historical cost. Rent is not dependent on historic building costs, and historic costs thus do not require that tenants pay rent to occupy the building. Again we must ask, why should rents be paid?

The answer lies in the word 'rationing'. If some useful commodity is fixed in supply, then it becomes important in both an economic and a business sense to use that commodity as fully and effectively as possible. If no rents were charged for the use of land or buildings, these commodities might be used by people who derive relatively little advantage from them to the exclusion of people who can use them most beneficially. The high rent asked for land near the centre of a city prices it out of the agricultural market and limits that land to business use, for which it is best suited. Without the rent payment, it might be used as a farm, greatly disrupting the business activities of the city. Economic rent rations a fixed resource by excluding all potential users except the one who derives maximum benefit from that resource. Very broadly, all market prices are rationing devices and economic rent is an important special type. Most prices are also related to resource costs, but there are no resource costs in rents to obscure the rationing function.

On this neo-classical economic analysis, the function of rent with its emphasis on rationing can be seen as an aspect of more general theories of land use (Harvey, 1973, p. 177). Marxist writers have criticized the limitations of the neo-classical approach, arguing that it ignores or disguises the nature of 'social relations' that exist between those who pay and those who receive rent (Massey & Catalano, 1978, especially ch. 2). From this perspective, the functions of rent are dependent on the political economic structures of particular societies. As Bierne puts it (1977, p. 56): 'Crucially the [neo-classical] model ignores the role of power in determining the origin and distribution of effective demand ... [The] level of rent at any moment is much more a function of the relative strength of those who receive and those who pay rent.'

There are, obviously, fundamentally different political implications to be derived from these contrasting analyses. The Marxist position is part of a more general analysis of the essential conflict between the bourgeoisie (including landowners) and the working class. The final solution to that conflict, which includes the power imbalance between landlords and tenants described above, can, it is argued, only be resolved by a confrontation with capitalism itself (Edel, 1977). However, since this position has not yet been the basis for widespread political action in Britain it will not be further discussed here.

What has happened in Britain is that, as we saw in chapter 1, the efficiency of the rationing function of rent has been frequently called into question, particularly as a basis for the allocation of housing to the poor. A series of political responses have been devised in attempts to encourage the rationing function to operate in a more equitable fashion. This has not, on the whole, been attempted by comprehensive measures designed to improve the overall financial position of the poor and the low-paid. Instead, there has been a complex series of measures designed in particular to subsidize housing costs. Some of these have been indirect, e.g. limiting the levels of rents chargeable by landlords; others have been direct, e.g. the provision of subsidized housing, or, more recently, means-tested rent rebates and allowances. Of course it is not just the poor, nor tenants, who have been subsidized. All owner-occupiers benefit from the tax rule that the sale of one's principal residence is exempt from capital gains tax; and for those buying on mortgage, interest payments may be set off against income tax. Indeed, it is widely argued that the present system of housing finance is extremely regressive, benefiting the better-off rather than the poor. (See, e.g., Kilroy, 1978; Grey, Hepworth & Odling-Smee, 1978.)

2. The legal obligation to pay rent

At common law, no rent had to be reserved for a valid lease to be created. This depends essentially on the intention of the parties, interpreted where necessary by the courts. However, the existence of a rent is often extremely helpful in determining whether a lease exists. (For tenancies within the Rent Acts, rent must be paid, see above, p. 176.)

If, as is usually the case, rent is reserved then it must be a profit. But it need not be a money payment: 'it may as well be in delivery of hens, capons, roses, spurs, bowes, shafts, horses, haws, pepper, cummin, wheat or other profit...' (Coke, 1670, p. 142a). Further, it must be certain, or capable of being reduced to certainty.

In *Greater London Council* v. *Connelly* [1970] 2 Q.B. 100, a council tenant (representing $2\frac{1}{2}\%$ of all GLC tenants who had been on rent strike) challenged a condition on his rent card which stated that the rent and other sums shown on the rent card 'are liable to be increased or decreased on notice being given'. Notice of increase had been given; but it did not comply with Prices and Incomes Act 1968, s. 12(3), which states that notices of increase of rent must tell the tenant of his right to terminate the tenancy. The tenants argued first that this section provided a procedure for all rent increases. The Court of Appeal disagreed. Secondly, it was argued that the notices issued by the GLC were to be regarded as invalid since the formulation of the rent was not sufficiently certain to meet the common law criteria. Not surprisingly, however, it was decided that the rent clause *was* certain. Lord Denning M.R. (*ibid.*, at 108) said: 'The courts are always loath to hold a condition bad for uncertainty. They will give it a reasonable interpretation whenever possible. It is possible here...' (See, too, *Brown* v. *Gould* [1972] Ch. 53, where an option to review a tenancy in 21 years' time at a rent 'to be fixed having regard to the market value of the premises at the time of exercising the option taking into account to the advantage of the tenant any increased value of such premises attributable to structural improvements made by the tenant during the ... present lease' was held to be valid by Megarry J.).

Where there is a formally documented lease or tenancy, the tenant's covenant to pay rent will invariably be one of the terms (see above, pp. 73, 75). Even where there is no such term, the courts will protect the right of the landlord by implying an obligation to pay rent. The full extent of this obligation was discussed in *Youngmin* v. *Heath* [1974] 1 W.L.R. 135.

LORD DENNING M.R.; Mr. Youngmin, the plaintiff, is the owner of a house – no. 31 Hartham Road, London, N.7. Some years ago his predecessor let two rooms furnished to Miss Reni at £3 a week. She shared the bath and w.c. with other tenants. Mr. Youngmin bought the house. Her tenancy continued. She paid rent to Mr. Youngmin regularly until October 3, 1970. Then she was taken ill and died on October 29, 1970. She had made no will and died intestate. Mr. Youngmin did not take possession of the two rooms. He left them as they were. His furniture remained there. Her clothing remained there. The rooms were left unoccupied. Miss Reni had no relatives living in this country. Her only relation was a sister who lived in Russia. This sister instructed a lawyer, a Mr. Heath, in London to take out administration of Miss Reni's estate. He took it out as attorney for the sister. The letters of administration were granted on May 24, 1972. The administrator claimed the clothing of Miss Reni. He also terminated the tenancy of the two rooms. On September 26, 1972, he gave to Mr. Youngmin a notice to terminate the tenancy on October 28, 1972.

Now Mr. Youngmin claims the rent of £3 a week from the last time it was paid by Miss Reni on October 3, 1970, up to the time of the expiry of the notice to quit on October 28, 1972. He claims the rent from Mr. Heath, the defendant, as the attorney administrator of the estate of Miss Reni. Mr. Youngmin admits that there are the clothes in the rooms and that Mr. Heath can take them. But the question is whether he is entitled to sue Mr. Heath for the rent. Mr. Heath says that the liability for rent ceased when Miss Reni died, and that he, as administrator, is not liable thereafter because he never entered into possession ... When there is an ordinary letting of premises furnished or unfurnished at a weekly rent the tenancy does not determine on the tenant's death. It is an implied term that the obligation to pay rent continues *during the currency of the tenancy*. This is a contractual obligation which binds the tenant and his personal representative to pay rent so long as the tenancy continues – that is, until it is determined by proper notice to terminate it. If the tenant dies and the executor does not take possession, the personal representative must fulfil the obligation to pay the rent, but only to the extent of the assets in his hands ... The administrator is liable for the rent to the extent of the deceased's assets until the tenancy is properly determined by notice to quit.

Stamp and Roskill L.JJ. agreed.

Legal recognition of the importance of the landlord's right to rent is also indicated in the wide range of remedies which are available to the landlord for breach of the covenant. Distress for rent, the recovery of rent by ordinary action for debt, compensation for use and occupation and, as a last resort, the right to forfeit the lease or tenancy are discussed below (pp. 301–3).

3. Statutory rent restrictions

We have already discussed (above, pp. 152–7) the circumstances in which control of housing rents was introduced in 1915. Before looking at the details of the law it is worth stressing that it is not just in the housing field that statutory rent regulation provisions operate. For example, under the Agricultural Holdings Act 1948, s. 8, there is a statutory procedure for referring the rents of agricultural tenancies to arbitration. Under the Landlord and Tenant Act 1954, s. 34, rent levels of business tenancies may be referred to the court. Admittedly the criteria on which such regulation is based are quite different. Broadly, the rent is to be the full market rent, but with the exclusion of certain matters such as the value of improvements made by the tenant. It is sometimes suggested that a similar formula be adopted for residential accommodation; what might be the arguments for or against this suggestion?

Latest estimates of the numbers of controlled and regulated tenancies may be found in Table 1.3, above, p. 14.

4. Rent control

The first method of restricting rent levels was Rent Control. Although the details of the scheme changed with great frequency (see above, pp. 153–6), the basic principle was that houses within the relevant rateable value limits had their rents controlled according to strict formulae and increases were only permitted in exceptional circumstances.

Since from a date to be specified after the passing of the Housing Act 1980 most controlled tenancies will be able to be converted into regulated tenancies (Housing Act 1980, s. 62(1)), the system of control will not be further discussed. (For an outline, see the first edition of this book, pp. 177–8.)

5. Rent regulation

The Rent Act 1965 introduced rent regulation, based on the principle of the 'fair rent'. The statutory definition of the 'fair rent' is to be found in Rent Act 1977, s. 70 (as amended by Housing Act 1980, Schedule 25).

70.—(1) In determining, for the purposes of this Part of this Act, what rent is or would be a fair rent under a regulated tenancy of a dwelling-house, regard shall be had to all the circumstances (other than personal circumstances) and in particular to –

    (a) the age, character, locality and state of repair of the dwelling-house, and

    (b) if any furniture is provided for use under the tenancy, the quantity, quality and condition of the furniture.

(2) For the purposes of the determination it shall be assumed that the number of persons seeking to become tenants of similar dwelling-houses in the locality on the terms (other than those relating to rent) of the regulated tenancy is not substantially greater than the number of such dwelling-houses in the locality which are available for letting on such terms.

(3) There shall be disregarded –

    (a) any disrepair or other defect attributable to a failure by the tenant under the regulated tenancy or any predecessor in title of his to comply with any terms thereof;

    (b) any improvement carried out, otherwise than in pursuance of the terms of the tenancy, by the tenant under the regulated tenancy or any predecessor in title of his;

    [(c) and (d) repealed (ed.)]

(e) if any furniture is provided for use under the regulated tenancy, any improvement to the furniture by the tenant under the regulated tenancy or any predecessor in title of his or, as the case may be, any deterioration in the condition of the furniture due to any ill-treatment by the tenant, any person residing or lodging with him, or any sub-tenant of his.

(4) In this section 'improvement' includes the replacement of any fixture or fitting.

Section 70[1] was examined by the Francis Committee (1971), whose report, despite subsequent changes in the law, contains the only detailed discussion of its operation. Many of the provisions are not thought to cause much difficulty, merely raising familiar points of valuation. The most controversial is the working of s. 70(2), on which the Committee had the following to say (Francis, 1971, pp. 57–61):

We have inquired fully into the operation of S. [70](2) – normally referred to as the 'scarcity' section – and the main points which have emerged in the course of the evidence are the following:

(a) We have received a good deal of evidence – mainly from persons or bodies who have not been actually engaged in the task – to the effect that the assessment of the scarcity element in the rent is an extremely difficult task and, indeed, that scarcity is incapable of measurement except by way of an intelligent guess. Even the Institute of Rent Officers tell us: 'Essentially it is a matter of opinion whether a rent is inflated by an excess of demand, and, if so, to what extent'. Certainly, it is now generally, if not universally, accepted that it is not possible to quantify the scarcity element directly. Initially, a practice arose of asessing the scarcity element in terms of a percentage of the market rent, such as 5, 15, 33⅓ or 40 per cent. But this practice has long since been abandoned. The method now generally adopted in assessing the fair rent involves a threefold approach, viz

(i) *To look at comparables*

Rent Officers have over the years built up a comprehensive register of rents for different types of properties in various localities in their area, and it is now possible to find comparable properties in the register whose registered rents were accepted by the parties without appeal, or were fixed on appeal by the Rent Assessment Committee. These rents are taken as a guide, subject to any necessary adjustment due to changes of circumstances which have occurred since the rents were registered.

(ii) *To look at market rents recently negotiated for properties in respect of which there is no scarcity*

It is clear that this is the method of approach favoured by professional

1. At the time it was Rent Act 1968, s. 46.

valuers. These properties will, as a rule, be properties of a much superior character to the subject dwellings and therefore a good deal of adjustment or 'extrapolation' will be required. No doubt, professional valuers are quite capable of doing this, and we think that Rent Officers, after gaining experience of this kind of exercise and with the guidance afforded by Rent Assessment Committees, should be able to do the same with a fair degree of accuracy. This method is clearly described by the President of the London Panel in his most helpful and comprehensive memorandum of evidence as follows:

'Furthermore, the London Rent Assessment Panel has always accepted the view that a valuer can, and as a matter of practice constantly does, compare for value dwellings and properties not themselves similar in detail but where, from experience, it is known that the value of the one can be a guide to the value of the other. Thus, in order to ascertain what is a fair rent for a dwelling where the supply falls far short of the demand, valuers can and do use the known values for dwellings where the supply and demand is in accordance with the balance in this sub-section and to make the necessary adjustments to arrive at a fair rent. The London Rent Assessment Panel consequently accepts the proposition that in that area of the residential dwelling market where the circumstances of supply and demand are broadly in line with this sub-section then the market rent and the fair rent will be close to each other and sometimes the same figure. Nevertheless, the fair rent can never be higher than the market rent. The fair rent will be lower than the market rent when, all the other factors in this whole section having been taken into account, the market rent is a higher figure than it would have been because of the excess of demand over supply. Thus, in cases where the assumptions have some effect, that effect is limited to certain factors, leaving all other factors (e.g. the cost of repairs or of the provision of services) to accord with the facts of the case and the current market at the relevant time.'

(iii) *To calculate what would be a reasonable rent on the basis of various conventional valuation criteria* e.g. fair return on capital value, economic cost, gross value.

The fair rent seems to be an amalgam of the results produced by these lines of approach. Where there is a scarcity element in the market rent, the fair rent thus arrived at will be less than the market rent. The difference represents the scarcity element.

EVIDENCE OF SCARCITY
(*b*) It appears that very little evidence is submitted to Rent Officers and Rent Assessment Committees on the issue of scarcity. Such evidence is hardly ever presented by tenants or individual landlords, although no doubt surveyor witnesses for the larger company landlords will often seek to show that the scarcity element in the market rent is small or non-existent. The result is that

Rent Officers and Rent Assessment Committees have to rely a great deal on their own knowledge of the locality. Rent Officers will often be better informed about local conditions than members of Rent Assessment Committees, and no doubt the latter for this reason will attach much weight to the Rent Officers' views on scarcity. It is obviously desirable, however, that at least one member of the Rent Assessment Committee should be reasonably familiar with housing conditions in the locality. Although Rent Officers and Rent Assessment Committees no longer attempt to quantify scarcity directly, they still have to decide as a preliminary matter whether or not the market rent for accommodation similar to the subject dwelling is affected by scarcity. The sort of evidence which is material to this enquiry will include the following:

(i) *Direct evidence of the demand for the subject dwelling, or for similar accommodation offered for letting on the same terms (except as to rent)*

If it is shown that there was a large demand for the accommodation, that might be evidence of scarcity. Conversely, a slight demand, or long delay in finding a tenant notwithstanding extensive advertisement, might well be evidence of no scarcity. It is clear, however, that evidence of the quantum of demand must be treated with caution. One specific criticism we have heard of section [70](2) is that the level of demand is not a reliable yardstick for measuring scarcity because the extent of the demand is affected by the level of the rent. It is said that if the landlord pitches his rent at a high level, he will thereby reduce the demand, and be able to argue that there is no scarcity. But it seems to us that, in such a case, the low level of demand, or the difficulty in finding a tenant, is no evidence of supply and demand being in balance. On the contrary, if the rent is excessive, the fact that nonetheless the landlord was able to find a tenant may be some evidence of scarcity. Conversely, if the rent is low, the fact that there was a large number of applicants for the dwelling is no evidence of scarcity. Evidence as to the level of demand is only relevant insofar as it is shown that the demand is related to the shortage of available accommodation of a similar character for renting.

(ii) *Movement of population*

A large influx of workers to the locality due to the establishment of new factories, or, conversely, the departure from the locality of a substantial number of workers due to the transfer of a large business to another part of the country, may be relevant evidence.

(iii) *Availability of local authority housing*

We have had evidence that, in certain provincial cities, local authority housing is available after a very short interval, if not almost immediately, not only for inhabitants of long standing but even for newcomers to the city. This would be pretty strong evidence of the absence of scarcity in the case of comparable accommodation. On the other hand, a long waiting list for local authority housing might well be evidence of scarcity although not necessarily so. Some local authorities allow anybody, including owner-occupiers, to put their names on the list, others require an applicant to possess residential and other qualifications. The significance to be attached to the waiting list will depend on the conditions of eligibility in the relevant area.

(iv) *Evidence of the prevalence of overcrowding or multi-occupation, or of the displacement of a large number of (say) furnished tenants* as the result of local authority or private re-development or road improvements, might also be evidence of scarcity.

EFFECT OF SCARCITY ON THE RENT OF SUBJECT DWELLING

(*c*) It is not, however, enough for the Rent Officer to find that there is scarcity of rented accommodation in the relevant locality in a general sense. He has further to decide whether the rent of the subject dwelling is affected by the scarcity. Scarcity is only relevant if it is related to the type of accommodation to which the subject dwelling belongs. The fact that there is scarcity of low-rented accommodation in a given locality does not mean that the market rents of a high grade block of flats in the same locality are affected by the scarcity. In this connection, two submissions were made to us by the Institute of Rent Officers in their written evidence, which perhaps call for some comment.

'(i) In our view if an Area is one of acute shortage of rented accommodation the excess demand will permeate the whole field of rented housing ... in conditions of acute housing shortage would-be tenants will usually be forced to enter a zone they would normally think beyond them.'

Whilst we would accept the latter part of this statement as a broad proposition (although 'usually' is a bit strong), we think the first part is too categorical.

'(ii) It seems to us there is danger in an assumption that one type or class of premises in an Area where rented accommodation is scarce can be taken in isolation and its fair rent determined without consideration of, or reference to, the fair rent levels of other types or classes of premises in that Area which have been determined as directed by the Statute.'

If this means that when fixing the fair rent for a high grade type of dwelling, one should have regard to the registered rents of inferior properties, then it seems to us that such a line of approach would contravene the directions contained in section 70, which enjoins (a) that regard shall be had to (inter alia) the character of the dwelling-house and (b) that the assessment has to be made on the assumption that supply and demand in respect of *similar* dwelling-houses is in approximate balance. The Institute of Rent Officers suggest that section 70 (2) should be amended by specifically providing that the would-be tenants referred to are seeking to become tenants at fair rents. This suggestion, if we understand it aright, seems to involve a misconception of the purpose of Section 70 (2). This subsection has nothing to do with the assessment of scarcity. It is concerned with the method of assessing the fair rent – for this purpose, it requires it to be assumed that there is no excess demand

for the type of accommodation under review which would have the effect
of inflating the rent. It is irrelevant for this purpose to consider what rents
the would-be tenants would be prepared to pay. The existence and extent
of scarcity are matters of fact, which the rent fixing authority has to determine
in the light of the evidence, and its own knowledge, of the actual circumstances of the particular case. It is concerned here not with notional demand,
but with actual demand, although, as a rule, the existence and extent of excess
demand will be a matter of inference from circumstantial evidence...

Comment on the impact of the fair rent formula on rent levels will
be found below (pp. 285–92).

The interaction of subsections (1) and (2) was discussed in *Metropolitan Property Holdings* v. *Finegold* [1975] 1 W.L.R. 349:

LORD WIDGERY C.J.: This is an appeal affecting a large number of flats
belonging to the appellants in a block known as South Lodge in St John's
Wood. [There] was recently built in St John's Wood a substantial school restricted in its entry to the children of American families in London. The
result of that school being built has undoubtedly rendered this part of St
John's Wood far more attractive to American families than it might otherwise
have been because of the facility of the education of their children which
this school provides. Although there is no specific finding to this effect on
the part of the committee, it is a reasonable inference, I think, from the
material which has been put before us that the presence of this school has
almost certainly put up the market rental values of flats and houses in the
neighbourhood. And it may be, although again there is no specific finding
to this effect, that this has produced locally an element of scarcity in the sense
that more Americans want to come and live in St John's Wood and have
the facility of having their children educated at that school than the accommodation vacant and to let in St John's Wood would permit. I think it only
right to approach the problem on the footing that both those assumptions
are good, namely, that the school in its own immediate surroundings has produced an increase in the number of Americans and, secondly, it may well
have produced an element of scarcity, or accentuated an element of scarcity
which previously existed...

[Looking] for the moment only at sub-s (1), any amenity (as the word has
been used frequently in this argument), any advantage which the premises
inherently have, either in their construction, their nature, their scale, their
situation, their proximity to a school, a zoo or a theatre, whatever it may
be, all those factors which would tend in the market to increase the rental,
are factors to be taken into account by the committee in fixing the fair rent.
To what extent they are taken into account is, of course, the duty of the committee to decide, but that these are matters which are eligible for consideration is beyond doubt. At this point, as I have already said, the presence of

the American school would, on the face of it, tend to put up the fair rent because it would be an amenity making the premises more attractive.

Then one comes to s [70](2) ... This is the provision which is intended to eliminate what is popularly called 'scarcity value' from the fair rent fixed by the committee, and it is a provision which has given rise to a great deal of difficulty in practice ... It seems to me that what Parliament is saying is this: if the house has inherent amenities and advantages, by all means let them be reflected in the rent under s [70](1); but if the market rent would be influenced simply by the fact that in the locality there is a shortage, and in the locality rents are being forced up beyond the market figure, then that element of market rent must not be included when the fair rent is being considered. Parliament, I am sure, is not seeking to deprive the landlord of a proper return on the inherent value and quality of his investment in the house, but Parliament is undoubtedly seeking to deprive a landlord of a wholly unmeritorious increase in rent which has come about simply because there is a scarcity of houses in the district and thus an excess of demand over supply.

The committee have come to the conclusion and expressed it in more than one way that the presence of the American school has created a local scarcity of premises. When I say 'local', I deliberately do not attempt at this stage to define it further. But what was in the committee's mind undoubtedly was that the attraction of the school has produced a local scarcity of houses, and that there is consequently in the premises now under review all the elements contained in s [70](2) of a scarcity which ought to be eliminated when the fair rent is assessed ... I do not think that Parliament was concerned with this kind of local scarcity when s [70] was passed. If one is looked for the unearned, unmeritorious increase in rent which might accrue to landlords if s [70](2) had never been passed, one must, I think, take a very much wider sweep than the sort of area to which the committee seems to have applied its mind in this case. Of course if you look at half a dozen streets round the American school, you may well find a scarcity. As you go out to a greater radius round the school, then the effect of the school is less and less. But, as I emphasised, we are not looking at the effect of the school as such; we are looking for scarcity in the locality which results from an excess of demand over supply.

It seems to me, with all deference to the committee, that they have somewhat lost sight of the fact that the sort of scarcity we are concerned with is a broad, overall, general scarcity affecting a really substantial area, and they wrongly focussed their attention on the extremely limited area which would not, I think, qualify as a 'locality' for the purposes of s [70](2) of the [1977] Act.

Mais and Croom-Johnson JJ. agreed. The case was referred back to the Committee. Cf. *Palmer* v. *Peabody Trust* [1975] Q.B. 604, in which

Lord Widgery C.J. emphasized that, in the normal case, it was for the Rent Assessment Committee to determine the extent of a 'locality'.

The procedures for fixing fair rents have occasionally come before the courts. The following materials illustrate the reluctance of the courts to interfere. They also show a variety of approaches to the fixing of fair rents. In *Mason* v. *Skilling* [1974] 1 W.L.R. 1437 (H.L. appeal from Scotland) Lord Reid said:

In my view, this section leaves it open to the rent officer or committee to adopt any method or methods of ascertaining a fair rent provided that they do not use any method which is unlawful or unreasonable. The most obvious and direct method is to have regard to registered rents of comparable houses in the area. In the initial stages this method may not be available but as the number of comparable registered rents increases the more likely it will be that it will lead to a correct result. Of course it must be open to either party to show that those comparable rents have been determined on a wrong basis but until that is shown it must be assumed that rents already determined have been rightly ascertained.

In the present case the committee did consider comparable rents and it is not said that they acted wrongly in this respect. Criticism is limited to the manner in which they dealt with the capital value of the house.

The committee were quite entitled and may well have been well advised to use other methods in addition to considering comparable rents. In particular they were entitled to have regard to the capital value. A fair rent should be fair to the landlord as well as fair to the tenant and it can be regarded as fair to the landlord that he should receive a fair return on his capital. We are not concerned in this case with the percentage which in present circumstances can be regarded as a fair return.

It is notorious that in existing circumstances the price which a house will fetch in the market is much higher if the buyer can get possession immediately, than if there is a sitting tenant with a statutory right to remain in possession. Admittedly the committee had regard to the capital value with vacant possession but the respondent argues that the only relevant capital value is the price which the appellants could get for the house today: as the respondent is a sitting tenant that would be much lower than if the appellants could give vacant possession. Their argument was accepted by the Second Division...

It is quite true that the fact that there is a sitting tenant is a 'circumstance' but in my opinion it is excluded by the Act. Section [70](1) directs that regard shall be had to 'all the circumstances (other than personal circumstances)' In my view the tenant's right to remain in possession is a personal circumstance. A right to possess a house (or anything else) appears to me to pertain to the person who has the right, whether the right is statutory or contractual. The house itself remains the same whoever is entitled to possess it. Moreover, under the Act the tenant's right to possess lasts so long, but only so long, as he complies with certain obligations. I am confirmed in this view by the fact that all the circumstances specified at the end of the subsection relate entirely to the house itself.

If this were not so it would lead to strange results. Suppose two identical adjacent houses one of which is vacant and the other occupied by a tenant with a regulated tenancy. If the respondent's argument is right then the fair rents would be different. No reasons have been suggested why two such houses should have different fair rents. Moreover, the Act appears to aim at uniformity but if the respondent is right there would be no uniformity and it would be difficult to find comparable cases. Of two similar houses one might be occupied by a tenant in the prime of life who has a wife and family who could succeed him in the event of his death. Then the selling price of the house would be low; it would be improbable that the purchaser could obtain vacant possession for a very long time. But the other house might be occupied by an aged, infirm tenant with no wife or family, or a tenant who was likely soon to leave. Then the selling price would be higher because the purchaser was likely to be able to get vacant possession quite soon. I find it impossible to believe that the statute contemplates different fair rents in these two cases...

Lord Morris of Borth-y-Gest commented: '[It] would not be appropriate to restrict a committee in its consideration of any relevant evidence that might be put before them provided it is evidence which, when considered in the light of the statutory directions, may be of help in assessing a figure of fair rent.'

Lord Kilbrandon implied that courts should not be too anxious to interfere: 'The fixing of a fair rent calls for a skilled estimate of a hypothetical figure, namely, the rent which a landlord could demand and a tenant would be prepared to pay if the market were roughly in a state of equilibrium ... [We] have here a valuation problem rather than a legal question of law ...'.

Lords Diplock and Cross of Chelsea agreed.

In *Crofton Investment Trust* v. *Greater London Rent Assessment Committee* [1967] 2 Q.B. 955, Lord Parker C.J., commenting on a complaint that the R.A.C. had no actual evidence of scarcity put before it, said (at 967):

I am quite satisfied that this committee, that is to say, a committee of this kind under a procedure which is clearly to be intended to be informal and not to be carried through with the precision of a court of justice, is fully entitled to act, as it has been said, on their own impression and on their own knowledge. It is idle in my view to think of gentlemen manning this committee and sitting maybe day after day without acquiring experience and knowledge of conditions in the locality, and to say that they should shut their eyes to what they know of their own knowledge, and act only on such evidence as may or may not be put before them, seems to me to reduce the matter to absurdity.

In *Metropolitan Properties Co. (F.G.C.) Ltd* v. *Lannon* [1969] 1 Q.B. 577, the Court of Appeal upheld Lord Parker's basic principle, though Lord Denning did remark (at 597) that if a committee is given evidence on a particular point, their freedom to act on their own knowledge 'does not mean that they should throw over the evidence altogether. At any rate, they should not throw over the evidence without saying why. That is what troubles me most about their written decision. They threw over the figure of the rent officer (himself an expert), the figures of the experts on each side, and the figure of the tenant himself. They fixed a much lower figure – without a word to say why they did it.'

One case where the Divisional Court did query the assessment of fair rent was *Anglo-Italian Properties* v. *London Rent Panel* [1969] 1 W.L.R. 731, where Lord Parker C.J. said:

The flat is in an old-fashioned house in a terrace which was acquired by the landlords, the appellants, in 1962 and converted into four flats, and this basement flat has the added attraction of a garden. The landlords let it to a Miss Cassidy, who applied then to the rent officer to determine and register the fair rent; the rent she was being charged was £600 per annum exclusive. The rent officer went into the matter, and in due course determined a fair rent of £335; whereupon the landlords objected and the matter was referred to the rent assessment committee.

The committee's reasons for determining the fair rent at £400 are contained succinctly in one paragraph of their decision and reasons, that is:

'We accepted Mr Tuckerman's valuation [he was for the landlords] of the purchase price in 1962 plus the cost of conversion, namely, £13,863; we considered that a fair yield would be 10 per cent of this capital and that a fair apportionment of this capital cost to the subject flat would be one-quarter. Thus we reached the figure of, say, £348 per annum as a basis for assessment of a fair rent for that flat. We did not dissent from the landlords' estimate of the average annual cost of repairs, namely, £250, and apportioning this to the subject flat in the same proportion as for the capital, we arrived at a total of £410.'

The committee then went on:

'But at the time of the purchase and conversion of the property, a developer would have obtained higher rents than those obtainable since the coming into effect of the Act of 1965, which excluded "scarcity value" from the assessment of fair rents. We put the "scarcity value" of the subject property at about 10 per cent. We therefore considered that a fair rent for the flat under reference would be £369 subject to some addition in respect of the tenant having the use and benefit of the landlords' furniture and effects. We did not agree the landlords' valuation of these items; we thought that a fair annual charge for them would be £31. Accordingly, we concluded that a fair rent within the meaning and for the purposes of section 46 of the 1968 Act would be £400 per annum,'

that is, adding the £31 to the figure of £369.

The point which is taken by Mr Wellings in this appeal is a very short one; the landlords do not quarrel with the calculation that the committee have done to arrive at £410 per annum. What he does say is that on this method of calculation there really is no room for any deduction in respect of scarcity value; accordingly he says that the true rent on this method of calculation would be the £410 plus the £31 for the use of the landlords' effects, in other words, £441.

I confess that for my part I can see no answer to Mr Wellings' contention. As I understand the calculation, a rent of £348 is first arrived at as a fair rent as at 1962 being 10 per cent of the capital cost in 1962. That being so, I cannot see that there is any room for deducting anything for scarcity. Of course, the committee might have said: 'true that capital cost in 1962 represents, let us say, £18,000 – because there is evidence of that – in 1968,' and then it would be right to deduct something for scarcity value, as compared with the position in 1962. Looking at it in that way, I can see no room for any deduction for scarcity value.

Having said that, however, I would for myself, and I do not claim to be an expert, voice the view that this is a quite novel method of valuation which the landlords put forward and the committee adopted. It is certainly one that I have never seen before. It is not arrived at on comparables, it is not based on square footage, it is certainly not based on the contractors' theory. But it is based on original cost, taking a percentage thereof as the fair rent. It may be, because there is no fixed yardstick by which a fair rent is to be arrived at, that this is a permissible method and that a just conclusion can thereby be arrived at. I only mention this because in my experience this method is a novel one. Bearing all these matters in mind I think that the proper course here is to allow this appeal, and send the case back to the committee with the opinion of this court. That would enable them to adhere, if they desire, to this method of calculation, but not eliminate scarcity value or to take into consideration any other method of calculation they desire.

However, in *Tormes Ltd* v. *Landau* [1971] 1 Q.B. 261, Lord Parker C.J. said:

The appellants in this case are a property company of which Mr Rambridge is director and main shareholder. The company in 1963 purchased premises known as 24, Belitha Villas, N.1, and in 1967 Mr Rambridge acquired control of the company. In 1967 and 1968 improvements were effected and the premises were converted into flats ... By October 1969 the appellants were desirous of letting flat no. 3 in these premises and on 6 October 1969, they made an application, as they were entitled to do, under section 45 of the Rent Act, 1968, asking for a certificate of fair rent in the sum of £565 on the basis of a seven-year lease, the tenant doing internal repairs and the appellants the rest. The only services to be supplied were those of lighting and cleaning the common parts of the premises at a charge of £8 per annum.

The matter was considered on 1 November 1969, by the rent officer, who, after going into the matter in great detail by reference to a number of alleged 'comparables', arrived at a figure of £330 per annum as the fair rent. The appellants were not satisfied with that. They appealed, as they were entitled to do, to a rent assessment committee, who heard the appeal on 17 February 1970, and certified £360 per annum, to include the £8 for heating and cleaning, as the fair rent on the terms suggested. The appellants now appeal to this court on what has to be a point of law.

I do not propose to go through the matter in great detail, but what the appellants did at the hearing through Mr Rambridge was to put forward a valuation on the basis of a reasonable return to the landlords. It has been said many times that the 'contractor's theory' based on building costs can do no more than set a ceiling when one is considering old premises. Equally, an adaptation of the contractor's theory to cover historic costs is something which may lead to very odd results according to the time when the costs were incurred, and, indeed, it may well be that a fair rent will show a landlord a loss on historic costs. What the appellants did was to prefer yet another adaptation, as it were, of the contractor's theory by starting with an estimate of replacement costs, allowing what was thought to be a reasonable interest on that cost and then adding management expenses, to use a general term, and something in respect of equipment provided ...

In my judgment, the committee were perfectly entitled to do what they did. Without criticizing the yardstick put forward by the landlords, it seems to me that the committee were perfectly entitled to reject it and to apply another, and, for my part, I cannot believe that, when one is approaching residential premises for which there are any number of comparables, as is the case here, much weight can properly be given to any version of the contractor's theory. As I have said, the true contractor's theory can only produce a ceiling. The adaptation based on historic costs may produce false results, and the present suggested adaptation based on replacement cost is an attempt to achieve indirectly something which can be achieved directly from market-rent comparables or in the fair rents of comparables which have been fixed. I myself think that there are great dangers in approaching the matter in the way in which the landlords approached it in the present case where, as here, undoubtedly there are comparable market rents and comparable fair rents. Accordingly, I do not think that the committee can be criticized for just saying that they were not going to go into this method of approach advanced by the landlords...

Could it be argued that permitting rent officers or Rent Assessment Committees to use their own expertise, without revealing their thinking to the parties, amounts to a breach of the rules of natural justice? (Watchman, 1979, especially pp. 207–10; see below, pp. 267–71.)

Since 1974, furnished tenancies have come within the jurisdiction of rent officers and Rent Assessment Committees. In *Metrobarn Ltd* v. *Gehring* [1976] 1 W.L.R. 776, the question arose as to whether a registered fair rent, relating to unfurnished premises, was to apply to a furnished tenancy of the same premises, brought within the scope of the fair rent scheme by the passing of the Rent Act 1974. The Court of Appeal decided that it did not so apply. Since the transitional provisions in the 1974 Act did not, in terms, deal with the point, their Lordships were not prepared to infer that this was an inevitable consequence of the passing of the Act.

In *Campbell* v. *Gardner* (1976) 238 E.G. 115, it was held that a rent assessment committee was entitled to view the premises as a whole, rather than first determining what a fair rent would be if the premises were unfurnished and then adding on something for furniture. Also, it was proper for the committee to take into account the fact that tenants of furnished accommodation generally stayed for shorter periods than those in unfurnished premises, so that the landlord's costs would be higher. (Is this not an example of taking personal circumstances into account, not allowed under the terms of s. 70?)

In *Dominal Securities Ltd* v. *McLeod* (1979) 39 P.&C.R. 411 (C.A.) a rent tribunal had, in 1972, fixed the 'reasonable rent' of a furnished tenancy at £52 a month, inclusive of rates. The landlords argued that when the furnished tenancy became fully protected under the Rent Act 1974, this rent should be deemed to be *exclusive* of rates. (See now Rent Act 1977, Sched. 24, para. 8.) The Court of Appeal rejected this argument. Although the £52 was deemed to be a fair rent registered under what is now Part IV of the Rent Act 1977, it was not to be deemed to be that which it was not, *viz.* a rent calculated as an exclusive rent.

Data on rents of furnished tenancies are set out below in Tables 5.6, 5.7 and 5.9.

6. Getting a fair rent registered

A The rent officer

The country has been divided into registration areas (Rent Act 1977, s. 62); and rent officers have been appointed to each area (*ibid.*, s. 63). They have the responsibility of maintaining a register of fair rents for each area; this is a public document, available for inspection (*ibid.*, s. 66). Applications for the registration of a fair rent may be made by the landlord, or the tenant, or both together (*ibid.*, s. 67). Local authorities may make application (*ibid.*, s. 68) but such applications can only result in confirmation or reduction of the privately agreed rent (*ibid.*, s. 68(2)).[2] Landlords who intend to let after improving or repairing accommodation may also apply for a certificate of fair rent (*ibid.*, s. 69, and Sched. 12). Applications may either be for first-time registration; or for re-registration as specified in s. 67(3) and (4), and as amended by Housing Act 1980, s. 60(1):[3]

(3) Subject to subsection (4) below, where a rent for a dwelling-house has been registered under this Part of this Act, no application by the tenant alone or by the landlord alone for the registration of a different rent for that dwelling-house shall be entertained before the expiry of 2 years from the relevant date (as defined in subsection (5) below) except on the ground that, since that date, there has been such a change in –

    (*a*) the condition of the dwelling-house (including the making of any improvement therein),

    (*b*) the terms of the tenancy,

    (*c*) the quantity, quality or condition of any furniture provided for use

2. This power was given to local authorities in 1972 when the compulsory scheme of rent allowances was introduced by the Housing Finance Act 1972. The 'rent eligible to be met by . . . all allowance' is defined in Housing Finance Act 1972, s. 25 and Sched. 4, para. 14. In cases where no fair rent is registered, the local authority is to estimate what the fair rent would be and any excess is to be ignored. The power to refer rents to the rent officer and avoid this question of local authority estimation seems not to be used, at least in Manchester (Yates (1979), who points out the consequences this may have for tenants).

3. The period of delay was formerly three years. This continues to apply to rents registered before the date of commencement of the Housing Act 1980; Housing Act 1980, s. 60(2).

under the tenancy (deterioration by fair wear and tear excluded),
or

(*d*) any other circumstances taken into consideration when the rent was
registered or confirmed,

as to make the registered rent no longer a fair rent.

(4) Notwithstanding anything in subsection (3) above, an application such
as is mentioned in that subsection which is made by the landlord alone and
is so made within the last 3 months of the period of 2 years referred to in
that subsection may be entertained notwithstanding that that period has not
expired.

(The 'relevant date' is usually the date of registration of the last
registered rent by the rent officer, *ibid*., s. 67(5) and (5A), as amended
by Housing Act 1980, s. 61(5).)

The effect of an application for re-registration was discussed in *London Housing Properties* v. *Cowan* [1977] Q.B. 148 (D.C.):

LORD WIDGERY C.J.: On 16th January 1973 application had been made
to the rent officer to fix a fair rent in respect of this flat. He had fixed a rent
of £295 per annum, which included £28 for services. The effective date for
that determination .. was 28th February 1973.

Shortly afterwards, the landlords took out a somewhat unreliable gas boiler
from the flat and substituted a modern electric boiler. It cost them £220 to
do it, and, having done it, they approached the rent officer with a view of
getting an increase in rent on account of this improvement ...

It seems to me, and I have no doubt about this, that the proper approach
to s. 67(3) is to ask whether there have been changes in the condition of the
house or in the other factors specifically referred to in the section, and, if
there have been, to ask the second question, which is whether as a result of
those changes the registered rent is no longer a fair rent. In other words, there
must be changes of a statutory kind before any question of review arises at
all. It must be shown that those changes have given rise to a situation
in which the rent is no longer a fair rent. Then the door is open for the
normal procedure to be followed and for an application to be made to the rent
officer ...

Given the circumstances to which I have already referred, there is jurisdiction for the rent officer to come in and reassess a fair rent for the house or
flat, and two alternative obligations have been canvassed in argument in that
situation. On the one hand, it is said that when he comes to assess the new
fair rent he must not increase the existing registered rent except to the extent
that an increase is warranted by the conditions which gave rise to the review.
In other words, it is said that the rent officer coming in within the three year
period, or as it has been put in argument in mid-term, to assess a new rent
must confine any increases in rental to those which follow from the alteration

in the condition of the house which itself gave rise to his right to come in mid-term.

For my part, I am quite satisfied that that is not the right answer. It seems to me perfectly clear that when the rent officer comes in to make an assessment of the fair rent he does so under s. [70] ... and under no limitations beyond the limitations contained in that section. I think it would have a very strange result if that were not so. It would mean that a further application in regard to the increase of the rent might be postponed for a new period of three years, and furthermore that might be done on a basis which resulted in only the smallest adjustment in the rent itself ...

Counsel for the tenant pleads that this attitude will be unfair to a tenant in conditions of inflation. He says, and he is absolutely right about this, that if an assessment is made mid-term it means that the tenant has to face a higher rent somewhat earlier in time than would otherwise be the case.

This is perfectly true, but again it must be remembered that, in my view, that all that is happening when a reassessment in mid-term is made is that the tenant in question is having his rent brought up to a fair rent somewhat earlier than he would otherwise have done. The three year limitation generally applied is not in my view intended to give the tenant a right to live on less than a fair rent for the better part of three years; its purpose is to supply an administrative limit within which in normal circumstances an application for a rent review cannot be made. But if under s [67](3) a review in mid-term is permissible, then, although it does in fact mean that the tenant is out of pocket to some degree compared with what would otherwise happen, it does not to my mind produce the kind of injustice which would make me wonder whether my construction of the section was the right one.

Comment

Farrand (1978, notes to s. 67) asks as a moot point whether inflation, on its own, could be a 'change in circumstance' justifying a new application? Whatever the answer to that, the *Cowan* decision effectively precludes tenants from taking any real advantage of s. 67(3), at least at current levels of inflation. For even if there has been a change of circumstances (other than inflation) which is detrimental to the tenant, the effect of inflation on the rent fixed is likely to be that it will be increased or confirmed, but certainly not reduced. The influence of inflation on ordinary re-registrations of fair rents can be seen below, p. 279, Table 5.5. (Note that special provisions relate to the ability of the landlord to pass on to the tenant increases in rates and the cost of the provision of services and furniture (Rent Act 1977, s. 71), so these would not usually need to be treated as 'changes in circumstance'.)

The application must be in proper form (*ibid.*, s. 74); model forms for applications and other matters are prescribed in the Rent Regulation (Forms etc.) Regulations 1978, S.I. 1978 No. 495. Attempts have been made to make these forms more comprehensible to the general public; it is worth studying them and asking whether this objective has been satisfied. One question that *has* to be completed by the applicant relates to the proposed rent for the property; failure to complete this renders the application invalid. (*Chapman* v. *Earl* [1968] 1 W.L.R. 1315; cf. *R.* v. *London Rent Assessment Panel, ex parte Braq Investments* [1969] 1 W.L.R. 970, where it was held that this requirement was satisfied if words are used from which the rent can be calculated with certainty.)

Once a valid application has been submitted the Rent Officer takes the following steps (Rent Act 1977, Sched. 11, paras. 1–6, now subject to further detailed amendment, Housing Act 1980, Sched. 6):

(i) The Rent Officer may and usually does request further information.

(ii) He notifies the other party (if only one applicant) or both if a local authority has applied.

(iii) If there are no representations from either party, he makes such inquiries as he thinks necessary and registers as a fair rent the rent mentioned in the application.

(iv) If he disagrees with the rent mentioned, or if there are representations, he must hold a 'consultation'.

In *R.* v. *Brighton Rent Officers ex parte Elliott* (1975) 29 P.&C.R. 456, Lord Widgery C.J. said:

... the rent officer, having received an application to fix a fair rent of the relevant properties, sent out a notice under paragraph 4 (2) of Part I of Schedule [11] calling the parties for a consultation. He made it clear that in his determination of a fair rent in this case he would be guided by other comparable rents which had already been determined or approved by the rent assessment committee ...

This produced a complaint from the present applicant on this basis: that it was unfair for him to be required to attend the consultation mentioned in paragraph 4 (2) of Schedule [11] without first being told what comparable properties the rent officer had in mind to rely on. His argument ... is that the consultation was the one and only opportunity which the landlord would have of seeking to influence the mind of the rent officer and that he could only effectively seek to influence the mind of the rent officer if he knew what was in the rent officer's mind, and particularly what comparable properties the rent officer was minded to rely on. The crunch, if one may use the word, comes at this point: that the rent officer is saying: 'No, I am not going to disclose in advance what comparable properties I may find of value and influence' and the applicant, through Mr. Galpin, is saying: 'You are denying me natural justice if you do not give me this information before the consultation takes place so that I can consider it and, if necessary, comment on it.' That is the short point.

The conception of a consultation is in my experience novel and I cannot think of another instance in which this kind of step is included in this kind of procedure. In many other instances, such as that of the valuation officer rating, no such step is provided by the legislation and the officer makes his determination and leaves the dissatisfied party to appeal.

Here, the step of consultation is brought in, and I think that it may have a number of purposes. One surely possible purpose is that it provides an opportunity for the parties to sit round the table with the rent officer and have an opportunity for a settlement of the matter by agreement. True, the rent officer's authority does not extend to requiring a settlement, but one can see that a potentially hard-fought case might in the course of the consultation lose much of its sting if the consultation was operated skilfully by the rent officer.

In any case, however, I think that a function, and a very important function, of the consultation must be to enable the rent officer to approach the problem of decision with the knowledge that he has heard what the parties want to say about this particular instant case. I do not take the view that the rent officer is expected to decide the matter in the course of the consultation, still less that he comes to the consultation with any sort of preconceived idea of what the rent ought to be. I think that an important function, as I have said, of the consultation is to enable the rent officer to pick up the atmosphere of the matter, make contact with the parties, listen to their observations and thus, one hopes, come to a conclusion which reflects what the parties have to say. I feel quite confident that there is no kind of obligation on the rent officer to determine what comparable properties he will rely on before he comes to the consultation. Indeed, I would have thought that it would be entirely wrong for him to do so because in this type of case, once the comparables are settled, the answer very often is only a matter of mathematics and if the rent officer came to the consultation with a firm decision in his mind to rely on certain particular comparables I think that he would be wrong.

It seems to me that the principal suggestion that he must disclose his comparables at or before the consultation is totally misconceived and quite inconsistent with the whole purpose of these provisions.

(v)   The Rent Officer registers a fair rent, at the same time informing the parties of their right to lodge an objection which will be referred to a Rent Assessment Committee. Such objection should be made within 28 days though the period is extendable (Rent Act 1977, Sched. 11, para. 6).

B The Rent Assessment Committee

Committees follow broadly similar procedures in order to get what information they need, though they have to seek it on prescribed forms. Failure to provide such information is a criminal offence (Rent Act 1977, Sched. 11, para. 7(2)). Further details are contained in Regulations (S.I. 1971 No. 1065). Thus they may decide cases by oral hearings or, if the parties agree, by written representations. The procedure of the Rent Assessment Committees (R.A.C.s) is relatively formal but less so than the courts'. Majority decisions are permitted. A feature of their procedure is the visiting of the property for which a fair rent is to be determined. They have no legal power to enter premises, but tenants have not been known to refuse entry (Francis, 1971, p. 45).

Representation is allowed but legal aid cannot be obtained. In London and recently extended throughout the country there exists a voluntary 'Surveyors Aid Scheme' run through the Citizens Advice Bureaux, which may provide representation for both landlords and tenants of limited means (Cutting, 1979, p. 124). The increasing range of neighbourhood law centres, community lawyers and pressure groups such as SHELTER and Child Poverty Action Group are also often able to help.

Committees have power to confirm or vary the rent officer's decision (Rent Act 1977, Sched. 11, para. 9). If they decide to vary, their task is to determine the fair rent at the time they find the property (and see *Western Heritable Investment Co. Ltd* (1978) S.L.T. 233). Given the delays inherent in such proceedings this almost invariably means they raise the level decided by the rent officer (see below, Table 5.9, p. 283). The decisions of Rent Assessment Committees are now effective from the date of registration (Rent Act 1977, s. 72(4) as amended by Housing Act 1980, s. 61(1)).

In *Hanson* v. *Church Commissioners* [1977] 2 W.L.R. 848 (C.A.), the question arose whether, once an objection had been referred to a Rent Assessment Committee, it could be withdrawn.

Lord Denning m.r.: There is a house in Chelsea which is owned by the Church Commissioners. It is 21, Bramerton Street. It has been let to Mr. John Hanson for the last ten years. In 1973 the rent was £600 a year. The landlords applied to the rent officer for the registration of a rent of £900 as being a fair rent for the house ... The rent officer said that he thought a fair rent would be £800 a year. The landlords' agents said that they would accept it. But the tenant did not agree. He thought £800 was too high. The rent officer, however, kept to his figure. On March 18, 1974, he determined a fair rent of £800 a year and notified both parties.

The landlords did not give any notice of objection, but the tenant did. On March 10, 1974, he objected. Thereupon it became a duty of the rent officer to refer the matter to a rent assessment committee, and he did so. On April 23, 1974, the rent assessment panel wrote to the tenant asking him if he wanted a hearing. On May 17, 1974, he replied saying that he would like to be assisted under the surveyor's aid scheme. He added that he would like to appear before a committee. He further said that the rent officer's report was fair. On July 9, 1974, the rent assessment committee gave notice to both sides that the objection would be heard on Thursday, August 15, 1974.

By this time the tenant had got the aid of surveyors, the well known firm of Debenham, Tewson & Chinnocks. The gentleman dealing with it for the tenant was a Mr. Newsom. These surveyors advised the tenant that he was unlikely to succeed in his objection to the £800 and they could not find themselves in a position to present a case on his behalf at the hearing.

The tenant was not very happy with this advice. He still thought £800 was too high, but he accepted the advice and told his surveyors that he did not wish to take his objection any further. This was on August 8. There was then only a week to go before the hearing on August 15. Thereupon Mr. Newsom of the tenant's surveyors telephoned to the clerk of the rent assessment committee. The evidence is somewhat conflicting but, as I read it, Mr. Newsom asked whether the tenant could withdraw his objection at a date so close to the hearing. The clerk said that it was in order for the tenant to withdraw and that a letter should be sent confirming the withdrawal. He suggested a form of words which Mr. Newsom used in a letter on that very day. It was as follows:

'August 8, 1974. Dear Sirs, No. 21 Bramerton Street; Objection to Rent Assessment. We write following our telephone conversation of this morning. Acting on behalf of Mr. Hanson of the above address, we confirm that we shall not be placing our objection before the London Rent Assessment Panel on Thursday August 15. W. Newsom.'

The landlords were told nothing about that letter. They were not told that the tenant had withdrawn his objection. The clerks of the panel did nothing about it either. They kept the case in the list of cases to be heard on August 15, 1974, by the rent assessment committee.

On that day, August 15, 1974, the committee and the landlords attended. They thought that the case was still effective. But the tenant did not attend. He thought that it was not effective. When the case was called on, the chairman treated it as a case where the tenant had made no withdrawal of his objection and had simply failed to turn up. According to a note we have, it would appear that the chairman asked Mr. Lowndes of Cluttons, the agents for the landlords: 'What do you want to tell us?' Mr. Lowndes acknowledged in effect that, after the consultation with the rent officer and the tenant, he had at that consultation accepted the £800 proposed by the rent officer, but now that he was present at the hearing he would like the committee to increase it to the £900 for which he had applied originally. He said that he had prepared a proof in support of the application for £900 and asked whether the committee would like him to read it. The chairman asked him to give it to them and they would read it for themselves. Mr. Lowndes handed it to them and they read it. No one challenged it because, of course, the tenant was not there.

In the afternoon the committee went to the house. The tenant had gone to work, but his wife was at home. The chairman of the committee telephoned the tenant at work. He asked if the committee could inspect the house. The tenant replied:

'I understood that my appeal had been withdrawn and the hearing would not proceed. I cannot agree to your inspecting the house in my absence. Would you wait half an hour until I can get home?'

The chairman said:

'We can't wait any longer as we have other properties to inspect. The hearing has already taken place. This is not a part of the hearing, but purely a visual inspection. We do not listen to further arguments at this stage. The case will have to go on without you. I will have to record that you refused the committee access for inspection.'

So the committee only looked at the outside of the house from the front.

The committee seem then and there to have agreed that a fair rent was £900 a year, but the chairman afterwards on September 7, 1974, gave a written decision and reasons. In it he expressed the indebtedness of the committee to the evidence of the landlords' agent contained in the proof, showing that they were much influenced by it...

I turn to the substantive points. Had the tenant any right to withdraw his objection? Upon this point Mr. Moshi before us has drawn our attention to the textbooks in which it is suggested that he had no right to withdraw. In *Megarry* (1967), pp. 405–406, it is said:

'There is no express provision for either or both of the parties to withdraw a reference to the committee; and it seems doubtful whether they can do so. For the reference is made not by the parties but the rent officer; and once either party has duly made an objection to the rent officer's determination, both the reference to the committee and the determination by the committee seem to be mandatory...'

Now that we have had the matter discussed before us, it seems to me that those statements go much too far. It is not right to say that there is no right whatever to withdraw an objection. We were told that in practice a limited right of withdrawal is always given to the tenant or landlord. Although he may have lodged an objection, he can withdraw it in this sense that, if he notifies the rent assessment committee that he withdraws his objection, the committee will get in touch with the other side and see whether they assent or not to the withdrawal or whether they object to it; and, if there is no objection to the withdrawal, the committee as a matter of practice do allow the withdrawal. So convenient is this practice that these committees have invariably allowed the withdrawal. In no case has a committee refused it. Thus reducing the work load of the committees. It seems to me that that practice is not only highly convenient but it is also in accordance with the true interpretation of the statute.

The legal position as shown by the cases is that in the ordinary way where there is a dispute before a tribunal in a civil matter, either party has a right to withdraw his application or objection, as the case may be, at any time before the decision is given. That is shown by *Boal Quay Wharfingers Ltd.* v. *King's Lynn Conservancy Board* [1971] 1 W.L.R. 1558, 1556, 1559.

But when the dispute is one in which there is a public interest involved, it may not be permissible for one of the parties to withdraw on his own without the assent of the other; and, even if they both agree, he may not be able to withdraw unless the tribunal consents. It all depends on the construction which the courts place on the statute setting up the tribunal. That seems to me to be the correct interpretation of *R.* v. *Hampstead and St. Pancras Rent Tribunal, ex parte Goodman* [1951] 1 K.B. 541 where *both* parties consented to the withdrawal of an application to pay the standard rent, and of the later case of *R.* v. *West London Rent Tribunal, ex parte Napper* [1967] 1 Q.B. 169 where there was an attempted withdrawal which was not upheld.

Applying that principle in the present case, it seems to me that the fixing of a fair rent is a matter in which the public interest is involved. The fair rent is to be registered for the house for the next three years, no matter in whose hands it comes. It normally affects the house itself. It also affects neighbouring houses, because the rent so registered will be taken into account in fixing their rent. It is a brake which stops landlords from demanding excessive rents or bringing undue pressure to bear on tenants. In these circumstances, it seems to me that the public interest is so much involved that no one party has a right on his own to withdraw an objection and stop the proceedings. He cannot withdraw if the other party objects; for the simple reason that once the matter has been referred to the rent assessment committee, the other party is entitled to have a decision upon it; but, if the other party does not object, then I think that the rent assessment committee can permit the proceedings to be withdrawn. The rent assessment committee need not go on with the hearing unless they think it is proper to do so. Accordingly, when one party wishes to withdraw the objection, either he or the panel should communicate with the other side and inquire whether they object to the withdrawal or not; and, if there is no objection, the committee can allow the case to be withdrawn in accordance with their practice. If the other side does object, of course, then the hearing must go on...

Now I will turn to the other point. Was there a failure of natural justice? ... If I may summarise it, the landlords agreed at the statutory consultation before the rent officer to a figure of £800. Yet the landlords before the rent assessment committee applied to increase it to £900 in the absence of the tenant and at a time when he had no warning that they were seeking an increase. He had no opportunity of dealing with it. It is one of the cardinal principles of natural justice that a matter should not be decided adversely to a man unless he has had a fair warning of the case against him and a fair opportunity of dealing with it.

Roskill and Lawton L.JJ. agreed.

This case also shows that Rent Assessment Committees are subject to the principle of judicial review. See too *Metropolitan Properties* v. *Lannon* [1969] 1 Q.B. 577, in which the Court of Appeal quashed a decision of the London Rent Assessment Committee. The chairman of the committee was a solicitor who resided with his parents in a block of flats called Regency Lodge. This was owned by a company in the same group as the appellant landlords. He was already advising his father and other tenants in Regency Lodge who were in dispute with their landlords. The Court of Appeal held that he should not have heard the case, even though it involved quite another block of flats, as there was a possibility of bias and 'justice must be rooted in confidence' (per Lord Denning M.R. at 599). This was a case of bias in the technical sense, *nemo index in sua causa*.

A more widespread complaint is sometimes heard that the type of person that sits on these committees is 'biased' in a general sense, by coming from a class or background more sympathetic to landlords than to tenants. Cavenagh and Hawker (1974) provide some social data:

Rent Assessment Panels [R.A.P.s] are made up of three categories of members: these are legally-qualified members, valuer members (both 'professional' members) and lay members. They are appointed by the Lord Chancellor and by the Secretary of State for the Environment. The Presidents appoint [R.A.P.s] on an *ad hoc* basis. ... Members ... sat only about six times a year ...

The Professional members of the R.A.P.s are clearly a distinct group. Most of the legally qualified members are solicitors. . . . Over a half had a net income of £100 per week or more, and almost a third were in the 35–55 age group . . . Valuer members similarly were high income earners in the solid upper reaches of their profession . . .

[It] is in some ways easier to find suitable professional than suitable lay members, for professionals come from a group which is already defined and about which obvious sources of information exist . . .

The [lay] members of R.A.P.s were in general of higher socio-economic status than Supplementary Benefit Appeal Tribunal (S.B.A.T.) [lay] members and were more highly educated . . . Those with professional qualifications made up 23% of the R.A.P. lay membership and 15% of the S.B.A.T., a difference accounted for almost entirely by the recruitment of academics to R.A.P.s . . . but not to S.B.A.T. . . .

An important difference between the two systems of tribunals [was that the] membership of S.B.A.T. was fairly homogeneous in terms of social background and public experience across the three regions we studied . . . [but the] lay membership of the R.A.P.s shows more variety within its own ranks. One Panel, for example, had almost double the average number of members claiming no formal education, another double the average earning over £100 per week, and another had more than double the average numbers of J.P.s . . . Whether the differences . . . have any significance for their day to day work may . . . be doubted; there is no evidence to suggest it. All the same, it seems inescapable that differences between the Panels owe something to the identity and character of the various Presidents . . .

What do the members themselves, especially the lay members, say about their membership? Some members experienced persistent personal dissatisfaction at the social conditions that their membership brought them into contact with . . . [They] generally agreed that laymen were 'a good cross section of the community' . . .

Lay and professional members of the R.A.P.s were agreed on the role of the layman. He should have commonsense (said 45% of respondents), an awareness of and interest in social problems (23%), should be impartial (28%) and have some experience of housing either from a landlord or tenant point of view (13%). For professional members, the emphasis was . . . on . . . impartiality (45%), a sense of justice and fair play (31%) patience (30%) and courtesy and consideration for other (28%) . . . [Both] lay and professional members see the layman bringing to his panel work a degree of social knowledge that operates in harmony with the more objective skills of the professional man . . .

A few wanted more 'working-class members' and 'poor people', which suggestions might well have political overtones if implemented, but a greater number, especially of Conservative voters, deprecated the appointment of what they saw as 'politically-minded persons' to the lay ranks . . .

Another aspect of judicial review discussed in a number of cases relates to the duty imposed on R.A.C.s to give written reasons for their decisions (Tribunals and Enquiries Act 1971, s. 12). In *Metropolitan Property Holdings Ltd* v. *Laufer* (1974) 29 P.&C.R. 172, Lord Widgery C.J. remarked:

So there is an obligation to state reasons, and it is necessary to say that this is a provision applicable to a wide range of tribunals, not merely the rent assessment committee, and it is, I think, obvious that the character of the reasons given, the nature of the reasons, the extent of the reasons, must in some measure be governed by the nature of the problem which the particular tribunal has been set to resolve . . .

[If], as so often happens in the typical simple case, the landlords' experts say that the rent should be X and the tenant's experts say that the rent should be X minus Y, if the committee thinks that neither figure is the right one not only can it choose a figure in between the two extremes but it should do so.

Now, what reasons should the committee give in that situation? The answer is that in the simply typical case to which I have referred there are no reasons which the committee can give, save that it was not satisfied with either of the alternatives put forward in evidence and on its own expert knowledge preferred another figure. If that is all that the decision was, a simple matter of valuation opinion and nothing else, that is all that the decision involves, and if the decision is based simply on the committee's own views, having regard to the evidence put before them, then there are no reasons which the committee can give save to say that they think that their figure is right. Great complication and trouble would ensue if it were sought to make committees give reasons in such a situation beyond the simple and single reason to which I have referred.

So, when one bears those considerations in mind and goes back to the notice of motion, it seems to me quite clear that the first three grounds of complaint, overlapping as they do, cannot be sustained. The committee did not fail to give reasons which deal with the substantial case made by the appellants because the substantial case made by the appellants was that Mr. Burrow's opinion of a certain rent being a fair one was correct. If the committee make it clear, as they have done, that they did not accept his rental figure, then they would be giving the only reason for that purpose, to deal with the substantial case made by the appellants.

The landlords also complain in their notice of motion that the committee overthrew highly qualified expert and other evidence. Perhaps they did. I hope that I have already made it clear that, if they took the view that that was necessary in order to give the right answer, they acted fully within their discretion.

In *Guppys (Bridport) Ltd* v. *Sandoe* (1975) 30 P.&C.R. 69, Lord Widgery C.J. was again called upon to adjudicate:

True to form, the tenant here based his claim principally, as the rent officer had done, on the proposition that other registered rents which were of comparable properties showed a rent equivalent or equal to that for which the tenant contended.

The landlord, on the other hand, as is the modern trend in these cases, sought to justify a higher figure by a variety of different approaches, some of which involved capital value and some, as I understand it, which did not. The landlords' case as summarised, and no doubt very briefly summarised, by the committee is a criticism of the reliance by the tenant on comparable rents.

Having discussed *Mason* v. *Skilling* and *Tormes Property Co.* v. *Landau* (above), he continued:

It is therefore indisputable, in my view, on those authorities that if the committee are faced with a landlord's case based on capital value, and a fair return thereon, and the tenant's case is based on other registered comparable rents, it is open to the committee, if they think it right in accordance with their judicial function, to choose the method of registered comparable rents. If they do choose that, then ... they can do it without criticising the landlord's approach on the basis of a capital value and a fair return on capital value.

Under the Tribunals and Inquires Act [1971] reasons are required to be given [s. 12 (1)], and Mr. Pryor says that if the committee do not explain in some detail and by means of analysis why they are not prepared to accept the landlord's figures then they fail to give the proper reasons. In so doing he recognises, I think, that he is putting up a submission ... which, in my view, is not to be found in the authorities at all.

There are plenty of judicial offices, not the least that of a High Court judge, where reasons undoubtedly have to be given for every decision, but that does not mean that if the judge has two conflicting opinions put before him in evidence he has to explain why he chooses one in preference to the other. Such explanations are not possible. They are matters of judgment, impression and sometimes even instinct, and it is quite impossible to give detailed reasons to explain how the system of decision has worked, and so with a rent assessment committee. If they have decided, having carefully weighed the evidence, that they must reject one approach and adopt another, then all they need to do is to say that in the exercise of their discretion and relying on their skill and judgment they prefer the method which in fact they do prefer. If they say that, it cannot be said against them that their decision is invalidated by the fact that no further or more detailed explanation of why they prefer method A and reject method B is given.

(Consider, too, *Mountview Court Properties Ltd* v. *Devlin* (1970) 21 P.&C.R. 689; cf. *Guppys Properties Ltd* v. *Knott* (1980) 124 S.J. 81.)

Does this approach of the Divisional Court represent robust common sense? Or is it a somewhat feeble stance in which they have failed to exercise the control one should expect from the Divisional Court? Interestingly, the approach of the English court is remarkably different from its Scottish equivalent where the Court of Session has not hesitated to quash decisions on the ground that inadequate reasons were given. (See Watchman, 1979, especially pp. 210–14, and *Albyn Properties* v. *Knox* (1977) S.L.T. 41.)

7. Conversion from rent control to rent regulation

When the Rent Act 1965 was first passed, rent controlled properties could only become regulated if let to a new tenant. In 1969 the Housing Act 1969, Part III provided that controlled tenancies could also be converted if landlords improved them to defined standards of repair and amenity. The complex procedures prescribed for such conversion meant that between 1969 and 1971 only 4,000 dwellings were so converted.

The Conservative Government's Housing Finance Act of 1972 laid down a timetable of automatic decontrol whereby all controlled properties, other than those unfit for human habitation, were to become regulated. To prevent rent officers being swamped with work, this process was to be carried out in stages. All controlled properties with a rateable value at the time of the passing of the Housing Finance Act 1972 of over £70 in Greater London and over £35 elsewhere were so converted. The policy was reversed in 1975 by the Labour Government who argued that landlords should receive the bonus of a fair rent only if all the 'standard amenities' (see below, pp. 331, 332) were first installed. A further reversal of policy by the current Conservative Government has resulted in the total abolition of controlled tenancies (Housing Act 1980, s. 64). Even those unfit for human habitation are to be decontrolled.

The likely impact of this move on the rent levels of persons living in some of the poorest quality property in the land may be seen from Table 5.8 (below, p. 282).

8. Effect of getting a fair rent registered

Once a rent has been registered, a number of possible consequences result:

(a) If there is no existing tenancy, the registered fair rent becomes the 'contractual rent limit' (Rent Act 1977, s. 44(1)) and is effective from the date of registration (*ibid.*, s. 72, as amended by Housing Act 1980, s. 61).

(b) If there is an existing tenancy, and the fair rent is lower than the originally agreed contractual rent, the registered fair rent becomes the 'contractual rent limit' (*ibid.*, s. 44 (1)) which is effective from the date of registration by the rent officer (*ibid.*, s. 72); any excess is irrecoverable from the tenant (*ibid.*, s. 44(2)).

(c) If there is an existing tenancy, but the registered fair rent is higher than the originally agreed contractual rent, this higher fair rent cannot be changed until the original contract has been brought to an end. This may be done by issuing a statutory notice of increase (*ibid.*, s. 49) which, if it shows a date which is *after* the date on which a valid notice to quit would operate to bring the contractual tenancy to an end, is deemed to have the effect of a notice to quit (*ibid.*, s. 49(4)) and thus to terminate the (contractual) regulated tenancy, and bring a statutory tenancy into existence. In such a case the higher fair rent is effective from that date. Thus, in the case of a weekly tenancy, the notice of increase cannot come into effect until at least twenty-eight days have elapsed. (For notices to quit, see below, pp. 412–13.)

(d) If there is an existing tenancy which has already become a statutory tenancy (e.g. because the term of a lease has expired, or a valid notice to quit has been issued and expired, or a notice of increase of rent to similar effect has been issued and expired) then, where a fair rent is registered which is lower than the existing rent, that fair rent is the rent limit and any excess is irrecoverable (s. 45(2)(b)). If the registered fair rent is higher than the existing rent, then the rent may be increased if a statutory notice of increase is served. Such a notice can, in these circumstances, be valid from up to four weeks *before* the date of service of the notice, or from the date of registration, whichever is the later (*ibid.*, ss. 45(3) and 72; and see *Avenue Properties (St John's Wood) Ltd* v. *Aisinzon* [1977] Q.B. 628 (C.A.)).

It is essential that any notice of increase be in the statutorily prescribed form (see now S.I. 1978 No. 495, Sched. 2, Forms 1–4) or in any form substantially to the same effect (Rent Act 1977, s. 61 (1)). Apart from details relating to the levels of rent which have been determined by the rent officer, such forms also contain information about rent allowances (see below, pp. 304–9) and phasing (see below, pp. 284–5). They are thus another example of a procedure designed to get information about legal rights over to tenants. The effectiveness of these procedures has not been adequately investigated. However the Francis Committee did state (1971, p. 117):

It is not an offence for the landlord of a regulated tenancy to charge more than the registered rent. The position under the present law is that (i) the landlord cannot recover by legal proceedings such part of the rent as is in excess of the registered rent, and (ii) the tenant can recover the excess payments within a period of two years after payment. By contrast, it is an offence for the landlord of a furnished tenancy to charge more than the registered rent. This distinction is, on the face of it, quite illogical. The rule with regard to excess payments under a regulated tenancy was presumably adopted by analogy to the rule governing excess rents for controlled premises. It has not been an offence to charge more than the recoverable rent for controlled premises. There was, however, a good reason for this, in that it might be difficult to ascertain the precise amount of the controlled rent. This, however, is not the case with a registered rent.

The 1970 Tenants Survey has unearthed the disquieting fact that a substantial proportion of regulated tenants appear to be paying rents in excess of registered rents. Table 5.1 below summarizes the results of the Survey in this respect.

Table 5.1   Percentages of tenants paying more than the registered rents

Amount of excess	Greater London		West Mid-lands		Clyde-side	S. Wales Coastal Belt
	c	s	c	s	s	
Tenants paying more by:						
£ 5–25	11	8	16	11	12	11
£25–50	7	3	4	4	–	5
£50–100	3	4	8	9	–	4
over £100	6	4	1	2	–	4
Number of tenants interviewed	235	316	106	82	105	110

c = conurbation
s = stress area

Source: Tenants' Survey (Appendix I), Chapter 2, Supplementary Table II (6).

Thus, in the Greater London conurbation, 27 per cent of the tenants in the sample paid a rent in excess of the registered rent, and 16 per cent paid over £25 per annum in excess. In the West Midlands conurbation 29 per cent, and in the South Wales Coastal Belt 24 per cent, paid rents in excess of the registered rents.

We have also received evidence from a number of witnesses that some landlords charge more than the registered rent, usually on re-letting to a new tenant, and this is sometimes done quite openly and with the concurrence of the tenant.

The Committee commented that: 'This practice ... constitutes a real danger to the effectiveness of the fair rents scheme.' They recommended that such a practice should be made an offence except where the parties had agreed on a rent higher than a registered one between the date of application for re-registration of rent and the actual determination of the application, but no action was taken on this recommendation.

Once a rent has been registered it continues to apply to the property, no matter who the tenant is. Registrations may, in defined circumstances, be cancelled. (Rent Act 1977, s. 73, as amended by Housing Act 1980, s. 62.)

If a fair rent has not been registered, it used to be the case that landlords were not legally entitled to alter existing rent levels. This 'rent freeze' was largely abolished on 1 January 1973 (for details see the first edition of this book, pp. 212–17). It is now, in general, permissible for landlords and tenants to re-negotiate rent levels on their own without using the rent officer. However, to prevent possible abuse of tenants resulting from any inequality of bargaining power, a number of complex procedural safeguards have been laid down, designed to inform tenants of their rights, e.g. to phasing, and to use the rent officer service (Rent Act, s. 51(4) as amended by Housing Act 1980, s. 68(1)). Failure to comply with these provisions renders any negotiated increase in rent irrecoverable from the tenant (*ibid.*, s. 54(2); see DoE Circular 77/72). If a tenant in fact pays rent which is in excess of that which is permitted under these provisions, he may recover the excess but only if he does so within one year of payment (*ibid.*, s. 57(3) as amended by Housing Act 1980, s. 68(3)). The extent to which these procedures are complied with is not known.

In the case of tenancies which have become regulated following conversion from being controlled tenancies, a 'rent freeze' has in effect been re-imposed (Rent Act 1977, s. 52, created by Housing Act

1980, s. 68(2)). Since this is an important provision it is set out in full:

52.—(1) This section applies to an agreement with a tenant having security of tenure which is entered into after the commencement of section 68(2) of the Housing Act 1980 if the tenancy has become or, as the case may be, the previous tenancy became a regulated tenancy by conversion.

(2) Any such agreement which purports to increase the rent payable under a protected tenancy shall, if entered into at a time when no rent is registered for the dwelling-house under Part IV of this Act, be void.

(3) If any such agreement constitutes a grant of a regulated tenancy and is made at a time when no rent is so registered, any excess of the rent payable under the tenancy so granted (for any contractual or statutory period of the tenancy) over the rent limit applicable to the previous tenancy, shall be irrecoverable from the tenant; but the subsection ceases to apply if a rent is subsequently so registered.

(4) For the purposes of this section a tenancy is a regulated tenancy by conversion if it has become a regulated tenancy by virtue of –

    (*a*) Part VIII of this Act, section 43 of the Housing Act 1969 or Part III of the Housing Finance Act 1972 (conversion of controlled tenancies into regulated tenancies); or

    (*b*) section 18(3) of this Act or paragraph 5 of Schedule 2 to the Rent Act 1968 (conversion on death of first successor); or

    (*c*) section 64 of the Housing Act 1980 (conversion of all remaining controlled tenancies).

(5) This section does not apply to any agreement where the tenant is neither the person who, at the time of the conversion, was the tenant nor a person who might succeed the tenant at that time as a statutory tenant.

(6) Where a rent is registered for the dwelling-house and the registration is subsequently cancelled, this section shall not apply to the agreement submitted to the rent officer in connection with the cancellation nor to any agreement made so as to take effect after the cancellation.

9. Data on use[4]

Table 5.2 shows the current levels of applications and determinations of fair rents by rent officers and Rent Assessment Committees. It can also be seen how relatively few cases are referred on to R.A.C.s.

Table 5.3 shows in more detail the effect of registration on the levels of rents. For first registrations of uncontrolled tenancies, the average rise has been substantial; and in the case of re-registration (after 3

---

4. The circulation of such data to rent officers and the possibility of DoE pressure to influence their decisions was discussed by Denim (1978).

Table 5.2 Rent registration: applications and determinations

	To Rent Officers[1],[2]			To Rent Assessment Committees[2]		
	Applications (net)	Registrations	In hand at end of period	References (net)	Determinations	In hand at end of period
Greater London[3]						
1972	46,373	39,536	16,588	2,532	1,831	2,007
1973	73,547	66,223	23,912	3,203	3,107	2,103
1974	48,745	56,054	16,603	4,398	3,735	2,766
1975	60,711	60,313	17,001	6,114	5,382	3,498
1976	86,769[4]	84,984	23,078	6,039[4]	7,371	2,166
1977	68,405	76,076	15,407	4,985	5,844	1,307
1978	66,276	66,483	15,200	3,803	3,760	1,350
Rest of England and Wales[3]						
1972	108,749	88,203	35,707	3,791	3,279	1,370
1973	186,249	163,415	58,541	4,769	5,416	723
1974	112,158	139,630	31,069	3,155	3,246	632
1975	167,657	156,113	42,613	5,255	4,975	912
1976	205,004[4]	198,140	53,051	5,699[4]	4,855	1,887
1977	162,030	183,607	31,474	4,061	4,987	961
1978	185,294	181,796	34,972	4,465	4,521	905

[1] Including cases subsequently referred to Rent Assessment Committees.

[2] Includes cases for re-registration.

[3] Cases under the Rent Act 1977 and corresponding earlier legislation.

[4] From 1st quarter 1976 includes applications for Certificates of Fair Rent and cancellation of registration.

Source: Housing and Construction Statistics No. 29 (1979), Table 44.

Table 5-3 Rent registration: average registered rents and change on previous rents (unfurnished tenancies)[1,2,3]

	First registrations				Re-registrations				All registrations			
	Mean registered rent £ p.a.	Mean change on previous rent[4] %	Median registered rent £ p.a.	Number of cases	Mean re-registered rent £ p.a.	Mean change on previous rent[4] %	Median re-registered rent £ p.a.	Number of cases	Mean registered rent £ p.a.	Mean change on previous rent[4] %	Median registered rent £ p.a.	Number of cases
Greater London												
1972	345	57	..	13,710	355	21	..	7,490	348	44	..	21,200
1973	344	65	..	8,860	380	25	..	5,740	358	49	..	14,600
1974[5]	402	58	322	10,630	397	23	357	15,940	399	33	349	26,570
1975	444	66	341	15,030	408	30	363	28,420	419	40	358	43,450
1976	531	87	398	11,610	471	38	397	36,440	485	50	397	48,050
1977	645	103	422	9,140	522	43	436	38,940	546	54	432	48,080
1978	622	126	460	6,480	591	44	490	32,430	596	58	485	38,910
Rest of England and Wales												
1972	190	92	..	27,250	212	29	..	8,290	196	77	..	35,540
1973	203	98	..	28,140	237	36	..	11,140	212	80	..	39,280
1974[5]	207	98	184	29,580	252	35	245	21,040	227	64	210	50,620
1975	253	117	227	42,440	268	44	255	59,920	262	67	246	102,360
1976	301	141	272	30,320	289	52	277	102,510	292	68	276	132,830
1977	342	160	311	23,280	309	57	286	106,900	315	76	288	130,180
1978	387	179	361	17,410	375	61	354	95,680	377	78	354	113,090

Notes: are at the bottom of Table 5.8, p. 282.

Source: Housing and Construction Statistics No. 29 (1979), Table 43(a).

Table 5.4 *Rent registrations[1] by Rent Assessment Panel area, 1977*

	Mean Rent Officer rent £ p.a.	Mean increase on previous rent %	Median Rent Officer rent £ p.a.	Mean ratio of Rent Officer rent to rateable value	Number of cases
Yorkshire	277	89	263	3.3	16,630
West Midlands	335	74	315	2.3	14,430
East Midlands	288	89	275	2.7	16,620
Bristol	404	89	384	3.0	3,510
Devon and Cornwall	413	113	397	3.4	2,830
Greater Manchester and Lancs.	255	64	230	2.4	11,010
Thames Valley	388	102	360	2.4	2,740
Beds., Herts., Cambs.	371	68	359	2.2	3,870
Eastern	400	92	390	2.7	6,200
Southern	379	65	346	2.5	6,700
Surrey and Sussex	428	69	401	2.7	9,110
Wales	291	82	280	3.3	4,930
Northern	256	66	250	2.9	9,980
Kent	356	78	333	3.1	5,750
Merseyside and Cheshire	247	53	234	1.9	15,820
Great London	546	54	432	2.1	48,080
England and Wales	377	70	323	2.5	178,210

[1] This table covers all unfurnished first and re-registrations except housing association cases and, on first registrations, formerly controlled tenancies.

Figures are comparable, but not identical, to those in Table 5.3.

Source: Housing and Construction Statistics No. 27 (1978), Supplementary Table XIV.

Table 5-5 Rent registrations: mean change on previous rent and number of cases by type of applicant

(a) Unfurnished: first registration[1]

	Landlord			Tenant			Joint			Local authority			All	
	Mean change on previous rent %	Number of cases	Percentage of all cases	Mean change on previous rent %	Number of cases	Percentage of all cases	Mean change on previous rent %	Number of cases	Percentage of all cases	Mean change on previous rent %	Number of cases	Percentage of all cases	Mean change on previous rent %	Number of cases
Greater London														
1975	79	9,251	83.1	−6	1,536	13.8	60	303	2.7	−27	45	0.4	66	11,135
1976	97	7,932	87.3	4	922	10.2	68	207	2.3	−28	20	0.2	87	9,081
1977	113	7,540	87.8	12	863	10.1	103	177	2.1	−22	6	0.1	103	8,586
Rest of England and Wales														
1975	127	24,215	89.0	17	2,061	7.6	106	868	3.2	−19	70	0.3	117	27,214
1976	155	19,765	87.1	20	2,069	9.1	114	797	3.5	−15	60	0.3	140	22,691
1977	179	18,121	86.2	22	2,280	10.9	136	560	2.7	−26	52	0.3	160	21,013

(b) Re-registration

	Landlord			Tenant			Joint			Local authority			All	
	Mean change on previous rent %	Number of cases	Percentage of all cases	Mean change on previous rent %	Number of cases	Percentage of all cases	Mean change on previous rent %	Number of cases	Percentage of all cases	Mean change on previous rent %	Number of cases	Percentage of all cases	Mean change on previous rent %	Number of cases
Greater London														
1975	30	24,786	94.4	23	154	0.6	21	1,315	5.0		—	—	30	26,255
1976	38	32,816	96.5	31	122	0.4	29	1,052	3.1		—	—	38	33,990
1977	43	34,802	97.4	40	141	0.4	39	798	2.2	−45	2	—	43	35,743
Rest of England and Wales														
1975	44	51,908	96.7	36	189	0.4	42	1,553	2.9	28	2	—	44	53,652
1976	52	91,793	98.0	44	295	0.3	46	1,591	1.7	34	5	—	52	93,684
1977	57	92,427	98.2	49	270	0.3	51	1,428	1.5		—	—	56	94,125

[1] Excluding housing association cases and, on first registrations, formerly controlled tenancies.

Source: Housing and Construction Statistics No. 27 (1978), Supp. Table XV.

Table 5.6 Rent registration: average registered rents and change on previous rents (regulated furnished tenancies[8])[1, 2, 3]

	First registrations				Re-registrations				All registrations			
	Mean regis-tered rent £ p.a.	Mean change on previ-ous rent[4] %	Median regis-tered rent £ p.a.	Number of cases	Mean re-regis-tered rent £ p.a.	Mean change on previ-ous rent[4] %	Median re-regis-tered rent £ p.a.	Number of cases	Mean regis-tered rent £ p.a.	Mean change on previ-ous rent[4] %	Median regis-tered rent £ p.a.	Number of cases
Greater London												
1975	549	−7	459	4,580								
1976	659	9	564	3,560								
1977	778	8	653	2,800	902	36	805	120	783	8	659	2,920
1978	826	13	703	2,380	867	40	757	820	837	20	721	3,200
Rest of England and Wales												
1975	406	8	367	7,540								
1976	466	10	418	5,640								
1977	521	8	466	4,900	575	52	542	330	524	10	471	5,230
1978	585	9	535	4,250	596	47	561	1,310	588	15	542	5,560

Notes: are at the bottom of Table 5.8, p. 282.

Source: Housing and Construction Statistics No. 29 (1979), Table 43(b).

Table 5·7 Rent registrations: mean change on previous rent and number of cases by type of applicant: regulated furnished, first registration[1]

	Landlord			Tenant			Joint			Local authority			All	
	Mean change on previous rent %	Number of cases	Percentage of all cases	Mean change on previous rent %	Number of cases	Percentage of all cases	Mean change on previous rent %	Number of cases	Percentage of all cases	Mean change on previous rent %	Number of cases	Percentage of all cases	Mean change on previous rent %	Number of cases
Greater London														
1975	40	610	17·3	−18	2,878	81·5	41	32	0·9	−32	13	0·4	−7	3,533
1976	64	900	30·5	−16	2,011	68·2	13	35	1·2	−24	4	0·1	9	2,950
1977	52	690	27·2	−9	1,816	71·5	31	18	0·7	−28	15	0·6	8	2,539
Rest of England and Wales														
1975	55	1,356	25·5	−9	3,605	67·8	32	146	2·7	−27	212	4·0	8	5,319
1976	64	1,161	25·9	−12	3,132	70·0	71	95	2·1	−29	88	2·0	9	4,476
1977	68	952	22·6	−11	3,043	72·3	22	152	3·6	−11	63	1·5	8	4,210

[1] Including housing association cases.

Source: Housing and Construction Statistics No. 27 (1978), Supp. Table XV.

Table 5.8 Rent registration: average registered rents and change on previous rents[1, 2, 3]:
First registrations of tenancies formerly rent controlled[9]

| | Decontrolled with qualification certificate[10] | | | | General decontrol (Housing Finance Act 1972 Part IV) | | | | | | | |
| | | | | | With all amenities[11] | | | | Lacking at least one amenity[11] | | | |
	Mean controlled rent £ p.a.	Mean registered rent £ p.a.	Mean change on controlled rent %	Number of cases	Mean controlled rent £ p.a.	Mean registered rent £ p.a.	Mean change on controlled rent %	Number of cases	Mean controlled rent £ p.a.	Mean registered rent £ p.a.	Mean change on controlled rent %	Number of cases
Greater London												
1974	76	270	312	850	88	286	252	6,660	80	248	232	11,370
1975	78	290	344	610	90	322	303	2,200	83	271	256	2,910
1976	82	337	389	590	95	379	364	1,420	91	319	308	1,540
1977	96	378	435	470	93	409	440	870	91	353	384	870
1978	100	413	502	300	121	464	486	370	106	395	447	370
Rest of England and Wales												
1974	50	182	357	6,140	59	190	248	32,440	52	165	225	28,050
1975	56	202	359	4,230	60	217	297	14,860	54	188	278	9,270
1976	68	238	377	3,550	66	260	361	7,690	59	220	323	4,670
1977	79	268	414	2,660	72	303	462	3,720	61	251	404	2,520
1978	92	321	509	1,660	82	342	502	1,620	74	294	488	1,160

[1] Cases under the Rent Act 1977 and corresponding earlier legislation.

[2] For England and Wales from the 2nd quarter 1974 the mean and median registered rents and numbers of cases are based on all registrations including non-comparable cases, i.e. those where there has been a material change to either the terms of the tenancy or the condition of the dwelling since the previous rent was set. Prior to the 2nd quarter 1974 all figures were based on comparable cases only.

[3] Unless there are substantial changes in circumstances, fair rents are fixed for a minimum of three years. With some exceptions rent increases up to the registered rent are now phased over three annual stages so that the full fair rent will only be paid from the beginning of the third year after registration.

[4] The mean change on previous rent is based on comparable cases only and is calculated as the average of the percentage changes for all individual registrations.

[5] Mean and median registered rents and mean change on previous rent relate to April–December only.

[6] Figures for first registrations of unfurnished tenancies in Scotland include qualification certificate and general decontrol cases.

[7] Cases under the Rent (Scotland) Act 1971 and the Housing (Financial Provisions) (Scotland) Act 1972.

[8] Rents include furniture and service charges.

[9] Controlled rents were fixed under the Rent Act 1957.

[10] Certificate of good repair and availability of a sink, a fixed bath or shower, a wash-hand basin, a hot and cold water supply to all three and

(a) Unfurnished tenancies

	First registrations							Re-registrations[3]						
				Number of cases	Rent Assessment Committee put Rent Officer rent						Number of cases	Rent Assessment Committee put Rent Officer rent		
	Mean Rent Assessment Committee rent £ p.a.	Mean change on Rent Officer rent %	Mean change on previous rent %	All cases Number	Down %	No change %	Up %	Mean Rent Assessment Committee rent £ p.a.	Mean change on Rent Officer rent %	Mean change on previous rent %	All cases Number	Down %	No change %	Up %
Greater London														
1976	708	17	90	2,522	5	16	79	569	11	48	2,701	6	16	78
1977	859	14	100	842	7	19	74	565	11	53	3,360	3	13	84
1978	829	9	101	736	7	26	67	709	8	53	2,166	6	23	71
Rest of England and Wales														
1976	365	7	135	1,556	15	35	50	333	7	57	1,855	7	29	64
1977	422	9	140	1,102	15	29	56	328	4	53	2,919	17	32	51
1978	462	3	114	896	28	33	39	420	5	59	2,416	11	30	59

(b) Furnished tenancies

	First registrations							Re-registrations[3]						
	Mean Rent Assessment Committee rent £ p.a.	Mean change on Rent Officer rent %	Mean change on previous rent %	All cases Number	Down %	No change %	Up %	Mean Rent Assessment Committee rent £ p.a.	Mean change on Rent Officer rent %	Mean change on previous rent %	All cases Number	Down %	No change %	Up %
Greater London														
1976	727	13	13	611	7	35	58							
1977	789	11	13	423	12	32	57	941	8	57	346	9	28	63
1978	809	8	34	549	7	42	51							
Rest of England and Wales														
1976	444	9	12	368	15	37	48							
1977	526	5	6	270	22	32	46							
1978	547	5	23	401	13	43	44	544	4	50	91	13	34	53

[1] Rent increases resulting from rent registration are normally phased over three annual stages under the Housing Rents and Subsidies Act 1975.

[2] The mean changes on Rent Officer and previous rents are calculated as the average of the percentage changes for all cases referred to the Rent Assessment Committee.

[3] At least three years after the previous registered rent. Furnished tenancies were brought within rent regulation by the Rent Act 1974. There were therefore no comparable re-registrations for furnished tenancies before August 1977.

Source: Housing and Construction Statistics No. 29 (1979), Supp. Table XXXI.

years) rises are noticeable. Increases tend to be proportionately higher outside London.

More detail of the impact of first registration on rent levels in different areas of the country is shown in Table 5.4. The data, which are for 1977 *only*, also show the average relationship between the fair rent and the rateable value of the property.

Table 5.5 shows who is using the fair rent system (1975–7 only). The figures reveal that landlords are by far the largest users of the fair rent scheme (for re-registrations they are overwhelming); that in the few cases taken by local authorities, rents have been reduced; and that even where tenants take cases, these usually result in rises, albeit relatively small.

Registration of furnished tenancies began after the enactment of the Rent Act 1974. The available data in Table 5.6 reveals that the numbers registered so far have been relatively few. Initial registrations were not, on average, much higher than existing rents; average re-registrations are more in line with those for unfurnished tenancies (above, Table 5.3).

However, the figures for first registrations by type of applicant (Table 5.7) reveal that at present a majority of applications are by tenants and on average these result in a rent reduction.

The conversion of tenancies from rent control to rent regulation not surprisingly results in massive percentage rent increases, as Table 5.8 shows. The table also shows how the numbers of registrations as a result of the automatic decontrol have fallen away, and the relatively small use of the old qualification certificate procedure (above, p. 271).

Table 5.2 gave the overall figures for the use of Rent Assessment Committees. The impact of their decisions on decisions taken by rent officers is shown in more detail in Table 5.9.

10. Phasing

One of the noticeable features of the data given above is that in most categories of case, applications to rent officers result in rent rises which are often substantial. To mitigate the burden on tenants, and because there is no adequate form of housing allowance for tenants, a piecemeal strategy has been introduced into the fair renting scheme whereby increases in rents may be phased. The details of these provisions need not be discussed in detail. They have been simplified somewhat by

the Housing Act 1980, s. 60(3)–(4). Since the date set for commencement of this section, increases in rents are in general to increase by
one-half of any authorized increase per annum, or 40 pence, whichever is the greater (Rent Act 1977, s. 55 and Sched. 8 as amended).
Phasing only applies to rent levels. Thus, increases in charges for services or for furniture may be passed on in full, as may rate increases,
if proper procedures are observed (Rent Act 1977, ss. 71(4), 71(3)).

It should perhaps be noted that Housing Act 1980, s. 60(5) and
(6) gives the Secretary of State extensive powers to further amend
or even to abolish the phasing provisions. This power is exercisable
by order.

11. The economic consequences of rent restrictions

Economic theorists have argued that the imposition of rent control
is inevitably going to reduce the amount of accommodation available
for letting. See, for example, Lansley (1979, pp. 117–19):

The impact of rent control is shown in theory [in Figure 5.1]. If the demand
and supply for rented accommodation is given by the curves denoted D and
S, the equilibrium market rent would be r_e and N_e the number of rented
dwellings provided. Suppose r_e was considered too high a rent for tenants
to pay and legislation set a maximum rent of r^*. Then each tenant receives
a subsidy of $(r_e - r^*)$ from his landlord. The initial effect of rent control is
to redistribute income from landlords to tenants. Further, lower rents will
expand the demand for rental accommodation from ON_e to ON_b. This will

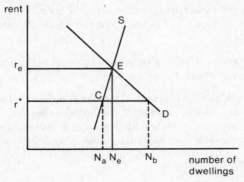

Figure 5.1   The impact of rent control

cause an initial excess demand of N_cN_b since the short run supply curve can be assumed to be fixed at N_cE. The excess demand will mean that some rationing device other than price will be needed to allocate the available supply of dwellings. An entry price in the form of 'key money' may develop, or overcrowding may increase.

In the longer run, the reduction in rents, while helping low income tenants, will discourage the supply of homes for renting. Supply will eventually fall to N_a, either by rented houses being sold, or by houses falling into disrepair. The new short supply curve will have shifted to the left at N_aC. The extent of the fall in supply will depend on the elasticity of supply. Since this is rather low, at least in the short run – a result mainly of the unfavourable tax treatment of landlords – the fall in supply may not be very great. Conversely, the effect of decontrol would not be to stimulate a very large increase in supply. To the extent that the elasticity of supply is greater in the long than the short run, however, decontrol would have a greater impact in the long run.

In general, therefore, the main impact of rent control has been to reduce the cost of housing to existing tenants, to redistribute income from landlords to tenants, to discourage new building of property to rent and to promote the deterioration in the quality of the existing rented stock, and its transfer into owner-occupation. But the precise extent of each of these effects is far from easy to establish, and is the subject of controversy. As a way of protecting tenants from the rents that would have emerged in a free market when rented accommodation is in short supply, rent control has been subject to a number of criticisms. First, because of the capricious nature of its distributional effects. Tenants are subsidised by their landlords, irrespective of their comparative incomes. By subsidising only one part of the rented market, rent controls also redistribute income away from landlords of controlled property to landlords of uncontrolled property and to existing owner-occupiers to whom unsatisfied demand is shifted. A fairer way of protecting tenants would have been by aid financed by taxation levied on the whole community. Secondly, because of its impact on the supply of accommodation to rent.

In more polemical vein, Pennance (1972, p. xi), introducing a set of essays on rent control, argues that:

Their common message is simple, but devastating in its criticism of policy. It is that in every country examined, the introduction and continuance of rent control/restriction/regulation has done much more harm than good in rental housing markets – let alone the economy at large – by

perpetuating shortages,
encouraging immobility,
swamping consumer preferences,

fostering dilapidation of housing stocks and eroding production incentives, distorting land-use patterns and the allocation of scarce resources

and all in the name of the distributive justice it has manifestly failed to achieve because at best it has been related only randomly to the needs and individual income circumstances of households.

and he continues (p. xv):

The economic fallacy – and economic incest

A 'fair rent', as defined by the statutory rules for determining it, is in effect what the market rent would be if supply and demand for homes in an area were broadly in balance, and taking into account age, character, quality and location. It thus specifically excludes from the reckoning the one economic factor likely to produce any easing of a situation of shortage. A 'fair' rent is therefore by definition a *restricted* rent, except in the peculiar circumstances where it is presumably unnecessary to bother with a fair rent! Unfortunately, there is also an inevitable tendency for 'fair' rents to be determined by the 'fair' rents already established for comparable properties in the area. This form of economic incest is common to most forms of valuation based on statutory rules. What it means in effect is that situations of shortage are not only perpetuated but also likely to be exacerbated unless further compensatory 'rules' are established.

In these circumstances there is little comfort to be drawn from the observed result that many applications to Rent Officers have produced increases in rent. What matters for investment incentives is the return achieved: not whether rent has been increased but by *how much*. A reduction in a rate of slide downhill does nothing much for morale if everyone else is climbing.

Control continues to creep

Moreover, the underlying and ill-formed notion of 'fairness' inevitably leads to extension of the area of control. The establishment of rent allowances for tenants of unfurnished accommodation has produced pressures to extend them to tenants of furnished accommodation, which means that furnished tenancies may eventually be brought into the ambit of rent regulation and 'fair' rent fixing. If this should produce a disincentive to supply furnished lettings, what is a 'fair' share of reduced opportunity worth?

The solution

The aim to relate subsidies to family need rather than indiscriminately to the fortunate occupants of some dwellings is laudable and welcome. With the flexible weapons of rent allowances and rent rebates available to cushion the impact of any marked change on individual family budgets, it is difficult to see what positive merit can possibly lie in the Government's attachment to rent control ...

In contrast, Donnison has argued that we should distinguish more clearly between rent control and rent regulation (1967, pp. 265–7):

A general system of rent regulation is now being established but its objectives deserve some clarification ...

Rent regulation is a more selective instrument, designed initially to deal with decontrolled unfurnished tenancies, other than the most expensive ones, and to restrain the more destructive effects of severe shortages. These shortages are created when the growth of employment and population outpace the growth of housing in centres where land scarcities and planning controls prevent a sufficient increase in the supply of housing. Discrimination, by private and public owners alike, against particular groups of the population – such as migrants and coloured people – may then impose hardships on such groups in the restricted corners of the market where they are able to secure a foothold. Complete decontrol of rents in face of such shortages inflict entirely pointless hardships which produce no solution or improvement. In every other country this has been recognized by procedures which have varied the extent and pace of decontrol according to the degree of shortage in the areas concerned.

But regulating rents does not mean freezing them. Where good houses are plentiful and supply and demand are already in balance and in places within areas of shortage where there is such a balance – typically the most expensive property – rents must be freely determined. Regulation is only designed to ensure that other rents which are subject to special scarcities are rationally related to those that are freely determined. If a purpose-built, centrally heated flat, standing in an attractive London neighbourhood, commands an annual rent of fifteen shillings per square foot, then a self-contained house, without central heating or bath, standing in a clean but unfashionable street, should command a lower rent; and two rooms opening off a landing in a house that stands in a sleazy quarter should command a yet lower rent. The fact that rents per square foot in our bigger cities do not follow this orderly pattern, and may actually be higher in the worst property than the best, is a measure of the scarcities operating in particular sectors of the market, and of the continuing distortions imposed by old-style rent controls.

Unlike rent *control*, which was designed to freeze a market, thus eventually depriving its prices of any systematic or constructive meaning, rent *regulation* is designed to recreate a market in which the over-all pattern of prices responds to changes in supply and demand, while the local impact of severe, and abnormal scarcities is kept within bounds. The general scarcity of housing throughout London being greater than the general scarcity throughout Birmingham, the whole pattern of rents should be higher in London than in Birmingham, just as Birmingham's rents will be generally higher than Oldham's, where the general level of scarcity is less severe still. But *within* each of these cities, differences in rents should represent differences in the value of the accommodation offered. The hardships such a change will inflict upon some tenants must be mitigated by government through housing allowances or other means, not by reductions in rent.

The first task of those responsible for regulating rents is to bring down some of the highest to a level that is rationally related to those that are freely determined in the open market. Their second task, when Parliament calls upon them to assume it, must be to help raise controlled rents to the same rational levels. It is this second phase which will be the most important numerically and the most difficult politically. In parts of the north of England and in other places where there is practically no shortage of housing, regulated rents may not differ greatly from controlled rents, for controlled rents of the older houses in these areas may not be far from the open market level for such property. But in areas of shortage, controlled rents will rise considerably. At the time the 1965 Rent Act was passed, few commentators grasped that it is in the longer run a measure for the raising rather than the lowering of rents. The second phase of its operation may never be brought into effect in areas of shortage unless a general system of housing allowances is first introduced to protect the poorer tenant involved.

There have been few attempts to assess the impact of rent regulation on the levels of rents. Perhaps, for the reasons advanced by Pennance, this is impossible. The Francis Committee wrote (1971, p. 62):

As regards registered rents, it seems we can conclude, generally speaking, that registered rents are on the average about 20 per cent lower than the related market rents. The London Panel told us that they examined 100 cases decided by Rent Assessment Committees, being cases in which reliable information as to the market rents was available, and they found that the registered rents were on average some 22 per cent below the market rents. The President of the Northern Panel, dealing with the North East, estimated that, in the case of dwellings in the lower rateable value bands, the registered rents were some 20 per cent below market rents. The President of the East Midland Panel, dealing with the East Midlands (where, we think, generally speaking, there is not a great deal of scarcity), estimated that the rents of dwellings in the low range of rateable value had been reduced by some 15 per cent. In the case of areas of stress, there is little doubt that the impact of Section 70(2) has been much greater. Thus, we are told that in Notting Hill, analysis of Rent Officer decisions during the early period of rent regulation showed an average reduction of 40 per cent on tenants' applications.

Many other witnesses have told us that the scarcity section has had the effect of reducing the level of registered rents to a substantial extent in areas of scarcity, and that even where the registered rent is higher than the previous rent, as is usually the case on landlords' applications, the increase is often substantially less than it would have been apart from section 70(2).

As regards unregistered rents, we have had a good deal of evidence that many landlords or their agents inspect the register, and we see no reason to doubt that in many instances the good landlord or agent will be guided by the pattern of registered rents.

Do these observations seem convincing in light of the data on rent levels now being set which were reproduced above (pp. 276–83)?

Another aspect of this question, revealed by Francis, and confirmed more recently by Paley (1978), is that substantial numbers of landlords and tenants do not use the rent regulation system at all. Table 5.2 shows that for England and Wales, for the years 1976–8 (three years being selected to allow for a complete cycle of rent registrations) some 650,000 applications for rent registration were made; yet Table 1.3 shows that there were an estimated 1,115,000 regulated tenancies in existence at the end of 1976.

The Francis Committee speculated on this and put forward six reasons why the scheme was not used more. Of these, they gave most emphasis to the suggestion that most tenants were quite happy with their rent levels (pp. 17–20):

[The] general impression we got from this evidence was that most landlords charge reasonable rents, and that a correspondingly high proportion of tenants acknowledge this fact. The grasping landlords who charge exorbitant rents are relatively few, and are to be found mainly in areas of unfit or nearly unfit houses, which are ripe or about to become ripe for clearance and likely to be acquired by the local authority for that purpose in a few years' time. In these areas, speculators tend to move in and buy up houses cheaply, and then let them off unconverted floor by floor or in rooms at high rents to several tenants, usually tenants who for one reason or another find it difficult to obtain better class accommodation and who are not in a position to obtain local authority accommodation or to buy a house. Two major categories of such tenants are newly arrived immigrants and 'problem' tenants. We were told that such tenants tend to gravitate to these areas because they cannot afford or find better accommodation. Of course, another class of tenants attracted to these areas consists of those who are lured by the prospect of being rehoused by the local authority when the area is cleared. All these tenants are susceptible to exploitation by unscrupulous speculators, and are unlikely to resort to the Rent Officer, even when they have good grounds for doing so, unless they are receiving regular payments of supplementary benefit which include provision for rent in the assessment of requirements and have been advised to do so by local officers of the Department of Health and Social Security (Supplementary Benefit Commission). We believe, however, that it would be a mistake to suppose that, even in these areas, all or even a majority of landlords charge exorbitant rents. Often the rents for accommodation in these areas are low, simply because the accommodation is of low standard, and many poor tenants seek accommodation in those areas for that reason.

In addition to those 'twilight' areas, there are also areas of acute housing stress – more particularly in London and the West Midlands – where there is scope for the unscrupulous speculator in the letting of unconverted multi-storey Victorian type houses. We have little doubt that a small minority but significant number of landlords in these areas charge rents which are well above those which Rent Officers would fix for the accommodation, but probably only in exceptional cases are these rents so high as to justify the description 'exorbitant'. These tenants are generally of a better type than those often found in the 'twilight' areas. They earn good money, and are able to pay a substantial rent, and are willing to do so for the sake of having accommodation near their place of work. These people constitute the speculative landlord's best customers, and he will be shrewd enough not to charge a rent which is so excessive as to be beyond their capacity to pay, or as to provoke them to go to the Rent Officer.

Apart from the speculator-type of landlord, there is another type who often charges excessively high rents, and that is the immigrant landlord who buys an old multi-storey house, wholly or partly vacant, for occupation by himself and his family, with the aid of a mortgage loan from a dubious source at a very high rate of interest, and who must perforce let off a part of the house at high rents to cover his financial commitments. Of course, not all immigrant landlords fall into this category, and for those who do there are circumstances of extenuation arising from the difficulties which face many immigrants in obtaining accommodation. It has to be borne in mind that these landlords often let to their own countrymen, who might otherwise be unable to obtain any accommodation. These tenants, unless they fall out with their landlord, are unlikely to resort to the Rent Officer, especially if they are aware of the circumstances which compel their landlord to charge high rents. The types of landlords referred to above are not typical of landlords in general. One of the things which has bedevilled the privately rented sector of housing for a long time is the tendency among some persons – often people with a deep social conscience who are rightly concerned about the housing conditions of the poor – to identify landlords as a class with the small minority of grasping landlords of the speculator type, and to assume or infer that any remedial action must be directed against landlords as such. It is only fair to add that the vast majority of our witnesses readily acknowledged that there were many good landlords, and that only a very small minority could be classified as 'bad'....

Other reasons they identified were: ignorance on the part of tenants; fear of their landlord retaliating; a sense of moral obligation to stand by an agreement; fear that the rent officer would put up the rent;

and finally that some tenants had an overriding concern to have repairs done rather than have their rents altered.

Notwithstanding these points, landlords' and tenants' *perceptions* of how they think the scheme works may be more important in determining their attitudes to rent regulation than detailed knowledge of how it actually works in practice. The following extract from Paley (1978, p. 19) gives some further information about this. For example:

> Where the landlord said that the rent for the letting was not registered, in 20% of cases he thought that it was not eligible for registration, either because the tenancy was controlled or because it was outside the scope of the Rent Acts for some other reason. In another 22% of cases he thought the rent officer (or tribunal) would reduce the level of rent or only confirm it at its current level if he applied to have it registered ... 5% specifically mentioned that they disliked getting involved with the council or with officialdom generally. A few, 4%, said that, even though they did not think that a registered rent would necessarily be lower than the current rent, it would not be financially worthwhile to them to have the rent registered because of the phasing of any future increases...

In the light of the data on the operation of the fair rent scheme presented in this chapter, consider how far these comments accurately reflect the law and practice relating to the scheme.

12. Rents for restricted contracts

A Jurisdiction and procedure

Jurisdiction over restricted contracts (defined above, p. 221) was given under Part V of the Rent Act 1977 to rent tribunals. The Housing Act 1980, s. 72, abolishes rent tribunals and provides that their functions are to be carried out by rent assessment committees. However, since the Act, almost unbelievably, proceeds to state that in carrying out those functions, the committees shall be known as rent tribunals, I shall continue to refer to them here as rent tribunals. Their task is to fix 'reasonable rents' (s. 78). The procedure of rent tribunals is governed by Rent Act 1977, s. 77(1): 'Either the lessor or the lessee under a restricted contract or the local authority may refer the contract to the rent tribunal for the district in question.'

The phrase 'under a restricted contract' has been interpreted to mean that there must be a valid contract, existing at the time of the application to the rent tribunal, that has not been brought to an end by (e.g.) a notice to quit or expiry of a fixed term. (See *R.* v. *East London Rent Tribunal, ex parte Schryer* [1970] 1 Q.B. 686.)

Where joint tenants refer a contract, all must join in the reference (*Turley* v. *Panton* (1975) 29 P.&C.R. 397). Surprisingly, perhaps, there is no statutorily prescribed application form.

In *R.* v. *Barnet and Camden Rent Tribunal ex parte Frey Investments* [1972] 2 Q.B. 342, the Court of Appeal held that a local authority could refer a number of contracts (in the case, twenty-two) simultaneously. However, in DoE Circular 48/73, local authorities were reminded of the restricted security available to such tenants:

> 22.   There will be cases where the rent eligible to be met by [rent] allowance is very low in relation to the rent being paid because that rent has not been registered and appears to be excessive. Authorities should ensure that the tenant concerned is aware of his right to apply to the Rent Tribunal to have a reasonable rent registered and they may wish in some cases to use their power under section [77 (1)] of the Rent Act [1977] to refer a contract to the Rent Tribunal. However authorities are strongly advised not to use this power if the tenant is unwilling. It is essential that no tenant applying for an allowance should as a result be forced to risk the possibly unfavourable consequences of a referral to the Tribunal.

Rent tribunals have a broad discretion as to the information they seek and the procedures they adopt. Failure on the part of the lessor (as defined in Rent Act 1977, s. 85(1)) to provide information is a criminal offence, though it can only be prosecuted by a local authority (*ibid.*, s. 77(2)–(4)).

In addition, Rent Act 1977, s. 80 (as amended) provides:

> **80.**—(1) Where the rent payable for any dwelling has been entered in the register under section 79 of this Act the lessor or the lessee or the local authority may refer the case to the rent tribunal for reconsideration of the rent so entered.
>
> (2) Where the rent under a restricted contract has been registered under section 79 of this Act, a rent tribunal shall not be required to entertain a reference, made otherwise than by the lessor and the lessee jointly, for the registration of a different rent for the dwelling concerned before the expiry of the period of 2 years beginning on the date on which the rent was last considered by the tribunal, except on the ground that, since that date, there has been such a change in –
>
> (a) the condition of the dwelling,
> (b) the furniture or services provided,

(c) the terms of the contract, or

(d) any other circumstances taken into consideration when the rent was last considered,

as to make the registered rent no longer a reasonable rent.

The tribunal's rent fixing powers are contained in Rent Act 1977, s. 78:

(1) Where a restricted contract is referred to a rent tribunal and the reference is not, before the tribunal have entered upon consideration of it, withdrawn by the party or authority who made it, the tribunal shall consider it.

(2) After making such inquiry as they think fit and giving to –

(a) each party to the contract, and

(b) if the general management of the dwelling is vested in and exercisable by a housing authority, that authority,

an opportunity of being heard or, at his or their option, of submitting representations in writing, the tribunal, subject to subsections (3) and (4) below –

(i) shall approve the rent payable under the contract, or

(ii) shall reduce or increase the rent to such sum as they may, in all the circumstances, think reasonable, or

(iii) may, if they think fit in all the circumstances, dismiss the reference,

and shall notify the parties and the local authority of their decision.

One difficulty noted by the Francis Committee was that the tribunal did not have power to reduce the rent on the ground that the landlord had broken his contractual obligations, e.g. to repair. This was the result of *R. v. Paddington etc Rent Tribunal, ex parte Bell Properties* [1949] 1 K.B. 666 where Lord Goddard C.J. stated: 'The Tribunal can only consider whether the rent is fair for what the landlord has contracted to give.' The Francis Committee noted that some tribunals did take into account the actual condition of the premises and the services provided by the landlord, irrespective of any contracual arrangements. But it was conceded that such practices were of doubtful legality. The suggestion to amend s. 78 has not been acted upon.

B Distinctions between rent tribunal and rent officer cases

(i) 'REASONABLE RENT' VS. 'FAIR RENT'

The question that arises is as to whether rent tribunals are required to exclude scarcity value. The Francis Committee stated (1971, pp. 146–7):

The question thus was whether the explicit basis for a 'fair rent' was appropriate to a 'reasonable rent', and in particular whether a 'reasonable rent' for the accommodation should discount any value attributable to scarcity. The Department's view was that this would be proper.

This view reflected the decision of the Court of Appeal in the case of *John Kay Ltd* v. *Kay*. This case arose under the Leasehold Property (Temporary Provisions) Act 1951, a forerunner to Part II of the Landlord and Tenant Act 1954, which enabled occupiers to apply to the county court for the grant of a new tenancy, 'at such rent on such terms and conditions as the court in all the circumstances thinks reasonable'. In the case of *Kay* v. *Kay* the rent fixed by the county court judge was £550 and the landlord, contending that a market rent would be £750, appealed. In giving judgment the Master of the Rolls said:

'The evidence before the court ... seems to me sufficient to justify the view that the figure of £750 is one that is derived not merely from the increase in general costs or the decrease in the value of money ... but is a figure further inflated by the particular and, one hopes, temporary circumstances of shortage of this sort of property; in other words, though £750 per annum is the market rent, the market figure is one inflated by the particular circumstances of shortage ... The judge has, and I think rightly, said that in so far as this figure has been inflated by that circumstance, it becomes an unreasonable figure; or at least, that it is unreasonable to impose on the tenant the obligation of having to pay that inflated sum.'

Lord Justice Jenkins said:

'If the only power the court has was to ascertain and fix the open market rent as the reasonable rent to be paid under a new tenancy, plainly this legislation ... would be in a great measure defeated because the whole difficulty which has to be met is that, in conditions of scarcity, the open market value may be forced up to a point which does exceed all reason; and it is essential in order to make legislation of this kind effective that the Tribunal which is to fix the rent should be able to discount contemporary market values to the extent necessary in its opinion to arrive at a fair result.'

The judgment in *Kay* v. *Kay* was quoted in 1965 by the then Minister of Housing and Local Government in the Second Reading debate on the Rent Bill. He said, 'There the Court of Appeal was precisely carrying out the fixing of a fair rent, less than the market rent, according to the principles of the Bill.'

The Department's letter of 4 August 1966 was criticized by Professor D.W. Elliott of the University of Newcastle in a letter to *The Times* but was defended in a reply by Mr C. D. Pilcher, Vice-President of the London Panel, so far as the relevance of s. [70] was concerned:

'We have endeavoured to ascertain to what extent Rent Tribunals have regard, so far as the accommodation is concerned, to registered rents for comparable unfurnished dwellings in the locality. In the process of determining the overall rent, Rent Tribunals first of all decide what would be a reasonable rent for the accommodation unfurnished, and, in this connexion, it appears that many Rent Tribunals – although, we think, by no means all – pay regard to registered rents for similar unfurnished accommodation. Some Rent Tribunal Chairmen have told us that they are not concerned with scarcity as such, but that, in determining a reasonable rent for the accommodation, they would incidentally eliminate any scarcity element in the rent to a large extent. Many Rent Tribunal Chairmen have expressed the view that it is in any event impossible to quantify scarcity, by which we think they mean that it is impossible to quantify it directly, and in this respect, as we have seen, we do not think that members of Rent Assessment Committees would now differ from them.'

Data on the work of rent tribunals since they were given jurisdiction over restricted contracts is to be found in Table 5.10. It is not possible to determine from this the extent to which scarcity is taken into account.

(ii) RECONSIDERATION

In *R.* v. *Fulham, Hammersmith and Kensington Rent Tribunal, ex parte Hierowski* [1953] 2 Q.B. 147, Lord Goddard C.J. said in part:

[The] landlord stated that the rates and other outgoings had increased. Thereupon, the tribunal seem to have regarded the increase in outgoings, which was the only change of circumstances alleged, as a change of circumstance enabling them to proceed on the tenant's application to reduce the rent. It is impossible to construe the Act of Parliament in this way. Counsel for the tribunal has strenuously argued that once any change of circumstance is shown, the matter is at large for the tribunal to deal with. If such a construction were placed upon this subsection, I think that it would be nothing more nor less than a trap, because a landlord applying to a tribunal to reconsider a rent already determined on the ground that there had been an increase in the rates might suddenly be met with the whole case being reopened and the tribunal reducing the rent although the rates had increased. That seems to me to be a most astonishing proposition ... [All] that the tribunal can consider is the change of circumstances alleged...

Lynskey and Parker JJ. concurred.

Is this case likely to be followed after the *Cowan* decision (above, p. 259)?

(iii) WITHDRAWAL OF REFERENCE

R. v. *Tottenham Rent Tribunal, ex parte Fryer* [1971] 2 Q.B. 681

Table 5.10 Rent tribunals: restricted contracts, Rent Act 1977: Applications for determination of reasonable rents (England and Wales)

	1976			1977			1978		
	Greater London	Rest of England and Wales	England and Wales	Greater London	Rest of England and Wales	England and Wales	Greater London	Rest of England and Wales	England and Wales
Number of applications									
Received	4,694	3,269	7,963	3,921	2,780	6,701	3,552	2,399	5,951
Withdrawn	607	805	1,412	543	784	1,327	511	609	1,120
Dealt with[1]	4,110	2,405	6,515	3,464	2,116	5,580	3,053	1,803	4,856
In hand at end of year	464	366	830	378	246	624	366	233	599
Decisions on rents[2]									
Determinations									
Rent reduced	800	574	1,374	671	472	1,143	569	416	985
Rent approved	472	263	735	400	231	631	286	196	482
Rent increased	921	488	1,409	802	529	1,331	827	528	1,355
All determinations	2,193	1,325	3,518	1,873	1,232	3,105	1,682	1,140	2,822
Other decisions									
Applications dismissed	502	470	972	429	410	839	440	267	707
No jurisdiction	531	301	832	395	244	639	349	197	546
All other decisions	1,033	771	1,804	824	654	1,478	789	464	1,253
All decisions on rents	3,226	2,096	5,322	2,697	1,886	4,583	2,471	1,604	4,075
Mean rent per week:									
All determinations:									
Registered rent £	9.13	7.88	8.66	10.53	10.32	10.45	11.59	10.92	11.32
Previous rent £	9.64	8.33	9.15	10.93	10.07	10.59	11.54	10.70	11.20

[1] Including cases not entertained or outside jurisdiction.

[2] Includes first applications for security where lessee has not previously applied on rent: such applications entail applying on rent as well as security. [This jurisdiction is now abolished, below, p. 440.]

Source: *Housing and Construction Statistics* No. 29 (1979), Supp. Table XXX.

LORD DENNING M.R.: Fryer Bros. (Properties) Ltd. are the owners of No. 7, Princes Avenue, Muswell Hill, London, N.10. On September 13, 1969, they let a flat in the house to a Mr. Penn at a rent of £6 3s. a week – furnished. On October 8, 1969, he referred the contract to the rent tribunal...

On receipt of the application the clerk to the tribunal looked to see whether it was within their jurisdiction. He made sure that it was within their district and that it was within the rateable limit. Having satisfied himself that there was jurisdiction, the clerk wrote to the landlords, asking them for information ... The landlords did not give the information.

On November 13, 1969, the clerk to the tribunal sent out notices both to the landlords and to the tenant, saying that the tribunal were going to hear the application on Monday, November 24, 1969, and would visit the premises during that morning.

Before the application was heard, however, the landlords sought to settle the matter by agreement. They approached the tenant and offered to reduce the rent from £6 3s. to £5 a week. He was reluctant to accept but thought they would turn him out unless he agreed. They also told him to write a letter to the tribunal withdrawing his application. He did so. Its terms show his state of mind. It is dated Friday, November 21, 1969. This is what he said:

'Dear Sir, I have today reached an agreement with the owner of this flat regarding rent and length of time I will be allowed to stay. I am sorry to cancel my application at this late date, but I had to compromise and accept their offer as I was assured I would be evicted if I let my application stand.'

It would appear that the tenant took that letter round by hand to the tribunal in the evening of Friday, November 21, 1969, but that the offices were then closed. So he put it through the letter-box. It was not opened until Monday morning, November 24, 1969, at about 9 a.m. when the staff arrived.

Meanwhile, however, the clerk to the tribunal had already, on the Friday afternoon, handed to the members of the tribunal the papers for Monday morning. They included the papers relating to Mr. Penn's flat. Over the weekend each member of the tribunal read his papers; and each of them completed a record sheet. In it each wrote down the particulars of the premises which they were to visit on the Monday morning. Each finished reading the papers by the Sunday evening. At that time none of the members had any idea that the tenant had withdrawn his application. His letter was still in the letter-box.

On the Monday morning at half past nine, Mr. Penn telephoned to the clerk of the tribunal. He asked whether the withdrawal of his application had been accepted. The clerk told him that the letter had been received too late to be shown to the members of the tribunal and that they would be visiting the premises at 10 o'clock that morning.

The members of the tribunal did not go first to the offices of the tribunal. They went straight to the flat. They intended to inspect it before holding the hearing. They could not get in. The tenant was not there. They visited other premises and then went to the tribunal offices. The clerk then told them of the letter which had been received from the tenant, Mr. Penn. The tribunal decided that the withdrawal was too late. They took the view that they had already 'entered upon consideration' of the reference, and that they would go on and consider it further. They adjourned it that day. But it was heard later – I think on December 12, 1969. The tribunal held that even the £5 was too high. They reduced the rent to £4 a week, for this one room.

Lord Denning noted that the tribunal might be said to have 'entered upon consideration' at various times, and continued:

The rival arguments are nicely balanced. If I were asked to say when this court 'enters upon consideration' of an appeal, I would say that we do not do so until we come into court and the case is called on for hearing. It may be that some members of the court will have read the papers beforehand. Some may have read the notice of appeal and the judgment in the court below. But, in so doing, they would not be 'entering on the consideration of the appeal'. They would only be preparing to enter upon the consideration of it. But, I think a rent tribunal is a very different body. They can and do act quite informally. They may come to a decision, if the parties so wish, merely on submissions in writing. In such a case, they may come to a decision on the papers without meeting at all, as, for instance, by agreeing in correspondence or by telephone. Seeing that it is such an informal tribunal, I think it proper to say that they 'enter upon consideration of' the reference when all three members of the tribunal have started to read the papers in it.

In order to withdraw the application, the party must 'withdraw' before that time. It is not sufficient for him to put a notice of withdrawal in the letter-box after office hours. A withdrawal is not complete until it is communicated to the clerk of the tribunal or his staff, which may be taken to be the time when it is received during office hours.

Salmon and Megaw L.JJ. agreed. Compare their analysis with the discussion in *Hanson* (above, p. 263).

(iv) EFFECT OF REGISTRATION

By the Rent Act 1977, s. 81, the 'reasonable rent' is effective from the date of registration. Further, it is a criminal offence to charge more than the registered rent, though only a local authority can institute proceedings (s. 81(4)).

Francis noted (1971, p. 158):

There is evidence that some landlords charge a rent in excess of the registered rent, notwithstanding that it is an offence to do so. Thus, out of 35 landlords interviewed for the purpose of the Study on Rent Tribunal Cases in London, being landlords of premises whose rent had been fixed by the Rent Tribunal, 4 were charging a rent in excess of the fixed rent for the same accommodation. In 2 of these cases, the landlord had decorated the premises since the registration, and presumably could have applied for reconsideration under section [80]. In the other 2 cases, there was no such excuse. We do not know whether in these 4 cases, the tenant had a rent book, or if he did, whether the rent book stated (as it should have done) that the rent had been fixed by the Rent Tribunal at a specified amount. It appears that a high proportion of weekly furnished tenants have no rent book – as many as 55 per cent, according to the Tenants' Survey, in Greater London. In the absence of a rent book, it is unlikely that a new tenant would know of the registration, there being no obligation on the landlord to inform him of that fact otherwise than by making the prescribed entry in the rent book. It seems to us that the best way of tackling this particular problem is by strengthening the law as to rent books ... It appears that overcharging is a good deal more common in regulated tenancies than in furnished. This may well be attributable to the fact that it is not an offence to charge more than the registered rent in the case of regulated tenancies.

Comment. In the light of these distinctions, which are largely the result of historical accident, not deliberate policy, it has frequently been suggested that the jurisdiction of Rent Officers and Rent Tribunals to fix rents should be amalgamated. The transferral of the Rent Tribunal's jurisdiction to the Rent Assessment Committee by the Housing Act 1980 may be seen as a first step in the eradication of the differences just discussed.

C A word on resident landlord cases

Restricted contracts will usually be resident landlord cases. Where a rent tribunal has assessed a reasonable rent in such a case, but the landlord ceases to be resident, the rent tribunal's rent becomes the registered 'fair rent' for the dwelling (Rent Act 1977, Sched. 2, para. 6). Such registration is deemed to be effective from the date the tenancy becomes protected; unwary landlords may thus find their right to reconsideration of the rent postponed.

The Paley study (1978, p. 3) found:

The indications are that the market for lettings by resident landlords was in a state of normal turnover. Those who did not intend to relet were approximately balanced numerically by owner-occupiers in these areas who thought they would decide to take in a boarder or tenant. Also the reasons given by the resident individual landlords and by owner-occupiers for not wishing to let most commonly reflected personal circumstances rather than an adverse reaction to rent levels or the law.

Estimates of the numbers of resident landlords are set out above, Table 1.6 (p. 17).

13. Remedies of the landlord for failure to pay rent

Failure by the tenant to pay rent may result in a number of legal (and thus social) consequences.

A Eviction

The ultimate sanction for non-payment of rent is eviction (discussed below, pp. 406, 424). The landlord may seek possession of the property in addition to the other remedies.

B Distress for rent

This is an ancient remedy, and an area of law of great complexity (Woodfall, 1978, pp. 317–404). In essence, it allows the goods of the defaulting tenant to be seized in lieu of payment of rent. Distress is usually levied by a bailiff, who has the protection of a warrant to distrain. Distress can only be levied after sunrise and before sunset. Over the years, various enactments have been passed to ensure that the basic necessities of life are not seized. In particular, distress for rent relating to a protected or a statutory tenancy shall only be levied with leave of the county court (Rent Act 1977, s. 147). The general discretions given to the court by Rent Act 1977, s. 100 (see below, p. 418) also apply to these decisions.

The law on distress is being examined, albeit in desultory fashion, by the Law Commission. They have reported that about 60% of applications for warrants to distrain are granted, 'but no information is obtainable of the grounds upon which leave was refused ...'. They give no information as to the actual extent of the use of this remedy. They comment that there is no evidence that wrongful distress is at all widespread, and they have found little evidence of abuse or hardship.

However, these conclusions are not based on a comprehensive social survey. They suggest that the mere process of bailiffs turning up and threatening to take a tenant's property away may have a galvanizing effect on a recalcitrant tenant. But they also concede that in many cases where rent is owed, the family have no goods worth taking anyway. They have not yet reached any conclusion as to whether this remedy should be allowed to continue. It may be noted, however, that in 1969, the Payne Committee (Payne, 1969, section 9) concluded that the priority effectively given to landlords over other creditors was no longer justifiable and argued that rent arrears should be treated on a par with other debts. No action has been taken on this proposal.

For some time the conventional wisdom was that this somewhat feudal remedy was only infrequently used. However, in 1978 it became apparent that many local authorities were using this remedy against council tenants on a more or less regular basis (Schifferes, 1979). Local authorities are able to levy distress without seeking the leave of the court. SHELTER discovered examples of abuse in the distraint process. More importantly, it frequently turned out to be a futile remedy since the value of the goods seized, after they had been sold, was often much less than the total arrears, which still remained to be paid off. SHELTER has therefore urged that the recommendation of the Payne Committee be brought into effect at once; so too has the National Tenants' Organization.

C A civil action for damages

Since failure to pay rent will usually amount to a breach of the covenant to pay rent, an ordinary civil action for damages for breach of contract can be brought. Since 1971 there has also existed a special procedure in the County Court – the 'Rent Action' – for the recovery of rent arrears while the tenant remains in occupation (County Court Rules, Order 26, Part II). Landlords who obtain judgment may also obtain an Attachment of Earnings order against the tenant. However, this is only effective against tenants who are in employment; it becomes very difficult to enforce against those who change employment.

In principle, a successful claim for rent (or for use and occupation or for mesne profits (below)) must be paid in full; the tenant is not usually allowed to set-off damages for breach of covenant against such claim. (*Hart* v. *Rogers* [1916] 1 K.B. 646; *Old Grovebury Manor Farm*

v. *W. Seymour Ltd* [1979] 1 All E.R. 573 (Ch. D).) See, though, pp. 364–7 below.

D Compensation for use and occupation

If no rent is agreed but the circumstances indicate that there was an implicit promise to compensate the landlord for the use of premises by a tenant, the law permits the owner of property to recover damages due on an implied agreement to pay for the use of the landlord's property (*Smith* v. *Eldridge* (1854) 15 C.B. 236). This implication is rebutted where the circumstances show that the occupation was to be without compensation (*Howard* v. *Shaw* (1841) 8 M.&W. 118).

As the right to compensation is based on the fact that no rent has been agreed, the landlord may recover a 'reasonable satisfaction' for the use and occupation (*Tomlinson* v. *Davy* (1821) 2 Brod.&B. 680).

E Mesne profits

After a tenancy has been finally determined (including any period of statutory protection), but the tenant remains in possession, the landlord may, if he wishes, claim 'mesne profits'. They are calculated according to the fair value of the premises which may or may not be the same as the rent under the preceding tenancy (*Clifton Securities* v. *Huntley* [1948] W.N. 267). Where the Rent Acts apply to property, the measure of damages is usually the regulated rent, even though a 'fair value' might be higher (*Rawlance* v. *Croydon Corporation* [1952] 2 Q.B. 803; *Newman* v. *Dorrington Developments* [1975] 1 W.L.R. 1642).

Question. Could the 'fair value' ever be *less* than the fair rent?

F Damages for trespass

Where no tenancy existed, but the landlord discovers trespassers on his property, he may sue for damages. In *Swordheath Properties* v. *Tabet* [1979] 1 All E.R. 240, the Court of Appeal held that damages could be claimed, even though the landlord did not prove that he could have let the premises during the period of occupation. The measure of damages, 'in the absence of anything special in the particular case, would be the ordinary letting value of the property' (*per* Megaw L.J.).

6
Other Financial Protections

Introduction

A fundamental problem, underlying the whole discussion of rent regulation contained in the last chapter, is the question of how can governments try to ensure that access to housing is available to all, including the poor, given that housing is provided largely through the operation of the private sector of the economy. In this chapter we examine briefly some of the other financial protections that have been created in attempts to support that basic policy. We shall see that, as with rent regulation, much of this law is not used in the ways in which politicians might have expected. Once again, therefore, the questions must be raised of whether greater use should be made of these laws and if so, how best may use of them be encouraged; and, more generally, it must be asked whether the policies themselves are wrong.

1. Rent rebates and allowances

In 1967 Donnison wrote (1967, p. 86):

Rent controls in this country have until recently taken a virtually unique pattern. Elsewhere in western Europe the private landlord has generally been regulated *and* subsidized; restrictions on his rents have been repeatedly modified and relaxed, and concentrated most heavily upon selected areas of shortage. In this way he has been employed, unwillingly maybe, as an instrument of housing policy, and in return has often been prepared to sustain or extend the contribution he makes to the housing market. In this country he has been treated in an altogether different way, sometimes as a parasite to be ruthlessly suppressed, sometimes as a paragon of free enterprise to be unleashed in haphazard and unselective fashion. Not surprisingly, he has extricated himself from the market whenever he gets the chance to escape with profit.

(See, too, Lawson & Stevens, 1974.)

However, it was not until 1 January 1973, when the Housing Finance Act 1972 came into force, that rebate and allowance[1] schemes have been available as of right throughout the country for both private (unfurnished) and council house tenants who are in full-time employment, and only since 1 April 1973 that they have been available to tenants of furnished accommodation. (Many local authorities took powers to run rent rebate schemes for their own tenants before that date; and the Birmingham Corporation Act 1968 gave that authority power to run the first rebate scheme for private tenants.)

The policy of bringing help to low-income families by way of means-tested benefits such as rent rebates/allowances is one of extreme controversy. Critics point out that means testing is fundamentally ineffective. People do not claim their rights perhaps because they do not know of them; because they do not understand them; because they are too proud to claim them. Thus rent rebates must be considered not only on their own but as a part of a wider strategy in social policy.

Scepticism has also been expressed at the desirability of this form of subsidy from an economic point of view. Nevitt has written (1966, p. 154): 'If every family with less than average national income were given a housing subsidy in cash, this would raise all rents and house prices and only landlords and sellers of land would benefit.'

A The model scheme

The Housing Finance Act, s. 20 provides that all schemes shall be at least as generous as the model set out in Schedule 3 (as frequently amended). Section 21 gives a local authority power to make larger rebates or allowances to people with exceptional personal or domestic circumstances. However, s. 22 states that the total paid out in rebates/allowances in any year must not be more than 110% of the 'authority's standard amount' of rebates or allowances.

The details of the means-test will not be reproduced here, but Schedule 3 should be studied so that the full complexity of the scheme

1. Rebates are made to council tenants, s. 18; allowances are paid to private tenants, s. 19.

Table 6.1 Rent rebates and rent allowances

	Rent rebates			Rent allowances to private tenants				
				Unfurnished			Furnished	
	Number granted (thous.)	Average weekly rebate (£)	Estimated percentage take-up	Number granted (thous.)	Average weekly allowance (£)	Estimated percentage take-up	Number granted (thous.)	Average Weekly allowance (£)
1970 March	350	0·87						
1971 March	350	1·04						
1972 March	270	1·21						
1973 May	700	1·99	60–70	48	2·08	10–15		
December	765	2·40		95	2·29			
1974 April	840	2·39		120	2·42	20–25	7	2·54
1975 January	820	2·42	70–75	135	2·30	30–35	12	2·58
April	870	2·68		150	2·41		10	2·80
October	940	2·85					11	2·80
1976 January	955	2·87		180	2·70	35–40	11	2·90
April	970	3·00	75–80	190	2·62	45–50	13	2·89
October	995	3·11		190	2·69	50–55	12	2·90
1977 January	990	3·15		190	2·75		11	3·08
April	1,000	3·31	80–85	200	2·84	55–60	11	3·06
October	1,005	3·32		200	2·92		10	3·15
1978 January	1,000	3·39		195	3·06		10	3·34
April	995	3·42		200	3·14		10	3·36
October	985	3·40		200	3·28		9	3·31

may be appreciated. The definition of 'rent' which is 'eligible' for rebate or an allowance is particularly confusing for tenants who are required to pay each week a sum which includes (say) amounts for rates, hire of garage, or payments for central heating equipment, some of which are 'eligible', others not. (See S.I. 1972, No. 1203.)

Administrative arrangements for dealing with applications are set out in Housing Finance Act 1972, Schedule 4 (as amended). Among other things, this gives local authorities power to require applicants to provide necessary information in writing (para. 2); prescribes the periods during which rebate will last (para. 4); sets out the situations in which a successful applicant must inform the local authority of changes in his circumstances (para. 5); provides that allowances may be paid direct to the landlord (para. 12(2)). Special rules relate to allowances paid to students (S.I. 1977 No. 1290).

The operation of the scheme has been kept under official review by the Advisory Committee on Rent Rebates and Allowances (1974, 1977). It has also been the subject of other studies (e.g. Legg & Brion (1976); Hetzel, Yates & Trutko (1978); Yates (1979)).

Table 6.1 gives some figures on the extent of take-up of rent rebates in England and Wales. These indicate that the schemes are reaching by no means all those potentially entitled. (This may be compared with the better-off who are buying housing on mortgage who receive their tax relief on interest payments automatically through the tax system.) Given the general pressures to raise rent levels in both the private and public sectors of the housing market, this failure to direct resources to those most in need must be a source of concern and call into question the suitability of this form of subsidy. It may further be noted that one objective of introducing rent allowances in the private sector, combined with the substantial relaxations in the rules relating to the regulation of rent levels discussed in the last chapter, was to encourage private landlords to spend more money on improvement of their properties. Yates (1979, p. 215) has found that this is not happening.

B Supplementary benefits and rent rebates/allowances

Table 6.2 shows the numbers of householders receiving supplementary benefit in the three main tenure categories.

Part II of Schedule 3 of the Housing Finance Act 1972 used to lay down rules for claimants who are in receipt of supplementary benefits (S.B.). Under administrative arrangements, most S.B. claimants were

Table 6.2   Householders receiving supplementary benefit

	Local authority tenants (thous.)	Privately renting tenants (thous.)	Owner-occupiers (thous.)
1970			
November	1,023	692	372
1971			
November	1,120	698	391
1972			
November	1,168	..	..
1973			
November	1,105	579	367
1974			
November	1,134	540	361
1975			
August	1,103	534	370
1976			
August	1,176	540	392
1977			
August	1,269	509	438
1978			
August	1,302	490	435

Source: Housing and Construction Statistics No. 28 (1979), Supplementary Table XX.

to be paid their rent rebate/allowance not by their local authorities, but by the Department of Health and Social Security (DoE Circular 154/73). However, because of the complex interaction of supplementary benefit rules and the rent (and also rate) rebate rules it was found that an increasing number of supplementary benefit claimants might be better off if they stopped claiming supplementary benefit and instead claimed rent and rate rebates. Initially it was up to the claimant to work out for himself which was the most financially advantageous. However, the difficulty of reaching this decision led central government to take the initiative and set in hand an exercise to find out which supplementary benefit claimants would be better off with rent rebates/allowances (DoE Circular 148/74). Despite this, it was estimated in 1979 that some 400,000 people were still receiving the wrong benefit (S.B.C., 1979, para. 5.21).

As a result of these administrative problems, the Housing Act 1980, s. 119 now provides that 'except in accordance with directions of the

Secretary of State' no rent rebates or allowances are to be paid to S.B. claimants. Thus those who would be better off on S.B. will benefit. However it appears that those who would have been better off on rent rebates and allowances will have to bear the burden of administrative convenience.

C A general housing allowance?

The complexities described above, combined with disquiet at the advantageous treatment of owner-occupiers, has led to a number of calls for a more comprehensive 'housing allowance' payable to everyone, possibly on the lines of Child Benefit. The details of this debate are beyond the scope of this work. In its Housing Policy Review, the last Labour Government was said to be against the idea (Housing Policy, 1977, paras. 5.13–5.17). However, it may be predicted that those critical of the present arrangements relating to housing finance will not allow the issue to die. (Donnison, 1979, p. 68; cf. Bradshaw & Bradley, 1979, p. 94; and see literature cited at p. 242 above.)

2. Illegal premiums

'By the end of the [19th] century, the asking for 'key money' ... was becoming very common in areas where houses were hard to find' (Gauldie, 1974, p. 159).

It is clear that it would have been futile for Parliament to try to control rent levels but not prohibit premiums. The three elements of the Rent Acts, control of rent, security of tenure and prohibition of illegal premiums, are all inter-related. When rent control legislation was first introduced in 1915, however, asking for premiums, though outlawed, was not made a criminal offence; this development occurred in 1920 (Salisbury, 1920, para. 24).

The current law on illegal premiums is to be found in Rent Act 1977, ss. 119–28 (as amended). Those provisions will not be set out in full, but the most important sections are discussed.

A Protected tenancies

119.—(1) Any person who, as a condition of the grant, renewal or continuance of a protected tenancy, requires, in addition to the rent, the payment of any premium or the making of any loan (whether secured or unsecured) shall be guilty of an offence.

(2) Any person who, in connection with the grant, renewal or continuance of a protected tenancy, receives any premium in addition to the rent shall be guilty of an offence.

(3) A person guilty of an offence under this section shall be liable to a fine not exceeding £100.

(4) The court by which a person is convicted of an offence under this section relating to requiring or receiving any premium may order the amount of the premium to be repaid to the person by whom it was paid.

Sections 120 and 121 deal with premiums on the assignment of protected tenancies. In such cases, certain sums may legitimately be passed on by the assignor to the assignee. (There is also special protection contained in s. 121 and Schedule 18 given in the case of tenancies which become regulated as a result of the Counter Inflation Act 1973.)

B Restricted contracts

122.—(1) This section applies in relation to any premises if –

(*a*) under Part V of this Act, a rent is registered for those premises in the register kept in pursuance of section 79 of this Act; and

(*b*) in a case where the approval, reduction or increase of the rent by the rent tribunal is limited to rent payable in respect of a particular period, that period has not expired.

(2) Any person who, as a condition of the grant, renewal, continuance or assignment of rights under a restricted contract, requires the payment of any premium shall be guilty of an offence.

(3) Nothing in subsection (2) above shall prevent a person from requiring –

(*a*) that there shall be paid so much of any outgoings discharged by a grantor or assignor as is referable to any period after the grant or assignment takes effect; or

(*b*) that there shall be paid a reasonable amount in respect of goodwill of a business, trade, or profession, where the goodwill is transferred to a grantee or assignee in connection with the grant or assignment or accrues to him in consequence thereof.

(4) A person guilty of an offence under this section shall be liable to a fine not exceeding £100.

(5) The court by which a person is convincted of an offence under this section may order the amount of the premium, or so much of it as cannot lawfully be required under this section, to be repaid to the person by whom it was paid.

C Treatment of furniture

123. Where the purchase of any furniture has been required as a condition of the grant, renewal, continuance or assignment –

(*a*) of a protected tenancy, or

(*b*) of rights under a restricted contract which relates to premises falling within section 122(1) of this Act, then, if the price exceeds the reasonable price of the furniture, the excess shall be treated, for the purposes of this Part of this Act, as if it were a premium required to be paid as a condition of the grant, renewal, continuance or assignment of the protected tenancy or, as the case may be, the rights under the restricted contract.

On this provision Megarry (1967, p. 438), adapting the judgment of Denning L.J. in *Eales* v. *Dales* [1954] 1 Q.B. 539, wrote:

'The reasonable price' means the price which in all the relevant circumstances was the reasonable price for the parties to have agreed; and this is a question of fact for the trial judge. It is not the price which would be realized if the articles were removed and sold by auction, but the price which an outgoing tenant who is willing to leave would agree with an incoming tenant who is willing to take them over; and this leaves much latitude. Fitted carpets are worth more *in situ* than removed, and furniture may be particularly suited to the premises. Where articles have a recognizable market value, this is important but not necessarily conclusive; but a price which exceeds the replacement cost cannot be reasonable. Extraneous elements must be excluded, such as the incoming tenant's desire to obtain a tenancy, or any payments for agent's commission or redecoration. The onus is on the tenant to establish that the price is excessive. This provision is confined to furniture, fittings and other articles; there is no corresponding provision to the effect that only the excess of any payment for other matters, such as repairs shall be treated as a premium.

Enforcement of s. 123 may be assisted in theory by a complex procedure laid down in s. 124. Among other things this gives power to local authority officials to enter premises and inspect furniture where the price asked is thought to be excessive.

D Rent in advance

126.—(1) Where a protected tenancy which is a regulated tenancy is granted, continued or renewed, any requirement that rent shall be payable –

    (*a*) before the beginning of the rental period in respect of which it is payable, or

    (*b*) earlier than 6 months before the end of the rental period in respect of which it is payable (if that period is more than 6 months),

shall be void, whether the requirement is imposed as a condition of the grant, renewal or continuance of the tenancy or under the terms thereof.

(2) Any requirement avoided by subsection (1) above is, in this section, referred to as a 'prohibited requirement'.

(3) Rent for any rental period to which a prohibited requirement relates shall be irrecoverable from the tenant.

(4) Any person who purports to impose any prohibited requirement shall be liable to a fine not exceeding £100, and the court by which he is convicted may order any amount of rent paid in compliance with the prohibited requirement to be repaid to the person by whom it was paid....

If 'irrecoverable' payments have in fact been made, they may be recovered for up to two years after the date of payment (s. 126(7)) either from the landlord or his personal representatives (s. 126(5)) or by deduction from rent (s. 126(6)). False entries in rent books are also punishable (s. 126(8) and (9); above, p. 62).

E Deposits

Rent Act s. 128(1)(c) (introduced by Housing Act 1980, s. 70):

'premium' includes – ...
(c) any sum paid by way of a deposit, other than one which does not exceed one-sixth of the annual rent under the tenancy and is reasonable in relation to the potential liability in respect of which it is paid.

(And see *R.* v. *Ewing* (1977) 65 Cr. App. R. 4.)

F Recovery of premiums

In addition to creating criminal offences, there is a general right given to those who have paid illegal premiums to recover them from those persons to whom they have been paid (s. 125).

G Notes on premiums

(a) Not all premiums are illegal. Only if the tenancy is within the Rent Act will any accompanying premium be unlawful. Thus most long leases with a very low ground rent fall outside these provisions. Special rules apply to long leases that also happen to be Rent Act protected: see s. 127 and Schedule 18, Part II (as amended by Housing Act 1980, s. 78).

(b) 'Person'. The meaning of this word was discussed in the important House of Lords decision in *Farrell* v. *Alexander* [1977] A.C. 59:

LORD WILBERFORCE: My Lords, the appellants, Mrs Farrell and her daughter, have brought an action to recover from the respondent, Mrs Alexander, a sum of money which was paid to her in order to obtain the tenancy of a flat. They claim that this money was a premium which it was illegal for the respondent to require or to receive and that they have the right to recover it...

The respondent had a protected tenancy of this flat with some four years unexpired from the Church Commissioners. There were negotiations with the appellants with a view to an assignment of it and the appellants were asked for a sum of £4,000 for the fixtures and fittings. Though the actual value of these fixtures and fittings has not been determined, it was certainly less than £4,000 so that the balance was a premium for the proposed assignment ... The transaction proceeded in this way. A formal agreement was drawn up under which the respondent agreed to surrender the lease subject to acceptance of the surrender by the landlords and to the simultaneous grant by them of a new lease to the appellants. On completion the new lessees were to pay to the respondent the sum of £4,000 for fixtures and fittings, and this money was in fact paid ... So the question to be decided is whether it is illegal for a lessee to require or to receive a premium as a condition of surrendering her lease, and in order that a new lease may be granted to the payer of the premium...

My Lords, I must say that, in relation to the facts which I have stated, these sections are to me, if not transparently clear, at least unambiguous in the legal sense. They refer to 'any person', words wide enough to include landlords, tenants, agents or middlemen. They apply to what was done here because the respondent required the premium as a condition of the grant of a protected tenancy (see the words 'subject to ... the simultaneous grant' mentioned above). The words 'any person' ... are words of wide generality and fit, without any strain whatever, the present facts.

Difficulties arose because two decisions of the Court of Appeal, *Remmington* v. *Larchin* [1921] 3 K.B. 404 and *Zimmermann* v. *Grossman* [1972] 1 Q.B. 167, had decided that 'person' meant 'landlord' only. Nonetheless, Lord Wilberforce decided that these decisions should not be followed and held that the sum demanded in the present case was recoverable. Viscount Dilhorne, Lords Simond, Edmund-Davies and Russell of Killowen all delivered concurring judgments. (Much of what their lordships had to say related to the proper method of interpreting consolidating Acts of Parliament, where the words of the legislation had not been changed.)

(*c*) Premium or rent: see above, pp. 183–8.

(*d*) Definition. Apart from the specific cases relating to furniture, rent in advance and deposits, discussed above, premium is defined (s. 128, as amended) as:

(*a*) any fine or other like sum;
(*b*) any other pecuniary consideration in addition to rent...

The scope for interpretation is obviously extensive though, surprisingly perhaps, the amount of judicial authority is small (see Megarry, 1967, pp. 418ff).

H Evidence of abuse of the law

Empirical evidence is hard to come by. The Milner-Holland report noted (1965, p. 171):

Many witnesses told us of sums demanded as 'key money', high prices for a few sticks of low grade furniture, advance payments for dilapidations, and deposits supposed to cover advance payments for gas and electricity. There is an infinite variety of labels applied to the sums thus demanded before tenancies are granted. If these payments result in reasonable security of tenure and were in due course properly accounted for, the practice might not be wholly objectionable. We were told, however, that all too often tenants who had paid sums of this kind in order to obtain a tenancy found it difficult or impossible to recover their deposits on the termination of their tenancies. We are quite unable to put any figure on the frequency of these practices; but we are satisfied that they occur. The activities of one operator, controlling forty-five properties ... were fully investigated by a committee formed by a St Pancras Borough Councillor ... Forty-three complainants came forward; except for one tenant who took proceedings in the High Court and recovered a deposit of £84, few, if any, got their money back ... Whether criminal proceedings would lie, seems doubtful ...

3. Agents' commission

It may be an offence for certain commission to be demanded from potential tenants. The Accommodation Agencies Act 1953 provides:

1.—(1) Subject to the provisions of this section, any person who, during the continuance in force of this Act, –

(a) demands or accepts payment of any sum of money in consideration of registering, or undertaking to register, the name or requirements of any person seeking the tenancy of a house;

(b) demands or accepts payment of any sum of money in consideration of supplying, or undertaking to supply, to any person addresses or other particulars of houses to let; or

(c) issues any advertisement, list or other document describing any house as being to let without the authority of the owner of the house or his agent,

shall be guilty of an offence.

(2) A person shall not be guilty of an offence under this section by reason

of his demanding or accepting payment from the owner of a house of any remuneration payable to him as agent for the said owner.

(3) A person being a solicitor shall not be guilty of an offence under this section by reason of his demanding or accepting payment of any remuneration in respect of business done by him as such.

(4) A person shall not be guilty of an offence under this section by reason of his demanding or accepting any payment in consideration of the display in a shop, or of the publication in a newspaper, of any advertisement or notice, or by reason of the display or publication as aforesaid of an advertisement or notice received for the purpose in the ordinary course of business.

(5) Any person guilty of an offence under this section shall be liable on summary conviction to a fine not exceeding one hundred pounds or to imprisonment for a term not exceeding three months, or to both such fine and imprisonment.

(6) In this section the following expressions have the meanings hereby assigned to them that is to say:—

'house' includes any part of a building which is occupied or intended to be occupied as a dwelling;
'newspaper' includes any periodical or magazine;
'owner', in relation to a house, means the person having power to grant a lease of the house.

Although one suspects that the Act is widely ignored (indeed an anonymous solicitor was reported in *The Guardian*, 12 August 1971, as saying it was 'one of those laws where nobody can believe what it appears to mean, so everybody ignores it'), it has been subject to some, not wholly consistent, judicial interpretation.

(a) McInnes v. Clarke [1955] 1 W.L.R. 102

[The headnote in that case reads as follows:] An estate agent carried on a business of finding for persons requiring it furnished accommodation. On a person making an enquiry for accommodation he would be told that the fee payable by him, if accommodated, was a sum equal to one week's rental of the premises and that a deposit of approximately half the weekly rental which he was willing to pay would be asked for. If the client was willing to pay the deposit an agreement was entered into between the client and the estate agent. Either before or after the agreement was signed a list of addresses would be given to the client. After a client had obtained accommodation, he would return and pay the balance of the fee due. Unsatisfied clients received their deposits back in full. *Held*, that, on the facts, the estate agent was demanding or accepting payment in consideration of supplying addresses contrary to section 1 (1) (b) [of the Act].

(b) *Crouch and Lees* v. *Haridas* [1972] 1 Q.B. 138

The plaintiffs' claim is for £90 commission due to them from the defendant under an agreement made orally in or about the month of March, 1968, between the Defendant and one Lees acting for the Plaintiffs. The Defendant was seeking particulars of a flat which was to let. The Plaintiffs, who are estate agents, were not retained by the landlords and informed the Defendant accordingly, who agreed that in consideration of the Plaintiffs supplying him with particulars of the said flat, he would pay the plaintiffs their commission in accordance with the scales authorized by the Chartered Auctioneers and Estate Agents Institute, namely 10 per cent of one year's rental in the event of his taking a lease of the said flat. In pursuance of the said agreement the plaintiffs supplied the defendant with particulars of a flat at 103 Bickenhall Mansions, Gloucester Place, London, W.1 and the defendant subsequently took the same on a five-year lease at a rental of £905 per annum...

DAVIES L.J. said (in part):

It seems to me that is perfectly clear on the facts found by the judge here that the plaintiffs in the present instance did demand payment of a sum of money in consideration of supplying or undertaking to supply to the defendant particulars of a flat to let. That is the whole contract as pleaded by them. The effect of the agreement was that the defendant was looking for a flat and they were going to supply him with the details of this flat at 103 Bickenhall Mansions in consideration of his agreement to pay 10 per cent of the first year's rent.

That is made clear by the case to which the judge himself referred in the other county court judgment, the case to which I have already alluded, *McInnes* v. *Clarke*. [above]...

It seems to me that that case is not distinguishable from the present one. It is true that there the estate agent demanded and received 50 per cent of the agreed commission in advance; but I think that is a distinction without a difference. There was no advance payment in the present case but only an agreement to pay when the defendant was satisfied. That makes no difference at all, because in each case, unless the defendant got a flat and was satisfied with it, in the event there would be no payment at all. As there, so here. I think that the case really is too clear for Argument...

EDMUND DAVIES and STAMP L.JJ. agreed.

(c) *Lawrence* v. *Sinclair-Taylor* (1973) 117 Sol. Jo. 815

The prosecutor, who was seeking accommodation, was told by the defendants, who were estate agents, that if he sought accommodation through them he would have to pay them a fee. They gave him the address of a flat; having liked its location he returned and paid them £18. The defendants then telephoned the lessor of the flat and arranged for the prosecutor to meet him at the flat; they then required the prosecutor to sign a form by which he agreed to deposit £18 in respect of services rendered by the defendants, subject to the proviso that the money was refundable if the accommodation was unacceptable to him. The defendants were convicted on informations charging that each of them accepted payment of £18 from the prosecutor contrary to s. 1 (1) (*b*) of the Accommodation Agencies Act 1953. They appealed. LORD WIDGERY CJ said that it was submitted for the defendants that, on the evidence, they had not accepted money in consideration of supplying the addresses as they were willing to refund it if the accommodation proved unsatisfactory; that they had accepted the money subsequent to the supply of the address; and that one could not describe the consideration as being substantially the giving of the address as the defendants had provided other services. His lordship said there was nothing in s 1 exempting agents merely because the money was refundable; if one looked at the facts of the present case and at the prohibition in the statute it could not be contended that money accepted in consideration of supplying the address was not within s 1. The fact that the actual payment was made after the provision of the address made no difference where, as in the present case, it was clear from the beginning that if the accommodation proved satisfactory the money had to be paid. Further, on any view the overwhelming consideration was the giving of the address to the prosecutor as in the circumstances, the most that the defendants did apart from that was telephoning the lessor. It was also contended for the defendants that there was no breach of s 1 unless an agent gave a number of addresses. His lordship said that the Interpretation Act 1889 provided that the plural meant the singular in the absence of any contrary intention. It would be very odd if there was a criminal offence on the provision of two addresses but not if only one address was provided.

Bridge and May JJ. agreed. Appeal dismissed.

(*d*) *Saunders* v. *Soper* [1975] A.C. 239 (H.L.)

VISCOUNT DILHORNE: My Lords, the appellant ... carries on and has carried on for some 6½ years a highly respectable agency under the name of Wilson's Accommodation Bureau. On 25th January 1973 a Miss Christine Nichols came to see her, wanting accommodation for herself and two friends. The appellant at that time did not know of any likely to suit but agreed to try and find some and asked Miss Nichols to call on her again. Miss Nichols did so on a number of occasions.

The appellant, or someone on her behalf, inspected premises at 27 Dawlish Drive, Southend-on-Sea, and thought they might suit Miss Nichols, and so Miss Nichols was given that address.

On 17th February 1973 Miss Nichols signed an agreement in writing which contained the following paragraph:

'In consideration of the services of Wilson's Accommodation Bureau in finding or introducing accommodation acceptable to me/us, I/We agree to pay to Wilson's Accommodation Bureau a Fee of the equivalent of one week's rent (minimum £5.25) for the accommodation accepted by me/us. No fee is payable to Wilson's Accommodation Bureau unless and until I or We become the tenant(s) of the accommodation found or introduced by Wilson's Accommodation Bureau to me/us.'

Miss Nichols, having inspected the premises, entered into an agreement to rent them for £7 a week. She thereupon under the agreement into which she had entered became liable to pay to the appellant £7 and she paid that sum on 20th February 1973.

Later Miss Nichols again came to see the appellant and again told her that she wanted accommodation for three persons. Again, the appellant had no suitable accommodation on her books and Miss Nichols was asked to call again. She did so on a number of occasions and on the last occasion was given an address, 34 Retreat Road, Westcliff-on-Sea. On 16th March 1973 she signed an agreement similar in all respects to that which she had previously made with the appellant. She became tenant of those premises at a weekly rent of £16 a week and so became liable under the agreement to pay the appellant £16. This she did not do and has not done although payment was demanded.

On 12th July 1973 the respondent, a police inspector, preferred two informations against her, the first alleging that she had on 20th February 1973 accepted from Miss Nichols £7 in consideration of supplying her with addresses of houses to let contrary to s 1 (1) (b) of the Accommodation Agencies Act 1953; and the second alleging that she had demanded £16 in consideration of supplying Miss Nichols with addresses of houses to let contrary to that subsection of that Act. The appellant was convicted of both offences and her appeal to the Divisional Court was dismissed. She now appeals to this House with the leave of that court.

That she accepted £7 from Miss Nichols and demanded payment of £16 by her is not disputed. The question to be decided is whether by doing so she committed offences against this subsection . . .

It is to be noted that the object of the Act is not stated to be the prohibition of the taking of all commissions in dealings with such persons but only of the taking of certain commissions . . .

The first matter to consider is what was the mischief at which this Act was aimed. One can only deduce that from its terms. Section 1 (1) was clearly directed to preventing persons desirous of accommodation being charged merely for the registration of their names or their requirements. Section 1 (1) (b) was, in my view, equally clearly directed to preventing charges being made just for supplying addresses. It is obvious what s 1 (1) (c) was intended to prevent.

Commission of any of the three offences created by this section does not in any way depend on the character of the agency. Whether the agency be reputable or bogus, the person who runs it and charges for supplying addresses to persons wanting accommodation, commits an offence against s 1 (1) (b).

The object of s 1 (2) is not at first sight easy to discern but if it was not there, a person who at the request of the owner, say, of a block of new flats, supplied the addresses of those flats to would-be occupants, would be unable to obtain from the owner or his agent any remuneration for his services.

It was not in this case contended that the agreements signed by Miss Nichols did not correctly and completely state the terms on which the bureau would become entitled to payment from her. The respondent, however, contended that if in the course of carrying out the contract made, the address of premises to let was supplied, then the demand or acceptance of payment, even though no payment was due unless and until acceptable accommodation had been found and rented by the client, was, inter alia, a demand or acceptance of payment for the supplying of the address.

If this be right, it follows that an agent employed by a prospective tenant to find for him, it may be, a large house or whose requirements are of an unusual character, cannot lawfully demand payment for his services from his client when he finds premises which suit his client and of which his client becomes the tenant. Counsel for the respondent in the course of his argument was unable to suggest that in such circumstances there was any mischief in the agent claiming commission which Parliament would want to prevent.

In my opinion, the mischief to which s 1 (1) (b) was directed was simply to prevent charges being made for supplying addresses and did not extend beyond that.

So, in my opinion, the question for decision in this appeal is simply, did the appellant accept or demand payment for supplying addresses? If instead of supplying one address on each occasion, she had supplied 100 or 1,000 addresses, under the agreements which she signed Miss Nichols would not have been liable to make any payment. She was not asked to pay nor did she pay for being given addresses. Under the agreements she became liable to pay not for the giving of addresses but for the finding of accommodation acceptable to her and accommodation of which she became the tenant.

On the facts of this case and in view of the terms of the agreements entered into, consideration of the terms of the section leads me to the conclusion that this appeal should be allowed; and as I read Lord Widgery CJ's judgment in this case, that would appear to have been his view were it not that he felt himself bound by some previous decisions to which I must now refer.

The first of these was *McInnes* v. *Clarke* [above]. In my opinion, the decision in that case was clearly right and is clearly distinguishable from this case ... The judgments in that case make it clear that the decision was founded on the payment of the deposit. In the present case there was no demand for or acceptance of payment just for supplying addresses.

The next case was *Crouch and Lees* v. *Haridas* [above] ... With the greatest respect, I do not think that it was accurate to say that the fact that there was no advance payment made no difference at all or that in each case there would have been no payment if the client was not satisfied. In *McInnes* v. *Clarke* there was a payment, which if the client was dissatisfied he might recover. In *Crouch and Lees* v. *Haridas* no payment of any sum was made or became due unless and until the client became a tenant of the premises of which the address had been supplied to him. In that case the other Lords Justices agreed with Davies LJ. I think that the decision was wrong for it does not appear to me from the facts set out in the report of the case that any payment was either accepted or demanded just for supplying addresses....

As in my view it was not proved in this case that any payment was demanded or accepted for the supplying of an address and as it was proved that the payments were accepted or demanded not for that but for finding Miss Nichols suitable accommodation and due only on her entering into a tenancy, in my opinion she was wrongly convicted and this appeal should be allowed...

For a note on this case see Partington (1975a). Note, also, that under the Estate Agents Act 1979, s. 3, there are now procedures whereby the Director General of Fair Trading may prohibit 'unfit persons' from doing estate agency work. Conviction of criminal offences, and discrimination are two circumstances that may lead to such prohibition.

4. Gas and electricity

Cutting (1979, pp. 40–44) writes:

	Gas	*Electricity*
	(All references are to Gas Act 1972, Schedule 4, unless contrary appears.)	(All references are to the schedule of Electric Lighting (Clauses) Act 1899 unless otherwise stated.)
1. What is the statutory power to supply energy?	Gas Act 1972, s. 2. Gas Corporation has a duty to develop and maintain an efficient, coordinated and economical system of gas	Electricity Act 1947, s. 1(2). It is the duty of area boards to carry out an efficient and economic distribution of bulk

	Gas	*Electricity*
	(All references are to Gas Act 1972, Schedule 4, unless contrary appears.)	(All references are to the schedule of Electric Lighting (Clauses) Act 1899 unless otherwise stated.)
	supply for Great Britain and to satisfy all reasonable demands for gas.	supplies of electricity obtained from the Central Generating Board.
2. Is there a duty to supply and to whom?	Para 2(1). Corporation shall; upon being required to do so by owner or occupier of any premises within 25 yards of a live gas main, give and continue to give a supply of gas to those premises.	Section 27(1). An area board shall, upon being required to do so by owner or occupier of any premises within 50 yards of any distributing main, give and continue to give a supply of energy for those premises.
3. How do I get supplies?	Para 2(5)(a). Give written notice to local office of Gas Corporation stating your name and address, that you are owner or occupier, and the day on which you require gas to be supplied to the premises.	Section 27(2). Serve notice on the area board specifying the premises, the minimum power required (e.g., the appliances using electricity – cooker, fires, storage heaters, etc.), and the day on which you require supply to commence. A simple form is available at local showrooms.
4. Do I have to pay for connection?	Para 2(2). If pipes have to be laid from the main to your house, you pay the cost of work on your land, the corporation pays for the rest. But, if your boundary is more than 30 ft from the main, you have to pay for the work after the first 30 ft, as well.	Section 27(1). Yes. You pay the cost of work on or over your property; the board pays the rest. If your boundary is more than 60 ft from the main you have to pay for the work after the first 60 ft as well.

	Gas	*Electricity*
	(All references are to Gas Act 1972, Schedule 4, unless contrary appears.)	(All references are to the schedule of Electric Lighting (Clauses) Act 1899 unless otherwise stated.)
5. Do I have to pay in advance for cables and pipes?	Para 2(5)(b). The corporation can require payment in advance for work and gas to be supplied.	Section 27(2). The board can require payment in advance for work and energy to be supplied.
6. How much do I have to pay for supply?	Para 12(1). An estimate for the charge for connecting and supplying gas should be obtained before any work is done; the charge for the actual supply of gas depends on where you live. The corporation is responsible for calculating the charge per therm; different tariffs may relate to different areas. For gas re-sold by landlords, the corporation fixes a maximum charge; get a leaflet from your consultative council telling you how to calculate it.	The charge for electricity is fixed by each area board. Electricity Act 1947, s. 37(3). Get a leaflet from your consultative council telling you how to calculate it.
7. Can they cut off supply without notice?	Para 17(1). No. You must pay for supply of gas within 28 days. In default, the corporation may give 7 days notice of its intention to cut off the supply. See [also] the Code of Practice on disconnection agreed by the gas industry.	Yes: Electric Lighting Act 1882 s. 21. If you owe the board money for electricity they may disconnect you without notice. However see the Code of Practice on disconnection agreed by the electricity industry.

	Gas	*Electricity*
	(All references are to Gas Act 1972, Schedule 4, unless contrary appears.)	(All references are to the schedule of Electric Lighting (Clauses) Act 1899 unless otherwise stated.)
8. What happens when supply is cut off?	The supply is disconnected. You remain liable to pay the outstanding amount and also the cost of cutting off.	The supply is disconnected. You remain liable to pay the outstanding amount and also the cost of cutting off.
9. Can I be made to pay for reconnection?	Para 17(2). Yes. The corporation is under no duty to reconnect supply unless all money outstanding is paid.	Yes. The board is under no duty to reconnect supply unless all money outstanding is paid. Electricity (Supply) Act 1926, s. 45.
10. What happens if they cut off supply by mistake or wrongly?	You are not liable for the cost of cutting off or reconnection. A criminal offence has been committed by the corporation – para 6.	You are not liable for the cost of cutting off or reconnection. A criminal offence has been committed by the board, s. 30.
11. Can they cut off supply because I have not paid for an appliance or for service?	Para 17(1). No. The Act specifically provides that you can only be disconnected for failure to pay for gas supplied.	No. The Electric Lighting Act 1882, s. 21, specifically provides that you can only be disconnected for failing to pay for electricity supplied.
12. What proceedings can be taken against me for debts?	Para 13. The money is recoverable as a simple contract debt. The corporation will issue a county court summons; invariably there is no defence and judgment will be obtained. This can be satisfied by: full payment; payment by	The debt is recoverable as a civil debt in the magistrates' court. Judgment is enforceable by: payment in full; instalments; distress on goods; or imprisonment.

Gas	*Electricity*
(All references are to Gas Act 1972, Schedule 4, unless contrary appears.)	(All references are to the schedule of Electric Lighting (Clauses) Act 1899 unless otherwise stated.)
instalments; attachment of earnings; bankruptcy; or execution upon goods.	

	Gas	*Electricity*
13. Do utility employees have a right to enter my premises?	No. Unless consent is given by or on behalf of the occupier, the corporation must obtain a warrant to enter from a magistrate. They can do this in an emergency, or if the occupier refuses them entry unreasonably, when they want to inspect any gas fitting, flue, etc., examine and test any gas appliance, service pipe, flue, etc., make sure that the Gas Safety Regulations (see question 14 below) are being followed, or disconnect and seal off any gas fitting or supply that they consider unsafe. The Gas Safety (Rights of Entry) Regulations 1976.	No. Unless consent is given by or on behalf of the occupier, the board must obtain a warrant to enter from a magistrate. In case of emergency, to take steps to avert danger to life or property, the board's officers can enter a house without notice and without a warrant. The Rights of Entry (Gas and Electricity Boards) Act 1954.
14. Do I have a duty to keep my appliances safe?	Yes. You have a duty: (i) to ensure that air is freely available to gas appliances, and (ii) to have gas appliances fitted by a competent installer (someone who has adequate technical knowledge and experience	There is no special requirement.

	Gas	*Electricity*
	(All references are to Gas Act 1972, Schedule 4, unless contrary appears.)	(All references are to the schedule of Electric Lighting (Clauses) Act 1899 unless otherwise stated.)

	Gas	*Electricity*
	of the type of work involved), and (iii) not to use a gas appliance that you know or suspect is unsafe, and (iv) if you suspect there is a gas leak, to shut off the supply and contact your local gas emergency service if the gas continues to escape. Failure to do any of these things is an offence carrying a fine of up to £400 (Gas Safety Regulations 1972).	
15. Who owns the meter?	Usually the Corporation. If you are a tenant living in furnished accommodation the meter may belong to your landlord.	Usually the board. If you are a tenant living in furnished accommodation the meter may belong to your landlord.
16. Who owns the money in the meter?	The Corporation. If the money is stolen, whether you pay or not depends on the terms of the actual hire agreement (if you are a party to it) and whether you negligently allowed the thief to enter. Most hire agreements contain a repayment clause. The landlord sustains the loss if he owns or hires the meter from the Corporation.	The board. If the money is stolen whether you pay or not depends on the terms of the actual hire agreement (if you are a party to it) and whether you negligently allowed the thief to enter. Most hire agreements contain a repayment clause. The landlord sustains the loss if he owns or hires the meter from the board.

	Gas (All references are to Gas Act 1972, Schedule 4, unless contrary appears.)	Electricity (All references are to the schedule of Electric Lighting (Clauses) Act 1899 unless otherwise stated.)
17. What do I do if I think the meter is wrong?	Tell the Corporation. The Gas Act provides for meters to be tested. You have to pay, but if the test shows that the meter was defective the Corporation must reimburse you (Gas Meter Regulations 1949, as amended.)	Tell the board. The Electricity Supply (Meters) Act 1936 provides for the appointment of examiners to test meters. You have to pay but if the test shows the meter was defective then the board must reimburse you.
18. If the landlord is over-charging for supply, can I recover excess payments by deducting them from the rent?	Yes. Give the landlord notice.	Yes. Give the landlord notice.
19. My landlord charges me rent for a meter; can he do this? (see question 6 for maximum charges for supply).	Yes. The maximum charge is laid down by the Corporation.	Yes. The board fixes a maximum charge.
20. Am I liable for the last tenant's account?	Para 14. No, unless you agreed with the previous tenant that you would be responsible.	No, unless you agreed with the previous tenant that you would be responsible (Electric Lighting Act 1882, s. 12).
21. Am I liable after I have left the premises?	Paras 15(1) and 16. Yes, for all gas you used. You must give at least 24 hours' notice to the Corporation that you	Yes, for all electricity used. You must give at least 24 hours' notice to the board that you intend to leave so they can

Gas	Electricity
(All references are to Gas Act 1972, Schedule 4, unless contrary appears.)	(All references are to the schedule of Electric Lighting (Clauses) Act 1899 unless otherwise stated.)
intend to leave so they can arrange a final meter reading. If you fail to pay the bill, the Corporation can refuse to supply you with gas at any other premises until you pay the outstanding account.	arrange a final meter reading. If you fail to pay the bill, the board can refuse to supply you with electricity at any other premises until you pay the outstanding account (Electric Lighting Act 1909.)

The Local Government (Miscellaneous Provisions) Act 1976, s. 33, may also be relevant in such cases:

(1) If any premises ... are occupied as a dwelling and the supply of water, gas or electricity to the premises –

(a) is cut off in consequence of the failure of the owner or former owner of the premises to pay a sum payable by him in connection with the supply; or

(b) is in the opinion of the council likely to be cut off in consequence of such a failure,

the council may, at the request in writing of the occupier of the premises, make such arrangements as it thinks fit with the undertakers who provided the supply for it to be restored to the premises or, as the case may be, for it to be continued to the premises ...

Any money paid out by the local authority is recoverable from the person who should have paid the bill. Section 33(2)–(5) prescribes the relevant procedures.

The extent to which local authorities have used this provision is not known.

5. Service charges

There has been some control over the level of service charges payable by tenants in blocks of flats since the Housing Finance Act 1972 came into force. However, the relevant provisions (Housing Finance Act 1972, ss. 90–91A) were not satisfactorily drafted. A new, rather broader set of provisions is now to be found in Housing Act 1980, s. 136 and Schedule 19. The intention of the provisions is to ensure that tenants are given detailed information about the cost of services, repairs, maintenance, insurance or landlord's management costs. It has been argued that unreasonable charges have in some cases been imposed. Thus procedures are laid down whereby, when a landlord is proposing to incur substantial costs (defined by a formula in the Act), at least two estimates must first be obtained and details of these estimates provided to the tenants. The provisions are interesting in that they specifically entitle 'recognized tenants' associations' to play a role in any negotiations as to what are, or are not, reasonable costs. Any dispute is, ultimately, to be resolved in the county court.

The provisions do not apply to service charges payable by the tenant of a flat the rent of which is registered under Part IV of the Rent Act, unless the amount registered is described as variable (Rent Act 1977, s. 71(4)); nor do they apply to service charges payable to an association or management company 'the membership of which is wholly or mainly restricted to persons who are tenants in the same block or blocks of flats'.

7
Repairs and Improvements

'The first object of landlord–tenant law should be the making of repairs and the general maintenance of property.'

(A.B.A. Model Residential Landlord–Tenant Code, cited Brown, 1970, p. 215.)

Introduction: Data on housing conditions

The state of Britain's housing leaves much to be desired. The findings of the 1976 English Housing Condition Survey are summarized in Table 7.1.

Table 7.1   Summary of housing conditions, 1976

Condition	Thousand dwellings	Percentage
Unfit dwellings	794	4.6
Fit dwellings lacking amenities	921	5.4
Fit dwellings with all amenities requiring repairs costing over £500	1,480	8.7
Satisfactory dwellings	13,920	81.3
All dwellings	17,115	100.0

Source: English Housing Condition Survey, 1976 (HMSO, 1978), Table A.

Drawing upon England only, Table 7.2 shows the close correlation between the age of the dwelling and its fitness[1] (or otherwise) for human habitation. The table also shows that 33% of unfit dwellings

1. Defined by Housing Act 1957, s. 4 (as amended), below, p. 389.

Table 7.2 Condition and age by tenure

Thousand dwellings/percentage

	Owner-occupied		Rented from local authorities or new towns		Private rented		Vacant		All tenures	
Built before 1919										
Unfit dwellings:										
In potential clearance areas	108	*1.1*	18	*0.4*	149	*6.5*	67	*13.5*	342	*2.0*
Not in potential clearance areas	148	*1.6*	20	*0.4*	175	*7.7*	76	*15.3*	419	*2.4*
All unfit dwellings	256	*2.7*	38	*0.8*	324	*14.2*	143	*28.8*	761	*4.4*
Dwellings not unfit:										
In or adjoining potential clearance areas	13	*0.1*	—	—	—	—	—	—	13	*0.1*
Not in potential clearance areas	2,596	*27.2*	140	*2.9*	1,245	*54.4*	202	*40.6*	4,183	*24.4*
All dwellings not unfit	2,609	*27.3*	140	*2.9*	1,245	*54.4*	202	*40.6*	4,196	*24.5*
All dwellings built before 1919	2,865	*30.0*	178	*3.7*	1,569	*68.6*	345	*69.4*	4,957	*29.0*
Built 1919 to 1976										
Unfit dwellings:										
In potential clearance areas	—	—	3	*0.1*	—	—	2	*0.4*	5	*0.0*
Not in potential clearance areas	7	*0.1*	5	*0.1*	10	*0.4*	6	*1.2*	28	*0.2*
All unfit dwellings	7	*0.1*	8	*0.2*	10	*0.4*	8	*1.6*	33	*0.2*
Dwellings not unfit:										
In or adjoining potential clearance areas	—	—	3	*0.1*	—	—	—	—	3	*0.0*
Not in potential clearance areas	6,674	*69.9*	4,596	*96.1*	708	*31.0*	144	*29.0*	12,122	*70.8*
All dwellings not unfit	6,674	*69.9*	4,599	*96.1*	708	*31.0*	144	*29.0*	12,125	*70.8*
All dwellings built 1919 to 1976	6,681	*70.0*	4,607	*96.3*	718	*31.4*	152	*30.6*	12,158	*71.0*
All dwellings	9,546	*100.0*	4,785	*100.0*	2,287	*100.0*	497	*100.0*	17,115	*100.0*

Source: English Housing Condition Survey, 1976 (HMSO, 1978), Table 3.

were owner-occupied and 42% were privately rented; only 6% were rented from local authorities.

Privately rented accommodation lacks proportionately more of the standard amenities,[2] as is shown by Table 7.3.

These figures suggest there has been an improvement in the state of England's housing, as compared with an earlier study in 1971. (*English Housing Condition Survey*, 1976 (1978), ch. 3.) However, there are fears that, with cutbacks in the numbers of slum clearance schemes, and doubts about the impact of improvement grant schemes and other measures, the overall state of British housing may begin to get worse again. Further, it must be remembered that the problem of housing conditions is a dynamic one, not one that can be solved once and for all.

To the lawyer, these figures may be particularly shocking since, as we shall see in this chapter, there is a great amount of law relating to housing conditions; yet none of it, particularly in the landlord–tenant sector, has worked particularly well.

For example, most leases contain repairing covenants. Yet they have not been enforced (**PEP** (1952), pp. 204–5):

In theory the covenants of a lease should be effective instruments for securing the maintenance of the houses. The lessor has an interest in seeing that the house that will come into his possession is well cared for ... [T]his control should work better than control through bye-laws.

In practice, repairing covenants often fail to prevent very serious deterioration of property. Both the Royal Commission on the Housing of the Working Classes, 1884–5 and the Minority Report of the Leasehold Committee, 1950 [Uthwatt-Jenkins], at widely separated points of time, record that leasehold tenure has done nothing to prevent slums. There are several reasons for this. There have been statutory limitations on the power of lessors to enforce repairing covenants ... Furthermore, property management is a skilled and therefore an expensive business. To detect disrepair and to remedy it quickly may require frequent and expert inspection. It is less costly and more conducive to a peaceful existence to allow lessees to go their own way until the lease expires and a formidable bill of dilapidations can be presented. This is a thoroughly bad practice from the standpoint of the community's interest in preserving the stock of houses, though it receives encouragement from some of the legislation designed to protect lessees from oppressive use of covenants. In houses as much as in anything-else a stitch in time saves nine ... and as the Leasehold Committee says, 'the expense involved may well be such as to cause serious embarrassment to the lessee' ...

2. Defined in Housing Act 1974, s. 58.

Table 7.3 *Lack of standard amenities by tenure*

Thousand dwellings/percentage

	Owner-occupied		Rented from local authorities or new towns		Private rented		Vacant		All tenures	
W.C. inside dwelling	360	3.8 (33.2)	157	3.3 (14.5)	437	19.1 (40.4)	129	26.0 (11.9)	1,083	6.3 (100.0)
Fixed bath in a bathroom	247	2.6 (30.9)	45	0.9 (5.6)	382	16.7 (47.8)	126	25.4 (15.8)	800	4.7 (100.0)
Wash basin	293	3.1 (29.6)	139	2.9 (14.0)	427	18.7 (43.1)	132	26.6 (13.3)	991	5.8 (100.0)
Sink	6	0.1 (14.0)	1	— (2.3)	11	0.5 (25.6)	25	5.0 (58.1)	43	0.3 (100.0)
Hot and cold water at 3 points	358	3.8 (30.5)	161	3.4 (13.7)	499	21.8 (42.5)	155	31.2 (13.2)	1,173	6.9 (100.0)
One or more of the amenities	473	5.0 (31.7)	269	5.6 (18.0)	585	25.6 (39.2)	166	33.4 (11.1)	1,493	8.7 (100.0)
All dwellings with or without amenities	9,546	100.0 (55.8)	4,785	100.0 (28.0)	2,287	100.0 (13.4)	497	100.0 (2.9)	17,115	100.0 (100.0)

Note: Figures in brackets show percentages of all dwellings in each row.

Source: *English Housing Condition Survey, 1976* (HMSO, 1978), Table 11.

The accumulation of dilapidations towards the end of a lease frightens away the *bona fide* lessee and encourages assignment to men of straw. It is often difficult for the purchaser of a lease to estimate what financial obligations will fall on him ... It is understandable that the only lessee to whom that kind of risk is likely to appeal is one who has no intention of fulfilling his obligations and no resources out of which he can be compelled to do it.

Public health legislation has a long history: the first major public health Act was passed in 1848. But, in so far as this area of law relates to housing conditions, it has always been concerned with patching up emergencies rather than enforcing long-term solutions. Under various Housing Acts, local authorities have been given powers to deal with housing conditions. However, they have not proved effective (CDP, 1975; Hadden, 1978; Balchin, 1979). More recently, the introduction of grants towards improvements in housing conditions has frequently not been taken up by those for whom they were designed, and their use appears to be declining (*Housing and Construction Statistics* No. 28 (1979), Tables 28–30).

In recent years, considerable energy has been spent on attempts to utilize the law. Law centres, housing aid centres, specialist advice agencies such as SHELTER, or Child Poverty Action Group (Hodge, 1979), or the now defunct Public Health Advisory Service have all gone to great lengths to take cases before the courts. In many individual cases a ruling favourable to tenants has been obtained (though this has not necessarily resulted ultimately in a favourable outcome to the case (Hadden, 1979, p. 86)). However, as the figures above show, huge problems remain.

There are many possible reasons for this apparent ineffectiveness in the use of law. Partly it may be said to derive from the law itself, much of which gives discretionary powers to local authorities rather than imposing absolute duties on them. The judges have on occasion interpreted laws so that their apparent scope has been reduced. More generally the economic climate has often not been encouraging. Public expenditure restraints have contributed to a fall in the numbers of improvement grants being made and prevented local authorities from acting as positively as they might in enforcing the law. Landlords have complained that low rent levels have made improvements and repairs financially impossible. (See Paley, 1978, ch. 3.)

The rest of this chapter will concentrate on an analysis of the relevant law. However, the problems of enforcement should constantly be borne in mind. What policy developments are needed which will result in effective improvements to housing being made? Should information about repairing obligations be put in rent books? Given the abolition of controlled tenancies, is it reasonable to expect landlords to spend some of their 'fair rents' on property maintenance? If so, how may this be achieved? Would the creation of a comprehensive housing code help to make the law on housing more effective (Arden, 1979a)?

Two further preliminary points should be noted:

(*i*) One argument that is being increasingly heard is that, while the remedies provided in the law may, if used, lead to some improvement in bad housing conditions, there is a lack of emphasis in the law on the prevention of bad quality housing from being erected in the first place. For example, it has been estimated that necessary repairs to local authority dwellings built only recently, in the 1950s and 1960s, total at least £200 million (Darwin (1979)). And the likelihood is that, with increasing economies in public expenditure, the erection of poor quality housing will continue (Benwell CDP (1978)). It may be possible to bring actions for breach of contract, or negligence, against those involved in the building process. Building regulations should ensure that basic standards of habitability are met. But are these adequate legal bases for the achievement of long-lasting, good-quality housing?

(*ii*) It should not be assumed that the law to be discussed in the following pages will deal with all problems relating to housing conditions. People's perceptions of what those problems are may well change. For example, it may not be possible at present to argue that the problems of families living in high-rise blocks of flats are within the legal regulation of housing conditions: but could this not come to be the case? As standards and expectations about the quality of life change, so attitudes as to what are, or are not, adequate housing conditions will also change. We should not assume that the standards embodied in the law that exists at present are the only possible legal standards by which to judge housing conditions.

1. Covenants to repair

A Express covenants

When a dispute arises as to the condition of a house, or indeed any other type of property that has been let, the first question will be: what are the terms of the lease, or tenancy agreement? At common law, the division of repairing obligations was often a matter of negotiation, or conveyancing practice (see Uthwatt-Jenkins, 1950, para. 228):

The landlord may by covenant undertake to do the repairs or some of them and it is not uncommon in short leases for the landlord to agree to be liable for external repairs. It is important to observe that except in so far as he expressly covenants to do so, he is generally speaking under no implied obligation to repair nor in general does he warrant that the premises are fit for occupation for any particular purpose. If therefore the lease is silent as to repairs the tenant must take the premises as he finds them ...

On the other hand (*ibid.*, paras. 216–17):

... in the case of a lease for say the typical building lease period of 99 years, containing, as is almost invariably the case, the usual 'full' repairing covenants, the aggregate liability over the whole period may amount to a formidable total ...

Put very shortly, the full repairing covenants normally entered into by the tenant under a typical long lease are:—

(i) To keep the premises in good repair both internally and externally.

(ii) To do certain specific works of repair at stated intervals – e.g. to paint inside once every 7 and outside once every 3 years.

(iii) To permit the landlord from time to time during the term to enter and view the state of repair; and to make good defects on notice.

(iv) To deliver up the premises in good repair at the expiration or sooner determination of the term.

Unless loss or damage by fire is excepted from the repairing covenants, the tenant under full repairing covenants such as these will be liable to reinstate the premises at his own cost. In leases of this type there is commonly a covenant by the tenant to insure the premises against loss or damage by fire, and to apply the moneys received under such insurance in reinstating the premises and sometimes also to make good out of his own pocket any deficiency in such insurance moneys as compared with the amount required to reinstate the premises.

Interpretation of repairing covenants has been the subject of much litigation. Given the expense frequently involved, this is not surprising. Some of the basic priciples that have been developed by the courts in these cases are outlined below. Consider how far they are likely to assist in determining liability in any given case. (See generally, Woodfall, 1978, pp. 591–618.)

(*a*) When a lessee has covenanted to repair and keep in repair premises at all times during the lease, it is implied that he must put them into repair if not in repair when the tenancy begins; otherwise they cannot be kept or left in repair according to the covenant (*Proudfoot* v. *Hart* (1890) 25 Q.B.D. 42). The same principle applies to a landlord's covenant to repair (*Saner* v. *Bilton* (1878) 7 Ch. D. 815; for covenants imposed on landlords by statute, see below, p. 350).

(*b*) The word repair is frequently qualified by an adjective such as 'good', or 'tenantable', or 'habitable'. In *Proudfoot* v. *Hart* (above) Lopes L.J. said this amounted to 'such repair as, having regard to the age, character and locality of the house, would make it reasonably fit for the occupation of a reasonably minded tenant of the class who would be likely to take it'. The standard for Belgravia would be different from that for Spitalfields. The term in this case was three years. However in *Calthorpe* v. *McOscar* [1924] 1 K.B. 716, premises were let on a 95-year lease. Originally the houses were in the country; at the time of dispute the district had become built up. It was argued that, since tenants were now only prepared to take short-term lettings, the proper standard of repair was what they would require now, i.e. minimal. The Court of Appeal rejected this, saying the premises had to be put into a reasonable state of repair to suit the type of tenant who would originally have taken a lease. (See also *Jaquin* v. *Holland* [1960] 1 W.L.R. 258.)

(*c*) Repair is said not to be the same as improvement, nor renewal. The difference between repairs and improvement was described by Denning L.J. thus (*Morcom* v. *Campbell-Johnson* [1956] 1 Q.B. 115):

> If the work which is done is the provision of something new for the benefit of the occupier, that is, properly speaking, an improvement; but if it is only the replacement of something already there, which has become dilapidated or worn out, then, albeit that it is a replacement by its modern equivalent, it comes within the category of repairs and not improvements.

and distinguishing between repairs and renewal, Buckley L.J. had this to say (*Lurcott* v. *Wakely and Wheeler* [1911] 1 K.B. 905):

> repair is restoration by renewal or replacement of subsidiary parts of a whole. Renewal, as distinguished from repair, is reconstruction of the entirety, meaning by the entirety not necessarily the whole but substantially the whole.

However, the practical difficulties of drawing such distinctions were acknowledged by Sachs L.J. in *Brew Bros.* v. *Snax (Ross) Ltd* [1970] 1 Q.B. 612. He said it was necessary 'to look at the particular building, to look at the state which it is in at the date of the lease, and then to come to a conclusion as to whether, on a fair interpretation of those terms in relation to that state, the requisite work can fairly be termed repair. However large the covenant is it must not be looked at *in vacuo*.' (See now also Forbes J. in *Ravenseft Properties Ltd* v. *Davstone (Holdings) Ltd* [1979] 1 All E.R. 929.)

One particular difficulty is who should be liable for inherent defects in a building. In *Lister* v. *Lane and Nesham* [1893] 2 Q.B. 212 at 216, Lord Esher M.R. had remarked: 'If a tenant takes a house which is such a kind that by its own inherent nature it will in the course of time fall into a particular condition, the effects of that result are not within the tenant's covenant to repair.' This defence was raised in the *Ravenseft Case* (above). The facts were that a 16-storey block of maisonettes, a modern rectangular structure made with a reinforced concrete frame, looking in the words of Forbes J. 'like a set of pigeon-holes, or . . . a flag locker', was erected between 1958–60 . . . The edges of the 'pigeon-holes' were veneered with a cladding of Portland stone about three inches thick and eight inches wide. For safety every third stone was L-shaped, having a projection which ran back into a channel in the main frame of the building and all the stones ought in addition to have been tied into the frame with metal straps, but some were not. Moreover, it was not appreciated when the building was constructed that the concrete frame and the stone cladding expanded at different rates and as a consequence emergency work had to be done in 1973 to prevent loose cladding from falling. Certain stones were bowing away from the concrete frame. When this remedial work was carried out it had become standard practice to include expansion joints in such cladding, using a plastic expansion absorbing material. This procedure was followed and metal dowels were used in addition to pin sections of the stone to the frame. The need for expansion joints was only made known by the Building Research Station's Annual Report issued in 1961. It cost £50,000 to remedy the original defective workmanship caused by the absence of ties and £5,000 for the expansion joints. The landlords claimed that this cost fell on the tenants under the repairing covenant but the tenants said that repairs, such as these, made necessary by an inherent defect of design or construction could not fall within the covenant to repair; if that proposition was incorrect they said that the *results* of an inherent defect could never be within the ambit of a covenant to repair.

Forbes J. denied that the tenants could raise the defence of 'inherent defect'. Rather he ruled (at 937) that '... It is *always* a question of fact and degree whether that which the tenant is being asked to do can properly be described as repair, or whether on the contrary it would involve giving back to the landlord a wholly different thing from that which he demised.' He conceded that repairs to the building could have been made without putting in expansion joints; but in light of the Building Research report, 'no responsible engineer would have allowed a rebuilding which did not include such expansion joints'. Thus the tenants were liable to pay the £55,000. (For further discussion of this case and the implications of the decision, see Wilkinson (1979), Hughes (1979), P. Smith (1979).)

(*d*) An exception for fair wear and tear is also frequently found in repairing covenants. This is another formula which has, inevitably, caused difficulty. In *Regis Property Co. Ltd* v. *Dudley* [1959] A.C. 370, the House of Lords approved the following statement of principle from the judgment of Talbot J. in *Haskell* v. *Marlow* [1928] K.B. 58–9.

> The meaning is that the tenant ... is bound to keep the house in good repair and condition, but is not liable for what is due to reasonable wear and tear ... If any want of repair is alleged and proved in fact, it lies on the tenant to show that it comes within the exception. Reasonable wear and tear means the reasonable use of the house by the tenant and the ordinary operation of natural forces. The exception of want of repair due to wear and tear must be construed as limited to what is directly due to wear and tear, reasonable conduct on the part of the tenant being assumed. It does not mean that if there is a defect originally proceeding from a reasonable wear and tear the tenant is released from his obligation to keep in good repair and condition everything which it may be possible to trace ultimately to that defect. He is bound to do such repairs as may be required to prevent the consequences flowing originally from wear and tear from producing others which wear and tear would not directly produce.

(See also *Warren* v. *Keen* (below, p. 346).)

B Covenants implied by the common law affecting landlords

(i) FURNISHED DWELLINGS

Notwithstanding the general 'freedom' of the parties to 'agree' terms, the common law did imply an obligation on landlords to let *furnished* dwellings in habitable condition. This implied that they might have to carry out certain basic repairs before a letting began; it did not imply any obligation to do anything during the period of the lease. The leading case is *Smith* v. *Marrable* ((1843) 11 M.&W. 5).

At the trial before Lord Abinger, CB, ..., it appeared that the action was brought to recover a balance of five weeks' rent of a furnished house at Brighton, which had been taken by the defendant of the plaintiff under the following agreement:—

Brighton, September 14, 1842.
Mr John Smith, of 24, St. James's-street, agrees to let, and Sir Thomas Marrable agrees to take, the house No. 5, Brunswick-place, at the rent of eight guineas per week, for five or six weeks at the option of the said Sir Thomas Marrable.

THOMAS MARRABLE.
JOHN SMITH.

The rent to commence on the 15th September.   T. M.
                                                      J. S.

Under this agreement, the defendant and his family entered into possession of the house on Friday the 16th of September. On the following day, Lady Marrable having complained to the plaintiff that the house was infested with bugs, he sent a person in to take means for getting rid of them, which however did not prove successful; and on the 19th, Lady Marrable wrote the following note to the wife of the plaintiff:—

'5, Brunswick Place, Sept. 19, 1842.
Lady Marrable informs Mrs Smith, that it is her determination to leave the house in Brunswick Place as soon as she can take another, paying a week's rent, as all the bedrooms occupied but one are so infested with bugs that it is impossible to remain.'

On the following Thursday, the 22nd, the defendant accordingly sent the key of the house, together with the amount of a week's rent, to the plaintiff, and removed with his family to another residence. Evidence was given to shew that the house was in fact greatly infested by bugs. The Lord Chief Baron, in summing up, stated to the jury, that in point of law every house must be taken to be let upon the implied condition that there was nothing about it so noxious as to render it uninhabitable; and that if they believed that the defendant left the plaintiff's house on account of the nuisance occasioned by these vermin being so intolerable as to render it impossible that he could live in it with any reasonable comfort, they ought to find a verdict for the defendant. The jury having found for the defendant,

Hayward now moved for a new trial, on the ground of misdirection ...

PARKE, B: This case involves the question whether, in point of law, a person who lets a house must be taken to let it under the implied condition that it is in a state fit for decent and comfortable habitation, and whether he is at liberty to throw it up, when he makes the discovery that it is not so. The case of *Edwards* v. *Etherington* [(1825) Ry. & Mod. 268] appears to me to be an authority very nearly in point. There the defendant, who held a house as tenant from year to year, quitted without notice, on the ground that the walls were in so dilapidated a state that it had become unsafe to reside in it; and Lord Tenterden, at Nisi Prius, held these facts to be an answer to an action by the landlord for use and occupation: telling the jury, that although slight circumstances would not suffice, such serious reasons might exist as would justify a tenant's quitting at any time, and that it was for them to say whether, in the case before them, such serious reasons existed as would exempt the defendant from the plaintiff's demand, on the ground of his having had no beneficial use and occupation of the premises. The jury found for the defendant, and the Court of King's Bench was afterwards moved for a new trial on the ground of misdirection, but they refused to disturb the verdict. There is also another case of *Collins* v. *Barrow* (1 M. & Rob. 112), in which Bayley, B., held that a tenant was justified in quitting without notice premises which were noxious and unwholesome for want of proper sewerage. These authorities appear to me fully to warrant the position, that if the demised premises are incumbered with a nuisance of so serious a nature that no person can reasonably be expected to live in them, the tenant is at liberty to throw them up. This is not the case of a contract on the part of the landlord that the premises were free from this nuisance; it rather rests in an implied condition of law, that he undertakes to let them in a habitable state ...

(See also *Bird* v. *Lord Greville* (1884) C. & E. 317; *Wilson* v. *Finch Hatton* (1877) 2 Ex. D. 336.)

In *Collins* v. *Hopkins* ([1923] 2 K.B. 617) MacCardie J. said, in part:

The result of the decisions as a whole seems to be that there is an absolute contractual warranty in the nature of a condition by the person who lets a furnished house or lodging to the effect that the premises and furniture are fit for habitation. What is the meaning of 'fit for habitation'? The meaning of the phrase must vary with the circumstances to which it is applied. In the case of unclean furniture or defective drains or a nuisance by vermin the matter is not, as a rule, one of difficulty. The eye or the nostrils can detect the fault and measure its extent. But in the case of a house lately occupied by a person suffering from an infectious disease, the eye and other senses are of no avail. The bacilli of infection are not apparent to the eye. Yet a peril is none the less grave because it is hidden.

This case before me definitely raises the question as to the contractual duty of a person who lets a furnished house lately occupied by one suffering from an infectious disease. It is not, of course, enough for the landlord to say that he honestly believes that the house is fit and proper for safe habitation. It must in fact be fit and safe. The mere belief of the landlord is not the point. Nor, on the other hand, can a tenant renounce his contract because of mere apprehension of risk or through mere dislike to the premises through the fact, e.g., that a person has died upon the premises of smallpox or scarlet fever. He must show more than mere apprehension or dislike. In my view the question in such a case as the present is this: Was there an actual and appreciable risk to the tenant, his family or household, by entering and occupying the house in which the infectious disorder had occurred? If the risk be serious, no one, I think, could doubt that the tenant may renounce. But in dealing with bacilli which may mean illness and death, I think further that an appreciable measure of actual risk justifies the tenant in throwing up his contract. A man should not be called on to expose his wife and children, household or himself to peril. . . .

In *Hart* v. *Windsor* ((1844) 12 M. & W. 68) it was held that the principle of *Smith* v. *Marrable* did not apply to lettings of unfurnished houses. In *Cruse* v. *Mount* ([1933] 1 Ch. 278) the question arose as to whether it applied to unfurnished flats. Maugham J. held:

It was argued here on behalf of the plaintiff that the case of a flat is midway between the two, and that in the case of a flat the same rule should be followed as that which applies in the case of furnished lodgings. It is pointed out that in the case of a flat it very often happens, as it did in the present case, that the landlord does not undertake to repair the inside of the flat, and it will be observed that the practice is not for intending tenants of flats to send a surveyor to examine the building, since a surveyor could not make a proper examination of the structure in a case where other flats are in the possession of other tenants. Further, it is to be noted that, if the building is structurally in bad repair, the tenant under an ordinary tenancy of a flat has no power to rebuild or reconstruct the premises. To do that he would have to go into flats which belong to other tenants and to attempt to do work on the premises which he has no power to do. I should not have felt any serious reluctance in holding, if it were open to me to do so, that the case of a flat is one of a special character, and that there was in this case an implied condition that the flat was fit for habitation, or, at any rate, that the flat was not part of a dangerous structure. I am, however, bound, as it seems to me, by the decision of the Common Pleas Division in *Manchester Bonded Warehouse Co.* v. *Carr* [(1880) 5 C.P.D. 507], a decision of Coleridge C.J. and Grove and Lindley JJ. The plaintiffs there had demised certain floors in a warehouse to the defendant, Mr Carr. The defendant covenanted, as the plaintiff did here, to repair and maintain the inside of the premises. The plaintiffs there covenanted to keep the walls, roofs and timbers of the premises in good and substantial repair and condition. Sublessees of the defendant overloaded a floor of the warehouse with flour, in consequence of which the whole building fell. The plaintiffs rebuilt it, and sued for rent during the time the building was unoccupied and for damages. The defendant denied liability, and claimed damages from the plaintiffs. It was held, first, that notwithstanding the fall the defendant was liable to pay the rent, and secondly, that there was no implied warranty by the plaintiffs that the building was fit for the purpose for which it was to be used.

The judgment of the Court on the question of warranty was simply based on the fact that no authority had decided that there was any such warranty, and what authority there was on the point was against its existence; and the Court held that no such warranty could be implied ... I am unable on any ground which seems to me to be satisfactory to distinguish that case from the present one. It was a lease of part of a building, where all the considerations I have mentioned as applicable in the case of a flat were, to some extent, applicable, and the Court ... came to the conclusion that it would be to extend the law to hold that any warranty could be implied in such a case. Accordingly I must hold, following that decision, that a landlord is entitled to let a flat in a building without being held to be giving such an implied warranty ...

The failure of the judges to extend the principle of *Smith* v. *Marrable* to other categories of property has been analysed and criticized by Reynolds who argues that precedent did not in fact impel the judges to develop the cases as they did. Further he castigates the judges for failing to respond to the social realities of the day (Reynolds, 1974, p. 378):

The judges were concerned about the effects of an implied duty to repair on agrarian leases,

'If (a demise) included any such contract as is now contended for, then, in every farming lease ... there would be an implied condition that the premises were fit for the purpose for which the tenant took them, and it is difficult to see where such a doctrine would stop' (*per* Parke B. in *Sutton* v. *Temple* (1843) 12 M.&W. 52 at 65).

The social reality was that the Industrial Revolution of the previous decades had seen the very structure of English society change from one dependent upon an agrarian economy to one based upon industry. One consequence of this had been the growth of the urban population; between 1801 and 1841, the populations of London, Birmingham, Leeds and Bristol had doubled whilst those of Manchester and Liverpool had trebled. Speculative builders arose to satisfy the housing needs of the new urban population. Houses were built without drains or privies, inferior materials were used and water was often available for only short periods from stand-pipes situated in narrow courts. Space was saved by thrusting families into cellar dwellings. It was at this crucial time of urbanization and slum formation that the judges looked to the agrarian lease as providing a justification for their decisions.

It is significant that these early cases were decided without reference to the accumulating evidence of social malaise.

(ii) GENERAL

More generally, the courts have from time to time been prepared to imply covenants into a letting agreement. An important attempt to formulate criteria to govern the circumstances in which it is proper to imply such terms was made by the House of Lords in *Liverpool City Council* v. *Irwin* [1976] 2 W.L.R. 562.

LORD WILBERFORCE: 50 Haigh Heights, Liverpool, is one of several recently erected tower blocks in the district of Everton. It has some 70 dwelling units in it. It was erected ten years ago, following a slum clearance programme at considerable cost, and was then, no doubt, thought to mark an advance in housing standards. Unfortunately, it has since turned out that effective slum clearance depends on more than expenditure on steel and concrete. There are human factors involved too, and it is these which seem to have failed. The appellants moved into one of the units in this building in July 1966; this was a maisonette of two floors, corresponding to the ninth and tenth floors of the block. Access to it was provided by a staircase and by two electrically operated lifts. Another facility provided was an internal chute into which tenants in the block could discharge rubbish or garbage for collection at the ground level.

There has been a consistent history of trouble in this block, due in part to vandalism, in part to non-cooperation by tenants, in part, it is said, to neglect by the corporation. The appellants, with other tenants, stopped payment of rent so that in May 1973 the corporation had to start proceedings for possession. The appellants put in a counterclaim for damages and for an injunction, alleging that the corporation was in breach of its implied covenant for quiet enjoyment, that it was in breach of the statutory covenant implied by s 32 of the Housing Act 1961 and that it was in breach of an obligation implied by law to keep the 'common parts' in repair . . .

I consider first the appellants' claim insofar as it is based on contract. The first step must be to ascertain what the contract is . . . We look first at documentary material. As is common with council lettings there is no formal demise or lease or tenancy agreement. There is a document headed 'Liverpool Corporation, Liverpool City Housing Department' and described as 'Conditions of Tenancy'. This contains a list of obligations on the tenant – he shall do this, he shall not do that, or he shall not do that without the corporation's consent. This is an amalgam of obligations added to from time to time, no doubt, to meet complaints, emerging situations, or problems as they appear to the council's officers. In particular there have been added special provisions relating to multi-storey flats which are supposed to make the conditions suitable to such dwellings. We may note under 'Further special notes' some obligations not to obstruct staircases and passages, and not to permit children under ten to operate any lifts. I mention these as a recognition of the existence and relevance of these facilities. At the end there is a form for signature by the tenant stating that he accepts the tenancy. On the landlord's side there is nothing, no signature, no demise, no covenant; the contract takes effect as soon as the tenants sign the form and are let into possession.

We have then a contract which is partly, but not wholly, stated in writing. In order to complete it, in particular to give it a bilateral character, it is necessary to take account of the actions of the parties and the circumstances. As actions of the parties, we must note the granting of possession by the corporation and reservation by it of the 'common parts' – stairs, lifts, chutes etc. As circumstances we must include the nature of the premises, viz a maisonette for family use on the ninth floor of a high block, one which is occupied by a large number of other tenants, all using the common parts and dependent on them, none of them having any expressed obligation to maintain or repair them.

To say that the construction of a complete contract out of these elements involves a process of 'implication' may be correct: it would be so if implication means the supplying of what is not expressed. But there are varieties of implications which the courts think fit to make and they do not necessarily involve the same process. Where there is, on the face of it, a complete, bilateral contract, the courts are sometimes willing to add terms to it, as implied terms; this is very common in mercantile contracts where there is an established usage ... In other cases, where there is an apparently complete bargain, the courts are willing to add a term on the ground that without it the contract will not work – this is ... the doctrine of *The Moorcock* [(1889) 14 P.D. 64]. This is, as was pointed out by the majority in the Court of Appeal, a strict test – though the degree of strictness seems to vary with the current legal trend, and I think that they were right not to accept it as applicable here. There is a third variety of implication, that which I think Lord Denning MR favours, or at least did favour in this case, and that is the implication of reasonable terms. But though I agree with many of his instances, which in fact fall under one or other of the preceding heads, I cannot go so far as to endorse his principle; indeed, it seems to me, with respect, to extend a long, and undesirable, way beyond sound authority.

The present case, in my opinion, represents a fourth category or, I would rather say, a fourth shade on a continuous spectrum. The court here is simply concerned to establish what the contract is, the parties not having themselves fully stated the terms. In this sense the court is searching for what must be implied.

What then should this contract be held to be? There must first be implied a letting, ie a grant of the right of exclusive possession to the tenants. With this there must, I would suppose, be implied a covenant for quiet enjoyment, as a necessary incident of the letting. The difficulty begins when we consider the common parts. We start with the fact that the demise is useless unless access is obtained by the staircase; we can add that, having regard to the height of the block, and the family nature of the dwellings, the demise would be useless without a lift service; we can continue that there being rubbish chutes built in to the structures and no other means of disposing of light rubbish there must be a right to use the chutes. The question to be answered – and it is the only question in this case – is what is to be the legal relationship between landlord and tenant as regards these matters.

There can be no doubt that there must be implied (i) an easement for the tenants and their licensees to use the stairs, (ii) a right in the nature of an easement to use the lifts and (iii) an easement to use the rubbish chutes.

But are these easements to be accompanied by any obligation on the landlord, and what obligation? There seem to be two alternatives. The first, for which the corporation contends, is for an easement coupled with no legal obligation, except such as may arise under the Occupiers' Liability Act 1957 as regards the safety of those using the facilities, and possibly such other liability as might exist under the ordinary law of tort. The alternative is for easements coupled with some obligation on the part of the landlords as regards the maintenance of the subject of them, so that they are available for use.

My Lords, in order to be able to choose between these, it is necessary to define what test is to be applied, and I do not find this difficult. In my opinion such obligation should be read into the contract as the nature of the contract itself implicitly requires, no more, no less; a test in other words of necessity. The relationship accepted by the corporation is that of landlord and tenant; the tenant accepts obligations accordingly, in relation, inter alia, to the stairs, the lifts and the chutes. All these are not just facilities, or conveniences provided at discretion; they are essentials to the tenancy without which life in the dwellings, as a tenant, is not possible. To leave the landlord free of contractual obligation as regards these matters, and subject only to administrative or political pressure, is, in my opinion, totally inconsistent with the nature of this relationship. The subject-matter of the lease (high-rise blocks) and the relationship created by the tenancy demands, of its nature, some contractual obligation on the landlord ...

(He then discussed *Lister* v. *Romford Ice & Cold Storage Co. Ltd* [1957] A.C. 555; *Miller* v. *Hancock* [1893] 2 Q.B. 177; *De Meza* v. *Ve-Ri-Best Manufacturing Co. Ltd* (1952) 160 E.G. 364; *Penn* v. *Gatenex* [1958] 2 Q.B. 210; and continued:)

I accept, of course, the argument that a mere grant of an easement does not carry with it any obligation on the part of the servient owner to maintain the subject-matter. The dominant owner must spend the necessary money, e g in repairing a drive leading to his house. And the same principle may apply when a landlord lets an upper floor with access by a staircase; responsibility for maintenance may well rest on the tenant. But there is a difference between that case and the case where there is an essential means of access, retained in the landlord's occupation, to units in a building of multi-occupation; for unless the obligation to maintain is, in a defined manner, placed on the tenants, individually or collectively, the nature of the contract, and the circumstances, require that it be placed on the landlord.

It remains to define the standard. My Lords, if, as I think, the test of the existence of the term is necessity the standard must surely not exceed what is necessary having regard to the circumstances. To imply an absolute obligation to repair would go beyond what is a necessary legal incident and would indeed be unreasonable. An obligation to take reasonable care to keep in reasonable repair and usability is what fits the requirements of the case. Such a definition involves – and I think rightly – recognition that the tenants themselves have their responsibilities. What it is reasonable to expect of a landlord has a clear relation to what a reasonable set of tenants should do for themselves ...

I would hold therefore that the corporation's obligation is as I have described. And in agreement, I believe, with your Lordships, I would hold that it has not been shown in this case that there was any breach of that obligation. On the main point therefore I would hold that the appeal fails ...

Lords Cross of Chelsea, Salmon, Edmund Davies and Fraser of Tullybelton delivered similar judgments.

Comment: Is this an example of judges giving with one hand and taking away with another? In what circumstances would this implied obligation be broken? (See also *Sleafer* v. *Lambeth B.C.* [1960] 1 Q.B. 43 (C.A.).)

Note. Any covenant implied by the common law may be excluded by an express provision to the contrary (cf. Housing Act 1961, s. 32 (below)).

C Covenant implied by the common law affecting tenants

The implied liability of tenants to look after premises was reviewed in *Warren* v. *Keen* [1954] 1 Q.B. 15 (C.A.):

Premises which were subject to the control of the Rent Restriction Acts had been let by the plaintiff landlord to the tenant on a weekly tenancy.

Various repairs had been carried out at times by the landlord. When she was served by the Heston and Isleworth local authority with a notice to remedy certain defects, which rendered the premises unfit for habitation by reason of their not being wind and water tight, she carried out the necessary repairs and in the present action claimed to recover from the tenant the cost of those repairs which amounted to £23 5s. By the particulars of claim the landlord contended that it was an implied term of the tenancy that the defendant would use the premises in a tenantlike manner, would keep them wind and water tight, and would make fair and tenantable repairs thereto. The tenant denied liability for repairs.

The county court judge, according to his written notes, held that there was an implied covenant that the tenant would keep the premises in a good and tenantable condition and do such repairs as were necessary to that end. He therefore gave judgment for the landlord.

The tenant appealed.

SOMERVELL L.J. said (in part):

The particulars of disrepair are important: '(*a*) First floor front room (Large). Walls – plaster damp – stained below window opening. (*b*) First floor front room (Small). Walls – plaster damp – stained and perished below window opening. (*c*) External. Front wall – rendering cracked and broken in parts. Front floor window opening – sills not weatherproof, joints and pointwork decayed. (*d*) Leak in hot water boiler.' ...

The case for the landlord before us was put as it appears in the particulars of claim. It was alleged that a tenant from year to year was under an obligation not only to use and cultivate the land or premises in a husbandlike or tenantlike manner but also to keep the buildings wind and water tight. That obligation will be found stated in the judgment of Swinfen Eady LJ in *Wedd* v. *Porter* ([1916] 2 K.B. 91) and in various other cases and in textbooks. On the other hand, the researches of counsel have failed to discover any case which throws light on the scope of that obligation, in other words, any case where a tenant has been held liable for failure to keep wind and water tight where the damage would not be covered by the obligation not to commit voluntary waste or the obligation to use the premises and land in a tenantlike manner ...

The argument is first that that obligation to keep wind and water tight applies to a weekly tenant as well as a tenant from year to year, and then, assuming that it does, the next submission is that the matters set out in the particulars of claim come within the covenant to keep the buildings wind and water tight. I think that submission fails at both stages. If there is a minor, but so far indefinite, obligation on a tenant from year to year to do certain minor repairs necessary to keep premises wind and water tight – and I will assume without deciding it that there is some such limited obligation – then

I see no ground in principle for applying that to a tenancy from week to week. It is quite true that under the Rent Restriction Acts many tenants from week to week are enabled to remain in premises year after year, and the landlord may find great difficulty in fulfilling the conditions which have to be fulfilled under those Acts if he is to get possession. But that does not to my mind affect the question of what are the implications of a weekly tenancy. It seems to me that it would be absurd to suggest that a weekly tenant was under an obligation to repair. It is difficult to think of repairs which would not in themselves cost more than the weekly rent in many cases and yet it is suggested that he is impliedly liable to expend that money although his right to the premises may be terminated in a week's time.

In the second place, I am myself quite clear that the matters particularized in the particulars of claim would not fall within the words 'wind and water tight'. It seems to me clear that the damage here was due to decay of the walls, and there is no suggestion that that was due to any other cause than fair wear and tear. There is no suggestion that the tenant started knocking the walls about or anything of that sort, but in the course of time they had become cracked and presumably required re-pointing, because water was seeping in through the cracks which had appeared. The same would appear to have applied to the wood of the window sills. That may have been due not only to age but also to the positive failure to have the external woodwork re-painted every three years, or whatever is the normal time. Those would be both matters which in my opinion could not on any construction come under this formula of keeping the building wind and water tight, having regard to the principles which are to be found in the cases with regard to the implied liability of a tenant from year to year. Therefore, for these reasons, I think this appeal succeeds and the claim made by the landlord fails.

DENNING L.J.: Apart from express contract, a tenant owes no duty to the landlord to keep the premises in repair. The only duty of the tenant is to use the premises in a husbandlike, or what is the same thing, a tenantlike manner... But what does 'to use the premises in a tenantlike manner' mean? It can, I think, best be shown by some illustrations. The tenant must take proper care of the place. He must, if he is going away for the winter, turn off the water and empty the boiler. He must clean the chimneys, when necessary, and also the windows. He must mend the electric light when it fuses. He must unstop the sink when it is blocked by his waste. In short, he must do the little jobs about the place which a reasonable tenant would do. In addition, he must, of course, not damage the house, wilfully or negligently; and he must see that his family and guests do not damage it: and if they do, he must repair it. But apart from such things, if the house falls into disrepair through fair wear and tear or lapse of time, or for any reason not caused by him, then the tenant is not liable to repair it.

The landlord sought to put upon the tenant a higher obligation. She said that the duty of the tenant was to keep the premises wind and water tight and to make fair and tenantable repairs thereto ... I do not think that is a correct statement of the obligation ...

After analysing the obligation, he concluded:

It was suggested by Mr Willis that an action lies against a weekly tenant for permissive waste. I do not think that that is so. It has been held not to lie against a tenant at will, and in my opinion it does not lie against a weekly tenant. In my judgment, the only obligation on a weekly tenant is to use the premises in a tenantlike manner. That does not cover the dampness and other defects alleged in the particulars of claim. The appeal should be allowed accordingly.

Romer L.J. agreed.

Note. Such an implied condition is excluded if there is an express covenant imposing obligations to repair on the tenant (*Marsden* v. *Edward Hayes* [1927] 2 K.B. 1). A tenant may also be liable under the law of waste, though this appears not to apply to weekly tenants.

Comment. The difficulty of deciding when covenants should be implied and when not has led the Law Commission to propose that an increased range of covenants should be implied into leases by statute (Law Commission, 1975, pp. 28–43). Some would be 'overriding' (similar in scope to those discussed in section D below); the rest 'variable', i.e. variable by the parties. These include many of the implied covenants discussed above.

D Covenants implied by statute

The dreadful housing conditions found in many urban areas in the nineteenth century, and the consequent social unrest that began to manifest itself, led to a number of official responses. In addition to the legal powers given to local authorities to take direct action on housing conditions (see now pp. 377–99 below), tenants were given by statute opportunities for taking legal action directly against their landlords. For example, the Housing of the Working Classes Act 1885, s. 12, gave the tenant power to recover damages for the landlord's 'neglect or default in sanitary matters'. After subsequent amendment it emerged as the Housing, Town Planning, etc. Act 1909, ss. 14, 15. Reynolds (1974, p. 380) notes: 'the intention of the Government introducing the provisions was that it was more than a mere technical

addition to landlord–tenant law and had a valuable role to play in
the fight against the slum'.

Two statutory provisions are currently in force.

(i) HOUSING ACT 1957, s. 6

This implies a condition that certain houses let at very low rents shall
be kept fit for human habitation. Since the abolition of rent controlled
tenancies (above, p. 245) it may be assumed that the section will be
of little practical importance, so will not be further discussed here.
(For details, see 1st edition of this book, pp. 268–9.)

(ii) HOUSING ACT 1961, ss. 32, 33

This was an attempt to stop unscrupulous landlords trying to impose
unreasonable repairing obligations on tenants: 'The right policy is
not only to relieve short term tenants of unreasonable obligations, but,
in the case of short term tenancies, to put definite obligations on the
landlord.' (Brooke, H.C. Deb., 1961, vol. 637 cols. 974–5.)

The provisions read:

32. Repairing obligations in short leases of dwelling-houses
   (1) In any lease of a dwelling-house, being a lease to which this section
applies, there shall be implied a covenant by the lessor –

   (a) to keep in repair the structure and exterior of the dwelling-house
        (including drains, gutters and external pipes); and
   (b) to keep in repair and proper working order the installations in
        the dwelling-house –
        (i) for the supply of water, gas and electricity, and for sanita-
             tion (including basins, sinks, baths and sanitary conveni-
             ences but not, except as aforesaid, fixtures, fittings and
             appliances for making use of the supply of water, gas or
             electricity), and
        (ii) for space heating or heating water,

and any covenant by the lessee for the repair of the premises (including any
covenant to put in repair or deliver up in repair, to paint, point or render
or to pay money in lieu of repairs by the lessee or on account of repairs by
the lessor) shall be of no effect so far as it relates to the matters mentioned
in paragraphs (a) and (b) of this subsection.

   (2) The covenant implied by this section (hereinafter referred to as the
lessor's repairing covenant) shall not be construed as requiring the lessor –

   (a) to carry out any works or repairs for which the lessee is liable
        by virtue of his duty to use the premises in a tenant-like manner,

or would be so liable apart from any express covenant on his part;

(*b*) to rebuild or reinstate the premises in the case of destruction or damage by fire, or by tempest, flood, or other inevitable accident; or

(*c*) to keep in repair or maintain anything which the lessee is entitled to remove from the dwelling-house;

and subsection (1) of this section shall not avoid any covenant by the lessee so far as it imposes on the lessee any of the requirements mentioned in paragraph (*a*) or paragraph (*c*) of this subsection.

(3) In determining the standard of repair required by the lessor's repairing covenant, regard shall be had to the age, character and prospective life of the dwelling-house and the locality in which it is situated.

(4) In any lease in which the lessor's repairing covenant is implied, there shall also be implied a covenant by the lessee that the lessor, or any person authorized by him in writing, may at reasonable times of the day, on giving twenty-four hours' notice in writing to the occupier, enter the premises comprised in the lease for the purpose of viewing their condition and state of repair.

(5) In this and the next following section the following expressions have the meanings hereby respectively assigned to them, that is to say:—

'lease' includes an underlease, an agreement for a lease or underlease, and any other tenancy, but does not include a mortgage, and 'covenant', 'demise' and 'term' shall be construed accordingly;

'lease of a dwelling-house' means a lease whereby a building or part of a building is let wholly or mainly as a private dwelling and 'the dwelling-house' means that building or part of a building;

'lessee' and 'lessor' mean respectively the person for the time being entitled to the term of a lease and to the reversion expectant thereon.

33. Application of s. 32 and restriction on contracting out

(1) Section thirty-two of this Act applies, subject to the provisions of this section and section 80 of the Housing Act 1980, to any lease of a dwelling-house granted after the passing of this Act, being a lease for a term of less than seven years.

(2) For the purposes of this section a lease shall be treated as a lease for a term of less than seven years if it is determinable at the option of the lessor before the expiration of seven years from the commencement of the term, and, except where the foregoing provisions of this subsection apply, shall not be so treated if it confers on the lessee an option for renewal for a term which, together with the original term, amounts to seven years or more.

(3) Where a lease of a dwelling-house (hereinafter referred to as 'the new lease') is granted –

    (a) to a person who when, or immediately before, the new lease is granted, is the lessee under another lease of the dwelling-house, or

    (b) to a person who was the lessee under another lease of the dwelling-house which terminated at some time before the new lease is granted and who, between the termination of that other lease and the grant of the new lease was continuously in possession of the dwelling-house or the rents or profits thereof,

the said section thirty-two shall not apply to the new lease if –

    (i) the new lease is a tenancy to which Part II of the Landlord and Tenant Act, 1954, applies and the other lease either is such a tenancy or would be such a tenancy but for section twenty-eight of the said Act; or

    (ii) the other lease is not a lease to which the said section thirty-two applies and, in the case of a lease granted before the passing of this Act would not have been such a lease if granted after that date.

(4) The said section thirty-two does not apply to any lease of a dwelling-house which is a tenancy of an agricultural holding within the meaning of the Agricultural Holdings Act, 1948.

(5) In the application of this section to a lease granted for a term part of which falls before the grant, that part shall be left out of account and the lease shall be treated as a lease for a term commencing with the grant.

(6) The county court may, by order made with the consent of the parties concerned, authorize the inclusion in a lease, or in any agreement collateral to a lease, of provisions excluding or modifying in relation to the lease the provisions of the said section thirty-two with respect to the repairing obligations of the parties if it appears to the court, having regard to the other terms and conditions of the lease and to all the circumstances of the case, that it is reasonable to do so; and any provision so authorized shall have effect accordingly.

(7) Subject to the last foregoing subsection, any covenant or agreement, whether contained in a lease to which the said section thirty-two applies or in any agreement collateral to such a lease, shall be void so far as it purports to exclude or limit the obligations of the lessor or the immunities of the lessee under that section, or to authorize any forfeiture or impose on the lessee any penalty, disability or obligation, in the event of his enforcing or relying upon those obligations or immunities.

(8) The county court shall have jurisdiction to make a declaration that section thirty-two of this Act applies, or does not apply, to a lease, whatever

the net annual value of the property in question and notwithstanding that the applicant for the declaration does not seek any relief other than the declaration.

A number of difficulties have arisen from the technique of using statutorily implied covenants.

(i) Parties
Since it is, in essence, a contractual remedy, only parties to the contract can sue. Thus a tenant's wife (*Middleton* v. *Hall* (1913) 108 L.T. 804) and daughter (*Ryall* v. *Kidwell* [1914] 3 K.B. 135) have both been held to fall outside the scope of the legislation.[3]

(ii) Extent of the covenant
Most cases will be relatively clear-cut. Consider, though, *Brown* v. *Liverpool Corporation* [1969] 3 All E.R. 1345:

Danckwerts L.J. said (in part):

The matter concerns the front access to the dwelling. There are, apparently, not steps down from the dwelling, as is usual in cases of houses of this type, which is a terraced house; instead there are about three flagstones, some 7 feet, and then there are four steps up, very shallow steps only about $1\frac{1}{2}$ inches each. The trouble arose in this case because one of the steps was broken and, therefore formed a danger for persons using the access to the house. The plaintiff in fact had a fall as a result of that and suffered injury.

The question is, simply, whether, for the purposes of s. 32 of the Housing Act 1961, the steps and the short bit of flagstones leading down to the entrance of the house are within the terms 'the structure and exterior of the dwelling-house (including drains, gutters and external pipes)'.

It is clear to me that this is not part of the structure of the dwelling-house. I think I have a very fair idea of what is meant by the structure of a dwelling-house, and this is not part, of course, of the structure. On the other hand it seems to me equally clear that the 7 feet of flagstones and the steps up do form part of the exterior of the dwelling-house. They are attached in that manner to the house for the purpose of access to this dwelling-house, and they are part of the dwelling-house which is necessary for the purpose of anybody who wishes to live in the dwelling-house enjoying that privilege. If they have not means of access of some sort they could not get there, and these are simply the means of access. The steps are an outside structure, and therefore, it seems to me they are plainly part of the building, and, therefore, the covenant implied by s. 32 of the Act of 1961 fits and applies to the obligations of the landlords in this case.

3. Though these cases were decided on the basis of earlier legislation, it is widely assumed that the same interpretation would be adopted in relation to the Housing Act 1961.

Compare *Hopwood* v. *Cannock Chase D.C.* [1975] 1 All E.R. 796:

CAIRNS L.J.: It was an action for damages for personal injuries which the plaintiff suffered when she fell in the back yard of the house and injured her knee.

The house is a terraced house; it is some 16 feet in width and at the back of it there is a little yard consisting first of a concrete area adjoining the house for the full width of the house and probably about five feet going out from the back of the house; then there is a row of nine paving slabs, again across the full width of the house; then next to them, on the other side, another concrete area, a rather narrower one, perhaps between two and three feet wide. Then, still further away from the house, is a garden.

At the time the plaintiff had come from the back door of the house and she had walked diagonally across the first concrete area; she was intending to go and have a chat with her neighbour at the next house. But when she came to one edge of the paving slabs – it is not clear whether it was the first edge that she came to or the second edge going up on to the other piece of concrete – but at one of those two places she tripped and fell; and it was common ground that there was a difference in height between the concrete and the paving slab of an inch and a half, the paving slab being lower than the concrete. It was found by the learned judge that the defendant, by their servants, well knew of this condition.

The judge had however to consider whether there was any obligation on the defendants to keep this part of the premises in repair. He held that there was no such obligation, and he gave judgment for the defendants, though he assessed the damages in case there should be a successful appeal ...

The plaintiff's case depended on whether there was an obligation on the defendants to repair this part of the premises, it being acknowledged that they were out of repair and it being found that they knew they were out of repair ...

(Cairns L.J. then discussed *Brown* v. *Liverpool Corporation* (above) and continued:)

One matter on which all three members of the court founded their judgments was that in that case the path and steps formed an essential part of the means of access to the house, in that it was the only way in. In this case that certainly was not so; the ordinary means of access to the house was from the front of the house and to my mind it is very doubtful whether this yard could be regarded as a means of access to the house at all. It is true that there was a way out from one side of the yard, apparently into an alley or lane, this house being at the end of the terrace of houses; and there was also a way through from the yard into the corresponding yard of the adjoining house. But that is very far from saying, as could be said in *Brown's* case, that it was necessary to the house as the means of access to it.

Sachs LJ in *Brown's* case went no further than to say that there were materials on which it was open to the county court judge to reach the conclusion that he did. Here, the county court judge has reached the opposite conclusion; he did I think approach it as a question of degree and of fact, and it appears to me that the facts were such as entitled him to reach that conclusion. I should be prepared to go still further and say that, treating it as Danckwerts and Salmon LJJ did, as a matter of law and construction of the section, in my view the section cannot be extended beyond what was held in *Brown's* case to include a yard of this kind.

For these reasons I would dismiss this appeal.

Stephenson L.J. and Brightman J. agreed.

Discussion of s. 32 is also to be found in *Campden Hill Towers* v. *Gardner* [1977] 2 W.L.R. 159. (This related to the same property which featured in *Ravenseft* v. *Davstone* (above, p. 337).) Clause 2 of the lease stated that what was let was:

ALL THAT flat ... numbered 20 and being on the third floor of the said Gate Hill Court ... (but so that this demise shall not include any part of the outside walls or roof thereof) TOGETHER with the Landlord's fixtures and fittings installed therein AND TOGETHER ALSO WITH the rights and privileges specified in the First Schedule hereto ...

The question arose as to what was within the scope of s. 32(1)(a). Megaw L.J. said, in part:

Anything which, in the ordinary use of words, would be regarded as a part of the structure, or of the exterior, of the particular 'dwelling-house', regarded as a separate part of the building, would be within the scope of para (a). Thus, the exclusion by the words of cl 2 of the underlease of 'any part of the outside walls' would not have the effect of taking outside the operation of para (a) that which, in the ordinary use of language, would be regarded as the exterior wall of the flat – an essential integral part of the flat, as a dwelling-house: that part of the outside wall of the block of flats which constitutes a wall of the flat. The paragraph applies to the outside wall or walls of the flat; the outside of inner party walls of the flat; the outer sides or horizontal division between flat 20 and flats above and below; the structural framework and beams directly supporting floors, ceilings and walls of the flat ...

On s. 32(1)(b) Megaw L.J. said:

The lessors contend that the words 'in the dwelling-house' have the effect of limiting the application of para (b) to installations of the prescribed types which are physically within the dwelling-house. Thus, to take an example debated in argument, if there is in the flat a hot-water radiator, the paragraph puts on the lessors the obligation to keep the radiator 'in repair and proper working order'. But it does not impose any obligation on the lessors in respect of, nor preclude them from making charges in respect of, repairs to anything outside the flat, for example a boiler in the basement which heats the water which is supplied to all the radiators in all the flats in the building.

The lessees contend that, despite the words of the paragraph 'installations *in* the dwelling-house', the paragraph applies to anything outside the flat, the proper functioning of which is required in order to enable the installation within the flat to function as it is intended to do. If it were not for the words 'proper working order' in para (*b*), it would, we think, be difficult to find any support for the lessees' contention. But the inclusion of those words does provide some possible support. It would, however, produce very odd results if that were so. First, there is nothing in s 32 which requires a lessor to provide such installations. Any such obligation would have to be derived from either non-statutory terms of the lease itself, which would be a matter of contractual negotiation, or from some other statute. Secondly, if 'proper working order' did include, for example, the necessity of a supply of hot water to a radiator, or water to a cistern there would be imposed by statute an absolute obligation, with no qualifications, which in some respects would be quite outside the lessors' control. For example, the central heating boiler in the basement may be operated by gas. The gas supply is cut off by the Gas Board for some reason outside the control of the lessors; or the water supply is cut off, or limited to certain times of the day, by the water authority. The hot water radiator, or the water cistern, while in perfectly good repair and perfectly good 'working order', cannot perform their function. If the covenant has the meaning suggested by the lessees, the lessors are liable for breach of the implied covenant.

In our judgment, the meaning of para (*b*) is as is contended for by the lessors. The installations in the physical confines of the flat must be kept in repair and capable, so far as their own structural and mechanical condition is concerned, of working properly. But no more than that. The lessors may be under additional obligations but, if so, they do not arise from this statute...

In *Sheldon* v. *West Bromwich Corporation* (1973) 25 P.&C.R. 360, a council tenant whose house was flooded when the cold water tank burst was entitled to damages against the council because of their failure to keep it in repair.

STEPHENSON L.J. said that there had been six inspections of the water supply in the house by the corporation's plumbers prior to the bursting of the cold water tank on July 6, 1970. The inspections were made after complaints by the tenant of water hammering – caused by a mysterious crossing of hot and cold water pipes. On the last inspection, on May 28, 1970, the plumber inspected the tank. He did so because the tank had become discoloured.

Discoloration was a sign of corrosion, which ultimately produced holes in the tank. Until holes appeared there was no immediate danger of a burst. The danger was usually shown by the tank weeping: weeping meant that there were already holes in it. On his inspection on May 28 the plumber found no weeping and considered that the tank did not require repair. A tank could be in a state of discoloration for years ...

Reversing the county court judge,

His Lordship could not accept that a landlord was under no obligation to carry out repairs to a discoloured tank unless a hole was actually made in it so that weeping had begun. In considering whether repairs were required, a reasonable landlord would take into account the age of the tank. The tank in question was 40 years old and had been discoloured for some time. In those circumstances the corporation's plumber ought to have realized that repair was needed.

Accordingly, the tenant was entitled to damages for breach of the statutory obligation ...

The House of Lords also had some terse comments to make on the nature of liability under s. 32 in *Liverpool City Council* v. *Irwin* [1976] 2 W.L.R. 562 (for facts see above, p. 343). See, for example, Lord Salmon:

It remains to consider whether the corporation was in breach of its obligations under s 32(1)(b) of the Housing Act 1961 ...

The judge found that every time a water closet was used, the water overflowed and was apt to flood the floor and escape on to the landing where it lay without any means of draining away. Whether the ballcock as fitted caused this tiresome fault or whether it was due to the design of the sanitary convenience is not clear – nor in my view does it matter. Some tenants tried using pails to catch the overflow. Others attempted to bend the ballcock down which stopped the overflow but did not allow sufficient water to flush the water closet efficiently. For my part I do not understand how on any acceptable construction of the section, it can be held that in the circumstances I have recited the corporation complied with its statutory obligations to keep the sanitary conveniences in proper working order. I can well understand that sanitary conveniences may be in proper working order even if they are too small or there are too few of them, but how can they be said to be in proper working order if every time they are used they may swamp the floor passes my comprehension.

My Lords, I would accordingly allow the appeal in relation to that part of the counterclaim based on the corporation's breach of the Housing Act 1961, and reduce the damages awarded from £10 to £5.

In disputed cases, the onus of proof that there have been breaches of the statutory covenants lies on the tenant (*Foster* v. *Day* (1968) 208 E.G. 495 (C.A.)).

(iii) Notice

It is a long-established principle of the common law that for a landlord to be liable under a covenant to do repairs the tenant must first give notice of want of repair (*Makin* v. *Watkinson* (1870) L.R. 6 Ex. 25). The question has arisen as to whether this principle should apply to statutorily implied covenants. This issue has come before the courts on a number of occasions. In *McCarrick* v. *Liverpool Corporation* [1947] A.C. 219 in the House of Lords, Lord Simonds said:

My Lords, this appeal ... is brought to test the correctness of *Morgan* v. *Liverpool Corporation* ([1927] 2 K.B. 131). The relevant facts are few and not in dispute in this House. The appellant was at all material times the tenant of the respondent corporation of a dwelling-house, No. 6, Brown Street, in the city of Liverpool. This house, which was subject to the provisions of the Housing Act, 1936, was by reason of the defective condition of two stone steps leading from the kitchen to the back-kitchen not 'reasonably fit for human habitation'. In consequence of this defect the appellant's wife fell and fractured her leg. The appellant suffered special damage assessed at £70. The question is whether this damage is recoverable in law from the respondents. They have so far successfully contended and contend before your Lordships that it is not recoverable, alleging that no notice of the defect was given to them and that notice is a condition precedent to their liability. It has been found as a fact, and your Lordships will not disturb that finding, that no notice was given. The question of law remains whether notice is a condition precedent to liability. So it was held in *Morgan's* case which must now be reviewed ...

The first question for consideration is what is the effect of a statutory provision that 'in any contract for letting ... there shall, notwithstanding any stipulation to the contrary, be implied a condition ...' In *Ryall* v. *Kidwell & Son* ([1914] 3 K.B. 135) it was held that the effect of the enactment was to import a new term into the contract of tenancy and no more. I think that this was manifestly right and respectfully adopt the language used by Lush J.: 'But the character and quality of the obligation which is imported by the statute are none the less contractual, although the contract is derived from and owes its existence to the statute.' To the same effect is the observation of Atkin LJ in *Morgan's* case: 'The clause in the Housing Act is imposed as a contractual term and as such it appears to be only available to the tenant because it is a term of the tenancy' ...

The rival contentions can now be stated. By the appellant it is said that the promise by the Landlord thus imported into the contract is an absolute one, by the respondents that the obligation is not absolute but that it is a condition of liability that notice of the material defect shall be given to them. My Lords, I find it impossible to approach a question of this kind as if similar questions had not for generations been the subject of decisions in the courts of this country and conveyancing practice had not grown up on the faith of them. On a long line of authority beginning with *Makin* v. *Watkinson* (1870) L.R. 6 Ex 25) it is clear that on a convenant by a lessor to keep demised premises in repair he cannot be sued for non-repair unless he has received notice of want of repair. In the case cited it appears that the lease did not reserve to the lessor the right to enter and inspect the demised premises and counsel for the appellant has urged that this makes all the difference and that the right of entry given by the imported term distinguishes the present from other cases. I think that this is not a valid distinction. In *London & South Western Ry Co.* v. *Flower* ((1875) 1 C.P.D. 77), the principle was applied though, as Brett J. said: 'I will assume also that by implication they had a right to go upon the railway for the purpose of examining the condition of the bridge and ascertaining whether or not it needed repair.' So also in *Hugall* v. *M'Lean* ((1884) 53 L.T. 94) (a case which was, I think, misunderstood in *Fisher* v. *Walter* ([1926] 2 K.B. 315), itself a decision which is, I think, inconsistent with higher authority and cannot stand). So also in *Torrens* v. *Walker* ([1906] 2 Ch. 166), where Warrington J., after referring to *Hugall* v. *M'Lean*, of which case he says: 'There, as here, the lease contained a covenant by the lessee to repair the inside of the premises, and to allow the lessor to enter and view the state of repair,' applied the same principle. I will refer finally to *Morgan's* case again. Atkin LJ closely examines the principle. I will cite only two short passages, he says: 'The result is, to my mind, that in all cases of that kind, speaking generally, it is a condition of the liability of the landlord that he should receive notice of the repairs,' and later: 'I think the power of access that is given, extensive though it may be, does not take the case away from the principle from which the courts have inferred the condition that the liability is not to arise except on notice.' The judgment that I have cited of Lord Atkin is the more valuable because it was given after the judgment of this House in *Murphy* v. *Hurley* ([1922] 1 A.C. 369), on which the appellant relies. There, the question being whether notice was a condition precedent to the liability of a landlord to keep in repair a sea-wall erected by him for the common protection of a number of holdings, it was held that it was not. The salient fact was that the sea-wall, so far from being in the exclusive occupation of any tenant was, as Lord Buckmaster said, 'intended to be within the control of the landlord.' It is, I think, true that in the speeches of Lord Buckmaster and of the other noble and learned Lords who heard the case there are observations which suggest that the principle has no application where the landlord has means of access and therefore means of knowing of the defect, but the ratio decidendi of the case is that the sea-wall was not in the exclusive occupation of any tenant, a fact always held sufficient to exclude the principle, see, e.g., *Melles & Co.* v. *Holme* ([1918] 2 K.B. 100). In none of the speeches is there any suggestion that the cases in which, though there was a right to enter and therefore means of knowledge, yet the principle was applied, were wrongly decided. It is on this footing that the Court of Appeal decided *Morgan's* case and in my opinion they were right. I conclude, then, that the provision imported by statute into the contractual tenancy must be construed in the same way as any other term of the tenancy and, so construed, does not impose any obligation on the landlord unless and until he has notice of the defect which renders the dwelling not 'reasonably fit for human habitation.' That is the only question which your Lordships have to decide and I do not think it desirable or necessary to consider what may constitute such notice ...

This principle was followed by the House of Lords in *O'Brien* v. *Robinson* ([1973] A.C. 912). Here the O'Briens were injured when their bedroom ceiling fell on them. It was found that this was the result of a latent defect, so they could not have given notice of it to the landlord, even if they had wanted to. The House of Lords held unanimously that the fact that no notice was given to the landlord was fatal to the O'Briens' claim. They felt that the rule requiring notice had to apply in circumstances where, *ex hypothesi*, no notice could be given: Lord Diplock did concede: 'An examination of the reasoning in the judgments in the cases on this subject during the last 100 years suggests that the law might easily have developed on different lines from those which it in fact followed. But, for my part, I am not persuaded that this development was clearly wrong or leads to results which are clearly unjust.'

Comment. These conclusions were criticized by Reynolds (1974). He referred to social studies on this question[4] which indicate (*a*) that many tenants do not complain about apparently trivial defects, but only exceptional damp, excessive rot and so on; and (*b*) that other tenants do not complain because they know their landlords would refuse to do anything (and indeed might start eviction proceedings). Reynolds comments, on point (*a*), that 'it seems unjust that tenants should have to bear the consequences of accidents caused by disrepair because their opinions as to the seriousness of the work needed turns out to be wrong'. On point (*b*) he asks: 'is the tenant to be penalized

4. Milner Holland, 1965, p. 382; Francis, 1971, p. 249; Coates & Silburn, 1970, p. 68.

because he has given up an apparently fruitless ritual?' (p. 393). However Robinson (1976, pp. 49–54) has suggested that the decisions on notice can be supported both in the light of precedent and on principle. He argues that landlords should not be made liable under these provisions where they are not at fault. What do you think? The Law Commission (1975, para. 131) has not recommended any change in the law, save to make it clear that notice may come from any source.

(iv) *Standard of repair (s. 32 (3)): London Borough of Newham* v. *Patel* (1979) J.P.E.L. 303 (C.A.)
A house in a redevelopment area in Newham had been let by the Council to Mr. Patel. It was acknowledged that the house was unfit for human habitation (see below, p. 389). Hence Mr Patel sought damages for alleged breaches of the landlord's covenant to repair. Templeman L.J. said in part:

The prospective life of the dwelling-house affected the duty of the council under section 32 and they were not bound to carry out repairs which would be wholly useless.

In his judgment also, the [county court] judge had been quite right when he had taken into account the low rent charged for 35 Prince of Wales Road and had come to the conclusion that the defendant had not suffered damage ... Mr. Patel could not have both the benefit of a low rent and an award of damages for the same reason, the condition of the house.

Therefore, it seemed to him that having regard to the damages which had been pleaded the learned judge had been quite right in coming to the conclusion that damages had not been made out.

ORMROD L.J. said that he agreed and added that it was conceded that the council was subject to section 32 of the 1961 Housing Act, but in construing that Act the court must have regard to the circumstances of the case and the general social conditions to which it was sought to be applied.

If Mr. Sedley's [counsel for Mr Patel] argument on this appeal was right, it would have the effect of greatly increasing the number of unfit houses which were standing empty, and correspondingly, of increasing the number of homeless persons in the stress areas of the cities of this country. It might be, of course, that that was a necessary consequence of the legislation which had to be accepted, although it was difficult to imagine that Parliament thought they were going to produce such a result. It was, however, a matter which the court was bound to bear in mind when it same to construing the section.

Subsection (3) was plainly put in to avoid the sort of absurdity that Mr. Sedley's argument leads to in this case. It was perfectly true, as Mr. Sedley had pointed out, that the terms of subsection (3) were almost, but significantly not entirely, in line with decisions relating to the construction of covenants for repair. In subsection (3) the crucially important addition was the phrase 'prospective life of the dwelling-house.' In his judgment that was an exceedingly important qualification. If the prospective life of the dwelling-house, as in this case, was short, then it was perfectly proper, sensible and reasonable to adjust the landlord's obligations accordingly and not to seek to impose a construction on the statute which could only be described as pedantic.

On the question of damages, it had been submitted that the fact that the tenant had been let into possession in the first place at a very low rent, (on the evidence about a third of the rent which would have been expected for such a house in reasonable condition) should be disregarded in assessing damages had there been a breach of the statutory obligation to repair. If this was right, local authorities had three alternatives when faced with a property like this. One was to spend a great deal of money on it and devote resources to it which would be plainly wasteful. One was to leave it empty, and one was to let it to the Mr. Patels of this world and pay them damages from the moment they entered. One only had to state the argument in that form to see how absurd it was ...

Orr L.J. agreed with both judgments.

Comment. Could it not be argued that, however low the rent, Mr Patel had suffered damage as a result of the landlord's failure to repair? Is the standard of repair required under sub-s. (3) always to be adjusted to 'nil' if the prospective life of the accommodation is short? If so, does this not make the repairing covenant worthless?

(v) *Miscellaneous*

(a) The statutory covenant is only implied into a lease; licensees cannot, therefore, take advantage of it (above, ch. 2).

(b) 'Term less than seven years'. In *Parker* v. *O'Connor* (*The Times*, 10 June 1974 (C.A.)) it was held that a lease of a dwelling-house for ninety years, subject to determination on three months' notice on the death of the landlord, was *not* within the scope of s. 33(2).

(c) 'Contracting out'. It is not possible to contract out of the obligations contained in s. 32 without permission of the county court (s. 33(6)). However, under the Housing Act 1980, s. 80, short-term leases to specified bodies (educational institutions, housing associations, local authorities, and the Crown) are deemed to fall outside the protection of s. 32.

2. Remedies for breach of covenant

A Tenants' remedies against the landlord

(i) DAMAGES

A tenant may have an action for damages against a landlord who is in breach of a covenant to repair, but only for damages suffered after he has given the landlord notice of want of repair (see above, p. 358). The measure of damages is the difference in value to the tenant between the premises as they are and as they would be if repaired in accordance with the covenant (*Hewitt* v. *Rowlands* (1924) 131 L.T. 757). If, after receiving the notice, the landlord fails to repair within a reasonable time, the tenant can sue without first incurring the expense of doing the repairs himself. The law implies a licence for the landlord to enter the property to do the repairs.

(ii) SPECIFIC PERFORMANCE

In *Jeune* v. *Queens Cross Properties* [1974] Ch. 97, Pennycuick V.C. appeared to hold that a tenant could ask for an order of specific performance against a landlord for breach of covenant. Woodfall (1978, para. 1-1509) has expressed some doubt as to the generality of this principle arguing that it goes against *Hill* v. *Barclay* (1810) 16 Ves. Jun. 402. However the court's jurisdiction is confirmed in the case of housing by Housing Act 1974, s. 125:

125.—(1) In any proceedings in which a tenant of a dwelling alleges a breach on the part of his landlord of a repairing covenant relating to any part of the premises in which the dwelling is comprised, the court may, in its discretion, order specific performance of that covenant, whether or not the breach relates to a part of the premises let to the tenant and notwithstanding any equitable rule restricting the scope of that remedy, whether on the basis of a lack of mutuality or otherwise.

(2) In this section –

'landlord', in relation to a tenant, includes any person against whom the tenant has a right to enforce a repairing covenant;

'repairing covenant' means a covenant to repair, maintain, renew, construct or replace any property;

'statutory tenant' has the same meaning as in the Rent Act [1977] and

'tenant' includes a sub-tenant and a statutory tenant but does not include a tenant under a tenancy to which Part II of the Landlord and Tenant Act 1954 (business tenancies) applies, and any reference to the premises let to a tenant means, in relation to a statutory tenant, the premises of which he is the statutory tenant...

In *Francis* v. *Cowcliff Ltd* (1976) 239 E.G. 977 (Ch. D.), the defendant landlords decided to install new lifts in a block of flats. However, they lacked adequate finance to complete the task. The plaintiff, a seventy-year-old widow living on the third floor, sought an order of specific performance. Judge Rubin said (in part):

If ever there was a case in which the defendants had brought the hardship on themselves, this must be it. They chose to purchase and embark upon an expensive scheme for development of the property without any or any adequate finance and without making any but the most speculative arrangements for such finance. Accordingly he (his Lordship) proposed to make the order for specific performance which the plaintiff sought. It was said that this would inevitably result in the company being wound up. Even if that were so, it did not seem to him to be any reason why the plaintiff should not have her order. In any event he was far from satisfied that the guarantors of the mortgage loan and others interested in the company would not provide the necessary money to do the requisite works and stave off the creditors of the company.

(iii) REPAIR AND DEDUCT

Lee-Parker v. *Izzett* [1971] 1 W.L.R. 1688 (Ch. D.). As part of a complex case relating to a contract for the sale of land, Goff J. said:

However, the third and fourth defendants further claim a lien for the cost of the repairs or alternatively for the value of any permanent improvement affected thereby, and they also claim a set-off against rent in their capacity as tenants. First, they say that insofar as the vendor was, as landlord, liable to do the repairs by the express or implied terms of the tenancy agreement, including the covenants imported by s 32 (1) of the Housing Act 1961, they, having done them themselves, are entitled to treat the expenditure as a payment of rent, for which reliance is placed on *Taylor v Beal* [(1591) Coo. Eliz. 222] ...

I do not think this is bound up with technical rules of set-off. It is an ancient common law right. I therefore declare that so far as the repairs are within the express or implied covenants of the lessor the third and fourth defendants are entitled to recoup themselves out of future rents and defend any action for payment thereof. It does not follow however that the full amount expended by the third and fourth defendants on such repairs can properly be treated as payment of rent. It is a question of fact in every case whether and to what extent the expenditure was proper.

For the sake of avoiding misunderstanding I must add that of course the *Taylor v Beal* right can only be exercised when and so far as the landlord is in breach and any necessary notice must have been given to him. Insofar as the repairs fall outside the landlord's covenants in the lease there can in my judgment be no set-off against the plaintiffs.

Some doubts have been expressed as to the correctness of this proposition. However, see now *British Anzani (Felixstowe)* v. *International Marine Management* [1979] 2 All E.R. 1063 (Q.B.D.), where Forbes J. said (in part):

On a consideration of these cases it seems to me that *Taylor v Beal* is authority for the proposition that there are at least two sets of circumstances in which at common law there can be a set-off against rent, one where the tenant expends money on repairs to the demised premises which the landlord has covenanted to carry out, but in breach has failed to do so (at any rate where the breach significantly affects the use of the premises), and the other where the tenant has paid money at the request of the landlord in respect of some obligation of the landlord connected with the land demised. To this proposition there must be added two riders. First, that as the landlord's obligation to repair premises demised does not arise until the tenant has notified him of want of repair, such notification must have been given before the set-off can arise; and secondly that the set-off must be for a sum which is not to be regarded as unliquidated damages, that is, it is a sum certain which has actually been paid and in addition its quantum has either been acknowledged by the landlord or in some other way can no longer be disputed by him, as, for instance, if it is the subject of an award on a submission to arbitration. The latest expression of opinion about this matter is in *Lee-Parker v Izzet* (above).

I do not think that there is any difference between the principle as seen by Goff J and that which I have set out above save for this. Goff J took the view that it was money properly expended which could form a subject of this right. My view is that the right is slightly more restricted, namely that it can only be exercised when the sum is certain and its amount cannot really be disputed by the landlord. This restriction which I think should be made arises from a consideration of the judgment of Lord Kenyon CJ in *Weigall v Waters* [(1795) 6 Term Rep. 488] which was not quoted to Goff J. In that case the tenant had in fact paid £30 but Lord Kenyon CJ still regarded the cross-claim as one for uncertain damages. It seems the quantum of the sum must have been either unchallenged or unchallengeable before it could be regarded as deductible....

See too *Asco Developments* v. *Lawes* (1978) LAG Bulletin 293; Arden (1979c).

The legitimacy (or otherwise) of tenants participating in a rent strike was discussed in *Camden Nominees* v. *Forcey* [1940] Ch. 352:

The plaintiffs are the owners of a block of flats known as Highstone Mansions, Camden Road. The flats are let on tenancy agreements which are in

a standard form, each agreement containing (*a*) an obligation on the tenant
to pay his rent, usually by monthly instalments in advance, and other usual
obligations; and (*b*) certain obligations on the landlord, including that of
lighting the staircase and landings and keeping them properly cleaned and
swept, and of maintaining constant hot water and central heating.

The defendant, Miss Forcey, is the tenant of flat No. 49, the defendant
Bennett, of flat No. 44, and there have at all material times been some sixty
other tenants in the block.

In the autumn of 1939 certain of the tenants complained that the landlords were not satisfactorily carrying out their obligations under the tenancy
agreements.

Miss Forcey decided not to pay her rent. Simonds J. said, of this
action, 'It is clear ... that it is no answer to a claim for rent for the
tenant to say that the landlord has not performed his obligation to
clean the staircase or furnish hot water...'

In addition, she and some of the other tenants decided to form a
tenants' association, which became affiliated to the St Pancras
Tenants' Defence League. She and another tenant, Mr Bennett, were
mainly responsible for trying to get all the tenants in the block to
act in a coordinated way, and in particular to refuse to pay their rent
until their grievances had been remedied. Simonds J. held, first, that
these defendants had knowingly interfered with the contracts between
the plaintiffs and their tenants. The further question that had to be
answered was whether the defendants were legally justified in so acting. Simonds J. said:

In the present case ... the defendants have pleaded that they are justified
in their otherwise actionable wrong on two grounds; the first, that they and
those whom they would persuade to break their contracts have a common
interest in making the landlords perform their obligations; and the second,
that there is such a state of affairs here existing, on the one side tenants who
are weak and on the other landlords who are strong and take advantage of
their strength, that it is justifiable for the defendants to use a weapon which
would otherwise be wrongful.

In my judgment, there is no validity in either of these contentions. The
defendants owed no duty to their fellow tenants; they sought their cooperation
for their own ends, though no doubt a successful campaign would have been
for the benefit of all alike. The end which they sought, namely, the performance by the landlords of their obligations, was one which could be reached
by process of law. If the landlords broke their contract the law gave the
defendants their remedy by way of damages, or in a proper case by way of
specific performance. There is neither reason nor authority for the suggestion

that in such circumstances a common interest can justify the interference with contractual rights ...

The second contention was one which appeared to be directed less to my reason than to my emotions. The case was put as something analogous to *Brimelow* v. *Casson* ([1924] 1 Ch. 302) in which any step that put an end to an intolerable position might be regarded as justifiable. *Brimelow* v. *Casson* stands alone, and has been the subject of a good deal of controversy. In a comparable case it would be my duty to follow it, though I would humbly suggest that on the facts stated in the judgment that case might have been simply disposed of by the application of the maxim Ex turpi causa non oritur actio. But, however that may be, there is no real analogy between the two cases. It is a dangerous proposition that inequality in wealth or position justifies a course otherwise actionable, and that tenants may against their landlord adopt measures of self-help because in their judgment the law does not afford them adequate remedy for his default.

I would only add, in deference to the argument addressed to me, which I think was intended to be founded on *Brimelow* v. *Casson*, that neither that case nor any other case supports the view that those who assume the duty of advising the withholding of rent or any other breach of contract can justify their action by protesting that they are performing a public service. Advice which is intended to have persuasive effects is not distinguishable from inducement, and there is no reason to suppose that the giving of such advice is justifiable except by those persons in whom the law recognizes a moral duty to give it.

In the result I hold that the defendants without justification interfered with the plaintiff's contractual rights and it is clear that at the date of the issue of the writ they intended to continue to do so. I must therefore grant an injunction as asked ...

B Landlord's remedies against the tenant

The Uthwatt-Jenkins Committee (1950, para. 222) noted:

Breach of a repairing covenant by the tenant may give the landlord a variety of remedies. If the lease so provides he may enter and repair at the tenant's expense, though he will not be granted a mandatory injunction or specific performance; if, as is usual, there is a proviso in the lease for re-entry he may, subject to the statutory restrictions mentioned below, forfeit the lease, or finally he may claim damages for the breach.

The statutory restrictions include:

(*i*) *Law of Property Act 1925*, s. 146(1) imposes a general limitation on the ability of landlords to forfeit leases. S. 146(2) contains a general power for the court to provide relief for a tenant against whom an action for forfeiture is brought (discussed below, pp. 406–12).

(*ii*) *Leasehold Property (Repairs) Act 1938*, as amended by Landlord and Tenant Act 1954, takes the above further. Section 1 provides:

1.   Restriction on enforcement of repairing covenants in long leases of small houses

(1) Where a lessor serves on a lessee under sub-section (1) of section one hundred and forty-six of the Law of Property Act, 1925, a notice that relates to a breach of a covenant or agreement to keep or put in repair during the currency of the lease [all or any of the property comprised in the lease], and at the date of the service of the notice [three] years or more of the term of the lease remain unexpired, the lessee may within twenty-eight days from that date serve on the lessor a counter-notice to the effect that he claims the benefit of this Act.

(2) A right to damages for a breach of such a covenant as aforesaid shall not be enforceable by action commenced at any time at which [three] years or more of the term of the lease remain unexpired unless the lessor has served on the lessee not less than one month before the commencement of the action such a notice as is specified in subsection (1) of section one hundred and forty-six of the Law of Property Act, 1925, and where a notice is served under this subsection, the lessee may, within twenty-eight days from the date of the service thereof, serve on the lessor a counter-notice to the effect that he claims the benefit of this Act.

(3) Where a counter-notice is served by a lessee under this section, then, notwithstanding anything in any enactment or rule of law, no proceedings, by action or otherwise, shall be taken by the lessor for the enforcement of any right of re-entry or forfeiture under any proviso or stipulation in the lease for breach of the covenant or agreement in question, or for damages for breach thereof, otherwise than with the leave of the court.

(4) A notice served under subsection (1) of section one hundred and forty-six of the Law of Property Act, 1925, in the circumstances specified in sub-section (1) of this section, and a notice served under subsection (2) of this section shall not be valid unless it contains a statement, in characters not less conspicuous than those used in any other part of the notice, to the effect that the lessee is entitled under this Act to serve on the lessor a counter-notice claiming the benefit of this Act, and a statement in the like characters specifying the time within which, and the manner in which, under this Act a counter-notice may be served and specifying the name and address for service of the lessor.

(5) Leave for the purposes of this section shall not be given unless the lessor proves –

(*a*) that the immediate remedying of the breach in question is requisite for preventing substantial diminution in the value of his reversion, or that the value thereof has been substantially diminished by the breach;

(*b*) that the immediate remedying of the breach is required for giving effect in relation to the [premises] to the purposes of any enactment, or of any byelaw or other provision having effect under an enactment, [or for giving effect to any order of a court or requirement of any authority under any enactment or any such byelaw or other provision as aforesaid];

(*c*) in a case in which the lessee is not in occupation of the whole of the [premises as respects which the covenant or agreement is proposed to be enforced], that the immediate remedying of the breach is required in the interests of the occupier of [those premises] or of part thereof;

(*d*) that the breach can be immediately remedied at an expense that is relatively small in comparison with the much greater expense that would probably be occasioned by postponement of the necessary work; or

(*e*) special circumstances which in the opinion of the court, render it just and equitable that leave should be given.

(6) The court may, in granting or in refusing leave for the purposes of this section, impose such terms and conditions on the lessor or on the lessee as it may think fit.

Section 1 (4) was discussed in *Middlegate Ltd* v. *Messimiris* ([1973] 1 W.L.R. 168) by Lord Denning M.R.: 'We should construe "not less conspicuous" so as to mean "equally readable" or "equally sufficient" to tell the tenant of his right to give a counter-notice.'

Megaw L.J. and Sir Gordon Willmer agreed.

Section 1 (5) was discussed in *Sidnell* v. *Wilson* ([1966] 1 All E.R. 681):

LORD DENNING, M.R.: This is an unusual case. In December, 1950, Mr Sidnell ('the landlord') who waa a tobacconist, owned a couple of shops at Sudbury in Suffolk. One of them, No. 11a, North Street, he occupied himself for the purpose of his tobacconist's business. The shop next door, No. 11, he let to a Mr Carver, who was a butcher, for twenty-one years at a rent of £156 a year. He took a covenant by the tenant to keep the premises in good and tenantable repair, damage by fire excepted. The landlord himself covenanted to keep the roof and the exterior of the premises in good and tenantable repair and particularly 'to do such structural repairs to the building as may be necessary for the convenient occupation thereof'. There was a covenant by the tenant to reside personally on the premises.

It appears that in June, 1962, there was a serious fire in some houses a little further along the street. When the fire brigade came and used their hoses, the water flowed down into the cellars beneath both the tobacconist's shop at No. 11a and also from there into Mr Carver's shop at No. 11. The fire assessors came round. They went into the cellars and found a lot of water there. They advised the landlord himself to leave the door open and dry out the cellar with heaters. He did so and there has been no trouble in his cellar since. We do not know whether the fire assessors told the same thing to Mr Carver who was next door in his butcher's shop; but it is said that Mr Carver himself or his successors did not take proper steps to get rid of the damp after this water got in from the hoses. So much so that it is suggested that the dampness in due course caused dry rot to develop. Mr Carver himself was only there a further six months when he assigned the lease to Mr Wilson, Mr Arnaudy and Mr Rollingson ('the tenants') together. They covenanted to reside personally on the premises and they took over the lease. Then it appears by the end of 1963 and the beginning of 1964 the landlord discovered that dry rot was rampant in the cellar of No. 11. He got the surveyors to look at it. They found that this dry rot was going through the cellar and might indeed spread to the landlord's premises, No. 11a. It has proved so bad that the floor of the butcher's shop has fallen through.

Under these circumstances, after considerable correspondence, the landlord's solicitors in October, 1964, served notice on the tenants under s. 146 of the Law of Property Act, 1925, alleging that there were breaches of covenant to keep in good and tenantable repair. The landlord required the tenants to dry out the cellar, replace the rotten timber, and so forth; and also to do other repairs, such as repairing patches of plaster and ceilings in other parts of the house ...

Thereupon the landlord applied for leave to bring proceedings in the county court to forfeit the lease. In order to get leave, the landlord had to bring himself within one of the clauses of s. 1 (5) of the Act of 1938. The relevant clauses here are (a) and (e) ...

Let me say at once that in the great majority of dilapidation cases when there is want of repair during the term, leave will not be given, for in most cases the reversion is not diminished much in value by the breach; but this case is out of the ordinary. It is clear that, if the breach which the landlord alleges is established, the value of the reversion has been substantially diminished. ...

The landlord does, therefore, bring himself within s. 1 (5) (a), provided always that he is right in saying that Mr Carver was in breach.

What has a landlord to prove in order to get leave? Has he actually to prove a breach by the tenant or has he to show only a prima facie case of breach? Counsel for the tenants admitted, as I think quite rightly, that the landlord need only show a prima facie case of a breach by the tenant ...

In this case I fear that the judge required the landlord to prove more. He required the landlord to prove that the tenant had been guilty of a breach of covenant. The judge was induced to do so, I think, by the way that counsel on both sides conducted the case. They called surveyors and so forth as if it were the trial. Naturally enough the judge treated it as such. He said: 'It is for the applicant *to show* that there has been a breach of covenant. As to the condition of the shop floor, which is the really serious defect in these premises, the applicant *has not shown* any breach of covenant to repair by the respondents.'

Counsel for the tenants urged us to treat this statement benevolently. Even so, I cannot help thinking that the judge treated this application almost as the trial of the action by requiring a breach to be proved. Whereas all the landlord had to show was a prima facie case. The evidence here for the landlord was as follows. The landlord's son said that there was no trace of dry rot in the cellar in 1962 immediately after the fire. But by the end of 1963 it was rampaging away. A surveyor said that it might be due to neglect to dry out the cellar. On the whole I think that this was a sufficiently prima facie case on which the judge might have given leave.

Cf. Diplock L.J.: 'It is sufficient that the landlord should show that there is a *bona fide* arguable case that the conditions or one or other of them set out in the paragraphs of the subsection are fulfilled, and that if he does that, it is no function of the county court judge on the application for leave to go into the merits of the matter and hear rebutting evidence, as if the trial were taking place then.'

(*iii*) *Law of Property Act 1925*, s. 147. This deals specifically with a notice relating to internal decorative repairs. Under this section:

The Court, if satisfied that the notice is unreasonable, having regard to all the circumstances of the case, including the length of the tenant's term remaining unexpired, may relieve the tenant wholly or partially from liability for such repairs. But if the notice relates to repairs required under an express covenant or agreement to put the property in a decorative state of repair, and the covenant or agreement has never been performed, or if it relates to any matter necessary or proper to put or keep the property in a sanitary condition, or for the maintenance or preservation of the structure, or to any statutory liability to keep a house fit for habitation, or to any covenant to yield up the house or other building in a specified state of repair at the end of the term, the Court has no power under the above provision to grant relief to the tenant (Hill & Redman, 1976, p. 248).

(*iv*) *Landlord and Tenant Act 1927*, s. 18(1) deals with the measure of damages:

Damages for a breach of a covenant or agreement to keep or put premises in repair during the currency of a lease, whether such covenant or agreement is expressed or implied, and whether general or specific, shall in no case exceed the amount (if any) by which the value of the reversion (whether immediate or not) in the premises is diminished owing to the breach of such covenant or agreement as aforesaid; and in particular no damage shall be recovered for a breach of any such covenant or agreement to leave or put premises in repair at the termination of a lease, if it is shown that the premises, in whatever state of repair they might be, would at or shortly after the termination of the tenancy have been or be pulled down, or such structural alterations made therein as would render valueless the repairs covered by the covenant or agreement ...

As the Uthwatt-Jenkins Report states (1950 para. 226):

The object of s. 18 (1) is in substance to prevent a landlord from making a profit out of the repairing covenants by recovering damages representing the cost of repairs which, if done, would add nothing to the value of the property without them, and the doing of which might indeed have been rendered wholly superfluous by the projected demolition or alteration of the premises. Its effect is that the landlord in order to recover damages must prove diminution in the value of the reversion occasioned by the failure to repair to an extent at least equal to the damages claimed. Evidence of the cost of doing the repairs is not necessarily evidence of such diminution (*Salisbury* v. *Gilmour* ([1942] 2 K.B. 38)) though it may be in some cases (*Jones* v. *Herxheimer* ([1950] 1 All E.R. 323)). There is no doubt that s. 18 (1) affords valuable protection to the tenant, and it is regarded by some as perhaps going further in that direction than is altogether fair to the landlord.

See *Hibernian Property* v. *Liverpool Corporation* [1973] 1 W.L.R. 751:

CAULFIELD J.: Subject to a compulsory order to which I shall refer later, the plaintiffs are the owners in fee simple of a piece of land known as 2, Uhlan Street, Liverpool, together with the buildings erected thereon. The said land was, by a lease dated February 17, 1875, demised by the Earl of Sefton to William Knapman for a period of 75 years from March 25, 1873. By divers assignments, the defendants became entitled to the residue of the lease on December 21, 1908. Upon the expiry of the lease by effluxion of time, the defendants held over upon the terms thereof and remained in possession. By the lease, William Knapman, for himself and his successors in title, covenanted at all times during the term to keep all the buildings which then were or should thereafter be erected or standing on the demised premises and their respective appurtenances in good and tenantable repair and condition and at the end or sooner determination of the said term to leave the same in such good repair and condition.

The plaintiffs allege that the defendants failed to keep the buildings in good or tenantable repair and, further, failed to leave the same in such repair upon the determination either of the said term or of the tenancy created by the defendants holding over.

On February 14, 1967, the Medical Officer of Health of the defendants certified, under section 42 of the Housing Act 1957, that a certain area of Toxteth Street – Clearance Area 196 – contained houses which were unfit for human habitation. The premises, 2, Uhlan Street, were designated within that area. The necessary formalities followed this notice. A notice to treat and a notice of entry were served on January 9, 1970. The plaintiffs served a schedule of dilapidations on May 19, 1970.

The plaintiffs' case is that the defendants, in breach of the repairing covenants, allowed the premises to reach such a state that they were declared unfit for human habitation. Because of this unfitness, the premises came to be included in the Toxteth Street Clearance Area. This designation resulted in compensation being restricted to the site value. The plaintiffs contend that if there had been compliance by the defendants with the covenants the house would not have been so designated and would either have remained as a dwelling house – that is, would have been excluded from the clearance area or, if included, the site and premises would have had an increased value ... [He read out Housing Act 1957, s. 52 and s. 4 and continued] The defendants say that because they intend to demolish the premises this claim is defeated by the terms of section 18 of the Landlord and Tenant Act 1927, [which he read out and continued]

The defendants therefore say that no sum is payable by the defendants to the plaintiffs, assuming breaches, other than site value. Secondly, say the defendants, on the facts, however well they had maintained the property, it would still have been designated as unfit for human habitation and if that be the true position the plaintiffs are only entitled to an agreed figure of £135 – the site value ... [He then discussed the facts and said:] By my fact findings, I am finding that compliance with the covenants to repair would have resulted either in the property being excluded from the clearance area or in its having a greatly enhanced value because it would have been habitable and in good repair ...

I may be stating too simply the situation as I see it, but, in effect, I think that this is a case where a lessee fails to comply with his covenant to repair, there is indeed continuing breach and, while he is still a lessee, he concludes by reason, on my findings, of his own breaches of covenant that the house should be demolished and then proceeds to purchase compulsorily, contending that the purchase price to him should only be site value.

I come now to deal with the law. I think that the proper test is to define the extent to which the value of the lesssor's reversion has been diminished. If the lessor intends to demolish the premises, there is no damage to the reversion. The most common example is that of the landlord who intends to demolish at the expiration of a lease and then to re-erect. The second part of section

18 beginning with the words, 'in particular' is not expressed to apply to breaches of a repairing covenant during the currency of the lease. In any event, on my findings of fact, I do not think that the second part of section 18 is applicable to the facts of this case. My first reason is that, on the facts, it has not been shown that these premises would at or shortly after the termination of the tenancy have been or be pulled down. Secondly, the last part of section 18 certainly, I think, contemplates the lessor making a decision to pull down or so structurally alter the premises that any repairs that would be shown to be necessary to achieve compliance with the covenants in the lease would be rendered nugatory. I do not, however, think that the section is even capable of being construed as enabling a municipal corporation, by its own failure to comply with covenants to repair so that the house has to be demolished, to contend that the second part gives it relief in a claim for damages for breach of covenant.

This is my view, whether the plaintiffs' claim is deemed to be made during the currency of the lease or at its termination. If I am wrong, it would, I think, mean that whenever a corporation was a lessee of property with an obligation to keep the property in repair, it could well find it more profitable to fail to comply with its contractual obligations than to discharge them. This, to my mind, does not make sense and I do not think that it is the law. I am fortified in this view because, if the corporation is satisfied that a certain area should be classified as a clearance area under section 42, it has a statutory duty to exlude from that area any building which is not unfit for human habitation. Obviously, in such a case the compensation to the owner of the property is much greater than site value.

Can it be the law that a local authority can allow property of which it is the lessee to fall into disrepair in breach of its own covenant, then, having gone through the formalities of compulsory purchase, pay only site value? I do not think that it can be. As I see it, the corporation would be rewarding itself for breach of its own obligation. I therefore conclude that there was damage to the reversion in this case and that the plaintiffs are entitled to recover damages.

(v) *Long Leaseholders at Low Rent.* Under Part 1 of the Landlord and Tenant Act 1954, long leaseholders at low rent may also gain some protection against landlords who seek to impose a heavy repair burden on them. The law is extremely complex but see ss. 3, 4, 7, 8, 12 and 16 in particular.

(vi) *Enforcement of Covenants and Estoppel.* In *Brikom Investments Ltd* v. *Carr and Others* [1979] 2 All E.R. 753 (C.A.), an interesting problem arose about liability for the cost of repairing a roof. Until 1971 the landlords had rented a block of flats; in that year they decided to sell the flats off to sitting tenants on 99-year leases. The leases expressly provided that the landlords would repair and maintain the structure of the building, including the roof; but that the tenants would pay an annual contribution towards excess maintenance expenses.

The roof was in a very bad state of repair; but the landlords were hoping to get planning permission to build another storey on top of the building, in which case it would have been pointless to repair the roof. In February 1972, the landlords told the tenants' association that if they failed to get the planning permission, they would repair the roof at their own cost. This assurance was repeated in 1973. Many tenants signed leases on the strength of these assurances.

In 1974, the roof was actually repaired at a cost of £15,000. In 1976 the landlords sought payment from the tenants, arguing that the express terms of the lease should prevail. The Court of Appeal unanimously rejected this argument. Lord Denning M.R. decided the case on the ground of his controversial doctrine of promissory estoppel (*Central London Property Trusts Ltd* v. *High Trees House Ltd* [1947] K.B. 130); Roskill and Cumming-Bruce L.JJ. on the basis of the following passage of Lord Cairns L.C. in *Hughes* v. *Metropolitan Railway Co.* (1877) 2 App. Cas. 439 at 448.

It was not argued at your Lordships' Bar, and it could not be argued, that there was any right of a Court of Equity, or any practice of a Court of Equity, to give relief in cases of this kind, by way of mercy, or by way merely of saving property from forfeiture, but it is the first principle upon which all Courts of Equity proceed, that if parties who have entered into definite and distinct terms involving certain legal results – certain penalties or legal forfeiture – afterwards by their own act or with their own consent enter upon a course of negotiation which has the effect of leading one of the parties to suppose that the strict rights arising under the contract will not be enforced, or will be kept in suspense, or held in abeyance, the person who otherwise might have enforced those rights will not be allowed to enforce them where it would be inequitable having regard to the dealings which have thus taken place between the parties.

In effect, therefore, it was held that the landlords had waived their strict contractual rights. (For further discussion of the principle of waiver, see above, p. 88.)

3. Liability in tort

Some of the problems relating to bringing actions in contract, in particular the principle that only parties to the contract can sue for breaches of it, could be avoided if there was liability in tort. The Law Commission (1970–71) recommended an extension of the law of tort, 'to provide that where the landlord has an obligation or right to repair ... he should in the discharge or exercise of that obligation or right be under a general duty of care to see that injury or damage is not suffered by those who are likely to be affected by any failure to discharge that obligation or exercise that right with reasonable diligence'.

The result was the Defective Premises Act 1972 (see North, 1973; Spencer, 1974). This has been operative since 1 January 1974. Section 4 is particularly relevant to the issues discussed in this chapter:

4.—(1) Where premises are let under a tenancy which puts on the landlord an obligation to the tenant for the maintenance or repair of the premises, the landlord owes to all persons who might reasonably be affected by defects in the state of the premises a duty to take such care as is reasonable in all the circumstances to see that they are reasonably safe from personal injury or from damage to their property caused by a relevant defect.

(2) The said duty is owed if the landlord knows (whether as the result of being notified by the tenant or otherwise) or if he ought in all the circumstances to have known of the relevant defect.

(3) In this section 'relevant defect' means a defect in the state of the premises existing at or after the material time and arising from, or continuing because of, an act or omission by the landlord which constitutes or would if he had had notice of the defect, have constituted a failure by him to carry out his obligation to the tenant for the maintenance or repair of the premises; and for the purposes of the foregoing provision 'the material time' means –

    (a) where the tenancy commenced before this Act, the commencement of this Act; and

    (b) in all other cases, the earliest of the following times, that is to say –

      (i) the time when the tenancy commences;

      (ii) the time when the tenancy agreement is entered into;

      (iii) the time when possession is taken of the premises in contemplation of the letting.

(4) Where premises are let under a tenancy which expressly or impliedly gives the landlord the right to enter the premises to carry out any description of maintenance or repair of the premises, then, as from the time when he first is, or by notice or otherwise can put himself, in a position to exercise the right and so long as he is or can put himself in that position, he shall be treated for the purposes of subsections (1) to (3) above (but for no other purpose) as if he were under an obligation to the tenant for that description

of maintenance or repair of the premises; but the landlord shall not owe the tenant any duty by virtue of this subsection in respect of any defect in the state of the premises arising from, or continuing because of, a failure to carry out an obligation expressly imposes on the tenant by the tenancy.

(5) For the purposes of this section obligations imposed or rights given by any enactment in virtue or a tenancy shall be treated as imposed or given by the tenancy.

(6) This section applies to a right of occupation given by contract or any enactment and not amounting to a tenancy as if the right were a tenancy, and 'tenancy' and cognate expressions shall be construed accordingly.

Comment

It does not appear, at least from reported cases, that this provision has been widely used. Has the problem of 'notice' been overcome (s. 4(2))? What is the extent of liability? What is reasonable (s. 4(1))? These are issues that remain to be considered by the courts.

(For further issues relating to liability of landlords in tort, see Defective Premises Act 1972, s. 3; and *Anns* v. *London Borough of Merton* [1977] 2 W.L.R. 1024.)

Although section 4 appears to have shifted much of the liability for damages suffered by third parties onto landlords, tenants may still be liable for damage caused by defects for which they are responsible and which fall outside the landlord's repairing obligations. Tenants are only liable for breaches of the 'common duty of care' imposed by the Occupiers' Liability Act 1957. (For full discussion see text books on the law of torts, e.g. Clerk & Lindsell, 1975, ch. 14.)

4. Public Health Acts and Housing Acts : an introductory note

The foregoing sections have described the basic common law principles relating to repairs, as amended in the case of many residential tenancies by statute law. However, in practice, most legal proceedings relating to housing conditions are taken under the two sets of statutory principles to be found in the Public Health Acts and the Housing Acts. These provisions have a long history and constituted the first legislative attempts to regulate the operation of the private sector of the housing market.

It cannot be said that the existence of these two sets of provisions is particularly satisfactory. Many of the provisions overlap; it may be difficult to know under which head to proceed. The case for a more comprehensive housing code is one that needs much more serious and urgent consideration than government, at present, appears prepared to give (see Hadden, 1978 and 1979).

From a practical point of view, Public Health Acts have the advantage that the procedures prescribed are relatively simple and can result in swift action; however they only relate to the elimination of the 'statutory nuisance' which may not result in any long-term improvement to housing conditions. Conversely, Housing Act procedures may result in permanent improvements, but the procedures involved (perhaps because of the expenses which house owners may be required to incur) are much slower. Indeed many authorities will not take action under the Housing Acts if the owner enters into a 'voluntary undertaking' to carry out repairs.

One legal problem that has arisen is whether action can be taken under, say, the Public Health provisions in relation to property which is already subject to action under the other set of rules. In *Salford* v. *McNally* [1976] A.C. 359 (H.L.), Lord Wilberforce said (in part):

Mrs McNally is living in a house which is 'unfit for human habitation' but which the council considers is, or could be rendered, adequate accommodation for the time being [Housing Act, 1957, s. 48].

The present proceedings arise, not under the Housing Acts, but under the Public Health Act 1936. Mrs McNally, as a person aggrieved, made a complaint against the council, as owners of the house, of a statutory nuisance ... Mrs McNally filled up a form, apparently supplied by some organisation, on which she ticked off various suggested defects and the stipendiary magistrate, after an inspection, found that there was rising damp and perished plaster, that the rear door was rotted and unhinged, that there was severe dampness in the first floor, and that the water closet pipe was cracked and insanitary. His finding continued that 'by reason of these defects, the premises were in such a state as to be prejudicial to health, or a nuisance' and therefore a statutory nuisance. He proceeded to make an order requiring the council to abate the statutory nuisance within two months.

On appeal by case stated, the Divisional Court upheld the magistrate's decision, but stated the following question for consideration by this House:

'Whether it is a lawful defence for a housing authority in proceedings brought against it by virtue of either s 93 or s 99 of the Public Health Act 1936 to prove that the house, the subject of the complaint, is one occupied by reason of s 48 of the Housing Act 1957 and maintained to the standard under s 48.'

My Lords, the answer to this question, in my opinion, is manifestly in the negative. It is only necessary to perceive the respective and different purposes of the Housing Acts and of the Public Health Act 1936 to see that they are dealing with different matters and setting different standards, which may in any individual case have to be separately met. The Housing Act 1957, in that part of it which provides for clearance and redevelopment, is concerned with fitness for human habitation ...

The Public Health Act 1936 on the other hand, is concerned with the general concepts 'prejudicial to health' and 'nuisance'; the former being defined as 'injurious, or likely to cause injury to, health'. And I do not doubt that the persons whose health is here in question may include occupiers of the house as well as members of the public. But it must be obvious that a house may well be 'unfit for human habitation' in the statutory sense without being either 'prejudicial to health' or a 'nuisance' and consequentially that the Housing Act 1957 when it authorises a house which is unfit for human habitation to be temporarily occupied as 'adequate for the time being' is not lending statutory authority to the use of a house which is prejudicial to health. In view, indeed, of the fact that houses may have to be used for accommodation, adequate for the time being, for considerable periods (in the present case seven years), it would be surprising if a local authority, in permitting such use, were held to be dispensed altogether for this period from the Public Health Act requirements.

There is therefore, in my opinion, no difficulty in reconciling the two legislative codes or in operating them side by side ...

Lord Edmund Davies delivered a concurring judgment; Lords Simon, Cross and Fraser of Tullybelton agreed.

R. v. *Kerrier D.C. ex parte Guppys* (*Bridport*) *Ltd* (1977) 75 L.G.R. 129 (C.A.). The facts are summarized in the headnote:

The owners of two adjacent houses which were unfit for human habitation within section 4 of the Housing Act 1957 but which were occupied by tenants protected by the Rent Act 1968 supplied the local authority with information as to the condition of the houses to enable them to exercise their duties as housing authority under sections 9 or 16 of the Housing Act 1957 in order that they, the owners, could obtain possession of the two houses and build one new house. The local authority in the exercise of their powers under the Public Health Act 1936 ordered the owners to repair the roofs of the two houses but refused to make an order under the Housing Act 1957, taking the view that the provisions of the Act of 1957 were not mandatory and that they had a discretion whether to exercise their powers under that Act of under the Public Health Act.

Orr L.J. said (in part):

The issue before this court on the appeal is therefore whether ... the word 'shall' in each of the sections 9 and 16 is imperative.

In support of the appeal two broad arguments were advanced. First, that if the construction adopted by the Divisional Court is right then great difficulties arise in relation to other provisions in the housing legislation, in particular those contained in that part of the Housing Act 1974 which provides for grants. It was claimed by Mr Sears that those provisions would be frustrated if it is correct that the provisions now in question are mandatory. It was further argued by Mr Sears that great difficulties are liable to arise for local authorities on the basis of the decision of the Divisional Court. There are in the country, we are told, over 1,000,000 houses unfit for human habitation, and it was suggested that there could be a great flood of applications for mandamus, with the result that local authorities would find it hopeless to obtain accommodation for displaced tenants.

On the narrower aspect of the construction of the word 'shall' in these two sections, it was argued that the word 'shall' has on at least two occasions been held to mean 'may'. (There are, of course, a number of cases in which, conversely, the word 'may' has been held to mean 'shall' but that is a different problem.) The first of these was *Howard v. Secretary of State for the Environment* [1975] Q.B. 235; where a section in a planning Act conferred a right of appeal and went on to provide that an appeal under the section should be made by notice in writing '... which shall indicate the grounds of the appeal and state the facts on which it is based; ...,' and it was held that 'shall' in that provision was directory only. I find that case, with great respect, of no assistance for present purposes.

Reliance was also placed on the decision of the Divisional Court in *Nottingham City Council v. Newton* [1974] 1 W.L.R. 923; where Lord Widgery C.J. took the view that in the particular context with which they were concerned the word 'shall' was not mandatory. The question there was one which arose under the Public Health Acts. I can sufficiently deal with that particular decision by saying that in my judgment it is clear from the speeches in the House of Lords in *Salford City Council v. McNally* ([1976] A.C. 359) that the view there expressed cannot be considered to be good law. It is true that in the House of Lords approval was expressed as regards another point in the judgment, but so far as concerns the point to which I have referred it appears to me to be inconsistent with the speeches and the decision in the House of Lords.

In my judgment, looking at the statute with which we are concerned, the Housing Act 1957, and looking at the word 'shall' in the context of that Act, it is very difficult indeed to see how it can be treated as other than imperative in either of the two sections to which I have referred, notwithstanding the use of the word 'Power' in the sidenotes to both sections. An examination of the Act itself (and Mr Pryor has referred us to a number of sections) shows that the Act frequently uses either the word 'shall' or the word 'may', plainly drawing a distinction between those words, and in my judgment the Divisional Court were entirely right in giving great weight to the imperative character of the word 'shall'.

Turning to the wider aspects of Mr Sears's argument, he claims that the provisions contained in the Housing Act 1974 as to improvement grants could in effect be stultified if the construction which the Divisional Court attributed to those sections were upheld. I have not been satisfied on the argument that those provisions would be stultified, but in my judgment it is impossible to treat the Act of 1974, enacted some 17 years after the Act with which we are concerned, as being in any way a guide to the construction of words used in the earlier Act. It is relevant, I would accept, to consider, in a case of real doubt or ambiguity, whether to put a particular construction on an earlier Act would have an untoward effect as regards subsequent legislation, but that aspect, in my judgment, can only be very minor compared with the proper application of canons of construction to the words used in the earlier Act ... The other general argument, which I have already mentioned, was that there would be a great danger, if the Divisional Court's construction of these words is upheld, of there being a vast number of applications for mandamus to compel local authorities to exercise their powers under section 9 or section 16. I have not been satisfied that that is likely to happen, having regard, among other things, to the consideration that the issue of mandamus is a discretionary matter. Be that as it may, however, in my judgment it is a matter for Parliament to deal with. The argument put forward about it is not one which persuades me to doubt the conclusion which I would otherwise reach in this case: that the word 'shall' in both sections can only be construed as imperative.

Comment. Whatever the interpretation of the law may be, it is clear from the data in Tables 7.1 and 7.2 (pp. 329, 330 above) that local authorities do not take proceedings in relation to each unfit house. These cases are illustrations of a much more general problem about the effectiveness of legal duties imposed by central government on local authorities, in particular where extra financial resources are not provided to encourage the execution of that duty. (See further below, on duties in relation to the homeless, pp. 482-96; generally, Griffith, 1966.)

5. **Public Health Act powers**

The Public Health Acts deal with many issues that could relate to housing issues: dangerous structures (Public Health Act 1961, s. 25); problems with sanitation (Public Health Act 1936, ss. 39, 44, 45, 52, 290(6)). The specific topic for discussion here is the procedure to abate 'statutory nuisances'.

A Definition of 'statutory nuisance'

Public Health Act 1936, s. 92:

92.—(1) Without prejudice to the exercise by a local authority of any other powers vested in them by or under this Act, the following matters may, subject to the provisions of this Part of this Act, be dealt with summarily, and are in this Part of this Act referred to as 'statutory nuisances', that is to say:—

(*a*) any premises in such a state as to be prejudicial to health or a nuisance ...

(*c*) any accumulation or deposit which is prejudicial to health or a nuisance ...

Section 343 states that 'prejudicial to health' means 'injurious, or likely to cause injury, to health'.

Coventry City Council v. *Cartwright* [1975] 1 W.L.R. 845 (D.C.)
Lord Widgery C.J. said (in part):

The facts on which the justices made an abatement order ... were these. There is a piece of vacant land where the houses in Arthur Street formerly stood. Arthur Street was demolished about three or four years ago and re-development has not yet taken place. The justices found that the local authority had allowed indiscriminate tipping to take place on the site since demolition, the local authority having taken no action to prevent tipping by either erecting fences or trenching or displaying official notice boards stating that the tipping of material and trespassing was prohibited. They found that the material deposited could encourage rodent infestation, this having been visible on the site in close proximity. They found that the items deposited consisted of large quantities of building materials, such as brick ends, tarmacadam, old reinforcements, earth, scrap iron, broken glass and household refuse.

The local authority had periodically removed the household refuse, but had taken no action to remove the other materials dumped to which I have referred ... The question which they put to us however is restricted. The question is whether inert matter, such as builder's rubble, without any putrescible matter attached to it is within the ambit of section 92(1) of the Public Health Act 1936 ...

The justices ... concluded that ... in their opinion the tipping of materials such as are referred to in this case was dangerous to health and limb and constituted a particular hazard, especially where children were concerned who had easy access to the site. In other words, they find a threat to health from these facts on the footing that people who went on to the site, and particularly if children went on to the site, might hurt themselves by reason of the physical properties present – broken glass, old tin cans and whatever it may be ...

For my part, I think that that is taking too wide a view of the section. The words are obviously very wide, and one should hesitate, in construing the section in proceedings such as the present, to lay down boundaries which may in another case prove to be unsitable. But I think that the underlying conception of the section is that that which it struck at is an accumulation of something which produces a threat to health in the sense of a threat of disease, vermin or the like ...

Ashworth J. agreed but noted:

For my part I regard this case as somewhere near the borderline, and if there had been more evidence, for example, about the effect of the refuse and whether that had set up infestation of rats, it may be that the justices would have been justified in reaching the conclusion they did, but on the material now before this court I agree with Lord Widgery C.J. that there is not enough to justify the order which they made. I would allow the appeal.

Michael Davies J. agreed.

National Coal Board v. *Neath B.C.* [1976] 2 All E.R. 478 (Q.B.D.)

Watkins J. : The appellants own premises known as 38 Roman Road, in the village of Banwen in South Wales. That village, for local government purposes, lies within the jurisdiction of the Neath Borough Council, the respondents in this appeal. The respondents have the duty under s 91 of the Public Health Act 1936 of inspecting from time to time property within their area for the detection of matters which need to be dealt with, under the provisions of Part III of the 1936 Act, as statutory nuisances.

At some time or other an officer of the respondents inspected 38 Roman Road and found the place to be in a state of disrepair in that there were two defective windows, there was no stop end for a rain water gutter and a defective skirting board. These were matters reported to the respondents. They determined that a nuisance was present in the premises and, using the power which they have under s 93 of the 1936 Act, they served on the appellants a notice to abate the nuisance, a notice which one supposes set out in terms the precise things which the appellants had to do in order to bring about an effective abatement. The appellants did nothing to abate the so-called nuisance. So an information was laid before the local justices. A hearing followed, the result of which was that on 4th April 1975 the justices found that an abatement notice had been served on the appellants on 9th January 1975 by recorded delivery and the requirements of the abatement notice had not been complied with by the appellants. So they decided that, having regard to those findings and the state of the law as they understood it to be, they had no alternative but to issue a nuisance order. The effect of issuing a nuisance order is to compel the person on whom it is served to comply with its terms under penalty. The penalty is laid down in the Act; it amounts nowadays to a maximum sum of £50.

Before, however, the appellants could be expected to carry out the terms of the nuisance order, they appealed. The appeal comes to this court by way of case stated.

The justices had addressed to them argument affecting the meaning to be attached to the word 'nuisance' as it appears in s 92(1) of the 1936 Act. Nothing was said at that hearing suggestive of the fact that there had been any injury or anticipated injury to the health of persons residing either in the premises or in any premises adjoining them. The information itself was laid simply on the basis that there was present at the material time at the premises a nuisance.

The short point therefore arising in this appeal is what is the meaning to be attached to the word 'nuisance'. *Betts v Penge Urban District Council* ([1942] 2 K.B. 154) has been referred to. What happened in that case was that the landlord of a flat, of which the rent was in arrears, made no application for possession but removed the front door and some of the window sashes thereby interfering with the personal comfort of the occupier, and it was held that there was a distinction between public and private nuisance which was material to the question whether a statutory nuisance under s 92(1) of the 1936 Act existed on the premises, and that it was sufficient in order to sustain a conviction of the appellant for permitting a statutory nuisance on the premises to prove that by his act or default they were in such a state as to interfere with the personal comfort of the occupiers, without necessarily being injurious to health. If the law is accurately stated in that case, then the justices in the instant case, it seems to me, cannot be criticised for issuing a nuisance order, since I see no basis for assuming that the justices came to conclusions of fact which were not properly founded on the evidence which came before them, and further on their findings of fact they were not entitled, assuming the law is correctly stated in the *Betts* case, to proceed as they did to make the nuisance order.

In his very able argument counsel for the appellants says that the word 'nuisance' cannot have and should not be understood to have the meaning attached to it by the *Betts* case, and that the word 'nuisance' as used in s 92(1) must be understood to equate with the same word as that is understood at common law in relation to nuisances, public or private. A public nuisance at common law has been expressed to be an act or omission which materially affects the material comfort and quality of life of a class of Her Majesty's subjects. A private nuisance has often been defined in this way: private nuisances, at least in the vast majority of cases, are interferences for a substantial length of time by owners or occupiers of property with the use or enjoyment of neighbouring property. The distinction which immediately springs to mind therefore between a private nuisance at common law and a nuisance of the kind as found by the justices in the instant case is this, that the justices, feeling compelled to follow the decision in the *Betts* case, found that a nuisance could exist in a dwelling-house in relation to the occupier of it, whereas the notion is obviously alien to the conception of a common law private nuisance ...

I welcome the opportunity of saying that what Lord Wilberforce said in *Salford City Council v McNally* ([1975] 3 W.L.R. 87) leads me to the conclusion that *Betts v Penge Urban District Council* unquestionably does not express the proper law on this question. Speaking for myself, I would adopt the words of Lord Wilberforce so as to state that a nuisance cannot arise if what has taken place affects only the person or persons occupying the premises where the nuisance is said to have taken place. A nuisance coming within the meaning of the Public Health Act 1936 must be either a private or public nuisance as understood by common law. For that reason, it seems to me that the proper course is to direct that the order of the justices should be quashed.

Lord Widgery C.J. and Kilner Brown J. agreed.

Comment

The Department of the Environment has commented (1979b, paras. 26–30) that this decision

may well have revealed an undesirable gap in local authorities' powers to deal with defective housing ... [But] it would be inappropriate to nullify it merely by extending the definition of statutory nuisance ... so as to include discomfort of occupiers, since it would be illogical to lay down a criterion less rigorous than prejudicial to health in a limb of the definition [in s. 92] and not in others.

Do you agree? Is it practical to argue, as the DoE does, that any gap in the law is a matter of housing policy? (See Davey, 1979).

Notwithstanding the difficulties revealed in the above decisions, there is no doubt that many types of bad housing condition fall within the definition of statutory nuisance. One particularly common problem is severe condensation. McQuillan and Finnis (1979) discuss this in some detail, and note how some local authorities try to evade potential legal liability by blaming the tenants for causing the dampness. (See also Blood (1979, p. 162), who describes the length of time procedures may take, but who also stresses the importance of using every means to fight such bad conditions.) It has been argued that existing legal definitions are inadequate to cope with this issue (DoE, 1979a).

B Procedures

(a) If the local authority decides there is a statutory nuisance they may serve an abatement notice under s. 93. If this is disregarded they may get a nuisance order from the magistrates under s. 94. Section 95 prescribes certain penalties for failure to comply with such an order. (See too Control of Pollution Act 1974, Schedule 2.)

(b) Where a local authority is satisfied that a statutory nuisance has occurred on premises and is likely to recur, it may issue a prohibition notice to prevent such recurrence (Public Health (Recurring Nuisances) Act 1969, s. 1). It need not wait for actual recurrence (*Peaty* v. *Field* [1971] 1 W.L.R. 387).

(c) Where premises are in a very defective state, a special nine-day procedure is available under Public Health Act 1961, s. 26:

26.—(1) If it appears to a local authority that –

(a) any premises are in such a state (in this section referred to as a 'defective state') as to be prejudicial to health or a nuisance, and

(b) unreasonable delay in remedying the defective state would be occasioned by following the procedure prescribed by sections ninety-three to ninety-five of the Public Health Act 1936,

the local authority may serve on the person on whom it would have been appropriate to serve an abatement notice under the said section ninety-three (if the local authority had proceeded under that section) a notice stating that the local authority intend to remedy the defective state and specifying the defects which they intend to remedy.

(2) Subject to the next following subsection, the local authority may, after the expiration of nine days after service of a notice under the foregoing subsection, execute such works as may be necessary to remedy the defective state and may recover the expenses reasonably incurred in so doing from the person on whom the notice was served.

(3) If, within seven days after service of a notice under subsection (1) of this section, the person on whom the notice was served serves a counter-notice that he intends to remedy the defects specified in the first-mentioned notice, the local authority shall take no action in pursuance of the first-mentioned notice unless the person who served the counter-notice either –

(a) fails within what seems to the local authority a reasonable time to begin to execute works to remedy the said defects, or

(b) having begun to execute such works fails to make such progress towards their completion as seems to the local authority reasonable.

(4) In proceedings to recover expenses under this section the court –

(a) shall inquire whether the local authority were justified in concluding

that the premises were in a defective state, or that unreasonable delay
in remedying the defective state would have been occasioned by following the procedure prescribed by sections ninety-three to ninety-
six of the Public Health Act 1936, and

(b) if the defendant proves that he served a counter-notice under subsection (3) of this section, shall inquire whether the defendant failed
to begin the works to remedy the defects within a reasonable time,
or failed to make reasonable progress towards their completion,

and if the court determines –

(i) that the local authority were not justified in either of the conclusions
mentioned in paragraph (a) of this subsection, or

(ii) that there was no failure under paragraph (b) of this subsection,

the local authority shall not recover the expenses or any part of them.

(5) Subject to the provisions of the last foregoing subsection, in proceedings
to recover expenses under this section the court may inquire whether the said
expenses ought to be borne wholly or in part by some person other than the
defendant in the proceedings, and the court may make such order concerning
the expenses or their apportionment as appears to the court to be just:

Provided that the court shall not order the expenses or any part of them
to be borne by any person other than the defendant in the proceedings unless
the court is satisfied that that other person has had due notice of the proceedings and an opportunity of being heard ...

(7) The power conferred on a local authority by subsection (1) of this section may be exercised notwithstanding that the local authority might instead
have proceeded under section nine of the Housing Act 1957.

The use made of this provision varies from local authority to local
authority (Hadden, 1979, p. 61).

(d) Public Health Act 1936, s. 99.

99. Complaint of the existence of a statutory nuisance under this Act may
be made to a justice of the peace by any person aggrieved by the nuisance,
and thereupon the like proceedings shall be had, with the like incidents and
consequences as to the making of orders, penalties for disobedience of orders
and otherwise, as in the case of a complaint by the local authority, but any
order made in such proceedings may, if the court after giving the local authority an opportunity of being heard thinks fit, direct the authority to abate
the nuisance.

This section has been widely used by individuals and housing aid
groups, particularly against local authorities. It may be noted that
proceedings under this section are criminal proceedings (*R.* v. *Newham
East JJ. ex parte Hunt* [1976] 1 W.L.R. 420).

(e) Effect of the Public Health rules. In *Salford C.C.* v. *McNally* (above, p. 378) the House of Lords stated clearly that action must be taken under these provisions, irrespective of any other action that might be being taken. However, the level of repair executed may be very limited; if the authority can show the house is about to be pulled down, no repairs may be carried out at all.

In *Nottingham Corporation* v. *Newton* [1975] 1 W.L.R. 371–2. Lord Widgery C.J. said:

This court made it perfectly clear that justices faced with this situation, although bound to make an order under the Act, can use their common sense and are entitled to take into account all the circumstances, and thus avoid the expenditure of public money unnecessarily in a case where the house is likely to be pulled down shortly in any event ... No doubt the existence of the s 48 resolution is one of the factors which will affect the magistrates' court when dealing with this difficult type of question, but that it is more than a factor and having such weight as the magistrate thinks right and no more, I find it impossible to say.

And this flexible approach was endorsed by Lord Wilberforce in *Salford C.C.* v. *McNally*:

In making the order the magistrate should take into account the circumstances in which the property is being occupied including, of course, the likely duration of the occupation. The shorter the period before probable demolition, the more severe must be the injury or likely injury to health or, as the case may be, the nuisance, to justify action by way of abatement. This aspect of the matter was well explained by the Divisional Court in *Nottingham Corpn v Newton* the keynote of which is the need, in making abatement notices, to use discretion and common sense.

Thus the operation of any abatement notice may be postponed until action under the Housing Acts has been taken. One result of these cases is that, at least where local authorities own the houses, notices to quite have been issued to the tenants. In most cases the houses would cease to be a statutory nuisance once the tenants had left. (See now, however, *Lambeth L.B.C.* v. *Stubbs* (1980) *The Times*, 15 May, where it was held that where premises are a nuisance, it is not abated merely by the owner obtaining vacant possession of them.)

Question. Is this solution still available to local authorities in view of the security of tenure provisions of the Housing Act 1980 (see below, p. 512)? If families are evicted, can they claim the protection of the Housing (Homeless Persons) Act 1977 (below, p. 482)?

6. Housing Act powers

A Definition of 'unfitness'

Housing Act 1957, s. 4 (as amended).

In determining for any of the purposes of this Act whether a house is unfit for human habitation, regard shall be had to its condition in respect of the following matter, that is to say –

(a) repair;
(b) stability;
(c) freedom from damp;
[(cc) internal arrangement];
(d) natural lighting;
(e) ventilation;
(f) water supply;
(g) drainage and sanitary conveniences;
(h) facilities for ... preparation and cooking of food and for the disposal of waste water;

and the house shall be deemed to be unfit for human habitation if and only if it is so far defective in one or more of the said matters that it is not reasonably suitable for occupation in that condition.

It will be appreciated that this 'definition' – the cornerstone of local authority action under the Housing Act – is extremely vague and leaves great room for interpretation and *ad hoc* decision-taking. Attempts to define the standard in more detail have not really been successful (MHLG Circular 69/67); and there has been little helpful judicial interpretation. In *Summers* v. *Salford Corporation* [1943] A.C. 283, a broken sash-cord which jammed open a bedroom window was held by the House of Lords sufficient to render the house unfit for human habitation. Lord Atkin noted: 'disrepair to a single room would not be sufficient [to make a house unfit] unless the effect was to render the whole house not reasonably fit for human habitation, as in the case before the court'. Cases will, therefore, tend to be decided on their individual facts.

B Rehabilitation : repair of unfit houses

Housing Act 1957, s. 9:

(1) Where a local authority, upon consideration of an official representation, or a report from any of their officers, or other information in their possession, are satisfied that any house is unfit for human habitation, they shall,

unless they are satisfied that it is not capable at a reasonable expense of being rendered so fit, serve upon the person having control of the house a notice

> (*a*) requiring him, within such reasonable time, not being less than twenty-one days, as may be specified in the notice, to execute the works specified in the notice, and
>
> (*b*) stating that, in the opinion of the authority, those works will render the house fit for human habitation ...

An appeal against such notice may be lodged within twenty-one days. The county court may determine whether the house is unfit; whether the prescribed works are excessive; and whether the expense is reasonable. The judge has a wide discretion to confirm, vary or quash the notice, depending on his findings (s. 11).

If there is no appeal, or the notice is confirmed, the works must be carried out within the prescribed period. Failure to do this leaves it open to the local authority to do the repairs in default, and charge the costs to the 'person having control of the house' (s. 10). Experience shows that permanent improvements in housing conditions are only achieved where authorities are prepared to exercise this power.

If the county court judge decides the works cannot be carried out at reasonable expense, the local authority may be authorized to purchase the house compulsorily (s. 12).

Hadden has shown (1978, 1979) that with the rising cost of building works, it has been increasingly difficult to meet the 'reasonable expense' criterion, which is defined in Housing Act 1957, s. 39(1) as follows:

> In determining for the purposes of this Part of this Act whether a house can be rendered fit for human habitation at a reasonable expense, regard shall be had to the estimated cost of the works necessary to render it so fit and the value which it is estimated that the house will have when the works are completed.

It will be realized that there is considerable potential for dispute over the estimated cost, and the question of 'value'. Some guidance may be found in *Inworth Property Co.* v. *Southwark L.B.C.* (1977) 34 P.&C.R. 186 (C.A.). Megaw L.J. said (in part):

> It was agreed, first, that the present price of the house on the open market was £1,300. It was agreed, secondly, that the price of the house on the open market if repaired would be £1,900. It was agreed, thirdly, that the cost of the required repairs, including value added tax, would be £1,800. So, taking

those figures, in order to bring the house into a state where, on the open market, it would have a value of £1,900, the expenditure required would be £1,800. That would produce a house the value of which, in the open market, was £1,900 compared with its present price, on the open market, of £1,300.

The principal argument put forward on behalf of the local authority by Mr. Sedley in this Court depends on the meaning to be given to the word 'value' in section 39 (1). Clearly, if 'value' in this subsection means 'open market value,' then the judge was right, on the agreed figures, to hold that, by reference to section 39 (1), so far as he 'had to have regard' to that, this house was not capable of being 'rendered fit for human habitation at a reasonable expense.' Therefore Mr. Sedley's argument must be, and I understand that it is, that 'value' in section 39 (1) has some meaning different from 'value on the open market.' To my mind, there is no justification for that argument. It is certainly not to be found in either of the two authorities to which we were referred: *Ellis Copp & Co.* v. *Richmond-upon-Thames London Borough Council* ((1978) 245 E.G. 931) and *Bacon* v. *Grimsby Corporation* ([1950] 1 K.B. 272 (C.A.)).

Mr. Sedley further argues that section 39 (1) provides only that for the purposes of section 9 (1) *'regard shall be had* to the estimated cost of the works necessary to render it so fit and the value which it is estimated that the house will have when the works are completed': therefore, other factors also fall to be taken into consideration for the purposes of deciding whether or not the local authority has arrived at the correct conclusion under section 9 (1) when the judge on appeal has to consider that matter under section 11.

That, in my judgment, does not arise in this case. I accept that 'regard' having to be 'had' to a matter indicates that it is not necessarily conclusive. In the present case, however, I have seen nothing to suggest that the judge was wrong in the view that he took, which was that: 'it may be that there are factors in individual cases to be taken into account' – that is, other than the section 39 (1) calculation – 'which will affect the result' but factors that in this case it was

'... unnecessary to take into account any of the other minor considerations which might be necessary in a borderline case, because none of these could, in my judgment, so adjust the figures as to show other than that these premises are not capable at a reasonable expense of being rendered fit for human habitation.'

Bridge and Waller L.JJ. agreed.

A particular difficulty is to know what is the 'value' of a house with sitting tenants. Hadden states (1979, p. 210) that it will 'lie somewhere between the "true" investment value, assuming that the tenancy will continue indefinitely, and the value with immediate vacant possession, and will vary according to the personal circumstances and age of the tenant'. But, again, how this formula will apply in any given case is hard to determine. At all events, the complexity of these provisions means that local authorities are reluctant to use the s. 9 procedures.

C Demolition or closure of condemned houses

Housing Act 1957, s. 16:

(1) Where a local authority, on consideration of an official representation, or a report from any of their officers, or other information in their possession, are satisfied that any house – (a) is unfit for human habitation, and (b) is not capable at a reasonable expense of being rendered so fit, they shall serve upon [any person interested in the house] notice of the time ... and place at which the condition of the house and any offer with respect to the carrying out of works, or the future user of the house, which he may wish to submit will be considered by them...

(4) The local authority may if, after consultation with any owner or mortgagee, they think fit so to do, accept an undertaking from him, either that he will within a specified period carry out such works as will in the opinion of the authority render the house fit for human habitation, or that it shall not be used for human habitation until the authority, on being satisfied that it has been rendered fit for that purpose, cancel the undertaking...

If the undertaking is not given, or is not acceptable to the authority, the authority must either make a closing or a demolition order (s. 17(1)) – in which case the occupants will be rehoused and compensated under the Land Compensation Act 1973 (see below, pp. 479–82); or purchase the house, voluntarily or compulsorily, if capable of being made suitable for temporary accommodation (s. 17(2) and s. 29).

Local authorities have an absolute discretion as to whether or not to accept an undertaking, though a county court judge has an equal discretion in determining any appeal to substitute his own decision for that of the authorities (s. 20(3)), as interpreted by Bridge L.J. in *Victoria Square Properties* v. *Southwark L.B.C.* (below). Section 16(5) provides that, where an undertaking has been given under s. 16, the security of tenure provisions of the Rent Acts do not protect tenants. Therefore, in areas where local authorities wish to prevent landlords getting rid of their tenants, it is likely that they will exercise their discretion against accepting an undertaking and in favour of using the powers of compulsory purchase. However, if a local authority is too blatant about its motives for adopting this course of action, any decision might be challenged in the courts (see *Dudlow Estates* v. *Sefton M.B.C.* (1979) 249 E.G. 1271 (C.A.)).

The importance of distinguishing between s. 9 and s. 16 was discussed in *Victoria Square Property Co. Ltd* v. *Southwark L.B.C.* [1978] 1 W.L.R. 463 (C.A.). Bridge L.J. said (in part):

The history of the dispute between the local authority and the owners in this case begins with the service of a notice under s 9 of the 1957 Act dated 26th June 1975, requiring them to carry out an extensive schedule of works on the house. The owners appealed to the county court [and] ... her Honour Judge Cooper allowed that appeal and quashed the s 9 notice ... The local authority decided to proceed by way of acquisition under s 12 of the 1957 Act and themselves carry out the scheduled works. There being no purchase by agreement, on 24th February 1976 the local authority made a compulsory purchase order. They then appreciated that they had not obtained from Judge Cooper at the hearing of the appeal an express finding under s 11(3) that the premises were not capable of being rendered fit for human habitation at a reasonable expense. Such a finding was a necessary foundation to support the compulsory purchase order they had made. Accordingly the local authority applied to the county court with a request for an express finding under s 11(3). For some reason which it is not easy to understand, this application was, on 30th April 1976, dismissed by her Honour Judge Cooper ... Recognising in fact that the compulsory purchase order could not now be confirmed, the local authority naturally withdrew it.

The second stage of the history begins with the service on 29th June 1976 of a notice specifying a time and place pursuant to s 16 at which the local authority would consider the condition of, and any offers with respect to, the house. The premise on which this notice was served was necessarily that the local authority were now satisfied, contrary to the view on which they had previously proceeded, that the house was not capable of being rendered fit for human habitation at a reasonable expense. No notice of an intention to carry out works was served by the owners pursuant to s 16(3). However, at the time and place specified in the s 16 notice the owners did offer a formal undertaking pursuant to s 16(4) that the house would not be used for human habitation until the local authority, being satisfied that it had been rendered fit for that purpose, cancelled the undertaking. This undertaking was not accepted by the local authority. On 28th September 1976 the local authority served on the owners pursuant to s 19 a notice of their determination to purchase the house under s 17(2). The owners appealed against this notice under s 20.

The hearing of the appeal before Judge McDonnell was on 21st April 1977. He delivered his reserved judgment in writing on 20th May. The essential facts were not in dispute. The local authority's intention was, as it has always been, that works to the house should be carried out to restore it to a state of fitness for human habitation. They were proposing on acquisition to rehouse the sitting tenant, who would require only single bedroom accommodation, and then to carry out at the house not only the works which had been specified in their original notice under s 9 but other works to bring the house to a still higher standard. After the works were carried out, the house, it was estimated, would have a useful life of not less than 30 years. The judge concluded, first, that the acquisition was not within the powers conferred on the local authority by s 17(2) ... The learned judge expressed his conclusion on the question of vires in these terms:

'I hold that a local authority are only entitled to purchase property under s 17(2) for the purpose of using it temporarily pending demolition ... In my judgment the local authority were not entitled to use their powers under the subsection for the purpose of obtaining a permanent addition to their housing stock.'

The first question we have to decide on this appeal is whether this was a correct conclusion on the true construction of the relevant provisions of the 1957 Act. It is quite clear that the primary purpose of an acquisition under s 17(2) is to enable the local authority to use a house to provide temporary housing accommodation notwithstanding that its condition falls short of the standard of fitness for human habitation prescribed by the Act. This emerges from consideration of the phrases in s 17(2) '*is* or can be rendered capable' and 'adequate for the time being', from the words in s 29(3) 'pending its demolition by the authority', and from the provision in s 29(4) excluding the statutory implied condition of fitness for human habitation from any letting of the house. But is the power conferred by s 17(2) limited to cases where the purpose of the local authority is to use the house only for a limited period and in a condition affording such a limited standard of accommodation? Counsel's argument in support of the appeal for the local authority is essentially a simple one. He submits that, once the authority have acquired the house under s 17(2), there is nothing in the statutory provisions to limit the scale of the works which the authority may carry out by way of repair or improvement of the house, the standard of accommodation which they may use it to provide, or the period of time for which it may be retained for use as housing accommodation 'pending demolition'. He relies in particular on the application by s 29(4) to houses acquired in this way of the powers of Part V of the 1957 Act. These include power under s 92(1)(*d*) to alter, enlarge, repair or improve any house which has been acquired by the local authority. It is said that the standard to which a house acquired under s 17(2) is to be repaired or improved and the length of time which it is to be retained are both matters of degree and that accordingly it would be impossible to draw a line at any point on the scale and to say that by proceeding beyond that point the local authority would be acting ultra vires. Thus it follows, so runs the argument, that even in a case where, as here, the declared purpose of the local authority which underlies the proposed acquisition is not to use the house to provide temporary accommodation of a standard falling short of fitness for human habitation but to bring it up to the full statutory standard of fitness and retain it as part of the local authority's permanent housing stock, it cannot be said that the purchase is beyond the power of the section . . .

Bridge L.J. then reviewed Part III of the Housing Act, dealing with slum clearance procedures, and in light of this decided to endorse the narrow interpretation of s. 17 that had been used by the county court judge . . .

Just as Parliament never contemplated under Part III that a temporary postponement of demolition could lead to a reversal of the original decision to demolish, so too, in the procedure under Part II beginning under s 16, it is, I think, implicit that Parliament regarded the initial decision that a house could not be rendered fit for human habitation at a reasonable expense as a decision necessarily leading to demolition or closure and a decision in that respect which would not be liable to be reversed, even though, as under Part III, the demolition or closure might properly be postponed for a limited period. This view of the practical working of Part II is really borne out by what happened in the instant case. The local authority always intended that either the owners or they themselves should carry out the works necessary to render this house fit for human habitation. But for the procedural mishap which unfortunately befell them in the first county court proceedings, they would, subject to obtaining confirmation of their compulsory purchase order, have achieved their objective perfectly normally under s 12. Finding that s 12 is tailor-made to empower an acquisition for the very purpose which the local authority are here seeking to achieve, I feel neither surprise nor regret to discover, as I hold, that the language of s 17(2), which contemplates quite a different purpose, cannot properly be stretched to cover the same ground as s 12.

Waller and Megaw L.JJ. agreed.

D Compulsory repair of fit houses

Housing Act 1957, s. 9(1A) (introduced by Housing Act 1969, s. 72)

(1A) Where a local authority, upon consideration of an official representation, or a report from any of their officers or other information in their possession, are satisfied that a house is in such state of disrepair that, although it is not unfit for human habitation, substantial repairs are required to bring it up to a reasonable standard, having regard to its age, character and locality, they may serve upon the person having control of the house a notice requiring him, within such reasonable time, not being less than twenty-one days, as may be specified in the notice, to execute the works specified in the notice, not being works of internal decorative repair . . .

The procedures are broadly similar to those relating to the rehabilitation of unfit houses. In contrast to s. 9(1), however, there is no explicit reference in s. 9(1A) to 'reasonable expense'. See now *Hillbank Properties Ltd* v. *London Borough of Hackney* [1978] 3 All E.R. 343 (C.A.). Lord Denning M.R. said (in part):

The cases are in the nature of test cases and for this reason: if the owners do not do the repairs, the houses will in due course become so dilapidated that they will be unfit for human habitation. Once they are unfit the owners will be in a position to evict the tenants by this means: they will give an undertaking to the local council that the houses will not be used for human habitation. On the owners giving such an undertaking, the tenants will no longer be protected by the Rent Acts; see s 16(5) of the Housing Act 1957. The owners will then get orders for possession of the houses. The local council will have to rehouse the tenants. The owners will get vacant possession; and then deal with the houses to their great advantage. They will do them up and sell them with vacant possession.

I should have thought that socially this was most undesirable. It means that the owners are at liberty to let houses get in a state of gross disrepair and use it as a means of depriving tenants of their homes . . . [In interpreting s. 9(1A)] the county court judge held that he was entitled to take into account the individual facts, including 'the value of the property, the capital cost of the works and the financial position of the owners'. Applying that principle, he said:

'I have no doubt that the house is not unfit for human habitation and that substantial repairs are required to bring it up to a reasonable standard, but it cannot be right in my view, that an individual owner can be required, on the say-so of the local authority to spend thousands of pounds when at no time were the individual facts considered. In the case of each house, a capital sum in excess of the value of the property will, if the local authority are right, have to be spent and still the value of the house after repairs will be less than the capital sum spent on the repairs. The notices will cause considerable financial loss to the owners. Money must be borrowed to carry out the work and still not be recovered by any increase of rent.'

The question is whether the county court judge directed himself aright in that passage ... In order to determine this question, I propose to consider the meaning of the word 'value' in s 39 of the Housing Act 1957. We all know that the value of a house depends greatly on whether it is sold with vacant possession or not. If the purchaser can get vacant possession, he will pay far more than if the house is occupied by a tenant who is protected under the Rent Acts. These two houses are excellent examples. Take 68 Glyn Road. It would cost £2,750 to put it into proper repair. If it was put into proper repair and sold with vacant possession, it would fetch £7,500. If sold with a protected sitting tenant, it would fetch only £2,300. Similarly with 48 Coopersale Road.

What is the 'value' that is spoken of in s 39? Is it the value with vacant possession? Or the value with a sitting protected tenant? Or something in between?

There is a sentence in *Bacon v Grimsby Corpn* ([1950] 1 K.B. 272) which looked as if it might be the value with a sitting tenant, but the matter was not discussed in that case, and I do not think it should be regarded in any way as binding. To my mind the value is primarily the value with vacant possession ...

In the case of these two houses, the value of each of them, when repaired, with vacant possession was so great that the local authority could not possibly have condemned them under ss 16 to 18. If the local authority had considered them *unfit* for human habitation, their duty would have been to compel the owner to do the repairs by serving a notice under s 9(1) and enforcing it by the measures stated in s 10.

But the local authority did not consider them *unfit* for human habitation. They considered them to be fit. They could not, therefore, condemn them under ss 16 to 18; nor could they require the owners to do the repairs under s 9(1); nor could they invoke the provisions of the Public Health Act 1936 to secure the doing of the repairs ... Their only recourse therefore, to secure the execution of the repairs, was section 9(1A).

There was much discussion before us as to the matters to which the judge should have regard. I would not myself limit his enquiry by any set limits. So long as the matters are relevant to the issue, he should consider them. Let me take a few instances.

(i) We are told that the local authority never serves notices under s 9(1A) on any owner-occupiers. This is no doubt a wise policy: but it should not be regarded as inflexible. They assume, no doubt, that every owner-occupier will do his best to keep his house in good repair to the extent of his resources.

So in many cases it would be unduly harsh to press him with a notice to do more. If, by some oversight or misunderstanding, a local authority did serve an owner-occupier with a s 9(1A) notice, the judge would be entitled to set it aside on appeal, if he thought it right to do so.

(ii) There was a question raised as to whether the judge could consider the means or financial position of the owner. Both sides seemed to think that he could not do so. But I would not limit the judge in this respect. I can envisage a poor widow who has only one house which she lets out to bring in some rent. If she could not afford to do the repairs, I think the judge could quash the notice or reduce the requirements so as to bring the cost within her means. So in this case, I think the judge could consider the financial position of these two companies. But I think he had too little evidence to form an opinion about them or their means. He should have torn aside the corporate veil and have seen the strength of the resources at their command. I should expect to find a strong property-owning company at the back of them.

(iii) Next, I think that the judge could consider the cost of the works as compared with the 'value' of the house. But in this respect I am inclined to think that the 'value' could in many cases be taken as the value with vacant possession (as in s 39), and not the 'value' with a sitting protected tenant. And on this reckoning of value, each house was well worth the cost of the works. The cost of the works to 68 Glyn Road was £2,750; and, when the work was done, the house would be worth, with vacant possession, £7,500. And very probably the company may have bought it at a very low figure.

It would, I think, be very mischievous to take the 'value' of the house with a sitting protected tenant. If that were taken, the owner could get the notice quashed, and then by good strategy deprive the tenant of the protection of the Rent Acts and sell with vacant possession. So its real value to him may be its value with vacant possession.

At any rate, the judge should not take, as the sole measure of value, the 'value' as the value with a sitting protected tenant in the house. For that is not its real value to the owner of the property. The sitting tenant may be old and soon die; or he may move elsewhere to live, and thus lose any protection. In one way or another the owner may soon get vacant possession, especially if he uses the device of letting the house get so bad that it is unfit for human habitation. So it may be very proper for the judge to consider the value as the value with vacant possession, or at any rate a value approaching it. Even if he took a midway value in this case, the house was of sufficient value to justify the cost of the repairs.

(iv) One final point. The judge said that, if public money had been expended on the property by way of improvement grants, it would be proper for the local authority to serve a notice under s 9(1A), but that, if no grant had been spent on it, the local authority should not put the owner to the expense of repairs. I do not think that an owner (who had received no grant) should be exempt from a notice under s 9(1A).

This case throws up a problem of great social importance. It seems to me that the policy of Parliament was to make the owners of houses keep them in proper repair. Not only so as to keep up the stock of houses, but also to see that protected tenants should be able to have their houses properly kept up. It would be deplorable if there were no means of compelling owners of old houses to keep them in proper repair, or if the owners could let them fall into disrepair as a means of evicting the tenants. Of course if the state of a house is so bad that it should be condemned, whoever was occupying it, then let it be demolished or closed or purchased. But if it is worth repairing, then it should be repaired, no matter whether it is occupied by a protected tenant or an unprotected tenant. The owners of these houses should not be allowed to evade their responsibilities under the cloak of the company law system. I think that the judge misdirected himself in taking the 'value' as it is, and when he said that the 'notice will cause considerable financial loss to the owners'. There was no evidence to warrant any such inference before him. If he had directed himself properly, on the evidence before him, it seems to me that there could only have been one answer. He should have upheld the notices. I would therefore allow the appeal and uphold these notices and not quash them.

Geoffrey Lane and Eveleigh L.JJ. delivered concurring judgments.

Comment. Do you regard the incorporation of s. 39 into s. 9(1A) as a desirable instance of judicial creativity? (See Morgan (1979); cf. *Buswell* v. *Goodwin* [1971] 1 W.L.R. 92 criticized by Reynolds (1974) and supported by Robinson (1976).) Do you think county court judges are the best people to deal with the problems of valuation and expense revealed in provisions of Part II of the Housing Act 1957? Would the presence of additional assessors be a good idea?

7. Improvement

We have already noted the common law distinction between repair and improvement (above, p. 336). Most of the foregoing discussion has related to basic questions of repair. However, repairs are essentially a method of retaining the *status quo*. Housing policy should also be engaged in encouraging improvements of the property. There is now a considerable amount of law on the circumstances in which improvements are permitted, or even required, the main features of which are discussed below.

A The common law

Leases frequently contain covenants prohibiting tenants from making alterations and improvements. They may be 'absolute' or 'qualified' (i.e. subject to the landlord's consent, see above, p. 80). In the latter case, by Landlord and Tenant Act 1927, s. 19(2), such consent is not to be unreasonably withheld, though the lessor may require as a condition of his consent payment of a reasonable sum in respect of damage to or diminution in the value of premises. (See generally Woodfall, 1978, paras. 1-1260–1-1267).

In order to encourage tenants to make improvements, and to take advantage of the new rules which permit payment of improvement grants to tenants, the Housing Act 1980, s. 81 now replaces Landlord and Tenant Act 1927, s. 19(2), so that in the case of most secure, protected and statutory tenancies, granted before or after s. 81 came into effect (s. 85), it is 'a term of every such tenancy that the tenant will not make any improvement without the written consent of the landlord' (s. 81(2)). Consent must not be unreasonably withheld (s. 81(3) and s. 82(1)). Any consent may be subject to conditions (s. 82(2)); failure to satisfy 'any reasonable condition' is regarded as a breach of an obligation of the tenancy (s. 83; for the potential impact of this rule on questions of security of tenure, see below, p. 424).

B Housing Act 1974: compulsory improvement of dwellings

(i) On the initiative of tenants

The Housing Act 1974, Part VIII, gives local authorities a general power to compel improvements. However, this can only operate after a tenant has made written representations to his local authority that the dwelling is without one or more of the standard amenities.[5]

On receipt of the written representations, the person having control of the dwelling must be told. The local authority has then to satisfy itself (s. 89(3)):

(a) that the person making the representations is, in fact, the tenant;
(b) that the dwelling is one to which the Act applies (i.e. lacks one or more standard amenities, was provided before 3 October 1961

5. Fixed bath/shower, wash-hand basin and sink, all with hot and cold water supply, and w.c.

and is not in a General Improvement Area or Housing Action Area);

(c) that the dwelling is capable of improvement at reasonable expense to the full standard or failing that to the reduced standard (s. 103A, introduced by Housing Act 1980, Sched. 25);

(d) that having regard to all the circumstances the dwelling ought to be improved, and is unlikely to be unless the local authority acts under the section.

The local authority then has to decide whether to issue a provisional notice (s. 89(4)). If the decision is no, the tenant must be told the reasons why; if it is yes, the provisional notice must be served on the tenant, the persons having control, and all others specified in s. 85(4). All these have the right to attend and hear the deliberations of the local authority when they discuss the provisional notice. At this stage a landlord may give a voluntary undertaking to do the repairs which, if accepted, avoids the need for compulsory procedures.

If an undertaking is not accepted, or not even made, the authority has twelve months within which to decide if the provisional notice should be followed by an improvement notice (s. 90). An appeal can be made by any interested party to the county court within six weeks of the service of this notice. A number of grounds of appeal are set out (s. 91). The court may confirm, quash or vary the notice as it thinks fit.

The notice becomes operative after six weeks if no appeal is launched, or on final determination of the appeal if there is one (s. 92). The local authority is given powers of enforcement if the notice is not acted upon within the time allowed (s. 93).

In order to facilitate the execution of the order, the person having control of the premises is given a statutory right to enter the premises (s. 96), and the local authority is under a broad duty to offer loans to meet the expenses of compulsory improvement (s. 100). Alternatively, the person having control of the dwelling may require the local authority to purchase his interest in the dwelling within six months from the improvement notice becoming operative (s. 101).

Whether an undertaking is accepted, or compulsion is used, the local authority must be satisfied that suitable 'housing arrangements' have been made between the landlord and the tenant; these must be in writing (s. 86). Hadden (1978, p. 38) has shown that from January 1975 to March 1977 some 4,500 improvement notices were issued in England and Wales; works were completed in less than one-third of the cases; and local authorities used their default powers in fewer than 100 cases. Nonetheless, he concludes that the power is a useful one. (And see *F.F.F. Estates* v. *Hackney L.B.C.* (1980) *The Times*, 2 August.)

(*ii*) *On the initiative of the local authority*
In Housing Action Areas and General Improvement Areas, use of the powers of compulsory improvement may be initiated by local authorities (s. 85).

C Landlord's right to improve

Under the Housing Finance Act 1972, s. 33, where a statutory tenant is refusing to give his consent to the carrying out of works which are to be grant-aided (see below, p. 403) a county court may, in certain circumstances, make an order empowering a landlord to enter and carry out the works.

(3) An order under subsection (1) of this section may be made subject to such conditions as to the time at which the works are to be carried out and as to any provision to be made for the accommodation of the tenant and his household whilst they are carried out as the court may think fit...

(4) In determining whether to make such an order and, if it is made, subject to what, if any, conditions, the court shall have regard to all the circumstances and, in particular to –

    (*a*) any disadvantage to the tenant that might be expected to result from the works, and

    (*b*) the accommodation that might be available for him whilst the works are carried out, and

    (*c*) the age and health of the tenant,

but the court shall not take into account the means or resources of the tenant.

Paley discovered (1978, para. 3.23) that about half the tenants in her sample who thought major repair work was necessary and nearly two-thirds of those who thought improvement work was necessary would be willing to pay a bit more rent if this work was done.

D Area improvement policies

Because of the difficulties of effecting improvements on an individual basis, there has been a shift of policy to allow local authorities to improve properties on an area basis. A number of General Improve-ment Areas (Housing Act 1969) and Housing Action Areas (Housing

Act 1974) have been designated. The details of the law will not be discussed here (see Hadden, 1979, ch. 7). The policies themselves have been widely criticized (see, e.g., Paris, 1977; CDP, 1977b; DoE, 1977; Paris & Blackaby (1979); *Roof*, 1979b; Monck, 1980).

E Grant aid

Finally, it may be noted that grant aid is available to assist with both improvements and repairs. The principal categories are:

(a) Intermediate grants: mandatory grants for the installation of standard amenities (see above, p. 400).
(b) Improvement grants: discretionary grants for the improvement of property.
(c) Repairs grant: discretionary grants towards repair of houses.
(d) Homes Insulation Grants: Power to award grants is limited to the amount of government finance available.

Again the details of the law (which have been further amended by Housing Act 1980, Sched. 12) are not considered here (Hadden, 1979, ch. 5). (For a brief critique of the improvement grant scheme see Wintour & Franey, 1978.) Whereas only the owners of houses used to be able to apply for grants, note that by Housing Act 1980, s. 106(1) many categories of tenant have now been given the right to apply. This raises a number of difficult questions: for example, how and on what terms is a tenant who has contributed to improvements to be compensated if he moves?

8
Security of Tenure

Introduction

By now we are familiar with the proposition that for a lease to exist, there must be a reversion (above, p. 401). At law, there is always the possibility that the tenant or leaseholder will have to give up his property and hand it back to the landlord, either because the term of the lease has expired, or because the tenant has broken the lease, or some such other reason. The social hardship that can result from this stage of affairs has resulted in the development of a large amount of protective law designed to assist tenants. One of the earliest developments of the law was that the courts of equity were often prepared to give relief from forfeiture (Megarry & Wade, 1975, pp. 664–5). The Rent Acts have long given additional security of tenure to residential tenants. Business tenants may have protection under Landlord and Tenant Act 1954, Part II. Tenant farmers may be protected by the Agricultural Holdings Act 1948. Certain long leaseholders have been given rights to extend their tenancies or even to enfranchise themselves under the Leasehold Reform Act 1967, a principle now extended to local authority tenants by the Housing Act 1980.

Discussion of housing issues in the press frequently suggests that statutory security of tenure is a unique feature of law on housing. This is not so. Further, it often seems to be suggested that security is the main reason why landlords will not let. This opinion seems somewhat at odds with the study by Paley (1978) who shows clearly that it is the low level of rents that concern landlords much more. Further the

British Property Federation has stated (1975) that it 'does not wish to press for any change in the law of security of tenure as it affects existing residential tenants [at least] where the landlord is primarily an investor'. Nonetheless, the new 'shorthold' tenancy (above, p. 205) has been added to the categories of tenancies (see below, pp. 433–9) which are designed specifically to avoid giving tenants security of tenure. It is argued that this will boost the accommodation available for short-term tenants, e.g. students or young couples waiting to buy a house; it remains to be seen what the actual social consequences of this new form of tenure will be.

A final point: because of the complexity of the law and the seriousness of eviction, a general requirement has been developed that, in the case of most residential occupiers, they should not be evicted without a court looking at the facts and deciding whether or not eviction is justifiable. Failure to follow these procedures can lead both to civil action and to criminal proceedings (below, pp. 444–56).

1. Methods of terminating leases/tenancies recognized by the common law

The common law recognized many different modes of determining tenancies. (For the consequences of failing to use one of them see, e.g., *Youngmin* v. *Heath*, above, p. 243.) The most important are:

(*a*) *Effluxion of Time* – a fixed-term lease ends when the time expires. This principle is now subject to many exceptions (see below, pp. 417–33).

(*b*) *Operation of Condition Subsequent* – e.g. the death/marriage of someone. This will only be relevant if the lease spells out the condition which is to terminate the lease.

(*c*) *By surrender* – where the tenant yields up his term to his immediate landlord, this may be done by the parties entering into a written agreement to surrender; or more commonly by the tenant performing some unequivocal act such as giving back the keys to the landlord and moving out. The parties must indicate an intention to terminate the lease. In *Hoggett* v. *Hoggett* (1979) 129 *New Law Jo.* p. cxliii (C.A.), it was held that where a husband attempted to surrender the lease without the knowledge of his wife, this did not operate as an effective surrender at common law since she retained rights of possession.

(*d*) *Under a power* – if the lease contains a power or option to determine which is validly exercised.

(*e*) *By merger* – when the reversion and the lease become vested in the same person, e.g. when the tenant buys out the landlord's interest. (*Rye* v. *Rye* [1962] A.C. 496, above, p. 43.)

(*f*) *By forfeiture* – a lessor may forfeit a lease either for breach of condition or for breach of covenant. In the latter case the lease must contain a proviso for re-entry for breach of the covenant. The nature of the distinction between a condition and a covenant will not be discussed in detail (see *Bashir* v. *Commissioner of Lands* [1960] A.C. 44 (P.C.)). Suffice to say that it will usually turn on the wording of the relevant provision in the lease (Megarry & Wade, 1975, pp. 655–6). The normal method of enforcing a forfeiture is for the landlord to issue a writ of possession.

(i) WAIVER

The landlord's right to forfeit may be lost if he 'waives' the breach of covenant (for an example see above, p. 88). Waiver will be implied if the landlord is aware of the acts or omissions of the tenant which make the lease liable to forfeiture and the landlord does an unequivocal act recognizing the continued existence of the lease (*Matthews* v. *Smallwood* [1910] 1 Ch. 777). The most clear-cut example of waiver is a demand by the landlord for rent, made after the breach, with knowledge of the facts constituting the breach (*David Blackstone* v. *Burnetts* (*West End*) [1973] 1 W.L.R. 1487; .cf. *Harvey* v. *Stagg*, above, p. 56). Where the breach of covenant is a continuing one (e.g. continued failure to repair), waiver extends only to the point of time at which the landlord knew that the breaches would last; later breaches afford a new right to forfeit (*Segal Securities Ltd* v. *Thoseby* [1963] 1 Q.B. 887).

(ii) FORFEITURE FOR NON-PAYMENT OF RENT

The Common Law Procedure Act 1852, ss. 210–12 provides that even where a landlord has obtained judgment for possession, the tenant may apply for relief – at the court's discretion – within six months of execution of the judgment. If relief is granted, no new lease need be executed (Supreme Court of Judicature (Consolidation) Act 1925, s. 46). (See generally, *Belgravia Insurance* v. *Meah* [1964] 1 Q.B. 436.) A similar (though by no means identical) jurisdiction to give relief is given to the county court under County Courts Act 1959, s. 191. (See too Administration of Justice Act 1965, s. 23; and *R.* v. *A Circuit Judge* (*sitting as Norwich County Court*) *ex parte Wathen* (1977) 33 P.&C.R. 423 (Div. Ct.).)

In *Wolmer Securities Ltd* v. *Corne* [1966] 2 Q.B. 243 (C.A.), Russell L.J. made it clear that where forfeiture is ordered, that only has the effect of terminating the original contractual tenancy. Thus a Rent Act protected tenancy will be converted into a statutory tenancy and the statutory tenant will have all the rights which are available under the Rent Act (see below, pp. 417–33). Russell L.J. also remarked that even if proceedings relating to a residential tenancy falling outside the Rent Acts resulted in a forfeiture order, the landlord's rights to recover possession were still subject to what is now Protection from Eviction Act 1977, s. 2:

Where any premises are let as a dwelling on a lease which is subject to a right of re-entry or forfeiture it shall not be lawful to enforce that right otherwise than by proceedings in the court while any person is lawfully residing in the premises or part of them.

These principles apply to all forfeiture cases, not just those relating to non-payment of rent. Failure to observe s. 2 is a criminal offence (see unlawful eviction, below, p. 448). (See too *Borzak* v. *Ahmed* [1965] 2 Q.B. 320.)

(iii) FORFEITURE FOR BREACH OF OTHER COVENANTS

Law of Property Act 1925, s. 146 reads (in part):

(1) A right of re-entry or forfeiture under any proviso or stipulation in a lease for a breach of any covenant or condition in the lease shall not be enforceable, by action or otherwise, unless and until the lessor serves on the lessee a notice –

  (a) specifying the particular breach complained of; and
  (b) if the breach is capable of remedy, requiring the lessee to remedy the breach; and
  (c) in any case, requiring the lessee to make compensation in money for the breach;

and the lessee fails, within a reasonable time thereafter, to remedy the breach, if it is capable of remedy, and to make reasonable compensation in money, to the satisfaction of the lessor, for the breach.

(2) Where a lessor is proceeding, by action or otherwise, to enforce such a right of re-entry or forfeiture, the lessee may, in the lessor's action, if any, or in any action brought by himself, apply to the court for relief; and the court may grant or refuse relief, as the court, having regard to the proceedings

and conduct of the parties under the foregoing provisions of this section, and to all the other circumstances, thinks fit; and in case of relief may grant it on such terms, if any, as to costs, expenses, damages, compensation, penalty, or otherwise, including the granting of an injunction to restrain any like breach in the future, as the court, in the circumstances of each case, thinks fit...

It is not possible to contract out of these provisions, and clauses in leases that have the effect of a forfeiture clause will be treated as forfeiture clauses, even though they do not look like a normal forfeiture clause (*Richard Clarke & Co.* v. *Widnall* [1976] 1 W.L.R. 845).

The question of whether a covenant is 'capable of remedy' under s. 146(1)(*b*) has been discussed on a number of occasions. Positive covenants (e.g. to repair) are clearly capable of remedy. Negative covenants have presented more problem. We have already seen (*Scala House Ltd* v. *Forbes*, above, p. 88) that unlawful sub-letting is not regarded as capable of remedy. There is also a line of cases that 'immoral user' is incapable of remedy (*Rugby School (Governors)* v. *Tannahill* [1935] 1 K.B. 87; *Egerton* v. *Esplanade Hotels* [1947] 2 All E.R. 88).

Thus in *Central Estates Ltd* v. *Woolgar* (No. 2) [1972] 1 Q.B. 48, the tenant had taken an assignment of a lease of a house. He paid a ground rent of £40 a year, payable quarterly. The lease contained a covenant against using the house so as to cause a nuisance etc. The tenant (a 60-year-old pensioner from the First World War) supported himself by letting furnished rooms in the house. In June 1970 he was convicted of keeping a homosexual brothel but was conditionally discharged for twelve months.

On 23 July 1970 the agents managing the house learned of the conviction and issued a notice under the Law of Property Act, s. 146. One of the agent's partners circulated a memorandum to his staff saying that no more rent should be collected from the tenant. In fact this message was not acted upon with the result that in September 1970 the quarter's rent due on 29th September was demanded from and paid by the tenant. The Court of Appeal held that this action constituted waiver of the breach of covenant which could have led to forfeiture. But Lord Denning M.R. was quite clear that 'when a tenant keeps a brothel in breach of covenant, that breach is one which is not capable of remedy'.

However, as we have also noted (above, p. 88), the fact that a breach is incapable of remedy does not preclude the court from exercising its jurisdiction under s. 146(2). As Lord Denning continued, in the *Woolgar* case:

... It has also been said that relief is not to be exercised in favour of persons who suffer premises to be used as a brothel: see *Borthwick-Norton* v. *Romney Warwick Estates Ltd* ([1950] 1 All E.R. 798). But I think that is going too far. In a somewhat parallel case under the Rent Acts, a county court judge allowed a tenant to remain in possession, and this court affirmed this decision: see *Yates* v. *Morris* ([1950] 2 All E.R. 577). It seems to me that in a proper case – I emphasize 'in a proper case' – the court can grant relief from forfeiture even for a breach of covenant against immoral user. After all, the statute does give a discretion to the court. It would not be right for the court to take away that discretion by applying a fixed rule of law that relief could never be given where a tenant has been convicted of keeping a brothel. It is true, as I said when this case was previously before us: 'Forfeiture was the almost inevitable consequence. Relief is rarely given for such a breach ...' But it may sometimes be given. Suppose there was a breach by a tenant four or five years ago – a conviction of immoral user – but never any breach since. The landlord did not know of it at the time. Then, after four or five years, he discovers it and he seeks to forfeit. I should say it was plain in such a case as that it would be open to the court to grant relief. The present case is not nearly so strong a case, but the judge, who saw the witnesses and considered the whole case, thought it was a case for relief. It is to be noticed that the past user has not affected the value of the premises. The stigma has not diminished the value of the landlords' estate. And there are many mitigating factors in favour of the tenant. The judge put it this way:

'The [tenant] is both sick and aged. There is no evidence suggesting that the immoral user to which he put these premises continued over a long period. There is no evidence that he persisted in such user after a preliminary warning, for example from his landlord as happened in the *Borthwick* case. There is no suggestion that his illegal user continued after 27th May 1970 which was the date offence proved against him. Indeed, all the evidence points to the opposite conclusion.'

He pointed out that –

'in terms of hard cash the [tenant] stands to lose and the [landlords stand] to gain a very substantial sum of money [it was £9,000 at that time, we are told much more now] which is as it seems to me wholly disproportionate to the harm actual or potential that the deplorable lapse that this otherwise respectable old man can be said to have occasioned to the [landlords].'

After considering all those matters, the judge came –

'to the conclusion that there are grounds upon which it would be proper for me to exercise my discretion and to give relief to the [tenant] from forfeiture.'

I have had some hesitation about this point, but on the whole I would not interfere with the judge's discretion. This old man has repented of his wrongdoing. He is doing all he can, and will do all he can, to keep the premises aright, and to see that they are properly used. There was material on which the judge could exercise his discretion to grant relief. I would affirm his decision on this point also...

BUCKLEY L.J., however, said:

For myself, I find it difficult to accept that those circumstances were sufficient ground for departing from the general principle that the court, in the exercise of its judicial discretion under s. 146 of the Law of Property Act 1925, ought not to grant relief to somebody who has been guilty of a breach of covenant in the lease of the kind which is involved in the present case. I feel myself to be in agreement with the views which were expressed by Hilbery J. in *Borthwick-Norton* v. *Romney Warwick Estates Ltd*, and what was said in the Court of Appeal by Lord Goddard CJ in the same case. In my judgment, exceptional circumstances need to be shown in a case in which the breach of covenant that is relied on is a breach of covenant of this nature. But that, of course, is not to say that the section does not confer a discretion on the court in such cases. It is merely an indication of the way in which courts in the past have thought it right to exercise that discretion in cases of this kind; and every case may be said to stand exclusively on its own facts. Left to myself, I do not think I should have taken the course which the learned judge took in the present case; I would I think have concluded that this was a case in which it was not right to grant relief from forfeiture; but the learned judge was exercising a discretion; he was exercising a discretion in a case in which the covenant which was breached was not a covenant in terms not to use the property for immoral purposes, but was a covenant against using the property so as to occasion a nuisance; and in all the circumstances of the case and particularly having regard to the view which Lord Denning MR has already expressed, I think perhaps it would not be right for me to say that I think the learned judge's discretion should be overruled. I content myself, therefore, with saying that it was a discretion which I myself would have exercised otherwise had I been trying this case at first instance.

Forfeiture was actually ordered in *Bathurst* v. *Fine* ([1974] 1 W.L.R. 905). Here, a country property of architectural and historical interest was let by Earl Bathurst to Herman Fine, an American, for 20 years. The rent was comparatively low (£450 per annum) since Fine had covenanted to keep the house in order and do considerable repairs. However, in 1973, Fine went to France and was banned by the Home Office from re-entering the country. Lord Denning noted:

In the ordinary way relief was almost always granted against forfeiture if a tenant could remedy the consequences of the breach: see *Hyman* v. *Rose* [1912] A.C. 623. Here the question was how far the tenant's personal qualifications were to be taken into account. In many cases they could not be taken into account, but in the case of a country house like Daneway House the personal qualifications of the tenant were important.

Despite the fact that Fine had spent some £5,000 on repairs, he continued:

The personal qualifications of the tenant were a legitimate consideration in other cases where relief was being considered. The present was essentially a case where the personal qualifications of the tenant were important. If the tenant was shown to be unsuitable personally to be tenant, then his personal qualifications were important. Here an American citizen had been banned from this country for an indefinite period. The appeal should be dismissed.

Special provisions relating to relief in respect of repairs (above, p. 368) and internal decorative repairs (above, p. 371) have already been mentioned.

(iv) GENERAL RULES OF EQUITY

Equity also developed wide powers to give relief. These were discussed by Lord Wilberforce in *Shiloh Spinners* v. *Harding* ([1973] A.C. 691). He noted that there was dispute as to whether equity would give relief only where the breach was of the covenant to pay rent or was broader based and concluded:

But it is consistent with these principles that we should reaffirm the right of courts of equity in appropriate and limited cases to relieve against forfeiture for breach of covenant or condition where the primary object of the bargain is to secure a stated result which can effectively be attained when the matter comes before the court, and where the forfeiture provision is added by way of security for the production of that result. The word 'appropriate' involves consideration of the conduct of the applicant for relief, in particular whether his default was wilful, of the gravity of the breaches, and of the disparity between the value of the property of which forfeiture is claimed as compared with the damage caused by the breach.

Both as a matter of history and by the nature of things, different considerations apply to different covenants.

On a further argument that the statutory provisions, such as those in the Law of Property Act 1925, had cut down the powers of the court, he said:

> I do not accept this argument. In my opinion where the courts have established a general principle of law or equity, and the legislature steps in with particular legislation in a particular area, it must, unless showing a contrary intention, be taken to have left cases outside that area where they were under the influence of the general law. To suppose otherwise involves the conclusion that an existing jurisdiction has been cut down by implication, by an enactment moreover which is positive in character (for it amplifies the jurisdiction in cases of leases) rather than negative.

In *Starside Properties* v. *Mustapha* ([1974] 1 W.L.R. 816) the Court of Appeal made it clear that in exercising its equitable jurisdiction to grant relief against forfeiture, a court is not limited to a once-for-all exercise of that jurisdiction. It may give whatever extensions of time seem necessary in all the circumstances. They emphasized that this principle applied generally and was not restricted to cases of relief from forfeiture for non-payment of rent.

(g) *By notice to quit* – the common law was, basically, that notice was for the same period as that for which rent was paid, except for yearly tenancies where the period was six months. This was subject to express terms in the lease, and even local custom (Woodfall, 1978, para. 1-1976).

In the case of periodic tenancies of residential accommodation the Protection from Eviction Act 1977, s. 5, states:

> 5.—(1) No notice by a landlord or a tenant to quit any premises let (whether before or after the commencement of this Act) as a dwelling shall be valid unless –
>
> > (a) it is in writing and contains such information as may be prescribed, and
> > (b) it is given not less than 4 weeks before the date on which it is to take effect...

The 'prescribed information' to be provided with notices to quit protected tenancies or restricted contracts is as follows (S.I. 1975 No. 2196, Schedule):

> 1. Even after the notice to quit has run out the landlord must get an order for possession from the court before the tenant can lawfully be evicted.
> 2. If the tenancy is a protected tenancy under the Rent Acts, the court can normally give the landlord such an order only on the grounds set out in those Acts...

4. If the tenant does not know whether his tenancy is a protected tenancy or is otherwise unsure of his rights, he can obtain advice from a solicitor. Help with all or part of the cost of legal advice and assistance may be available under the Legal Aid Scheme. He can also seek information from a citizens' advice bureau, a housing aid centre, a rent officer or a rent tribunal office.

Failure to provide this information renders the notice invalid.

In *any* periodic tenancy, the notice to quit must expire either at the end of the current period or on the first day of any period (*Crate* v. *Miller* [1947] K.B. 946). These principles apply equally to notices issued in accordance with Protection from Eviction Act 1977 (*Schnabel* v. *Allard* [1967] 1 Q.B. 627), and to statutory notices of rent increases which are to operate as notices to quit (see above, p. 272).

In relation to notices to quit given by statutory *tenants*, Rent Act 1977, s. 3(3) provides:

Subject to section 5 of the Protection from Eviction Act 1977 (under which at least 4 weeks' notice to quit is required), a statutory tenant of a dwelling-house shall be entitled to give up possession of the dwelling-house if, and only if, he gives such notice as would have been required under the provisions of the original contract of tenancy, or, if no notice would have been so required, on giving not less than 3 months' notice.

See *Boyer* v. *Warbey* [1953] 1 Q.B. 234 (C.A.) for the enforcement of this provision.

Note also Rent Act 1977, s. 3(4) which applies to statutory tenancies:

(4) Notwithstanding anything in the contract of tenancy, a landlord who obtains an order for possession of a dwelling-house as against a statutory tenant shall not be required to give to the statutory tenant any notice to quit...

(*h*) Other methods known to the common law were: disclaimer; and (possibly) by the operation of the doctrine of frustration.

(*i*) Leases may also be terminated as the result of various statutory procedures: e.g. compulsory purchase; enfranchisement under the Leasehold Reform Act 1967; the imposition of a demolition order (or in some cases a closing order) under the Housing Act 1957.

2. Lawful eviction

As has already been mentioned, the foregoing methods of terminating a lease bring the contractual lease to an end. This will not, however,

Table 8.1 County court actions for recovery of possession of residential premises, England and Wales, 1977–8[1]

	1977	1978 All actions	Private landlords against tenants Resident	Private landlords against tenants Absentee Mandatory grounds	Private landlords against tenants Absentee Alternative accommodation	Private landlords against tenants Absentee Discretionary grounds	Social landlords against tenants	Agricultural tied cottages	Other types of action[2]
Greater London									
Orders for possession refused by Court:	460	350	100	20	10	120	60	—	40
Orders for possession made by Court:	19,720	18,010	1,860	1,050	100	2,490	10,670	10	1,830
of which									
Made forthwith, or suspended 28 days or less:	18,480	17,000	1,760	980	100	2,290	10,250	10	1,610
Suspended for over 28 days:	1,240	1,010	100	70	—	200	420	—	220
All applications determined:	20,180	18,360	1,960	1,070	110	2,610	10,730	10	1,870
Rest of England and Wales									
Orders for possession refused by Court:	410	530	50	20	10	80	170	10	200

Orders for possession made by Court: *of which*	16,480	140	33,520	3,440	100	930	2,760	57,370	63,600
Made forthwith, or suspended 28 days or less:	14,520	120	30,390	2,900	80	760	2,520	51,290	54,910
Suspended for over 28 days:	1,960	20	3,130	540	20	170	240	6,080	8,690
All applications determined:	16,680	140	33,690	3,520	110	950	2,810	57,900	64,010
England and Wales									
Orders for possession refused by Court:	240	—	230	200	20	40	150	880	870
Orders for possession made by Court: *of which*	18,310	150	44,190	5,930	200	1,980	4,620	75,380	83,320
Made forthwith, or suspended 28 days or less:	16,130	130	40,640	5,190	180	1,740	4,280	68,290	73,390
Suspended for over 28 days:	2,180	20	3,550	740	20	240	340	7,090	9,930
All applications determined:	18,550	150	44,420	6,130	220	2,020	4,770	76,260	84,190

[1] 1978 figures are based on a three months' sample, and may be revised.

[2] 'Other actions' cover actions to recover possession from defaulting mortgagors and former licensees (including occupants of non-agricultural tied accommodation), and all actions brought, whether by private or by 'social' landlords, under Order 26 of the County Court Rules against alleged trespassers.

Source: *Housing and Construction Statistics*, vol. 30 (1979), Supplementary Table XXXVIII.

usually destroy a tenant's statutory rights. Before looking at the details of those rights it is important to stress that many thousands of lawful evictions take place each year, as Table 8.1 shows. A majority of these are taken by 'social landlords' (e.g. local authorities, housing associations), but a substantial number of private sector tenancies are also brought to an end by the courts. Presumably the balance of these figures will alter with the coming into force of security of tenure for local authority tenants.

The adequacy of the court procedures, as a method of reviewing cases and filtering out doubtful claims, has been challenged in two small-scale studies of eviction proceedings in a few London county courts (Cutting, 1975; Leevers *et al.*, 1977). The latter stated (p. 52):

> The results of the study indicate that the majority of defendants in possession hearings often did not realise the need to defend their cases, and rarely knew how to. Where the defendant did not appear the judge was not presented with the two sides of the case and therefore had no real basis on which to make a decision. Defendants who represented themselves found the court procedure intimidating and confusing. Their defence was often inadequate because of unfamiliarity with the procedures. The court form, designed to provide a basis for defence, bewildered rather than helped defendants. Most of these defendants had to contend with plaintiffs having expert legal representation, and in such circumstances their defences were understandably inadequate. Only in those few cases where the litigants were equally represented was it possible for the judge to arbitrate between two equal adversaries. Defendants could not understand the complex legislation or the machinery which enforces it. They felt that justice had not been done. On occasions this was seen to be so.

It is also frequently claimed that delays in obtaining a hearing are extensive. Table 8.2 provides some information on this.

Table 8.2   Average delays in county court hearings

	1977	1978
Average interval in days between issue and hearing when no expedition granted:	41	41
Formal applications for expedited hearings: granted:	262	252
refused:	15	12
Average interval in days when expedition granted:	17	15

Source: As Table 8.1.

A further issue relating to delay, frequently argued by landlords, is that even when an order for possession has been obtained, its effect is postponed by the courts. As a result of Housing Act 1980, s. 89, the courts' discretion has been substantially curtailed:

89.—(1) Where a court makes an order for the possession of any land in a case not falling within the exceptions mentioned in subsection (2) below, the giving up of possession shall not be postponed (whether by the order or any variation, suspension or stay of execution) to a date later than fourteen days after the making of the order, unless it appears to the court that exceptional hardship would be caused by requiring possession to be given up by that date; and shall not in any event be postponed to a date later than six weeks after the making of the order.

(2) The restrictions in subsection (1) above do not apply if –

    (*a*) the order is made in an action by a mortgagee for possession; or

    (*b*) the order is made in an action for forfeiture of a lease [see above, p. 406]; or

    (*c*) the court had power to make the order only if it considered it reasonable to make it [see below]; or

    (*d*) the order relates to a dwelling-house which is the subject of a restricted contract (within the meaning of section 19 of the 1977 Act) [see below, p. 440]; or

    (*e*) the order is made in proceedings as mentioned in s. 88(1) above [see p. 235].

3. Security of tenure under the Rent Act 1977

The basic powers of the court are set out in Rent Act 1977, ss. 98 and 100 (as amended by the Housing Act, 1980). (Section 99 deals with jurisdiction over dwellings let to agricultural workers.)

98.—(1) Subject to this Part of this Act, a court shall not make an order for possession of a dwelling-house which is for the time being let on a protected tenancy or subject to a statutory tenancy unless the court considers it reasonable to make such an order and either –

    (*a*) the court is satisfied that suitable alternative accommodation is available for the tenant or will be available for him when the order in question takes effect, or

    (*b*) the circumstances are as specified in any of the Cases in Part I of Schedule 15 to this Act.

(2) If, apart from subsection (1) above, the landlord would be entitled to recover possession of a dwelling-house which is for the time being let on or subject to a regulated tenancy, the court shall make an order for possession if the circumstances of the case are as specified in any of the Cases in Part II of Schedule 15.

(3) Part III of Schedule 15 shall have effect in relation to Case 9 in that

Schedule and for determining the relevant date for the purposes of the Cases in Part II of that Schedule.

(4) Part IV of Schedule 15 shall have effect for determining whether, for the purposes of subsection (1)(a) above, suitable alternative accommodation is or will be available for a tenant.

(5) Part V of Schedule 15 shall have effect for the purpose of setting out conditions which are relevant to Cases 11 and 12 of that Schedule [below, p. 456].

100.—(1) Subject to subsection (5) below, a court may adjourn, for such period or periods as it thinks fit, proceedings for possession of a dwelling-house which is let on a protected tenancy or subject to a statutory tenancy.

(2) On the making of an order for possession of such a dwelling-house, or at any time before the execution of such an order (whether made before or after the commencement of this Act), the court, subject to subsection (5) below, may –

(a) stay or suspend execution of the order, or

(b) postpone the date of possession,

for such period or periods as the court thinks fit.

(3) On any such adjournment as is referred to in subsection (1) above or any such stay, suspension or postponement as is referred to in subsection (2) above, the court shall, unless it considers that to do so would cause exceptional hardship to the tenant or would otherwise be unreasonable, impose conditions with regard to payment by the tenant of arrears of rent (if any) and rent or payments in respect of occupation after termination of the tenancy (mesne profits) and may impose such other conditions as it thinks fit.

(4) If any such conditions as are referred to in subsection (3) above are complied with, the court may, if it thinks fit, discharge or rescind any such order as is referred to in subsection (2) above.

(4A) Subsection (4B) below applies in any case where –

(a) proceedings are brought for possession of a dwelling-house which is let on a protected tenancy or subject to a statutory tenancy;

(b) the tenant's spouse or former spouse, having rights of occupation under the Matrimonial Homes Act 1967, is then in occupation of the dwelling-house; and

(c) the tenancy is terminated as a result of those proceedings.

(4B) In any case to which this subsection applies, the spouse or former spouse shall, so long as he or she remains in occupation, have the same rights in relation to, or in connection with, any such adjournment as is referred to in subsection (1) above or any such stay, suspension or postponement as is referred to in subsection (2) above, as he or she would have if those rights of occupation were not affected by the termination of the tenancy.

(5) This section shall not apply if the circumstances are as specified in any of the Cases in Part II of Schedule 15.

There is very little helpful guidance as to the meaning of 'reasonable' in s. 98; however in *Cumming* v. *Danson* [1942] 2 All E.R. 653 (C.A.) Lord Greene M.R. remarked:

> In considering reasonableness . . . , it is, in my opinion, perfectly clear that the duty of the judge is to take into account all relevant circumstances as they exist at the date of the hearing. That he must do in what I venture to call a broad, common-sense way as a man of the world, and come to his conclusion giving such weight as he thinks right to the various factors in the situation. Some factors may have little or no weight, others may be decisive, but it is quite wrong for him to exclude from his consideration matters which he ought to take into account.

A Exceptions

(*i*) Rent Act 1977, s. 101

101.—(1) At any time when a dwelling-house to which this section applies is overcrowded, within the meaning of the Housing Act 1957, in such circumstances as to render the occupier guilty of an offence, nothing in this Part of this Act shall prevent the immediate landlord of the occupier from obtaining possession of the dwelling-house.

(2) This section applies to a dwelling-house which consists of premises used as a separate dwelling by members of the working classes or of a type suitable for such use.

(*ii*) Housing Act 1957, s. 16(5)

Nothing in the [Rent Act 1977] . . . shall prevent possession being obtained of any premises by any owner thereof in a case where an undertaking has been given under this section that those premises shall not be used for human habitation.

(See above, p. 392.)

(*iii*) Housing Act 1957, s. 22(5) creates a similar exception where a demolition order has been made; and also, *ibid.*, s. 27(5).

The possibility for abuse created by sections such as these was discussed by Lord Denning in the *Hillbank Properties Case* (above, p. 396).

B Suitable alternative accommodation

Table 8.1 gives some indication of the frequency of use of this head (above, p. 414). Schedule 15, Part IV, which further defines what is suitable alternative accommodation, provides:

3. For the purposes of section 98(1)(a) of this Act, a certificate of the housing authority for the district in which the dwelling-house in question is situated,

certifying that the authority will provide suitable alternative accommodation for the tenant by a date specified in the certificate, shall be conclusive evidence that suitable alternative accommodation will be available for him by that date.

4. Where no such certificate as is mentioned in paragraph 3 above is produced to the court, accommodation shall be deemed to be suitable for the purposes of section 98(1)(a) of this Act if it consists of either –

(a) premises which are to be let as a separate dwelling such that they will then be let on a protected tenancy (other than one under which the landlord might recover possession of the dwelling-house under one of the Cases in Part II of this Schedule), or

(b) premises to be let as a separate dwelling on terms which will, in the opinion of the court, afford to the tenant security of tenure reasonably equivalent to the security afforded by Part VII of this Act in the case of a protected tenancy of a kind mentioned in paragraph (a) above.

and, in the opinion of the court, the accommodation fulfils the relevant conditions as defined in paragraph 5 below.

5.—(1) For the purposes of paragraph 4 above, the relevant conditions are that the accommodation is reasonably suitable to the needs of the tenant and his family as regards proximity to place of work, and either –

(a) similar as regards rental and extent to the accommodation afforded by dwelling-houses provided in the neighbourhood by any housing authority for persons whose needs as regards extent are, in the opinion of the court, similar to those of the tenant and of his family; or

(b) reasonably suitable to the means of the tenant and to the needs of the tenant and his family as regards extent and character; and that if any furniture was provided for use under the protected or statutory tenancy in question, furniture is provided for use in the accommodation which is either similar to that so provided or is reasonably suitable to the needs of the tenant and his family [see above, pp. 211–20].

(2) For the purposes of sub-paragraph (1)(a) above, a certificate of a housing authority stating—

(a) the extent of the accommodation afforded by dwelling-houses provided by the authority to meet the needs of tenants with families of such number as may be specified in the certificate, and

(b) the amount of the rent charged by the authority for dwelling-houses affording accommodation of that extent,

shall be conclusive evidence of the facts so stated.

6. Accommodation shall not be deemed to be suitable to the needs of the tenant and his family if the result of their occupation of the accommodation would be that it would be an overcrowded dwelling-house for the purposes of the Housing Act 1957...

For possible meanings of 'family' in para. 5, see above, pp. 211–20.

Macdonnell v. *Daly* [1969] 3 All E.R. 851 (C.A.)

LORD DENNING, M.R.: The landlord is a stockbroker's clerk. In August 1966, he bought a house, no. 15 Kempson Road, London, S.W.6. It is a six-roomed house. Three of the rooms were occupied by an artist, the tenant. He had been there for 20 years. He was paying a rent of £2 18s a week. The tenant was a bachelor. The three rooms were filled with all his artist's things; his easels, paints, frames and so forth. He had no kitchen, only a gas ring in one room. He had some rugs in another on which he slept. He made his living by teaching at a school of art and by doing some painting on commission and for sale. The landlord had a wife and two small children. He asked the tenant to give up one of his rooms. He wanted the room on the first floor which the tenant used a great deal for his work as an artist...

Counsel for the landlord submitted to us that alternative accommodation may consist of part only of the premises which are let to the tenant. For that proposition he cited *Thompson* v. *Rolls* ([1926] 2 K.B. 426) and *Parmee* v. *Mitchell* ([1950] 2 K.B. 199); but those cases are quite distinguishable. In each case the tenant occupied only part of the house and sublet the rest. He was offered the whole of the part which he himself occupied. That was held to be suitable alternative accommodation. But those cases do not extend to the present. The landlord here does not offer the tenant all the three rooms which he occupies. He offers him only two of them. That is not good enough. The tenant is protected in respect of all these three rooms...

In my opinion, when a tenant is protected for combined dwelling and professional purposes, the alternative accommodation must be suitable for his needs which include not only his living, cooking and sleeping, but also his professional needs, including his studio. Insofar as the earlier cases express a different view, I cannot agree with them. The overriding consideration is that the tenant here is entitled to protection in regard to all three rooms which he occupies. It is not suitable accommodation to offer him only two of them. Even if it were suitable alternative accommodation, there is still another consideration. No order is to be made against the tenant unless it is 'reasonable' to make it.

Mykolyshyn v. *Noah* [1971] 1 All E.R. 48

WIDGERY L.J.: Number 32 Newton Avenue, Acton, is a conventional dwelling-house built on two floors. The top floor has been in the occupation of the tenant, Mrs Noah, for a very long time, and she is a lady of 78 years at the present time. She occupies that floor under a tenancy which is admittedly protected by the rent restrictions Acts. The top floor comprises four rooms and a lavatory ... The use to which the tenant puts these rooms is as follows. She seems to spend her life in the bedroom, the kitchen and the scullery. In the sitting-room there is, according to her evidence, a three-piece suite, a dining table and four chairs, a piano and a sideboard; but she uses that room, apart from the facility which it gives to her to put that furniture in it, very little. It has no heating, no gas and no electric power. She says that she cannot go into it in winter and that she uses it in summer not very often ... Wishing for more space and particularly wishing for a means of giving their children separate bedrooms instead of having them sleeping with their parents, the landlords have sought to obtain possession of the tenant's sitting-room...

In my judgment there is nothing in *MacDonnell* v. *Daly* [above] to disturb the long-accepted proposition that 'alternative accommodation' may include part of that previously let; and if Lord Denning MR had wished to express a different view on that proposition he would, I feel sure, have used far more positive language. Accordingly I would reject counsel for the tenant's first submission and would accept that the judge was right in saying that this accommodation was 'alternative' for the purposes of the Rent Act [1977] and then move on to the second question, which is whether it was 'suitable' alternative accommodation.

That is a matter which depends on the facts of every case, in the light of the relevant legislation. In the Rent Act [1977, Sch. 15], Part IV, one has a code defining 'Suitable Alternative Accommodation'.

In deciding whether the accommodation offered was reasonably suitable to the tenant's needs, the judge had to consider, amongst other things, whether it would take her furniture so far as that furniture was required to enable her to live in reasonable comfort. He would, I think, have been right to conclude that the premises were not rendered unsuitable merely because there was no accommodation for additional furniture for which the tenant had no foreseeable need. This is in effect what the judge has done, because he has adopted the tenant's own conduct as the best test of what furniture she really requires and has come to the conclusion that the furniture in the sitting-room is surplus to those requirements and, therefore, the alternative offered is not unsuitable merely because it cannot provide a storage place for that furniture.

Accordingly, as it seems to me, and reminding myself that we are concerned only with points of law, I can find nothing wrong in the learned judge's direction of himself on the issue whether the accommodation was 'suitable'...

Redspring Ltd v. *Francis* [1973] 1 All E.R. 640

BUCKLEY L.J. said (in part): The tenant, Mrs Francis, who is the appellant in this court, had lived for, I think, some 30 years in premises at 47 Lisburne Road, London NW3, which was a small flat in a converted house, in connection with which she had a share only of a bathroom with another tenant who had accommodation in the same house, and while she enjoyed the use of the garden she had no legal right in that respect.

The landlord company, Redspring Ltd, served a notice to quit and offered as alternative accommodation premises in Fleet Road, London NW3, which is a busy traffic thoroughfare not far distant from Lisburne Road. The accommodation offered was again a flat in a converted house, rooms on the top floor, somewhat larger in size than the rooms which the tenant had occupied, and still occupies, in Lisburne Road, which included a bathroom of which she would have had exclusive possession. But the house had no garden. Not only is Fleet Road a busy traffic thoroughfare, but immediately next door to no 108, in which the accommodation was offered to the tenant, there is a fried fish shop; there is a hospital in the neighbourhood, a cinema and a public house close by, and it is an area where at all hours of the day and night there are people coming and going and where there is a lot of traffic. The fried fish shop emits smells of a kind which one would expect to be emitted from an establishment of that sort. Lisburne Road, on the other hand, is a quiet residential road, as I gather, and at the back of the house there is the garden which the tenant is permitted to use. At the back of 108 Fleet Road there is a yard or open space, previously occupied by a tram shed, but which the local authority are proposing to use as a transport depot, where presumably there would be large motor vehicles coming and going from time to time. It is conceded on the part of the tenant that the physical accommodation offered at 108 Fleet Road is more spacious and better in respect of the bathroom than the accommodation enjoyed by the tenant in Lisburne Road. But it is said that because of the environment in which it stands it does not satisfy the tenant's needs...

The contention of the tenant has been that in considering the character of alternative accommodation not only the physical characteristics of the premises containing the accommodation fall to be considered, but also such matters as neighbourhood, noise, smell and other considerations of a kind which one can perhaps best describe as environmental considerations; and we have been referred to certain authorities bearing on that aspect of the matter, with none of which do I think it necessary to deal in any detail in this judgment because it is conceded on the part of the landlords that environmental questions are matters relevant to the character of the proposed alternative accommodation. That concession was, in my judgment, properly made. For if a tenant who occupies accommodation in a residential area is offered other accommodation which may be physically as good as or better than the accommodation which he is required to vacate, but is situated in an area which is offensive as the result of some industrial activity in the neighbourhood, which perhaps creates offensive smells or noises, or which is extremely noisy as a result of a great deal of traffic passing by, or in some other respect is clearly much less well endowed with amenities than the accommodation which the tenant is required to vacate, then it seems to me that it would be most unreal to say that the alternative accommodation is such as to satisfy the needs of the tenant with regard to its character. What he needs is somewhere where he can live in reasonably comfortable conditions suitable to the style of life which he leads, and environmental matters must inevitably affect the suitability of offered accommodation to provide him with the sort of conditions in which it is reasonable that he should live.

The Court of Appeal held that the alternative accommodation here was not suitable. Orr and Sachs L.JJ. agreed.

See too *Heglibston Establishment* v. *Heyman* (1978) 246 E.G. 567, where the Court of Appeal held that, where a tenant was offered accommodation in a flat with his estranged wife, this was not 'suitable alternative accommodation'. Also *Yewbright Properties Ltd* v. *Stone* (1980) 254 E.G. 863; *Siddiqui* v. *Rashid* (1980) L.S. Gaz. 623.

C The discretionary grounds

Schedule 15, Part 1 :

Case 1

Where any rent lawfully due from the tenant has not been paid, or any obligation of the protected or statutory tenancy which arises under this Act, or –

   (*a*) in the case of a protected tenancy, any other obligation of the tenancy, in so far as is consistent with the provisions of Part VII of this Act, or

   (*b*) in the case of a statutory tenancy, any other obligation of the previous protected tenancy which is applicable to the statutory tenancy,

has been broken or not performed.

Breach of any of the terms of tenancy agreement is always a potential ground for eviction. Payment of rent into court after the date of commencement of proceedings will not take the tenant out of this case, but it may make it unreasonable for the court to order possession (*Dellenty* v. *Pellow* [1951] 2 K.B. 858 (C.A.); *Hayman* v. *Rowlands* [1957] 1 W.L.R. 317 (C.A.)). (For other remedies in relation to rent arrears, see above, pp. 301–3.)

As regards the other terms of the lease/tenancy they may be contained in formal documents, rent books, or be implied. (See above, pp. 72–9.) In the case of statutory tenancies, the terms of the original tenancy are incorporated (above, p. 79). The importance of looking carefully at the details of such terms and construing them carefully was stressed by the Court of Appeal in *Heglibiston Establishment* v. *Heyman* (1978) 246 E.G. 567.

Case 2

Where the tenant or any person residing or lodging with him or any subtenant of his has been guilty of conduct which is a nuisance or annoyance to adjoining occupiers, or has been convicted of using the dwelling-house or allowing the dwelling-house to be used for immoral or illegal purposes.

This is another very widely drawn Case. It was discussed in *Abrahams* v. *Wilson* [1971] 2 Q.B. 88 (C.A.):

EDMUND DAVIES L.J.: The landlady sought possession on several grounds, only two of which need now be referred to. The first was that the tenant and a Mr Cleghorn, who under a separate tenancy occupied a room in that house, had each been convicted for using the rooms the subject of the tenancy, or allowing them to be used, for criminal or illegal purposes namely, the smoking of cannabis resin. By way of particulars of that allegation, it was pleaded that on 9th May 1969 the tenant and Mr Cleghorn were each convicted at the court of quarter sessions held at the Guildhall in Westminster of being in possession of 66 grains of cannabis resin without being duly authorized. That each of those defendants was so convicted was admitted in the defence...

What is more difficult, however, is the claim that the tenant has been convicted (in the words of case 2) of 'using the dwelling-house or allowing the dwelling-house to be used for immoral or illegal purposes'. Now the evidence in relation to this matter is, in my view, extremely unsatisfactory. The certificate of conviction itself simply recites that the tenant was on 10th March of last year 'in possession of a drug, namely, 66 grains of cannabis resin, without being duly authorized'. The certificate itself makes no reference to 10 Chamberlayne Road as being connected in any way with the charge preferred. But it has emerged – in, I repeat, an unsatisfactory way – that those premises did play some part in relation to the prosecution case which found favour with the jury. It seems that a police witness testified that he had found under a cupboard in one of the rooms let to the tenant 66 grains of cannabis resin. As I understand, the tenant did not challenge that this quantity of cannabis resin was found in one of her rooms, but she vehemently denied having any knowledge of its existence or of being a party to its being placed there. Nevertheless the jury convicted her. Counsel for the tenant has, if I may say so, been extremely helpful to the landlady's case by conceding as much as that. But I think that, in cases (such as the present) where the user of the premises is the focal point of the claim to possession, evidence should be called as to what actually transpired in the criminal trial, so that the civil judge may know with precision the basis of the conviction.

But, having said that the certificate of conviction itself makes no reference to any particular premises, it emerges from a series of cases that this fact does not prevent the circumstances which led to the conviction from being adduced in evidence. The matter was dealt with at length by this court in *Schneiders & Sons Ltd* v. *Abrahams* ([1925] 2 K.B. 301) in which a tenant had been convicted under the Larceny Act 1916 of receiving at the demised premises certain property well knowing it to have been stolen. The place where the act of receiving occurs is in general of no materiality in law; but there it was held that the tenant, having made use of the premises in order to commit that crime, must be regarded as having been convicted of 'using' the premises for an illegal purpose within the meaning of the statutory provision then applicable, i.e. s. 4 of the Rent and Mortgage Interest Restrictions Act 1923. But there must be some link between the criminal conviction and the premises which are the subject-matter of the proceedings for possession; and the test that was applied by Bankes L.J. is one which I would respectfully adopt for the purposes of the present case. He said:

'... I reject the argument that the section includes only offences in which user of the premises is an essential element. But I think it is necessary to show that the tenant has taken advantage of his tenancy of the premises and of the opportunity they afford for committing the offence. In this view the tenant who uses the demised premises as a coiner's den, or as a deposit for stolen goods, and is convicted of counterfeiting coin or receiving goods, would be "convicted of using the premises for an ... illegal purpose" within the meaning of s. 4.'

Scrutton L.J. applied this test:

'Were the words meant to have their strict meaning or were they meant to cover all cases where a tenant is convicted of a crime and had used the premises to facilitate the commission of it?'

He later said:

'Giving the case the best consideration I can, I come to the conclusion that the *conviction* need not be for using the premises for one or another immoral or illegal purpose, and that it is enough if there is a conviction of a crime which has been committed on the premises and for the purpose of committing which the premises have been used; but that it is not enough that the tenant has been convicted of a crime with which the premises have nothing to do beyond merely being the scene of its commission.'

Applying that test to the present case, I for my part would put it in this way. In proper and clear circumstances – which must be established, of course, by the landlord – a conviction of using premises for an illegal purpose, within the meaning of case 2, can be established by proof that in the demised premises a quantity of cannabis resin was found. One must, however, look at the circumstances very carefully before an isolated finding on a single occasion is held to constitute proof of such user. The evidence produced in the civil proceedings was very unsatisfactory regarding what transpired at the criminal trial and I am not prepared to hold that user was established. But, even if it were, my conclusion in relation to case 2 must ultimately turn on the overriding requirement imposed by s. [98] (1) of the Act, that no order for possession may be made by the court (even though the circumstances are such as to bring the matter clearly within any other of the cases set out in Part I of Sch. 3) 'unless the court considers it reasonable to make the order' ...

I do not think that the learned judge failed to take into consideration those matters which were relevant to determining whether the overall requirement of 'reasonableness' had been established. He was, notwithstanding that this was a case [9] matter, entitled to consider the purposes for which the landlady was seeking to obtain possession; he was entitled to have regard to the past behaviour of the tenant as presented by the landlady; and he was, as I think, entitled to have regard to the proof that the tenant had been convicted of the possession of cannabis. I think that he did bear those matters in mind. He also made reference to the evidence that the tenant had on occasion been under the influence of drink. It is complained that the judge ignored the position of the daughter, who, if she went to live in these premises, might be cheek-by-jowl with those who certainly on one occasion had been convicted of the unlawful possession of cannabis; and there was also the binding over in 1969 of the tenant, to which he expressly made reference. But at the end he said:

'I cannot conceive that any judge who has one day's experience of rehousing poorer classes would hold that it would be right to throw out the [tenant]. Unable to work, daughter aged 15 not yet working, a former professional dancer, lives on the State.'

Then he referred to the fact that the learned deputy chairman who had tried the criminal case at quarter sessions had disposed of it by making a conditional order for 12 months against the tenant, and continued:

'This court thinks that the chairman of quarter sessions, having considered the evidence, could not have been more lenient. The suggestion now is that the additional very severe penalty of eviction should be imposed.'

He expressed incredulity that 'any judge in the United Kingdom' would make an order for possession in such circumstances. Having considered all those matters, he came to the conclusion that the reasonableness of making an order had not been made out. Who is to say he was wrong? There were competing considerations but he clearly bore them all in mind. It might be that I personally would have weighed those considerations in a different manner and possibly arrived at a different conclusion; but, even so, that would not be enough for this appeal to succeed. It must further be shown that the learned judge was disentitled to conclude that reasonableness had not been established. I do not think his error in that regard has been demonstrated, and accordingly for my part I would dismiss this appeal.

WIDGERY LJ: Applying Scrutton LJ's test, the position in regard to the finding of dangerous drugs on the demised premises I think is simply this. If the drugs are on the demised premises merely because the tenant is there and has them in his or her immediate custody, such as a pocket or a handbag, then I would say without hesitation that that does not involve a 'using' of the premises in connection with the offence. On the other hand, if the premises are employed as a storage place or hiding place for dangerous drugs, a conviction for possession of such drugs, when the conviction is illuminated by further evidence to show the manner in which the drugs themselves were located, would I think be sufficient to satisfy the section and come within case 2. One must not forget that at the present time landlords may incur heavy penalties if their premises are used for the smoking of cannabis, and one must not lightly deprive a landlord of an opportunity of obtaining possession against a tenant who runs the landlord into that kind of risk.

In *Heglibiston Establishment* v. *Heyman* (1978) 246 E.G. 567, the Court of Appeal stated that a father who permitted his son and girlfriend to live in his flat as man and wife was not using the flat for immoral purposes. Roskill L.J.: '[If] that user is to be interpreted as using premises for an immoral purpose there must be a great many breaches of covenant being committed in London and elsewhere today...'

Case 3

Where the condition of the dwelling-house has, in the opinion of the court, deteriorated owing to acts of waste by, or the neglect or default of, the tenant or any person residing or lodging with him or any sub-tenant of his and, in the case of any act of waste by, or the neglect or default of, a person lodging with the tenant or a sub-tenant of his, where the court is satisfied that the tenant has not, before the making of the order in question, taken such steps as he ought reasonably to have taken for the removal of the lodger or subtenant, as the case may be.

Case 4

Where the condition of any furniture provided for use under the tenancy has, in the opinion of the court, deteriorated owing to ill-treatment by the tenant or any person residing or lodging with him or any sub-tenant of his and, in the case of any ill-treatment by a person lodging with the tenant or a sub-tenant of his, where the court is satisfied that the tenant has not, before the making of the order in question, taken such steps as he ought reasonably to have taken for the removal of the lodger or sub-tenant, as the case may be.

These two cases may be seen together and reflect the common law obligations of a tenant to behave in a tenant-like fashion (above, p. 346).

Case 5

Where the tenant has given notice to quit and, in consequence of that notice, the landlord has contracted to sell or let the dwelling-house or has taken any other steps as the result of which he would, in the opinion of the court, be seriously prejudiced if he could not obtain possession.

Tenants are not allowed to change their minds. The requirements of a valid notice are discussed above (p. 412).

Case 6

Where, without the consent of the landlord, the tenant has, at any time after –

(*b*) 22nd March 1973, in the case of a tenancy which became a regulated tenancy by virtue of section 14 of the Counter-Inflation Act 1973;

[(*bb*) added by Housing Act 1980]

(*c*) 14th August 1974, in the case of a regulated furnished tenancy; or

(*d*) 8th December 1965, in the case of any other tenancy,

assigned or sublet the whole of the dwelling-house or sublet part of the dwelling-house, the remainder being already sublet.

It has been held that consent must be given, even though the tenancy itself contains no covenant against assignment (*Regional Properties* v. *Frankenschwerth* [1951] 1 K.B. 631; above, p. 79). Statutory tenants cannot assign (Rent Act 1977, s. 2, above, p. 207).

Case 7 (repealed, Housing Act 1980)

Case 8 (discussed below, p. 460)

Case 9

Where the dwelling-house is reasonably required by the landlord for occupation as a residence for –

(*a*) himself, or

(*b*) any son or daughter of his over 18 years of age, or

(*c*) his father or mother, or

(*d*) if the dwelling-house is let on or subject to a regulated tenancy, the father or mother of his wife or husband,

and the landlord did not become landlord by purchasing the dwelling-house or any interest therein after –

(i) 7th November 1956, in the case of a tenancy which was then a controlled tenancy;

(ii) (8th March 1973, in the case of a tenancy which became a regulated tenancy by virtue of section 14 of the Counter-Inflation Act 1973;

(iii) 24th May 1974, in the case of a regulated furnished tenancy; or

(iv) 23rd March 1965, in the case of any other tenancy.

Note carefully the dates before which the landlord must have come to own the property. Schedule 15, Part III, para. 1, provides:

1. A court shall not make an order for possession of a dwelling-house by reason only that the circumstances of the case fall within Case 9 in Part I

of this Schedule if the court is satisfied that, having regard to all the circumstances of the case, including the question whether other accommodation is available for the landlord or the tenant, greater hardship would be caused by granting the order than by refusing to grant it.

See *Thomas* v. *Fryer* [1970] 1 W.L.R. 845 C.A.

LORD DONOVAN: This appeal arises out of a contest for the possession of a dwelling-house. The house is 47 Queens Road, London, N11. The tenant, Alice Fryer, a widow aged 60 or 61, has lived in this house with members of her family for over 30 years. She has a controlled tenancy. Possession of the house is now sought by the landlord, Mildred Elizabeth Thomas. She does so pursuant to case [9] ...

Miss Thomas became the landlord of this house in the following circumstances. It was owned by her mother, who died on 26th June 1961. In her will she disposed of the house by a residuary gift in these words: 'The residue of my Estate I give and bequeath in equal shares unto my four children, Barbara, Owen, Geoffrey and Mildred if living at my death ...'

Mildred is the landlord to whom I have already referred. All four children survived their mother. All four were named as executors. The eldest child alone, however, i.e. Mr Owen Thomas, proved the will on 5th October 1961. Besides the house the testatrix left some £4,500 in stocks and shares. After making specific bequests of certain chattels, and leaving some pecuniary legacies to others, she disposed of the residue in the terms I have already quoted. The residuary gift therefore comprised the house and such of the investments as were not required to meet the legacies ...

The landlord had made an unsuccessful attempt to get possession of the house in 1968. The county court judge who tried that case decided no more than this, that greater hardship would be caused by granting the order than by refusing it ...

The present proceedings represent a second attempt by the landlord. The case was heard by his Honour Judge Moylan, sitting at Edmonton County Court, and on 5th June 1969 he made an order for possession in the landlord's favour but postponing its operation for six months. Counsel on behalf of the tenant in the county court took a preliminary objection which the judge disposed of first. It was that the circumstances in which the landlord acquired the house involved the consequence that she could not discharge the onus which was on her of proving that she had become landlord otherwise than by purchasing the house or an interest therein after 7th November 1956. Accordingly, she could not bring herself within case [9] and her application for possession must therefore fail. The judge rejected this contention. His broad reason was this. This was a family arrangement between beneficiaries under the will by which the landlord was allowed to have the house as part of the residue, whilst at the same time making compensatory payments to her fellow residuary legatees in order to achieve equality of benefit. Such a family arrangement was not, he decided, equivalent to becoming a 'landlord by purchasing the dwelling-house or any interest therein' within the meaning of case [9].

In this appeal from that decision, counsel for the tenant, in a strenuous argument, insisted that it was wrong. A family arrangement and a purchase are not, he said, mutually exclusive terms. So much may be conceded. The motive for a transaction does not determine its legal character. Again, no one would dispute that. Counsel then went on to say, in effect: 'Here is the house. The landlord was left by will an undivided fourth share in it. She wanted, however, the whole. Her fellow residuary legatees let her have it. She agreed to pay compensatory payments to them, and indeed paid them £750. That was equivalent to the three-quarters' interest which they had in it. What is that except the purchase of an interest in the dwelling-house?' Despite the attraction of the argument, I find myself after due consideration unable to accept it. One has to decide what is meant by 'purchasing the dwelling-house' in the context of the Rent Act ... This particular provision has a history going back at least to the Rent and Mortgage Interest Restrictions (Amendment) Act 1933 ...

In *Baker* v. *Lewis* ([1947] K.B. 186) Morton L.J. said:

'I am well aware that the word "purchaser" and the words "by purchase" have in certain contexts a technical meaning which is well-known to all lawyers, but I am not aware of any case in which the words "by purchasing a dwelling-house" have been given any technical meaning. For my part I feel no doubt that they simply refer to a transaction of purchase or buying.'

That, of course, by itself does no more than rule out the technical meaning of 'purchase' in the law of property.

In *Littlechild* v. *Holt* ([1950] 1 K.B. 1) Denning L.J. said:

'The intention of the legislature was that people should not be able to buy houses over the heads of the tenants and then turn them out without giving them alternative accommodation ... The acquisition of the reversion, whether it be a freehold or a leasehold, for money or money's worth, and whether payable in a lump sum or by instalments, is plainly a "purchase", but the acquisition of it under a will is not a purchase: *Baker* v. *Lewis* (above).'

There are certain cases under the Stamp Act 1891 where family arrangements involving the transfer of assets to a beneficiary for a consideration have been held to be 'conveyances on sale' ... There are other stamp duty cases dealing with such family arrangements where the opposite conclusion has been reached ... In those circumstances I do not myself get much help from the cases under the Stamp Act 1891.

One returns to what the county court judge said was the root question: Would the ordinary and reasonable person call this transaction a purchase and sale of the house? I think he would not. He would call it a domestic arrangement between members of a family for the division of their mother's estate in a manner which did justice to all of them. The landlord, if asked how she got the house would, I think, instinctively reply: 'I got it as my share under my mother's will, although I had to get my brothers and sister to agree, and I made adjusting payments so as to achieve fairness'. I think that is the true view, and that the learned county court judge was therefore entitled to rule as he did on the preliminary point ...

Counsel for the tenant then contended that greater hardship would be caused by granting than by refusing the order. On this point the judge went with great care into the relevant circumstances of both parties and decided against the contention. This is a finding of fact against which there would ordinarily be no appeal. But it has been argued that it is vitiated because the judge took into account in favour of the landlord evidence which he should have ignored. This was evidence given on her behalf by Dr William Gooddy, a well-known neurologist. He said that the landlord's failure to obtain possession of the house in the proceedings which she brought in 1968 had worried and depressed her ever since; that in consequence she has not been able to keep up with her teaching work, despite her high qualifications. He gave an instance of her failure to complete the marking of certain Cambridge University examination papers; and eventually expressed his opinion thus:

'I am quite sure that her preoccupation with the situation which I have outlined is having an adverse effect on her health. I do not say that the situation is necessarily entirely responsible for her present state of health; but in a person of her age and background, who might any way suffer from severe depression, her housing problem is damaging her to a serious degree medically. For these reasons, I am quite sure that [the landlord] is undergoing great hardship on medical grounds. Her general health will, in my opinion, deteriorate quite rapidly, if she is unable to obtain possession of her property. I feel it is most important for the future welfare of this conscientious and valuable teacher that, if her case is reconsidered in a county court, this medical point should be considered when assessing the degrees of hardship likely to be experienced by the contending parties.'

Counsel for the tenant then said that, if this sort of evidence is to be admitted, where is the line to be drawn? Is it to be contended, for example, that a bad loser will suffer hardship whereas a good loser will not? Is a party to be allowed to say: 'If I lose this case all sorts of things may happen to my state of mind which will cause me hardship?' I recognize the danger that evidence may be given on these lines which could be without real weight, or even be spurious; but the trial judge will normally, I think, be able to recognize truth as distinct from falsehood or exaggeration. In the present case, where it was proved that the health of one of the parties was already suffering, and that her health was likely to deteriorate rapidly if possession were refused,

I can see no reason whatever why the judge should not have taken this evidence into account, even though such deterioration had its origin in mental suffering.

In my opinion, therefore, this appeal fails and should be dismissed.

In *Rowe* v. *Truelove* (1977) 241 E.G. 535, the Court of Appeal held that a landlord who sought to regain possession of a flat so that he could sell it and thereby get out of financial difficulties could not do so under Case 9. See too *Cumming* v. *Danson* [1942] 2 All E.R. 653 (C.A.) where Lord Greene M.R. remarked that it was not just hardship to the tenant that was to be considered, but also to all those who were living with the tenant.

Case 10

Where the court is satisfied that the rent charged by the tenant –

    (*a*) for any sublet part of the dwelling-house which is a dwelling-house let on a protected tenancy or subject to a statutory tenancy is or was in excess of the maximum rent for the time being recoverable for that part, having regard to Part II or, as the case may be Part III of this Act, or

    (*b*) for any sublet part of the dwelling-house which is subject to a restricted contract is or was in excess of the maximum (if any) which it is lawful for the lessor, within the meaning of Part V of this Act to require or receive having regard to the provisions of that Part.

See too Rent Act 1977, s. 139 (above, p. 89).

D The mandatory grounds

Schedule 15, Part II sets out the mandatory grounds on which a court must order possession. Note the reduction in the discretion allowed to the court regarding the postponement of the date for giving up of possession in such cases (Housing Act 1980, s. 89; above, p. 417). The County Court Rules Committee is also actively considering amendments to County Court Rules Order 26 Part II which if adopted should help to speed up the time taken to deal with cases under Part II. 'Relevant date' is further defined in Schedule 15, Part II, para. 2.

Case 11 (as amended)

Where a person who occupied the dwelling-house as his residence (in this Case referred to as 'the owner-occupier') let it on a regulated tenancy and –

    (*a*) not later than the relevant date the landlord gave notice in writing

to the tenant that possession might be recovered under this Case,
and

(b) the dwelling-house has not, since –

(i) 22nd March 1973, in the case of a tenancy which became
a regulated tenancy by virtue of section 14 of the Counter-Inflation
Act 1973;
(ii) 14th August 1974, in the case of a regulated furnished
tenancy; or
(iii) 8th December 1965, in the case of any other tenancy,

been let by the owner-occupier on a protected tenancy with respect
to which the condition mentioned in paragraph (a) above was not
satisfied, and

(c) the court is of the opinion that of the conditions set out in Part V
of this Schedule one of those in paragraphs (a) and (c) to (f) is
satisfied.

If the court is of the opinion that, notwithstanding that the condition in
paragraph (a) or (b) above is not complied with, it is just and equitable to
make an order for possession of the dwelling-house, the court may dispense
with the requirements of either or both of those paragraphs, as the case may
require...

(Part V of Sched. 15 is set out below, p. 456.) In *Kennealy* v. *Dunne*
[1977] 1 Q.B. 837, the landlords had a residence in Hayling Island,
and access to their daughter's flat in London. They sought possession
of the flat that had been let under Case 11. For the tenants, it was
argued that the word 'required' must mean 'reasonably' required.
STEPHENSON L.J., having analysed Case 11 and compared it with
Case 9, said:

That leads me to the inescapable conclusion that 'required' in *Case* [11]
does not mean 'reasonably' required: it means no more than bona fide wanted
and genuinely intended to be occupied as a residence at once, or at any rate
within a reasonable time, but so wanted and intended whether reasonably
or unreasonably, even from the landlord's point of view.
There is force in counsel for the landlords' submission that the purpose
of *Case* [11] is that a landlord who is living in his own house should be free
to take up a post in another part of the country or abroad and let his home
to a tenant, secure in the knowledge that when the job is finished and he
wants to return home he can, on giving the proper notice, come back and
resume life in his own home, without being confronted with all the difficulties
which a landlord who seeks possession under *Case* [9] has to overcome. If

that is the purpose of *Case* [11], it explains the apparently deliberate omission of the qualifying adverb 'reasonably'.

I agree with the way the matter is put in *Megarry on The Rent Acts*. Dealing with 'Unrestricted Grounds for Possession' and 'Required', the author says (1967, p. 309):

'In each case the word "required" is used, without being prefixed by "reasonably" the dwelling-house must be "required" as a residence for the owner-occupier, or for occupation by a minister of religion, or for occupation by an agricultural employee. Though "required" is ambiguous, the absence of any qualifying adverb removes most of the difficulty. It appears that all that the landlord need establish is that he genuinely (and not merely colourably) seeks possession in order to use the dwelling-house for the stated purpose; and if he does this it seems to be immaterial that other and more reasonable courses of action are open to him. In short, the issue is merely whether the requirement is genuine, not whether it is reasonable; and sometimes the genuine may be far from reasonable.'

For these reasons, the learned judge was in my opinion wrong in saying that 'requires' means more than 'wants' and more than bona fide 'intention', and in saying that there was 'something objective as well'. There is nothing more objective about this provision than that it must be a genuine requirement and there must be a present intention; and, if the landlord proves that, he is entitled to possession under *Case* [11].

Browne and Megaw L.JJ. agreed.

Tilling v. *Whiteman* [1979] 1 All E.R. 737 (H.L.)

LORD WILBERFORCE: The appellant, Mrs Tilling, owns a small house in Canterbury jointly with Miss Dossett. She claims to have been in occupation of it immediately before 19th February 1975. On that date the joint owners let it to the respondent, Miss Whiteman, for two years. The tenancy agreement contained a clause whereby Miss Whiteman agreed to yield up the premises at the end of the tenancy. There was a statement, signed by the joint owners, addressed to Miss Whiteman that under the Rent Acts 1968 and 1974 '. . . the Landlord [sic] may recover possession of the premises under the provisions of Case 10' [now Case 11].

Miss Whiteman did not yield up possession as she had agreed, so the owners brought proceedings in the Canterbury County Court for possession and other relief . . .

Case [11], and s [98] of the [1977] Act on which it is based, say nothing about joint owners, or joint occupiers. To read, or not to read, the singular expressions 'person' and 'landlord' as including the plural, gives rise to difficulties, as the judgments below well demonstrate. In my opinion our task must be to attribute that reasonably admissible meaning to the language which will best carry out what appears to be the legislative intention.

The two alternative views are clearly and forcefully set out in the judgments of the Court of Appeal. The first is that, for an order for possession to be made, the house must be required for the residence of both co-owners. This commended itself to Stephenson and Shaw LJJ. There is no doubt that a powerful case can be made for it on the language used, and some further support may be derived from the Court of Appeal decision in *McIntyre* v. *Hardcastle* ([1948] 2 K.B. 82), decided on what became Case [9] in the same schedule.

The second alternative is that there is no such requirement, and that each of the three conditions stated in Case [11] are on the agreed or assumed facts satisfied in the present case. First, Mrs Tilling occupied the dwelling-house as her residence. Secondly, she let it on a regulated tenancy. Third, she requires it as a residence for herself. On these facts, the court must make an order for possession. This was the opinion of Eveleigh LJ.

My Lords, I propose to do little more than to say that, having to the best of my ability compared the weight of these rival arguments, and having carefully considered Miss Whiteman's printed case, I have come to the conclusion that on balance, the judgment of Eveleigh LJ is to be preferred. The arguments in its favour are so clearly stated in his judgment that nothing would be gained, and something might be lost, by my restating them in my own language. I will only add two observations.

First, the purpose of this piece of legislation, added to the bulky corpus of rent legislation in 1965, was to induce occupiers of dwelling-houses, who for some temporary reason desired, or had, to reside elsewhere for a time, to make their premises available for letting to others, on the basis that on their return they would be able, without dispute, to regain possession. The emphasis is on occupation: the person concerned must have occupied the dwelling-house as his residence, and must require it as his residence, or that of a member of his family who resided with him when he last resided there. As compared with this emphasis on occupation and residence, ownership plays a subsidiary part. It enters into the matter only because of the inherent fact that the dwelling-house is let, and letting is effected by a landlord. But Case [11], and the policy behind it, is not, if I may personalise, interested in the landlord: he is not, as such, the key figure: that is the 'owner-occupier'. This consideration, to my mind, provides justification for avoiding a strict interpretation of the words 'let it on a regulated tenancy', the words which mainly, if not wholly, support the argument that one of two or more joint owners cannot satisfy the Case unless they both also require to reside in the house. I find it therefore possible to say that Mrs Tilling, being at the time the occupier, when she decided to go to live elsewhere for a time, let her house on a regulated tenancy, even though, for the letting to be effective,

Miss Dossett had to join in. This interpretation might, to a conveyancer, appear loose, but it is one which might easily appear in common parlance. For the reasons I have given I do not think that the strict conveyancing meaning is intended to be imposed.

Secondly, as regards *McIntyre* v. *Hardcastle* the wording in Case [9] ... [indicates that there is an] identity between the person who has let the house and the person who requires it. There must then be great strength in the argument that if for one purpose the plural is deemed to be included in the singular, so it must for the other: plural landlords must require the house for themselves, not for one of them. This was the argument accepted by the Court of Appeal in *McIntyre*'s case. But assuming the correctness of this (and I agree that the question remains open in this House), the argument under Case [11] is different. There is no imposed identity between occupier and landlord: there may be a plurality of landlords, but only one occupier, and it may be possible to say that one of these landlords has let. I find therefore no necessity, or indeed attraction, in following the earlier case ...

Lords Diplock, Salmon, Scarman and Fraser of Tullybelton delivered concurring judgments.

Under the Rent (County Court Proceedings) (Case 11) Rules 1979, a special procedure for dealing with Case 11 cases was created, designed to speed up such hearings. If changes in the County Court Rules Ord. 26 Part II (currently under discussion) are brought into effect, this special procedure will be subsumed under the new Rules.

Case 12 (as amended)

Where the landlord (in this Case referred to as 'the owner') intends to occupy the dwelling-house as his residence at such time as he might retire from regular employment and has let it on a regulated tenancy before he has so retired and –

    (*a*) not later than the relevant date the landlord gave notice in writing to the tenant that possession might be recovered under this Case; and

    (*b*) the dwelling-house has not, since 14th August 1974, been let by the owner on a protected tenancy with respect to which the condition mentioned in paragraph (*a*) above was not satisfied; and

    (*c*) the court is of the opinion that of the conditions set out in Part V of this Schedule [below, p. 456] one of those conditions in paragraphs (*b*) to (*e*) is satisfied.

If the court is of the opinion that, notwithstanding that the condition in paragraph (*a*) or (*b*) above is not complied with, it is just and equitable to make an order for possession of the dwelling-house, the court may dispense with the requirements of either or both of those paragraphs, as the case may require.

Farrand (1978) suggests this was introduced in 1974 'somewhat sentimentally'. The problems of interpretation he identified were not the subject of any reported litigation. Possible explanations are, either that landlords who acquired property under this head have not yet retired; or that the head is simply not well known. The new wording is, no doubt, intended to be simpler. (See generally, Karn, 1977.)

Case 13

Where the dwelling-house is let under a tenancy for a term of years certain not exceeding 8 months and –

(a) not later than the relevant date the landlord gave notice in writing to the tenant that possession might be recovered under this Case; and

(b) the dwelling-house was, at some time within the period of 12 months ending on the relevant date, occupied under a right to occupy it for a holiday.

For the purposes of this Case a tenancy shall be treated as being for a term of years certain notwithstanding that it is liable to determination by re-entry or on the happening of any event other than the giving of notice by the landlord to determine the term.

This Case is the converse of the rules relating to holiday lets (above, pp. 197–202). The very real hardships that families who take 'winter lets' can suffer are discussed by Burrows (1979, p. 42). In particular, some local authorities have refused to accept those who have been evicted as homeless, arguing that they are 'intentionally homeless' (see below, p. 492).

Case 14

Where the dwelling-house is let under a tenancy for a term of years certain not exceeding 12 months and –

(a) not later than the relevant date the landlord gave notice in writing to the tenant that possession might be recovered under this Case; and

(b) at some time within the period of 12 months ending on the relevant date, the dwelling-house was subject to such a tenancy as is referred to in section 8 (1) of this Act.

For the purposes of this Case a tenancy shall be treated as being for a term of years certain notwithstanding that it is liable to determination by re-entry or on the happening of any event other than the giving of notice by the landlord to determine the term.

This is designed to allow specified educational institutions (see above, p. 194) to let accommodation to non-students during the vacations without giving security of tenure.

Case 15 deals with ministers of religion.

Cases 16–18 deal with various aspects of agricultural tenancies (cf. now Rent (Agriculture) Act 1976, below, pp. 462–3).

Case 19 (introduced by Housing Act 1980, s. 55)

Where the dwelling-house was let under a protected short hold tenancy (or is treated under section 55 of the Housing Act 1980 as having been so let) and –

(*a*) there either has been no grant of a further tenancy of the dwelling-house since the end of the protected shorthold tenancy or, if there was such a grant, it was to a person who immediately before the grant was in possession of the dwelling-house as a protected or statutory tenant; and

(*b*) the proceedings for possession were commenced after appropriate notice by the landlord to the tenant and not later than 3 months after the expiry of the notice.

A notice is appropriate for this Case if –

(i) it is in writing and states that proceedings for possession under this Case may be brought after its expiry; and

(ii) it expires not earlier than 3 months after it is served nor, if, when it is served, the tenancy is a periodic tenancy, before that periodic tenancy could be brought to an end by a notice to quit served by the landlord on the same day;

(iii) it is served—

(*a*) in the period of three months immediately preceding the date on which the protected shorthold tenancy comes to an end; or

(*b*) if that date has passed, in the period of three months immediately preceding any anniversary of that date; and

(iv) in a case where a previous notice has been served by the landlord on the tenant in respect of the dwelling-house, and that notice was an appropriate notice, it is served not earlier than 3 months after the expiry of the previous notice.

Housing Act 1980 s. 55(2) further provides: If, in proceedings for possession under Case 19 set out above, the court is of opinion that, notwithstanding that the condition of paragraph (*b*) or (*c*) of section 52 (1) above is not satisfied, it is just and equitable to make an order for possession, it may treat the tenancy under which the dwelling-house was let as a protected shorthold tenancy.

For the basic definition of shorthold tenancy, see above, pp. 205–6. Note also, under Housing Act 1980, s. 53, a specific right is given to tenants to terminate their shorthold tenancies prematurely: on one month's notice if the term is for two years or less; three months if more than two years. Tenants are entitled to exercise this right without penalty or other disability.

Case 20. A new case relating to lettings by servicemen has been introduced by Housing Act 1980, s. 67.

4. Restricted contracts

These used to be referable to Rent Tribunals who had power to postpone any notice to quit. (See 1st edition of this book, pp. 330–34.) This jurisdiction has been abolished except for contracts entered into before the coming into force of Housing Act 1980, s. 69. The courts are given a special jurisdiction to decide such cases under Rent Act 1977, s. 106A (introduced by Housing Act 1980, s. 69(2)):

106A.—(1) This section applies to any dwelling–house which is the subject of a restricted contract entered into after the commencement of section 69 of the Housing Act 1980.

(2) On the making of an order for possession of such a dwelling-house, or at any time before the execution of such an order, the court may –

(a) stay or suspend execution of the order, or
(b) postpone the date of possession

for such period or periods as, subject to subsection (3) below, the court thinks fit.

(3) Where a court makes an order for possession of such a dwelling-house, the giving up of possession shall not be postponed (whether by the order of any variation, suspension or stay of execution) to a date later than 3 months after the making of the order.

(4) On any such stay, suspension or postponement as is referred to in subsection (2) above, the court shall, unless it considers that to do so would cause exceptional hardship to the lessee or would otherwise be unreasonable, impose conditions with regard to payment by the lessee of arrears of rent (if any) and rent or payments in respect of occupation after termination of the tenancy (mesne profits) and may impose such other conditions as it thinks fit.

(5) Subsection (6) below applies in any case where –

(a) proceedings are brought for possession of such a dwelling-house;
(b) the lessee's spouse or former spouse, having rights of occupation under the Matrimonial Homes Act 1967, is then in occupation of the dwelling-house; and

(*c*) the restricted contract is terminated as a result of those proceedings.

(6) In any case to which this subsection applies, the spouse or former spouse shall, so long as he or she remains in occupation, have the same rights in relation to, or in connection with, any such stay, suspension or postponement as is referred to in subsection (2) above, as he or she would have if those rights of occupation were not affected by the termination of the restricted contract.

5. Shorthold tenancies

See above, pp. 205–6 and 439–40.

6. Assured tenancies

For definition, see p. 204 (above). As regards security of tenure, Landlord and Tenant Act 1954, Part II is made to apply to them (with some important modifications: Housing Act 1980, s. 58 and Schedule 5). An outline follows.

7. Security of tenure under Landlord and Tenant Act 1954, Part II

The security of tenure provisions for business tenancies (and now, also, for assured tenancies) differ in fundamental respects from the Rent Act protections described above. Two principal differences may be noted: first, the tenant himself has to take procedural steps within certain time limits to protect his position; second, the grounds on which a landlord may seek to repossess are somewhat wider. A question that is sometimes raised is whether this regime would be suitable for residential tenancies. What do you think? Would ordinary residential tenants be able to cope with the prescribed procedures?

The main features of the law are as follows (for full details, see, e.g., Woodfall, 1978, ch. 22):

(i) There must be a true tenancy (cf. above, p. 43, and chapter 3).

(ii) Under s. 24 (1), a tenancy within the scope of the Act continues until brought to an end by a special statutory notice issued by the landlord under s. 25; or by a notice issued by the tenant under s. 26 seeking a new tenancy; or by a notice to quit issued by the tenant; or by forfeiture; or by surrender (see above, p. 405).

A contractual tenancy brought to an end by any other means (e.g. effluxion of time) continues under the terms of s. 24. However, unlike the Rent Act statutory tenancy, which is a mere 'personal privilege' (above, p. 55), a continuation tenancy under the Landlord and Tenant Act 1954 is a full estate in land which may therefore be assigned (if the terms of the lease so permit) and, in the event of breach of covenant, is subject to forfeiture.

(iii) The landlord's notice, under s. 25 must, to be valid, together with certain other rules:

(a) state a date for the termination of the tenancy;

(b) be in the prescribed form;

(c) require the tenant, within two months after the giving of the notice, to notify the landlord in writing whether or not, at the date of termination, the tenant will be willing to give up possession;

(d) state whether the landlord will oppose an application for a new tenancy under Part II of the Act, and if so, on what grounds, mentioned in s. 30, he would do so. (This section is vital, since these are the only grounds the landlord is permitted to advance at any court hearing.)

(iv) The tenant *must* respond within two months and indicate he is *unwilling* to give up the tenancy; otherwise he cannot apply for a new tenancy (s. 29(2)).

(v) Certain tenants are entitled, of their own volition, to request a new tenancy under s. 26. If they do so, a landlord cannot issue a notice under s. 25. If they do not, or are not entitled to, they can still apply for a new tenancy under s. 29.

(vi) Applications for a new tenancy must be made not less than two nor more than four months after the s. 25 notice or the s. 26 request has been issued (s. 29(3)). The court will be the county court where the rateable value is less than £5,000; transfer to the High Court is in the discretion of the High Court.

(vii) The landlord may oppose a new tenancy on the following grounds (s. 30(1)):

(a) where under the current tenancy the tenant has any obligations as respects the repair and maintenance of the holding, that the tenant ought not to be granted a new tenancy in view of the state of repair of the holding, being a state resulting from the tenant's failure to comply with the said obligations;

(*b*) that the tenant ought not to be granted a new tenancy in view of his persistent delay in paying rent which has become due;

(*c*) that the tenant ought not to be granted a new tenancy in view of other substantial breaches by him of his obligations under the current tenancy, or for any other reason connected with the tenant's use or management of the holding;

(*d*) that the landlord has offered and is willing to provide or secure the provision of alternative accommodation for the tenant, that the terms on which the alternative accommodation is available are reasonable having regard to the terms of the current tenancy and to all other relevant circumstances, and that the accommodation and the time at which it will be available are suitable for the tenant's requirements (including the requirement to preserve goodwill) having regard to the nature and class of his business and to the situation and extent of, and facilities afforded by, the holding;

(*e*) where the current tenancy was created by the sub-letting of part only of the property comprised in a superior tenancy and the landlord is the owner of an interest in reversion expectant on the termination of that superior tenancy, that the aggregate of the rents reasonably obtainable on separate lettings of the holding and the remainder of that property would be substantially less than the rent reasonably obtainable on a letting of that property as a whole, that on the termination of the current tenancy the landlord requires possession of the holding for the purpose of letting or otherwise disposing of the said property as a whole, and that in view thereof the tenant ought not to be granted a new tenancy;

(*f*) that on the termination of the current tenancy the landlord intends to demolish or reconstruct the premises comprised in the holding or a substantial part of those premises or to carry out substantial work of construction on the holding or part thereof and that he could not reasonably do so without obtaining possession of the holding;

(*g*) subject as hereinafter provided, that on the termination of the current tenancy the landlord intends to occupy the holding for the purposes, or partly for the purposes, of a business to be carried on by him therein, or as his residence.

It will be noted that some of these grounds differ substantially from Rent Act grounds.

(viii) The court may dismiss the application (s. 31) or make an order for a new tenancy (s. 29(1)). Sections 32 to 35 define what is to be the property let, the duration, rent and other terms, in the absence of agreement between the landlord and the tenant.

(ix) In certain cases where a new tenancy is refused, compensation is payable to the tenant (s. 37) ; compensation for improvements may also be payable (ss. 47–50 and Landlord and Tenant Act 1927, s. 1).

(x) Contracting out of these provisions is not usually permitted, unless the court agrees (s. 38).

8. Prohibition of eviction without due process of law : tenancies not statutorily protected

Protection from Eviction Act, s. 3 (as amended by Housing Act 1980, s. 69(1)) and Schedule 25:

3.—(1) Where any premises have been let as a dwelling under a tenancy which is not a statutorily protected tenancy and –

    (*a*) the tenancy (in this section referred to as the former tenancy) has come to an end, but

    (*b*) the occupier continues to reside in the premises or part of them,

it shall not be lawful for the owner to enforce against the occupier, otherwise than by proceedings in the court, his right to recover possession of the premises.

(2) In this section 'the occupier', in relation to any premises, means any person lawfully residing in the premises or part of them at the termination of the former tenancy.

(2A) Subsections (1) and (2) above apply in relation to any restricted contract (within the meaning of the Rent Act 1977) which –

    (*a*) creates a licence; and

    (*b*) is entered into after the commencement of section 69 of the Housing Act 1980;

as they apply in relation to a restricted contract which creates a tenancy ...

[(3) Deals with the owner's right to recover possession on the death of the statutory tenant.]

Note

(i) This section applies to 'restricted contract licences' (see above, pp. 222–5) as well as tenancies. They are to come under the new jurisdiction of the county court created by Rent Act 1977, s. 106A (above, p. 440). Service licensees come within s. 3 because of s. 8(2) (below, p. 461). This is discussed in *Warder* v. *Cooper* (below).

(ii) By s. 3(2), the 'occupier' must be *lawfully* on the premises. What about the position of the unlawful sub-tenant? *Bolton Building Society* v. *Cobb* [1966] 1 W.L.R. 1 (C.A.) held that a tenant of a mortgagor was a lawful occupier, but only if such occupation began before the mortgage was entered into. Those who became tenants after the mortgage was executed were covered by the prohibition against letting contained in all properly drawn mortgages and thus were not 'lawful occupiers'. Pettit argues (1978, p. 229) that this principle should extend to all unlawful sub-tenants (see above, p. 90; also see the unsatisfactorily reported case of *Maley* v. *Fearn* [1946] 2 All E.R. 583 (C.A.); and *Fleming* v. *House* (1972) 224 E.G. 2020 (Ch. D.)).

(iii) Failure to observe these rules is a criminal offence (see unlawful eviction, below, p. 448).

(iv) Breach of s. 3 may also give rise to civil liability in tort. See *Warder* v. *Cooper* [1970] Ch. 495:

STAMP J.: Coopers Garages (Aldermaston) Ltd has a garage and filling station business on the Bath Road at Beenham, in Berkshire. The property, which includes a bungalow, is let on a lease to the company and the lease contains an unqualified covenant against underletting. The bungalow was erected so that it might be used to house a garage employee. The garage is rather isolated and it is difficult to get employees unless accommodation can be offered. The defendant, Denis Roy Cooper, has authority to grant, on behalf of the company, a licence to occupy the bungalow to persons employed in the garage business, but he says that neither he nor the company has any permission from the landlord to create a tenancy in respect of the bungalow.

Towards the end of September 1969 the defendant, who is the managing director and the majority shareholder of the company, acting on behalf of the company, engaged the first plaintiff as foreman. It is the defendant's evidence that he told the first plaintiff that the bungalow would be available for the first plaintiff while he was working for the defendant. The defendant was desperate for a foreman and took on the first plaintiff without a reference.

The terms of the employment are recorded in a document dated 15th October 1969, which states:

'TERMS OF EMPLOYMENT. HOURS. Monday to Friday, 8 a.m. to 5.30 p.m. Lunch hour 1 p.m. to 2 p.m. Saturdays. 8 a.m. to 1 p.m. Wages. £25. per week, overtime above the hours stated, 12/6 per hour. Bungalow. Rent free, whilst employed. Holidays. Two weeks paid holiday a year with the normal bank holidays. Notice. Two weeks notice to be served either way.'

In the meantime, the first plaintiff had commenced his duties and had moved himself, his wife, the second plaintiff, his family and his furniture into the bungalow. Shortly before 19th November, the defendant gave the first plaintiff oral notice to terminate employment on Friday, 5th December. On 19th

November, the company gave the first plaintiff a written notice, which, for the purposes of this motion, I must take to have been in these terms:

'Dear Sir, With reference to our conversation of last week wherein it was promised that you would get Notice to Quit we herein give you this notice. After a month's trial we have decided that you are unsatisfactory. As per our agreement you have two weeks' notice to date from 21st November 1969. We also remind you that the bungalow is to be vacant on December 5th 1969.'

5th December, the day on which the notice expired, was a Friday. On that day, the first plaintiff and his family left the bungalow and remained away until the following Monday evening. The defendant asserts that he had grounds which he specifies, for thinking that the first plaintiff had left permanently. But his goods and furniture were still there. At some time prior to the evening of Monday, 8th December, the defendant changed the locks on the bungalow and moved some of the first plaintiff's furniture into the garage. When, on 8th December, in the evening, the first plaintiff returned to the bungalow, he could not get in. He asks for an injunction designed to secure access to the bungalow.

The first plaintiff puts forward three grounds on which he claims such an injunction. First, he urges that he became, and is, a statutory tenant of the bungalow and that, therefore, no valid notice to quit has been served. Given the premise, no doubt the conclusion follows. The first plaintiff has not, however, in my judgment, made out a prima facie case that his occupation was occupation as a tenant. The fact that no rent was specified to be payable, that the landlord could not, without breaking his covenant in the lease under which he held the bungalow, sublet the bungalow, and that the employment was liable to be determined on two weeks' notice, suggests that it may turn out otherwise at the trial that the occupation was under a licence rather than as a tenant...

However, in view of s. 8(2) he was deemed to be a tenant for the purposes of protection under s. 3.

Counsel for the defendant invited me to find, for the purposes of this motion, that before the lock on the bungalow was changed the first plaintiff had ceased to reside in the premises, so that s. [3 (1) (b)] was not satisfied. But the first plaintiff was unquestionably resident at the bungalow on 5th December. He did not remove his furniture, and on the facts at present before the court, again it may turn out otherwise at the trial, I can only find that the first plaintiff has made out a prima facie case of residence at the time of his exclusion. The fact that the lock was changed suggests that the defendant did not think that residence had ceased.

On the facts before me, I therefore find that, in locking the first plaintiff out, the defendant was in breach of s. [3] (1) of the [Protection from Eviction

Act 1977]. Ought I then to grant the injunction sought? Counsel for the defendant, pointing to the fact that s. [3] does not confer any rights on the first plaintiff – not even a right to remain in occupation – urged that an injunction ought not to be granted. Much reliance was placed by the first plaintiff on the recent decision of the Court of Appeal in *Luganda* v. *Service Hotels Ltd* ([1969] 2 Ch. 209). The plaintiff in that case, who was, as the court held, entitled to six months' security of tenure under the Act, was locked out of his residence by the landlord and obtained an injunction against the landlord to give him access. But, as counsel for the defendant pointed out, the distinction between that case and this is that in that case the Rent Act 1968 conferred a right to six months' security of tenure[1] whereas there is nothing like that conferred by s. [3]. And, indeed, Edmund Davies LJ, in holding the plaintiff entitled to the injunction which he sought, pointed to this right to remain in the premises for six months and distinguished the case from *Thompson* v. *Park* ([1944] K.B. 408), where the Court of Appeal held that where a licence to use certain premises had been wrongfully revoked the licensee could be restrained from entering on or using the premises and must content himself with a claim for damages for breach of contract. In *Thompson* v. *Park*, the expelled party, having no interest in the land, was, after revocation of the licence, a trespasser, whereas in the *Luganda* case he was not; so tested, the present case falls within *Thompson* v. *Park* and outside *Luganda* v. *Service Hotels Ltd*. But I distinguish *Thompson* v. *Park* from the present case on another ground. There, what the owner of the land was assumed to have done was to break the terms of the licence under which the defendant claimed to use it – a mere breach of contract – whereas here, what the defendant has done is to infringe the terms of an Act and so committed a tort. For although s. [3] conferred on the first plaintiff no proprietary interest in the bungalow, the breach of its terms by the defendant was, in my judgment, a tort. The first plaintiff was clearly one of the class of persons whom the section was intended to protect, the injury – the evidence is that the first plaintiff is homeless – is of the kind that the section is intended to prevent and it is the breach of the statutory duty which is causing the damage to the first plaintiff.

However much sympathy I may feel for a defendant who has taken on a servant whom he finds unsatisfactory and cannot really recover the accommodation required for another employee who is to replace him, I feel bound to grant the injunction sought. The intention of Parliament that possession of premises occupied by a person in the position of the first plaintiff, may not be obtained except by proceedings in the court, is clear from s. [3]. The first plaintiff is entitled to the benefit of the section. If the court were to refuse the injunction, leaving the first plaintiff to a remedy to damages for the tort, it would be allowing just the mischief which the section was designed to

1. This right to protection from the rent tribunal has now been abolished; see above, p. 440.

prevent. If the matter had come before the court on a threat by the defendant to lock out the first plaintiff, I entertain no doubt that an injunction would have been granted. And to quote Lord Denning M.R. in the *Luganda* case, 'They should not be in a better position by wrongfully locking him out'.

9. Unlawful eviction and harassment

If any person attempts to circumvent the protections described above he may be liable under the Protection from Eviction Act 1977, s. 1:

1.—(1) In this section 'residential occupier', in relation to any premises, means a person occupying the premises as a residence, whether under a contract or by virtue of any enactment or rule of law giving him the right to remain in occupation or restricting the right of any other person to recover possession of the premises.

(2) If any person unlawfully deprives the residential occupier of any premises of his occupation of the premises or any part thereof, or attempts to do so, he shall be guilty of an offence unless he proves that he believed, and had reasonable cause to believe, that the residential occupier had ceased to reside in the premises.

(3) If any person with intent to cause the residential occupier of any premises –

(a) to give up the occupation of the premises or any part thereof; or
(b) to refrain from exercising any right or pursuing any remedy in respect of the premises or part thereof;

does acts calculated to interfere with the peace or comfort of the residential occupier or members of his household, or persistently withdraws or withholds services reasonably required for the occupation of the premises as a residence, he shall be guilty of an offence.

(4) A person guilty of an offence under this section shall be liable –

(a) on summary conviction, to a fine not exceeding £400 or to imprisonment for a term not exceeding 6 months or to both;
(b) on conviction on indictment, to a fine or to imprisonment for a term not exceeding 2 years or to both.

(5) Nothing in this section shall be taken to prejudice any liability or remedy to which a person guilty of an offence thereunder may be subject in civil proceedings.

[(6) Deals with the liability of corporate landlords.]

Note

(i) The concept of 'residential occupier' is considerably wider than 'tenant'. In certain circumstances a trespasser may be a 'residential occupier' because the Criminal Law Act 1977, s. 7 restricts the rights of owners to recover possession of their premises. Licensees who are not protected by Protection from Eviction Act, 1977, s. 8(2) (below, p. 461) or s. 3(2A) (above, p. 444) will be 'residential occupiers' during the period of the licence; but after a licence has been properly ended (above, p. 149) the licensee becomes a trespasser (*R.* v. *Blankley* [1979] Crim. L.R. 166) and is thus unprotected subject to the limited protection afforded to trespassers. Statutory tenants protected by the Rent Act are covered (Rent Act 1977, s. 98, above, p. 417), as are tenants outside the Rent Acts (Protection from Eviction Act 1977, s. 3, above, p. 444). Deserted spouses may be protected by the 'rule of law' contained in the Matrimonial Homes Act 1967, s. 1. (For further discussion, see Arden & Partington, 1980, ch. 5.)

(ii) The offences can be committed in relation to 'premises', which have been held to be wider than 'dwelling' (Rent Act 1977, s. 1, above, p. 158). It thus includes a caravan which, though not attached to the ground, had been static for ten years and could not easily be towed away (*Norton* v. *Knowles* [1969] 1 Q.B. 572). One room was sufficient to constitute premises in *Thurrock U.D.C.* v. *Shina* (1972) 23 P.&C.R. 205.

(iii) The facts that constitute unlawful eviction or 'acts calculated to interfere . . .' or persistent withdrawal or withholding of services will obviously vary widely. (For examples, see Arden & Partington (1980), p. 65.)

(iv) The average penalties imposed under s. 1(4) have been derisory; indeed the numbers of prosecutions have been very small, as Table 8.3 shows.

Table 8.3 *Prosecutions for harassment and illegal evictions in England and Wales, 1973–5*

	Prosecutions		Convictions		% success rate		Average fine (£)		Sentences of imprisonment (months)		Average length of sentence (months)	
	H	IE	H	IE	H	IE	H	IE	H	IE	H	IE
73	206	172	132	109	64	64	N/A	N/A	6	–	6	–
74	100	92	59	56	59	61	63	39	0	0	–	–
75	124	158	53	98	43	62	53	71	0	8	–	5

=Harassment. IE=Illegal Eviction.
urce: (1973–1975) Parliamentary Question, March 1977.

Notwithstanding these figures, there have been occasions when severe sentences have been imposed, e.g. *R.* v. *Bokhari* (1974) 59 Cr.App.R. 303 (two years' imprisonment, £1,600 compensation, and £400 costs; see Atiyah (1979)).

Police practice in such cases was discussed by the Francis Committee (Francis, 1971, ch. 14):

In England and Wales before the passing of the Protection from Eviction Act 1964 and the Rent Act 1965, police responsibilities in disputes between landlord and tenant were confined to preventing breaches of the peace. In investigating allegations of offences under Part III of the 1965 Act the police are faced with some difficulties. These difficulties are broadly as follows:

(*a*) Eviction – A residential occupier is protected but not a trespasser or a person with no valid right to remain in occupation. A constable on the spot is in obvious difficulty in distinguishing between these categories or dealing with a situation in which the intricacies of sub-tenancy agreements are involved.

(*b*) Harassment – Allegations that there may have been acts calculated to interfere with the peace and comfort of a residential occupier, or a persistent withdrawal of services take time to investigate and a constable is in no position to take immediate action.

The police have no power to arrest for offences under the Rent Act. Even if the legal situation between the parties were to be clearly established a constable cannot take any person into custody; he can only make a report on the case.

The police, therefore, act as follows when complaints are made to them (apart from any action that might be necessary to prevent or deal with a breach of the peace):

(*a*) if called to the scene of a dispute between landlord and tenant, or if there are allegations of unlawful eviction or harassment, the police make such investigations as are possible on the spot;

(*b*) where it appears from these investigations that there may have been, or may be, a breach of the Act the investigating officer warns the landlord about the provisions of Part III and about the possibility of prosecution;

(*c*) whether or not such a warning is issued, a full report of the incident is sent to the local authority;

(*d*) in appropriate cases, the police inform the complainant in writing that the complaint has been passed to the local authority.

The forms of activity that come under this head were discussed by the National Citizens' Advice Bureaux Council, who noted the following problems:

Harassment

Except in cases of actual or threatened violence or cutting off essential supplies it is extremely difficult to prove harassment in the sense that it is behaviour deliberately designed to cause the tenant to give up his tenancy. Bureaux receive many complaints about so-called harassment but say that in some cases the behaviour referred to may be the result of people's differing standards. Some bureaux say that it is sometimes no more than the irritation caused by people having to live in multi-occupation of accommodation not originally designed for that purpose. The stories of the two parties to the event are often so different that it would be difficult to determine who is more to blame – landlord or tenant. Noise is frequently mentioned as harassment and this may vary from noisy parties to noisy children but except in the most blatant cases (as in an example quoted of a landlord who, when his tenants appealed to the rent tribunal and were given six months security of tenure, used abusive language and stamped on the floor of his bedroom to keep them awake at night) it is very difficult to judge whether this is deliberate harassment. Apparently valid examples of harassment quoted by one bureau include:

> tenant bolted out (temporarily)
> essential services being turned off
> landlord assaulting tenant with knives
> landlord taking up floor boards every weekend on pretext of doing
>   electric wiring
> taking slates off the roof to let the rain in
> throwing petrol bombs through the letter box

Harassment is not however confined to acts by the landlord against the tenant. There are some quite horrifying stories reported of tenants harassing landlords particularly if they are elderly or women on their own. As this is not an offence against the Rent Act the only remedy for the landlord is to seek possession through the county courts and it is in these situations that fear of court procedures and their slowness as well as the need for special provisions for people letting rooms in their own home is emphasized.

Illegal eviction

There is some evidence that this does take place. Several bureaux state that it is more likely to happen in connection with furnished accommodation than unfurnished because it is easier to pack up the belongings of a tenant of furnished accommodation and to lock him out.

Although it is clear that in some cases the action is a deliberate flouting of the law, there is a good deal of experience that ignorance of the requirements of the law is the root cause. Bureaux say that ignorance is particularly acute amongst small landlords. There are particular areas of difficulty where the landlords and tenants are immigrants unaccustomed to the law of this country. Many an immigrant buys a house with a sitting tenant and is genuinely surprised when he finds he cannot evict him.

(See also House of Commons Expenditure Committee (1972–3) which, *inter alia*, discussed the relationship between harassment and improvement (or 'gentrification'): and Caplan (1975).)

Much of the 'enforcement' is undertaken by local authority Tenancy Relations Officers who tend to prefer to conciliate between parties rather than initiate prosecutions. (As many TROs are ex-policemen, they may be aware of the hazards of prosecution.)

(v) For many years it was assumed that s. 1(5) created a separate tort of unlawful eviction (e.g. *dicta* of Sachs L.J. in *Mafo* v. *Adams* [1970] 1 Q.B. at 557; and J. Smith (1974)). However, in *McCall* v. *Abelesz* [1976] 2 W.L.R. 151, an unanimous Court of Appeal held that this was not so. Thus, someone who has been unlawfully evicted or harassed and who wishes to take civil proceedings has to fit the facts into a recognized head or tort law or breach of contract. While this will often be easy, it will not necessarily be so. (See further next section.) Compare the interpretation of s. 3 in *Warder* v. *Cooper* (above).

10. Civil proceedings

The primary objective of most civil proceedings in cases in this area is to obtain an injunction from the court ordering the landlord to put the 'residential occupier' back into the premises. Many law centres and advice agencies are now very adept at the procedures for doing this, and may obtain injunctions within a very short space of time.

The principal causes of action that will be utilized are:

(i) Breach of the covenant for quiet enjoyment.

Like other covenants, e.g. to repair, this covenant may be an express covenant. But if the lease/tenancy agreement does not mention it, then the common law will still *imply* it into a true landlord–tenant relationship. If it is so implied, it is an absolute covenant; the landlord is absolutely bound by it. The basic idea is that the landlord must not disturb the tenant's possession either legally or physically. The tenant must usually suffer physical interference with his enjoyment of the property; it does not in fact cover a landlord who simply annoys a tenant, e.g. by making a noise. (See *Perera* v. *Vandiyar* [1953] 1 W.L.R. 672; *Kenny* v. *Preen* [1963] 1 Q.B. 499 (C.A.).)

(ii) Breach of Protection from Eviction Act 1977, s. 3 (*Warder* v. *Cooper* above).

(iii) Trespass to land.

(iv) Assault and battery : trespass to the person.

(v) Trespass to goods.

(vi) Nuisance.

Despite the attempt to keep criminal law proceedings separate from civil law proceedings, in practice they have become somewhat muddled. Besides *R.* v. *Bokhari* (above), see *Jennison* v. *Baker* [1972] 2 Q.B. 52, in which the Court of Appeal confirmed that county court judges had power to commit to prison for contempt of court a landlady who flagrantly broke an injunction not to break her implied covenant of quiet enjoyment.

A further example arises from the fact that, in addition to obtaining an injunction, a plaintiff in a civil action may also be able to obtain damages. An important distinction between actions in contract and actions in tort is that, in the latter only, it may be possible to seek exemplary damages. In *Cassell* v. *Broome* [1972] A.C. at 1079, Lord Hailsham made this remark about the application of exemplary damages to harassment and eviction:

> How ... about the late Mr Rachman, who is alleged to have used hired bullies to intimidate statutory tenants by violence or threats of violence into giving up vacant possession of their residences and so placing a valuable asset in the hands of the landlord? My answer must be that if this is not a cynical calculation of profit and cold-blooded disregard of a plaintiff's rights, I do not know what is ...

In *Drane* v. *Evangelou* [1978] 2 All E.R. 437,

> LORD DENNING M.R. said: Mr George Evangelou is the owner of a leasehold house, 172a Bowes Road, New Southgate. He let a maisonette in it to a young man, Mr Anthony Malcolm Drane, who lived there with a woman, Ann Watts, not his wife, but who lived with him as if she was his wife. The maisonette was let to them furnished at a rent of £25 a week inclusive of rates from 31st August 1974.
>
> On 11th July 1975 the tenant, Mr Drane, applied to the rent officer for a revision of the rent. This annoyed the landlord, Mr Evangelou, greatly. So on 21st August 1975 the landlord gave the tenant notice to quit. That was not effective because the tenant was protected by statute from eviction. On 8th October 1975 the rent officer fixed the rent and adjudged it be £16 a week exclusive.
>
> Six days later, on 14th October, the landlord behaved atrociously. He

waited until the young couple were out, when the tenant had taken Ann Watts to college in the morning, and then got three men to invade the maisonette. The judge described what the tenant found on his return:

'When he came back a little later, I think at 9.30, there he found that a large Greek Cypriot was barring the entrance; all his belongings had been put outside in the backyard; the lock of the door had been hammered in; the door was bolted on the inside; about four to five people were inside his premises and two women among them ... some of their belongings were broken and books were damaged.'

The tenant called the police. They told Mrs Evangelou, the landlord's wife, that she was committing an offence and that it would be reported to the town hall. Nevertheless she did not let the tenants back into their maisonette. They had to go and stay with friends. They stored some of their belongings in their friends' garage, and slept on the living room floor of their friends' house.

The tenant went to the county court and asked for an injunction so that he and Ann Watts could be restored to their premises. The judge on 31st October 1975 granted an injunction against the landlord. But the landlord did not obey it. He had moved his wife's father and mother into the maisonette. The landlord or his in-laws appealed to this court. This court heard the appeal on 27th November 1975 and rejected it. Lawton L.J., giving the judgment of the court, said:

'I am surprised that this appeal has been made to this court. The defendant's behaviour was reprehensible ... it is right and just that the plaintiff should be put back where he is entitled to be ... this court should take every step it can to see that landlords who behave like the defendant in this case has behaved should get no benefit whatsoever from what they have done.'

So the appeal was dismissed on 27th November 1975. Still the landlord did not go out. The tenant had to apply again for an injunction to the county court on 19th December 1975. The landlord and his in-laws were ordered to leave by 6 pm on Saturday, 21st December. They gave the tenant a key, but it did not fit. So he could not get in. On 23rd December the tenant applied to commit them for contempt. That at least brought results. The in-laws left. It was only then, on 23rd December, that the in-laws and the landlord went out. The tenant had been kept out for ten weeks. The tenant eventually moved in on 1st January 1976. He found everything dirty and damaged and went on with his action for damages. He was awarded exemplary damages in the sum of £1,000.

Now there is an appeal to this court ... Counsel for the landlord submitted that it was not open to the judge to award exemplary damages. He has taken us through Lord Devlin's judgment in *Rookes* v. *Barnard* [[1964] A.C. 1129]. He said that the general principle nowadays is that in a civil action damages are awarded by way of compensation for damage actually done or for any aggravation by way of injured feelings of the plaintiff; but the court cannot in the ordinary way award punitive damages over and above that which is compensation: because punishment is the prerogative of the criminal courts and should have no place in the civil courts.

Lord Devlin acknowledged that there are some categories of tort in which exemplary damages may still be awarded. This case seems to me to come within the second category. Lord Devlin said (at 1227):

> 'This category is not confined to moneymaking in the strict sense. It extends to cases in which the defendant is seeking to gain at the expense of the plaintiff some object, – perhaps some property which he covets, – which either he could not obtain at all or not obtain except at a price greater than he wants to put down. Exemplary damages can properly be awarded whenever it is necessary to teach a wrongdoer that tort does not pay.'

To my mind this category includes cases of unlawful eviction of a tenant. The landlord seeks to gain possession at the expense of the tenant, so as to keep or get a rent higher than that awarded by the rent tribunal, or to get possession from a tenant who is protected by the Rent Acts. So he resorts to harassing tactics. Such conduct can be punished now by the criminal law. But it can also be punished by the civil law by an award of exemplary damages...

11. Summary proceedings for possession

In 1970 the High Court was faced with the problem of how to deal with squatters. (For background to the rise in squatting in the 1960s, see Bailey, 1973 and 1977; Kinghan, 1977.) A new summary procedure was created by Rules of the Supreme Court Order 113. It is available:

1. Where a person claims possession of land which he alleges is occupied solely by a person or persons (not being a tenant or tenants holding over after the termination of the tenancy) who entered into or remained in occupation without his licence or consent or that of any predecessor in title of his, the proceedings may be brought by originating summons in accordance with the provisions of this Order.

An identical jurisdiction was created for the county court in Order 26, Part I.

Although initially intended to be used against trespassers, it has been successfully used against licensees whose licence has been withdrawn (*Bristol Corporation* v. *Persons Unknown* [1974] 1 W.L.R. 365; *G.L.C.* v. *Jenkins* [1975] 1 W.L.R. 155 (C.A.)); and against unlawful sub-tenants (*Moore Properties (Ilford)* v. *McKeon* [1976] 1 W.L.R. 1278 (above, p. 91)). In *Department of Environment* v. *James* [1972] 3 All E.R. 629, it was held that R.S.C. Order 113 did not permit a court to suspend a possession order made under Order 113, unless the plaintiff consented. This was confirmed by the Court of Appeal in *McPhail* v. *Persons, Names Unknown* [1973] Ch. 447. The same position was held to exist under the county court jurisdiction in *Swordheath Properties Ltd* v. *Floydd* [1978] 1 All E.R. 721 (C.A.). (For criticism of these developments, see Griffith, 1978, pp. 120–21.)

Proposals to amend Order 26 are currently before the County Court Rules Committee which if adopted would restrict the operation of Order 26, Part I to those who entered property as trespassers only. Ex-licensees would thus be dealt with under the speedier but non-summary procedure which would be found in Order 26, Part II.

Appendix: Rent Act 1977, Sched. 15, Part V, para. 2; introduced by Housing Act 1980:

   2. The conditions referred to in paragraph (*c*) in each of Cases 11 and 12 are that—

   (*a*) the dwelling-house is required as a residence for the owner or any member of his family who resided with the owner when he last occupied the dwelling-house as a residence;

   (*b*) the owner has retired from regular employment and requires the dwelling-house as a residence;

   (*c*) the owner has died and the dwelling-house is required as a residence for a member of his family who was residing with him at the time of his death;

   (*d*) the owner has died and the dwelling-house is required by a successor in title as his residence or for the purpose of disposing of it with vacant possession;

   (*e*) the dwelling-house is subject to a mortgage, made by deed and granted before the tenancy, and the mortgagee—

         (i) is entitled to exercise a power of sale conferred on him by the mortgage or by section 101 of the Law of Property Act 1925; and

         (ii) requires the dwelling-house for the purpose of disposing of it with vacant possession in exercise of that power; and

   (*f*) the dwelling-house is not reasonably suitable to the needs of the owner, having regard to his place of work, and he requires it for the purpose of disposing of it with vacant possession and of using the proceeds of that disposal in acquiring, as his residence, a dwelling-house which is more suitable to those needs."

9
Miscellaneous Occupational Groupings

Introduction

Discussion of the landlord–tenant relationship has been held, so far, largely in the context of the most obvious categories of residential occupation. Here we look briefly at three additional areas where there are signs that pressure may grow for changes in the law. In none of these cases will the details of the existing law be discussed; there is insufficient space for that. However, attention will be drawn to points of interest. And, in so far as in each of these topics there is pressure for changes in the law, it does offer an indication of the continuing reliance many people place on using law as a means of social reform. The topics discussed are: tied accommodation; mobile homes; and gypsies.

1. Tied accommodation

A surprisingly large number of people still live in tied accommodation. This section discusses the important, but frequently neglected, legal points relating to their accommodation. It does not deal with the potential employment protection aspects of such cases, save to remind readers that complex questions of labour law may be involved as well. (See, generally, Hepple & O'Higgins, 1979.) In this section we first look at the most recent estimates of numbers in tied accommodation; then turn to the distinction between service tenants and service occupiers (licensees) and the special statutory provisions that apply to each category; briefly discuss the Rent (Agriculture) Act 1976; and finally mention other proposals for reform that have recently been made.

A Estimates of numbers in tied accommodation

Table 1.3 (above, p. 14) estimates there is a total of 700,000 people in tied accommodation which represents 25% of the total private rented sector in England and Wales at the end of 1976. Table 1.5 (above, p. 16) estimates the figure for England only at the end of 1977 as 481,000, or 20% of the total renting privately. Put another way, tied accommodation, as the *General Household Survey 1977* (1979, p. 26, Table 3.1) shows, represents 3% of the total of households. (This represents a decline from 5% of households being in tied accommodation in 1971.) The same survey (*ibid.*, pp. 26 ff) now gives a considerable amount of detail about the characteristics of this group, the nature of the accommodation occupied, and so forth. What the *GHS* does not do to give any guide as to the extent of tied accommodation in particular industries. Unofficial estimates have now been provided by Ramsey (1979, Appendix 1) who suggests (somewhat out of line with the totals given above) that some 404,000 are public sector employees (including the armed services, school caretakers, priests, etc.) and a further 353,000 are private sector employees (including hotel staff, retail staff, and agricultural workers). The details of these figures are not too important for present purposes. What is important is to draw attention to the existence of this not insubstantial minority. (See now also Schifferes, 1980b.)

B Legal position of tied employees

Leaving aside, for the moment, agricultural workers, the legal position of tied employees and the extent of any protection they are afforded under the Rent Acts depends on the question already discussed of the distinction between the lease and the licence (above, chapter 3). However, in the case of tied employees, the distinction between the existence of a tenancy and a mere licence will not depend simply on the nature of the accommodation and the circumstances in which it was let, but also on the nature of the employment. The question was rather confusingly discussed by Denning L.J. in *Torbett* v. *Faulkner* [1952] 2 T.L.R. 659.

DENNING L.J.: In 1948 the plaintiff, Mr Torbett, having won £8,000 in a football pool, was minded to form a company to carry on business. He needed someone to help him in it, and to this end he came into touch with the defendant, Mr Faulkner. Mr Faulkner was then living in a council house at Pontypridd, whereas the new business was to be at Cardiff. Mr Faulkner agreed to work for the new company if a house were found for him at Cardiff. Mr Torbett told him to look for one, and told him the house would be provided by the company. Mr Faulkner found a house of the value of £2,500 or thereabouts. It was bought by Mr Torbett in his own name, and at Christmas, 1948, Mr Faulkner was let into occupation of it. The company was formed on 24 January 1949, and as from that date Mr Faulkner was paid by the company a salary of £12 a week less 30s. deduction for the house, and Mr Faulkner paid the rates on the house. There is no evidence that Mr Faulkner paid any rent for the house for the three or four weeks he was in occupation before the company was formed. After some six months or so, the company got into difficulties, and eventually on 19 November 1949, Mr Faulkner left the employment of his own accord and took another job. He said he would leave the house but he did not do so because he did not find other accommodation. The company afterwards went into liquidation and Mr Torbett sought possession of the house. Mr Faulkner claimed the protection of the Rent Restrictions Acts. The issue depends on whether Mr Faulkner was a tenant or only a licensee. If he was a tenant, he is protected by the Acts. If he was only a licensee, he is not protected.

This question – whether a man is a tenant or a licensee – is continually arising nowadays. There have been several cases in this Court quite recently on it. The impact of the Rent Acts has had a marked effect on the law on the matter. Previously the holding of a servant was classified either as a service occupation or as a service tenancy. There was no third category. But nowadays it is recognized that there is an intermediate position. He may be a licensee. A service occupation is, in truth, only one form of licence. It is a particular kind of licence whereby a servant is required to live in the house in order the better to do his work. But it is now settled that there are other kinds of licence which a servant may have. A servant may in some circumstances be a licensee even though he is not required to live in the house, but is only permitted to do so because of its convenience for his work – see *Ford* v. *Langford* (1949) 65 T.L.R. 138 *per* Lord Justice Asquith, and *Webb Ltd* v. *Webb* unreported – and even though he pays the rates, *Gorham Contractors Ltd* v. *Field* (1952) C.P.L. 266, and even though he has exclusive possession, *Cobb* v. *Lane* [1952] 1 All E.R. 1199. If a servant is given a personal privilege to stay in a house for the greater convenience of his work, and it is treated as part and parcel of his remuneration, then he is a licensee, even though the value of the house is quantified in money; but if he is given an interest in the land, separate and distinct from his contract of service, at a sum properly to be regarded as a rent, then he is a tenant, and none the less a tenant because he is also a servant. The distinction depends on the truth of the relationship and not on the label which the parties choose to put upon it; see *Facchini* v. *Bryson* [1952] 1 T.L.R. 1368. The distinction is essentially one for the county court Judge, with which this Court will not interfere unless he has misdirected himself or there are no reasonable grounds for his decision . . .

In this case I think the Judge has found in effect that Mr Faulkner was a licensee, and I see no reason for disturbing his decision. He uses a somewhat ambiguous phrase that it was 'not an ordinary tenancy', but I think he meant that Mr Faulkner had only a personal privilege to stay in the house, and was not a tenant at all. The house was bought specially for him to live in to be near his work and it was part and parcel of his remuneration, being quantified at 30s. a week.

Apart from this finding, I would point out that Mr Faulkner seems to have occupied the house under an agreement with the company and not with Mr Torbett personally. Now, the company had no estate or interest in the land at all. It had nothing out of which it could carve a tenancy. It was in this respect in the same position as a requisitioning authority. It could only grant a licence and not a tenancy. This is another reason for holding Mr Faulkner to be a licensee only.

In these circumstances, I think that the appeal fails.

Comment. First, is there really a 'third category' as Denning L.J. suggests? Are not service occupiers simply licensees?[1] Secondly, how is one actually able to distinguish between the 'personal privilege' and the 'interest in land'? Is this not another example of the judges using imposing language in an apparently principled way in order, in fact, to reserve a very broad discretion to decide cases as they see fit? Ramsey (1979, p. 3) suggests that since this decision it has been virtually impossible for service employees to show they have tenancies as opposed to licences. See too, *Mathew* v. *Bobbins* (1980) *The Times*, 21 June.

C Service tenants

Assuming that an occupier has been classified as a service tenant, he may then be a fully protected tenant, or a restricted tenant under the Rent Act; this will depend on all the usual tests. (See *Crane* v. *Morris* [1965] 1 W.L.R. 1104 (C.A.).) One particular problem that may occur is whether, if the accommodation is rent free, but his wages or salary have been reduced, he is a tenant paying rent for the purposes of Rent Act 1977, s. 5(1) (see above, p. 176). In the case of service tenants, within the Rent Acts, there is nonetheless a special discretionary ground on which a landlord may seek possession (Rent Act 1977, Schedule 15, Case 8):

Where the dwelling-house is reasonably required by the landlord for occupation as a residence for some person engaged in his wholetime

1. Pettit (1978, pp. 12–13) attempts, somewhat half-heartedly, to sustain the threefold classification; cf. Cutting (1979, p. 174).

employment, or in the whole-time employment of some tenant from him or with whom, conditional on housing being provided, a contract for such employment has been entered into, and the tenant was in the employment of the landlord or a former landlord, and the dwelling-house was let to him in consequence of that employment and he has ceased to be in that employment.

It will be appreciated that there are a number of conditions that must be satisfied before this case can be used. The employment must be 'whole-time'; the original letting must have been 'in consequence of that employment'. (See further Pettit (1978, pp. 202–4); and *Fuggle* v. *Gadsden* [1948] 2 K.B. 236 (C.A.).) The court also has a special power to award compensation to a tenant against whom a possession order has been made, if the landlord obtained the order by misrepresentation or the concealment of material facts; there is no power of reinstatement, however (Rent Act 1977, s. 102).

Special cases

(*i*) Tenancies of pubs fall wholly outside the Rent Act (Rent Act 1977, s. 11; Landlord and Tenant Act 1954, Part II, s. 43(1) (*d*); Housing Act 1980, Sched. 3, para. 10).

(*ii*) Parsonages of the Church of England are subject to the Pluralities Act 1838. In the case of other religions, clergy have, effectively, no security of tenure (Rent Act 1977, Schedule 15, Case 15) though they could take advantage of other Rent Act protections.

(*iii*) Under the Housing Act 1980, many local authority employees remain without the statutory security of tenure granted to other public sector tenants.

D Service occupants

Assuming that service occupants are to be regarded as licensees, they will for the most part have no Rent Act protection unless they are 'restricted licensees' (see above, p. 221). However the Protection from Eviction Act 1977 (s. 8(2)) provides that: 'For the purposes of Part I of this Act a person who, under the terms of his employment, had exclusive possession of any premises other than as a tenant shall be deemed to have been a tenant...' Thus, service licensees can only be lawfully evicted after a court has ordered possession, since they fall within Protection from Eviction Act 1977, s. 3 (above, p. 444).

As we have seen (*Warder* v. *Cooper*, above, pp. 445–8) failure to obtain the requisite court order is a tort.

E Rent (Agriculture) Act 1976

The agricultural tied cottage has long been a highly emotive political issue.[2] The lengthy struggle between the National Union of Agricultural and Allied Workers and the farmers' and landowners' lobby was reflected right to the end during the stormy passage of the bill through Parliament (Newby, 1977b). A number of points about it may be briefly made.

The first is that the Act does not abolish the tied cottage system (Hennah, 1979). What it provides is that, before any farmer can turn a worker, protected by the Act, out of his house, in circumstances where he needs the house for another worker, proper steps must be taken to get the original worker rehoused. The primary responsibility for rehousing is placed on local authorities. It is not an absolute duty but a duty to 'use their best endeavours' (Rent (Agriculture) Act 1976, s. 28(7)), a reflection, perhaps, of the frequent scarcity of council housing in rural areas. Furthermore this duty arises only where the evicting farmer can show that the authority should provide housing 'in the interests of efficient agriculture' (*ibid.*, s. 27(1)(c)) and if there is urgent need (*ibid.*, s. 28(3)). Advice on these questions may be sought from a new, very informal tribunal, the Agricultural Dwelling House Advisory Committee (*ibid.*, s. 29). In 1977, employers requested alternative accommodation in 1,180 cases; a housing duty was accepted by local authorities in 925 cases. 710 (69%) of the cases were referred to ADHACs; in only 60 was agricultural need not found (*Housing and Construction Statistics No. 26* (1978), Table XXXVII).

In cases where there is no question of repossession on grounds of agricultural efficiency, workers are given protections similar to those contained in the Rent Acts. There is a right to get a fair rent registered (*ibid.*, ss. 13–16); pending registration, rents may be agreed between farmer and worker but must be limited to 1.5 times the rateable value of the dwelling house (*ibid.*, s. 12). Security of tenure is also granted (*ibid.*, s. 6 and Schedule 4), so that possession can only be ordered by a court on the basis of a similar mix of discretionary and mandatory grounds as those in the main Rent Act.

Finally, one notable feature of the legislation is that its provisions

2. The literature is cited and reviewed in Newby (1977a and b).

apply to all relevant occupation situations, i.e. licences as well as tenancies (*ibid.*, s. 1 and Schedule 2; see above, p. 151).

F Further reform proposals

In view of the apparent success of this legislation, it seems highly likely that more extensive protections for other groups of tied employees will be sought. The Labour Party (1979) has already put out a discussion paper; and so has Ramsey, for the Centre for Environmental Studies (1979). His argument is based on an analysis of 224 cases involving tied employees that came to the SHELTER Housing Aid Centre in 1978. Useful information is provided about the difficulties tied employees face, including insecurity of tenure for the majority of tied employees; unreasonable work levels being demanded by employers of their tied employees by threatening them with the loss of their accommodation; low wages, and the inability of tied employees to question the amount charged for their accommodation; unfair dismissal from a job can be challenged, but the loss of accommodation that accompanies it cannot; and compensation for unfair dismissal or redundancy is not also awarded for loss of tied accommodation; it is difficult for a tied employee to change his job without first finding alternative accommodation; older employees and those nearing retirement age in particular find it difficult to cope with the loss of both their job and their accommodation; tied employees who resign, either voluntarily or under pressure, are most commonly classed as intentionally homeless by local authorities, who will refuse to rehouse them; a tied employee's relationship with his employer is complicated by the additional relationship of tenant to landlord, and disagreements either at work or over the accommodation can threaten the employee with loss of both; furthermore, occupiers of tied accommodation are not entitled to rent rebates or allowances.

In light of these issues Ramsey argues that policy changes are needed to give tied employees security of tenure under the Rent Acts; to extend the priority groups under the Housing (Homeless Persons) Act; to amend the Employment Protection Act to give additional compensation for loss of tied accommodation; and to discourage employers, and particularly public employers, from using tied housing to meet what is basically a housing rather than an employment need.

2. Mobile homes

Mobile homes, usually factory-built, single-storey dwellings installed on a concrete slab and connected to mains electricity and water and sewage systems, and thus not in fact movable, are used as a relatively cheap form of accommodation by many people (Bird & O'Dell, 1977). They are particularly attractive to small households, especially the retired, younger people on low incomes, and single people (DoE Circular 12/78, para. 6). (See, generally, Arden & Parish, 1979.)

Since 1968 (Caravan Sites Act 1968) persons who have been granted a licence or contract entitling them to station on a caravan site a caravan which they occupy as a permanent residence have had limited legal protections as against the owner of the caravan site. They must be given four weeks notice to quit (*ibid.*, s. 2); they must not be unlawfully evicted or harassed, and it is a criminal offence for any person to do this (*ibid.*, s. 3; discussed in *Hooper* v. *Eaglestone* (1977) 34 P.&C.R. 311); and a county court is given a broad discretion to suspend any eviction order for up to twelve months (*ibid.*, s. 4).

The Mobile Homes Act 1975 extended these protections by providing, broadly speaking, that where the owner of a caravan site proposes to permit someone to station a mobile home[3] on that site or to take over a home already on the site, and before that person moves in he notifies the owner of his intention to occupy the home as his only or main residence, it is the statutory duty of the site owner to enter into a written agreement with the prospective occupier (*ibid.*, s. 1). The agreement is to run for at least five years (*ibid.*, s. 2(1)), which may be extended by up to another three years, unless the site owner only has a shorter interest in the site. The terms of the agreement must satisfy the requirements of s. 3. The county court is given a wide discretion to review the terms of such agreements (s. 4). The scope of these sections was discussed in *Taylor* v. *Calvert* [1978] 1 W.L.R. 899; *Grant* v. *Allen* [1980] 1 All E.R. 720 (C.A.).

There is some evidence that these provisions are not working. Furthermore, because of the wording of the legislation, the Act of 1975 only applies to those who already own their mobile home, and are merely seeking a site on which to station it. It does not apply to those who rent their mobile home. Thus in 1978, an Official Review of the legislation recommended a strengthening of the law. Instead

3. For the purposes of the legislation, 'mobile home' and 'caravan' are treated synonymously: Mobile Homes Act 1975, s. 9.

of revising the system of agreements just discussed, they recommended that a set of implied terms should be imposed by statute on all residential contracts covering the right to occupancy, maintenance obligations, undertakings about payments, quiet enjoyment, access, assignment of the contract, resale rights and the reasonableness of charges. No action has so far been taken on this recommendation.

3. Gypsies

Part II of the Caravan Sites Act 1968 imposed a broad duty on local authorities 'to provide adequate accommodation for gypsies residing in or resorting to their area' (*ibid.*, s. 6(1) and see s. 7). This was intended to be done by ensuring that a sufficient number of permanent sites and pitches were available on which gypsies could install their caravans. Six and a half years after the Act came into force it was reported (Cripps, 1977) that provision existed for only one-quarter of the estimated total number of gypsy families with no site of their own. (The total estimate was 8,000–9,000 families containing approximately 40,000 persons (Cripps, para. 319; for a more general discussion see Adams *et al.*, 1975).)

In response to the Cripps report, the government offered larger grants to assist local authorities with the capital costs of equipping sites with basic facilities (DoE Circular 11/79). The extent to which these grants have been utilized is not yet clear. However, it may be noted that this is yet another example of the difficulty of ensuring that legal duties imposed on local authorities, which involve politically very sensitive issues, are enforced.

10
Local Authorities and Housing Associations

Introductory note : the structure of the chapter

In this chapter, I wish to discuss the role of 'social landlords' and the law that regulates them. It has been a difficult task deciding how to structure this chapter, for there are many differences between local authority tenancies and housing association tenancies. Yet, since the enactment of the Housing Act 1980, much of the law governs both types.

The solution that has been adopted is that in Part One there is discussion of specific issues realting to local authority housing; in Part Two there is a brief discussion of the same issues as they relate to housing association housing; in Part Three, the common statutory law is presented.

Part One : Local Authority Housing

Introduction

The fundamental difficulties of providing accommodation for the very poor through the medium of the private sector of the housing market led to the development of policies whereby housing was provided directly by local authorities (Housing Policy (1977) (1) ch. 1 and (3) ch. 8; Merrett (1979)). Growth in this sector of the housing market is revealed in Tables 1.1 and 1.2 (above, pp. 11, 12)

The continued growth of this sector of the housing market is now, however, a matter of considerable controversy. For a number of years there have been cutbacks in the levels of finance available for new housing; the state of repair of much public sector housing is a matter of considerable concern; slum clearance policies together with re-development have largely been abandoned; the improvement pro-gramme is argued to be inadequate; and the more recent introduction of the right of council tenants to buy a council house are all issues which have raised considerable doubts as to the future of this sector of the housing market. While these issues will not be pursued in detail, it is nonetheless important to be aware of the general political and economic climate in which local authority housing policies are being carried out; for these policies will have considerable impact on the availability of council housing, and on the conditions in which council tenants live.

From a legal point of view, one of the most dramatic changes in the area of landlord–tenant law in the last three or four years has been the speed with which council tenancies have become the subject of legal regulation. From a position where there was relatively little law, save for basic common law principles (cf. Hoath (1978)), and the assumption was that local authorities were model landlords who ran their affairs in a benevolently paternalistic way, the situation is now changed, with important new laws relating to duties to house the homeless and grant security of tenure. An important question to ask is: why has this happened?

At first glance it might be thought that those changes in the law are the result of numerous campaigns against the alleged injustices of social policy being administered on the basis of discretion, which, it is said, leads to arbitrary decision-taking, undesirable levels of power in the hands of officials, and so on. (See, generally, Davis (1971) and CDP (1977a, ch. 6).) This has led to a movement arguing for more carefully defined legal 'rights' with standards and procedures being laid down on a national rather than local basis. On this interpretation, it is likely that many individual tenants will be able to take advantage of the new laws, though the extent to which this law is utilized will clearly depend on additional factors such as the quality of local advice agencies and the willingness of authorities to respond to this new legal framework.

However, what is the importance of the political and economic con-text in which these changes have occurred? As already noted, these legal developments have been introduced during periods of restraints and cutback in public expenditure on public sector housing. Although local authorities have long asserted the right to local control over their housing provision (Griffith, 1966, ch. 4), central government has equally been anxious to reduce levels of local autonomy, particularly in relation to housing finance, so that it has greater control over the level of resources that are devoted to council housing. Seen in this light, may not the measures contained in Part 1 of the Housing Act 1980 (relating to sale of council housing and the establishment of security of tenure for local authority tenants), combined with the legal duties towards the homeless created in 1977, be as much to do with these struggles between central and local government as with concern for the creation of rights for individual tenants?

Indeed, may it not be plausible to argue that these changes in the law may be seen as a rather cheap policy substitute for the more expensive task of providing adequate resources for the building of new homes and for the renovation and improvement of existing ones? If that view is taken, apparently radical changes in legal form may be nothing, or not much more than a diversionary tactic drawing attention away from the severe restrictions that governments have imposed on the scope of housing policy. (See, e.g., CDP (1976).)

1. Local housing authorities and their administration

Local housing authorities vary greatly in size and structure. In London, under the London Government Act 1963, both the Greater London Council and the individual London boroughs shared housing responsibilities. The exact demarcation is a matter of negotiation, shifts in policy, and dispute (particularly with some of the outer London boroughs). In recent years, the G.L.C. has effectively reduced its involvement in housing provision. In the rest of England and Wales, under the Local Government Act 1972, housing is mainly the responsibility of the district councils with the county councils having only limited reserve powers.

The functions of housing departments may include house design and building; repairs and maintenance; improvement schemes; housing management and 'welfare'; control of houses in multiple occupation; provision of housing advice agencies and tenancy relations officers; and so on. The relationship between housing departments and public health departments may also be very important in practice.

Most councils will have a separate housing committee, and the administration of housing policy will be a matter for local directors of housing. But detailed administrative structures vary from authority to authority. It should be remembered that while much of the work of such departments relates to the administration of local authority housing, housing departments (and environmental health departments) also have substantial powers to regulate the private sector, particularly in relation to housing conditions (see ch. 7, above).

2. The assessment of 'housing need'

In 1969, the Central Housing Advisory Committee wrote (Cullingworth, 1969, p. 148):

> Our review of current local policies convinces us that local authorities need to have a clearer, deeper and more detailed understanding of the housing situation in their areas. The development of national housing information has had a major impact on national policy formulation. *But we no longer have a single 'national' housing problem: we have a large number of local housing problems of great variety.* It is therefore essential that local policies be based on a well-informed understanding of the problems of individual areas and the context in which they arise. Our first recommendation is, therefore, that local authorities should take steps to ensure that they are better informed of the housing situation of their areas.

> After reviewing the current statutory provisions in this connection we conclude that amending legislation is needed. The responsibilities of local housing should extend far beyond providing for the needs of those who are actually to be housed by them; they should be looking for hidden needs, for needs which are not being met elsewhere, and for needs which may arise in the future...

Despite these recommendations the law has not been substantially amended.

A Statutory provisions

(i) *Housing Act 1957, s. 91* (as amended)

It shall be the duty of every local authority to consider housing conditions in their district and the needs of the district with respect to the provision of further housing accommodation and for that purpose to review the information which has been brought to their notice, either as a result of inspections carried out under [section 70 of the Housing Act 1969] or otherwise.

(The Chronically Sick and Disabled Persons Act 1970, s. 3(1) requires authorities who act under s. 91 to have regard to the special needs of the chronically sick and disabled.)

(ii) *Housing Act 1969, s. 70* (as amended)

It shall be the duty of every local authority ... to cause an inspection of their district to be made from time to time with a view to determining what action to take in the performance of their functions under Part II or III of the (Housing) Act of 1957, Part II of the Housing Act, 1961, Part IV of the Housing Act, 1964, Part II of this Act [or Part IV of the Housing Act 1974], and for the purposes of carrying out that duty the authority and their officers shall comply with any directions the Minister may give and shall keep such records and supply him with such information as he may specify.

(iii) *Housing Act 1957, s. 76*

If it appears to a local authority that occasion has arisen for a report on over-crowding in their district, or any part thereof, ... or the Minister so directs, it shall be the duty of the authority to cause a further inspection to be made and to prepare and submit a report showing the result of the inspection and the number of new houses required to abate overcrowding in the district or the part of the district and, unless they are satisfied that the required number of new houses will be otherwise provided, to prepare and submit to the Minister proposals for the provision thereof.

(iv) *Local Government Act 1972, s. 194(6)*

The Council of a County may undertake any activity for the purposes of or incidental to establishing the needs of the whole or any part of the county with respect to the provision of housing accommodation.

The extent to which these legal duties are performed is not known. Local authority practice varies widely, depending on factors such as available resources and expertise, the nature of local housing problems, and the political complexion of the authority. Nonetheless it was somewhat surprising to read Glasgow District Council's statement that 'The Scale of Need is so great against any realistic possibility of meeting the need in the short term that a survey into the precise requirements ... is not required at the present' (*Roof*, 1979a, p. 138).

In practice, assessments of local authorities' housing needs are likely to be found in two principal sources: (*a*) the local authority waiting list; and (*b*) the housing investment programme (HIP).

Table 10.1 Persons registered on council house waiting lists, 1977

Region	Member of household registered						No one		All households
	Head of household		Other person		HoH and other person				
	'000s	%	'000s	%	'000s	%	'000s	%	
North	80	7.1	12	1.1	17	1.5	1,012	90.3	1,120
Yorkshire/Humberside	109	6.2	23	1.3	28	1.6	1,581	90.8	1,741
East Midlands	64	4.7	20	1.4	18	1.3	1,269	92.6	1,371
East Anglia	23	3.4	7	1.1	9	1.3	638	94.2	678
South East	313	5.1	65	1.0	85	1.4	5,741	92.5	6,203
Greater London	173	6.5	27	1.0	55	2.1	2,405	90.4	2,660
Rest of South East	140	4.0	38	1.1	30	0.9	3,336	94.1	3,544
South West	59	3.7	15	1.0	21	1.3	1,489	94.0	1,583
West Midlands	90	5.0	21	1.2	30	1.7	1,650	92.1	1,792
North West	111	4.8	23	1.0	23	1.0	2,179	93.3	2,336
England	848	5.0	186	1.1	232	1.4	15,558	92.5	16,824

Source: National Dwelling and Housing Survey (1978), Table 42.

B Waiting lists

There are, however, a number of problems with these lists. It is likely that many people are on them who have subsequently rehoused themselves and who no longer need council accommodation. To that extent, waiting lists may overstate the demand for council housing. Secondly, and by contrast, such lists only represent articulated demand; they do not represent a positive effort on the part of housing authorities to search out hidden housing needs. Further, some authorities impose restrictions on the housing list, for example by demanding that a person reside in the housing authority's area for a specific period before he can go on the housing list. Such rules seriously affect the value of the housing list as a measure of housing need. Again, there are possible categories of need, e.g. single people or the old, who are often not catered for by local authorities, and who therefore do not trouble to put themselves on the housing list. Waiting lists are, therefore, a somewhat crude instrument for increasing housing need. (See, generally, Watson *et al.*, 1973; Murie, 1976; Holmes, 1976; Gregory, 1975.)

C Housing investment programmes

Since 1977, levels of local authority expenditure on housing have been determined by central government in the light of Housing Investment Programmes which have been submitted by local authorities (DoE Circular 63/77; see also Crine & Wintour, 1980). HIP documentation includes a brief narrative of the authorities' general housing strategy; a fuller statistical statement on existing housing, households and population and likely changes over a four-year period; and a financial statement including expenditure proposals for the next four years.

The quality of the data submitted in HIP documents varies widely from authority to authority. Further, the fact that needs have been identified by no means results in adequate central government funding, which is dependent on overall economic strategy. Nonetheless, the intention, at least, of HIPs is to provide some indication of the extent of local housing needs. (For criticism of HIPs, and the distortions they appear to cause in relation to housing provision, see, e.g., Murie & Wintour, 1978; Paris, 1979; Stoker, 1978.)

3. Local authority housing finance : expenditure

The bulk of local authority expenditure on housing is classified as capital expenditure. Capital sums are raised in the money markets either for new building projects or for improvement schemes for existing housing (Housing Act 1974, s. 105). The income that is generated from rents, subsidies and the rates (see below) will then go to pay the charges that result from those debts. The details of these procedures need not concern us here (though see Hepworth (1978, ch. 7)). However, since raising capital will involve the local authority in borrowing large sums of money, we may note the central government's powers of veto called 'loan sanction'. Originally these powers were to ensure that local authorities only borrowed for lawful purposes. Today they are used more broadly by central government to try to ensure that local authority borrowing fits in with other aspects of official monetary and economic policies.

The central government used to use borrowing controls to ensure that new houses were up to modern standards. To qualify for loan sanction all dwellings submitted for approval had to comply with space and heating standards recommended by the Parker Morris Report *Homes for today and tomorrow* (1961). However, the link between loan sanction and housing standards has now been broken.

4. Local authority housing finance : income

As we have just noted, there are three main sources of income for local authority housing: rents, subsidies from central government, and payments from the rates. What is regarded as a 'proper' mix between those three sources has for a number of years been a matter of acute political controversy, for the general trend of government to seek to cut levels of public expenditure has resulted in a number of tactics designed to ensure that levels of rents increase, so that levels of subsidy may be reduced, or at least contained. A further issue has been the desire of government to try and ensure a broad equality of treatment between the direct subsidies provided for local authority tenants and the indirect subsidies (in the form of tax relief) payable to owner-occupiers buying with a mortgage. (See, generally, Housing Policy (2), 1977, chs. 5 and 6; Wintour, 1979; also reading cited above, p. 242.)

Table 10.2 gives an indication of levels of local authority rents.

Table 10.3 presents a broad comparison between local authority annual rent levels and private sector rent levels.

At first sight, it would appear that local authority tenants are paying rather more than those in the unfurnished private sector. However, since figures for the unfurnished private sector include *controlled*

Table 10.2   Average weekly rents of local authority dwellings, England and Wales

£

	Average weekly unrebated rents		
	Greater London	Rest of England and Wales	England and Wales
1973			
May	4.40	3.24	3.44
October	4.75	3.50	3.70
1974			
January	4.80	3.55	3.75
October	4.88	3.61	3.81
1975			
April	4.95	4.01	4.16
October	5.39	4.21	4.40
1976			
April	5.78	4.57	4.77
October	6.04	4.85	5.05
1977			
April	6.50	5.31	5.52
October	6.75	5.41	5.64
1978			
April	6.99	5.62	5.85
October	7.16	5.71	5.95

Source: Housing and Construction Statistics No. 28 (1979), Suppl. Table XIX.

rents (see above, p. 245), it is frequently argued that a more realistic comparison should be between local authority rents and 'fair rents' registered by the Rent Officer (see, e.g., Table 5.3 above, p. 277).

As regards rent levels, formally, local authorities have complete legal discretion as to the levels of rents they charge (Housing, Rents and Subsidies Act 1975). However, the Housing Act 1980, Part VI introduces a new system of housing subsidy (effective from the financial year 1981/2) which is based on the principle of deficit financing. The new subsidy will be paid on the basis of costs incurred. Subsidy will be determined by the central government taking the amount of subsidy each local authority received in the previous year (the 'base amount' (s. 98)), adding on increased costs (the 'housing costs differential' (s. 99)); and then subtracting the amount by which central government expects rents and rates to have increased (the 'local contribution differential' (s. 100)). Thus it can be seen that, by

Table 10.3   Annual rent (less rebate or allowance, excluding rates) by tenure, Great Britain, 1972–7

Households in rented accommodation*

	Tenure											
	Renting from local authority or New Town†				Renting privately, unfurnished†				Renting privately, furnished†			
	Lower quartile	Median	Upper quartile	Base	Lower quartile	Median	Upper quartile	Base	Lower quartile	Median	Upper quartile	Base
	£	£	£	No.	£	£	£	No.	£	£	£	No.
1972‡	99	137	178	3708	31	63	117	1261	142	217	332	336
1974	137	177	218	3166	52	97	185	926	217	327	500	288
1975	159	.203	248	3711	59	121	220	991	221	328	583	316
1976	187	237	288	3701	65	148	261	871	257	369	529	263
1977	211	271	326	3731	83	183	304	783	278	425	630	296

*Data for 1974–7 exclude households paying nil rent and those unable to distinguish rent rebate/allowance from rate rebate. Estimated median rents in 1972 excluding those not paying rent are: local authority £137, unfurnished £227.

† Excluding those renting with a job or business or from a housing association or co-operative.

‡ Rent before deduction of rebate/allowance.

Source: General Household Survey, 1978 (HMSO, 1979), Table 3.7.

this indirect means, local authorities are effectively being pressured at least to keep rent and rate increases of local authority tenants in line with other price increases (see s. 100(5)). Local authorities seeking to protect tenants against rent increases will have to subsidize any additional amounts from the general rate funds. Some protection for poorer tenants against the impact of rent increase is achieved by the rent rebate scheme (discussed briefly above, pp. 304–7). However, as Table 10.4 reminds us, there are always problems in ensuring adequate take-up of such means-tested benefits.

Furthermore, comparing the number of rebates granted with the total number of local authority dwellings (Table 1.1 above) it

Table 10.4   Rent rebates (England and Wales)

	Number granted (thous.)	Average weekly rebate (£)	Estimated percentage take-up
1972			
March	270	1.21	
1973			
May	700	1.99 ⎫	
December	765	2.40 ⎭	60–70
1974			
April	840	2.39 ⎫	
1975			70–75
January	820	2.42	
April	870	2.68 ⎭	
October	940	2.85 ⎫	
1976			
January	955	2.87	
April	970	3.00 ⎬	75–80
October	995	3.11	
1977			
January	990	3.15 ⎭	
April	1,000	3.31 ⎫	
October	1,005	3.32 ⎭	80–85
1978			
January	1,000	3.39	75–80
April	995	3.42	
October	985	3.40	
1979			
January	975	3.47	
April	975	3.53	

Source: Housing and Construction Statistics No. 30 (1979), Suppl. Table XXXVI.

can be seen that, for example, in 1976 the rents of some 17 per cent of tenancies are already rebated. What implications might this have for attempts to raise rent levels still further? To what extent is sensible to fix rent levels in the public sector by relating them to 'fair rents' in the private sector? Is such a policy realistic, given the data on council tenants? (see above, pp. 22–3).

5. Allocation of council tenancies

This is clearly one of the most important issues in relation to council housing. Until 1949, housing authorities were statutorily limited to providing housing for 'the working classes'. This concept had originally entered English law in the nineteenth century in legislation 'which was not primarily concerned with the supply of additional houses: but with the enforcement of minimum building codes and housing standards' (Nevitt, 1968). It was a vague and increasingly anachronistic concept, only once defined by statute. The Housing of the Working Class Act 1903, Schedule 1, para. 12(*e*) read:

> Working class includes mechanics, artisans, labourers and others working for wages; hawkers, costermongers, persons not working for wages, but working at some trade or handicraft without employing others, except members of their own family, and persons other than domestic servants whose income in any case does not exceed an average of 30/- a week, and the families of any such persons who may be residing with them.

(The 30/- limit was altered to £3 by the Housing Act 1936, Schedule II.)

After the Second World War, the concept came under attack even in the courts. Thus, in *Green and Sons* v. *Minister of Health* (*No. 2*) [1948] 1 K.B. 34, Denning L.J. remarked:

> These words 'working-classes', have appeared in a number of Acts for the last hundred years. I have no doubt that in former times it had a meaning which was reasonably well understood. 'Working-classes' fifty years ago denoted a class which included men working in the fields or the factories, in the docks or the mines, on the railways or the roads, at a weekly wage. The wages of people of that class were lower than those of most of the other members of the community, and they were looked upon as a lower class. That has all now disappeared. The social revolution in the last fifty years has made the words 'working-classes' quite inappropriate to-day. There is no such separate class as the working classes. The bank clerk or the civil servant, the school teacher or the cashier, the tradesman or the clergyman, do not earn

wages or salaries higher than the mechanic or the electrician, the fitter or the mineworker, the bricklayer or the dock labourer. Nor is there any social distinction between one or the other. No one of them is of a higher or a lower class. In my opinion, the words 'working-classes' used in the Acts are quite inappropriate to modern social conditions. Nevertheless, the words are used in an Act in 1936, and I must do my best to interpret them. 'Working-classes' there certainly include the classes of persons who, fifty years ago, would have been included in that term. They include all the persons who are, for a special purpose, mentioned in sch. XI to the Act of 1936. They include 'mechanics, artisans, labourers and others working for wages'. They include 'hawkers, costermongers and persons not working for wages, but working at some trade or handicraft without employing others'. Besides these, 'working-classes' include a larger number of other persons not specified in the schedule. That large number is left quite indefinite in the Act, and is, I suspect, incapable of definition.

More importantly the concept was becoming administratively embarrassing. Nevitt (1968, pp. 442–3) notes:

> The economic and housing situation which formed a background to the debates was an acute shortage of accommodation, the emergency requisitioning powers of local authorities and the control of all new building and conversion works by a licensing system. These policy measures effectively reduced the power of individuals to obtain vacant accommodation unless they could prove housing need. These administrative rationing arrangements made it equitable to remove the limitation on local authority housing powers and allow them to provide accommodation to all those in housing need. Another factor which may have been an important influence was the expansion of local authority employment. Many authorities complained that they were unable to appoint teachers, mid-wives and professional workers unless they could offer accommodation.

A Powers and duties of local authorities

The law which now sets out the powers of housing authorities to provide accommodation is the Housing Act 1957, s. 113(2) which lays down, in broad terms, that they 'shall secure that in the selection of their tenants a reasonable preference is given to persons who are occupying insanitary or overcrowded houses, have large families or are living under unsatisfactory conditions [and to persons towards whom they are subject to a duty under s. 4 or 5 of the Housing (Homeless Persons) Act 1977].' In addition, the provisions of the Land Compensation Act 1973 must be considered.

(i) THE LAND COMPENSATION ACT 1973, S. 39

This provides:

39.—(1) Where a person is displaced from residential accommodation on any land in consequence of –

    (*a*) the acquisition of the land by an authority possessing compulsory purchase powers;

    (*b*) the making or acceptance of a housing order, or undertaking in respect of a house or building on the land;

    (*c*) where the land has been previously acquired by an authority possessing compulsory purchase powers or appropriated by a local authority and is for the time being held by the authority for the purposes for which it was acquired or appropriated, the carrying out of [any improvement to a house or building on the land or of] redevelopment on the land;

    [(*d*) the service of an improvement notice, within the meaning of Part VIII of the Housing Act 1974, in respect of premises in which that accommodation is situated],

        and suitable alternative residential accommodation on reasonable terms is not otherwise available to that person, then, subject to the provisions of this section, it shall be the duty of the relevant authority to secure that he will be provided with such other accommodation.

There are a number of exceptions to this general position. For example, subsection 2 states that s. 39(1) shall not apply to those served with blight notices. To overcome difficulties which may arise when squatters move into empty property, s. 39(3) states: 'Subsection (1) above shall not apply to any person who is a trespasser on the land or who has been permitted to reside in any house or building on the land pending its demolition [or improvement].'

Further, s. 39(6) provides:

For the purposes of subsection (1) above a person shall not be treated as displaced in consequence of any such acquisition[, improvement] or redevelopment as is mentioned in paragraph (*a*) or (*c*) of that subsection unless he was residing in the accommodation in question–

    (*a*) in the case of land acquired under a compulsory purchase order, at the time when notice was first published of the making of the order prior to its submission for confirmation or, where the order did not require confirmation, of the preparation of the order in draft;

    (*b*) in the case of land acquired under an Act specifying the land as subject to compulsory acquisition, at the time when the provisions of the Bill for the Act specifying the land were first published;

(c) in the case of land acquired by agreement, at the time when the agreement was made;

and a person shall not be treated as displaced in consequence of any such order or undertaking as is mentioned in paragraph (b) of that subsection [or of such an improvement notice as is mentioned in paragraph (d) of that subsection] unless he was residing in the accommodation in question at the time when the order was made, the undertaking was accepted, [or the notice was served].

Section 29(7), which extends to the foregoing states:

In this section 'a housing order, or undertaking' means –

(a) a demolition, closing or clearance order under Part II or III of the Housing Act 1957, [or] section 60 of the Housing Act 1969;

(c) an undertaking accepted under section 16(4) of the said Act of 1957, [or] section 60(2) of the said Act of 1969 or [section 87 of the Housing Act 1974].

Section 40 creates a similar duty to rehouse certain caravan dwellers.

The extent of the duty was discussed in *R.* v. *Bristol Corporation ex parte Hendy* [1974] 1 All E.R. 1047:

LORD DENNING M.R.: In Bristol a Mr Hendy, his wife and two daughters, were occupying basement rooms at 164 Lower Cheltenham Place. He was a weekly tenant at some £4 a week. He had security of tenure. But it turned out that these basement rooms were quite unfit for human habitation. They could not be made fit at reasonable expense. They came within the Housing Act 1957. Accordingly, under ss 16 and 18 of the 1957 Act, the local authority were under a duty to make a closing order. On 16th October 1972 they made a closing order. That meant that the tenant had no longer any protection under the Rent Acts. The landlord was entitled to turn him out. The landlord did so. He went to the county court and got an order for possession of those basement rooms.

It is plain that when this Act came into operation Mr Hendy was displaced under a housing order. So a duty was cast on the corporation to secure that he was provided with housing accommodation . . .

At first the corporation offered temporary accommodation at a flat at 19 Mina Road, Bristol. It had two bedrooms, one living room, kitchen, bathroom and toilet. He got it all for £4.55 a week; and for that sum, he also was provided with lighting and the laundry of his bed linen. That would seem very suitable accommodation, but he or his advisers took exception to it because it was only temporary. It was called a 'short stay accommodation'.

So Mr Hendy or his advisers applied to the Divisional Court for a mandamus; but it was refused. The Divisional Court said Mr Hendy was housed already at the moment, and so they would not make an order.

Now a counsel on his behalf applies to this court. We have had the advantage of a very clear argument by her and also much help from counsel for the corporation. The corporation are anxious to know what the legal position is under this new Act; does it mean that, if a person is displaced under a housing order, he immediately goes to the top of the queue of people waiting for council houses? Does it mean that he is to be treated more favourably than other persons whom they wish to house?

The town clerk stated that this is what the corporation are prepared to do:

'The Corporation are prepared to fulfil their duty by (a) offering to the Applicant as soon as practicable a tenancy of suitable residential accommodation on the terms normally offered by the Corporation to prospective tenants and (b) lodging the Applicant and his family in temporary accommodation until a suitable dwelling house becomes available.'

Counsel for Mr Hendy suggested that that offered was not sufficient to fulfil their duty. She pointed out that the words of the statute are – 'it shall be the duty of the relevant authority to secure that he will be provided with such other accommodation'. She said that this was a higher duty than they owed to other persons on their housing list; and so Mr Hendy should be given priority over them. I cannot accept that submission. I think that the corporation fulfil their duty when they do their best, as soon as practicable, to get him other accommodation. No doubt they can take into account the fact that he has been displaced under a closing order; but it does not mean that he takes priority over everybody else in the housing list. His circumstances must be considered along with the others and a fair decision made between them.

Counsel next pointed out that Mr Hendy was previously protected by the Rent Acts, whereas in a council house he will not be protected. Counsel admitted that in practice a council house tenant has virtually as much security of tenure as a Rent Act tenant. So long as he pays his rent and fulfils the conditions of his tenancy, they will not turn him out. In these circumstances, I think that the corporation have done enough. They fulfil their duty if they let him have a council house on the terms normally offered to prospective tenants.

Counsel then mentioned the town clerk's reference to 'temporary accommodation until a suitable dwelling house becomes available'. She said that might mean that Mr Hendy might be moved every three weeks from one place to another. I do not think that there is anything in that point. If Mr Hendy does have frequent moves, that cannot be helped. The corporation have only to do the best they can until a council house is available. They do not have to go further and give Mr Hendy priority over everybody else. I think the corporation have made a very proper offer. There is no case for a mandamus. I would dismiss the application.

Stamp and Scarman L.JJ. agreed.

Comment. Compare the interpretation of this section with that of Rent Act 1977, s. 98 (above, pp. 419–24).

(ii) HOUSING (HOMELESS PERSONS) ACT 1977

This Act – a Private Member's Bill, passed in the teeth of considerable local authority opposition (see generally Partington, 1978) – is important for a number of reasons.

(*a*) It is extremely interesting as an attempt to use legal means to solve a pressing social problem, *viz.* homelessness. Some local authorities have, not without some justification, complained that the Act made no further resources for housebuilding available. It is worth considering in this context the general question of the 'limits of the law' to solve social problems.

(*b*) The resistance of some local authorities to the legislation is worthy of note and must call into question the ability of legal rules to alter administrative practices. (For critical accounts see, e.g., SHELTER, 1978; Finnis, 1978; Berry, 1979.) The effectiveness of using the courts as the principal means of enforcing the legal duties is another issue to be considered in this context.

(*c*) More generally, the Act may be seen as the culmination of an extended struggle between central government, anxious that local authorities allocate housing strictly in accordance with 'housing need', and the practice of local authorities who have frequently taken other issues into consideration, e.g. length of time on a waiting list. For example, in 1968 the Seebohm Report noted (1968, paras. 396–9):

Families in greatest need

396. In addition to a broader interpretation of their housing responsibilities we consider housing departments should pay more attention to families in greatest need. Some families are at greater risk than others of becoming homeless or grossly ill-housed; for instance, the very young family, the large family with a low income or the fatherless family. They are not numerous; for example, only 8 per cent of all households in England and Wales contain three or more children and only 2 per cent five or more. About 2 per cent of households comprise fatherless families and many of them, and many large families as well, are already adequately housed. Although the proportion of families who are particularly vulnerable is small the problem is urgent. If it is set aside by local authorities, not only may families be endangered but considerable social costs incurred to the community.

397. At present there are particular difficulties facing such families in obtaining a council house. Two are especially important. First, they tend to be

mobile (or, as with immigrants, they have been mobile) and to gravitate to areas of greatest housing need which are also generally areas with a high demand for labour. As a result they may find it difficult to get on to a housing list, or be given a low priority, because they lack residential qualifications. Second, because they are often poor, they may not be able to afford the rents of the council houses offered them.

398. We recognize that the Housing Act 1957 requires local authorities to give reasonable preference to large families, amongst other groups, when allocating houses. Successive Ministers of Housing and Local Government, endorsing recommendations of the Central Housing Advisory Committee, have also urged local authorities to look critically at allocation schemes involving residential qualifications, to introduce rent rebate schemes to assist poorer tenants, and to provide for special groups such as unmarried mothers. Nevertheless, the problem remains of vulnerable families who have little hope of getting (or, in some cases, keeping) a council house for a long time. The problem is not solved by leaving certain families to fend for themselves, or shuttle between accommodation for homeless families, 'half-way housing', unlicensed caravan sites, unsatisfactory lodgings and the streets.

399. The problem of the family which cannot really afford council housing, or which is not thought fit or qualified to have it must be faced. The present methods of subsidizing housing do not necessarily help families to obtain accommodation appropriate to their needs. The distribution of subsidies is inequitable and in large measure accidental, being based on categories of housing rather than need. Within local authorities the adoption of rent rebate arrangements can help if they are framed to give maximum benefit to the poorer tenants; we hope such schemes become more widespread.

These comments were endorsed by Cullingworth (1969). The clear implication is that not all authorities follow such principles. The Housing (Homeless Persons) Act may therefore be seen as an attempt to force local authorities to allocate on the basis of social need. Is this desirable?

The contents of the Act itself are extremely complex. The main provisions only will be discussed, together with some of the cases on the Act. (For procedures and a full summary of cases decided at the time of writing, see Arden, 1979d, 1980a & b.)

SECTION I. DEFINITION OF HOMELESS PERSON

(1) A person is homeless for the purposes of this Act if he has no accommodation, and a person is to be treated as having no accommodation for those purposes if there is no accommodation –

    (*a*) which he, together with any other person who normally resides with him as a member of his family or in circumstances in which the housing authority consider it reasonable for that person to reside with him –

(i) is entitled to occupy by virtue of an interest in it or of an order of a court, or

(ii) has, in England or Wales, an express or implied licence to occupy, or

(iii) has, in Scotland, a right or permission, or an implied right or permission to occupy, or

(b) which he (together with any such person) is occupying as a residence by virtue of any enactment or rule of law giving him the right to remain in occupation or restricting the right of any other person to recover possession of it.

(2) A person is also homeless for the purposes of this Act if he has accommodation but –

(a) he cannot secure entry to it, or

(b) it is probable that occupation of it will lead to violence from some other person residing in it or to threats of violence from some other person residing in it and likely to carry out the threats, or

(c) it consists of a movable structure, vehicle or vessel designed or adapted for human habitation and there is no place where he is entitled or permitted both to place it and to reside in it.

(3) For the purposes of this Act a person is threatened with homelessness if it is likely that he will become homeless within 28 days.

Comment. It will be seen that whether or not a person is homeless may involve complex questions relating to that person's legal status. To what extent are housing officials trained to deal with the complexities of the law? For possible meaning of the word 'family', see above, p. 211; would such interpretation be used here?

In *R.* v. *Beverley B.C., ex parte McPhee* (*The Times,* 27 October 1978; noted *LAG* Bulletin (1978) at 293) it was held by the Divisional Court that once a local authority had decided a person was homeless, the court should not interfere with such a decision.

In *R.* v. *Hillingdon L.B.C., ex parte Streeting* (*The Times,* 11 July 1980) the Court of Appeal held that any duty to house homeless persons applied to all homeless persons lawfully in this country and was not limited to those who had or had had a local connection with the area of a housing authority in Great Britain. A local authority such as Hillingdon which had London Heathrow Airport within its boundaries was thus obliged to accept anyone as homeless, wherever they came from. It was noted that Britain's very strict immigration laws and their administration would prevent such authorities from being swamped with cases.

SECTION 2 : DEFINITION OF PRIORITY NEED

(1) For the purposes of this Act a homeless person or a person threatened with homelessness has a priority need for accommodation when the housing authority are satisfied that he is within one of the following categories:—

  (*a*) he has dependent children who are residing with him or who might reasonably be expected to reside with him;

  (*b*) he is homeless or threatened with homelessness as a result of any emergency such as flood, fire or any other disaster;

  (*c*) he or any person who resides or might reasonably be expected to reside with him is vulnerable as a result of old age, mental illness or handicap or physical disability or other special reason.

(2) For the purposes of this Act a homeless person or a person threatened with homelessness who is a pregnant woman or resides or might reasonably be expected to reside with a pregnant woman has a priority need for accommodation . . .

(The Secretary of State has power to alter these categories; the power has not yet been exercised.)

THE DUTIES

Once an application has been made to a local authority, it is required to make 'appropriate inquiries' (s. 3). These are designed to satisfy the authority that the applicant is homeless, within s. 1; if he is, whether or not he has priority need (s. 2); whether or not he became homeless, or threatened with homelessness 'intentionally' (as defined in s. 17); and whether the applicant has a 'local connection' (as defined in s. 18) with another area.

Pending completion of inquiries, local authorities are under a duty to house those who appear to be homeless and have a priority need (s. 3(4)). The consequences of breaching this duty were discussed in *Thornton* v. *Kirklees M.B.C.* [1979] 3 W.L.R. 1 (C.A.). Although seeking an administrative law remedy from the High Court (R.S.C. Ord. 53) is a legal possibility, the practicalities of court procedure are such that actions in the county court are usually simpler and speedier. In this case, the Court of Appeal was asked to decide whether breach of the duty under s. 3(4) gave right to a cause of action for damages in the county court. The Court of Appeal (Megaw and Roskill L.JJ.) unanimously decided that it did. An important practical result of that decision is that since a claim for damages can be made in the county court, it is also possible to ask for an injunction from the county court (County Courts Act 1959, s. 74). Once an applicant has been given temporary accommodation, no further duty to make inquiries arises if the new application is based solely on matters relied on for the first application (*Delahaye* v. *Oswestry B.C.* (1980) *The Times*, 29 July).

Further duties are prescribed in s. 4.

4.—(1) If a housing authority are satisfied, as a result of inquiries under section 3 above, that a person who has applied to them for accommodation or for assistance in obtaining accommodation is homeless or threatened with homelessness, they shall be subject to a duty towards him under this section.

(2) Where –

  (*a*) they are not satisfied that he has a priority need, or
  (*b*) they are satisfied that he has a priority need but are also satis-fied that he became homeless or threatened with homelessness intentionally.

their duty is to furnish him with advice and appropriate assistance.

(3) Where –

  (*a*) they are satisfied that he is homeless, and
  (*b*) they are subject to a duty towards him by virtue of subsection (2) (*b*) above,

they shall secure that accommodation is made available for his occupation for such period as they consider will give him a reasonable opportunity of himself securing accommodation for his occupation.

(4) Where –

  (*a*) they are satisfied –
    (i) that he is threatened with homelessness, and
    (ii) that he has a priority need, but
  (*b*) they are not satisfied that he became threatened with homelessness intentionally,

their duty, subject to subsection (6) below, is to take reasonable steps to secure that accommodation does not cease to be available for his occupation.

(5) Where –

  (*a*) they are satisfied –
    (i) that he is homeless, and
    (ii) that he has a priority need, but
  (*b*) they are not satisfied that he became homeless intentionally, their duty, subject to section 5 below, is to secure that accommodation becomes available for his occupation.

(6) Nothing in subsection (4) above shall affect any right of a housing authority to secure vacant possession of accommodation, whether by virtue of a contract or of any enactment or rule of law.

(In *Lally* v. *Kensington* (1980) *The Times*, 27 March, it was held unlawful for an authority to decide as a matter of policy that, for cases under s. 4(3), accommodation would only be provided for 14 days.)

5.—(1) A housing authority are not subject to a duty under section 4(5) above –

    (*a*) if they are of the opinion –

        (i) that neither the person who applied to them for accommodation or for assistance in obtaining accommodation nor any person who might reasonably be expected to reside with him has a local connection with their area, and

        (ii) that the person who so applied or a person who might reasonably, be expected to reside with him has a local connection with another housing authority's area, and

        (iii) that neither the person who so applied nor any person who might reasonably be expected to reside with him will run the risk of domestic violence in that housing authority's area, and

    (*b*) if they notify that authority –

        (i) that the application has been made, and

        (ii) that they are of the opinion specified in paragraph (*a*) above...

'Local connection' is further defined in s. 18. The procedures to be followed in reaching decisions under s. 5 are to be found in the Housing (Homeless Persons) (Appropriate Arrangements) Order 1978 (SI 1978 No. 69) and in an extra-statutory 'agreement' drawn up by local authorities (Culley, 1978, p. 188).

It should be stressed that, even where the duty is to 'secure that accommodation becomes available', this does not mean that the authority has to provide a brand new council house.

Section 6(1) provides:

A housing authority may perform any duty under section 4 or 5 above to secure that accommodation becomes available for the occupation of a person – (*a*) by making available accommodation held by them under Part V of the Housing Act 1957 or Part VII of the Housing (Scotland) Act 1966 or under any other enactment, or (*b*) by securing that he obtains accommodation from some other person, or (*c*) by giving him such advice and assistance as will secure that he obtains accommodation from some other person.

Indeed many authorities still put families into temporary accommodation (Billcliffe, 1979, p. 118). Could this be regarded as unlawful? (Cf. the *Hendy* case, above, p. 480.) In *Attorney General, on the relation of Tilley* v. *Wandsworth L.B.C.* (*The Times*, 21 March 1980) it was held that a Council resolution that housing for those 'intentionally homeless' (see below) should never be provided under Children and Young Persons Act 1963, s. 1, was invalid.

In *R.* v. *Bristol City Council, ex parte Browne* [1979] 3 All E.R. 345 (Div. Ct.), Lloyd J. said (in part):

The applicant arrived in this country from Limerick in Eire on 12th March 1979. She was accompanied by her seven children. She is now 29. She was married in 1967 and lived with her husband at Tralee in County Kerry. According to her affidavits, of which we have two before us, her husband is a man given to violence. She refers to a number of incidents of violence culminating in November 1978. As a result of that incident she was advised by her doctor to leave the matrimonial home and go to the Women's Aid Hostel in Limerick where she remained with her children for some four and a half months. She left that hostel in March 1979, and she says she did so because her husband had discovered her whereabouts.

At all events, the people who run the hostel in Limerick made arrangements for her to come to Bristol where they put her in touch with the Bristol Women's Aid office. She arrived by air in Bristol on 12th March. They had paid her air fare of £152. She was met by a representative of Bristol Women's Aid at the airport, and she spent her first night in England at their hostel.

The next day at 11 am she visited the Bristol Council's housing aid centre, accompanied by two representatives of Bristol Women's Aid. There she was presented as a homeless person. She was interviewed by two of the council's officers, Mr Jeremy Ball and Mr Rex Hodgkinson, and they started enquiries at once as provided by s 3 of the 1977 Act. They also booked accommodation for her and for her children at a local guest house, initially for one night, while they completed their enquiries.

There was a further discussion on the afternoon of the same day with representatives of Bristol Women's Aid. Mr Hodgkinson asked why the applicant in this case had been brought to England when they had no accommodation for her. The explanation they gave us was that the accommodation which they hoped to provide for her had been taken up by three emergency admissions over the weekend.

On the next day, 14th March, Mr Ball telephoned a Mr Burke, who is the community welfare officer in Tralee and is the man responsible for homeless families in that part of Ireland. Mr Burke said that if the applicant were to return to Tralee he would make provision for her and her children.

The next day, 15th March, Mr Hodgkinson spoke to Mr Burke in order to satisfy himself as to what the position was. I think it is best that I should quote from his affidavit in which he describes that conversation. He says:

'Following Mr Ball's telephone conversation with Mr Burke, the community welfare officer in Tralee on 14th March 1979, I subsequently spoke to Mr Burke on 15th March 1979 and he assured me that if the applicant returned to Tralee accommodation would be secured for her and her children upon her arrival. He indicated to me that he was fully aware of the applicant's background and volunteered information concerning her husband's illegal activities. I again asked for confirmation that should the applicant return to Tralee he would make provision for her, and he confirmed that he would. In the light of this discussion, I concluded that any accommodation which Mr Burke arranged for the applicant would be arranged in the full knowledge of her husband's violent nature and that Mr Burke would have regard to the possibility of violence in arranging that accommodation.'

The case was then considered by Mr Martin, the principal assistant in charge of housing aid . . . [who] came to the following decisions, which I quote from Mr Martin's affidavit:

'(a) That the applicant was homeless. (b) That the applicant had a priority need. (c) That the applicant had not become homeless intentionally. (d) That the applicant did not have a local connection with the City of Bristol but that it would not be appropriate to transfer responsibility to another housing authority under section 5 of the Act as there was no relevant housing authority in England, Wales or Scotland.'

He concluded on the basis of those findings that the council were under a duty to secure that accommodation became available for the applicant. Those findings and that conclusion were subsequently set out in a written notification dated 15th March which was given to the applicant in accordance with s 8 of the 1977 Act.

Mr Martin then gave consideration to the question how the council should perform their duty under the Act. Again it is best to give Mr Martin's reasons in his own words. I quote from his affidavit:

'I concluded that the authorities in Tralee in Eire had with full knowledge of the facts surrounding her case indicated their willingness to accept responsibility for the applicant and that the community welfare officer charged with the responsibility for securing the health and well-being of the inhabitants of the area would not have agreed to the applicant returning if he was not able to make arrangements for the applicant to be adequately protected against any risk of violence. I therefore concluded that as the primary responsibility for the applicant rested with the Irish authorities in the country from which she had originated, and as the authorities were prepared to take responsibility for the applicant, the city council could properly carry out its duty under the Act by advising the applicant to return to Tralee and to contact the community relations officer there and by arranging for travel assistance to be available to enable the applicant to return. I was satisfied that the city council could properly carry out its duties in this way under the provisions of section 6(1)(c) of the Act, i.e. by giving such advice and assistance as would secure the applicant to obtain accommodation from some other person.'

[This decision was subsequently ratified by the Council] . . .

Thus the question comes down to this very narrow point: is Mr Burke a 'person' within the meaning of s 6(1)(c) of the 1977 Act? In my judgment, he is. Indeed, counsel, who has appeared on behalf of the applicant, did not suggest the contrary, or at any rate did not suggest it very strenuously. Putting the question of violence on one side, counsel for the applicant accepted that the council could fulfil their duty under the Act by assisting the applicant and her children to go back to Tralee, even though Tralee is outside the jurisdiction. It may well be that in most cases the person referred to in s 6(1)(c) of the Act will be a person within the area of the housing authority in question. But there is nothing in the Act which expressly so confines it; and, as I say, counsel did not strenuously argue that it should be so confined.

The real point which counsel makes is that the applicant should not, on the special facts of this case, be asked to go back to Tralee, because that is the place where she has suffered the domestic violence in the past. In that connection counsel for the applicant referred us to s 5(3) and (4) of the Act . . .

It is not of course argued that Tralee is itself a housing authority within the meaning of the 1977 Act; nobody suggests that the conditions set out in s 5(4) apply as such. But what is argued is that s 5(4)(b) can and should be applied, as it were, by analogy.

There is, I think, a short answer to that submission. The fact that Tralee is the place from which the applicant has come and the place where she has suffered violence in the past does not mean that she would necessarily suffer any risk of violence if she goes back. Obviously she will not go back to the same house; but there is other accommodation in the same area. The risk involved in her going back was, in my judgment, a matter for the council to consider together with the community welfare officer in Tralee. The passages from the affidavits which I have read show that that risk was considered very carefully by the council. The view which they have formed is quite clear, namely that accommodation can be provided in Tralee without risk to the applicant or her children. There is no material on which this court can possibly interfere with that conclusion or say that it was not justified. Counsel's main point, therefore, fails . . .

Lord Widgery C.J. agreed.

When the authority has come to a decision, there is, as we have seen, an extensive duty imposed on the authority to notify the result to the applicant. In the case of decisions adverse to the applicant, reasons for the decision must be stated (s. 8). In *R.* v. *Beverley B.C.*, *ex parte McPhee* (above, p. 484), Wein J. held that a local authority cannot postpone its obligations under s. 4 until after a notification under s. 8 has been provided.

Section 9(1) provides:

Where a housing authority –
  (*a*) request –
      (i) another housing authority;
      (ii) the Greater London Council;
      (iii) a development corporation;
      (iv) the Commission for the New Towns;
      (v) a registered housing association; or
      (vi) the Scottish Special Housing Association
    to assist them in the discharge of their functions under section 3, 4 or 5 above, or
  (*b*) request a social services authority or a social work authority to exercise any of their functions in relation to a case with which the housing authority are dealing under section 3, 4 or 5 above,
they shall co-operate with the housing authority in rendering such assistance in the discharge of the functions to which the request relates as is reasonable in the circumstances.

It has been suggested (Arden, 1980a) that in light of the *Browne* case (above, p. 488) a local authority may use s. 9 as the basis for lawfully transferring a homeless person to another local authority area. (Cf. *Wyness* v. *Council of the Borough of Poole* (1979) *LAG Bulletin* 166, where a county court judge considered, *obiter*, that an offer of accommodation in the area of another authority so far away that the applicant would have had to give up his job, when the local connection provisions did not apply, would not discharge the authority's duty under s. 4.)

There can be no doubt, however, that in practice the most difficult problem in relation to the operation of the Act is the definition of 'intentional homelessness'. Section 17 provides:

17.—(1) Subject to subsection (3) below, for the purposes of this Act a person becomes homeless intentionally if he deliberately does or fails to do anything in consequence of which he ceases to occupy accommodation which is available for his occupation and which it would have been reasonable for him to continue to occupy.

(2) Subject to subsection (3) below, for the purposes of this Act a person becomes threatened with homelessness intentionally if he deliberately does or fails to do anything the likely result of which is that he will be forced to leave accommodation which is available for his occupation and which it would have been reasonable for him to continue to occupy.

(3) An act or omission in good faith on the part of a person who was unaware of any relevant fact is not to be treated as deliberate for the purposes of subsection (1) or (2) above.

(4) Regard may be had, in determining for the purposes of subsections (1) and (2) above whether it would have been reasonable for a person to continue to occupy accommodation, to the general circumstances prevailing in relation to housing in the area of the housing authority to whom he applied for accommodation or for assistance in obtaining accommodation.

This definition gives considerable room for 'interpretation' and authorities who are unwilling or reluctant to comply with the Act are often able to use this section to get out of their apparent obligations.

Further guidance on the interpretation of the Act is to be found in a separate Code of Guidance, to which the authority is required to have regard (s. 12). Notwithstanding this, the Court of Appeal in *De Falco* v. *Crawley B.C.* ([1980] 1 All E.R. 913 (C.A.)) stressed that the Code did not have statutory force. In that case, two Italians had come to Britain. One had stayed with his family, but could no longer do so; the other had arranged private accommodation before leaving Italy, but the arrangement fell through. The Code of Guidance's interpretation of 'intentional homelessness' (see paras. 2.13–2.19) at para. 2.18 stated: 'In assessing whether a person has become homeless intentionally it will be relevant to consider the most immediate cause of that homelessness rather than events that may have taken place previously . . .' Nonetheless the Court of Appeal held that both applicants were intentionally homeless, since they had left Italy without first making adequate housing arrangements. (It may be noted that the reasoning of Lord Denning in this case is strikingly similar to his judgment in *London Borough of Southwark* v. *Williams* [1971] 1 Ch. 734 at 743. Should the new legislation have justified a different approach?)

More recently *Youngs* v. *Thanet D.C.* (Ch. D.) (*The Times*, 21 February 1980) again discussed the issue of 'intentional homelessness'. Judge Mervyn Davies:

Mr Youngs, a security guard, was 26, married and now had three young children. He was not a native of Thanet, but his wife had lived there all her life. The Youngs married in March, 1975, and made their home in Margate. On April 5 he applied for council housing accommodation and in August, 1976, became the tenant of a council house in Toddy Gardens, Margate, at an inclusive rent of £13.07 a week. At that time he was working and earning about £50 a week. Arrears of rent soon mounted up despite substantial payments by the Department of Health and Social Security when Mr Youngs was unemployed. As at December 31, 1976, the arrears were £175.74.

The council served a notice to quit on February 7, 1977, with a letter of explanation and advice. Mr Youngs offered to pay arrears in instalments but did not do so and he was notified that he would be receiving a county court possession summons.

On August 1 a possession order was made in Thanet County Court together with an order for payment of £395.41 rent and mesne profits and £25 costs. The council did not immediately enforce that order. Mr Youngs was treated with every consideration. The arrears continued to rise. On November 24 a council official saw Mr Youngs, who gave no explanation for the non-payment of his rent save that his money had been spent on other things such as curtains, a car and turf for the garden. At that time Mr Youngs had started work again, but that had not improved his financial position because the benefits he received while he was unemployed amounted to much the same as any wages he could earn.

Mr Youngs's case was considered by the council sub-committee concerned with housing matters. It was decided that, in view of a promise to pay £15 a week, no action would be taken to implement the possession order.

Mr Youngs was informed that if the promise was not kept a warrant for eviction would be issued.

Mr Youngs did not keep his promise. Four months later he was told that, on the instructions of the housing committee, arrangements were being made for the issue of a warrant for his eviction. There was no immediate eviction. Mr Youngs applied to the county court registrar to suspend the issue of the warrant of possession. On June, 1978, the application was dismissed, and the court bailiff executed a warrant of possession on June 29.

At that time Mr Youngs's arrears amounted to £608. The Youngs immediately went into occupation of temporary accommodation provided by the council in Albert Terrace. The council's housing officials had his plight well in mind and on the day he was evicted he applied for emergency housing assistance on a printed council form which referred to the 1977 Act.

The council's principal housing officer concluded that Mr Youngs was homeless within the meaning of section 1, he had priority need under section 2 but that he was 'homeless intentionally'. Thus the council came under the duty not only of furnishing him with advice and appropriate assistance: section 4(2)(b), but also of securing that accommodation was made available for his occupation for such period as they should consider would give him a reasonable opportunity of himself securing accommodation for his own occupation: section 4(3).

The Youngs remained at Albert Terrace until October 16. After a meeting with the housing committee on October 11 Mr Youngs was given a week's notice by letter (on October 12) to leave. He owed £275.67 rent for that accommodation. The council made it clear that they regarded their obligation to him under the 1977 Act as at an end.

After seeing a shop window advertisement, he found accommodation in Addington Square, Margate, at a weekly rent of £15. The rent was paid to the resident landlady direct by the Department of Health and Social Security. That accommodation was used for holiday lettings. The landlady said that she had explained to Mr Youngs – which he denied – that he would be required to vacate by April 1, 1979, at the latest. When he was asked he refused to go. The landlady took other steps, and she eventually obtained from the county court an order for possession in 14 days from July 18.

Mr Youngs immediately sought advice – and help from the housing department. He was informed that the council would not be offering him any permanent occupation but if he should be evicted the council would try to secure bed and breakfast accommodation for him in the private sector; and if that was not possible the council would as a last resort take the Youngs into a council unit for a short period. Mr Youngs was strongly advised to look for his own accommodation.

Once the possession order of July 18 was obtained Mr Youngs became a person threatened with homelessness within section 1(3). As soon as he left Addington Square he made an application under the Act to the council for emergency housing assistance. The view the council's officer took was that his homelessness was a continuation of the original state of homelessness that had occurred in June, 1978. Accordingly, advice only was given to Mr Youngs, and he was eventually advised to go to the Hotel Louise, which he did. He was not happy there. Its charges were £108 a week.

The next step was another application under the Act. Mr Youngs's solicitors wrote to the council in effect asserting that the council was under a duty to consider an application for accommodation for him as being a person with priority need who was homeless or threatened with homelessness, and further that pending inquiries he was entitled to have interim accommodation if he was put out of the hotel. The council replied stating that Mr Youngs's predicament arose 'out of his original problem of homelessness' and therefore the council had fully carried out the statutory requirements under the Act.

On September 4 Mr Youngs issued a writ seeking various orders and declarations, but the main issue was whether or not the council did what they ought to have done at the time when Mr Youngs left Addington Square, ie, in response to the application of August 3, 1979.

Going through the evidence, his Lordship thought that the application was considered to be enough for them to give such advice and assistance as would secure that he obtained accommodation from some third party; see section 6(1)(c) and *Reg v Bristol City Council Ex parte Browne* ([1979] 1 WLR 1437).

On that view of the council's obligations they were discharged. But Mr Youngs's homelessness was not a continuation of his earlier homelessness. When he left Albert Terrace for Addington Square he found his own accommodation within the meaning of that word as used in section 1(1)(a). The homelessness that arose on June 29, 1978, came to an end. He became once again a person who could once again become homeless with section 1. That he did on August 3, 1979, and on that occasion he became homeless unintentionally for the reasons in section 17. Homelessness under the Act was a matter of fact and not a matter of status.

Mr Youngs was ordered to pay £401 arrears of rent.

Cf. now *Dyson* v. *Kerrier D.C.* (1980) *The Times*, 1 July. In *Miller* v. *Wandsworth L.B.C.* (*The Times*, 19 March 1980) Walton J. said:

that the Millers were living in rented accommodation in Churchfield Road, Acton, in Ealing London borough up to August 4, 1979...

On August 4, during the night, there was an explosion in the kitchen due to an electrical fault in the water heater. The damage caused was comparatively minor, being limited to internal decorations and the heater, which was completely burnt out. They spent the rest of the night at the house of Mrs Miller's parents in Wandsworth.

Mr Miller, who earned £75 a week, stated that the landlady had asked them to stay elsewhere while the flat was being repaired, but was unable to say when the repairs would be done. They were unhappy about returning to the flat, and on August 5 he told the landlady that they did not intend to return. Shortly after he instructed solicitors to try to recover a month's rent of £130 paid as a deposit.

That explained why, when on August 9 the Millers had an interview with the homeless persons unit in Wandsworth, Mrs Blyth, the local government officer concerned, formed the impression that they had no intention of returning to the flat. She had advised them to retain the tenancy until it was known what was the extent of the damage and whether it could be repaired for them to move back in. The information conveyed by the Millers was that there was no reason why they could not remain in the flat once the repairs were done and provided they paid the rent, and that pending such repairs, if the work took place within a short time, they had accommodation with Mrs Miller's mother.

On the basis of that information the council wrote on August 10 advising them to maintain payments of rent and warning them that failure to safeguard the tenancy would mean that if at a later date they presented themselves as homeless, the council would be unable to assist since they could be considered 'intentionally homeless'. Implicit in the advice was that it was reasonable to go on paying the rent for a short period while repairs were carried out. The work was in fact done in September.

On December 20 the Millers again presented themselves as homeless indicating that Mrs Miller's mother could not house them after Christmas. After further inquiries the council wrote on January 25, stating that the council had decided that the Millers were 'in priority need and homeless' but that they were 'intentionally so' as they had failed to retain their tenancy of the flat, and that in those circumstances the council took no responsibility for permanent rehousing and could only offer bed and breakfast accommodation for 28 days expiring on February 23. The Millers therefore sought a mandatory injunction for the local authority to secure that accommodation was made available to them until the hearing of the action.

Mrs Miller's baby was born shortly after the fire, and they clearly had a priority need for accommodation. The council had made the appropriate inquiries and were satisfied that they had become homeless intentionally. The Act placed the responsibility for making the relevant findings as to homelessness, priority need and intentional homelessness on the council as the housing authority, and it was well settled that the court was in no sense a court of appeal from their decisions unless it appeared that decision was one which no reasonable authority, having made the proper inquiries, could have made.

The decision in the present case was that the Millers either deliberately gave notice to quit or to terminate their licence, or deliberately neglected to pay the rent of premises which were available for their continued occupation and which it was reasonable for them to continue to occupy. Was that conclusion unreasonable? His Lordship thought not.

Mr Blake [counsel for the Millers] had criticized the council for not having made more inquiries before the letter of August 10, but such criticism could not be justified. The council had obtained from the Millers themselves all the necessary information – that they were not homeless. To obtain further information would have been wholly unnecessary, and his Lordship was the last person to seek to impose a duty to obtain unnecessary information upon an already hard pressed local authority. In the matter of housing Wandsworth was indeed extremely hard pressed.

Doubtless immediately after the fire the premises were in a poor state and would have required cleaning. The absence of hot water was temporary and something which a reasonable man or woman had to put up with from time to time. Information from Ealing London Borough Council was that the electrical wiring was satisfactory. At the end of the day it was quite impossible to criticize Wandsworth council's decisions.

De Falco v Crawley Borough Council (*The Times*, December 13) showed that the code of guidance, which had been relied on by Mr Blake, was something which the council must have regard to, but it did not have statutory effect...

B General allocation of council housing

(i) THE WAITING LIST (see also above, p. 471)

First, a family or person seeking a council tenancy has to get on to the Housing List. One problem is that some authorities do not allow new applicants to join the list unless they have resided in their area for a specific period.

As long ago as 1955 CHAC recommended (1955, p. 21):

3. Until applications are accepted for investigation and consideration, there can be no assurance that houses will in fact be let to those in the greatest need ...

5. The desire to give preference to residents of long standing should not lead local authorities to interpret their statutory responsibilities for housing too narrowly.

6. Residential qualifications are sometimes used to deter newcomers from entering the district and overcrowding accommodation, thus gaining priority for a house. Local authorities can prevent deliberate overcrowding by other and better means.

7. The length of the waiting list should not be restricted by the use of residential qualifications. The cost of maintaining the list, however long, should be regarded as a legitimate charge on public funds ...

11. Waiting lists should not be closed ...

17. The time has now come for the removal of all residential qualifications in a large number of districts ...

In 1969 the CHAC carried out a sample survey of local authorities and found (Cullingworth, 1969, p. 45):

17% had no residential qualifications whatsoever – whether for acceptance on the housing list or for consideration for rehousing. 38% allowed unrestricted entry to the housing list of any applicant already living in the area and non-residents working in their area. A further 28% accepted registrations from residents but not from people working in the area. There were only 17% of authorities who required a specific period of residence (or employment) in the area before acceptance on the housing list. Residential qualifications for acceptance on the housing list varies from less than a year to more than four years.

The Committee concluded (*ibid.*, p. 54):

Conditions differ so greatly between different areas that absolute uniformity is not possible. Nevertheless, we are firmly of the conviction that there should be no barrier to acceptance on a housing list. We regard this of importance both in relation to the rights of applicants and the need of local authorities to have as full information as possible on the demand for council housing in their area. We therefore recommend that there should be no residential qualifications for admission to a housing list. Indeed, we go further and hold it to be fundamental that no one should be precluded from applying for, or being considered for, a council tenancy on any ground whatsoever ... *We think that this rule should be made a statutory obligation.*

Despite this clear recommendation, there is still no statutory duty. And evidence suggests that local authority practice has not changed (Winyard, 1978, p. 107).

(ii) ASSESSMENT OF APPLICANTS

Once on the housing list, the applicants have to be assessed. This will usually be done by a member of the housing staff. The Cullingworth Committee Report described the procedures used (1969, pp. 30 ff):

Most (but not all) local authorities pay home visits to applicants. We think these visits constitute an important and potentially very valuable tool. But more emphasis needs to be laid on giving information and advice, rather than assessing housing standards and 'suitability' for different standards of council housing. From an analysis of the replies to our questionnaire it is clear that there is a wide variety of practice. Some local authorities go to great lengths to allocate houses which are 'suitable', grading applicants according to their suitability for houses of different ages and standards. A housing visitor may be required to assess general standards on a scale, e.g. very good/good/fair/ poor/bad/unsuitable. Some local authorities only require housing visitors to make 'general remarks on standards' on the record sheet, others have a list of questions to be filled in, covering 'type', or 'standard' of family, state of rooms, e.g. tidiness, cleanliness in bedrooms and living rooms, state of furniture, state of decoration and repair, and personal cleanliness. Many visitors are required to look at the bedding to assess its cleanliness and quantity. Some have to indicate whether standards are likely to improve or whether supervision would be needed.

Alternatively, the emphasis may be different, and the essential purpose of the visit is to discuss with the applicant the types and locations of houses which are likely to be available, the direct costs (rent and rates) and indirect costs (travel to work) involved, and so forth.

We have found considerable variation not only in the extent to which local authorities 'grade' their tenants, but also in the reasons why grading is thought to be necessary. On a very limited scale the justification for grading is that some tenants will not take care of a new house: at the extreme they may wreck it. It would not be sound policy to allocate a high standard house to such an 'unsatisfactory tenant'. But such families are very few in number, though they pose problems for the local authority out of all proportion to their numbers. It is a far cry from allocating specially selected houses to unsatisfactory tenants to grading all according to their 'fitness' for particular types of houses. We were struck by the simple fact that the approach of a number of local authorities to this seemed to vary according to the range of house types they had available. A local authority with a small range (e.g. all postwar houses) see no need for careful grading. On the other hand, a local authority with a great range tend to see a necessity for fine grading ...

We were surprised to find some housing authorities who took up a moralistic attitude towards applicants: the underlying philosophy seemed to be that council tenancies were to be given only to those who 'deserved' them and that the 'most deserving' should get the best houses. Thus unmarried mothers, cohabitees, 'dirty' families, and 'transients' tended to be grouped together as 'undesirable'. Moral rectitude, social conformity, clean living and a 'clean' rent book on occasion seemed to be essential qualifications for eligibility – at least for new houses. Some attitudes may reflect public opinion – in the same way that they induce policies unfavourable to newcomers (white and non-white), but this is a case where local authorities must lead public opinion.

Whatever justification such attitudes may have had when council housing was on a small scale (which is by no means self-evident), they cannot be upheld in a situation where council housing forms a large and ever-increasing proportion of the available rented accommodation. The simple fact is that it is becoming increasingly difficult for those excluded from publicly-provided housing (on whatever grounds) to find satisfactory alternatives. Indeed, one feature of current housing policy (which it is not for us to question) is the concentration of effort on clearance and redevelopment. This has the effect of reducing the alternatives for those ineligible for council housing. There is thus a severely practical reason why local housing authorities should be paying particular attention to the needs of those who face acute social problems.

Local electorates may resent this. Certainly, 'respectable' families whose names have been on a housing list for many years feel aggrieved if they see 'less deserving' families being rehoused. Nevertheless, these are the families who have the greatest difficulty in obtaining good accommodation elsewhere and they should, as we have already stressed, be given special priority for council housing ...

Quite apart from these issues of principle there is a severely practical issue of the ability of housing visitors to make assessments, particularly if (as is typically the case) the visit is a brief one. Without wishing to impugn the good will and good sense of the majority of housing visitors, we believe that the system leaves too much scope for personal prejudice and unconscious bias to be acceptable ...

Despite these views, it is frequently claimed that local authority housing staff are still not adequately trained to carry out what may be a very sensitive task (Legg, Brion & Bieber, 1978, p. 84). And from the applicant's point of view, the home visit may be a confusing and incomprehensible experience (Lambert, Paris & Blackaby, 1978, ch. 3).

(iii) SELECTION SCHEMES

Finally, applicants are actually selected for council houses. Again there is an enormous variety of schemes, reviewed by C.H.A.C. (Cullingworth, 1969, pp. 40 ff):

We have undertaken no comprehensive review of types of selection scheme ... Nevertheless, we feel it is incumbent on us to comment on the main types of schemes, though in practice each type can shade imperceptibly into another type.

Date order schemes ... In situations where there is little or no backlog of housing need there appears to be widespread acceptance of the equity of allocating houses in order of date-application

In a paper submitted to us by one local authority the following advantages were among those listed in favour of such a scheme:

   (i) The scheme is very simple and easily understood.
  (ii) Applicants appreciate the fairness of the scheme and its simplicity.
 (iii) The scheme is easy to administer and reduces clerical time.
 (iv) The scheme simplifies investigation of applicants' circumstances.
  (v) It is easier to estimate the date when accommodation could be offered. The knowledge of the length of the waiting period may induce some applicants to solve their own housing problems.
 (vi) Applicants who improve their circumstances by, for example, obtaining better accommodation after application, are not penalized, provided they still have a housing need.
(vii) Applicants who limit the size of their families have an equal opportunity of housing.
(viii) The time of Committees is saved to some extent. In particular, this dispenses with the need to review points schemes from time to time.

Our view is that where there is no real housing problem *and as long as individual hardship cases and key workers are dealt with separately*, a date-order allocation scheme has many merits, appears to be generally acceptable, and may well be appropriate. We would certainly deprecate a scheme under which houses were allocated strictly according to the date order in which applications were lodged without any reference being made to, or account being taken of, the degree of housing and social need. But in areas where there is no backlog of need and where applicants are being housed within, say, eighteen months of registration, a date-order allocation scheme is simple, popular and acceptable as being fair. In all such schemes, however, there should be an assessment of need and applicants suffering hardship should be rehoused outside the scheme. This is the general practice in areas operating date-order schemes.

A variation on a date-order scheme is one in which applicants are grouped according to their circumstances. If the effect of such a grouping is to give priority to those with greater need we think this is preferable to a general date-order scheme. The type of grouping we have in mind is one in which applicants are grouped, for example, into:

  (i) Evictions
 (ii) Severe ill-health or 'social need'
(iii) Overcrowding and sharing
 (iv) All other applicants

In this example, the first three groups would have priority over the remainder...

Points schemes

130. Points schemes, of widely varying degrees of complexity, are widely used. They constitute an attempt to weigh the relative claims of applicants in greatly different circumstances. They are excellent in concept but exceedingly difficult to devise in detail with fairness. They need continual review (in the light of changing conditions) if they are not to become outdated...

'Merit' schemes

We use this fine-sounding term for schemes which attempt to treat each application 'on its merits'. As a general approach, particularly in larger authorities, this approach would appear to be unworkable – though some quite large authorities apparently do not find it so. One authority, for example, with 5,000 council houses, informed us that 'the preparation of the short list for consideration by the Lettings Committee is left to the discretion of the Housing Officer, who prepares his lists from the investigations carried out in each individual case'. These schemes also have the fundamental drawbacks that they cannot be published, and that consistency and impartiality is difficult to achieve and virtually impossible to demonstrate.

On the other hand, a merit scheme does permit the exercise of judgement on factors which it is difficult to 'point'. It is noteworthy that points schemes characteristically deal with easily measurable, objective factors such as overcrowding, lack of amenities and sharing. These factors are capable of statistical treatment. Health, social and economic factors are much less amenable to this.

Combined schemes

Some authorities use a combination of schemes, for example a merit scheme for 'priority' cases (e.g. for severe ill-health, homelessness and eviction); a points scheme for 'ordinary' applicants (families); and a date-order scheme

for single people. All authorities deal with cases of 'exceptional hardship' outside their normal scheme, though the definition of 'exceptional' varies. Many
authorities deal with their rehousing obligations for clearance and redevelopment separately, though a number award a large number of points thus
technically bringing such households within the points scheme...

Comment

(*a*) It can be seen from the above that certain aspects of the schemes
used have been heavily criticized. Notwithstanding criticism of the
use of merit schemes, in particular, central government has not felt
able to intervene directly (see, too, Housing Services Advisory Group
(1978)); Winyard (1978, p. 175) states that 10% of authorities still
use this method of allocation. The Labour Government's Housing
Bill 1979 (which fell with that government) did propose to prohibit
certain local authority practices, such as taking into account place
of birth, residence, or employment in the local authority's area when
making allocation decisions (clause 27). But the Conservative Party's
Housing Act 1980 has dropped this proposal.

(*b*) Many local authorities have long refused to publish details of
their allocation schemes so that it is impossible for potential tenants
to gain any idea of whether they would be likely to qualify for accommodation. Under Housing Act 1980, s. 44, local authorities will be
obliged to publish their allocation schemes, and the principles on
which transfers operate.

(*c*) The whole process places considerable discretionary power in
the hands of local officials. Lawyers should be interested in this to
see if there are ever grounds for bringing cases for abuse of such discretion. This point was reviewed by JUSTICE (1969) who stated:

Complaints are made about local authority administration, some of which
may allege some element of maladministration, while others may be concerned only with the 'merits' of a discretionary decision. In our examination
of this subject we found that complaints of both kinds are commonest in relation to such topics as the allocation of 'benefits' of various kinds, [such as]
... the granting of tenancies of council houses ... In these and similar cases,
a complaint about maladministration is not, we feel, always redressed.

In fact, the courts have shown great reluctance to intervene to control these discretionary powers (see *Hendy*, above; *Bristol District
Council* v. *Clark* [1975] 3 All E.R. 976). However, since the Commissioners for Local Administration began work, a number of cases of
alleged maladministration in housing allocation (and transfer) have

been investigated, a considerable proportion of which were upheld (analysed by Hughes & Jones (1979), p. 277). Indeed, in some cases it was suggested by the Commissioners that the general guidelines of Housing Act 1957, s. 113(2) (above, p. 478) were being ignored. (See, e.g., Case Inv. 4537C: Hughes & Jones, p. 281.) Hughes and Jones conclude:

Although bias is much more difficult to prove than, say, delay or sheer incompetence, the cases discussed above do seem to show that bias can be shown to exist. From the cases studied it would seem that Council Officers adopt a professional attitude to applications, but bias is likely to creep in where Council members are concerned in the application.

The forms of personal bias revealed in this investigation are varied. Decisions appear to have been affected by the following 'improper' considerations:

(1) unsubstantiated hearsay evidence;
(2) over-reliance on local knowledge of the individuals involved to the exclusion of relevant considerations;
(3) anger;
(4) hostility to persons in receipt of state aid;
(5) allowing annoyance at the unpleasant behaviour or character of an applicant to influence judgment;
(6) a lack of sympathy with the marital problems of an applicant and allowing this to affect judgment.

It does seem that personal bias is likely to affect the processing of applications where too much reliance is placed on local knowledge and when the personalities involved are identified. Members may tend to allow their own moral values and social position to cloud their judgment and this is particularly so when there is little or no firm procedure or where agreed procedure is not followed...

To assist applicants who wish to check that local authorities are taking all the correct particulars into account, Housing Act 1980, s. 44(6) requires local authorities to make available to the applicant all the information they have recorded as relevant. (More general discussions of problems of control of discretion in allocation procedures are to be found in Lewis, 1976; Grant, 1976; Gray, 1976; Lewis, 1977; Lewis & Livock, 1979; Welsh Consumer Council, 1976.)

(*d*) One particular problem concerns the impact on allocation policies of discrimination on racial grounds. Notwithstanding the Race Relations Act 1976, s. 21 and earlier legislation which attempted to outlaw discrimination, a number of studies reveal that black families are being located on poorer, older, less desirable estates (Lomas & Monck, 1975; G.L.C., 1976; Smith & Whalley, 1975). This issue has been discussed on a number of occasions by the Community Relations Commission (now Commission for Racial Equality) (C.R.C. 1976; 1977a; 1977b; see, too, Franey (1979b), p. 56).

(e) More generally, the question of allocation of council housing goes to the root of the social function of council housing. Consider the following passage from Cullingworth (1969, paras. 56–62):

In our view it is not sufficient that local authorities should give priority to 'housing need' as measured by objective factors such as overcrowding, sharing and the like. These indices, important though they are, give only a partial picture. Different economic and social situations in which different families live must also be taken into account. We are not suggesting that more affluent council tenants should be evicted or that council housing should be reserved for the poor. There are social advantages in having a broad spectrum of social classes living in a community and we certainly would not wish to see an official encouragement to a policy of income segregation. (The actual rents paid by tenants with different incomes is quite a different matter). Our point is simply that in allocating council houses local authorities should give particular attention to those with incomes which are low in relation to their needs.

More difficult in some ways is the problem of the family occupying adequate accommodation which is too expensive for them. Such a family might be helped by a housing advice service to obtain cheaper accommodation, but (especially in London) such accommodation might be difficult or even impossible to obtain outside the council house sector. It is not easy for a local authority to allocate scarce housing to such families when there are so many others living in inadequate housing. Yet the problem facing the adequately housed family may be greater than that facing the inadequately housed, and their ability to solve their problem themselves may be less.

There is no simple way of judging conflicting claims such as this ... But an issue on which it is difficult to adjudicate cannot for that reason be ignored. We cannot lay down in detail how individual cases should be judged: what we do wish to do is to state clearly that factors such as the economic circumstances of a family should be taken into consideration by local authorities in determining their allocation policies. In many areas of the country, outside London, there are increasing opportunities for house purchase and even for renting from other bodies at a reasonable rent. In London, the competition for all types of housing is such that the situation is different in kind. This makes the principle we are seeking to establish much more difficult to apply, but at the same time it makes it more important ...

Our wider conception of 'housing need', however, embraces more than economic circumstances. There are also social circumstances which, though often complicated by inadequate income, demand attention in their own right – the fatherless family, the family with a mentally ill mother, and that highly diverse group which are termed 'problem families'. Such families frequently lack the social skills required to obtain and keep good housing in the private sector. And, in any case, those with the power of choosing who shall live in the private sector may well not want them. Unfortunately, publicly account-able local authorities may not want them either: it is not easy for a council to justify to its electorate the rehousing of families in arrears of rent, unmarried mothers or, indeed, any group which does not conform to the accepted canons of good behaviour. Yet these are often the very people (and electors) whose social needs demand attention by local authorities. Unlike others who may be judged to have a stronger moral claim on the local authority, their only opportunity to obtain good housing may be via the local authority.

At the same time, to the extent that their mode of life is judged to be in-adequate and in need of change, the tenancy of a council house provides a base on which the personal social services can build. It is unfortunate that all too often our society unwittingly raises unsurmountable barriers for those whom we seek to assist...

Perhaps more persuasive than principles is finance. We hold no simple-minded views on the effect of good housing on behaviour, but we do point out that bad housing greatly increases the difficulties facing families who are unable to cope with the every-day problems of maintaining a home and rear-ing children. Such families need more help than those better able to cope. Without good housing their problems tend to increase and, as a result, their calls on the personal social services mount. The financial implications of this can be serious. It is good financial policy as well as good social policy to ensure that priority in the allocation of council houses is given to the most socially needy groups.

There is a widespread fear among housing managers that policies of this type will encourage others to worsen their position or discourage some from improving their position. (The same argument is heard in relation to liberal policies for the homeless and even to the publication of points schemes). We are convinced that these fears are greatly exaggerated. The fear of 'queue-jumping' can paralyse effective action in the very areas where it is most needed. So far as discouraging some from improving their conditions is con-cerned, we suspect that this is also exaggerated; and to the extent that it is true it constitutes a sad commentary on our housing policies. Policy should be directed towards helping people to improve their housing situation. The allocation of a council house should be only one of the means of doing this. The paradox today is that though there is greater choice in an increasing range of goods and services, choice in housing is declining. For a family wish-ing to rent (or unable to buy) a good quality house the position is rapidly approaching when there is no alternative to a council house. Hence the impor-tance of establishing a claim for a council house and the temptation to wait and not to jeopardize the chance of a council house by improving one's situation. It is difficult to say how prevalent deliberate 'waiting' is, but clearly there is always this possibility. The implications are far wider than we can encompass within our restricted inquiry...

Do you agree with these sentiments? To what extent will the policy of sale of council houses assist or hinder the achievement of the objectives outlined above?

(*f*) Data on council tenants are given in chapter 1 (pp. 22–3).

Part Two: Housing Associations

(Discussion in this Part reflects, albeit more briefly, the topics covered in Part One.)

Introduction

Housing associations have existed for many years. Indeed, many have their origins in the philanthropic housing movement of the Victorian era, which substantially pre-dated the development of council housing (Cohen, 1971; Stedman-Jones, 1976, ch. 9). However, it is only in recent years that they have been specially encouraged to develop by the provision of increasingly generous grants and subsidies, in particular since the passing of the Housing Act 1974.

1. Administration

Some indication of the variety of housing associations, and their relationship with the Housing Corporation, has already been given (see above, pp. 23–4). One feature of Housing Association administration is that associations complying with Rent Act 1977 s. 15 (as amended) are not protected tenancies though they are subject to 'fair rent' procedures (below, p. 508) and to the new system of security of tenure for public sector dwellings (below, p. 512):

15.—(1) A tenancy shall not be a protected tenancy at any time when the interest of the landlord under that tenancy belongs to a housing association falling within subsection (3) below; nor shall a person at any time be a statutory tenant of a dwelling-house if the interest of his immediate landlord would belong at that time to such a housing association.

(2) A tenancy shall not be a protected tenancy at any time when the interest of the landlord under that tenancy belongs to –

(*a*) the Housing Corporation; or

(*b*) a housing trust which is a charity within the meaning of the Charities Act 1960;

nor shall a person at any time be a statutory tenant of a dwelling-house if the interest of his immediate landlord would belong at that time to any of those bodies.

(3) A housing association falls within this subsection if –

(*a*) it is for the time being registered in the register of housing associations established under section 13 of the Housing Act 1974; or

(*b*) it has made an application to the Housing Corporation, before 1st April 1975, for registration in that register and the application has not been disposed of by the Corporation; or

(*c*) it is for the time being specified in an order made by the Secretary of State under section 80 of the Housing Finance Act 1972 or paragraph 23 of Schedule 1 to the Housing Rents and Subsidies Act 1975; or

(*d*) it is a registered society within the meaning of section 74 of the Industrial and Provident Societies Act 1965 and its rules restrict membership to persons who are tenants or prospective tenants of the association and preclude the granting or assignment of tenancies to persons other than members.

In this subsection 'housing association' has the same meaning as in section 189(1) of the Housing Act 1957.

('Housing Trust' is defined in s. 15(5) as amended by Housing Act 1980, s. 74(2).) In *Goodman* v. *Dolphin Square Trust Ltd* (1979) 38 P. & C.R. 257 the Court of Appeal held that a housing association registered with the Housing Corporation was to be presumed to be validly registered. If doubts arose as to the validity of the registration, these were to be resolved by the Housing Corporation using its statutory powers of control under the Housing Act 1974. Thus here, the tenant, against whom a possession order had been made, could not challenge in court the effective exemption of the Trust from the security of tenure provisions of the Rent Acts.

2. Assessment of housing need

Unlike local authorities, housing associations are under no general legal obligation to assess or provide for particular housing needs.

Many, particularly the specialist associations (see above, p. 24), have, however, been established with particular groups in mind, e.g. the elderly, single persons or one-parent families. Further, in the case of new projects, applications for the 'Housing Association Grant' (see below) will only be approved by the Department of the Environment if the association can demonstrate that the housing to be provided is 'for people whose needs and circumstances justify the provision of housing to be substantially subsidized by the taxpayer' (DoE Circular 170/74, para. 29).

3. Housing association finance : expenditure

Expenditure on housing association projects, whether new building or renovation, obviously involves heavy capital expenditure. It must be remembered that, since 1 April 1975, only associations registered with the Housing Corporation are entitled to receive statutory grants and loans (Housing Act 1974, s. 17). Initial funding of projects will be provided by loans which may come from local authorities (Housing Act 1957, s. 119) or from the Housing Corporation (Housing Act 1974, s. 9). (Under the Housing Act 1980, s. 120, the Housing Corporation's own borrowing limits have been increased from £400 million to £2,000 million, which can be increased to £3,000 million by Order in Council.)

Once the project has been completed, registered housing associations may receive a substantial subsidy towards the costs of the project – the Housing Association Grant (Housing Act 1974, ss. 29–30). (Applications for grants must be made to the body providing the loan finance, before the project is started.) The details of the methods of calculating the Housing Association Grant need not concern us; but typically they amount to between 70 and 80 per cent of the total costs of a scheme (Holmes, 1978, p. 111).

4. Housing association finance : income

(i) *Rent*
It is a condition of the receipt of Housing Association Grant that the housing association's rents must be 'fair rents' fixed by the rent officer acting under Rent Act 1977, Part VI (as amended by Housing Act 1980, s. 69 and Schedule 7).

Table 10.5 Rent registration: average registered rents and change on previous rents: housing association tenancies

	First registrations				Re-registrations				All registrations			
	Mean regis-tered rent	Mean change on prev-ious rent	Median regis-tered rent	Number of cases	Mean regis-tered rent	Mean change on prev-ious rent	Median re-regis-tered rent	Number of cases	Mean regis-tered rent	Mean change on prev-ious rent	Median regis-tered rent	Number of cases
	£ p.a.	%	£ p.a.		£ p.a.	%	£ p.a.		£ p.a.	%	£ p.a.	
Greater London												
1974	342	54	313	12,520	209	22	191	280	336	54	308	12,800
1975	378	66	333	9,380	319	37	308	880	373	63	331	10,260
1976	430	31	392	14,250	383	41	366	21,450	401	39	376	35,700
1977	490	30	448	11,820	432	43	403	9,950	463	37	420	21,770
1978	536	33	491	12,540	513	39	469	7,490	527	36	484	20,030
Rest of England and Wales												
1974	320	71	277	14,740	240	23	241	440	317	71	272	15,180
1975	380	54	303	16,880	294	37	263	1,460	373	52	295	18,340
1976	427	68	363	17,440	378	47	331	25,080	397	53	337	42,520
1977	495	29	497	25,270	431	48	403	13,940	472	39	475	39,210
1978	542	26	537	31,740	488	46	468	16,730	523	38	523	48,470

Source: Housing and Construction Statistics (1979), No. 29, Table 43.

Table 10.5 provides details of the levels of rents.

Even with the assistance of rent allowances (see ch. 6), these rent levels have been causing alarm. A survey published in October 1976 indicated that fair rents for newly built housing association accommodation were between 25 and 96% higher than reasonable rents for council houses (Weir, 1976, p. 130); see also Tunney (1978, p. 68). The Housing Corporation has argued that the fair rent formula, as applied to housing association dwellings, should be amended so that rent officers should consider local authority rent levels as part of the process of fixing the fair rent. (Cf. pressures for increasing local authority rent levels, discussed above, p. 474.)

(ii) *Subsidies*

In addition to Housing Association Grant (see above), certain other subsidies are also payable:

(*a*) Management grants (Housing Act 1974, s. 31)
(*b*) Revenue deficit grants (*ibid.*, s. 32)
(*c*) Hostel deficit grants (*ibid.*, s. 33)

The details will not be discussed here. See, though, DoE Housing Association Notes 2/75; 3/75.

5. Allocation of tenancies

See the discussion above (pp. 24–7).

Part Three : Public Sector Housing Rights

1. The 'secure tenancy'

The principal concept on which the new public sector housing law is based is the 'secure tenancy'. This is defined by Housing Act 1980, s. 28:

(1) A tenancy under which a dwelling-house is let as a separate dwelling is a secure tenancy at any time when the conditions described below as the landlord condition and the tenant condition are satisfied, but subject to the exceptions in Schedule 3 to this Act and to subsection (5) below and sections 37 and 49 of this Act.

(2) The landlord condition is that –

(*a*) the interest of the landlord belongs to one of the bodies mentioned in subsection (4) below; or

(*b*) the interest of the landlord belongs to a housing association falling within subsection (3) of section 15 of the 1977 [Rent] Act; or

(*c*) the interest of the landlord belongs to a housing co-operative and the dwelling-house is comprised in a housing co-operative agreement; or

(*d*) the interest of the landlord belongs to a county council and the tenancy was granted by it in the exercise of the reserve powers conferred on county councils by section 194 of the Local Government Act 1972.

(3) The tenant condition is that the tenant is an individual and occupies the dwelling-house as his only or principal home; or, where the tenancy is a joint tenancy, that each of the joint tenants is an individual and at least one of them occupies the dwelling-house as his only or principal home.

(4) The bodies referred to in subsection (2)(*a*) above are –

(*a*) a local authority;

(*b*) the Commission for the New Towns;

(*c*) a development corporation;

(*d*) the Housing Corporation;

(*e*) a housing trust which is a charity within the meaning of the Charities Act 1960; and

(*f*) the Development Board for Rural Wales.

(5) Where a secure tenancy is a tenancy for a term certain and the tenant dies, the tenancy remains a secure tenancy until either –

(*a*) the tenancy is vested or otherwise disposed of in the course of the administration of the tenant's estate; or

(*b*) it is known that when the tenancy has been so vested or disposed of it will not be a secure tenancy.

Note. (*a*) Notwithstanding the apparent similarity with Rent Act 1977, s. 1 (above, p. 157), Housing Act 1980 attempts to avoid some of the problems of interpretation by providing that certain licenses should come within the scope of s. 28 (*ibid.*, s. 48).

(*b*) Rent Act 1977, s. 15(3) covers housing associations registered with the Housing Corporation, or registered under the Industrial and

Provident Societies Act 1965. However, under Housing Act 1980, s. 49, tenancies granted by housing associations that are both registered with the Corporation *and* registered under the Industrial and Provident Societies Act 1965 are not secure tenancies; and associations which are merely registered under the Act of 1965 are exempt from sections 35 to 46 of the 1980 Act. (They deal with the 'tenants' charter', below, p. 528.)

(*c*) Under the Act of 1980, s. 37, a secure tenancy which is assigned ceases to be secure, unless assigned under Matrimonial Causes Act 1973, s. 24 (which is a common occurrence in divorce proceedings); or unless the assignment was to a spouse or a member of the tenant's family. Further, if the *whole* of a dwelling-house is sub-let, the secure tenancy ends.

(*d*) Schedule 3 provides that the following categories of tenancy are not secure: long leases (for a fixed period of twenty-one years or more); premises occupied under a contract of employment (see ch. 9, above, pp. 457–62); tenancies of dwellings on land acquired for development; tenancies of accommodation which has been provided under the Housing (Homeless Persons) Act (unless the tenant remains in the property for over six months); tenancies granted temporarily to someone seeking employment; tenancies of dwellings leased to the landlord on a short-term basis; tenancies of dwellings provided temporarily during the completion of building works; agricultural holdings lettings; lettings of pubs; lettings to students; business tenancies; lettings by almshouse charities.

(*e*) On the death of the secure tenant, there is provision for *one* succession only to a member of the tenant's family (Housing Act 1980, ss. 30 and 31).

(*f*) The following principles apply to secure tenancies created before as well as after the passing of the Housing Act 1980 (s. 46).

2. Security of tenure

The most substantial right granted by the 1980 Act (though subject, as we shall see, to a large number of exceptions) is security of tenure. Housing Act 1980, s. 32:

32.—(1) A secure tenancy which is either –

    (*a*) a weekly or other periodic tenancy; or

    (*b*) a tenancy for a term certain but subject to termination by the landlord;

cannot be brought to an end by the landlord except by obtaining an order of the court for the possession of the dwelling-house or an order under sub-section (2) below; and where the landlord obtains an order for the possession of the dwelling-house the tenancy ends on the date on which the tenant is to give up possession in pursuance of the order.

(2) Where a secure tenancy is a tenancy for a term certain but with a pro-vision for re-entry or forfeiture, the court shall not order possession of the dwelling-house in pursuance of that provision; but in any case where, but for this section, the court would have made such an order it shall instead make an order terminating the secure tenancy on a date specified in the order.

(3) Section 146 of the Law of Property Act 1925 (restriction on and relief against forfeiture), except subsection (4) (vesting in under-lessee) and any other enactment or rule of law relating to forfeiture shall apply in relation to proceedings for an order under subsection (2) above as if they were proceed-ings to enforce a right of re-entry or forfeiture.

(Rights of forfeiture are discussed above, pp. 406–12.)

In order to obtain such order as is specified in s. 32, proceedings must be begun by a special notice of intended proceedings (s. 33). This replaces the common law requirements relating to notices to quit, s. 33(3). It must be in a specified form (s. 33(2)). Possession will be granted only on the grounds defined in the legislation. The similari-ties and differences between these provisions and Rent Act provisions (above, ch. 8, pp. 417–40) should be carefully noted.

3. Grounds for eviction

34.—(1) The court shall not make an order for the possession of a dwelling-house let under a secure tenancy except on one or more of the grounds set out in Part I of Schedule 4 to this Act and shall not make such an order on any of those grounds unless the ground is specified in the notice in pursuance of which proceedings for possession are begun; but the grounds so specified may be altered or added to with the leave of the court.

(2) The court shall not make the order–

(a) on any of grounds 1 to 6, unless the condition in subsection (3)(a) below is satisfied;

(b) on any of grounds 7 to 9, unless the condition in subsection (3)(b) below is satisfied; and

(c) on any of grounds 10 to 13, unless both those conditions are satisfied.

(3) The conditions are–

(a) that the court considers it reasonable to make the order; and

(b) that the court is satisfied that suitable accommodation will be avail-able for the tenant when the order takes effect.

(4) Part II of Schedule 4 has effect for determining whether suitable accommodation will be available for a tenant.

Ground 1

Any rent lawfully due from the tenant has not been paid or any obligation of the tenancy has been broken or not performed.

Comment. The question of rent arrears, particularly in local authority dwellings, is a matter of acute controversy. Many local authority housing managers see it as a crucial problem to be dealt with by harsh measures, including distraint (see above, pp. 301–2) and eviction. It is feared that failure to take firm action will encourage others not to pay, and is done out of fairness to those who do pay. Others argue that the imposition of draconian remedies fails to take account of the wider causes of rent arrears. These may be found in the far more fundamental reasons of inadequate incomes, frustration at the inability to get repairs done, inadequate advice so that rent and rate rebates are not taken up, and other such reasons. Furthermore, harsh measures fail to solve the problem. Distraint of goods is frequently insufficient to pay off any arrears; eviction may simply result in the local authority having to rehouse, because of its duties under the Housing (Homeless Persons) Act 1977 (above, p. 482). In any event, it is suggested that local housing authorities as, effectively, the last source of housing for many people have a social responsibility not to evict, except in the most exceptional cases. What do you think? (There is a considerable literature on this topic: see, e.g., Harvey, 1969, and citations therein; Popplestone, 1980; Ungerson & Baldock, 1978; *Lamsac*, 1978; Alpren, 1977; Porter, 1978, p. 141; Downey, 1978.)

Further detail on alternative procedures for enforcing payment of rent arrears can be found above (pp. 301–3); see, too, DoE Circular 83/72:

6. In cases, however, when rent arrears do still arise, the attention of your Council is invited to the Attachment of Earnings Act 1971 which makes provision for the attachment of earnings as a means of enforcing the payment of judgment debts and other monetary obligations. In addition a simple and speedy means of preventing rent arrears from accumulating is now available through the new procedure of rent action in the county courts introduced by Rule 17 of the County Court (New Procedure) Rules 1971 (SI 1971 No 2152 (L.53)), which came into operation on 1 March 1972 and introduced a new Part II into Order 26 of the County Court Rules.

7. This new procedure makes possible the recovery of rent from a tenant still in occupation. Upon application being made to the county court a summons for rent in County Court Form 410 will be issued against a tenant in arrears requiring him to attend to answer the claim. It is anticipated that the hearing of the summons will follow quickly and judgment will be given at the hearing whether the defendant appears or not. The only exception to this will be when the defendant appears and raises some substantial defence or objection to the claim. Once judgment has been entered, the defendant will be able to pay money into the court either in satisfaction or on account of the claim. If, however, he fails to comply with the judgment, an authority will be able to proceed to enforcement.

8. In general, therefore, Ministers are confident that those local authorities who have not hitherto applied to the county court to obtain orders for possession will, in practice, find this new system both satisfactory and, where necessary, expeditious. In relation to rent cases in particular, it is their view not only that there should be less occasion in the future for tenants to fall into arrears but also that there is an alternative means of recovering arrears where they do arise which offers a better solution to this problem than recourse to eviction.

and the Appendix to Circular 18/74:

3. Rent arrears are a serious problem. Local authorities are right to use every endeavour to prevent them arising and to recover them when they do. The help available to tenants through rent and rate rebates and, for those in receipt of supplementary benefit, through the rent element of such benefit should enable all tenants to meet their financial obligations towards the authority. For the majority who do, with or without such help, meet their obligations, the knowledge that no action would be taken in respect of those with rent arrears, would be resented. This does not mean, however, that rent arrears should be treated simply as a financial problem attracting as routine penalties the issue of an eviction notice with the possible execution of any subsequent possession order. To create homelessness with which the local authority itself will have to deal, can only make matters worse both for the tenant and his family and for the local authority.

4. Cases of rent arrears call for a variety of approaches, including the use of social services work. Some of the methods which have been used by local authorities are set out below. These measures, including the more serious possibilities in (vii) and (viii), should be seen as ways of helping a tenant and his family to manage their financial affairs better, and to improve their chances of meeting their obligations, and not as punishments.

    i. The number of missed payments, as well as the total of the outstanding debt, may give early warning of difficulties and enable special arrangements for rent collection to be made, and for social services advice to be sought.

ii. As soon as it becomes apparent that rent arrears are accumulating, the housing authority should check that the tenant is getting the benefit of any rent or rate rebates to which there is an entitlement.

iii. The vigorous pursuit of rent arrears, including selective visiting in suitable cases, will help to prevent the amount outstanding becoming substantial.

iv. In suitable cases, while family or social problems are being dealt with, financial support by social service departments or authorities might be appropriate by means of rent guarantees (with payments attached direct to the housing authority if necessary) or, by means of payments of rent arrears, using the powers in section 1 of the Children and Young Persons Act 1963.

v. Direct payment of the rent element in supplementary benefit in suitable cases. Local social security offices should be consulted as soon as it seems likely that direct payment might be appropriate.

vi. DOE Circular 83/72 explains some of the possibilities for recovery of rent arrears, including civil proceedings to recover the debt and subsequent attachment of earnings where a person has regular employment. A watch needs to be kept on current rent accruing after a Court decision.

vii. Transfer to cheaper accommodation may help reduce a tenant's financial difficulties, but care needs to be taken not to create a concentration of families with financial or social problems.

viii. If (vii) fails e.g. because the tenant refuses to move without a Court order for possession, an eviction notice might be issued followed by proceedings for possession but only if the authority is satisfied, or can arrange, that other accommodation is available.

5. Arrangements to provide early warning of homelessness will enable authorities to forestall some homelessness. Potential sources of information about tenants in difficulty include the County Courts, Housing Associations, Probation and Social Workers, Housing Aid Centres, Citizens Advice Bureaux and other places to which people may bring their housing troubles. Since virtually all possession orders leading to evictions originate in the County Courts, authorities should examine their arrangements for liaison with the Court so as to receive early warning of cases to be considered there and of any possession order. This may enable help to be given to prevent eviction and so avoid another claim on local authority resources. An early step should be to ensure that any entitlement to rent allowances or rate rebates is being taken up. Rent guarantees or payment of rent arrears might be appropriate to help some families in difficulties.

Consider also the views of an economist (Culyer, 1973, p. 160):

Cost-benefit analysis can, as we have seen, be a useful exercise even though it is not possible fully to quantify every cost or benefit. A good example of a case where many effects cannot be quantified but where the technique gives quite positive guidance to social policy makers at the local level is in the treatment of council house tenants in arrears.

Arrears are frequently symptomatic of a far deeper social problem than irregularity of payment and this alone is sufficient for local authorities to exercise caution, before bringing in the bailiffs, by involving local social services departments at an early stage. An entirely different type of concern is also embodied in the Home Office and Department of Health circulars on this matter among which the potential burden on the rates of homelessness is one. The standard cost-benefit framework with its unitary weights system regards these, however, as purely interpersonal transfers – the tenant's benefit or the rate-payer's cost – which cancel out. The most plausible alternative assumptions about weights would normally place a higher value on the tenant's than the rate-payer's pound which makes one feel even less inclined to think that social welfare is much impaired by a shift of burden from tenant to rate-payer. A recent study in Reading, however, of the costs and benefits of eviction for rent arrears should make the problems raised by transfers clearer.

The number of evictions in Reading for rent arrears was small – six in 1966/67 with outstanding arrears of £670 from former tenants – and the total collectors' arrears owed by current tenants varied quite substantially around £2,000. The choice facing the authorities is simply between eviction, once tenants become persistently and seriously in arrears, and non-eviction.

The pattern of pure transfer payments created as a result of eviction is broadly as follows:

Rent of temporary accommodation for evicted tenants
Rent of vacated dwelling from new tenants
Supplementary Benefits
Rent of husband's lodging

Real resource costs and benefits are shown in Table [10.6], together with an item by item comparison of the net benefit (+ or −) of eviction compared with non-eviction. [*MV*=marginal value.]

Even though it was not possible to measure all the items, it is quite clear that, with the single possible exception of the care of the family (especially the children), eviction imposed net social costs upon the evicted family. Possible benefits not so far included are chiefly (a) the replacement of an irregularly paying tenant by a regularly paying tenant and (b) the incentive effect that eviction may have on neighbouring tenants. If eviction is to be justified at all, it will needs have to be justified on either or both of these two counts.

Previous analysis has established a fundamental point about the provision of social services, that the socially optimal quantity is where the sum of all *MV's* is equal to marginal social cost. A second point, that the individual

Table 10.6   Costs of eviction and non-eviction (£)

	Category	Policies		Net social benefit of eviction
		Eviction	Non-eviction	
1.	Direct costs of Eviction	25	0	−25
2.	Preparation for new tenants (redecoration)	5	0	− 5
3.	Allocation of new tenants	5	0	− 5
4.	Consumers' surpluses lost of temporarily vacant property	+	0	−
5.	Removal and storage of furniture	5	0	− 5
6.	Provision of temporary accommodation for one month	10	0	−10
7.	Social Services	10	0	−10
8.	Tenant's loss of earnings while searching for new accommodation	10	0	−10
9.	Effect on evictees	+	0	−
10.	Risk of permanent split in family	+	0	−
11.	Damage to tenant's property	+	0	−
12.	Care of family	−(?)	0	+(?)

subsidies should vary (for income elastic services) according to income, will be derived in chapter 10 but is of relevance here. For our present purpose, the first of these conditions implies that the sum of *MV's* should be set equal to the *open market potential rent* of local authority housing this representing its social opportunity cost, not to either per unit historical cost or per unit replacement cost. If we assume an optimal stock of local authority housing in any area the differential between open market rent and the rent paid by tenants is the *MV* of the rest of society. If every tenant paid the same rent for the same type of dwelling any tenant falling in long term arrears would signal a permanent fall in his *MV* and, if there were no excess demand for the optimal stock of subsidised housing, would imply a case both for eviction, if it were costless, and a reduction in the subsidised housing stock. If the social costs of eviction are positive, as they are, the greater the shortfall of the tenant's *MV* (as indicated by arrears) and the *difference* between open market rent and the rest of society's *MV*, the greater the likelihood that eviction is a socially optimal policy. However, only if the social costs of eviction are zero does it follow that *any* permanent arrears require eviction.

Identical rents for all tenants implies, however, that all tenants have identical *MV's* – supposing subsidising policy to be efficient. The fact that *MV's* differ implies modifying the conclusion of the previous paragraph for an accumulation of arrears may now be evidence for the need for a larger subsidy to the family in question – especially if it is due to a change in the family's financial circumstances. Essentially, this amounts to an assessment of the comparative urgency of 'need' of the family in arrears and the family with the highest priority on the waiting list. Since in practice priorities on the waiting list are usually based on arbitrary criteria such as length of wait it seems unlikely that the new tenants would, on average, necessarily represent more urgent cases in the sense of imposing an externality on the rest of the concerned community than those who have got themselves into chronic difficulties with arrears. In such circumstances, the adjustment of rent would be a natural and consistent corollary, the case for non-eviction being strengthened by the positive social costs of eviction.

The incentive effect of eviction is mainly an empirical matter which we do not propose to explore in detail. The Reading study indicated that the effect of eviction on other tenants in arrears was small, was confined to tenants in the immediate neighbourhood and was, anyway, temporary. Viewed purely as an incentive effect eviction is almost certainly an inefficient policy. Given both the small number of evictions in Reading and the relatively small size of outstanding arrears it does not seem likely that even the *existence* of the eviction right supplies much in the way of an incentive to pay, especially by comparison with the many ordinary social pressures on tenants not to default on payments.

But implicit in the foregoing is a criticism of the standard treatment of transfer payments as merely cancelling items, for transfers, like prices, provide a measure (though frequently a very poor one) of individual and social valuations. If, for example, neither an individual tenant nor the rest of society is prepared to pay (possibly only implicitly in the case of the rest of society) enough to keep the tenant in a council dwelling in the public sector of the housing market, that is evidence for the potential optimality of either reletting the dwelling in the public sector at a suitable rent or for selling it. In this way transfers can be used as the basis for shadow pricing to achieve both a socially optimal stock of local authority housing and a socially optimal mix of tenants occupying it.

Ground 2

The tenant or any person residing in the dwelling-house has been guilty of conduct which is a nuisance or annoyance to neighbours, or has been convicted of using the dwelling-house or allowing it to be used for immoral or illegal purposes.

This ground relates to the question of the so-called 'problem' family, or 'difficult tenants'. Again this raises controversial questions of housing management. Some argue that if tenants were treated more responsibly, they would behave more responsibly; others argue that severe action is needed to keep 'the problem' under control. Following a survey of policy in six local authorities Popplestone (1979) came to the following conclusion:

Few housing officials appear to have any good ideas about what to do with unsatisfactory tenants. Some officials bemoan the erosion of sanctions brought about by legislation and government circulars. But unsatisfactory tenants tend not to respond to treatment, and no amount of new sanctions will do anything to change this. Most approaches still concentrate attention on them as the problem that needs to be dealt with. But often they are the victims rather than the cause of the problems.

Behind complaints about neighbouring tenants often lie a host of other grievances that have not been dealt with. They often stem from the lack of choice available to council tenants over the question of who to live next to. People with similar life styles and outlooks are likely to get on better with people who share those outlooks, than people who live radically differently. Also, tenants are often obliged to live in housing patently inadequate for their needs. In the course of the research we came across complaints which stemmed from the stressful conditions brought about by physical densities as well as the high child population of some estates. Few estates cater adequately for the needs of young or teenage children. Families living in stressful circumstances at very high densities cannot be expected to tolerate disruptive families. This is the nub of many of the intractable problems. Unsatisfactory tenants are often the scapegoats for intolerable conditions.

No amount of thought about how to deal with difficult tenants will bring results until the cause of stress in some estates is substantially reduced by adequate play and nursery provision, realistic opportunities for families to transfer out, adequate provision for teenagers and more imaginative use of public and semi-public space in order to create a richer environment.

Another difficulty that has a bearing on this issue stems from blocked aspirations. We found tenants who resent the way that, once allocated a dwelling, they cannot aspire to something better (like owner-occupiers), and many who do not like their initial allocations may feel trapped. In such circumstances, difficult neighbours may appear intolerable. It is also easy to get rid of frustrations by complaining about the neighbours.

The issue of difficult tenants needs to be put in this wider context if tenants' complaints are ever to be tackled realistically. Disruptive behaviour and stressful conditions may be two sides of the same coin.

Do you agree? Consider *Smith* v. *Scott* [1972] 3 All E.R. 645:

PENNYCUICK V.-C.: By this motion ... the plaintiff, Cecil Edward Smith, seeks against the mayor and corporation of the London Borough of Lewisham an injunction restraining them 'from allowing or permitting any person licensed or permitted by them to occupy use or dwell in the said premises situate at and known as No. 25 Walpole Road aforesaid from doing' certain acts, those acts being, as set out in the notice of motion, entering on the plaintiff's adjoining premises, 27 Walpole Road, doing damage there and creating disturbance by noise.

Mr Smith and his wife are the registered proprietors of the dwelling-house known as 27 Walpole Road, New Cross ... in the London Borough of Lewisham. Mr and Mrs Smith are an elderly couple, and until the events which I will recount, lived at 27 Walpole Road with their son, Mr John Smith. Walpole Road lies in an area scheduled for demolition and reconstruction as an open space.

The defendant corporation has acquired a number of other houses in Walpole Road, and intends to acquire the remaining houses, including no. 27 if necessary, by the exercise of compulsory powers. For the time being it is using certain of these houses as short-term accommodation for homeless families. It is the policy of the corporation to place homeless families in council accommodation on a short-term basis in order to ascertain what type of permanent accommodation is appropriate for them...

In July 1971 ... the corporation moved ... Mr and Mrs Scott, into no. 25. The Scotts have a large and unruly family. I am satisfied beyond doubt, indeed it is not challenged, that the conduct of the Scott family as a whole was altogether intolerable both in respect of physical damage and of noise. The Smiths found it impossible to live next door to the Scotts and went to live elsewhere with relatives, where they still remain. The corporation, notwithstanding protests on the part of the Smiths, has taken no effective steps to control the Scotts, nor has it taken any step to evict them ...

The corporation let the Scotts into possession of no. 25 on the terms of certain printed conditions of tenancy. These include cl. 6: 'THE TENANT(s) SHALL: ... (h) Be responsible for the orderly conduct of all persons (including their children) who occupy the premises, their own and other occupants' visitors on any part of the estate...'

Then cl. 8: 'THE TENANT(s) SHALL NOT: ... (d) Overcrowd the premises or do or permit or suffer anything to be done on the premises which in the opinion of the Council may be or become a nuisance or annoyance to other persons...'

Then cl. 12: 'The tenant shall be responsible for ensuring that members of his family, his visitors and other persons who occupy the premises or any part thereof comply with conditions 7 and 8 hereof and accordingly any infringement of such conditions by such persons will be deemed to be and be treated as an infringement thereof by the tenant.'

A considerable volume of evidence was filed on both sides, and most of the deponents were cross-examined. I need not go into particulars of the conduct on the part of the Scott family which was flagrant and, as I have said, unchallenged.

A great part of the Mr Smith's evidence was concerned to establish by inference from the circumstances that the corporation must have been actuated by some improper motive in placing the Scotts in no. 25, the collateral purpose advanced being to get the Smiths out of no. 27 by agreement and at an under-value. There is no doubt that there was ill-feeling between the Smiths and certain of the corporation officials.

After hearing Mr Smith's witnesses it seemed to me that there was a case for the corporation to answer in this respect. Mr Davy, the assistant housing manager to the corporation, and the principal deponent on its behalf, did not himself adequately meet this case. He admitted that he knew before July 1971 that the Scotts were the sort of people who did not appear to be good tenants and were likely to be guilty of anti-social behaviour and was unable himself to explain why no. 25 had been selected for the Scotts. However, at a later stage in the hearing counsel for the corporation, with the consent of counsel for Mr Smith, called a Mrs Hand, the allocation officer who actually made the allocation of no. 25 to the Scotts on her own initiative. Mrs Hand had not been informed by Mr Davy that the Scotts had given trouble before. She gave a satisfactory account of the reasons which had led her to allocate no. 25 to the Scotts.

On the evidence of Mr Davy and Mrs Hand, I find, (1) that the corporation had knowledge when it placed the Scotts in no. 25 that they were likely to cause a nuisance, but (2) that the corporation was not actuated by any improper motive in making the allocation...

I must then consider the law applicable to the foregoing conclusions of fact. Apart from the allegation of improper motive, counsel for Mr Smith based his case on three propositions of law, namely (1) the corporation in placing the Scotts in no. 25 with knowledge that they were likely to cause a nuisance to their neighbours itself committed the wrongful act of nuisance; (2) the corporation brought on to its land a 'thing', namely the Scotts, likely to do mischief if it escaped; (3) the corporation had a duty of care to Mr Smith, as owner of no. 27, and failed in that duty by placing the Scotts in no. 25. I will consider those propositions in the same order.

(1) It is established beyond question that the person to be sued in nuisance is the occupier of the property from which the nuisance emanates. In general, a landlord is not liable for nuisance committed by his tenant, but to this rule there is, so far as now in point, one recognized exception, namely, that the landlord is liable if he has authorized his tenant to commit the nuisance: see *Harris* v. *James* ((1876) 45 L.J.Q.B. 545). But this exception has, in the reported cases, been rigidly confined to circumstances in which the nuisance has either been expressly authorized or is certain to result from the purposes for which the property is let: ... and see generally Clerk and Lindsell on Torts, [13th edn, 1969, p. 805, para. 1426].

I have used the word 'certain', but 'certainty' is obviously a very difficult matter to establish. It may be that, as one of the textbooks suggests, the proper test in this connection is 'virtual certainty' which is another way of saying a very high degree of probability, but the authorities are not, I venture to think, altogether satisfactory in this respect.

Whatever the precise test may be, it would, I think, be impossible to apply the exception to the present case. The exception is squarely based in the reported cases on express or implied authority – see in particular the judgment of Blackburn J. in *Harris* v. *James*. The exception is not based on cause and probable result, apart from express or implied authority. In the present case the corporation let no. 25 to the Scotts as a dwelling-house on conditions of tenancy which expressly prohibited the committing of a nuisance and notwithstanding that the corporation knew the Scotts were likely to cause a nuisance, I do not think it is legitimate to say that the corporation impliedly authorized the nuisance.

(2) The rule in *Rylands* v. *Fletcher* ((1868) L.R. 3 (H.L.) 330) was applied in *Attorney-General* v. *Corke* ([1933] Ch. 89), against a defendant who had brought caravan dwellers on to his land as licensees, but so far as counsel has been able to ascertain, the rule has never been sought to be applied against a landlord who lets his property to undesirable tenants and I do not think it can be properly applied in such a case. The person liable under the rule in *Rylands* v. *Fletcher* is the owner or controller of the dangerous 'thing', and this is normally the occupier and not the owner of the land ... A landlord parts with possession of the demised property in favour of his tenant and could not in any sense known to the law be regarded as controlling the tenant on property still occupied by himself. I should respectfully have thought that *Attorney-General* v. *Corke* could at least equally well have been decided on the basis that the landowner there was in possession of the property and was himself liable in nuisance for the acts of his licensees: see *White* v. *Jameson* ((1874) L.R. 18 Eq. 303).

(3) The principle of the duty of care has been evolved in a series of modern cases, commencing with *Donoghue* v. *Stevenson* ([1932] A.C. 562). If this were virgin territory it might be argued that a landowner owes a duty of care to his neighbours when selecting the person to whom he will let as a tenant, but I do not think it is open to the court, certainly a court of first instance, to apply the principle in such circumstances.

I will quote a passage from the speech of Lord Reid in the recent case of *Home Office* v. *Dorset Yacht Co Ltd* ([1970] A.C. 1004):

'In later years there has been a steady trend towards regarding the law of negligence as depending on principle so that, when a new point emerges, one should ask not whether it is covered by authority but whether recognized principles apply to it. *Donoghue* v. *Stevenson* may be regarded as a milestone, and the well-known passage in Lord Atkin's speech should I think be regarded as a statement of principle. It is not to be treated as if it were a statutory definition. It will require qualification in new circumstances. But I think that the time has come when we can and should say that it ought to apply unless there is some justification or valid explanation for its exclusion. For example, causing economic loss is a different matter; for one thing it is often caused by deliberate action. Competition involves traders being entitled to damage their rivals' interests by promoting their own, and there is a long chapter of the law determining in what circumstances owners of land can, and in what circumstances they may not, use their proprietary rights so as to injure their neighbours.'

In the last words which I have cited from that passage, Lord Reid treats the rights and liabilities of landowners as determined by a long chapter of the law, and that passage seems to me strongly to support the view that the law cannot in this respect now be reshaped by a reference to the duty of care. I should add that the relationship of landowner, tenant and neighbour is, in its nature, of the most widespread possible occurrence and the introduction of the duty of care in this connection would have far-reaching implications in relation to business as well as to residential premises.

I come, therefore, to the conclusion that the corporation has not committed a wrong against Mr Smith which is actionable under the general law.

The conclusion reached by Pennycuick V-C has been criticized, e.g., by Merritt (1973) who thought that a different conclusion could have been reached, particularly on the issue of whether the authority was liable in nuisance. Having cited *Brew Bros. Ltd* v. *Snax (Ross) Ltd* ([1970] 1 Q.B. 612) and the judgment of Sachs L.J., Merritt asks:

Is it not to apply a 'rational consideration' to say that an owner of property on which a tenant or licensee is so misbehaving as to cause a nuisance, if it is within the owner's power without unreasonable difficulty to get rid of the person so misbehaving, is held by the law subject to an obligation to persons affected by the nuisance to exercise that power of control and is liable to them if he does not?

Ground 3

The condition of the dwelling-house or of any of the common parts has deteriorated owing to acts of waste by, or the neglect or default of, the tenant or any person residing in the dwelling-house and, in the case of any act of waste by, or the neglect or default of, a person lodging with the tenant or a sub-tenant of his, the tenant has not taken such steps as he ought reasonably to have taken for the removal of the lodger or sub-tenant.

In this paragraph 'the common parts' means any part of a building comprising the dwelling-house, and any other premises, which the tenant is entitled under the terms of the tenancy to use in common with the occupiers of other dwelling-houses let by the landlord.

Note the interaction of this ground with situations such as those discussed in *Liverpool C.C.* v. *Irwin* (above, pp. 343–6). This appears to throw much greater responsibility on tenants to prevent vandalism, and failure to do so may result in eviction.

Ground 4

The condition of any relevant furniture has deteriorated owing to ill-treatment by the tenant or any person residing in the dwelling-house and, in the case of any ill-treatment by a person lodging with the tenant or a sub-tenant of his, the tenant has not taken such steps as he ought reasonably to have taken for the removal of the lodger or sub-tenant.

In this paragraph 'relevant furniture' means any furniture provided by the landlord for use under the tenancy or for use in any of the common parts (within the meaning given in ground 3).

Ground 5

The tenant is the person, or one of the persons, to whom the tenancy was granted and the landlord was induced to grant the tenancy by a false statement made knowingly or recklessly by the tenant.

Ground 6

The dwelling-house was made available for occupation by the tenant or his predecessor in title while improvement works were carried out on the dwelling-house which he previously occupied as his only or principal home and –

(a) he (or his predecessor in title) was a secure tenant of that other dwelling-house at the time when he ceased to occupy it as his home;

(b) he (or his predecessor in title) accepted the tenancy of the dwelling-house of which possession is sought on the understanding that he would give up occupation when, on completion of the works, the other dwelling-house was again available for occupation by him under a secure tenancy; and

(c) the works have been completed and the other dwelling-house is so available.

Ground 7

The dwelling-house is overcrowded, within the meaning of the 1957 Act, in such circumstances as to render the occupier guilty of an offence. (Compare Rent Act 1977, s. 101, above, p. 419.)

Ground 8

The landlord intends, within a reasonable time of obtaining possession of the dwelling-house –

> (*a*) to demolish or reconstruct the building or part of the building comprising the dwelling-house; or
>
> (*b*) to carry out work on that building or on land let together with, and thus treated as part of, the dwelling-house;

and cannot reasonably do so without obtaining possession of the dwelling-house.

Ground 9

The landlord is a housing trust which is a charity within the meaning of the Charities Act 1960 and the tenant's continued occupation of the dwelling-house would conflict with the objects of the charity.

Ground 10

The dwelling-house has features which are substantially different from those of ordinary dwelling-houses and which are designed to make it suitable for occupation by a physically disabled person who requires accommodation of a kind provided by the dwelling-house and –

> (*a*) there is no longer such a person residing in the dwelling-house; and
>
> (*b*) the landlord requires it for occupation (whether alone or with other members of his family) by such a person.

Ground 11

The landlord is a housing association or housing trust which lets dwelling-houses only for occupation (alone or with others) by persons whose circumstances (other than merely financial circumstances) make it especially difficult for them to satisfy their need for housing; and –

> (*a*) there is no longer such a person residing in the dwelling-house; and
>
> (*b*) the landlord requires the dwelling-house for occupation (whether alone or with other members of his family) by such a person.

Ground 12

The dwelling-house is one of a group of dwelling-houses which it is the practice of the landlord to let for occupation by persons with special needs and –

> (*a*) a social service or special facility is provided in close proximity to the group of dwelling-houses in order to assist persons with those special needs;

(b) there is no longer a person with those special needs residing in the dwelling-house; and

(c) the landlord requires the dwelling-house for occupation (whether alone or with other members of his family) by a person who has those special needs.

Ground 13

The accommodation afforded by the dwelling-house is more extensive than is reasonably required by the tenant and –

(a) the tenancy vested in the tenant, by virtue of section 29 of this Act, on the death of the previous tenant;

(b) the tenant was qualified to succeed by virtue of subsection (2)(b) of that section; and

(c) notice of the proceedings for possession was served under section 32 of this Act more than six months, but less than twelve months, after the date of the previous tenant's death.

Since Grounds 7 to 13 essentially relate to questions of housing management, suitable accommodation must be provided (but not *alternative* accommodation in the Rent Act sense, above, pp. 419–24). See Housing Act 1980, Sched. 4, Part II:

1.—(1) For the purposes of this Part of this Act, accommodation is suitable if it consists of premises –

(a) which are to be let as a separate dwelling under a secure tenancy, or

(b) which are to be let as a separate dwelling under a protected tenancy (other than one of a kind mentioned in sub-paragraph (2) below) within the meaning of the 1977 Act,

and, in the opinion of the court, the accommodation is reasonably suitable to the needs of the tenant and his family.

(2) The kind of protected tenancy referred to in sub-paragraph (1) above is one under which the landlord might recover possession of the dwelling-house under one of the Cases in Part II of Schedule 15 to the 1977 Act (cases where court must order possession).

2. In determining whether it is reasonably suitable to those needs regard shall be had to –

(a) the nature of the accommodation which it is the practice of the landlord to allocate to persons with similar needs;

(b) the distance of the accommodation available from the place of work or education of the tenant and of any members of his family;

(c) its distance from the home of any member of the tenant's family if proximity to it is essential to that member's or the tenant's well-being;

(d) the needs (as regards extent of accommodation) and means of the tenant and his family;

(e) the terms on which the accommodation is available and the terms of the secure tenancy;

(f) if any furniture was provided by the landlord for use under the secure tenancy, whether furniture is to be provided for use in the other accommodation and, if it is, the nature of that furniture;

but where possession is sought on ground 7, accommodation otherwise reasonably suitable to the needs of the tenant and his family shall not be deemed not to be so by reason only that the permitted number of persons, computed under Schedule 6 to the 1957 Act in relation to the number and floor area of the rooms in it, is less than the number of persons living in the dwelling-house of which possession is sought.

3. Where the landlord is not a local authority for the purposes of Part V of the 1957 Act, a certificate of such an authority certifying that the authority will provide suitable accommodation for the tenant by a date specified in the certificate shall be conclusive evidence that suitable accommodation will be available for him by that date, if the dwelling-house of which possession is sought is situated in the district for supplying the needs of which the authority has power under that Part of that Act.

4. Terms of secure tenancies

The Housing Act 1980 prescribes a number of conditions relating to secure tenancies. These represent the results of the recent campaign for a 'Tenants' Charter'. (See National Consumer Council, 1976; Welsh Consumer Council, 1977.) In particular:

(a) Secure tenants are given the right to take in lodgers or sub-let *part* of the dwelling-house. In the case of members of the family this is an absolute right; in the case of others, consent must be obtained, but must not be unreasonably withheld (Housing Act 1980, ss. 35 and 36). (For sub-letting of the whole house, see above, p. 512.)

(b) Where a secure tenant has made improvements to the dwelling 'the landlord shall (in addition to any other power to make such payments) have power to make, at or after the end of the tenancy, such payment to the tenant (or his personal representatives) in respect of the improvement as the landlord considers to be appropriate' (*ibid.*, s. 37(2)). It will be very interesting to see how this particular discretion is used. Rents are not to be increased because of improvements lawfully made (though rates may be increased) (*ibid.*, s. 39). The right of tenants (both private sector and secure) to improve is to be found in Part III of the Act of 1980 (ss. 80–85; above, p. 400).

(*c*) Variation of the terms of a tenancy is not to be permitted without the completion of certain formalities allowing tenants to comment on proposed changes. These procedures do not apply to changes in rent, payments for services, or rates. The tenant has the right to issue a notice to quit if he so wishes (*ibid.*, s. 40). Furthermore, and somewhat surprisingly, any variation of the premises let under a tenancy is not to be regarded as a variation to which the statutory formalities apply (*ibid.*, s. 40(9)).

(*d*) Information about the terms of secure tenancies must be published, but landlords have two years from the date when this part of the Act comes into force to comply with this (*ibid.*, s. 41). Publication is to be:

in such form as [the landlord] considers best suited to explain in simple terms and so far as it considers appropriate, the effect of –

(*a*) the express terms of its secure tenancies;

(*b*) the provisions of this Part, and Part III of this Act; [This includes the right to buy; rights to security and other terms discussed here; and the right to improve.]

(*c*) the provisions of sections 32 and 33 of the Housing Act 1961. [This relates to repairing obligations; above, pp. 350–62.]

5. Consultation

For a number of years, the argument has been advanced that tenants should have greater involvement in the management of estates (Ward, 1974). This idea has gained widespread support (Richardson, 1977) since it is seen to be as much a means for local authorities to control what goes on on their estates as a method of giving tenants further democratic control over their lives. However, the terms of the Housing Act, on this issue, are a somewhat watered down version of the original idea:

42.—(1) In this Chapter 'landlord authority' means –

(*a*) a local authority;

(*b*) subject to section 49 of this Act, a housing association which falls within section 15(3) of the 1977 Act;

(*c*) a housing trust which is a charity within the meaning of the Charities Act 1960;

(*d*) a development corporation; or

(*e*) the Development Board for Rural Wales;

but neither the Development Board for Rural Wales nor a development corporation is a landlord authority for the purposes of this Chapter if an exemption certificate has been issued to it by the Secretary of State under section 45 of this Act.

(2) A matter is one of housing management for the purposes of this Chapter if, in the opinion of the landlord authority concerned, it –

(a) relates to the management, maintenance, improvement or demolition of dwelling-houses let by the authority under secure tenancies, or to the provision of services or amenities in connection with such dwelling-houses; and

(b) represents a new programme of maintenance, improvement or demolition or a change in the practice or policy of the authority; and

(c) is likely substantially to affect its secure tenants as a whole or a group of them.

(3) A matter is not one of housing management for the purposes of this Chapter in so far as it relates to the rent payable under any secure tenancy or to any charge for services or facilities provided by the landlord authority concerned.

(4) In this section 'group' means a group of secure tenants who –

(a) form a distinct social group; or

(b) occupy dwelling-houses which constitute a distinct class (whether by reference to the kind of dwelling-house concerned or the housing estate or other larger area in which they are situated).

(5) In the case of a landlord authority which is a local authority, the reference in subsection (2)(a) above to the provision of services or amenities is to be taken as referring only to the provision of services or amenities by the authority acting in its capacity as landlord of the dwelling-houses concerned.

43.—(1) Every landlord authority shall, within 12 months of the commencement of this Part of this Act, make and thereafter maintain such arrangements as it considers appropriate to enable those of its secure tenants who are likely to be substantially affected by a matter of housing management –

(a) to be informed of the authority's proposals in respect of that matter; and

(b) to make their views known to the authority within a specified period.

(2) It shall be the duty of a landlord authority, before making any decision on a matter of housing management, to consider any representation made to it in accordance with arrangements made by the authority under this section.

(3) Every landlord authority shall publish details of the arrangements which it makes under this section and a copy of any document published under this subsection shall –

(*a*) be made available at the authority's principal office for inspection at all reasonable hours, without charge, by members of the public; and

(*b*) be furnished, on payment of a reasonable fee, to any member of the public who asks for one.

(4) A landlord authority which is a housing association falling within section 15(3)(*a*) of the 1977 Act (registered with Housing Corporation) may, instead of complying with paragraph (*a*) of subsection (3) above, send a copy of any document published under that subsection to the Housing Corporation, which shall make it available, at its appropriate regional office, for inspection at all reasonable hours without charge by members of the public.

(5) Where a copy of any document is sent to the council of a district or London borough under subsection (4) above, the council shall make it available at its principal office for inspection at all reasonable hours, without charge, by members of the public.

Comment: It will be interesting to see whether these provisions have any effect in encouraging tenants' organizations to act more collectively in the running of public sector estates, and whether local authorities respond positively or negatively to these provisions (cf. above, pp. 27–8).

BIBLIOGRAPHY

Abel, R. (1973), 'Law Books and Books About Law', 26 *Stanford Law Rev.*, 175–228.

Abel, R.L. (1979), 'The Rise of Professionalism', 6 *British Journal of Law and Society*, 82–98.

Abel-Smith, B., Zander, M. and Brooke, R. (1973), *Legal Problems and the Citizen* (Heinemann, London).

Adams, B. *et al.* (1975), *Gypsies and Government Policy in England* (Heinemann, London).

Adams, J.E. (1976), 'Rent Act Problems of Sharing and Multi-Occupation', 120 *Solicitors Journal*, 125–6.

Advisory Committee on Rent Rebates and Allowances (1974, 1977), *Reports* (HMSO, London).

Aldridge, T.M. (1974), 'Flat Sharing', 118 *Solicitors Journal*, 3–4.

Alpren, L. (1977), *The Causes of Serious Rent Arrears* (Housing Centre Trust, London).

Ambrose, P. and Colenutt, B. (1975), *The Property Machine* (Penguin, Harmondsworth).

Anderson, J.S. (1979), 'Of Licences, and Similar Mysteries', 42 *Modern Law Review*, 203–7.

Arden, A. (1976), 'The Rent Acts: A Personal View', 126 *New Law Journal*, 319–21.

Arden, A. (1978a), *Housing: Security and Rent Control* (Sweet & Maxwell, London).

Arden, A. (1978b), 'Non-Exclusive Occupation Agreements', *LAG Bulletin*, 138–40.

Arden, A. (1979a), 'The Case for a Housing Code', *LAG Bulletin*, 79–82.

Arden, A. (1979b), 'High Court Guerrillas', 3 *Roof*, 78–82.

Arden, A. (1979c), 'A Note on Set-Off against Rent', *LAG Bulletin*, 210–11.

Arden, A. (1979d), 'Enforcing the Homeless Persons Act: 1. General Principles', *LAG Bulletin*, 283–6.

Arden, A. (1980a), 'Enforcing the Homeless Persons Act: 2. Courts and Cases', *LAG Bulletin*, 14–17.

Arden, A. (1980b), 'More on Enforcing the Homeless Persons Act', *LAG Bulletin*, 64–5.

Arden, A. and Parish, J. (1979), 'Mobile Homes', *LAG Bulletin*, 233–6.

Arden, A. and Partington, M. (1980), *Quiet Enjoyment* (LAG, London).

Atiyah, P. (1979), 'Compensation Orders and Civil Liability', *Criminal Law Review*, 504–9.

Bailey, R. (1973), *The Squatters* (Penguin, Harmondsworth).

Bailey, R. (1977), *The Homeless and the Empty Houses* (Penguin, Harmondsworth).

Balchin, P.N. (1979), *Housing Improvement and Social Inequality* (Saxon House, Farnborough).

Barnett, M.J. (1969), *The Politics of Legislation* (Weidenfeld & Nicolson, London).

Bean, J.M.W. (1968), *The Decline of English Feudalism 1215–1540* (Manchester University Press, Manchester).

Benwell CDP (1978), *Slums on the Drawing Board* (Benwell Community Project, Newcastle-upon-Tyne).

Berry, F. (1979), 'Anomalous Treatment of the Homeless', 4 *Roof*, 23.

Bierne, P. (1977), *Fair Rent and Legal Fiction* (Macmillan, London).

Billcliffe, S. (1979), 'Dumped in the Interim', 4 *Roof*, 118–21.

Bird, B. and O'Dell, A. (1977), *Mobile Homes in England and Wales* (Building Research Establishment, Watford).

Blood, C. (1979), 'One Woman's Fight for a Damp-Free Home', 4 *Roof*, 162–3.

Bradshaw, J. and Bradley, K. (1979), 'Can a Housing Allowance Work?', 4 *Roof*, 94–6.

British Property Federation (1975), *Policy for Housing* (BPF, London).

Brown, L.N. (1970), 'Comparative Rent Control', 19 *International and Comparative Law Quarterly*, 205–15.

Burrows, L. (1979), 'One Man's Holiday: Another Man's Home', 4 *Roof*, 42–4.

Byles, A. and Morris, P. (1977), *Unmet Need* (Routledge & Kegan Paul, London).

Caplan, D. (1975), *People and Homes* (British Property Federation, London).

Cavenagh, W.E. and Hawker, G.N. (1974), 'Laymen on Administrative Tribunals', *Public Administration*, 209–22.

CDP, *see* Community Development Project.

Central Housing Advisory Committee (1955), *Residential Qualifications* (HMSO, London).

CHAC, *see* Central Housing Advisory Committee.

Chalklin, C.W. (1968), 'Urban Housing Estates in the Eighteenth Century', 5 *Urban Studies*, 67–85.

Chalklin, C.W. (1974), *The Provincial Towns of Georgian England* (Edward Arnold, London).

Chambers, J.D. and Mingay, G.E. (1966), *The Agricultural Revolution: 1750–1880* (Batsford, London).

Clerk, J.F. and Lindsell, W.A.B. (1975), *On Torts* (14th ed. by A. Armitage and others) (Sweet & Maxwell, London).

Coates, K. and Silburn, R. (1970), *Poverty: The Forgotten Englishmen* (Penguin, Harmondsworth).

Cohen, Sir K.C. (Chairman) (1971), *Housing Associations* (HMSO, London).

Coke, Sir E. (1670), *A Commentarie upon Littleton* (London).

Community Development Project (1976), *Whatever Happened to Council Housing?* (CDP Information and Intelligence Unit, London).

Community Development Project (1977a), *Limits of the Law* (CDP Inter-Project Editorial Team, London).

Community Development Project (1977b), *The Poverty of the Improvement Programme* (revised ed.) (CDP Political Economy Collective, Newcastle-upon-Tyne).

Community Relations Commission (1976), *Housing in Multi-Racial Areas* (CRC, London).

Community Relations Commission (1977a), *Race and Local Authority Housing* (CRC, London).

Community Relations Commission (1977b), *Housing Choice and Ethnic Concentration* (CRC, London).

Constable (Chairman) (1925), *Report of the Committee on the Rent Restriction Acts* (Cmd. 2423) (HMSO, London).

Corrigan, P. and Ginsberg, N. (1975), 'Tenants' Struggle and Class Struggle' in *Political Economy and the Housing Question* (Political Economy of Housing Workshop, London).

CRC, *see* Community Relations Commission.

Crine, A. and Wintour, J. (1980), 'HIPs: The Vital Statistics', 5 *Roof*, 52–4.

Cripps, J. (1977), *Accommodation for Gypsies* (HMSO, London).

Crossman, R.H.S. (1975), *The Diaries of a Cabinet Minister*, Vol. 1 (Michael Joseph, London).

Culley, L. (1978), 'Council Referral Procedures', 3 *Roof*, 188–91.

Cullingworth, J.B. (1963), *Housing in Transition* (Heinemann, London).

Cullingworth, J.B. (Chairman) (1969), Central Housing Advisory Committee Report: *Council Housing: Purposes, Procedures and Priorities* (HMSO, London).

Cullingworth, J.B. (1979), *Essays on Housing Policy* (Allen & Unwin, London).

Culyer, A.J. (1973), *The Economics of Social Policy* (Martin Robertson, Oxford).

Cutting, M. (1975), *Tenants in the County Court* (Catholic Housing Aid Society, London).

Cutting, M. (1979), *A Housing Rights Handbook* (Penguin, Harmondsworth).

Darwin, J. (1979), 'Build Cheap Now – Pay More Later', 4 *Roof*, 82–4.

Davey, M. (1979), 'Bridging the Nuisance Gap', 4 *Roof*, 163.

Davis, K.C. (1971), *Discretionary Justice* (University of Illinois Press, Urbana, USA).

Dawson, I.J. and Pearce, R.A. (1979), *Licences relating to the Occupation or Use of Land* (Butterworths, London).

Denim, S. (1978), 'DoE's Suggestive Remarks about Rents', 3 *Roof*, 143–4.

Department of the Environment (1977), *Improvement Research Note 3/77* (DoE, London).

Department of the Environment (1979a), *Domestic Energy Notes 4* (DoE, London).

Department of the Environment (1979b), *Consultation Paper: Review of the Law of Statutory Nuisance and Offensive Trades* (DoE, London).

de Smith, S.A. (1980), *Judicial Review of Administrative Action* (4th ed.) (Sweet & Maxwell, London).

DoE, *see* Department of the Environment.

Donnison, D.V. (1967), *The Government of Housing* (Penguin, Harmondsworth).

Donnison, D.V. (1979), 'Benefit of Simplicity', 4 *Roof*, 68.

Douglas, R. (1976), *Land, People and Politics: A History of the Land Question 1878–1952* (Allison & Busby, London).

Downey, P. (1978), *Rent Arrears in Local Authority Housing: A Discussion Paper* (Housing Development Directorate, Occasional Paper 1/78) (DoE, London).

Dunn, A.T. and White, G.C. (1979), 'Trends in Sales of Land and Buildings', *Economic Trends*, 100–12.

Economist (1979), 'Move in Now, Pay Later', 5th May.

Edel, M. (1977), 'Rent Theory and Working Class Strategy: Marx, George and the Urban Crisis', 9 *Review of Radical Political Economics*, 1–15.

Eversley, D. (1975), 'Landlords' Slow Goodbye', 31 *New Society*, 119–21.

Farrand, J. (1978), *The Rent Act 1977* (Sweet & Maxwell, London).

Finnis, N. (1977), 'The Private Landlord is Dead but he Won't Lie Down', 2 *Roof*, 109–12.

Finnis, N. (1978a), 'Students Wrinkle the Rent Act', 3 *Roof*, 38.

Finnis, N. (1978b), 'Courting Rent Act Disaster', 3 *Roof*, 74–6.

Finnis, N. (1978c), 'The Heartless and the Homeless', 3 *Roof*, 138.

Fisher, J.R. (1978) 'The Farmers' Alliance: An Agricultural Protest Movement of the 1880's', 26 *Agricultural History Review*, 15–25.

Francis, H. (Chairman) (1971), *Report of the Committee on the Rent Acts* (Cmnd. 4609) (HMSO, London).

Franey, R. (1979a), 'Making Tenants' Charter Work', 4 *Roof*, 20–2.

Franey, R. (1979b), 'Long Playing Records', 4 *Roof*, 56–7.

Franey, R. (1980), 'The Homeless are Normal – New Shock!', 5 *Roof*, 6–7.

Gallacher, W. (1936), *Revolt on the Clyde* (Lawrence & Wishart, London).

Garratt Lane Law Centre (1978), *Laws That Leak* (Garratt Lane Law Centre, London).

Gauldie, E. (1974), *Cruel Habitations* (Allen & Unwin, London).

Ginsburg, N. (1979), *Class, Capital and Social Policy* (Macmillan, London).

GLC (1976), *Colour and the Allocation of GLC Housing* (GLC, London).

Grant, M., *Local Authority Housing: Law, Policy and Practice in Hampshire* (Hampshire LAG, Southampton).

Gray, F. (1976), 'Selection and Allocation in Council Housing', 1 *Transactions of the Institute of British Geographers (NS)*, 41.

Gregory, P. (1975), 'Waiting Lists and the Demand for Public Housing', 3 *Policy and Politics*, 71–87.

Grey, A., Hepworth, N.P. and Odling-Smee, J. (1978), *Housing Rents, Costs and Subsidies* (Chartered Institute of Public Finance and Accountancy, London).

Griffith, J.A.G. (1966), *Central Departments and Local Authorities* (Allen & Unwin, London).

Griffith, J.A.G. (1978), *The Politics of the Judiciary* (Fontana, London).

Hadden, T. (1978), *Compulsory Repair and Improvement* (Centre for Socio-Legal Studies, Wolfson College, Oxford).

Hadden, T. (1979), *Housing: Repairs and Improvement* (Sweet & Maxwell, London).

Harloe, M., Issacharoff, R. and Minns, R. (1974), *The Organization of Housing: Public and Private Enterprise in London* (Heinemann, London).

Harloe, M. (1976) with Minns, R. and Stocker, J., *Housing Advice Centres* (Centre for Environmental Studies, London).

Harrison, A. and Lomas, G. (1980), 'Tenure Preference: How to Interpret the Survey Evidence', 8 *C.E.S. Review*, 20–4.

Harvey, A. (1964), *Tenants in Danger* (Penguin, Harmondsworth).

Harvey, A. (1979), *Remedies for Rent Arrears* (SHELTER, London).

Harvey, D. (1973), *Social Justice and the City* (Edward Arnold, London).

Harwood, M. (1977), *Cases and Materials on English Land Law* (Professional Books, Abingdon).

Hawkins, A.J. (1971), *Law Relating to Owners and Occupiers of Land* (Butterworths, London).

Hayton, D. (1977), *Registered Land* (2nd ed.) (Sweet & Maxwell, London).

Hennah, J. (1979), *The Agricultural Tied Cottage* (unpublished student paper, LSE).

Hepple, B.A. and O'Higgins, P. (1979), *Employment Law* (3rd ed. by B.A. Hepple) (Sweet & Maxwell, London).

Hepworth, N. (1978), *The Finance of Local Government* (4th ed.) (Allen & Unwin, London).

Hetzel, O., Yates, D. and Trutko, J. (1978), 'Making Allowances for Housing Costs: A Comparison of British and US Experiences', 1 *Urban Law and Policy*, 229–74.

Hill, H.A. and Redman, J.H. (1976), *Law of Landlord and Tenant* (16th ed. by M. Barnes) (Butterworths, London).

Hilton, R. (1978), *The Transition from Feudalism to Capitalism* (Veso, London).

Hoath, D.C. (1978–9), 'Rent Books: The Law, Its Uses and Abuses', *Journal of Social Welfare Law*, 3–13.

Hoath, D. (1978), *Council Housing* (Sweet & Maxwell, London).

Hodge, H. (1979), 'A Test Case Strategy', in Partington and Jowell (eds.), *Welfare Law and Policy* (Pinter, London).

Hoggett, B.M. (1972), 'Rental Purchase', 36 *Conveyancer (NS)*, 325–39.

Hoggett, B.M. (1975), 'Houses on the Never-Never: Some Recent Developments', 39 *Conveyancer (NS)*, 343–54.

Holderness, B.E. (1974), 'The English Land Market in the Eighteenth Century; the Case of Lincolnshire', 27 *Economic History Review* (2nd Ser.), 557–76.

Holdsworth, W.S. (1923), *History of English Law* (3rd ed.) (Methuen, London).

Holmans, A.E. (1979), 'Housing Tenure in England and Wales: the Present Situation and Recent Trends', 10 *Social Trends*, 10–19.

Holmes, C. (1976), 'Clampdown on Council Housing', 1 *Roof*, 113–16.

Holmes, C. (1978), 'The Elusive Panacea', 3 *Roof*, 110–12.

House of Commons Expenditure Committee (1972–73), *House Improvement Grants* (H.C. 349–I/1972–73) (HMSO, London).

Housing Corporation (1979), *Housing Association Tenants* (Housing Corporation, London).

Housing Development Directorate (1977), *Canvassing Rent Allowances in Bristol and Westminster* (DoE, London).

Housing Policy (1977), *A Consultative Document* (Cmnd. 6851) (HMSO, London).

Housing Policy (1) (1977), *Housing Policy Technical Volume Part 1* (HMSO, London).

Housing Policy (2) (1977), *Housing Policy Technical Volume Part 2* (HMSO, London).

Housing Policy (3) (1977), *Housing Policy Technical Volume Part 3* (HMSO, London).

Housing Services Advisory Group (1978), *Housing for People: The Allocation of Council Housing* (DoE, London).

Hughes, D.J. (1979), 'Saga of Campden Hill Towers', 129 *New Law Journal*, 691–2.

Hughes, D. and Jones, S.R. (1979), 'Bias in the Allocation and Transfer of Local Authority Housing', *Journal of Social Welfare Law*, 273–95.

Hunter/Scott (1915), *Departmental Committee on Increases in the Rentals of Small Dwelling-Houses in Industrial Districts in Scotland* (Cd. 8111) (HMSO, London).

Hunter/Scott (1916), *Evidence to Hunter/Scott Committee* (Cd. 8154) (HMSO, London).

Hunter, Lord (1918), *Report of Committee on the Increase of Rent and Mortgage Interest (War Restrictions) Acts* (Cd. 9235) (HMSO, London).

Interdepartmental Committee on Rent Control (Ridley Committee) (1945), *Report* (Cmd. 6621) (HMSO, London).

Johnson, T.J. (1972), *Professions and Power* (Macmillan, London).

JUSTICE (1969), *The Citizen and His Council* (Stevens, London).

Kahn-Freund, O. (1977), *Labour and the Law* (2nd ed.) (Stevens, London).

Karn, V. (1977), *Retiring to the Seaside* (Routledge & Kegan Paul, London).

Karn, V. (1979), 'Pity the Poor Home Owners', 4 *Roof*, 10–14.

Kilroy, B. (1978), *Housing Finance – Organic Reform?* (Labour Economic Finance and Taxation Association, London).

Kinghan, M. (1977), *Squatters in London* (SHELTER, London).

LAG, *see* Legal Action Group.

Lambert, J., Paris, C. and Blackaby, B. (1978), *Housing Policy and the State* (Macmillan, London).

LAMSAC (1978), *Report II, Rent Arrears* (for Association of District Councils, London).

Lansley, S. (1979), *Housing and Public Policy* (Croom Helm, London).

Law Centres' Working Group (1977), *Rent Act 1978?* (LCWG, London).

Law Commission (1970), *Working Paper No. 25* (Law Commission, London).

Law Commission (1970–71), *Civil Liability of Vendors and Lessors for Defective Premises* (H.C. 184/1970–71) (HMSO, London).

Law Commission (1975), *Obligations of Landlords and Tenants* (H.C. 377/1974–75) (HMSO, London).

Law Commission (1978), *13th Annual Report* (H.C. 87/1978–79) (HMSO, London).

Lawson, R. and Stevens, C. (1974), 'Housing Allowances in West Germany and France', 3 *Journal of Social Policy*, 213–34.

Leevers, M. *et al.* (1977), *A Fair Hearing? Possession Hearings in the County Court* (SHAC, London).

Legal Action Group (1977), *The Review of the Rent Acts: Submissions to the DoE* (LAG, London).

Legg, C. and Brion, M. (1976), *The Administration of the Rent Rebate and Rent Allowance Schemes* (DoE, London).

Legg, C., Brion, M. and Bieber, M. (1978), 'Time for a Great Leap Forward', 3 *Roof*, 84–6.

Lewis, J.R. and Holland, J.H. (1968), *Landlord and Tenant* (Sweet & Maxwell, London).

Lewis, N. (1976), 'Council House Allocation: Problems of Discretion and Control', *Public Administration*, 147–60.

Lewis, N. (1977), 'Council House Tenants, Time for a Change?', *Journal of Planning Law*, 155–62.

Lewis, N. and Livock, R. (1979), 'Council House Allocation Procedures: Some Problems of Discretion and Control', 2 *Urban Law and Policy*, 133–74.

Lomas, G. and Monck, E. (1975), *The Coloured Population of Great Britain: A Comparative Study of Coloured Households in Four County Boroughs* (Runnymede Trust, 1975).

Marley, Lord (1931), *Report of Inter-Departmental Committee on the Rent Restriction Acts* (Cmd. 3911) (HMSO, London).

Martin, J. (1978), 'Joint Landlords and Tenants: Some Problems', 42 *Conveyancer*, 436–48.

Massey, D. and Catalano, A. (1978), *Capital and Land – Landownership by Capital in Great Britain* (Edward Arnold, London).

Maudlsey, R. and Burn, E. (1975), *Land Law: Cases and Materials* (3rd ed.) (Butterworths, London).

McDonald, I.J. (1969), 'The Leasehold System: Towards a Balanced Land Tenure of Urban Development', 6 *Urban Studies*.

McKay, D.H. and Cox, A.W. (1979), *The Politics of Urban Change* (Croom Helm, London).

McQuillan, J. and Finnis, N. (1979), 'Ways of Seeing Dampness: When Houses Can't Cope with Being Lived In', 4 *Roof*, 85–9.

McQuiston, J.R. (1973), 'Tenant Right: Farmer against Landlord in Victorian England, 1847–1883', 47 *Agricultural History*, 95–113.

Megarry, R.E. (1967), *The Rent Acts* (10th ed.) (Sweet & Maxwell, London).

Megarry, R.E. and Wade, H.W.R. (1975), *The Law of Real Property* (4th ed.) (Stevens, London).

Merrett, S. (1979), *State Housing in Britain* (Routledge & Kegan Paul, London).

Merritt, E.J. (1973), 'Liability of Landlords for Nuisances Committed by their Tenants', *Journal of Planning and Environment Law*, 154–8.

Miller, E. and Hatcher, J. (1978), *Mediaeval England: Rural Society and Economic Change 1086–1348* (Longman, London).

Milner-Holland (1965), *Report of the Committee on Housing in Greater London* (Cmnd. 2605) (HMSO, London).

Milsom, S.F.C. (1969), *Historical Foundations of the Common Law* (Butterworths, London).

Monck, E. (1980), 'HAAs and GIAs: Actual and Potential Declarations', 8 *C.E.S. Review*, 51–5.

Monroe, J.G. and Nock, R.S. (1976), *Law of Stamp Duties* (5th ed.) (Sweet & Maxwell, London).

Morgan, D. (1979), 'Unfit Housing: The Issue of "Reasonable Cost"', 43 *Conveyancer* (*NS*), 414–22.

Murie, A. (1976), 'Estimating Housing Need – Technique or Mystique?' 25 *Housing Review*, 54–8.

Murie, A. and Wintour, J. (1978), 'The Problems with HIPs', 3 *Roof*, 42–3.

Mylan, D. (1979), *Housing Aid and Advice Centres* (Association of Housing Aid, Birmingham).

National Consumer Council (1976), *Tenancy Agreements* (NCC, London).

National Dwelling and Housing Survey (1978), *Report* (HMSO, London).

Nevitt, A.A. (1966), *Housing, Taxation and Subsidies* (Nelson, London).

Nevitt, A.A. (1968), 'Conflicts in British Housing Policy', 39 *Political Quarterly*, 439–50.

Nevitt, A.A. (1970), *The Nature of Rent Controlling Legislation in the UK* (C.E.S. University Working Paper No. 8, London).

Newby, H. (1977a), *The Deferential Worker* (Allen Lane, London).

Newby, H. (1977b), 'Tied Cottage Reform', 4 *British Journal of Law and Society*, 94–103.

Niner, P. (1979), 'Associations Match Council Selection', 4 *Roof*, 125–6.

Noble, D. (1979), 'Policing Voluntary Housing', 4 *Roof*, 122–5.

North, P.M. (1973), 'Defective Premises Act, 1972', 36 *Modern Law Review*, 628–38.

Onslow, Lord (1923), *Final Reports of the Departmental Committee on the Increase of Rent and Mortgage Interest (Restrictions) Act 1920* (Cmd. 1803) (HMSO, London).

Paish, F.W. (1950), 'The Economics of Rent Restriction', *Lloyds Bank Review* reprinted in *Verdict of Rent Control* (1972) (Institute for Economic Affairs, London).

Paley, B. (1978), *Attitudes to Lettings in 1976* (HMSO, London).

Paris, C. (1977), 'Housing Action Areas', 2 *Roof*, 9–14.

Paris, C. (1979), 'HIPs and Housing Need: The Oxford Experience', 5 *C.E.S. Review*, 19–27.

Paris, C. and Blackaby, B. (1979), *Not Much Improvement: Urban Renewal Policy in Birmingham* (Heinemann, London).

Partington, M. (1974), 'Furnished Accommodation and the Rent Acts', 124 *New Law Journal*, 913–15.

Partington, M. (1975a), 'Accommodation Agencies and the Law', 125 *New Law Journal*, 148.

Partington, M. (1975b), 'Rent Fixing: Problems of Jurisdiction', *LAG Bulletin*, 214–16.

Partington, M. (1978), *The Housing (Homeless Persons) Act 1977* (Sweet & Maxwell, London).

Partington, M. (1979), 'Non-Exclusive Occupation Agreements', 42 *Modern Law Review*, 331–8.

Partington, M. (1980a), 'Landlord and Tenant: The British Experience', in E. Kamenka (ed.), *Law and Social Control* (Edward Arnold, London).

Partington, M. (1980b), 'Collective Bargaining in Landlord and Tenant Law', *Urban Law and Policy* (forthcoming).

Payne, the Hon. Mr Justice (1969), *Report of the Committee on the Enforcement of Judgment Debts* (Cmnd. 3909) (HMSO, London).

Pennance, F.G. (1972), *Verdict on Rent Control* (Institute of Economic Affairs, London).

PEP (1952), 'The Future of Leasehold', 18 *Planning* No. 338, 201–11.

Perkin, H. (1969), *The Origins of Modern English Society 1780–1880* (Routledge & Kegan Paul, London).

Pettit, P. (1977), 'The Question of Jurisdiction in Relation to Rent Tribunals, Rent Officers and Rent Assessment Committees', 41 *Conveyancer (NS)*, 379–88.

Pettit, P. (1978), *Landlord and Tenant Under the Rent Act 1977* (Butterworths, London).

Popplestone, G. (1979), 'Difficult Tenants: Who They Are and What To Do About Them', 5 *C.E.S. Review*, 35–40.

Popplestone, G. (1980), 'Managing Rent Arrears', 8 *C.E.S. Review*, 34–40.

Porter, G. (1978), 'Rent Arrears – Asking the Right Questions', 3 *Roof*, 141–3.

Porter, G. (1979), 'Associated Failings', 4 *Roof*, 18–19.

Public Accounts Committee (1979), *5th Report* (H.C. 327/1978–1979) (HMSO, London).

Ramsey, E. (1979), *Caught in the Housing Trap: Employees in Tied Housing* (C.E.S., London).

Rex, J. and Moore, R. (1967), *Race, Community and Conflict* (Oxford University Press, Oxford).

Reynolds, J.I. (1974), 'Statutory Covenants of Fitness and Repair: Social Legislation and the Judges', 37 *Modern Law Review*, 377–98.

Richardson, A., (1977), *Tenant Participation in Council Housing Management* (H.D.D. Occasional Paper 2/77) (DoE, London).

Robinson, M.J. (1976), ' "Social Legislation" and the Judges: A Note by Way of Rejoinder', 39 *Modern Law Review*, 43–54.

Roof (1979a), editorial, 4 *Roof*, 138.

Roof (1979b), 'Housing in Action Areas', 4 *Roof*, 151–3.

Royal Commission on Legal Services (1979) (Sir H. Benson, Chairman), *Report* (Cmnd. 7648) (HMSO, London).

Salisbury, Lord (1920), *Report of the Committee on the Increase of Rent and Mortgage Interest* (War Restrictions) Acts (Cmd. 658) (HMSO, London).

S.B.C., *see* Supplementary Benefits Commission.

Schifferes, S. (1979), *In Distress over Rent* (SHELTER, London).

Schifferes, S. (1980a), 'Housing Bill 1980: The Beginning of the End for Council Housing', 5 *Roof*, 10–14.

Schifferes, S. (1980b), *The Forgotten Problem* (SHELTER, London).

Seebohm, F. (Chairman) (1968), *Report of the Committee on Local Authority and Allied Personal Social Services* (Cmnd. 3703) (HMSO, London).

Select Committee on Race Relations and Immigration (1971), *Housing* (H.C. 508-1/1970–71) (HMSO, London).

Select Committee on Town Holdings (1889), *Report* (H.C. 251/1889) (Hansard, London).

SHAC, *see* Shelter Housing Aid Centre.

SHELTER (1978), *Where Homelessness means Hopelessness* (SHELTER, London).

Shelter Housing Aid Centre (1977), *Private Rented Housing: A Policy for the Future* (London Housing Aid Centre, London).

Shelter Housing Aid Centre (1979), *Shorthold Tenancies: Policy Paper 1*.

Sherrin, C.H. (1980), 'Note', 43 *Modern Law Review*, 77.

Shutt, J. and Stewart, A. (1976), 'Instalment Mortgages in Birmingham: Another Way of Evading the Rent Acts?', 126 *New Law Journal*, 217–19.

Simpson, A.W.B. (1961), *Introduction to the History of Land Law* (Oxford University Press, Oxford).

Smith, D. and Whalley, A. (1975), *Public Housing and Racial Minorities* (PEP, London).

Smith, J. (1974), 'Section 30, Rent Act 1965: Remedies in Tort', *LAG Bulletin*, 54.

Smith, P. (1979), 'Repair, Renewal and Improvement', 43 *Conveyancer* (*NS*), 429–35.

Smith, R.B. (1970), *Land and Politics in the England of Henry VIII: The West Riding of Yorkshire, 1530–40* (Clarendon Press, Oxford).

Smith, Wallace F. (1970), *Housing: The Social and Economic Elements* (University of California Press, Berkeley).

Spencer, J.R. (1974), 'The Defective Premises Act 1972: Defective Law and Defective Law Reform', *Cambridge Law Journal*, 307–23; (1975) *ibid.*, 48–78.

Stedman-Jones, G. (1976), *Outcast London* (Penguin, Harmondsworth).

Stein, P. and Shand, J. (1974), *Legal Values in Western Society* (Edinburgh University Press, Edinburgh).

Stoker, G. (1978), 'Manchester Grapples with HIP Targets', 3 *Roof*, 76–7.

Supplementary Benefits Commission (1979), *Annual Report for 1978* (Cmnd. 7725) (HMSO, London).

Tapper, C. (1974), *Computers and the Law* (Weidenfeld & Nicolson, London).

Thompson, F.M.L. (1963), *English Landed Society in the Nineteenth Century* (Routledge & Kegan Paul, London).

Tunney, J. (1978), 'Fair Rents on the Up and Up', 3 *Roof*, 68–9.

Twining, W. and Miers, D. (1976), *How to Do Things with Rules* (Weidenfeld & Nicolson, London).

Tyler, E.G.L. (1971), 'Rental Purchase', 121 *New Law Journal*, 427–8.

UK Government (1953), *Government Policy on Leasehold Property in England and Wales* (Cmd. 8713) (HMSO, London).

Ungerson, C. and Baldock, J. (1978), *Rent Arrears in Ashford* (University of Kent, Canterbury).

Uthwatt-Jenkins (1950), *Committee on Leasehold, Final Report* (Cmd. 7982) (HMSO, London).

Ward, C. (1974), *Tenants Take Over* (2nd ed.) (Architectural Press, London).

Watchman, P. (1979), 'Fair Rents and the Judicial Control of Administrative Discretion', 43 *Conveyancer* (*NS*), 205–14.

Watchman, P. (1980), 'The Origin of the 1915 Rent Act', 5 *Law and State*, 20–50.

Watson, C. *et al.* (1973), *Estimating Local Housing Needs* (Centre for Urban and Regional Studies, Occasional Paper 24, Birmingham).

Weir, S. (1976), 'Associations' Alarm at High Fair Rents', 1 *Roof*, 130–2.

Welsh Consumer Council (1976), *Council Housing: A Survey of Allocation Policies in Wales* (WCC, Cardiff).

Welsh Consumer Council (1977), *A Bargain for Tenants* (WCC, Cardiff).

Whitehead, C. (1979a), 'The Role of the Resident Landlord', 5 *C.E.S. Review*, 16–18.

Whitehead, C. (1979b), 'Why Owner Occupation', 6 *C.E.S. Review*, 33–42.

Wilkinson, H.W. (1979), 'The Lessons of Ravenseft', 129 *New Law Journal*, 839–40.

Winkler, J.T. (1975), 'Law, State and Economy', 2 *British Journal of Law and Society*, 103–28.

Wintour, J. (1979), 'Raising Passions on Council Rents', 4 *Roof*, 114–15.

Wintour, J. and Franey, R. (1978), 'Are Improvement Grants Tied Up in the Town Halls?' 3 *Roof*, 81–3.

Winyard, S. (1978), 'Points to a Good Policy', 3 *Roof*, 106–8.

Wohl, A.S. (1971), 'The Housing of the Working Classes in London, 1815–1914' in S.D. Chapman (ed.), *History of Working Class Housing* (David & Charles).

Woodfall (1978), *Law of Landlord and Tenant* (28th ed. by V.G. Wellings) (Sweet & Maxwell, London).

Yates, D. (1979), 'Rent Allowances – Six Years On', *Journal of Social Welfare Law*, 195–215.

Zander, M. (1978), *Legal Services for the Community* (Temple Smith, London).

INDEX